"Out of his broad experience of expounding the Scriptures, Dr. Fernando has given us a commentary that will appeal to all those who preach the Word. The work breathes a love for God, a deep understanding of Biblical theology, and a warmly poignant grasp of human nature—with its failings and its potentials. His applications of Deuteronomy's teaching are both perceptive and relevant. While showing an awareness of scholarly treatments, the work is very accessible to those who do not have scholarly training. It is highly recommended."

John Oswalt, Distinguished Professor of Old Testament,
Asbury Theological Seminary

"Vintage Fernando. Like all of his preaching, this book is a model of the wonderful gift that God has given to Ajith Fernando for simple, clear, and challenging exposition of the Word of God. Without evading the more difficult questions and problems that scholars have wrestled with in the book of Deuteronomy, he does not allow them to dominate but stays close to the thrust of the text, patiently explaining and applying it step by step. The rich infusion of illustrations that are mostly drawn from the challenges and stresses, joys and sorrows of his own experience in ministry add a wonderful earthy texture to the whole book as we constantly weave between the Biblical world and today's world in a way that listens to and engages with both. This book is a deep well of Biblical study, ethical challenge, practical advice, pastoral wisdom, and spiritual warmth. It breathes love for God, God's Word, God's world, and God's people."

Christopher J. H. Wright, International Director,
Langham Partnership International; author, *Old Testament Ethics for the People of God*

DEUTERONOMY

PREACHING THE WORD
Edited by R. Kent Hughes

Genesis | R. Kent Hughes

Exodus | Philip Graham Ryken

Leviticus | Kenneth A. Mathews

Numbers | Iain M. Duguid

Deuteronomy | Ajith Fernando

Joshua | David Jackman

Judges and Ruth | Barry G. Webb

1 Samuel | John Woodhouse

2 Samuel | John Woodhouse

1 Kings | John Woodhouse

Job | Christopher Ash

Psalms, vol. 1 | James Johnston

Proverbs | Raymond C. Ortlund Jr.

Ecclesiastes | Philip Graham Ryken

Song of Solomon | Douglas Sean O'Donnell

Isaiah | Raymond C. Ortlund Jr.

Jeremiah and Lamentations | R. Kent Hughes

Daniel | Rodney D. Stortz

Matthew | Douglas Sean O'Donnell

Mark | R. Kent Hughes

Luke | R. Kent Hughes

John | R. Kent Hughes

Acts | R. Kent Hughes

Romans | R. Kent Hughes

1 Corinthians | Stephen T. Um

2 Corinthians | R. Kent Hughes

Galatians | Todd Wilson

Ephesians | R. Kent Hughes

Philippians, Colossians, and Philemon | R. Kent Hughes

1–2 Thessalonians | James H. Grant Jr.

1–2 Timothy and Titus | R. Kent Hughes and Bryan Chapell

Hebrews | R. Kent Hughes

James | R. Kent Hughes

1–2 Peter and Jude | David R. Helm

1–3 John | David L. Allen

Revelation | James M. Hamilton Jr.

The Sermon on the Mount | R. Kent Hughes

(((PREACHING *the* WORD)))

DEUTERONOMY

LOVING OBEDIENCE
to a LOVING GOD

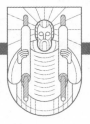

AJITH FERNANDO

R. Kent Hughes
Series Editor

WHEATON, ILLINOIS

Royalties from the sale of this book have been assigned to staff education and literature projects of Youth for Chris t, Sri Lanka.

Library of Congress Cataloging-in-Publication Data

Fernando, Ajith.
    Deuteronomy : loving obedience to a loving God / Ajith Fernando.
      p. cm. (Preaching the Word)
    Includes bibliographical references and index.
    ISBN 978-1-4335-3100-2 (hc)
    1. Bible. O.T. Deuteronomy—Commentaries. I. Title.
BS1275.53.F47   2011
222'.1507—dc23   2011025566

To
Genga and Lakshi Arulampalam
Loran and Merle Grant
Brian and Lilly Stiller
With gratitude to God for
over three decades of friendship.

Love is . . . kind.
1 Corinthians 13:4

"Hear, O Israel: The LORD our GOD, the LORD is one.
You shall love the LORD your God with all your heart
and with all your soul and with all your might.
And these words that I command you today shall be on
your heart. You shall teach them diligently to your children,
and shall talk of them when you sit in your house,
and when you walk by the way, and when you lie down,
and when you rise. You shall bind them as a sign
on your hand, and they shall be as frontlets between
your eyes. You shall write them on the doorposts of
your house and on your gates.

"And when the LORD your God brings you into the land
that he swore to your fathers, to Abraham, to Isaac,
and to Jacob, to give you—with great and good cities
that you did not build, and houses full of all good things
that you did not fill, and cisterns that you did not dig,
and vineyards and olive trees that you did not plant—
and when you eat and are full, then take care
lest you forget the LORD, who brought you out of
the land of Egypt, out of the house of slavery.
It is the LORD your God you shall fear.
Him you shall serve and by his name you shall swear."

DEUTERONOMY 6:4–13

Contents

Frequently Used
Reference Materials

The Christian community is blessed with some wonderful commentaries and expositions of Deuteronomy. Some of these are not only useful for extracting scholarly information but can also be read as edifying devotional material. In my study of Deuteronomy I found the commentaries listed below particularly helpful. In this book I will refer to them only by the names of the authors. The assumption is that the quotation or citation is taken from the comment on the particular passage I am commenting on at the time.

Brown, Raymond. *The Message of Deuteronomy: Not by Bread Alone*. The Bible Speaks Today. Leicester, UK and Downers Grove, IL: InterVarsity Press, 1993.

Chianeque, Luciano C., and Samuel Ngewa. "Deuteronomy." In *Africa Bible Commentary: A One-Volume Commentary Written by 70 African Scholars,* edited by Tokumbo Adeyemo. Nairobi, Kenya: WordAlive Publishers and Grand Rapids, MI: Zondervan, 2006.

Clarke, Adam. *A Commentary and Critical Notes on the Holy Bible: Old and New Testaments*. WORDsearch 7.0 Software.

Craigie, Peter C. *The Book of Deuteronomy*. The New International Commentary on the Old Testament. Grand Rapids, MI: Eerdmans, 1976.

Hall, Gary H. *The College Press NIV Commentary: Deuteronomy*. Joplin, MO: The College Press Publishing Co., Inc., 2000. Logos Bible Software.

Henry, Matthew. *Matthew Henry's Commentary on the Whole Bible*. Grand Rapids, MI: Zondervan, 1999. Zondervan Interactive, 2007. Pradis 6.0 Software.

Kalland, Earl S. "Deuteronomy." In *The Expositor's Bible Commentary,* edited by Frank E. Gaebelein. Grand Rapids, MI: Zondervan, 1992. Zondervan Interactive, 2007. Pradis 6.0 Software.

Keil, C. F., and F. Delitzsch, *Commentary on the Old Testament: Numbers-Ruth*. Albany, OR: Ages Software, 1999. Ages Digital Library 1.0 Software.

McConville, J. G. *Deuteronomy*. Apollos Old Testament Commentary. Leicester, UK and Downers Grove: InterVarsity Press, 2002.

———. "Deuteronomy." In *New Bible Commentary: 21ˢᵗ Century Edition*. Edited by G. J. Wenham, J. A. Motyer, D. A. Carson and R. T. France. Leicester, UK and Downers Grove, IL: IVP Academic, 1994. Logos Library System: The Essential IVP Reference Collection. Software. (Referred to as McConville, NBC.)

McIntosh, Doug. *Deuteronomy*. Holman Old Testament Commentary 3. Nashville, TN: B&H, 2002.

Merrill, Eugene H. *Deuteronomy*. The New American Commentary, vol. 4. Nashville, TN: B&H, 1994. WORDsearch 7.0, 2005. Software.

Payne, David F. *Deuteronomy*. The Daily Study Bible. Edinburgh, UK: The Saint Andrew Press and Philadelphia, PA: Westminster, 1985.

Thompson, J. A. *Deuteronomy: An Introduction and Commentary*. Tyndale Old Testament Commentaries. Leicester, UK and Downers Grove, IL: InterVarsity Press, 1974. Logos Bible Software.

Biblical Illustrator: Old Testament, Deuteronomy. Edited by Joseph Exell. Rio, WI: Ages Software, 2002. Ages Digital Library: Christian Library Series Software.

Deuteronomy. Pulpit Commentary: Old Testament. Edited by H. D. M. Spence and Joseph Exell. Rio, WI: Ages Software, 2002. Ages Digital Library: Christian Library Series Software.

Wesley, John. *Notes on the Old Testament*, 1765. WORDsearch 7.0, 2005. Software.

Wiersbe, Warren W. *Be Equipped: Acquiring the Tools for Spiritual Success (Deuteronomy)*. Colorado Springs, CO: Chariot Victor, 1999. Logos Bible Software.

Work, Telford. *Deuteronomy*. Brazos Theological Commentary on the Bible. Grand Rapids, MI: Brazos Press, 2009.

Wright, Christopher J. H. *Deuteronomy*. The New International Biblical Commentary. Peabody, MA: Hendrickson, 1996.

Abbreviations and bibliographical details for other reference works that I used frequently are given below. I used the electronic version of these resources.

BBC-OT—John H. Walton, Victor H. Matthews, and Mark W. Chavalas, *The IVP Bible Background Commentary Old Testament*. Leicester, UK and Downers Grove, IL: InterVarsity Press, 2000. Logos Library System: The Essential IVP Reference Collection Software.

ESVSB—*The ESV Study Bible*. Wheaton: Crossway, 2008. WORDsearch, 2008. Software.

Heb-Eng Lexicon—*Hebrew-English Lexicon of the Old Testament*. Zondervan Interactive, 2007. Pradis 6.0 Software.

Merriam-Webster—Merriam-Webster's Collegiate Dictionary, Version 2.5, 2000. Software.

NBC—*New Bible Commentary: 21st Century Edition*. Edited by G. J. Wenham, J. A. Motyer, D. A. Carson, and R. T. France. Leicester, UK and Downers Grove, IL: IVP Academic, 1994. Logos Library System: Essential IVP Reference Collection Software.

NIDCH—*New International Dictionary of the Christian Church*. Edited by J. D. Douglas. Grand Rapids, MI: Zondervan, 2002. Zondervan Interactive, 2007.

Pradis 6.0 Software. (Most of my historical notes and dates are from this resource.)

NIDOTTE—*The New International Dictionary of Old Testament Theology and Exegesis*. Edited by Willem A. VanGemeren. Grand Rapids, MI: Zondervan, 1997, 2002. Zondervan Interactive, 2007. Pradis 6.0 Software.

NIVSB—*The New International Version Study Bible*. Edited by Kenneth Barker. Grand Rapids, MI: Zondervan, 1995. Zondervan Interactive, 2007. Pradis 6.0 Software.

TWOT—*Theological Wordbook of the Old Testament*. Edited by R. Laird Harris, Gleason L. Archer Jr., and Bruce K. Waltke. Chicago: Moody Publishers, 1980. WORDsearch 7.0, 2004. Software.

ZIBBC-OT—*Zondervan Illustrated Bible Backgrounds Commentary: Old Testament*. Edited by John H. Walton. Grand Rapids, MI: Zondervan, 2009. Logos Library System Software. (Comments on Deuteronomy are by Eugene E. Carpenter.)

ZPEB—*The Zondervan Pictorial Encyclopedia of the Bible*. Edited by Merrill C. Tenney. Grand Rapids, MI: Zondervan. Zondervan Interactive 2007. Pradis 6.0 Software.

Acknowledgments

I need to first express my gratitude to God for the way in which he spoke to me through studying the book of Deuteronomy. I was often convicted of sin and unfaithfulness to God. I received many instructions on the pathways of repentance and obedience. I was specifically ministered to by the vision of God's greatness that pervades this book and by the way it addressed some tough situations I faced while writing this book. I agreed to write this book because God has spoken to me clearly through Deuteronomy over the years. The opportunity to concentrate on it in order to write this book intensified that process.

I am grateful to my friends Dr. Lane Dennis, President of Crossway Books, and Dr. Kent Hughes, the general editor of the Preaching the Word series, for honoring me with the invitation to contribute to this series that I have grown to value highly. After my long struggle to complete this book, my admiration of Dr. Hughes increased even more. I am amazed that he has been able to maintain his consistently high standard of brilliant exposition in his treatment of so many of the volumes in this series. It is also a joy to work again with editor Ted Griffin.

The Board of Youth for Christ (YFC) granted me two short sabbaticals-of-sorts to work on this book. The first was canceled because of the massive relief operation following the devastation caused by the December 2004 tsunami. Needs in the YFC ministry resulted in my doing much less study than I had planned during the second sabbatical. I am grateful for God's grace to complete this project despite that and for YFC's willingness to let me squeeze in whatever opportunity I could get to work on this book. The exhaustion of trying to combine active ministry and expository study and writing is more than compensated by the refreshment from spending time delving into the riches of the Word. And what a rich book Deuteronomy is!

My basic approach to the passages was to first do an inductive study of them using only the Biblical text with a very wide margin and my lead pencil and color pencils. Only after this did I check the commentaries for clarification, correction, and enrichment. I am so grateful to Drs. Robert Traina and Daniel Fuller who introduced me to the thrill of discovering riches from the Word through inductive study. Another teacher, Dr. John Oswalt, who vividly communicated to his students the glory of Old Testament study, graciously read the first three parts of the first chapter. I harvested the godly scholarship of the unusually large number of superb Deuteronomy commentaries that I consulted. I am grateful to the scholars who wrote these commentaries, for their labors of love on behalf of us preachers. In terms of usefulness for preaching, my favorite commentary was that by Christopher Wright.

I am grateful to the many friends who opened up their homes for me to hide (sometimes with my wife) and work on this book. God used their kindness and friendship to help me bear the terrible loneliness I felt, especially during the times I was away from my wife and family. This book was written in the homes of so many friends, I decided that the list of their names is too long to include here. I find it difficult to write while in Sri Lanka because of the complication of involvement in so many ministries. However, the YFC Youth Guidance drug rehabilitation center provided me with a wonderful atmosphere for study and writing, while ministering to the staff and students there on the side.

This book took me more than eight years to write, and no one encouraged me during this time as much as my family. During these eight years my daughter Nirmali married a YFC worker and subsequently joined YFC staff. My son Asiri went to seminary and then also joined YFC staff. If I were to identify the primary human contributory factor to their love for the Lord and for Christian ministry, despite having to pay the price of having a father who was so busy in ministry, it would be their mother. Nelun's contagious love for God, his Word, and his ways and for our family must surely have contributed to the joy my children have in following and serving Christ. I join that happy band of Christian workers who declare, "Thank God for the gift of family!"

A Word to Those Who Preach the Word

There are times when I am preaching that I have especially sensed the pleasure of God. I usually become aware of it through the unnatural silence. The ever-present coughing ceases, and the pews stop creaking, bringing an almost physical quiet to the sanctuary—through which my words sail like arrows. I experience a heightened eloquence, so that the cadence and volume of my voice intensify the truth I am preaching.

There is nothing quite like it—the Holy Spirit filling one's sails, the sense of his pleasure, and the awareness that something is happening among one's hearers. This experience is, of course, not unique, for thousands of preachers have similar experiences, even greater ones.

What has happened when this takes place? How do we account for this sense of his smile? The answer for me has come from the ancient rhetorical categories of *logos*, *ethos*, and *pathos*.

The first reason for his smile is the *logos*—in terms of preaching, God's Word. This means that as we stand before God's people to proclaim his Word, we have done our homework. We have exegeted the passage, mined the significance of its words in their context, and applied sound hermeneutical principles in interpreting the text so that we understand what its words meant to its hearers. And it means that we have labored long until we can express in a sentence what the theme of the text is—so that our outline springs from the text. Then our preparation will be such that as we preach, we will not be preaching our own thoughts about God's Word, but God's actual Word, his *logos*. This is fundamental to pleasing him in preaching.

The second element in knowing God's smile in preaching is *ethos*—what you are as a person. There is a danger endemic to preaching, which is having your hands and heart cauterized by holy things. Phillips Brooks illustrated it by the analogy of a train conductor who comes to believe that he has been to the places he announces because of his long and loud heralding of them. And that is why Brooks insisted that preaching must be "the bringing of truth through personality." Though we can never perfectly embody the truth we preach, we must be subject to it, long for it, and make it as much a part of our ethos as possible. As the Puritan William Ames said, "Next to the Scriptures, nothing makes a sermon more to pierce, than when it comes out of the inward affection of the heart without any affectation." When a preacher's *ethos* backs up his *logos*, there will be the pleasure of God.

Last, there is *pathos*—personal passion and conviction. David Hume, the Scottish philosopher and skeptic, was once challenged as he was seen going to hear George Whitefield preach, "I thought you do not believe in the gospel." Hume replied, "I don't, but he does." Just so! When a preacher believes what he preaches, there will be passion. And this belief and requisite passion will know the smile of God.

The pleasure of God is a matter of *logos* (the Word), *ethos* (what you are), and *pathos* (your passion). As you preach the Word may you experience his smile—the Holy Spirit in your sails!

R. Kent Hughes

Preface:
Why I Am Excited about
Deuteronomy

In my thirty plus years of ministry I have worked primarily among first-generation Christians from other faiths both in Youth for Christ and in the church where my wife and I serve. We have faced three huge challenges in this work. The first is that of making contact with these people who have no contact with the church so that they would have an opportunity to hear the gospel. The second is communicating the gospel in such a way that they would not only understand it but also be persuaded to leave their past allegiances to accept the salvation it offers. I have addressed these two challenges in two books, *The Supremacy of Christ*[1] and *Sharing the Truth in Love*.[2]

The third challenge is nurturing people who have not learned to view life using Biblical categories—that is, those with a worldview that is not Christian—and helping them move into a godly life. This is also becoming an increasingly important challenge in the West where those outside, and sometimes inside, the church have attitudes that are alien to the religion of the Bible. Around twenty years ago, while walking along the beach and praying, I told God that one day I would like to write a comprehensive theology of the Christian life, especially focusing on how to move people on to holiness. I think this book is God's answer to that prayer.

When my friends found out that I was writing a preaching commentary on Deuteronomy, I usually got one of three responses. Some responded with enthusiasm, pointing out that it is such an important book. I share their enthusiasm. Others pointed to what a tough assignment this would be, and I agree with them too. When I started on this project I had not realized what a large book Deuteronomy is and how much I had to learn about its background in order to do this project justice. The third type of response I received seemed to imply that this is a dry book, with a lot of difficult and irrelevant material, which does not seem to have much to teach us today. I take strong exception to that sentiment!

Deuteronomy is an exciting book that is very relevant today. I first realized this about twenty-five years ago when, early in my ministry, I read the book for my devotions. I found that there was so much I can learn about the Christian life and ministry that I began to list it all. I ended up with a huge list that has had a huge impact on my ministry. For example, I made a list of 142 incentives to obedience from Deuteronomy. So when I was asked by my friends at Crossway whether I would be interested in writing the Deuteronomy commentary in the series I responded with an enthusiastic yes.

Why am I so excited about Deuteronomy? Primarily because in this book Moses is attempting to do something that is still so important for all Christians. He is close to death, and they are close to entering the promised land without him, the one who led them for forty years. Deuteronomy gives Moses' farewell addresses to them. His aim is to motivate them to go forward and conquer the land and to help them to be faithful to God amidst all the challenges to such faithfulness that they will face. He warns them of challenges, he encourages them to a life of holiness, and he tells them the consequences of living and of failing to live such a life. All the time Moses was aware of the temptation the people would have to compromise their faith by assimilating aspects of Canaanite religion.

Are these not some of our greatest challenges today? How can we remain faithful to God? How can we avoid compromise when the lure of the society around us is so powerful? And how can we help our children and the people we lead to be faithful? Deuteronomy tells us how Moses tackled these challenges. After citing a story that appears in Deuteronomy, Paul writes, "Now these things happened to them as an example, but they were written down for our instruction" (1 Corinthians 10:11).

Therefore I have approached every passage of Deuteronomy as having significance to Christians today. Because all of Deuteronomy is part of God's inspired Word, that affirmation should be accepted without question. But it is often not, for many Christians think that in this era of grace many of the teachings of the Old Testament are not significant for us. Indeed we may not use some of the laws and regulations that are given there because they apply only to the Jewish nation. But the religion of this nation had the same basic ingredients that the Christian religion has today. Their life was to be a response of faith and obedience to the God who had graciously acted to redeem them. So even the laws that are specific to Israel have principles behind them that help us in the life of faith today.

When I studied Deuteronomy this time around with a view to writing this book, I found another feature that makes it extremely helpful. Many consider Moses to be the greatest national leader in history. From what Moses says and does in Deuteronomy we can learn many important lessons on leadership. Perhaps this has been to me the most thrilling aspect of this present study that

I have done of Deuteronomy. This book has also had a chastening influence in my life because often through it the Lord showed me areas where I have been slack in my Christian commitment.

The Biblical writers seem to have considered Deuteronomy to be a very important book; they used it all the time. Gordon Fee and Douglas Stuart say that "Deuteronomy has perhaps had more influence on the rest of the biblical story (both Old and New Testaments) than any other book of the Bible." They point out that "Deuteronomy . . . had considerable influence on Israel's and Judah's prophets, especially Isaiah and Jeremiah, and through them influenced the major figures of the NT (especially Jesus and Paul)."[3] Chris Wright says, "The book of Deuteronomy lies close to the very heartbeat of the Scriptures. It is to the Old Testament something like the book of Romans to the New Testament. It deals with many of the key themes that inform the rest of the Bible."[4] It is quoted over eighty times in the New Testament, and references to it occur in all the New Testament books except John, Colossians, 1 Thessalonians, 2 Timothy, and 1 and 2 Peter. Thus it belongs to a small group of four Old Testament books—Genesis, Deuteronomy, Psalms, and Isaiah—to which early Christians made frequent reference.[5] When Jesus was tempted, he quoted from Deuteronomy in each of his three responses to Satan.

We must never forget that when the New Testament was written, the only Bible that the Christians had was the Old Testament. When they "studied the Word," they studied the Old Testament. Therefore it was not necessary for some of the things emphasized in the Old Testament to be emphasized again in the New Testament. The New Testament takes it for granted that Christians were very aware of these emphases. Some of these emphases are not very strong in the thinking of Christians today. Therefore it is especially important that we study the Old Testament, because the failure to do that would result in our not being influenced by a key aspect of God's thinking.

Let me list some of those things that are very important for the Christian life but that the New Testament does not emphasize as much as the Old Testament because they already have a good emphasis there. Each of these is an emphasis found in Deuteronomy also.

- The importance of order and the attention to detail especially in connection with worship.
- The importance of visual and symbolic reminders of Biblical truth, such as festivals.
- The importance of constantly being aware of the holiness of God and how it influences a faithful life. In fact, in the Old Testament the life of faith is often described as walking in the fear of the Lord, an emphasis

that may be much needed today when people tend to be careless about sticking to Christian principles in every sphere of life.

- The need for discipline and disciplining people when serious disobedience occurs.
- The need to have a vital relationship with the Word through memorization, meditation, discussion, and obedience.

Deuteronomy is particularly important because it records a series of sermons given to help people in their day-to-day lives. It begins with the words, "These are the words that Moses spoke to all Israel . . . " (1:1). Deuteronomy 1:5 says, "Beyond the Jordan, in the land of Moab, Moses undertook to explain this law. . . ." So it is an expository sermon. Paul Barker points out that "apart from chapter 34 there are only five major paragraphs in the book which are not reported speech."[6]

Because it consists of sermons, Deuteronomy would also give us helpful models for preaching today.

- The sermonic style is found here with its sense of urgency, with frequent pleading and exhorting, and with calls to action.
- The laws are not simply listed, they are preached.
- Deuteronomy is full of imperatives to love, fear, serve, obey, walk after, and hold fast.
- The two main ways Moses tries to motivate the people to faithfulness are reviewing history and retelling the Law. Surely that has something to teach us about good preaching!
- "Almost every time Moses talks about the land, he is seeking to motivate Israel."[7] Therefore, when he mentions the land he qualifies it with terms like "which the Lord your God gave you," "the good," "flowing with milk and honey," or "which the Lord your God swore (or promised) to give you."

I must confess that usually I get excited about any book in the Bible I am studying at a given time. The study of all of Scripture is a thrilling exercise. But I needed to give reasons why Deuteronomy is exciting because I have found that many people, assuming that this is a boring book that is difficult to understand, avoid studying it and preaching from it. This is a serious error.

1

Deuteronomy:
Highly Relevant History

DEUTERONOMY 1:1–3, 5

THE BOOK OF DEUTERONOMY consists primarily of speeches that Moses gave to the Israelites shortly before he handed over the leadership to Joshua. They aim to prepare the people to conquer Canaan and live faithful lives in their new land. The speeches give some strong teaching that would be somewhat unpopular today. Our natural tendency would be to dismiss this teaching as not being relevant to our lives. However, this book claims to contain the very thoughts of God. Deuteronomy 1:3 says, "Moses spoke to the people of Israel according to all that the LORD had given him in commandment to them." If these are indeed God's words, we are forced to take them seriously. Therefore, I will give a brief defense of the historical reliability of this book. This study is more technical than the others in this book.

The Name Deuteronomy

The Israelites usually used the first two words in the Hebrew text of Deuteronomy, "*elleh haddebarim*," meaning "these are the words," as their title for the book. Sometimes they simply used the shortened form *debarim* ("words"). The name that has become popular in English comes from a translation of Deuteronomy 17:18 in the Septuagint, the most important ancient Greek translation of the Old Testament, usually abbreviated as LXX. Here Moses is asked to make "a copy of this law," and the LXX translated that as "second law" or "repetition of the law." The Latin Vulgate version of the Bible, which was completed by Jerome in AD 405, titled the book

Deuteronomium meaning "second law." And that is from where we get our English title.

This strange history of the name should not trouble devout Bible students too much, as the claims we make for the Scriptures are for the text of the Bible, not the titles. Besides, the title is not entirely inappropriate because it is a second version of the one law given at Sinai and originally recorded in Exodus, Leviticus, and Numbers and because it is structured along the lines of the renewing of the covenant that was originally done at Sinai.

Are These Really the Words of Moses? (1:1)

Deuteronomy begins with the statement, "These are the words that Moses spoke to all Israel beyond the Jordan in the wilderness . . . " (1:1a). In other places too, the book often claims to have a record of the words of Moses (1:5; 31:30). There are references to Moses writing parts of it (31:9, 22, 24). "Other OT books similarly assert Mosaic authorship of Deuteronomy (1 Kings 2:3; 8:53; 2 Kings 14:6; 18:6, 12), as do Jesus and others in the NT."[1] Over the past 200 years or so there has been a strong (but misguided) challenge to the claim that Moses is the main person behind Deuteronomy.

Verse 1 uses the expression "beyond the Jordan" to describe the place from which Moses spoke the words of Deuteronomy. This expression came into use only after the Jordan was crossed, that is, after Moses had died. This points to the hand of an editor in the composition of Deuteronomy. Chapter 34 records the death of Moses, which again is from the hand of someone else. Sometimes there are explanatory notes added to the words of Moses that seem to come from an editor (e.g., 2:10–12, 20–23; 3:11, 13b–14). In this book we will view Deuteronomy as essentially coming from Moses though it contains several editorial touches by others. That is, we believe that Moses really did say what Deuteronomy says he said.

From the beginning of the nineteenth century there was among Biblical scholars a growing acceptance of "higher critical" approaches to the study of Scripture. Along with this came the view that Deuteronomy came from the time of the righteous king Josiah. Some asked whether Deuteronomy was "the book of the Law" that was found around 621 BC during the reign of Josiah, as recorded in 2 Kings 22:8. Some even said that Deuteronomy was a "pious fraud"; that is, that someone had placed the book in the temple so that it would be "found" accidentally. Many said that the writing of Deuteronomy was part of the seventh-century reforms under Josiah.

Josiah clearly seems to have been acting under the influence of the teaching found in Deuteronomy. What is controversial is the claim that

Deuteronomy was written in the time of Josiah. Those who hold this view say that Deuteronomy has a tone like that of the prophets and even opens like the prophetic books that were written during the time of the kings (Isaiah 1:1; Amos 1:1; etc.). In answer we would ask, could not the prophets have been influenced by Deuteronomy rather than vice versa? After all, the influence of Deuteronomy is found in many other sections of the Bible too, including the New Testament. We contend that Josiah and the prophets were influenced by Deuteronomy, which is a much earlier document. After all, the book does claim to contain the words of Moses.

Gordon McConville has given several arguments in support of the view that Deuteronomy came from a time much closer to the time of Moses than claimed by the critics.[2] "First, Deuteronomy shows no knowledge of the main institutions of Israel's political and religious life during the period of the kings, namely the kings themselves and the Jerusalem temple." McConville further points out that Deuteronomy is also unenthusiastic about the idea of a king (17:14–20), merely permitting such a thing, and trying to ensure that the king would not become a tyrant. This law is unlikely to have come from the time of Josiah.

"Secondly," McConville says, "Deuteronomy knows only a single, united Israel, and shows no acquaintance with the division of the nation into two kingdoms following the reign of Solomon, around 930 BC (1 Kings 12)."

"Thirdly, the book warns again and again about the dangers of Canaanite religion (*e.g.* chs. 7, 13)." While this remained a problem until the time of the exile, it was a seriously urgent problem immediately after setting foot in the promised land. And Deuteronomy claims to contain material that prepares the people for their life after they enter the promised land.

"Fourthly, certain laws make best sense in relation to imminent (or recent) occupation of the land." According to Leviticus 17, all slaughter of animals was to be sacrificial and carried out in the tent of meeting, which is where the Israelites worshipped and sacrificed until the temple was built. After settling in the land it would have been too difficult for the people to travel to the tent of meeting every time they wanted to consume meat. Therefore, Deuteronomy permits the secular eating of meat also (12:15–25), indicating that it is talking about a new situation to be faced by the people.

"Fifthly, Deuteronomy shares the concerns of the prophets, namely, the need for heartfelt religion, and a love of justice and the rights of the poor (14:28–29). Yet," says McConville, "it is different from the prophetic books in the sense that it does not address particular occasions and individuals. It has much more the appearance of a programme for the future." McConville says that it is likely "that the prophets take their cue from Deuteronomy, as well as from other parts of the Pentateuch."

McConville's last point is that "it has been shown that Deuteronomy formally resembles certain political treaties made by Hittite kings with weaker states, as well as certain ancient law-codes, such as that of the famous Babylonian king and lawgiver, Hammurabi." Of the eighty or ninety documents of law codes that have been found by archaeologists, Deuteronomy resembles the Hittite treaties from 1400 to 1200 BC, which according to more conservative scholars is the time that Moses lived.

Kenneth A. Kitchen, an esteemed expert in ancient Near Eastern studies from the University of Liverpool, has recently written a 662-page book, *On the Reliability of the Old Testament*, in which he painstakingly presents evidence for the historical reliability of the Old Testament. In his discussion of the Sinai covenant (of which Deuteronomy is a record), he shows how a comparison of the Sinai treaty, as described in the Pentateuch, with ancient Near Eastern treaties gives strong evidence for a dating of the records of the Sinai covenant in the era when Moses is said to have lived. He divides the history of treaties, laws, and covenants into six phases covering 2,000 years. He says, "It is vitally important to understand that the documents of each phase are sharply different in format and full content from those in the phases before and after them. There is no ambiguity."[3]

Kitchen's observations cause him to place Deuteronomy and other records of the Sinai covenant squarely within the fifth phase, which includes the Hittite treaties. This phase covers roughly 1400 to 1200 BC He shows how there is a "glaring contrast" between the Hittite and Sinai treaties on the one hand and the treaties of phase VI which covers roughly 900 to 650 BC and includes Assyrian treaties.[4] His conclusion is:

> The impartial and very extensive evidence (thirty Hittite inspired documents and versions!) sets this matter beyond any further dispute. It is *not* my creation, it is inherent in the mass of original documents *themselves*, and cannot be gainsaid, if the brute facts are to be respected.[5]

The six arguments given above give us confidence to say that the contents of Deuteronomy can be traced to the time of Moses. This is very important in determining our approach to Deuteronomy. Some scholars think it is not important. Recently there has been a return in Biblical studies to studying Biblical books as a whole in the way they are found in the Bible—that is, in their canonical form—without chopping the books up according to the various sources from which different parts of a book are said to have been derived. This chopping up was done a lot in the twentieth century in the heyday of what was known as form criticism. The canonical approach (called canon criticism) is being advocated even by those who would not call themselves evangelical Christians. They study a book as a whole to see what it teaches. This has been a welcome trend, and it has produced some outstanding and helpful studies of Biblical texts.

However, some (not all[6]) people advocating this canonical approach would say that it does not matter if the words attributed to Moses were not said by Moses himself. They say that what we need to learn is the teaching of the book without bothering with historical details. I find that approach unsatisfactory. If Deuteronomy contains God's clear teaching to his people, and if it is inspired so as to become a definite infallible source of authority for our belief and practice, shouldn't we expect its basic historical premise—that these are indeed Moses' words—to be true? After all, it claims to contain the speeches that Moses gave to the Israelites and claims that God is the one who is behind those speeches (1:3)! If the claims it makes for itself are inaccurate, I do not think we could come to the book as being a bearer of ultimate and trustworthy teaching that will have an exclusive and authoritative claim on our thinking and behavior.

The Scriptures contain many radical teachings that run contrary to popular thinking, and embracing those teachings is not easy today. In this environment I cannot see how the Bible could become our reliable and ultimate source of authority for faith and practice if we do not accept some of the things it claims for itself. We could drop things that we don't like by claiming that those statements are not historically reliable and that they do not reflect the mind of God. This is what many have done with radical statements of Christ that present him as divine and absolute Lord. These claims go against the pluralist mood of the present day, and they are rejected on the grounds that they come from a period much later than Jesus and therefore should not be attributed to him.[7] I believe it is not necessary for us to jettison statements in the Bible because of a suspicion that they are not historically accurate. A strong case has been made by several writers in recent years for the historical reliability of both the Old and the New Testaments.[8]

Today people who call themselves Christians are discarding some teachings of the Bible and accepting lifestyles that are contrary to these teachings. For example, homosexual practice, which is explicitly prohibited in Leviticus 18:22; 20:13, is accepted as a legitimate alternate lifestyle by some who call themselves Christians. If we really believed that God gave those commands to Moses, we would be more cautious about discarding them. Deuteronomy clearly teaches that sex belongs within marriage (22:13–29) and that adultery is prohibited (5:18). But adultery is publicly and shamelessly flouted by famous people and reported in the news media as something quite normal. Sadly, the statistics seem to show that the incidence of extramarital sex is quite high among those who call themselves Christians. If Christians understood that God himself gave those prohibitions to Moses, they would be much more reluctant to violate them. And that is the claim that Deuteronomy makes. Deuteronomy 1:3 says, "Moses spoke to the people of Israel according to all that the LORD had given him in commandment to them."

Deuteronomy and Hittite Treaties

Moses' aim in his final speeches is to ensure that the people will remain faithful to God. He reminds them that they are a people under a covenant with God. It probably is not accidental then that the book takes a form somewhat similar to the covenants made by people at that time. We should be cautious about attaching too much significance to the similarities between Deuteronomy and the ancient Hittite treaties that have been discovered. However, the two listings below show the parallels between the parts of a Hittite treaty and the contents of Deuteronomy. Deuteronomy, of course, is not a political treaty like the Hittite treaties but a document describing the covenant between God and his people.

Scholars differ about the precise ways in which the parts of a Hittite treaty should be described. We know for sure that the treaties in Moses' time generally had the six parts (see the column on the left in the chart below). The right column shows Deuteronomy structured according to a pattern that shows remarkable similarities to the Hittite treaties.

Figure 1.1: Hittite Treaties and Deuteronomy

Hittite Treaties	Pattern of Deuteronomy
1. A preamble: announcing the treaty and those who are a party to it	1. Preamble (1:1–5)
2. A historical prologue: remembering the previous relations between the parties	2. Historical prologue (1:6 – 4:49)
3. General stipulations (conditions): setting out the nature of the future relationship between the two parties	3. General stipulations (chs. 5 – 11)
4. Specific stipulations: the detailed requirements applicable to the weaker party	4. Specific stipulations (chs. 12 – 26)
5. Witnesses: gods were called to witness the treaty	5. Witnesses (ch. 32). Calls on heaven and earth to witness the words of Israel
6. Blessings and curses: these are pronounced for loyalty and disloyalty respectively	6. Blessings and curses (chs. 27, 28)

The six features in the pattern of Deuteronomy introduce us to six very important features in a healthy life of faith. We will have occasion to look at them in some detail in the rest of this book.

Disobedience Slows Us Down (1:1–3)

The first three verses of Deuteronomy give some introductory historical and geographical notes. Verse 1 says that the words of this book were spoken by Moses "beyond the Jordan in the wilderness, in the Arabah opposite Suph. . . ." The Arabah was a rift valley running from the Sea of Galilee in the north all the way to the Gulf of Aqaba, which is some distance south of the Dead Sea. Verse 5 also gives the historical context: "Beyond the Jordan, in the land of Moab, Moses undertook to explain this law. . . ." God's people are in the northern part of the Arabah. The promised lands east of the River Jordan have been conquered. Now it is time to go into the main portion of the promised land west of the Jordan.

Verse 2 makes a strange observation: "It is eleven days' journey from Horeb by the way of Mount Seir to Kadesh-barnea." Horeb is another name for Sinai and is the preferred name in Deuteronomy (Deuteronomy uses the word Sinai only once [33:2]). Kadesh-barnea is where they camped after leaving Horeb. This is at the border of the promised land, and it is from here that they sent the twelve spies to check out the land (Numbers 13; Deuteronomy 1:19–25). They had left Horeb a long time ago. Verse 3 even gives the time that these events took place: "In the fortieth year, on the first day of the eleventh month . . . " This is the only time specification in the whole book. And "fortieth year" refers to the time calculated from when they left Egypt.

There seems to be a reason for mentioning the eleven-day journey just before mentioning the fortieth year. It takes eleven days to travel from Horeb to the border of Canaan. But it took forty years for the whole journey from Egypt to Canaan. They traveled for about two years before coming to Kadesh. This means it took about thirty-eight years to go from the border of Canaan to Canaan itself and only eleven days to go from Horeb to the border. That is the price of disobedience! The thirty-eight-year wilderness wandering was a punishment for the stubborn disobedience of the people. Deuteronomy will refer to this many times. Disobedience never pays. God will forgive us when we repent, but the consequences of sin make it sheer folly to disobey. Disobedience slows down our progress!

Verse 3 says that "Moses spoke to the people of Israel according to all that the LORD had given him in commandment to them." The book consists of God's words given in a specific historical setting. Here it differs in style from the Qur'an, which contains absolute statements that claim to be directly given by God. In the Bible the style of the writers and the contents of their writings differ according to their personalities, experiences, and the specific cultural situations in which they lived. If we are to fully understand the meaning of a text we must work hard to understand the context from which it arose. This makes for an exciting lifelong pilgrimage of discovery as we seek to understand the Bible.

The fact that Deuteronomy was written to a specific context adds a freshness and relevance to it. The places, people, and experiences mentioned in Deuteronomy are real. This is why the Bible is so relevant to everyday life. I will never forget a conversation I had one day with a colleague working in our drug rehab ministry while we were traveling to our rehab center. We were talking about the things of the Lord, and suddenly my colleague said, "When I read Paul's epistles, I feel that Paul himself may have been a drug addict at some time." He told me that the struggle with sin that Paul records in Romans 7 is very similar to the experience of drug dependents. Our study of Deuteronomy will show how relevant it is to our lives today.

Moses Gives the People God's Word (1:3b, 5, 6)

A Practically Relevant Word from God (1:3b, 5)

Moses is an aged leader who has led his people from slavery to the brink of possessing a land that will be permanently theirs. He knows he is soon going to die. Now he speaks for the last time to these people whom he has led for forty years. He is considered by many to be the greatest national leader in history. You can imagine the eager anticipation of the audience. These messages will need to be motivational in tone because the people have a river to cross and a few battles to win before they take possession of the land. They will also need to be exhortational, because the people will face many temptations to disobedience, and remaining faithful to God is going to be a big challenge.

What approach would Moses take? Would he dazzle the people with creativity and brilliance that would elicit praise from them for his eloquence? That is what many consider to be a great speech today. Moses' intention is not to leave an impression of his brilliance. He has a far more important task before him. He has to give people the word of God that will mediate to the people the health and stability they need in order to face their challenges successfully.

Verse 3b says, "Moses spoke to the people of Israel according to all that the LORD had given him in commandment to them." Verse 5 explains this further: "Beyond the Jordan, in the land of Moab, Moses undertook to explain this law." What the people needed most was not eloquence or attractive speeches. They needed a word from God.

A short while later, when commissioning Moses' successor Joshua, God told Joshua, "This Book of the Law shall not depart from your mouth, but you shall meditate on it day and night, so that you may be careful to do according to all that is written in it. For then you will make your way prosperous, and then you will have good success" (Joshua 1:8). The path of prosperity and success for Joshua was the path of obedience to the Word of God. It would be so for Joshua's people too. So when Moses addresses them, just before Joshua is appointed, he expounds God's Word to them.

When will we learn that our great responsibility as leaders is to get our people into the Word? That is what will help them successfully tackle the challenges they face. I think one reason for the woeful statistics, showing that Christians are not behaving very differently from non-Christians today, is that the church has focused much on keeping the people entertained and much less on making them strong through the Word. In this marketing-oriented era we have concentrated on providing people a program they will like and have neglected our responsibility to give them "the whole counsel of God" (Acts 20:27). Jesus asked God to "sanctify them in the truth; your word is truth" (John 17:17). People who are not properly fed the Word will not be sanctified.

I am amazed at how many Christian leaders today think that it is not appropriate to expound the Scriptures in their regular preaching to their people. A prominent evangelical leader once told me that he exegetes society more than exegeting the Scriptures so that he can give a relevant message to the people. But wouldn't the message of the Creator to his creation be most relevant to people? Indeed, because the Bible is a message for all time we will need to work hard at applying its eternal message to a particular context. Yes, we must exegete society, but it is even more important to exegete Scripture because that is where the power to change lives lies.

The challenge to exegete both Scripture and society and then integrate the results into an attractive and powerful message calls for hard work. But our desire to faithfully fulfill our call would make us take on this tough challenge. I believe a primary reason for the scarcity of relevant expository preaching in the church today is that preachers are not willing to devote the time needed to do that well.

Another reason is that we live in a postmodern society where the value of objective truth has been greatly diminished. This affects us because objective truth is basic to Christianity, and it is given to us in the Bible. Therefore, today we need evangelists for objective truth. Earlier we had the challenge of convincing people that the gospel is the truth. Now we have the more basic challenge of convincing people that truth is valuable, necessary, and appealing.

Some people say that Biblical preaching does not attract people anymore. The answer to that is not to stop doing Biblical preaching. It is to do it in a way that is attractive. We may use creative means of communication and the new methods that are currently popular in society. We can use things like story, drama, film, PowerPoint, dialogue, and discussion. But the driving force should be the Scriptures. That should never be dethroned by the methods we are using. All the methods are servants of the truth of the Word that needs to be communicated.

A Year of Equipping the People (1:6)

The major job of equipping the people with God's Word took place at Horeb (Sinai) when God gave Moses the Law and Moses explained it to the people. In Deuteronomy, Moses reminds the people of the things they were taught at Horeb. Moses' first speech begins with God telling the people that they had stayed long enough at Horeb and that now it was time for them to move on (1:6). They had to spend approximately a year (see Exodus 19:1; Numbers 10:11) at Mount Horeb[9] learning from God before they went any farther. After that year God says, "You have stayed long enough at this mountain" (1:6) and commands them to proceed with the journey. This long stay follows the pattern of God giving people an extended period of preparation before they launch out into difficult projects.

Moses started his leadership of the Israelites at the ripe old age of eighty years. It would look like a waste of time for him to be hidden for so long while there was the urgent need of delivering his suffering people. Need or no need, we must let people be spiritually prepared for the challenges they face before giving them the huge responsibility of leadership. So Jesus started his public ministry only when he was "about 30 years of age" (Luke 3:23). Paul became an evangelist immediately after his conversion, but several years elapsed before he joined Barnabas to begin what would become his life's work.

Paul asks Timothy not to appoint recent converts to leadership in the church, because they could get conceited and become prey to Satan's devices (1 Timothy 3:6). Some new believers seem eminently qualified for leadership, because they have the personality and gifts that go into making a good leader. Others have so much enthusiasm for the work that, given the shortage of leaders, we see them as the answer to our need for people to carry out our programs. But until the Word has taken solid root in their lives they are too immature to handle the challenges of Christian leadership. They will be forced to become something they are not. They begin to live beyond their resources and are vulnerable to Satan's tricks. One of the most important ingredients of nurturing leaders is feeding them with the Word and developing them into people of the Book. By that we mean that they should know the Word (2 Timothy 3:14–17), know how to handle the Word (2 Timothy 2:15), and depend on the Word for guidance (Psalm 109:105).

2

Keys to Launching out into Fresh Exploits

DEUTERONOMY 1:4–8

DEUTERONOMY BEGINS WITH an introduction that explained when and where Moses gave the speeches that formed the bulk of the book (1:1–5). His first speech (1:6—4:43) will major on the history of the people up to that point. The historical section charts the progress of the people after the time they spent in Horeb (or Sinai) where God gave them the Law. The start of Moses' speech gives God's command to the people to launch into what should have been the last leg of their journey to the promised land after a year at Mt. Horeb. Sadly, their disobedience made it only a penultimate stage of the journey. Yet we see some interesting features of Moses' strategy to motivate them to move forward on this crucial journey. It gives us some keys to launching out into fresh exploits.

The Inspiration: Past Victories (1:4, 5)

First, however, we will look at verse 4, which is part of the introduction of the book of Deuteronomy before the record of Moses' first speech. The whole book is also intended to motivate the people to enter the promised land and to live faithfully to God in the land, and what is found in verse 4 will help motivate them to do this. It says that Moses gave the speeches of Deuteronomy "after he had defeated Sihon the king of the Amorites, who lived in Heshbon, and Og the king of Bashan, who lived in Ashtaroth and in Edrei." The next verse shows that because of these two victories the people have now come to the brink of the main part of the promised land and have even taken over the lands east of Jordan that God had planned to give them: "Beyond the Jordan, in the land of Moab, Moses undertook to explain this law" (1:5).

The significance of the victory over the kings Sihon and Og is evidenced by the fact that, apart from the two basic descriptions of this event in Numbers and Deuteronomy (Numbers 21:21–26; Deuteronomy 2:26—3:11), the victory is mentioned four other times in Deuteronomy (1:4; 4:46–47; 29:7–8; 31:4) and eleven times in other parts of the Old Testament,[1] yielding a total of seventeen occurrences. The victory appears as part of a song of praise three times (Numbers 21:27–32; Psalm 135:10–12; 136:17–22).

The reason for the frequent repetition is that God's intervention in giving us victories in the past gives us confidence and the assurance of God's similar intervention as we face present challenges. This is well expressed in the promise God gave to Joshua when he commissioned him: "No man shall be able to stand before you all the days of your life. Just as I was with Moses, so I will be with you. I will not leave you or forsake you" (Joshua 1:5). The same idea appears in the frequent way in which God and Biblical writers describe God as the God of Abraham and of Isaac and of Jacob or the God who made a covenant with those three patriarchs. I found twenty-two occurrences of this idea in the Bible, one of them in the present passage (Deuteronomy 1:8).[2]

The tragedy is that after all the Israelites saw of God's provision, intervention, and victory, when they were faced with big challenges they almost always lost heart and rebelled against God. Unfortunately, we do the same thing! When there is a tough challenge we grumble and say that God is not looking after us. I am writing this in the USA where I am spending five weeks during a writing break. Owing to some practical problems my wife is not with me. I have three such times of separation on this trip. And sometimes I revolt against the idea and act as if God has failed me. It is hard to travel alone. But hardship is an essential part of the Christian life. I need to keep telling myself that the Lord who has looked after me all these years will do so this time too.

Sometimes when things are not working out as we wish and we are faced with huge challenges, we reject the idea of waiting on God to act, and we try to solve our problems our way. In Sri Lanka it is sometimes very difficult for Christian women to find spouses who are committed to Christ. As they get older and are still unmarried, some of them say they have waited long enough and take matters into their own hands and marry an unbeliever.

I have heard many Christians say that God has not looked after them even though they were faithful to God. This is something we must not say. We are people who were headed for an eternal Hell, and that was because we deserved it. And God has given us an eternal home in Heaven. How small our momentary troubles are in comparison with our eternal reward (2 Corinthians

4:17)! But even during our brief life as Christians God has helped us so many times, and he has helped others we know. And what about all that the Bible tells us about how God looks after his people?

The mention of the victory over the two kings Sihon and Og seventeen times in the Bible encourages us also to use our past victories, which demonstrated God's faithfulness and power, as encouragements to pursue God's way in anticipation of final victory.

The Occasion: God's Guidance (1:6, 7)

The God Who Guides (1:6)

Moses' first speech begins with God's summons to the people to leave Horeb and proceed northward toward the promised land: "The LORD our God said to us in Horeb, 'You have stayed long enough at this mountain. Turn and take your journey, and go to the hill country of the Amorites and to all their neighbors in the Arabah'" (1:6, 7). Note that Moses refers to God as "the LORD our God" (1:6). This way of identifying God points to the covenant relationship between God and the people. The word "LORD" is a translation of the Hebrew word probably spelled as "*Yahweh*,"[3] which is the covenant name of God. (The usual Hebrew word for Lord, *adonay*, is translated as "Lord" in most English translations.) The Israelites seem to have been reluctant to pronounce the distinctive name of God and chose to use the word *Lord* when reading the Old Testament. The expressions "LORD our God" or "LORD your God" appear 260 times in Deuteronomy. We belong to him, and in a sense he belongs to us in a covenant relationship. That is the most important thing about us. We are his, and he is ours.

As we face challenges in our lives, as we launch into challenging exploits—like a new job or a difficult project—often all we have to fall back on is the knowledge that the Lord is *our God*. Things may look bleak. The task may be very difficult. It may seem like a huge risk to launch out into the dark unknown. But we know that he has promised to look after us and that we have tried to be obedient to him. As our God, he has been with us before and has seen us through, and we can trust him to see us through again. Sometimes when problems come we are tempted to give up. Then we brace ourselves because of the promises, and we persevere.

As leaders we must spur people along the path of obedience, when they get discouraged and want to give up, by pointing them to the God who is with them. Some who have faced many tough experiences and failures in life may tend to lose hope when the going gets tough. They can't believe that God will look after them. A timid Christian is buying a house, and he faces many obstacles along the way. When the problems keep mounting, he considers giving up and going on living in rented housing without purchasing his own house. A Christian friend spurs him on to believe in God and persevere so that he ultimately experiences God's good provision. A woman doing a difficult ministry faces so many obstacles, failures, and disappointments that she is considering giving up the work. A friend urges her to accept the truth of 1 Thessalonians 5:24: "He who calls you is faithful; he will surely do it."

A word of prayer with such people, an exhortation, or a gentle rebuke will help them stay on course. Moses motivated the people by constantly reminding them that the Lord of the universe is their God in a covenant relationship.

The Time to Move Forward (1:6, 7)

Before commanding the people, God says, "You have stayed long enough at this mountain" (1:6). This refers to their yearlong stay at Horeb. Then he tells them to start journeying and gives a long list of places they are to go to: "Turn and take your journey, and go to the hill country of the Amorites and to all their neighbors in the Arabah, in the hill country and in the lowland and in the Negeb and by the seacoast, the land of the Canaanites, and Lebanon, as far as the great river, the river Euphrates" (1:7). This is a command to go and occupy the land originally promised on oath to Abraham and his descendants (Genesis 15:18–21).

After a year of being taught by God at Mt. Horeb (Sinai), now the time has come to move forward. The preparation time is over; now is the time to act. They are asked to "turn" or "break camp" (NIV). The Hebrew word translated "turn" (*panah*) is used sixteen times in Deuteronomy. It appears seven times in connection with the record of the journey from Horeb to Moab in chapters 1—3.[4] McConville says that the word "carries the connotation of decision, a leaving behind and setting the face to the new destination." After a period of learning, they need to launch out into the active path of progress.

Often in life we have to make decisions to move away from where we are and travel in another direction. When the time to do that has come, we cannot delay. We have to "break camp," say good-bye to the things and people we are comfortable with, and decisively move forward. In this process we need to be very sensitive to God so that we sense what his mind is on this launch forward. Often he gives us a sense that the time is ripe for us to move.

Sometimes when we know that we need to do a certain action, we delay doing it. I find that when I am writing a book, one of the hardest things is to start writing a new chapter. I may have taken a break from writing after completing the previous chapter in order to read or take a rest. The laziness regarding starting may cause me to think of many other things that need to be done so that I "cannot" start the writing. I may do further study even though I have read enough to start writing. I may decide that my desk needs to be cleared up or that I need to do some visiting.

Sometimes when we should be moving forward decisively we keep asking questions, claiming that we want to clear our doubts, but in reality they are tactics to delay doing something difficult. When the powerful King Nebuchadnezzar found out that Shadrach, Meshach, and Abednego refused to bow down before the great image that he had built, he lectured them and said he was giving them one more chance to save their lives. They faced the prospect of being thrown into a fiery furnace. The king taunted them with his final challenge: "But if you do not worship, you shall immediately be cast into a burning fiery furnace. And who is the god who will deliver you out of my hands?" (Daniel 3:15). The young men calmly replied, "O Nebuchadnezzar, we have no need to answer you in this matter" (Daniel 3:16). The king already knew about their God and his power, so there was no need to talk any more about this. This was not the time for discussion; this was time for action. Their decision had been made. They were going to obey God rather than the king!

The founder of Operation Mobilization, George Verwer, is credited with having said, "Some people say they are waiting for a call. What they need is not a call. That they have already received. What they need is a kick in the pants!" Once the decision to move forward is made, then there is no turning back.

The Motivation: The Promise of God (1:8)

Promises Contingent on Obedience

The command is followed by an encouragement to persevere based on the promise that God had made to the fathers of the Israelite nation. "See, I have set the land before you. Go in and take possession of the land that the LORD swore to your fathers, to Abraham, to Isaac, and to Jacob, to give to them and to their offspring after them" (1:8). First he says, "See, I have set the land before you." What the ESV translates as "set" the NIV translates as "given," though the more literal "set" may be more appropriate here. The NASB translates the expression as, "I have placed the land before you." It's there for the taking, but the people have to go in and take it. So God continues, "Go in and take possession of the land that the LORD swore to your fathers."

The generation that was given this command refused to obey God and did not take hold of the promise. Therefore, only their children entered the promised land. Earl Kalland explains, "The promise . . . was irrevocable, but the fulfillment in time and personnel was contingent on the people's obedience to the Lord's directives to enter, conquer, and take possession of the land." The blessing that God gives his people is freely available for us to take hold of, but we must obey. If we turn away from God's path, these promises are going to be fulfilled in the lives of others. Churches that were vibrant at one time may die spiritually, but God will raise up other groups to demonstrate vital Christianity to the nation.

There is a warning for us here. Though the promises of God are there for us to take hold of and enjoy, we could forfeit the blessing by disobeying even though we, like Moses' generation, have experienced many blessings in the past. We must not take the promises for granted. We must always be alert lest the place of blessedness that God intended for us is taken away from us and given to another. That this does happen is evidenced by the fact that many who showed great potential at one time end their lives in defeat and fruitlessness, while others from whom we did not expect much end up being mightily used by God. Paul said, "But I discipline my body and keep it under control, lest after preaching to others I myself should be disqualified" (1 Corinthians 9:27).

The verb translated "take possession" (*yarash*) "appears about fifty times in Deuteronomy relative to Israel's occupation of the land."[5] Important but difficult tasks could be neglected or not done owing to disobedience; therefore they need to be reiterated. Jesus did this with the Great Commission, which appears at least seven times in the record of the last week of his life and the events that followed the resurrection.[6]

The Promises Are Repeated

Perhaps an even greater motivation to obedience is the promise of God. So the land they are to possess is described as "the land that the LORD swore to your fathers, to Abraham, to Isaac, and to Jacob, to give to them and to their offspring after them" (1:8). T. W. Cartledge points out that "in the OT, any promise of God is tantamount to an oath."[7] So the use of the verb "swear" for God's promises is most appropriate. This verb (*shaba*) appears thirty-three times in Deuteronomy—twenty times in connection with the promise of the land, eight times in connection with God's promise to show his covenant love and care for Israel, three times to refer to God's swearing that Moses and his generation will not enter the land, and twice to refer to human oaths.

There is no doubt about God keeping his promises. The problem is that we lose hope, give up on God, and try to get what we want by another route. We need to be reminded over and over about the promises of God. When God first spoke to Abraham he promised him three things—a large nation arising from him (Genesis 12:2), a land (Genesis 12:1, 7), and that he would be a blessing (Genesis 12:2, 3). These three promises appear in verses 10, 8, and 11 respectively in Deuteronomy 1.

According to the Bible the promises of God are a great aid to obedience. Peter says, ". . . he has granted to us his precious and very great promises, so that through them you may become partakers of the divine nature, having escaped from the corruption that is in the world because of sinful desire" (2 Peter 1:4). When our sinful desires threaten to take us away from God's path, we remind ourselves of the promises. When we think that we need to watch something unclean on the Internet or on TV in order to get pleasure, we remind ourselves of the promise that "no good thing does he withhold from those who walk uprightly" (Psalm 84:11). God will give us the pleasure we need if we obey him. So disobedience is both unnecessary and harmful to us. Those who start an affair giving the excuse that their spouses do not satisfy them also make this mistake and a serious error in judgment.

Our passage gets the speeches of Moses off to a very positive start. The future is as bright as the promises of God. How sad that those who first heard the words of verses 6–8 in their original context did not see those promises fulfilled in their lifetime. But their children did, because they believed the promises and heeded God's command to obey him. They conquered the opposition and occupied the land. Those struggling with the challenge of obedience, perhaps discouraged by the behavior of their leaders and spiritual ancestors, do not need to give up. The promises of God come over and over to them. God's promises are like oaths; they are sure. "He who calls you is faithful; he will surely do it" (1 Thessalonians 5:24).

3

Leadership and Growth

DEUTERONOMY 1:9–15

MANY CONSIDER MOSES TO BE the greatest national leader in history, an opinion with which I concur. So the story of Moses would be a good source for learning about great leadership. This study will look at two key issues that leaders of growing movements deal with: stress and delegation. Our passage (1:9–15) is part of Moses' first speech (1:6—4:43) given at the gateway to the main portion of the promised land to the west of the River Jordan. In this speech Moses gives a historical survey of what had happened to the people from the time they left Horeb (Sinai) up to the point where they were at that time.

Here he talks about how he appointed leaders to take over some of his burden. The parallel account in Exodus 18 says that this was initiated by Moses' father-in-law Jethro. Here it looks like Moses initiated it. This does not mean that one account is right and the other wrong. The difference in the two accounts shows the difference in perspective. In the Deuteronomy passage the focus is on Moses and his relationship with the people. There is no need to mention Jethro's role here. Though it is not mentioned, neither is it denied. Jethro initiated the idea, and Moses fully accepted it and made it his own.

Growth and Stress (1:9–12)

Stress Is Inevitable in a Growing Movement (1:9, 10)

After recording how God asked the people to leave Horeb (Sinai) and travel toward the promised land, Moses says, "At that time I said to you, 'I am not able to bear you by myself. The LORD your God has multiplied you, and behold, you are today as numerous as the stars of heaven'" (1:9, 10). The time Moses is speaking of is the period prior to the departure from Horeb. Moses says that the stress he is experiencing is because the people have multiplied so rapidly.

Any leader of a growing movement will face stress. Paul tells the Corinthians, "And, apart from other things, there is the daily pressure on me of my anxiety for all the churches. Who is weak, and I am not weak? Who is made to fall, and I am not indignant?" (2 Corinthians 11:28, 29). Christians are not perfected this side of Heaven. Leaders who love their people, as Paul gives evidence of doing in this passage, will experience stress over the people's imperfections. That is an aspect of love: concern for the imperfect object of love.

Yet there can be unnecessary stress. As we shall shortly see, some of Moses' stress was unnecessary.

We Must Talk about Our Stress (1:9–12)

Moses and Paul did not keep their stress to themselves and suffer alone. Our passage and the passage from Paul quoted above show that they talked about the problem openly. Leaders need to talk about their problems, wisely and in the right setting, so they can find solutions to those problems. In this way we involve God and other people in finding a solution to the problems.

Some people who bear their stress alone without sharing the pain of it with anyone end up angry with the church or organization they serve in and angry with the people with whom they work. They don't make good leaders because their anger gets in the way of acting in a healthy manner. Leaders sometimes need to be angry with their people and with situations so they can be motivated to bring about change. But unshared anger soon turns to bitterness that is destructive to people and organizations.

Bitter leaders usually cause others to lose their motivation and enthusiasm because they say things that hurt and dampen that enthusiasm. Their attitude also often fosters disunity in the body. Without the security of having a stable leader, the people also get insecure, and in their insecurity they do things that hurt others and break unity. Their bitterness makes them become bad Christians because they lack the joy of the Lord, which is a key ingredient of Christian character.

Good leaders are change agents. They have an ambition to see their group healthy, mature, and fruitful. When they see themselves losing their motivation, they realize that this will be a huge obstacle to healthy growth. So they talk about the problems with a view to finding solutions to them.

The People's Problems Become the Leader's Problems (1:12)

In verse 12 Moses gives another reason for his stress: "How can I bear by myself the weight and burden of you and your strife?" Three causes are given here: their "weight," their "burden," and their "strife."

It is difficult to say what the exact difference is between "weight" and "burden." The NIV and certain other translations render "weight" as "problems." The only other time this Hebrew word appears in the Old Testament is in a very negative context: ". . . they have become a burden to me; I am weary of bearing them" (Isaiah 1:14b). These people were certainly a headache to Moses. They grumbled constantly; they rebelled so often that the term "stiff-necked" (meaning "stubborn") is used of them eight times in Exodus and Deuteronomy (NIV). Yet when people grumble, leaders cannot just ignore it. They must respond. It hurts them, as we see in the case of Moses who sometimes overreacted to their grumbling. These overreactions cost him the opportunity to go into the promised land.

The second word is translated "burden" by both the ESV and NIV, and it appears thirty-four times in the Bible, often in a positive way. In most of these occurrences it refers to the burdens that one must carry as one's duty. The dictionary defines it as "burden, load, cargo, that which is lifted up/ carried."[1] This fits in with our understanding of this word as referring to the duties of leadership. Keil and Delitzsch explain, "The burden and cumbrance of the nation are the nation itself, with all its affairs and transactions, which pressed upon the shoulders of Moses." Few aspiring for the position of leadership realize the responsibility that leadership entails. Perhaps if they see that before becoming leaders, they would not aspire to leadership so eagerly.

The third cause for stress in verse 12 is described as "your strife." This must refer to the legal disputes about which we are told in verses 16, 17. Here is another factor that saps the energy of leaders: disunity. The psalmist says, "Behold, how good and pleasant it is when brothers dwell in unity!" (Psalm 133:1). But when there is no unity, it is not good and it is not pleasant. Disunity affects the morale of all who are actively involved. And it drains the energy of the leader.

Often today leaders ignore unity issues that crop up in their work. Sometimes they get a specialist to handle it. Sometimes they simply dismiss the person who is alleged to be the cause of the problem from the group to which he or she belongs. But that is not the Biblical method. Paul's epistles, especially 1 Corinthians and Philippians, show that he got actively involved in solving unity problems. Leaders have to confront the issues and work toward unity. I can say that in my thirty-four years in the leadership of Youth for

Christ/Sri Lanka, nothing sapped my emotional strength more than disunity among the leaders. I did not like to face the issue, as it is usually very unpleasant, but I had no choice.

What this passage goes on to say, however, is that one leader does not need to confront all the problems alone. Some responsibilities can be delegated to others.

Delegation (1:11, 13, 15)

We Must Not Stop Growth (1:11)

In Moses' case we see that his stress was caused by growth, and growth is a blessing. As McConville says, "The 'problem' is actually a function of blessing." When a movement grows, new problems will arise. Some will complain about these and keep talking about the "good old days." Usually those who complain about the "good old days" were complainers during the supposedly good old days, too! Change does come with growth, and we cannot avoid that.

One solution to this problem is to have things nice and small, so that the leader can control everything. Usually micromanagers—leaders who want to be in control of every little detail—cannot lead large and growing groups. Usually micromanaging leaders are insecure people who are afraid to risk entrusting major responsibilities to others. Their insecurity causes them to be threatened by capable and creative people. It is dangerous to hand over the leadership of growing movements to such people.

Moses had no regrets about the growth of Israel, even though he had to face huge challenges because of that growth. So he says, "May the LORD, the God of your fathers, make you a thousand times as many as you are and bless you, as he has promised you!" (1:11). He wishes for the growth to take place even more rapidly. Similarly, leaders today must be very careful about stifling a growing segment of the group of which they are leaders.

For us the numerical growth of the church means that many people who were lost are saved, unless the church specializes in stealing the sheep belonging to other flocks! The vision of the lostness of people without Christ gives us a passion for numerical growth. The passion for the lost is well expressed by Paul: "For it is all for your sake, so that as grace extends to more and more people it may increase thanksgiving, to the glory of God" (2 Corinthians 4:15). The greatest affront to God is that people who were created to live under his lordship live in rebellion against him. Therefore, the glory that comes to God through lost people who find Christ is immense. We have the privilege of playing a part in enhancing the glory of God through evangelism. So when people come to Christ we are thrilled, not primarily because we have grown, but because lost people have found salvation and God has been glorified.

So we must not stop growth. But with growth comes new problems, and we need to deal with those.

Delegation: A Key to Conquering Stress (1:13, 17c)

The stress that Moses had was unnecessarily aggravated by the fact that he had not delegated some of his responsibilities. This problem had become acute because the people had multiplied. Indeed, the leadership must confront the problems of the people. But one leader does not need to do all the confronting. We are not messiahs; we do not need to do everything that needs to be done by the leadership of a group. We need to find leaders who can share the burden with us. This is what Moses does. He tells the people, "Choose for your tribes wise, understanding, and experienced men, and I will appoint them as your heads" (1:13). From now on only the extreme cases will be brought to Moses who will act as something like the Chief Justice. In verse 17c Moses says, "And the case that is too hard for you, you shall bring to me, and I will hear it."

Delegation is a key to overcoming un-Biblical stress in the life of a leader. Before that, of course, we need to invest in people so that they understand the inside workings of our group. Clearly the Israelites had such people who could be appointed to the role. We have to open up ourselves and our dreams to others. Then we have to trust them to carry the ball and move forward. Unfortunately, the controlling type of micromanager may not have people available to take on such responsibilities. Often they have young and enthusiastic workers who are excited by the program and are willing to work under the controlling leader. But once they become mature and have visions of their own, they find the environment too restricting, and they leave. This is usually very painful because often controlling leaders have cared for their people sacrificially. So it is very painful to see them depart.

In our passage it is implied that Moses is not going to know many of the problems faced by the people. Leaders need to keep in touch with the people and ensure that the organizational structure does not isolate them from contact with the rank and file. But they are not going to know everything that is happening like they did when the group was small. This is part of the surrender that takes place with appointing leaders and trusting them to lead.

That Moses was willing to surrender control is evidenced through an incident that may have taken place at the same time that the leaders were appointed. It was when the Spirit fell on seventy elders resulting in their prophesying (Numbers 11:16–30). Moses is informed that two individuals, Eldad and Medad, were prophesying in their camp apart from the group that met under Moses. Moses' loyal assistant Joshua says, "My lord Moses, stop them" (Numbers 11:28). Moses' response shows that he was not worried that good things were happening without his knowledge or control: "Are you jealous for my sake? Would that all the LORD's people were prophets, that the LORD would put his Spirit on them!" (Numbers 11:29).

Nine verses after this statement we read the words, "Now the man Moses was very meek, more than all people who were on the face of the earth" (Numbers 12:3). The secret of his greatness was that he was not a self-serving leader. Leadership was not a thing that he used to boost his status. As movements grow, leaders will need to let go of some of their control and let others do things that they once did and liked doing.

Sometimes the new leaders may do things differently than the way we did them. Because personalities differ, leadership styles and methods of doing things will also differ from leader to leader. But if the basic principles are not violated, we must give the new leaders the freedom to do things their way. Even God included the respect for personality differences in the forming of Scripture. This is why we have four different Gospels recording the life and work of Jesus in four different styles. The Muslims find this difficult to understand because they see the Qur'an as inspired in the sense that Muhammad was only a passive recipient of the words of God—like a typewriter. When God gave us the Bible, he permitted the personality of the authors to be stamped on the material they wrote, a factor that makes Bible study so much more exciting.

I had the great privilege of speaking at the International Conference of Operation Mobilization (OM) at which the leadership mantel of OM was passed on from its founder George Verwer to Peter Maiden. Verwer had led the movement for forty-five years. Among the tributes given at this gathering was one by Alfy Franks, a close associate of Verwer and the first leader of the work in India. He said that Verwer had told him that he did not agree with about 25 percent of the financial and administrative decisions that the movement took as it grew. But he allowed the administrative people to go the way they felt was best for the organization. I think these disagreements were not on basic principles but on how to apply those principles.

Great people focus on the grand task and impart the vision of this to others. They allow these other leaders to implement the vision they imparted in the way that they (the other leaders) think is best. Under such a leadership structure Operation Mobilization was able to have an amazing impact for the kingdom of God. An estimated one billion people have been touched by this work through book exhibitions on the ships, literature evangelism, ministry teams, and other projects. They now have about 100,000 workers worldwide.

The Small Group Method (1:15)

The method of delegation adopted by Moses was somewhat similar to the small group method popular in growing churches today. Verse 15 says, "So I took the heads of your tribes, wise and experienced men, and set them as heads over you, commanders of thousands, commanders of hundreds, commanders of fifties, commanders of tens, and officers, throughout your tribes." Usually one cannot really care properly for over ten to fifteen people. If we have too many people to supervise, some will get neglected. You cannot see to the needs of everyone, and even if you do address these needs you cannot do much about them as you are overstretched.

When Jesus, the Savior of the world, lived on earth with many of the limitations of humans, he too needed to narrow his focus to concentrate on a smaller group of people to whom he could hand over the leadership of his work. "He called his disciples and chose from them twelve, whom he named apostles" (Luke 6:13). Mark gives two reasons for appointing these twelve apostles: "And he appointed twelve (whom he also named apostles) so that *they might be with him* and *he might send them out to preach*" (Mark 3:14). He loved the whole world and died for everyone, but when he lived on earth he could "be with" and train only a few people to send out as preachers.

Today we are seeing different structures that are trying to apply this small group principle. They are called by different names—cell groups, house groups, home fellowships, class meetings, home cells, G-12—and there is a variation in the culture of the different groups. But hopefully the principle that it is a means of caring for the flock is present in all the groups.

Appointing Leaders (1:13–15)

Qualifications for Leadership (1:13)

In verse 13 Moses gives the qualifications needed for being chosen to the leadership role he is proposing: "Choose for your tribes wise, understanding, and experienced men, and I will appoint them as your heads." Leaders must be "wise" and "understanding." These two qualities are similar, though the second seems to have more of the meaning of discernment.[2] Putting together two similar words like this strengthens the meaning, giving the resultant meaning of "very wise" (a literary device known as hendiadys).[3] Leaders have to make many important decisions that impact many others and give advice in crucial situations. Therefore, we need to ensure that the persons appointed as leaders have sufficient practical wisdom.

Seniority alone is an insufficient qualification for this position. Leaders need to have the abilities required for the job. Zeal and talent alone are not enough. They must be able to direct that zeal and talent in wise ways. Some people are particularly gifted with wisdom. But even for them wisdom is fine-tuned through experience. At least three requirements are needed for that fine tuning. First, they must know God's Word. The importance of this is underscored in the commissioning of Joshua when God told him, "This Book of the Law shall not depart from your mouth, but you shall meditate on it day and night, so that you may be careful to do according to all that is written in it. For then you will make your way prosperous, and then you will have good success" (Joshua 1:8).

The second ingredient in fine-tuning wisdom is knowledge of the world in which we live. Jesus, with his true-to-life parables, and Paul, with his knowledge of the ideas and laws of the Gentiles he went to, showed that they knew about the inner and outer lives of the people with whom they were dealing. The Swiss theologian Karl Barth (1886–1968) is credited with having said that the preacher must have the Bible in one hand and the newspaper in the other. This knowledge of the world also comes by simply being observant—watching what goes on in the world around us with the interest of a professional. John Wesley was walking with one of his preachers when they encountered two women quarreling. The preacher suggested that they walk on, but Wesley checked him. "Stay, Sammy, stay," he said, "and learn to preach!"[4]

The third ingredient needed for acquiring wisdom is personal work. Skill in putting the knowledge of the Word and of the world into effective use comes from practicing its application in our lives and in the lives of those with whom we live and work. This is why working with people is so important, though it may be time-consuming and seemingly takes us away from what looks like our primary call. For example, a preacher may complain about having to visit hospitals as that takes him away from his sermon preparation. But the hospital is a good place to learn how to apply what we know of Christianity. This is why even specialists need to do some personal work. This is not a world in which machines and productivity are most important. Machines and productivity are servants of the most important factor in this world—human beings. Therefore leaders in the field of ideas, like theologians, and organizational leaders, like pastors and executives, should be skilled in dealing with people.

The next qualification for leadership is what the ESV, NASB, and McConville translate as "experienced" and the NIV and NRSV as "respected" and "reputable" respectively. This Hebrew word is found 873 times in the Old Testament and takes a wide variety of meanings that must be decided on based on the context.[5] This accounts for the divergent translations here. The basic meaning of this word is "know" and may refer to knowing through intimate knowledge, perception, recognition, etc.

The underlying meaning is that these people must have a proven track record. This is why Paul counsels Timothy not to appoint "a recent convert" as a leader in the church because "he may become puffed up with conceit and fall into the condemnation of the devil" (1 Timothy 3:6). He has not developed an inner foundation of spiritual life that can handle the challenges of leadership. So he will become puffed up—trying to show that he is what he is not—and end up becoming prey to Satan's attacks.

It is interesting that in the record in Exodus of this same selection of elders, the qualifications given by Moses' father-in-law Jethro focus more on character: "Moreover, look for able men from all the people, men who fear God, who are trustworthy and hate a bribe" (Exodus 18:21). However, the qualifications given here in Deuteronomy focus more on wisdom and ability. The two are not mutually exclusive. In fact, Jethro first mentions ability and then goes to focus on character. In the Hebrew holistic idea of the human personality, ability without character was not acceptable ability.

The combination of character, wisdom, ability, and reputation as the basic criteria for the selection of leaders is one that is found often in the Bible. Seniority is a factor to consider, but it is only one factor (see Acts 6:3; 1 Timothy 3:2–13; Titus 1:5–9). On the ability side wisdom has a very high place. Some leaders may not be able to do some things that leaders are usually expected to do. But wise leaders will know the need and their lack of ability to meet the need, and they will ensure that this need is met through others compensating for their weaknesses.

Securing the Agreement of the People (1:14)

The people agreed with Moses' suggestion. Moses tells the people, "And you answered me, 'The thing that you have spoken is good for us to do'" (1:14). Working for agreement with our people is the ideal situation when it comes to decision-making. This is not an absolute principle because sometimes leaders have a prophetic role where they have to rebuke people and redirect them back to the path of God after they have strayed. Sometimes God gives them a work to do that others do not understand. The disciples did not understand or agree with Jesus' prediction of his death. The churches Paul visited on his way to Jerusalem did not understand or agree with his decision to go to that city because they knew he was going to suffer there.

Still, the ideal situation is when all the parties concerned can come to a point of agreement. Luke says that when the apostles presented a resolution to the problem pertaining to rations for the Grecian widows, "what they said pleased the whole gathering" (Acts 6:5). At the Jerusalem Council after much debate and discussion the whole gathering was able to say, ". . . it has seemed good to the Holy Spirit and to us . . . " (Acts 15:28). Leaders must work at unanimity among the group. Sometimes this may take a lot of time to achieve, but the lost time is compensated for by a motivated team.

Even when we have to pursue a vision from God that others do not understand, we must do our best to get them to understand. Jesus talked many times to the disciples about his death and why it was necessary. Acts 21:12–14 has a moving description of the way Paul dealt with Luke and the loving Christians in Caesarea who were given a prophecy by Agabus about his impending arrest. Luke says, "When we heard this, we and the people there urged him not to go up to Jerusalem" (Acts 21:12). Their gentle, perplexed, and dedicated shepherd replies, "What are you doing, weeping and breaking my heart? For I am ready not only to be imprisoned but even to die in Jerusalem for the name of the Lord Jesus" (Acts 21:13). They did not understand Paul's reasoning, but they finally released him to do what he felt he needed to do: "And since he would not be persuaded, we ceased and said, 'Let the will of the Lord be done'" (Acts 21:14).

Leaders Are Appointed (1:15)

Verse 15 tells us that Moses, having secured the agreement of the people, appointed leaders ensuring that a practical way was there for every person in the Jewish nation to be led by someone: "So I took the heads of your tribes, wise and experienced men, and set them as heads over you, commanders of thousands, commanders of hundreds, commanders of fifties, commanders of tens, and officers, throughout your tribes." Note that they are called "commanders." This points to the authority of the leader, which is a factor that we will discuss in the next chapter.

This passage shows a pattern that occurs often in the Bible. When a need for structural change is revealed, God's people must act immediately to bring that about. Sometimes this may involve a lot of study and discussion. But the important point is that we must ensure that our movements have structures that help the movement grow and also ensure that all in the groups are cared for adequately.

4

Basic Training for Judges

DEUTERONOMY 1:16–18

WE ENDED THE LAST CHAPTER with a report on how Moses appointed heads of the tribes as commanders over groups of people. Deuteronomy 1:16 talks about instructions given to judges. There is some question whether the judges were a different group of people than the commanders. Our exposition will not be greatly changed if the commanders and judges were two different groups of leaders or the same group. From the description that follows it seems that judging is the primary work of the judges described here. In the book of Judges the judges were primarily military leaders raised up for a crisis, though some, like Deborah, did judge (Judges 4:5).

Judging, of course, is an awesome responsibility. Therefore, the new judges need to be trained in this work. Verses 16, 17 give a brief summary of the training they were given by Moses. The training itself must have been much more comprehensive. Considering that that the Law had only recently been given to the people, they would have needed to master the Law if they were going to judge properly. What we have here are moral guidelines for enforcing the Law.

The Leader Gives a Charge to His Leaders (1:16)

Moses explains that he "charged [their] judges at that time" (1:16a). This possibly was at a ceremony involving an oath.[1] Such ceremonies are helpful because they point to the seriousness of the responsibilities of the people appointed. The word translated "charged" occurs 496 times in the Old Testament, of which 252 occurrences are in the Pentateuch and eighty-eight in Deuteronomy. The word means "order, command, charge, direct, appoint, commission, forbid (when negated). . . . It denotes the action of a superior stating something with authority and/or force to a subordinate with the purpose of eliciting a response."[2] Of the 496 occurrences of the verb, God is the subject 280 times, Moses eighty-five times, and Joshua fourteen times. Just as God gives charges to people, the leaders who represent him also do that.

From the above evidence it is clear that charging people is a necessary aspect of leadership. Paul often charged his readers, especially Timothy, with certain responsibilities (1 Corinthians 7:10; 1 Timothy 1:18; 5:21; 6:13; 2 Timothy 4:1). He also asked Timothy to charge others (1 Timothy 1:3; 6:17; 2 Timothy 2:14). Once Paul gives a charge to Timothy about the responsibility to charge others: "I charge you in the presence of God and of Christ Jesus, who is to judge the living and the dead, and by his appearing and his kingdom: preach the word; be ready in season and out of season; reprove, rebuke, and exhort, with complete patience and teaching" (2 Timothy 4:1, 2).

Today the practice of leaders, as God's representatives, exhorting people has gone out of fashion. Fearing that people will react negatively to such exhortation, the church focuses on doing things that will keep the people satisfied. Even the sermon will lack an urgent summons to discipleship. I think one reason for this is that Christians have lost the sense of living under submission to God. Therefore they react negatively to any strong language by Christian leaders. The calling for leaders to charge the people places a huge responsibility on them. They need to ensure that they are qualified to do so. The main challenge is to ensure that what they tell the people is in harmony with the mind of God.

Toward that end we must ensure that we remain close to and obedient to God. Then there is a greater likelihood of our thoughts being in harmony with his.

Another way is to master God's Word, which today is the equivalent of Moses' words. Moses' authority was derived from God. So is ours. Moses received a revelation from God, and he directly gave that to the people. We have this revelation recorded in the Scriptures, and our authority is derived from it. Therefore, we have the responsibility to study the Scriptures and to ensure that what we tell the people is indeed in harmony with God's Word.

Because our authority is derived and only God is the ultimate authority to whom all the glory will go, we must ensure that, like Moses, we are humble people (Numbers 12:3). Great harm can come to the cause of Christ when exhortation is done by leaders who are proud and dictatorial.

There is a great need to restore exhortation in church life today. May we who are leaders perform this task faithfully. May we do so in such a way that exhortation will once more be acceptable as an important part of the life of a vibrant Christian community. The call to charge people places us with an awesome responsibility, but that is a necessary aspect of leadership.

How to Judge (1:16, 17)

Moses' charge to the judges is about how they are to judge.

Righteous Judgment (1:16b)

First Moses says, "Hear the cases between your brothers, and judge righteously between a man and his brother or the alien who is with him" (1:16). The lexicon describes the word translated "righteously" as "righteousness, justice, rightness, acting according to a proper (God's) standard, doing what is right, being in the right."[3] "Righteously" seems to be a better rendering than "fairly" (NIV). As McConville puts it, "Judges must not be deterred from a decision by any consideration other than the truth." The leader's response to allegations of wrongdoing is one of the best ways to demonstrate the righteousness of God.

In our minds the word *righteousness* has become associated with coldly rational decisions, usually involving punishment. McConville says that righteous "judgment should be according to the true merits of a case, and ordinary human compassion." We must not forget that it is because of his righteousness that God saves us even though we are sinners (Psalm 71:2). In order to bring us that salvation, a great price had to be paid. God is not coldly rational without compassion in the exercise of his righteousness. Essentially, judging with righteousness is presenting the best solution to the problem so that it is in line with all of God's nature as holy love. Sometimes the poor are helplessly left without resources and help because the law does not allow any help to them. But in places like Deuteronomy 15 we see extensive regulations given to protect and help the poor and needy.

Verse 16 goes on to state that the same righteous principles are to be used for disputes "between a man and his brother or the alien who is with him." Aliens must not be deprived of their rights. Applying this to the life of the church or nation today, it would mean that sometimes a judgment may be made against a loyal member for the benefit of an outsider. In our cultures there is a strong sense of community solidarity that goes to the extreme of protecting one's own when outsiders are involved. To do otherwise is considered an act of disloyalty and betrayal. But Moses instructs the judges to judge against members of their own group if necessary.

Pronouncing judgment against one's own and in favor of an outsider is very hard for leaders as sometimes it looks like ingratitude and disloyalty to one who has worked so loyally and hard. But though there will be hurt at first, in the long run such thoroughgoing commitment to justice will reap good results. The people will have a security that gives them the sense that here right is right and wrong is wrong. It would also act as a deterrent to unrighteous living, for they know that the law is practiced here in a thoroughgoing manner.

Today political leaders often know about illegal things that people under them are doing, but they ignore them until the person falls out of line. At that time their indiscretions are brought up and the people are silenced. It is well known that certain heads of state keep dossiers against members of their cabinet, to be used when "appropriate." Because of this type of behavior, even in the church, when a person is accused of wrongdoing, immediately a dishonorable motive is attributed to the accusation. You hear things like, "He is bringing this up because she opposed the building project." The best way to take such dishonor from the church is thoroughgoing and serious application of Biblical principles of justice.

Christian judges in places where the judiciary is shackled by the intervention of unjust rulers must be willing to pay the price of commitment to righteousness and impartiality. Christians should support righteous judges, whatever their religion, with their prayers and other public affirmations of support, such as letters to newspapers in support of them. Christians should be in the forefront of creating a groundswell of popular opinion in their nation that says, "Enough is enough. We want pure justice in our land."

No Partiality (1:17a)

Verse 17 prohibits partiality in judgment: "You shall not be partial in judgment. You shall hear the small and the great alike." The call to treat "the small and the great alike" comes often in the Bible. James uses similar language in connection with Christian community life: "My brothers, show no partiality as you hold the faith in our Lord Jesus Christ, the Lord of glory" (James 2:1). That passage talks about the seats one is given when believers gather together (James 2:2–4).

In many societies, and sadly in some churches too, people with influence are considered immune to prosecution. Sometimes you hear statements like, "Do you know who I am?" when a person is stopped by a policeman. When I have been stopped sometimes I think, "I will tell them I am a religious worker, and then he will let me go." But if I am a religious worker and have done wrong, I should receive a higher penalty because I was supposed to be an example to others!

Because the rich and powerful are immune to prosecution and condemnation, those who are prosecuted get the message that they are not influential and powerful people. The law thus reminds them of their weakness, and therefore they begin to resent the law. This is a sad state of affairs: the thing that is supposed to bring security and stability to their lives becomes the thing they resent. People will long for the day when they are powerful enough that they too can break the law and escape prosecution and condemnation. A nation where the people do not respect the law is a sick nation. One of the best ways to bring an attitude of respect for the law among our people is for those who enforce the law to act without partiality.

Of course, when we apply the law we need to follow the systems of respect and the etiquette of our society. For example, Paul tells the young leader Timothy, "Do not rebuke an older man but encourage him as you would a father" (1 Timothy 5:1a). In this passage Paul is talking about how Timothy should deal with different groups in the church. He is not saying that if an older person does wrong, the wrong should be overlooked. His point is that leaders cannot rebuke older people the way they would rebuke a younger person. If the person has done some wrong that requires disciplinary action, then the younger person should talk to the older person with the respect that is due to him.

No Fear of People (1:17b)

Next Moses says, "You shall not be intimidated by anyone, for the judgment is God's" (1:17b). If we are in a position that gives us the responsibility to judge, then we are acting on behalf of God who is the ultimate judge. Paul says that even non-Christian judges in society are doing God's work on earth when they punish wrong and reward right (Romans 13:1–7).

Sometimes we may suffer because of righteous judgment. But we should not be afraid because we are doing God's work. He is ultimately the only one we should fear. Jesus uses this argument when he warns the disciples of the persecution that will come to them because they preach the gospel. He asks the disciples not to be afraid: "And do not fear those who kill the body but cannot kill the soul. Rather fear him who can destroy both soul and body in hell" (Matthew 10:28). Disobedience is the only thing that we should fear. Many wilt under the strain of pressure and give in to the corrupt systems that control public life. They do so because of fear of the forces of evil. We should not fear them because God is Lord of the universe, and ultimately his greatness over them will be revealed. Therefore the only one we should fear is God.

Know Your Limitations (1:17c)

Moses' final word to the judges is, "And the case that is too hard for you, you shall bring to me, and I will hear it" (1:17c). When it comes to judging, it is essential that a fair and competent trial is given; therefore those who are not qualified for that particular case should not be given it to judge. In the legal system today some are automatically disqualified from judging a case if there are unhelpful connections between the parties involved in the case and the prospective judge. It would be best to follow that procedure in the church too. For example, it would be best for us to assign dealing with a discipline problem relating to a family member to someone else.

The particular situation mentioned here is a case that is too hard for us to handle. This required the judge to accept that he was not competent to handle the case. How hard it is for leaders to accept that! This applies in all areas of leadership. All of us know there are things that we cannot do well. Sometimes we cannot avoid working in areas of incompetence. But when there is a situation involving serious consequences it is best to admit our lack of ability and see that someone else does the job. Some refuse to accept that, and often the result is a discrediting of the person and also damage to others.

In our text the final court of appeal is Moses. Moses was "God's faithful mediator." J. A. Thompson further explains, "It was common practice in the ancient Near East to refer difficult cases to the monarch. In Israel God was the Monarch, but acted through his representative." Today this reminds us that all our authority is derived. God is the ultimate leader. Our attitudes and actions should aim at buttressing God's leadership, not ours.

Teach the People to Live under Authority (1:18)

Moses ends his discussion about leadership by stating, "And I commanded you at that time all the things that you should do" (1:18). There is some question about whether this continues the discussion on training for judges or whether this is referring to instructions given to all the people. The expression "all the things that you should do" suggests that all the people are meant here. Moses is giving instructions for all of life, which is what the Old Testament Law intended to do.

We should never forget the comprehensiveness of Scripture. Sometimes we can get bogged down with all the ceremonial, national, social, and family regulations in the Old Testament and think that all of this is not relevant to us. These passages tell us that God is Lord of all of life and that all we do is encompassed in our devotion to God. We have the responsibility to send all our thinking and acting through the sieve of God's Word. A few years after

Martin Luther began proclaiming his reformation message, he was brought before the Diet of Worms in 1521 and asked whether he would recant. He expressed his refusal to do so in these words: "I am bound by the Scriptures I have quoted, and my conscience is captive to the Word of God. I cannot and will not retract anything, since it is neither safe nor right to go against conscience."[4] All the time we must ask, how do I respond to this situation Biblically? And we must follow the Bible whatever the cost.

This is why at Joshua's commissioning God told him, "Only be strong and very courageous, being careful to do according to *all* the law that Moses my servant commanded you. Do not turn from it to the right hand or to the left, that you may have good success wherever you go" (Joshua 1:7). The way for Joshua to be courageous is to be faithful to the Word in all his actions. Because the Word is so important for his life and work, God tells him that he must be saturated in the Word: "This Book of the Law shall not depart from your mouth, but you shall meditate on it day and night, so that you may be careful to do according to all that is written in it. For then you will make your way prosperous, and then you will have good success" (Joshua 1:8).

So leaders must be people of the Word, and like Moses they must teach the Word to the people they lead. In Paul's list of criteria for the selection of overseers (1 Timothy 3:1–7), only one has to do with ability in ministry. The rest have to do with character and reputation. The one ability-related criterion is that an overseer must be "able to teach" (v. 2). All leaders must introduce those they lead to the truths in the Word. I do not think this means that they must be great orators. There are different ways in which we can lead people to the truths of the Word. Chatting with them about the things in the Word, advising them, leading discussions on issues, leading a small-group Bible study, and directing them to things that they can read and learn from are all methods of communicating the Word, in addition to the traditional classroom type of teaching.

Note how Moses said that he taught them "*all* the things that [they] should do" (1:18). Paul said something similar to the elders of the church in Ephesus: "I did not shrink from declaring to you the whole counsel of God" (Acts 20:27). We have the responsibility to be comprehensive in our teaching. We must try to ensure that we have not left out any essential things in our communicating truth to our people. It is necessary for preachers and leaders to keep note of what they have taught their people, so that they know that within a given period of time they would have covered most of the main teachings and emphases of Christianity.

Our two studies on Deuteronomy 1:9–18 have shown that leadership is an issue that we must approach with utmost seriousness. We change leadership structures according to the needs that growth brings. We ensure that the leadership structure is such that everyone in the congregation is adequately cared for. We have criteria for the selection of leaders. We are careful to train them and tell them what their responsibilities are and how they should carry out their work.

5

Faith versus Fear

DEUTERONOMY 1:19–33

MOSES' FIRST SPEECH to the people in preparation for his death started with God's command to the people to leave Horeb (Sinai) and travel northward in order to enter the land he promised them (1:6–8). Then Moses went on to explain how, along with the growing stress he faced, leaders were appointed to take over various responsibilities in managing the people (1:9–18). With verse 19 Moses picks up from where he stopped in verse 8 by reporting how the people followed God's command to depart from Horeb. That they did, but afterward when they needed to launch out in faith they ended up being overcome by fear.

Launch out in Faith (1:19–21c)

Moses first describes how the people responded obediently to the command to leave Horeb. Verse 19 says, "Then we set out from Horeb and went through all that great and terrifying wilderness that you saw, on the way to the hill country of the Amorites, as the LORD our God commanded us." It was a journey of about 100 miles through a dusty, dreary desert described by Moses as a "great and terrifying wilderness." This description of the desert points to the people's obedience and to God's guidance.

Moses goes on to say, "And we came to Kadesh-barnea" (1:19b). Finally they have come to the border of the promised land. Moses relates how he addressed the people when they arrived there: "And I said to you, 'You have come to the hill country of the Amorites, which the LORD our God is giving us'" (1:20). Though "the Amorites" were an ethnic group, the designation was also used to refer to all the people of Canaan and of the land east of the Jordan River.

Note how Moses says that this is the land "which the LORD our God is giving us." The conquest of the land is presented as a foregone conclusion. Now they are at the threshold of the great conquest, and Moses buttresses their faith even more by saying, "See, the LORD your God has set the land before you" (1:21a), or as *Today's English Version* (TEV) puts it, "Look, there it is!" Now they have to enter in faith. So Moses says, "Go up, take possession" (1:21b). So that they may not hesitate with this command Moses adds, ". . . as the LORD, the God of your fathers, has told you" (1:21c). God has given them the great privilege of being the instruments through whom he is going to fulfill a promise that was made and renewed for 500 years!

Don't Be Afraid (1:21d)

The people's fear, however, was a problem. So Moses urges them, "Do not fear or be dismayed" (1:21d). This was a very real problem for the Israelites. Therefore, this advice is recorded ten times in Deuteronomy.[1] When Joshua was commissioned, God told him three times to be "strong and courageous" (Joshua 1:6, 7, 9), without being afraid (Joshua 1:9). In the resurrection narratives five times we are told that Christ's followers were afraid (Mark 16:5, 8; Luke 24:5, 37; John 20:19). Twice Jesus (Matthew 28:10; Luke 24:38) and twice the angels tell them not to be afraid (Matthew 28:5; Mark 16:6). Earlier as Jesus advised his disciples before sending them out to preach, he told them, ". . . do not fear those who kill the body but cannot kill the soul" (Matthew 10:28).

If fear is mentioned so often in the Bible it must be a real problem that we need to be aware of and the reality of which we need to face squarely. Fear is the natural reaction of humans to danger. As such it is a helpful thing, for it prompts us to take note of and be prepared for the danger. It becomes sin when it paralyzes us and prevents us from launching out in obedience to God. The Christian response to fear is to address it with our belief in the sovereignty of God, because of which God will give us victory over what causes it if we are obedient to him. We find out what God's will is concerning the fear-causing situation, and we concentrate on doing that will, believing that God will see us through. The prayer that the disciples prayed, after the Great Commission was declared illegal by the authorities, gives us a good example of how Christians should face up to fear. Most of the prayer is a reflection on the sovereignty of God (Acts 4:24–28). Then there is a cursory glance at their problem—"And now, Lord, look upon their threats" (Acts 4:29a)—followed by a request to help them boldly obey the Great Commission—"and grant to your servants to continue to speak your word with all boldness" (Acts 4:29b). The prayer closes with a request to God to intervene with healing, signs, and wonders (Acts 4:30).

If the Bible urges people so often not to fear, then we should similarly urge ourselves and others. This helps people face their fears and take steps to apply the principle of sovereignty to that which causes fear so they can respond in bold obedience to the will of God.

One Christmas eve I was getting ready to go to America for the Urbana Student Missionary Conference. I was a little nervous because I had been very busy and had lost sleep because of all the things I had to do during that time. I was afraid that the lack of sleep and the jet lag would leave me so disoriented that I would not be able to speak well at the conference. I was also scheduled to preach at the Christmas service at our church the next morning. I finished preparing the sermon around 2:00 A.M. and went to sleep hoping for at least four hours of sleep.

Shortly after I fell asleep there was a knock at our door. An infant in a poor Hindu family living near our home was sick with a stomach illness. They did not have electricity in this home, and in the low light from an oil lamp they mistook some skin lotion for the medicine used for the child's ailment. When they realized their error they came to our home hoping that we would take the child to the hospital, which I did.

As the poor are sometimes neglected in government hospitals I stayed with them until I was sure they had been properly cared for. By the time I came home, it was time to get ready to go to church. I decided that I would try to get some sleep after Christmas lunch. So we put our van in the garage and closed our windows, hoping that people would think no one was at home. (We do not have air-conditioning, and our windows usually open out; so when they are closed it usually means no one is at home.) I had slept only for a few minutes when a visitor came. I went back to sleep, and a few minutes later I was awakened by another visitor. I decided that Christmas afternoon was not a good time to sleep! I played some games with my children instead.

But I needed sleep! At midnight I went to the airport. The plane that took me from Colombo to Amsterdam had about 350 seats, but only about fifty passengers. I had four seats to myself, which became a very comfortable bed. I have never slept on a flight as much as I slept on that memorable Christmas night! When we launch out in faith in obedience to his call, God will indeed look after us! We address our fear with our belief that God is sovereign and concentrate on obedience to his will.

Doubting God's Faithfulness (1:22–25)

Verse 22 shows that despite Moses' word to the people not to be afraid, they were afraid and looked for some security instead of launching out in faith as Moses had told them to do. Moses recounts the story: "Then all of you came near me and said, 'Let us send men before us, that they may explore the land for us and bring us word again of the way by which we must go up and the cities into which we shall come" (1:22). Twice in this chapter Moses says, "the LORD your God who goes before you" (1:30, 32–33). But they say, "Let us send men before us." They are looking to people to give them the security that only God can give.

From the human point of view, the proposal to send spies seems to be a wise one. But God had rendered this step unnecessary by promising to give them victory without the spies. Often when God asks us to act in one way believing in him, we disobey and act in a way that seems safer from a human perspective. When Abraham went to Egypt with his beautiful wife, he was afraid he might be killed because of her, so he describes his wife as his sister (Genesis 12:10–20). Then he got impatient when the promise of a son was unfulfilled, and he followed a cultural practice prevalent in that time and had a son through his wife's servant (Genesis 16).

I am writing this in Singapore where the ratio of believing young adult males to females is estimated to be 1:2. This means that many believing young women are going to find it very difficult to find a spouse. Some who want to get married may need to remain single. Some of these young women may turn their backs on God's will and go ahead and marry a person who does not share their commitment to Christ. By solving their problem in this way they miss out on the beautiful plan God has for them.

Moses says, "The thing seemed good to me, and I took twelve men from you, one man from each tribe" (1:23). Numbers 13:1, 2 says that it was God who asked them to send the spies. What seems to have happened is that the people requested Moses to send the spies. Moses asked God, who approved the idea and explained to Moses the way he should go about putting it into practice.

This is another instance that we find in the Bible of God making a concession when the people are afraid to obey because of weak faith.

- When Moses said he couldn't speak, God gave him a spokesman, Aaron, as a concession, even though God did not think that was necessary (Exodus 4:10–16).
- Gideon saw the angel of the Lord cause fire to spring up and burn up his sacrifice (Judges 6:21). But before he launched out in obedience, leading the people into battle, he wanted still more evidence that God would

surely be with him and give him victory. So he kept a fleece out at night and asked God to wet the fleece alone with dew without wetting the surrounding floor. When that was done, he wanted God to do the opposite, to wet the ground and not the fleece. That also God did (Judges 6:36–40).

These extra evidences or securities were not needed, but they were given by God to buttress the weak faith of his servants. The great British architect Christopher Wren was asked to draw plans for a city hall in England. He drew a plan where the weight of the roof was distributed in such a way that there was no pillar in the large hall. The city councillors were nervous about this and asked Wren to include a pillar in his plan. When he refused to do this, the matter was taken to the people of the city, who also voted for a pillar. Wren reluctantly added a pillar to the plan, and the building was completed along with the pillar. Many years later when some refurbishing was being done on the building someone who was working near the top of the pillar found that it ended about two inches short of the wood of the roof! This space, of course, was not visible from the ground.[2] Wren satisfied the fearful people by including a security item that was not really needed. In the same way God also makes concessions for our weak faith. This is a great comfort to us. There is hope for us cowards!

However, some people have what the Bible calls "an evil, unbelieving heart" (Hebrews 3:12) and do not want to obey. They will keep looking for excuses and bringing up objections and reasons for being afraid. This is what the Israelites did with the report of the spies. The spies did as they were told and traveled north: "And they turned and went up into the hill country, and came to the Valley of Eshcol and spied it out" (Deuteronomy 1:24). They returned and reported some good news: "And they took in their hands some of the fruit of the land and brought it down to us, and brought us word again and said, 'It is a good land that the LORD our God is giving us'" (1:25). Numbers 13:28 tells us that the spies also talked about the power of the people and their cities: "However, the people who dwell in the land are strong, and the cities are fortified and very large. And besides, we saw the descendants of Anak there."

The Israelites were faced with two different bodies of evidence. One was positive: the land was as good as God had said it would be, and God had said he would help them conquer the land. The other evidence was negative: the cities were well-fortified, and the people were strong. Why, even the descendants of Anak, who were giants, lived there. We face similar challenges. We sense that God asks us to move forward in faith. But there are a lot of negatives too. "If I do this, all the people in my office will disagree with me, and

I will be all alone." "I do not think I could handle the terrible weather in the place where God is sending us." "What about the children? Will they get a good education there?" We choose what body of evidence we will focus on and determine our course of action.

When we launched our drug rehabilitation ministry in Youth for Christ there were clear evidences that God wanted us to do this work. After some years funds were raised to purchase property for the work. It took us about a year to find suitable land. My colleagues looked at over 125 sites, often traveling hours in dreary weather on their motorcycles. When we found suitable land, the government department under which we are registered did not give us permission to buy it. We appealed the decision, and the matter was sent to the Attorney General's department. They accepted our appeal and directed the department to give us permission to buy the land, which was almost nine acres in extent. But the department gave us permission to purchase only two acres!

We had to set up a separate trust to purchase the land. Many of our first students ran away before their rehabilitation period was complete. One of our workers got assaulted during a wave of attacks against Christians in the country. There were so many discouragements that some began to ask, "Are all these problems signs from God that this was not his will?" Others said, "God clearly led us to start this work. These problems are signs that Satan does not like what we are doing. Probably God wants to do something very significant through this ministry." Fortunately the latter group prevailed! And I believe that over the years something really significant has happened. Jesus said, "No one who puts his hand to the plow and looks back is fit for the kingdom of God" (Luke 9:62). Problems will come, but our trust in God, our experience of past providence, and the belief that he has asked us to move forward will help us go on without giving up.

I have found that some people constantly lose heart when problems come—not because they have "an evil, unbelieving heart" but because they are naturally timid. Some of them have experienced failure all their life, and they find it difficult to believe that God will help them come victoriously through the crisis they are now facing. We need to encourage such people to believe in God. Sometimes when they are thinking of giving up, we may need to pray with them or urge them or rebuke them or gently hold their hand and guide them along so they will move forward without giving up. As they experience God's deliverance on several occasions, they will begin to believe that things can go right for them.

Rebellion Against God (1:26–28)

The report of the spies described the goodness of the land and the greatness of the people. The account in Numbers adds that, except for Caleb and Joshua, the spies added "a bad report" to the original report, focusing on the power of the opposition (Numbers 13:31–33). The people chose to go with the majority report. Moses says, "Yet you would not go up, but rebelled against the command of the LORD your God" (Deuteronomy 1:26). Note that to refuse to obey by launching out in faith is rebellion against God.

Murmuring as an Expression of Rebellion (1:26, 27)

The rebellion expressed itself in murmuring: "And you murmured in your tents and said, 'Because the LORD hated us he has brought us out of the land of Egypt, to give us into the hand of the Amorites, to destroy us'" (1:27). This is different from the laments and questioning of faithful but timid or discouraged believers, as we find in the Psalms, Jeremiah, and Lamentations. Those are cries of obedient people who are suffering despite their obedience. In our passage the people who murmur do not want to obey. Moses says, "Yet you would not go up, but rebelled against the command of the LORD your God" (1:26). In the Bible there is great sympathy for the tears and laments of faithful people who are suffering. The murmuring of the disobedient belongs to a completely different category.

The accusation the people make against God is amazing: "Because the LORD hated us he has brought us out of the land of Egypt, to give us into the hand of the Amorites, to destroy us" (1:27). A book could be written about all the wonderful things that God did for these people. Through some amazing plagues and other interventions he delivered the people miraculously from crushing slavery. The Red Sea was parted, they were fed and were given drink miraculously, and God led them miraculously with a pillar of fire by night and a pillar of cloud by day. But when they saw the power of the Canaanites, they forgot everything and said that God hated them and had brought out of Egypt just to let them die! People say some amazing things when they turn their backs on God.

The Unbelieving Heart Magnifies the Problem (1:28)

Those who look at a challenge to faith with the heart of unbelief see the problem in a much larger light than it deserves. This is what the rebellious Israelites did. They exaggerated the problem and said, "Where are we going up? Our brothers have made our hearts melt, saying, 'The people are greater and taller than we. The cities are great and fortified up to heaven. And besides, we have seen the sons of the Anakim there'" (1:28). The cities were not "fortified up to heaven." Perhaps it was a figure of speech, but it was one that magnified the problem. They looked only at the negative features, and when you do that, the situation does seem to be really tough. And we give it exaggerated importance.

Some are natural grumblers who automatically panic when there is a crisis. But God is eventually able to break into their lives with his peace. These are not rebellious people. They want to be obedient, but they are naturally timid or have a complaining personality. God can work with such and use them despite their weakness. Not so with the people who keep looking for things to complain about, people who do not want to obey. You answer one problem they have, and they bring up a new problem. And the sequence of problem-raising and problem-solving continues—on and on—so that they can go on having excuses for avoiding obedience. God's verdict on such people is that they have rebelled against God.

The complaint of the people that God hated them after so many miraculous provisions reminds me of Polycarp, Bishop of Smyrna, who was martyred in the middle of the second century. He was brought to a stadium to be killed, but the officials did not want to kill him because he was an old man. The proconsul told him, "Have respect to your old age" and other similar things. He said, "Swear, and I will set you at liberty, reproach Christ." Polycarp's memorable response was, "Eighty and six years have I served Him, and He never did me any injury: how then can I blaspheme my King and my Savior?"

The proconsul pressed him again and said, "Swear by the fortune of Caesar." Polycarp answered, "Since you are vainly urgent that, as you say, I should swear by the fortune of Caesar, and pretend not to know who and what I am, hear me declare with boldness, I am a Christian. And if you wish to learn what the doctrines of Christianity are, appoint me a day, and you shall hear them."

After more dialogue the proconsul said, "I have wild beasts at hand; to these will I cast you, unless you repent." But he answered, "Call them then, for we are not accustomed to repent of what is good in order to adopt that which is evil; and it is well for me to be changed from what is evil to what is righteous." Again the proconsul said to him, "I will cause you to be consumed by fire, seeing you despise the wild beasts, if you will not repent." But Polycarp said, "You threaten me with fire which burns for an hour, and after a little is extinguished, but are ignorant of the fire of the coming judgment and of eternal punishment, reserved for the ungodly. But why are you tarrying? Bring forth what you will." When Polycarp was bound to be burned, he looked up to Heaven and prayed a memorable prayer thanking God for the privilege of being a martyr for Christ.[3]

The Fear of Giants (1:28)

Verse 28 mentions three things as being causes for the rebellious refusal of the people to obey. "[1] The people are greater and taller than we. [2] The cities are great and fortified up to heaven. [3] And besides, we have seen the sons of the Anakim there." They were intimidated by the size and strength of the people and the cities. "The sons of Anakim" probably referred originally to a tribal or ethnic group. Later it came to be used as a general term for giants.

How different is this attitude to that of David as he faced the challenge of Goliath. There all the people, including the king, were terrified. But this young man, who was not yet even a soldier, declared, "For who is this uncircumcised Philistine, that he should defy the armies of the living God?" (1 Samuel 17:26b). He carried his faith to its logical end. That is what we must do: we must apply the implications of what we believe about God to every situation we face. Then we can conclude, "If God is God and I am obedient to him, he will see me through." That is the logic of faith. Believing God's goodness, power, and love for us helps us to be obedient.

The God Who Fights for Us (1:29–33)

Speaking to reassure the people and boost their faith, Moses repeats what he has already said in verse 21: "Do not be in dread or afraid of them" (1:29). Then, to stop them from fearing, Moses makes an affirmation and substantiates the advice just given: "The LORD your God who goes before you will himself fight for you" (1:30a). What an amazing thought this is! A poor person who needs a good lawyer to appear on behalf of him would not be able to secure the lawyer he needs, because of the lack of resources. A woman who has been falsely accused may not have an independent person to confirm her story. A small boy being bullied by older students at school may be defenseless in the face of their attacks. But they could have the Lord of the universe going before them and fighting for them! In the case of the Israelites he went before them in a most vivid and evident way—with a pillar of cloud by day and a pillar of fire by night. What an awesome sight this would have been!

But that is not all. Moses says, "God . . . will himself fight for you" (1:30). He appears on our behalf, like the best lawyer appearing for the poor person, or the most reliable witness vouching for the woman's story, or the strongest person in school responding to the bullies on behalf of the child. The difference with God's battle for us and the situations I just mentioned is that God is perfect in strength and ability, unlike humans who appear on behalf of us. Goliath taunted David saying, "Am I a dog, that you come to me with sticks? . . . Come to me, and I will give your flesh to the birds of the air and to the beasts of the field" (1 Samuel 17:43, 44). David's response was, "You come to me with a sword and with a spear and with a javelin, but I come to you in the name of the LORD of hosts, the God of the armies of Israel, whom you have defied" (1 Samuel 17:45).

The statement that God fights for us appears twelve times in the Old Testament.[4] The frequent use of this one thought is surely very significant. Shortly before he died Joshua told the people, "One man of you puts to flight a thousand, since it is the LORD your God who fights for you, just as he promised you" (Joshua 23:10).

Having made the affirmation that God will go before them and fight for them, Moses substantiates it, saying, ". . . just as he did for you in Egypt before your eyes, and in the wilderness, where you have seen how the LORD your God carried you, as a man carries his son, all the way that you went until you came to this place" (Deuteronomy 1:30b, 31). God had acted on behalf of them with incredible power and commitment, and they had seen it with their own eyes. Moses says that God had carried them "as a man carried his son, all the way" from Egypt to where they were at the time that Moses commanded them to go and take the land.

When Moses returned to Egypt to win freedom for his people, God told him to tell Pharaoh, "Thus says the LORD, Israel is my firstborn son, and I say to you, 'Let my son go that he may serve me'" (Exodus 4:22, 23). Now Moses reminds them about how God had treated them like a son. The figure of a father carrying his son has a beautiful combination of love, security, and provision. But because of their evil heart of unbelief they did not rest secure in the fact that God was their Father. They refused to believe that God would look after them. And by refusing to move forward they missed out on the blessing for which they had been waiting for so long.

Second Chronicles 20 records an event in which the people trusted in God against all odds and won a great victory. Jehoshaphat, the godly king of Judah, is told that a great army is coming against them (vv. 1, 2). The king's first reaction is to be "afraid." But in response to that fear he "set his face to seek the LORD, and proclaimed a fast throughout all Judah" (v. 3). The people gathered together, and then Jehoshaphat spoke to them (vv. 4, 5). This is followed by a great prayer. It starts by affirming that God is sovereign over all creation (v. 6). Then he describes how God drove out the inhabitants of Canaan and gave them the land and how they have made a sanctuary for God in that land (vv. 7, 8). Then he mentions how when they have crises they could go to God in this sanctuary and cry out to him, and God would hear and save them (v. 9). Then he placed their present problem before God: the countries that God asked them not to invade when they came with Moses toward Canaan were now coming against them and trying to drive them out of the possession that God gave them (vv. 10, 11).

Next Jehoshaphat makes his famous request from God: "O our God, will you not execute judgment on them? For we are powerless against this great horde that is coming against us. We do not know what to do, but our eyes are on you" (2 Chronicles 20:12). The result is a great victory.

There are remarkable parallels between Jehoshaphat's response to the crisis and the prayer, discussed at the start of this chapter, that the apostles prayed when they were first told they must not preach the gospel (Acts 4:18–31). The same story could have been told of the Israelites' response to the report of the spies if they had believed God and obeyed him. From these three passages a pattern emerges that we could follow each time we are faced with a difficult challenge.

- The problem is shared among God's people.
- The leader takes a lead in taking the people to the throne of God in united prayer or he speaks to them describing the God who is with them.
- The prayer or the description focuses on the sovereignty of God, especially as it is evidenced generally in his sovereignty over creation and specifically in his victorious intervention on behalf of his people in history.
- The people obey, and a great victory results.

Sadly, our passage lacks the last point, and the paragraph ends with Moses' pathetic words, "Yet in spite of this word you did not believe the LORD your God, who went before you in the way to seek you out a place to pitch your tents, in fire by night and in the cloud by day, to show you by what way you should go" (Deuteronomy 1:32, 33). The consequence of such unbelief resulting in rebellion is that they had to wander in the desert for thirty-eight years until that rebellious generation died.

Moses gives the answer to four questions people ask when they are afraid to launch out in obedience to God.

- *How will we know what to do?* "The LORD your God . . . goes before you" (v. 30a) just as he "went before you in the way to seek you out a place to pitch your tents, in fire by night and in the cloud by day, to show you by what way you should go" (v. 33).
- *Do we have the ability to overcome such a huge challenge?* "The LORD your God . . . will himself fight for you" (v. 30b).

- *How do we know he will fight for us?* He has already done this "in Egypt before your eyes, and in the wilderness" (vv. 30c, 31a).
- *What assurance do I have that God will really look after me?* ". . . the LORD your God carried you, as a man carries his son, all the way that you went until you came to this place" (v. 31b). He is committed to us like a father is committed to his son.

This passage shows us that fear is a reality that we should combat with our belief in the sovereignty of God. And to encourage us to believe, we have a whole history of God's glorious dealings with his people. Fear is a reality, but it does not need to overcome us and lead to defeat. We can overcome it with our faith in God's sovereignty.

6

The Seriousness of God's Severity

DEUTERONOMY 1:34–46

MOSES HAS BEEN TALKING about the journey of the Israelites. He relates how God asked them to leave Mt. Horeb (Sinai) after the Law had been given and to go to the land God had promised them (Deuteronomy 1:6–8). Then, after a slight detour where he talks about how leaders were appointed (1:9–18), Moses tells how they came to Kadesh-barnea bordering the promised land (1:19). There he tells them to go forward and take the land, but they ask for spies to be sent to survey the land, a request to which Moses accedes (1:20–24). Yet the report of the spies causes them to rebel against God and refuse to go forward (1:25–33). That is where this new study begins.

God's Anger and Pleasure (1:34–38)
Anger with the People (1:34, 35)
Moses says, "And the LORD heard your words and was angered, and he swore, 'Not one of these men of this evil generation shall see the good land that I swore to give to your fathers, except Caleb the son of Jephunneh . . .'" (1:35, 36). We will discuss the issue of wrath as being part of the nature of God in our discussion of 9:7, 8, but now we will note that the word "swore" appears twice here. This dual swearing shows the nature of God as holy love. As the *loving* God he swore to give the promised land to their fathers, but as *holy* God he swore not to give it to the present generation. This shows how we must hold these two aspects of God's nature together without separating them as many do. We sometimes say things like, "God loves you unconditionally and will not leave you whatever you do." That is not true. We are told that "the Spirit of the LORD departed from Saul" (1 Samuel 16:14) because he had

become disobedient to God. We cannot expect God to bless us if we disobey. Of course, if we repent, then we open ourselves again to God's blessings.

It has been said that there are more references to the wrath of God than to his love. Possibly this is because we tend to ignore wrath because it is an unpleasant topic. We constantly need to heed Paul's advice: "Note then the kindness and the severity of God: severity toward those who have fallen, but God's kindness to you, provided you continue in his kindness. Otherwise you too will be cut off" (Romans 11:22).

The promises of God are to a righteous nation. I think this should influence the way we look at modern Israel. I am convinced from passages like Romans 9—11 that even though the church is now the representative of the kingdom of God, God has a plan for Israel, especially for a large number of its people turning to Christ. However, this does not mean that we should support everything that Israel does. The promises of God are to a just nation. If we think they are doing something unjust, for example, to the Palestinians, we must oppose that.

We must all take note of this dual truth. Some of us may have some wonderful gifts and show great potential for being used by God. But that does not guarantee that we will remain victorious to the end. God can withdraw his hand from us because of our disobedience. As Paul says, "God's kindness" is given "provided you continue in his kindness. Otherwise you too will be cut off" (Romans 11:22b). This is why Paul said, "I discipline my body and keep it under control, lest after preaching to others I myself should be disqualified" (1 Corinthians 9:27).

Pleasure with Caleb (1:36)

Caleb, who spoke against the negative report of his fellow spies, escaped God's punishment. God said, "Not one of these men of this evil generation shall see the good land that I swore to give to your fathers, except Caleb the son of Jephunneh. He shall see it, and to him and to his children I will give the land on which he has trodden, because he has wholly followed the LORD!" (Deuteronomy 1:35, 36). From Joshua 14:12–15 we find that this land is Hebron, which had been inhabited by the Anakites, the giant people whom Caleb said Israel should not fear—a great honor to a great man.

We know that Caleb received the land because he and Joshua stood alone, refusing to bow down to fear and disbelief. But the reason given in Deuteronomy is ". . . because he has wholly followed the LORD!" This must be a very significant feature of Caleb because three times similar things are said of him. Numbers 14:24 says he "followed [God] fully," and Joshua 14:14

says, "he wholly followed the LORD." Peter Craigie explains that the wording in our Deuteronomy verse literally translates as "he completely filled himself after the Lord." Caleb was saturated with God. Always all that mattered to him was, "What does God want me to be and do?"

When faith is challenged, those with a halfhearted commitment will wilt. They have become used to following God selectively. They have entertained sinful attitudes and actions that may not show in their public behavior. The ten spies who gave the negative report were handpicked men, and each of them was described as "a chief among [their tribes]" (Numbers 13:2). But in a time of crisis when costly obedience is called for, or when obedience involves trusting God to do what seems to be so difficult, or when temptation hits powerfully, the real person is revealed. Those who have given Satan a foothold will wilt and fall.

Sometimes we are shocked by news that a prominent Christian has fallen into serious sin. But the fall was not as sudden as it seems. Sinful attitudes and/or practices had been secretly entertained. They had not wholly followed God. Is there an area in your life where the lordship of Christ is not total? Beware, and I say this to myself, too! That could be a vulnerable place where Satan hits us.

Displeasure with Moses (1:37)

Next Moses says, "Even with me the Lord was angry on your account and said, 'You also shall not go in there'" (1:37). Moses would not go to the promised land. We know he did get to Heaven and even continued to have a special place in the history of God's dealings with humanity. When Jesus needed encouragement about his coming death, Moses was one of the two chosen to talk to him on the Mount of Transfiguration. But he had to pay the price for letting the people influence his actions.

Moses had to bear the responsibility for his action even though it was their sin that prompted it. The event is described in Numbers 20:10–13. God asked him to speak to a rock to yield water when the people were grumbling for lack of water. But Moses struck it twice instead. A summary of what happened in Psalm 106:32, 33 suggests that he also used rash words at that time: "They angered him at the waters of Meribah, and it went ill with Moses on their account, for they made his spirit bitter, and he spoke rashly with his lips."

Today, too, leaders respond to crises with rash words and actions. A leader is directing a very important and public program, and suddenly something goes very wrong, possibly because of the carelessness of a member of his team. And he erupts like a volcano. The team member did something wrong, but that is no excuse for the leader to do wrong. When Paul lists qualifications for leadership in the Pastoral Epistles he says that "an overseer must be . . . self-controlled" (1 Timothy 3:2) and that "an overseer . . . must not be . . . quick-tempered . . . but . . . self-controlled" (Titus 1:7, 8). Sometimes our eruptions cause us to lose credibility with those we lead. It also causes nervous and inexperienced younger colleagues to panic because our behavior suggests that God is not in control of the situation. Leaders have to control their anger and vent it only when it is appropriate to do so.

In thirty-four years of marriage my wife and I have tried to follow the principle of Ephesians 4:26: "Be angry and do not sin; do not let the sun go down on your anger." In other words, if we are upset with each other we will not go to sleep until the air had been cleared. Many think this is not practical in marriage. We still believe it is practical and necessary. After these many years there is only one modification that we have made to this principle, and that is that if we are really angry about something, it may be best to delay expressing ourselves because in our rage we may say things we really don't mean and will regret saying. Often our rash statements get so embedded in the hearers' memories that they can adversely affect them for many years. A man who was happily married for over fifty years was asked the secret of his happy marriage. He said that every day there was at least one thing he did not say! He was referring to unnecessary statements that come to the mind but are stopped before they leave the mouth.

The punishment given to Moses seems to be severe considering that he had been a faithful leader for a long time. I think the reason for this is that leaders are supposed to be examples, and therefore their sins are more serious than those of others and they are judged with a more severe measure than others (James 3:1). We tend to ignore or hide the sins of leaders today because of their position. Often too much is at stake when such sins are exposed. A huge and thriving program may suddenly have to come to a grinding halt. Or there may be divisions in the body as there are people who are very loyal to the leader. In order to keep the machinery moving smoothly, we choose to let the matter pass without being properly confronted. The Bible has the opposite approach to this problem. Paul says, "As for [elders] who persist in sin, rebuke them in the presence of all, so that the rest may stand in fear" (1 Timothy 5:20).

Pleasure with Joshua (1:38)

After mentioning that Moses will not go into the promised land, God tells Moses, "Joshua the son of Nun, who stands before you, he shall enter.

Encourage him, for he shall cause Israel to inherit it" (1:38). Joshua gave the minority report, along with Caleb, after his spying expedition (Numbers 14:6–9). The term "who stands before you" is a technical term for servant or minister; hence the NIV renders it, "your assistant." Joshua is often described as Moses' assistant (Exodus 24:13; 33:11; Numbers 11:28; Joshua 1:1). Numbers 11:28 describes him as "the assistant of Moses from his youth." He did this for more than thirty-eight years, for we first encounter him leading the people in battle against the Amalekites, even before they came to Mt. Sinai (see Exodus 17). We know that he was very devoted to Moses. Once when he feared that Moses' authority was being undermined because two people were prophesying independently of Moses, he said, "My lord Moses, stop them" (Numbers 11:28). One of the things that made him great was that he was devoted to Moses over such a long period.

Some cannot work under a leader for a long time. So after a time they launch out on their "own" ministry. This may sometimes be God's will because it is necessary to enable that person to achieve his or her fullest potential under God. But the key to God's doing great things is not primarily by working through individuals but by working through the body consisting of committed individuals. Often people can do the greatest good by sticking to the same group and doing a work of depth with that group. Perhaps the person may not get too much recognition on earth, but in God's annals of the kingdom he or she will be known to have contributed to a truly significant work.

If people are to work for a long time to assist a leader, the leader also needs to be truly concerned for the assistant. Moses must surely have cared for Joshua in this way. I believe that one of the most important callings of a leader is to care for those he or she leads. When the people are cared for, they will be motivated to serve the group faithfully and sacrificially. So the group doesn't suffer because the leader spends so much time and energy caring for the people. Sometimes people get the idea that what their leaders want from them is for them to look after the leaders and help fulfill their goals. Often in such situations the junior people leave and launch out on their own the moment they get an opportunity to be leaders themselves.

Isn't it interesting that God asks Moses to "Encourage [Joshua], for he shall cause Israel to inherit [the land]." Moses often mentions how much he wished he could perform that task. He asked God for permission to go into the land (3:25). Now God is asking him to encourage the person who is going to do what he had wanted to do. We will look more closely at that in our discussion of 3:28.

Pleasure with Innocent Children, but Not with Their Parents (1:39)

Though the rebellious generation that set out of Egypt would not see the promised land, God said that their children would: "And as for your little ones, who you said would become a prey, and your children, who today have no knowledge of good or evil, they shall go in there. And to them I will give it, and they shall possess it" (1:39). The children were innocent of the rebellion of their parents. They had "no knowledge of good or evil"; that is, they did not understand the rebellious actions of their parents, and they were not punished for those acts.

It is interesting that the parents used these children as an excuse for their disobedience. They said that their "little ones . . . would become a prey" if they tried to enter the land. How often parents use the welfare of their children as their excuse for moving away from the tough call of God! Now I must emphasize that looking after children is an important service one does for God. A mother who reduces her involvement in church so she can give more time to her children is not giving up God's service for family duties. She is replacing one form of Christian service for another.

However, there are times when people move away from God's call using their children as an excuse. I know that while there are great leadership needs in poorer nations, there are capable leaders from those nations who are languishing in rich countries doing unfulfilling work. They left their native countries because they said they were concerned for their children. Some did not return after studies in an affluent country because their children would have found it difficult to adjust back in their home country. Indeed, this is a valid reason. For this reason my wife and I decided that we will not take our children to the West after they are about nine years old. When a sabbatical came up for me, I took it in Sri Lanka. And I could not have a real sabbatical that time because I was forced to fill a sudden vacancy that cropped up for an acting head of Colombo Theological Seminary in Sri Lanka!

Perhaps out of consideration for our children we may need to forgo a chance of studies abroad. If, for example, a leader goes for doctoral studies in the West when the children are in their teens, they would have a tough time adjusting back in their home country after the studies. It would perhaps be better to forgo the doctorate. We cannot make hard and fast rules here. Sometimes people can legitimately leave the land of their birth because their children (especially those with handicaps) would have opportunities they would not otherwise have.

When God calls us to difficult vocations that seem to affect our children negatively, we need to carefully work out ways of serving our children adequately as their parents while at the same time being faithful to our call. If we conscientiously carry through with this dual commitment to vocation and family, I believe the Lord will compensate and provide what our families need.

Sin Takes Us Back, Never Forward (1:40)

God told these rebellious people, "But as for you, turn, and journey into the wilderness in the direction of the Red Sea" (1:40). They are to journey southward, in the opposite direction of the promised land toward the Red Sea, the Gulf of Aqaba, which is a fingerlike projection on the north part of the Red Sea. Their progress would be halted because of their sin. From being at the brink of the promised land they will be made to wander in the wilderness for thirty-eight years. God's people needed to be taught that sin never takes people forward, only backwards. Even though God may forgive our sins, we may need to face unpleasant consequences of sin. Soon the Israelites would experience a humiliating defeat that would show them they could not bypass God's discipline (1:41–43). We always step back when we sin. It is never worthwhile sinning!

Accepting Sin, but Bypassing Discipline (1:41–43)

The Israelites, after God pronounces his discipline following their rebellion, accept that they were wrong and say, "We have sinned against the LORD," but they do not accept God's discipline. Instead they tell Moses, "We ourselves will go up and fight, just as the LORD our God commanded us" (1:41). This is like a person who apologizes because he has to, in order to get back to the program in which he is active. The people apologize and prepare to do what God had originally asked them to do. Now that they know they were wrong, what is there to prevent them from getting back on track with the plan of God? So they say they will proceed "just as the LORD our God commanded us." The original plan of God was clear, but they could not follow the plan now because this was discipline time.

In the same way, when we are under discipline there may be great needs around us that we may have the ability to meet. But we cannot do so because it would break the conditions of the discipline. A brilliant worship leader may have to go through the agony of being at the service when someone who can't sing in tune leads worship. God's work always faces a setback when God's people sin. And sometimes things will have to be left undone even though we know we can do them. Let's be careful about talking about the urgent task ahead when it is God's time to deal with us.

Our inaction is part of the pain of discipline that God uses to bring healing to us. It cannot be bypassed. Though the sin was forgiven, it revealed a
weakness in our lives. Forgiveness does not automatically heal the weakness.
The discipline helps do that. Three crucial passages about discipline in the
New Testament describe how discipline helps people along the path to obedience. Paul told the Corinthians that the person guilty of serious sexual sin
must be delivered to Satan, that is, deprived of the blessings of belonging to
God's covenant community, "for the destruction of the flesh, so that his spirit
may be saved in the day of the Lord" (1 Corinthians 5:5). A similar action
is recommended for Hymenaeus and Alexander, "that they may learn not to
blaspheme" (1 Timothy 1:20). Hebrews 12:11 says discipline is "painful,"
but "it yields the peaceful fruit of righteousness to those who have been
trained by it." Note how the last two references speak of the learning that
takes place as a result of the discipline. Painful discipline helps direct people
to healthy living.

But the arrogant Israelites are not willing to bow down to the discipline.
So, as Moses says, "And every one of you fastened on his weapons of war and
thought it easy to go up into the hill country" (Deuteronomy 1:41c). As they
were busy getting ready for war, God tells Moses, "Say to them, Do not go up
or fight, for I am not in your midst, lest you be defeated before your enemies"
(1:42). But they are too busy working to listen to the voice of God. Moses tells
them, "So I spoke to you, and you would not listen; but you rebelled against
the command of the LORD and presumptuously went up into the hill country"
(1:43). This is typical of people who are trying to find security from their
activity after they have sinned! They get themselves into a frenzy of activity
to try and silence the voice of God who wants to do a deep working of healing in their lives. They do not want to sit still, so that the Divine Surgeon can
remove the sinful flesh in their body. They want to avoid the humiliation of
having to acknowledge their wrongdoing before others by submitting to the
discipline. So they get busy. They may even be doing "God's work," but that
work is an expression of disobedience to God. Not everything that passes off
as Christian service meets God's approval!

Moses' verdict about this action was that by this action they "rebelled
against the command of the LORD" and acted "presumptuously." It looked
like obedience, but in God's sight it was "arrogance" (NIV). That is how
God regards the bypassing of discipline through doing what we would call
Christian service. Let us be warned! Sadly, as the Bible says, "Pride goes
before destruction, and a haughty spirit before a fall" (Proverbs 16:18). When
people arrogantly bypass discipline they are prime candidates for bigger traps
of Satan than the original trap that triggered the discipline.

Today people break discipline by not following the terms of the disciplinary procedure set out for them. Some move to another church or group. And, sadly, there are Christian groups who will welcome such people, especially if they are gifted and useful to their program. Some modify the constraints placed on them. For example, if they are asked not to preach for six months, they start preaching after three months. If they have been asked to go for regular counseling for a period of three months, they stop after one month.

I have found that many who do not fulfill the terms of the discipline commit the same sin again after a time. The sin revealed a weakness in their lives. The discipline was aimed at healing the weakness. When they encountered a similar situation to what led to the fall the last time, they didn't have the strength to overcome it. If they had followed the discipline, when the temptation came they would have remembered the severe pain that the discipline caused them. That would have acted as a check that helped them overcome the temptation.

God's Angry Silence (1:44–46)

So the Israelites disobeyed God and battled the Amorites. Moses says, "Then the Amorites who lived in that hill country came out against you and chased you as bees do and beat you down in Seir as far as Hormah" (1:44). What a humiliating defeat! Now they have shed their arrogance, and they cry out to God: "And you returned and wept before the LORD, but the LORD did not listen to your voice or give ear to you" (1:45). I am reminded of something a Buddhist classmate told me in high school: "You Christians are lucky guys! You sin and go to church and get God's forgiveness and then go back and do the same thing again, and again you get God to forgive you." It is not so simple, because sin is a very serious thing. We cannot take it lightly like my Buddhist friend said we did.

Weeping when we face the consequences of our sin is not the same as repentance. People can cry with what seems to be deep sorrow over sin without a willingness to change their ways. God will never be deaf to the cry of sinners who are willing to change their ways. What the Israelites needed now, more than weeping, was a sincere desire to obey. And because they did not have that, God would not even listen to their prayers. Verse 46 says, "So you remained at Kadesh many days, the days that you remained there."

This study, like many others from the book of Deuteronomy, shows that following God is serious business. Those who disobey God meet with his displeasure. How sad that the statement my high school friend made represents the way many people think about Christianity. This was the opinion of the Indian leader Gandhi. He was very impressed by the life of Christ, whom he considered the best example of the perfect man. But he said that the Christian doctrine of grace opened the door for irresponsible behavior. He cited examples of irresponsible behavior by people who had abused grace in this way.

7

Provision in the Wilderness

DEUTERONOMY 2:1–23

IN THE FIRST CHAPTER OF DEUTERONOMY Moses recounted some rebellious decisions that caused great setbacks to the progress of the Israelite people on their way to the promised land. Chapter 2 recounts some of their victories that came as a result of their obedience to God. The errors we make warn us so that we avoid the paths that led to them. The victories encourage us to follow the path of obedience. Because we need to remember both the errors and the victories, we have both types of stories in the Bible.

Discipline as a Wilderness Learning Experience (2:1–3)

Deuteronomy 1 tells us how the people rejected God's command to move forward and were told that their generation would not enter the land (1:19–39). Then when God asked them to travel south as a discipline, they traveled north and were roundly defeated (1:40–46). Chapter 2 begins with the words, "Then we turned and journeyed into the wilderness in the direction of the Red Sea, as the LORD told me" (2:1a). After the defeat they obeyed God and traveled south, away from the promised land. The Red Sea mentioned here seems to be what we now know as the Gulf of Aqaba, that is, a fingerlike projection on the north part of the Red Sea. This stage of the journey of the Israelites has been called the "Anti-Exodus" (see McConville). But it opened the door to two great victories against the kings of Heshbon and Bashan (2:24 — 3:11), which must have been very significant because they were later referred to often when encouraging the people.

But before these two victories, they had to go to the wilderness. Moses simply says, "And for many days we traveled around Mount Seir" (2:1b).

Verse 14 informs us that these many days were actually thirty-eight years: "And the time from our leaving Kadesh-barnea until we crossed the brook Zered was thirty-eight years, until the entire generation, that is, the men of war, had perished from the camp, as the LORD had sworn to them." For thirty-eight years they wander without a land. They must learn that God will not accept disobedience, that though he will forgive and restore their covenant relationship with him, it is never worthwhile to sin.

In the earlier wilderness travel God gave them the Law. This time they are going to learn how importance obedience to that Law is. That is going to take place through discipline. The Law would be powerless if the people did not have a will to obey. The discipline will, through its pain, help them develop such a will. Let me say here that churches that have no disciplinary procedures are going to find it difficult to nurture Christians who fear God and live holy lives.

The time finally came when the discipline period was over. Moses says, "Then the LORD said to me, 'You have been traveling around this mountain country long enough. Turn northward . . . '" (2:2, 3). The wilderness learning time is over; now it is time for them to change direction and start marching toward the promised land.

Don't Attack Hostile People without God's Orders (2:4–6)

They would first go through the territory of Esau, known as Edom (Numbers 20:14–21). Moses says, "You are about to pass through the territory of your brothers, the people of Esau, who live in Seir; and they will be afraid of you. So be very careful" (2:4). Strict instructions are given about not fighting with these people: "Do not contend with them, for I will not give you any of their land, no, not so much as for the sole of the foot to tread on, because I have given Mount Seir to Esau as a possession" (2:5). But they must try to get supplies from there: "You shall purchase food from them for money, that you may eat, and you shall also buy water of them for money, that you may drink" (2:6). In the account in Numbers (20:14–21) we see what really happened with Edom. The Israelites asked for food, water, and safe passage, but the Edomites refused. In fact they came up against Israel. But Israel obeyed God's command not to attack them, even though they may have had a much larger army than the Edomites.[1] Instead they took a somewhat circuitous route north without going through Edomite territory.

The command not to attack the Edomites is prefaced by the words, "So be very careful" (2:4b). The Hebrew word translated "careful" is *shamar*, which appears sixty-five times in Deuteronomy (out of 440 in the Old Testament).

We will look at this word in other studies. But let me say now that the word essentially means, "pay careful attention to."[2] Fearful people can act rashly, and wisdom is needed to know how best to respond to their action. The natural reaction would be to attack a weaker opponent who is afraid of them but is coming to attack them. Holding back was unusual because in the ancient Near Eastern culture, as in many cultures today, when one group dishonors another group like this, they are expected to protect their honor and hit back. Asian converts to Christianity find that not hitting back is a very difficult task. Therefore they needed to be especially careful.

During the exodus and conquest several groups of people were destroyed, but that was because it was necessary for the ultimate good (see our discussion on Deuteronomy 7). But this is not the same as attacking our enemies. Not only the New Testament but also the Old Testament teaches us to show kindness to our enemies (Exodus 23:4, 5; Proverbs 25:21, 22). Victory in war is never simply for the sake of victory. One cannot, from Deuteronomy, build a case for colonizing militarily weaker countries with a view to expanding an empire. They are permitted to destroy only those who seriously threaten their existence. Their existence was very important for the greater good of the whole human race.

Actually often when Christians do not hit back when they could have, as here, they give evidence of true Christianity. A colleague working in our drug rehab ministry was once assaulted by a gang just outside the center. The students at the center wanted to hit back. He had himself been a gang leader before his conversion, and that is what he would have done in his pre-Christian days. But not only did he stop the students from hitting back, he found that he did not have even a desire to hit back. Later he told me that the fact that he did not desire to hit back was a great encouragement to him. It assured him that God had indeed done a definite work in his life. He told me, "Now I know I am a real Christian."

Care During Discipline Time (2:7)

The wilderness wandering period included thirty-eight years when the people were under discipline. But Moses says this was a time when God blessed them and cared for them: "For the LORD your God has blessed you in all the work of your hands. He knows your going through this great wilderness. These forty years the LORD your God has been with you. You have lacked nothing" (2:7). The punishment or discipline included negative consequences on earth. Sin does hinder our progress. But if we are open to God during this time, we know that he will look after us and meet our needs. Discipline is a lonely time, and sometimes even God seems to be silent. But God is working in the midst of these experiences. Our job is to be obedient and to follow his instructions. If we are faithful to his covenant, he will be faithful to us. We must not attempt to bypass the discipline. The Israelites had tried to do that, and they experienced a huge defeat (1:41–46).

Hebrews 12:11 says, "For the moment all discipline seems painful rather than pleasant." We will be hurt by reactions of people to us. We will interpret innocent statements of others negatively and be hurt by them. Because of this sensitive situation others do not know how to best relate to us and sometimes tend to avoid meeting us or speaking to us. This makes us feel rejected and causes more pain. Then there is the humiliation of the discipline, the wagging tongues that say untrue things about us. We can go on and on. How can we say we lacked nothing in such a situation?

A plea of David in his famous psalm of repentance gives us a clue to solving this puzzle. After his sin with Bathsheba he had painful things happen to him until the day he died. The baby born from his adultery died shortly after being born. Much pain came to him from the behavior of his children. But in his psalm twice he asks for joy. He prays, "Let me hear joy and gladness; let the bones that you have broken rejoice. . . . Restore to me the joy of your salvation, and uphold me with a willing spirit" (Psalm 51:8, 12). If we have the joy of the Lord we will be able to endure all the pain in the world. "The joy of the LORD is [our] strength" (Nehemiah 8:10). "Strength" here means "stronghold" or "fortress."[3] That is, the joy of the Lord is what enables us to withstand all the painful things we encounter. The most important things in our lives are that God loves us, that no pain can destroy our relationship with him, and that he will look after us because his love and power are greater than the hatred and power of all other forces. Love, of course, is the source of the deepest joy. Whatever happens to us, we have a joy deep down that is greater than all the negative things we have to endure.

So we will desperately battle to ensure that we always have the joy of the Lord. John Stam and his wife Betty were missionaries in China who were martyred in 1934 when they were twenty-seven and twenty-eight years old. Their tragic death motivated many young people to missionary service. John once said, "Take away everything I have, but do not take away the sweetness of walking and talking with the King of glory."[4]

Applying this to the lives of those who have been disciplined, we can say that they may have joy amidst the pain because they know God is with them, caring for them, providing for them, and turning even the painful experiences into good. This helps them persevere along the path of obedience and, by doing that, to experience all the good that God intended for them through the discipline. Then when they come out of their discipline period, their hearts will not be filled with anger, which is how many come out and thus do not have spiritual freedom to live a vibrant Christian life.

Don't Keep Grudges Against Those Who Oppose (2:8)

Verse 8a says, "So we went on, away from our brothers, the people of Esau, who live in Seir, away from the Arabah road from Elath and Ezion-geber." They had to take a somewhat circuitous route. The Edomites had refused to help them and instead had come out with a large and strong army to fight them (Numbers 20:17–21). But Moses refers to them as "your brothers," and he doesn't mention their bad actions. Instead he says that they proceeded on their journey, as God has asked them to, without harming the people: "And we turned and went in the direction of the wilderness of Moab" (Deuteronomy 2:8b). There was no need to dwell on these unpleasant past conflicts. The main thing is that through all of it, God had worked to bless them.

In Paul's love chapter he says, "[Love] keeps no record of wrongs" (1 Corinthians 13:5, NIV). The Greek verb used here, *logizomai*, is often translated as "reckon" or "count." To reckon something is to consider it still as an important factor that influences our attitudes and actions. Paul uses the same word in 2 Corinthians 5:19: ". . . in Christ God was reconciling the world to himself, not *counting* their trespasses against them." Because of Christ and his work God does not reckon or count our sin against us; he does not take our sins into account in his attitude toward us. Similarly because God turns everything to good, we do not hold grudges against those who refuse to help us and oppose us. We have no need to because the unpleasant action has become something that God used to benefit us.

Is this the way we respond to those who reject our requests for help and who oppose us? We do not need to be resentful and hurt that we were not helped. If God permitted that person to refuse to help us, it is because God has something better in store for us. Why should we be angry over an action that opened the door to great blessings from God? We can feel sorry for the other person. We can regret that we do not have a loving relationship with that person. But we do not need to constantly keep bringing up this matter and meditating on the fact that we were not helped. That is bitterness. And if God is sovereign there is no reason for those who love him to be bitter. They know that "for those who love God all things work together for good" in their lives (Romans 8:28).

Christians don't keep grudges because they have no need to, considering that God turned the evil done to them into good. Indeed, when love is rejected, there will be hurt. But the hurt does not grow into bitterness because we know God will turn it into something good. We may feel sorry for the person, we may be sad that our loving overtures were rejected, but we will not be bitter. Some Christians live with the sense that they have been wronged. They are carrying a huge and unnecessary burden that takes away their joy.

Remember That God Directs History (2:5, 9–12, 16–23)

Verses 9, 19 contain more commands from God not to harm the nations they will encounter on their way to the promised land. This time they are asked to pass without harming two nations that descended from Lot: Moab and Ammon. Earlier a similar command was given about Edom, which descended from Esau (2:5):

> Do not harass Moab or contend with them in battle, for I will not give you any of their land for a possession, because I have given Ar to the people of Lot for a possession. (2:9)

> And when you approach the territory of the people of Ammon, do not harass them or contend with them, for I will not give you any of the land of the people of Ammon as a possession, because I have given it to the sons of Lot for a possession. (2:19)

Verses 10–12 and 20–23 are presented as parentheses in most Bibles. They describe the previous inhabitants of these lands and report on how these lands were taken over by their present inhabitants. Verse 12 compares the way the people of Esau took hold of their land with the way Israel took over her land. Israel took over the land after Moses died, and this leads us to the conclusion that all or parts of these two parentheses were not in Moses' speech but were probably inserted by an editor later on.

An important truth emerges from the description of how these three nations, which are not to be harmed, received their lands. Each time we are told that God is the one who gave them their lands. God says, "I have given Mount Seir to Esau as a possession" (2:5). "I have given Ar to the people of Lot for a possession" (2:9). "I have given [Ammon] to the sons of Lot for a possession" (2:19). Verse 21 talks of "a people great and many, as tall as the Anakim [giants]" and goes on to say, "but the Lord destroyed them before the Ammonites." God is dealing with these three nations, who did not acknowledge him, in a way similar to the way he dealt with Israel. Earlier Pharaoh was told that the whole earth belongs to God (Exodus 9:14, 16, 29). Later we find God using Assyrians, Babylonians, and Persians to carry out his purposes. Chris Wright describes this theme as "God's ultimate, universal direction of the nations (Deut. 32:8; Jer. 18:1–10; 27:1–7)." These nations who were given their land by God were not righteous nations. Moab and Ammon did a lot of evil and were often a problem to Israel. But we affirm that nothing happens without God knowing and permitting. Even the evil that nations do will be ultimately turned by God to fulfill his good purposes. All nations, even those that rebel against God and his ways, owe their existence and lands to God's sovereignty over history (see Acts 17:26).

Today we may be quite bewildered by what is happening in our nations. The day I studied this text, something I viewed as terrible was going to take place in Sri Lanka. A pact was going to be signed between two political parties, one of them strongly anti-Christian, that I felt would really hurt the country. When I got up in the morning my wife reminded me of this. I had a strong sense of despair, and I told her, "What a sad day this is." Then I studied this passage. I realized that we do not need to lose heart. God is in control of history and is working out his sovereign will through all the different events in the world. We will concentrate on obedience to God even in the darkest night and believe that ultimately God will do what is good.

Remember That God Was against His People (2:13–18)

After the parenthesis (2:10–12) we come back to Moses' speech in verse 13. He mentions how God commanded the people to go over the brook Zered, which separated Edom (with Esau's descendants) and Moab (with Lot's descendants): "Now rise up and go over the brook Zered." And they obeyed: "So we went over the brook Zered." Next Moses gives a sober reminder that the generation that started off from Egypt did not reach the promised land: "And the time from our leaving Kadesh-barnea until we crossed the brook Zered was thirty-eight years, until the entire generation, that is, the men of war, had perished from the camp, as the LORD had sworn to them" (2:14). Why? Moses says, "For indeed the hand of the LORD was against them, to destroy them from the camp, until they had perished" (2:15).

God was against them! What strong words to use about the people who had experienced such marvelous blessings from God: the ten plagues, the exodus, the crossing of the Red Sea, the pillar of cloud by day, the pillar of fire by night, the manna from heaven for so many years. But they were not going to see the land because they were stubborn and rebellious in spite of all the blessings that God gave them.

The promise that they would not see the land was made thirty-eight years earlier. But it was fulfilled after they had wandered in the wilderness for all that time. We may forget our promises after some years, but God does not. That includes his promises to bless and to punish. We have a very interesting paradox here. Verse 7 says that God was with these people and provided for them all this time. Verse 15 says that at the same time he was "against them." They were still God's people, but they will not get the blessing of entering the land. Putting it in today's language, they were saved people, but because of their disobedience they would not receive the honors and fruitfulness that should have been theirs. They were disqualified from receiving the prize (1 Corinthians 9:27).

Paul had in mind these same events described in Deuteronomy when he wrote his famous words of warning in 1 Corinthians 10. Paul lists the great blessings of God that they received (vv. 1–4). "Nevertheless," says Paul, "with most of them God was not pleased, for they were overthrown in the wilderness" (v. 5). Twice he says that the Old Testament records these events so that we may be warned and instructed (vv. 6, 11). Then comes his famous warning: "Therefore let anyone who thinks that he stands take heed lest he fall" (v. 12). Thank God, Paul does not end with that warning. The very next statement is a word of encouragement that we do not need to live defeated lives: "No temptation has overtaken you that is not common to man. God is faithful, and he will not let you be tempted beyond your ability, but with the temptation he will also provide the way of escape, that you may be able to endure it" (v. 13).

This passage has two paradoxes. The first is that God provides for us but does not make us immune to wilderness experiences. Life is not always easy. But God is with us and will work out his purposes for us even through the wilderness. Second, God will bless us and give us great victories for him, but even after that we can disobey and forfeit his final blessing. Let us be encouraged by God's presence and power and be warned about the dangers of rebellion and stubbornness.

I will close this discussion with a word of encouragement to anyone who may be going through a wilderness experience. God's providences are sometimes mysterious. But there is no doubt about his ability and willingness to turn the most terrible situations into good. It may be very humiliating because these experiences do not give external evidence that God is blessing us. People may even question our commitment. Therefore be faithful!

A very saintly missionary went to an unreached area and ministered there for several decades but did not see any visible fruit from his work. He finally died among those people. A young inexperienced missionary was sent to replace him. He was surprised when large numbers of people came to Christ shortly after he arrived there. He asked the people how it is that they did not become Christians when that saintly man was among them. They replied that this missionary had told them that if you are a Christian you do not fear death. They said they wanted to see him die to know whether what he said was true. After they saw him die, they realized it was true. And they accepted the message as soon as his replacement came.

8

Doing Battle with God's Help

DEUTERONOMY 2:24—3:11

WE ARE FOLLOWING MOSES' first speech made to the Israelite people before his death (1:6—4:43). This speech consists primarily of a retelling of the story of the journey to the promised land. Moses has just explained how they passed by the lands inhabited by the descendants of Esau and Lot without warring with them because those lands were allotted to those people by God (2:1–23). Now we come to the first lands that the Israelites are going to own. This means that the people living there will be replaced by the Israelites. This land, which is east of the Jordan River, is usually called the Transjordan territory, as it is on the other side of Jordan when viewed from the mainland of Israel.

Moses' description of the battles with the two kingdoms in this passage gives us some valuable principles of doing battle with God's help that could be applied to our lives today, too.

The Victory Is Won before the Battle Starts (2:24, 25)

We Must Take Hold of the Victory (2:24)

God commanded the people, "Rise up, set out on your journey and go over the Valley of the Arnon" (2:24a). The valley of the Arnon River served as the border between Moab, where Lot's descendants lived, and the region of the Amorites. It flows west into the Dead Sea at a point near the middle of its eastern shore. God is asking them to go to the border of the land of the Amorites where they will encounter a hostile king. Yet in God's mind victory is already an accomplished fact. He says, "Behold, I have given into your hand Sihon the Amorite, king of Heshbon, and his land" (2:24b).

When the parents of this generation of Israelites refused to obey God and go north to take the land, they said, "Because the LORD hated us he has brought us out of the land of Egypt, to give us into the hand of the Amorites, to destroy us" (1:27). They accused God of giving them into the hand of the Amorites. But what God says here is, "I have given into your hand Sihon the Amorite." Unbelief can warp our minds so that we see the opposite of what would happen if God were with us. Sometimes because of our disobedience this opposite of blessing is finally what happens. Then we say, "See, I told you that God would not look after me." But the reason for the defeat was not God's inability to look after us; it was our refusal to accept God's help.

I have seen some people come to Christ from poorer backgrounds who are unwilling to totally commit themselves to God's ways. They continue to lie, sometimes rob a little from their employers, and not do their job conscientiously. But they come to church regularly and claim to be Christians. Usually these people are never freed from the bondage of poverty. They continue to depend on handouts from other Christians who help them because otherwise they and their children would starve. When they are confronted about their unrighteous ways, they say they have to resort to these ways in order to feed their children. How we wish that they would trust God and look to him to provide as he has promised to do!

I have seen others, also from poorer backgrounds, who decide to follow God totally and give up their past behavior. I have seen them start earning money through hard work. Their homes are transformed from places ruined by alcohol and poverty into places reflecting the beauty of Christ. They obeyed God and saw how God blesses the faithful.

God Prepares the Way; We Work Hard (2:24c, 25)

The victory is won in God's eyes, but the people have to obey in order to practically take hold of it. So God tells them, "Begin to take possession, and contend with him [King Sihon] in battle" (2:24c). The words, "*Begin* to take possession" show that they are beginning the process of taking possession of the promised land. They are to overthrow the kingdom of Heshbon under King Sihon (2:24b). This and the next kingdom they are to overthrow—Bashan under King Og (3:1–11)—are both relatively small kingdoms.

God did miraculous things for them, like parting the Jordan River and destroying the walls of Jericho. But they, too, had to work hard. They must "contend with [Sihon] in battle." It is the same with the victories that God will give us. God has prepared the victory, but he has made humans with the capacity for hard work. It is as we work hard that we reach our fullest potential as human beings. So he chooses our hard work as a means by which he will grant us the victory he has already won.

God works, ahead of our work, to prepare the way for our work. Here he causes fear in the hearts of the enemies. Verse 25 says, "This day I will begin to put the dread and fear of you on the peoples who are under the whole heaven, who shall hear the report of you and shall tremble and be in anguish because of you." Nearly forty years before this battle against Sihon, in Moses' song after the crossing of the Red Sea, he said that particular victory would cause terror among the people of Canaan (Exodus 15:14–16).

We may not be involved today in physical "holy wars" ordained by God. But we have numerous battles against those who have convictions opposed to ours. I think of the battles against numerous moral sins such as class, caste and race prejudice, exploitation of the poor, abortion-on-demand, same-sex marriage, pornography, selfish individualism, and greed. Then there are the battles for the souls of individuals trapped in unbelief and sin. We can be assured that God goes before us and prepares the way for us. Sometimes as we go to a place to battle, we are surprised that God has been there preparing the people for our work. For example, someone has already spoken to the person to whom we are to speak and made the person much more receptive to what we say.

But we know that this is not always so. How is it that our opponents seem to have no fear of us so that we are the ones who are intimidated by their arrogance and confidence? Two thoughts come to mind.

First, their show of confidence may be a mask hiding their lack of confidence. Numbers 20:14–21 says that the Edomites came up to battle the Israelites who wanted to pass through their land because they were afraid. Anyone living against the way God intends for him to live will be insecure. Their conscience bothers them, and their humanity revolts against their unholy lifestyle. You cannot go against the way you were intended to live and expect to have peace and joy. Psalm 119:165 says, "Great peace have those who love your law; nothing can make them stumble." As a great American preacher from an earlier generation, Henry Clay Morrison, said, "God never fixed me up so that I could not sin. He fixed me up so that I could not sin and enjoy it."

I think our youths (and adults too) need to be told this as they are bombarded by an approach to life that says that personal desires must be met even if they are morally wrong. The Western media aggressively presents the idea that not only is it okay to have sex outside of marriage, one owes it to oneself to be gratified in this way. We need to remind ourselves that not only is this abhorrent to God, it also takes away the real pleasure and joy that God intends us to have through costly, lifetime commitment to a spouse. We must remind ourselves that though immorality is flaunted as an enjoyable way to live, it is not so; rather, it leaves people restless and unfulfilled.

We may feel very small as we face powerful forces whose influence and power we cannot seem to match. But we must remember that if these powerful forces are rebelling against God's way, they are insecure and restless. Their confidence may be a mask to hide massive insecurity. We will face the enemy with the quiet confidence of a prince or princess in the kingdom of the King of kings. Earlier we described the quiet confidence of Bishop Polycarp as he faced death (see my comments on 1:28).

This is why the contemporary caricature of fundamentalists does not fit in with Biblical Christianity. According to this caricature, fundamentalists are sour people with one-track minds who treat their opponents with disrespect, who do not try to understand them, and who refuse to listen to reason. They are seen as loveless individuals intent on destroying their enemies. These are all signs of insecurity. These are people who are threatened by the show of confidence by their opponents. We do not need to act that way because we belong to God. Believing in the power of truth, we will contend for it using whatever means possible to engage those with different views. But we will do so with gentleness and respect (1 Peter 3:15, 16).

Second, we must remember that the God who won his battles then will win them now also. However, his means to victory is often the way of the cross. For a time the opponents of God's truth may seem to be very powerful while we seem to be very weak. We may go through what temporarily looks like defeat. The early Christians may often have felt like a defeated bunch of people when they were being hounded and martyred by the Roman authorities. But even their martyrdom became an occasion for witness. People saw that Christianity was so powerful that it gave Christians the strength to suffer joyfully. They realized Christianity had an answer to something that they were afraid of: suffering. And within three centuries Rome had bowed its knee to Christ.

God's Mysterious Providence (2:26–30)

Peace Terms to a Group Destined for Destruction (2:26–29)

Verse 26 introduces a section that leaves the modern reader very puzzled. It says Moses "sent messengers from the wilderness of Kedemoth to Sihon the king of Heshbon, with words of peace." How could one send a message of peace to a people who are going to be overthrown and destroyed? Gordon McConville explains that the "words of peace" here "represent a conventional diplomatic opening, which implies the possibility of war (cf. Deut. 20:10).

They are presenting a challenge to Sihon to submit to Israel's, and Yahweh's, terms—though Moses knows . . . that he will not." Deuteronomy 20:10–14 says that with such cities, if they respond positively to the peace overture, the people should be made to do forced labor. If they respond negatively, they are to be destroyed.

The messengers are to ask for safe passage, citing what happened with Edom and Moab:

> Let me pass through your land. I will go only by the road; I will turn aside neither to the right nor to the left. You shall sell me food for money, that I may eat, and give me water for money, that I may drink. Only let me pass through on foot, as the sons of Esau who live in Seir and the Moabites who live in Ar did for me, until I go over the Jordan into the land that the LORD our God is giving to us. (2:27–29; see 2:1–19)

The idea is that this land is to be like the lands they went through because their real destination is on the west side of the Jordan.

How could they give a message like this if they were planning to occupy this land? J. A. Thompson, who agrees that "the problem is complex," suggests a possible solution. He says it is true that in later centuries Israel regarded these Transjordan lands as rightfully theirs and later fought wars to retain them. But this territory was not "part of the land of promise defined in Genesis 12 and 15:18–20." I would add that when they were offered peace it could be that the intention was to do what Deuteronomy 20:10–14 stated. That is, they would become forced labor if they accepted the terms or would be destroyed if they did not. They did not accept the terms; therefore they were destroyed. We note that according to 2:32, it was Sihon who "came out against" the Israelites. He was the initiator of the battle, the aggressor. We come back to Thompson who says, "Once conquered, however, areas in Transjordan were regarded as Israelite territory and were allotted to the two and a half tribes."

What we see here is one aspect of the mystery of God's providence. He knows what will happen—that they will reject the offer of peace. But the offer of peace is genuine and a very real possibility. As in many issues involving divine sovereignty and providence and human choice, the two streams will need to be kept in tension in a way our finite minds find difficult to fully resolve. I present the above explanation only as a suggested resolution, rather than a firm position, on a difficult problem.

God Hardens a King's Spirit (2:30)

Verse 30a says, "But Sihon the king of Heshbon would not let us pass by him." That by itself would harmonize with the above suggested resolution to the problem. However, this verse goes on to say regarding Sihon's action, ". . . for the LORD your God hardened his spirit and made his heart obstinate, that he might give him into your hand, as he is this day." Was he then like a mindless puppet who had no say in the decision? Again we come to the mystery of God's providence. This kind of language is used to describe the way God works through people's sin to achieve his purposes. Ten times Exodus says that Pharaoh hardened his heart.[1] And ten times it says that God hardened Pharaoh's heart.[2]

Both these truths should be kept side by side without diluting either. Pharaoh and Sihon were responsible for their actions. They did not want to help Israel, and God was going to work through that. The all-knowing God confirmed them in their decision so that it could be said that God hardened their hearts. Which came first, their decision to rebel or God hardening their heart? I do not think the Bible gives us sufficient evidence to answer that question with confidence. I prefer to leave such questions unanswered without going into speculation that could lead us to deny some truth that is found in the Scriptures.

An interesting argument is found in Romans 1:18–32, where three times Paul uses the expression "God gave them up" to describe how humans were let loose by God to do grossly sinful deeds following their rejection of God (vv. 24, 26, 28). God's giving them up is viewed as punishment for the more basic act of rejecting God. God confirmed them in their rejection by giving them up so that they can now sin without restraint. This could be the type of thing that happened with King Sihon. He first rejected God's way. Then God helped carry through that rejection to its ultimate end by hardening the king's heart.

The Battle That Completes the Victory (2:31–37)

Earlier we said that the battle is won even before the actual battle starts, because God wills for it to happen (2:24). But this has to be completed through an actual physical battle where humans are physically involved. That battle is now described.

Once More: "Begin to Take Possession" (2:31)

Once more, as in verse 24, Moses mentions God's command to go and possess the land that God has already acted to give them: "And the LORD said to me, 'Behold, I have begun to give Sihon and his land over to you. Begin to take possession, that you may occupy his land'" (2:31). God has "*begun* to give Sihon and his land," so they must "*begin* to take possession" of the land. God acts to prepare the way. We must obey in order to reap the benefits of his action. Again both God's providence and human obedience are needed for victory.

God Gives Victory, We Obey (2:32, 33)

The battle was initiated by Sihon: "Then Sihon came out against us, he and all his people, to battle at Jahaz" (2:32). The divine-human synergy is well expressed in Moses' description of the battle: "And the LORD our *God gave* him over to us, and *we defeated* him and his sons and all his people" (2:33). God gives victory, but we must launch out in obedience. This is the key to fruitfulness. Often the Israelites refused to launch out, and not only did they lose, they were also punished for their disobedience.

What God needs from us is faithfulness. Paul says that we are "stewards of the mysteries of God" (1 Corinthians 4:1). The word "steward" is used for the "manager of a household. . . . Often a trusted slave was put in charge of the whole household. The word emphasizes that one is entrusted with great responsibility and accountability."[3] Paul goes on to say, "Moreover, it is required of stewards that they be found trustworthy" (1 Corinthians 4:2). Paul says about himself that Jesus "judged me faithful, appointing me to his service" (1 Timothy 1:12). That is the key: not brilliance but faithfulness.

Anyone examining the life of William Carey (1761–1834), the former shoe repairer, would agree that he was a brilliant man. He personally translated the Bible into several languages. But he did many other things also.

> He himself served as professor of Sanskrit, Bengali, and Marathi [three Indian languages] at the College of Fort William; he supervised and edited translations of the Scriptures into thirty-six languages, produced a massive Bengali-English dictionary, pioneered social reform, and founded the Agricultural and Horticultural Society of India. Carey has generally been acclaimed as "the Father of Modern Missions."[4]

But when you look at Carey's life and the amazing obstacles with which he worked, you realize that the key to his effectiveness was his persevering in what God called him to do. Once during a felicitation for him, after many eloquent things had been said about him and his work, Carey responded by simply saying, "I am just a plodder." If we simply say, "Lord, I want to do what you want me to do," there is no telling what God can do through us!

Total Destruction (2:34, 35)

Next Moses says how there was total destruction of the people: "And we captured all his cities at that time and devoted to destruction every city, men, women, and children. We left no survivors. Only the livestock we took as spoil for ourselves, with the plunder of the cities that we captured" (2:34, 35). This brings out another feature in God's dealings with humans in the Old Testament that is difficult to understand. Why does God ask for everyone to be destroyed? We will discuss it in some length in our discussion on Deuteronomy 7, which focuses on the issue of what some people call "holy wars."

No City Was Too High (2:36, 37)

Next Moses describes the extent of the victory: "From Aroer, which is on the edge of the Valley of the Arnon, and from the city that is in the valley, as far as Gilead, there was not a city too high for us. The LORD our God gave all into our hands" (2:36). Their fathers, refusing to go forward and take the land, had said, "The cities are great and fortified up to heaven" (1:28). Now Moses says, "there was not a city too high for us."

Often people refuse to obey, saying the challenge is too great or the cost is too much. "If I don't tell a lie or slander a colleague, I could never progress in my job." "There are no committed Christians around. So what can I do? God has not given me a believer, so I will marry an unbeliever." "This calling is too difficult. I need to take another job." "These people are too resistant to the gospel. There is no point in my continuing to work among them." "This place is too unsafe for me and my family to live in. I need to serve somewhere else."

Others obey, sometimes reluctantly, even though they have real concerns about the situation. And God sees them through to victory. Then they can say things like what Moses said in 2:36: "It was not as difficult as I thought." "God did give me the strength to complete this project." "God did look after me." This is the thrill of obedience. We launch out in faith while others, and sometimes we ourselves, think we are fools. But God provides our every need. There is temporary fear, but that is replaced by permanent joy over God's deliverance! If we never got into difficult situations, how could God ever have an opportunity of delivering us? How boring life would be without a few crises and nail-biting happy endings!

Verse 37 says, "Only to the land of the sons of Ammon you did not draw near, that is, to all the banks of the river Jabbok and the cities of the hill country, whatever the LORD our God had forbidden us" (2:37). They were obedient not only in attack but also in sparing people whom God had asked them to spare. The Ammonites were the descendants of Lot to whom God had given the land they were occupying. God had told Israel, "Do not harass them or contend with them" (2:19).

A Repeat Victory (3:1–11)

One Victory Encourages Us to Anticipate Another (3:1–7)

After the victory over King Sihon (2:24–37), God leads them to victory over King Og of Bashan (3:1–11). Bashan is the area north of Heshbon. The Hebrew word points to the meaning "fertile" or "fruitful." This is probably where the modern Golan Heights is, directly east of the Sea of Galilee. It was known for its wealth and fertility and for land suitable for grazing. The Bible often refers to its fertility, high-grade cattle, oaks, and mountains. Once conquered it became the northernmost district of the Transjordan region.

Here, too, the king initiates the war against Israel: "Then we turned and went up the way to Bashan. And Og the king of Bashan came out against us, he and all his people, to battle at Edrei" (3:1). Again God reassures Moses that they will have victory, but this time he adds a word asking them not to fear: "But the LORD said to me, 'Do not fear him, for I have given him and all his people and his land into your hand'" (3:2a).

God also says that this battle will be victorious like the previous one was: "And you shall do to him as you did to Sihon the king of the Amorites, who lived at Heshbon" (3:2b). One victory gives us the courage to look hopefully to another. The victories over Heshbon and Bashan are going to be used often in the rest of the Old Testament as evidences of God's ability to see us through the battles we face. I found thirteen such places where this victory is used as a ground for encouragement or praise.[5] There are important lessons for us here. We must recall God's acts in history and in our own personal lives so that we will be encouraged to believe that God will see us through present crises (see the discussion on 4:9–14).

Like before, the victory in battle and how the people were devoted to destruction is described (3:3–7). This time there is no statement similar to what was said in 2:36: "there was not a city too high for us." Instead, there is a more detailed description of the height of the cities: "All these were cities fortified with high walls, gates, and bars, besides very many unwalled villages" (3:5).

Why Details of God's Workings Are Important (3:8–10)

Verses 8–10 describe the extent of the land acquired through battle. This description is conspicuous for its many details:

> So we took the land at that time out of the hand of the two kings of the Amorites who were beyond the Jordan, from the Valley of the Arnon to Mount Hermon (the Sidonians call Hermon Sirion, while the Amorites call

it Senir), all the cities of the tableland and all Gilead and all Bashan, as far as Salecah and Edrei, cities of the kingdom of Og in Bashan. (3:8–10)

I want to glean two implications from this attention to detail. First, the comprehensiveness of the description shows how important it is for us to be careful to note all of God's goodness to us. The time will come when we will have problems and will be tempted to lose heart. A firm hold of all of God's goodness over the years will help us keep hoping for deliverance during the hard times. The familiar song by Johnson Oatman Jr. puts it well:

When upon life's billows you are tempest tossed,
When you are discouraged, thinking all is lost,
Count your many blessings, name them one by one,
And it will surprise you what the Lord hath done.
Count your blessings, name them one by one,
Count your blessings, see what God hath done!
Count your blessings, name them one by one,
And it will surprise you what the Lord hath done.

Second, would you expect so much detail in a description in which the author was not sure whether the events happened exactly as mentioned in the description? I think not. I think the way that Old Testament (and New Testament) history is written drives us to the conclusion that the authors really believed that the events took place just as they described them. If it was not so, they would be frauds. It is significant that one of the views that discount the historicity of Deuteronomy has been described with the words, "Pious Fraud." I believe that one who wrote history as a service to God would avoid fraudulent methodology.

The End of a Line of Heroes (3:11)

Next there is what may not be a part of the speech but an editorial insertion that explains that Og was the last of the great ancient hero figures known as the Rephaim: "For only Og the king of Bashan was left of the remnant of the Rephaim. Behold, his bed was a bed of iron. Is it not in Rabbah of the Ammonites? Nine cubits was its length, and four cubits its breadth, according to the common cubit" (3:11). His greatness is mentioned to serve as a reminder for generations to come of the greatness of the victory that God won for them over their enemies. As McConville puts it, "The monument to the hero king's memory ironically becomes an eloquent witness to the power of Yahweh over all such giants (cf. 1:28)."

9

Preparing a Community to Live Harmoniously

DEUTERONOMY 3:12–29

THE PASSAGE WE WILL NOW STUDY (3:12–29) gives us some hints on how a leader can prepare a community to live harmoniously long-term. Moses has been recounting the story of their journey to the promised land. He has come to the stage where some lands east of the River Jordan have been conquered. After some time spent looking back to the past, the time has come for Moses to prepare them for what is ahead. This is what will occupy the rest of this first speech of Moses.

Clarity in the Distribution of Assets (3:12–17)

First Moses describes how the lands conquered by the Israelites east of the River Jordan were given to a section of the Israelite community. Moses cannot enter the mainland of the promised land. The distribution of that land will be done by Joshua. He is given the task of supervising the division of the Transjordan lands. The northern border of the land was Chinnereth, which refers either to a city on the Sea of Galilee or to the Sea itself (3:17). The southern border is about halfway down the Sea of the Arabah, which was also called the Salt Sea or the Dead Sea (3:17). The tribe of Reuben will get the southernmost region; the region north of that will go to Gad (3:12, 16). The northernmost region will go to the half-tribe of Manasseh (Joseph's son) (3:13).

Two of Manasseh's sons are specifically mentioned. Verse 14 says, "Jair the Manassite took all the region of Argob, that is, Bashan, as far as the border of the Geshurites and the Maacathites, and called the villages after his own name, Havvoth-jair, as it is to this day." Jair was a leading warrior in the conquest of Gilead by Moses (Numbers 32:40, 41). The expression "as it is to this day" in Deuteronomy 3:14 gives evidence of an editorial hand at work in the composition of the book of Deuteronomy. We said in our discussion of 1:1 that the content of Moses' words seem to have been touched up by an editor or editors here and there, and this seems to be one of those places. Verse 15 says, "To [Manasseh's eldest son] Machir I gave Gilead."

Numbers 32 gives us some background that sheds more light on this passage. The tribes of Reuben and Gad asked for this land because it was good grazing land, and these two tribes had a lot of livestock. Moses became alarmed, thinking that they might settle here and not participate in the conquest of the land west of Jordan. Once they gave assurance that they would indeed go to battle, Moses allotted these lands east of Jordan to them.

It would be pertinent to ask at this stage why so much space is given to the report of the demarcation of land, a description that is rather boring to read and that does not make much sense unless we have a map in front of us. This type of tedious description is found often in the Old Testament. The thought that came to me was that when it comes to the distribution of possessions and land there needs to be clarity on the part of the donor or the leader. Otherwise there could be a lot of unpleasantness, with some saying that one person or group took more than their rightful share. One can cite many stories of siblings, respected Christians, who fought among themselves after their parents handed over the family business to them. The sad phenomenon of families battling over property after a father or mother dies, without leaving instructions for the distribution of the property, has not escaped the Christian church.

Sometimes leaders assume that we can simply leave it to the people to distribute responsibilities or property among themselves. But when it comes to the distribution of assets, even Christians can forget their Christian values as greed clouds out better sense. Often the anger over such situations surfaces in the form of a battle for justice. Therefore, good leaders carefully allot responsibility before leaving. Good parents make sure that instructions are given (usually through a will) for the distribution of their wealth. I can write about this with some feeling because I have sometimes not done this in connection with my leadership role. I have come to view this as a failure to lead properly.

Join in the Battles of Others (3:18–20)

The next paragraph (3:18–20) describes how Moses told the people who were settled in the lands east of Jordan to join the rest of the nation in its battle for the rest of the land west of the Jordan. Numbers has a more detailed description. The people of Reuben and Gad told Moses that this land was suited for them because it is "a land for livestock" and they had a lot of livestock (Numbers 32:4). Their request is: "If we have found favor in your sight, let this land be given to your servants for a possession. Do not take us across the Jordan" (Numbers 32:5). Moses was alarmed by this request and responded with strong words, even comparing their not joining in with the rebellion of the people after the episode in Kadesh-barnea. He said that they could be punished for their non-involvement in the battle just as the people were after the spy episode (Numbers 32:8–15). The Transjordan tribes agreed to join in the battle, and Moses approved their request for the land, while permitting them to make provision for the care of their families and flocks (Numbers 32:16–27).

Our Possessions Are Given by God (3:18a, 20b)

A major point in Moses' exhortation to the Transjordan tribes to join in the battle of their fellow Israelites is the statement that this land has been given to them by God. So the statement by Moses begins and ends with that affirmation. He begins saying, "And I commanded you at that time, saying, 'The LORD your God has given you this land to possess. All your men of valor shall cross over armed before your brothers, the people of Israel'" (3:18). He ends by saying that after the conquest is complete, "Then each of you may return to his possession which I have given you" (3:20).

The Bible proclaims that the whole earth belongs to God. Therefore, whatever we have is given to us by God. Deuteronomy 8:18 says, "You shall remember the LORD your God, for it is he who gives you power to get wealth." As J. L. Kelso says, "Wealth is the gift of God. . . . The believer is only the administrator of God's wealth."[1] An awareness of this truth has a marked influence on the way we look at our possessions. We will always seek God's will in the use of them. When we see needs in the community, we ask God whether he would have us share something of our possessions in order to meet that need. This is not to say that private ownership of possessions is wrong. What is wrong is for us to think that because what we have is ours, we can do whatever we wish with it.

Moses tells the Transjordan tribes that because God gave them what they have, now they must help others to also get what they need to have. Some may think this is a terrible bondage that makes it impossible for us to enjoy what we have. Let me assert the exact opposite. When we assert that all we have is from God, we are not afraid of losing what we have. We are free to fully enjoy it. Some people are so protective of what they have that they cannot be free to enjoy life. In this enjoyable life under God one of the greatest joys is helping others. Those who have the love of God in their hearts want to express love. Giving time, energy, and resources for others is a thrill to them. It activates God's love and lets it flow out of our lives, and in the process God's love in us does its work of giving us a deep joy. St. Francis of Assisi is a Christian who exemplified the sheer joy of giving to others. He knew what the Bible meant when it spoke of eager (2 Corinthians 8:3, 4), extravagant (1 Timothy 6:18), and "cheerful" (2 Corinthians 9:7) giving.

Caring for Family While Battling for God (3:18b, 19)

Verse 18 presents the responsibility to join the brothers in the conquest as a command: "And I commanded you at that time, saying, ' . . . All your men of valor shall cross over armed before your brothers, the people of Israel.'" Allowance is made for the care of the rest of their families: "Only your wives, your little ones, and your livestock (I know that you have much livestock) shall remain in the cities that I have given you" (3:19). The wives and the little ones are not needed in the battle, and they can look after the land and the livestock. The command is done in a realistic way so that the families are looked after and the battle is won.

This is the way of the kingdom. We look after our families, and we battle in the broader agenda of the kingdom. Doing both may not be easy for us. But both are essential responsibilities. We cannot neglect our families, saying that we have "God's work" to do. Neither can we neglect the service of the kingdom, saying we have our families to look after. Often people choose one or the other. That is wrong.

The Need of Our Fellows Is Our Responsibility (3:20)

In verse 20 Moses tells the Transjordan tribesmen that they need to be in the battlefield "until the LORD gives rest to your brothers, as to you, and they also occupy the land that the LORD your God gives them beyond the Jordan. Then each of you may return to his possession which I have given you." We do not have rest until our fellows have rest.

It is in connection with this dialogue between Moses and the Transjordan tribes about their joining the rest of the people in battle that a famous statement in Scripture appears. Moses told them, "But if you will not do so, behold, you have sinned against the LORD, and be sure your sin will find you out" (Numbers 32:23). The failure to help our fellows in their time of need is a serious sin. Some Christians are known to be nice and harmless people. They do what they are supposed to do, but they do not concern themselves with the needs of other people. They may be nice people, but if they are not helping those in need, they are living in sin. We note that in Jesus' parable of the sheep and the goats the sin of those who are condemned to eternal punishment was the failure to help the needy:

> Then he will say to those on his left, "Depart from me, you cursed, into the eternal fire prepared for the devil and his angels. For I was hungry and you gave me no food, I was thirsty and you gave me no drink, I was a stranger and you did not welcome me, naked and you did not clothe me, sick and in prison and you did not visit me." (Matthew 25:41–43)

Christians, especially in the West, have emphasized personal initiative and independence so much that this idea of community solidarity is sometimes lacking. In Christianity if a fellow Christian is in need we should immediately ask, "Is there something I can do about this need?" Indeed, a need should not be automatically regarded as a call to action from God. There is so much need in the world that we cannot meet all the needs we encounter. But when people within the community to which we belong are in need, a Christian almost automatically asks, "Do I need to do something about this?"

In the Numbers passage Moses says that if the Transjordan tribes did not join in the battle the others would be discouraged: "Shall your brothers go to the war while you sit here? Why will you discourage the heart of the people of Israel from going over into the land that the LORD has given them?" (Numbers 32:6, 7). Those who are struggling with a tough challenge get discouraged when their fellows see them struggle and do nothing to help.

We often face this type of situation in our own lives. One division in our workplace may have a lot of work while another may not have so much. When persons from the division with less work see the others toiling and struggling to keep up with the load of work, they should try to help them. In our organization we have found that if the others do not help, those with the heavy load of work can get very discouraged. Sadly, this happens sometimes. Some people seem to have developed immunity to the needs of others. They do their job well, but they do not concern themselves with the job of another. That is not the Christian way.

Handing over Leadership When One Does Not Want To (3:21–29)

The last section of chapter 3 is painful to read. The great leader Moses is denied his desire to lead the people to the mainland of Canaan and he is asked to prepare Joshua to do this job.

The God Who Helped in the Past Fights for You (3:21, 22)

Verse 21 says that Moses "commanded Joshua," but what he says is more an encouragement to persevere than a command. The word translated "command" comes three times in this chapter (3:18, 21, 28 [NKJV; ESV, "charge"]), and we will discuss it below. Moses words to Joshua follow a pattern that is well used in Deuteronomy. First Moses' gives Joshua a reason to be hopeful about the future by appealing to experiences of victory in the past: "Your eyes have seen all that the LORD your God has done to these two kings. So will the LORD do to all the kingdoms into which you are crossing" (3:21; see the discussion on 1:4). Then he points to the fact that God fights for them: "You shall not fear them, for it is the LORD your God who fights for you" (3:22; see the discussion on 1:29–33).

Right Theology but Wrong Request (3:23–26)

Next we have a really sad account of Moses pleading with God to let him enter the promised land. Moses says, "And I pleaded with the LORD at that time . . . " (3:23). The word translated "pleaded" is used in connection with acts of kindness, mercy, and pity.[2] Moses is pleading with God to have mercy on him. Then he says, "O Lord GOD, you have only begun to show your servant your greatness and your mighty hand. For what god is there in heaven or on earth who can do such works and mighty acts as yours?" (3:24). Just as Luke described his Gospel as dealing "with all that Jesus began to do and teach" (Acts 1:1), Moses says here, "You have only begun to show your servant your greatness and your mighty hand." This is only the beginning. The best is yet to be. Then he affirms that no God could do what God has done.

The theology of Moses here is correct, and on this theology he bases his request. He says, "Please let me go over and see the good land beyond the Jordan, that good hill country and Lebanon" (3:25). Going to this land was the goal that had propelled him throughout the forty tough years that he led this difficult people. The request seems to be very reasonable, but it was not God's will. "But the LORD was angry with me because of you and would not listen to me" (3:26a). He had to suffer the consequences of a rash action of his, because of which he was barred from entering the land (see the discussion on 1:37). God's response to Moses' request is, "Enough from you; do not speak to me of this matter again" (3:26b). Moses' theology was right, but his request was not in keeping with God's will. He needed therefore to stop asking for this.

When the child born out of David's adulterous relationship with Bathsheba was deathly ill, David prayed for his healing with great earnestness. "David therefore sought God on behalf of the child. And David fasted and went in and lay all night on the ground. And the elders of his house stood beside him, to raise him from the ground, but he would not, nor did he eat food with them" (2 Samuel 12:16, 17). Then the child died. His servants were afraid to tell him, thinking that if he behaved so intensely when the child was sick, he would be uncontrollable if he knew that the child was dead. David, sensing their unease, asked, "Is the child dead?" They replied, "He is dead" (v. 19).

David's response to the news of his son's death surprised the servants: "Then David arose from the earth and washed and anointed himself and changed his clothes. And he went into the house of the LORD and worshiped. He then went to his own house. And when he asked, they set food before him, and he ate" (v. 20). His words in response to the servants' questions show that he had submitted to God's sovereignty and accepted his verdict.

These two stories from the lives of two of God's great servants have much to teach us. Some Christians quote passages that suggest that God will give us whatever we ask. For example, Jesus said, "And whatever you ask in prayer, you will receive, if you have faith" (Matthew 21:22). Other Scriptures would cause us to qualify that statement by saying that God will give only what is best for us—that is, what is in keeping with his will. James 4:13–15 speaks directly to this situation. It talks about people making business plans with profits in view. James says to such, ". . . yet you do not know what tomorrow will bring. What is your life? For you are a mist that appears for a little time and then vanishes" (v. 14). Therefore he says, "Instead you ought to say, 'If the Lord wills, we will live and do this or that'" (v. 15).

It is not a lack of faith to add, "If it is your will" after a making a request in prayer. It is an acknowledgment that God knows what is best for us. Those with special gifts, such as the gift of healing, may make confident proclamations because they have received a revelation that something is God's will. But most people do not have such discernment, and it would be best for them to combine intensity and earnestness in prayer with an attitude of glad submission to the will of God.

It is interesting that Jesus quoted the same incident that resulted in Moses' being disqualified in his response to the temptation by Satan to jump from the pinnacle of the temple (Matthew 4:7). The fuller quotation goes like this: "You shall not put the LORD your God to the test, as you tested him at Massah" (Deuteronomy 6:16). They put the Lord to the test by demanding water. God gave them the water, but he was displeased by their demanding attitude. Referring to this event Psalm 78:18 says, "They tested God in their heart by demanding the food they craved." The word "craved" suggests the idea of desire out of control. We must always humbly submit to God and affirm that God knows what is best for us.

Recently I prayed in the home of a wonderful Christian woman of faith whose mother was very ill. In my prayer I asked God to heal that mother if it was his will. A few weeks later she died. Later her daughter told me she was at first a little disappointed that I had qualified the request for healing with a submission to God's will. But she said that God used that to prepare her for her mother's death. One thing we can be thankful about is that God's will for us is best. So even though Moses was unable to go into the land, we can affirm that God did what was best for him, given his past action that disqualified him from what he wanted. One who has fully surrendered to God will accept that and move forward.

God had to tell Moses not to bring up the matter again because it seemed as if he had not accepted God's verdict and kept bringing it up. Sometimes we find people bringing up the same issue over and over again, and sometimes this goes on for years. We need to grapple with God and keep grappling until we come to a sense that this is what God wants. Then we should accept that as best and stop going back over and over the same issue. If we remain unhappy with something that God has decreed for us, we forfeit the joy and freedom that should be ours.

God's Gracious Concession (3:27)

Moses asked to be able to "go over and see the good land" (3:25). God refused the first part of that request but in his kindness granted the second. He says, "Go up to the top of Pisgah and lift up your eyes westward and northward and southward and eastward, and look at it with your eyes, for you shall not go over this Jordan" (3:27). Life after repentance from sin results in a restored relationship with God, which includes a restoration of the joy of salvation (Psalm 51:12) and a return to usefulness in God's Word. But the consequences remain. For Moses it meant that he would not go into the land. For David it meant that the sword would never depart from his house (2 Samuel 12:10). But we are still in relationship with God. He is sufficient for every crisis. And the sin does result in several crises (making sin never worthwhile!).

While the consequences remain, so does the tender care of God. Within the context of the disciplinary situation ordained by God, there will be numerous examples of God's acts of kindness to us that bring freshness to our lives. Moses' seeing the promised land could be taken as one of these gracious acts of God. This is an example of the holy love of God. The thoroughgoing application of the discipline shows God's holiness. But within that discipline God acts graciously to give us ample opportunity to experience his special care and to find joy in that.

He Must Charge His Successor (3:28a)

Next God tells Moses, "But charge Joshua . . . " The leader is asked to give specific instructions to his successor. The Hebrew word translated "charge" (*tsavah*) appeared twice earlier in our passage translated as "commanded." In those verses Moses is talking about how he commanded the people (3:18) and Joshua (3:21). This is a word that appears 496 times in the Old Testament, of which eighty-eight times are in Deuteronomy. It means "to command, order, instruct, give direction."[3] It is a strong word. About 280 times in the Old Testament the subject doing the charging is God. Moses is the subject about eighty-five times and Joshua about fourteen times.[4] The leader has been given authority by God to act on his behalf. So when he gives God's thoughts to those he leads, he can and must speak with authority.

Paul uses several similar words in his epistles. His advice to Timothy, who in some sense had a relationship with Paul similar to what Joshua had with Moses, is interesting. For example, different Greek words translated "charge" appear in the ESV in 1 and 2 Timothy. Paul gives Timothy a charge five times (1 Timothy 1:5, 18; 5:21; 6:13; 2 Timothy 4:1), and he asks Timothy to charge others three times (1 Timothy 1:3; 6:17; 2 Timothy 2:14).

From this evidence it is clear that leaders should give authoritative instructions to those they supervise. We have already addressed this in our study of Deuteronomy 1:16, but this is a topic that needs repeating today. This is because actions such as charging people and giving exhortations are going out of fashion today. A lot of preaching is aimed at making people feel good. Truth is presented in an entertaining and appealing fashion, but people are not urged to follow God's ways with the earnestness that characterized all good preaching and leading through the centuries.

The distaste for objective truth in the postmodern era seems to have influenced the church so much that people are not encouraged to speak authoritatively on anything. Paul's words to Timothy should act as a corrective to this approach to communication: "I charge you in the presence of God and of Christ Jesus, who is to judge the living and the dead, and by his appearing and his kingdom: preach the word; be ready in season and out of season; reprove, rebuke, and exhort, with complete patience and teaching" (2 Timothy 4:1, 2).

Of course, those charging others need to do it with all humility. The authority leaders have is derived from God who has communicated an authoritative word to us through the Scriptures. So we will speak with authority only if we know that what we say is well backed by the authority of Scripture. Besides, charging is one of many ministries. The verses from 2 Timothy quoted above have Paul adding "with complete patience and teaching" after "reprove, rebuke, and exhort." Similarly here, after telling Moses to charge Joshua, God says, ". . . and encourage and strengthen him" (3:28b). Exhortation without encouragement and patience gives exhortation a bad name. Some say that their personalities go well with exhortation and not with encouragement. But if they want to be leaders, they must learn to do both. Otherwise they will be disqualified from leading God's people.

Encouraging One's Replacement (3:28b)

As we just noted, God goes on to tell Moses, ". . . and encourage and strengthen [Joshua], for he shall go over at the head of this people, and he shall put them in possession of the land that you shall see" (3:28b). "Encourage" and "strengthen" are almost synonyms. Joshua will face various obstacles along the way. He was a brave warrior, but he needed encouragement to persevere. Not only did Moses do this, God also did this when he commissioned Joshua (Joshua 1:1–9). We must equip those we prepare for leadership to face discouragement without giving up.

Many great people would point to words of encouragement from others that were keys to their pursuing the difficult path that made them heroes. They were discouraged and wanted to give up, and a simple word of encouragement helped them see things from God's perspective. The Russian writer Aleksandr Solzhenitsyn (1918–2008) spent part of his life in a Soviet Siberian prison. At one point he was so physically weak and discouraged that he hoped for death. The hard labor, terrible conditions, and inhumane treatment had taken its toll. He knew the guards would beat him severely and probably kill him if he stopped working. So he planned to expedite his death by simply stopping his work and leaning on his shovel. But when he stopped, a fellow Christian reached over with his shovel and quickly drew a cross at the feet of Solzhenitsyn, then erased it before a guard could see it. He would later record that his entire being was energized by that little reminder of the hope and courage we find in Christ.[5]

In this passage God is asking Moses to encourage the person who was going to do what he had wanted to do—take the people across the Jordan to the promised land. Christians are often asked to act in that way. Moses did it well. It is clear from his speech that he is boosting Joshua before the people. He wants them to accept Joshua as the new leader. Our personal agendas are less important than the agenda of the kingdom. We may be hurt by the fact that something we wanted to do has been given to someone else, as Moses seems to have been. But our commitment to God causes us to overcome the hurt and help the other person.

Because of our hurt, we may be biased about the person. We may think that we are more suitable for the job and start focusing on our strong points in comparison to the weak points of the other person. Some Christians boycott the person who got the job instead of them. They refuse to help him and sometimes even put obstacles in his way. They claim they are acting with the best interests of the group as they seek to "right his wrongs" and point out his shortcomings. But in matters like this it is so easy for us to make huge mistakes because of the unreliability of our emotions when we are hurt. So it is "better to be safe than sorry" and give the fullest possible support to the person who got the job.

How sad it is when predecessors often do not help their successors. Some take their "personal mailing list" and refuse to give it to the successors, who have the daunting task of raising funds for the organization. How can we talk of "personal mailing lists" when we are serving the kingdom in which the method of all ministry is working through the body!

This type of behavior violates the spirit of God's kingdom to which we belong. It is a clear indication that the person's hurt has resulted in his or her acting in the flesh. We may leave an organization, we may hand it over to someone else, but that work belongs to God's kingdom, and despite personal hurt we must always seek the welfare of the kingdom. There are so many stories of bad leadership transitions in Christian organizations and churches that we need to address this as a matter of some urgency. Leaders who give a hard time to their successors are sinning. Sin must be rebuked and not tolerated in the church!

Actually when we help the person who has been given the task we wish we were doing, we are following Paul's advice: "Do not be overcome by evil, but overcome evil with good" (Romans 12:21). We overcome the evil of hurting the kingdom through jealousy by helping the person of whom we are envious. F. B. Meyer (1847–1929) was recognized as one of the greatest Bible teachers of his era. He used to speak regularly at Bible conferences organized by evangelist D. L. Moody in Northfield, Massachusetts. Large crowds would attend his Bible studies. Then a younger Bible teacher, G. Campbell Morgan (1863–1945), came onto the scene, and soon there would be more people listening to Campbell Morgan than to Meyer. Meyer confessed that he was tempted to be envious of Morgan. "The only way I can conquer my feelings," Meyer said, "is to pray for him daily, which I do."[6] He overcame envy by asking God to bless the one who ultimately took on his mantle as the most prominent Bible teacher in the world.

Moses ends his historical review by saying, "So we remained in the valley opposite Beth-peor" (3:29). Moses' second speech is also made from there

(4:46), and Moses was buried close to Beth-peor (34:6). While we are not certain where this is, we know it was east of the northern tip of the Dead Sea and the southern tip of the Jordan.

Our passage has given us some important principles of Christian community life:

- Leaders need to carefully explain the way assets are going to be distributed. Otherwise there could be unnecessary unpleasantness between those among whom the assets are distributed.
- Members cannot think only of their needs; the needs of their fellows become their responsibility.
- We can do this if we remember that all we have is ultimately a gift from God and belongs to God. We act only as stewards of this gift.
- While we care for others we must also fulfill our responsibilities to our own families.
- We may sometimes need to hand over to others things that we would have liked to do.
- Even when we hand over, we must instruct and encourage our successors.

10

Nurturing People Who Cling
to God and His Word

DEUTERONOMY 4:1–14

CHAPTER 4 BRINGS US TO the end of the first address of Moses. Up to this point he had been recounting the history of the Israelite journey from Egypt. Most scholars include 4:1–43 along with chapters 1—3 in the first speech of Moses. But what we get in this section is an exhortation that follows the historical review.[1] Moses has given the people the history of God's goodness to them despite their rebellious and stubborn attitudes. Now he will give some principles of how to remain faithful to God and obedient to the Law and how to stay away from idolatry.

Faithfulness to the Word (4:1–3)

Introduction: Listen and Do (4:1)

The first verse is a summary of Deuteronomy 4, which is essentially about the attitude the people should have toward the Law: "And now, O Israel, listen to the statutes and the rules that I am teaching you, and do them, that you may live, and go in and take possession of the land that the LORD, the God of your fathers, is giving you." The Law is described as "the statutes and the rules." These two words appear together eleven times in Deuteronomy. Eugene Merrill thinks this is what is called a hendiadys where two nouns are used to express a single idea. The exact difference between the two terms is difficult to pinpoint, but together they indicate comprehensiveness. We are to listen not just to a part of but to all of the Law.

But listening is not enough. Moses goes on to say, ". . . and do them"

115

(4:1b). As James 1:22 puts it, "But be doers of the word, and not hearers only, deceiving yourselves." We deceive ourselves by thinking we are doing fine because we know the Scriptures when actually we are headed for a crash. This is a trap into which even mature Christians can fall. We begin to look at the Bible for knowledge, often to find material for our ministry of teaching, preaching, or counseling. We need to develop the habit of reading the Bible with a view to learning more about obedience. Bible knowledge is worthless without obedience. Someone has said, "The only part of the Bible you truly believe is the part you obey."[2] Members of religions other than Christianity often defend and expound the moral prescriptions in their scriptures but consider them impractical to carry out in daily life (e.g., the prohibition on lying). Not so the Christian Scriptures. One way to develop this habit is to keep a devotional journal where you record what God taught you from your reading of the Bible.

Next Moses gives a consequence of listening and doing: ". . . that you may live, and go in and take possession of the land that the LORD, the God of your fathers, is giving you" (4:1c). Here is the formula for success in life: expose yourself to the Word and obey what it says, and God will bless you with success. In light of the powerful pull of earthly values that lure us into compromising on Biblical principles, we must constantly remind ourselves that the lonely path of total obedience to God is the only path worth following. One method the Bible uses repeatedly to convince us of this is to refer to the blessings of obedience.

Don't Add to or Take from the Law (4:2a)

Verse 2a says, "You shall not add to the word that I command you, nor take from it." This verse is not saying there will be no more revelation after the Law of Moses. We know that God spoke later and revealed much more to his people, supremely through the person and work of Jesus Christ. This verse is talking about submission to the Word, not about the comprehensiveness of this particular word. Not adding to or subtracting from the Word means having it as our sole authority; living under it. This is such an important command that it is repeated often in the Bible. Deuteronomy 12:32 says, "Everything that I command you, you shall be careful to do. You shall not add to it or take from it." In Revelation 22:18, 19 a curse is attached to those who add to or subtract from the Word (see also Proverbs 30:5, 6).

We can add to the Law by introducing practices that are against the spirit of the Law. We do this when we give another book, such as the Book of Mormon, the status of being a primary source of authority. We do this when we legitimize practices such as homosexual marriage that are clearly contradictory to what is in the Law. We can take from it when we try to dismiss its value and relevance. For example, we might say that we cannot practice some of the things it teaches, such as honesty, truthfulness, and sexual purity.

Adam Clarke (1762–1832), writing before liberalism had really hit the church, said this verse includes giving "any comment that has any tendency to corrupt, weaken or destroy any part of this revelation." I have had occasion to dialogue with many people who reject the absolute uniqueness of Christ. They do this by denying the historical trustworthiness of the Gospels and thus dispensing with the statements where Christ is said to claim to be absolutely unique. Sometimes we hear people highlighting with delight the supposed contradictions in the Bible or rejecting things like miracles or the virgin birth. They may sound scholarly when they do this. They seem to think that graduating in this way from their "Sunday school faith" is a necessary step along the path to maturity.

The true servant of God bows in submission to the Word, acknowledging his or her fallibility and approaching the Scriptures like a child hungry to be fed. This is not bibliolatry, as some claim; it is a humble recognition that the Bible is the Word of God. So, out of devotion to its author we carefully study its texts so as to get at its meaning and are careful to obey what it commands.

Some claim the academic freedom to say things that undermine the Word. This becomes a problem when such statements come from academics in institutions governed by some ideas of academic freedom that must be followed to maintain their accreditation. That should not make others complacent and unwilling to confront statements that undermine the Bible. Every Biblically legitimate effort should be made to uphold the authority of the Scriptures in the church, whatever the cost. That is an implication of what Deuteronomy says about the importance of God's revealed Word.

Within the attitude of submission to the Word, of course, is a strong place for scholarship. Sometimes we cannot understand something in it; or we encounter statements that seem to be in error or that seem to contradict other statements. At such times we will grapple to find a solution to the problem. Until a solution is found we will keep the issue in suspense. We do not discard what the Scriptures state, saying they are erroneous, as some seem delighted to do today. Rather, we humbly acknowledge our finiteness and our inability to solve the problem at that point and continue to grapple for an answer.

There are several people in the history of the church whose scholarly inquiries caused them to discard the scholarly consensus and change their views in order to be more accepting of the Biblical record. This happened to the noted Scottish archaeologist Sir William Ramsey (1851–1939). He looked into the New Testament only because he had to, since it was a document that came from the period he was studying. He found a place in Acts 14 with a geographical note that went against the scholarly consensus. Like many scholars of his day he assumed that the writer of Acts had made a mistake. While he was lecturing at Oxford University he went to Asia Minor on an archaeological expedition and was surprised to find out that Luke was right and the scholarly consensus was wrong. This triggered a process that made him change his views about the Bible and ultimately led to his conversion.[3] He ended up writing ten books on Paul and Luke, including his *magnum opus* entitled *St. Paul: Traveler and Roman Citizen*.[4] Many consider him one of the leading archaeologists of the modern era.

Be Careful to Keep the Law (4:2b)

Verse 2 goes on to tell why it is so important not to add to or subtract from the Law: ". . . that you may keep the commandments of the LORD your God that I command you." The Hebrew word translated "keep" (ESV, NIV, NASB) or "obey" (NLT) or "carry out" (REB) is a familiar word (*shamar*) which appears sixty-five times in Deuteronomy. The word essentially means "pay careful attention to."[5] The particular way that is done in this verse is by obeying the Law. But the idea is that of being careful to obey. This is something we do with utmost dedication and care. We are to study the Word carefully in order to find out how it can be practiced in today's world. The Bible is not primarily a book we go to for an emotional kick each day. Indeed, that is often the by-product of Bible reading. But the primary reason for reading the Bible is for instructions on how to think and act.

Remember the Punishment for Disobedience (4:3)

Verse 3 says, "Your eyes have seen what the LORD did at Baal-peor, for the LORD your God destroyed from among you all the men who followed the Baal of Peor." Moses tells the people that they must constantly remember that when they sinned they were punished. There is no doubt about the fact that in the Bible one of the strong motivations to obedience is the prospect of punishment for sin. This is true of the Old Testament, but many forget that it is also true of the New Testament.

Peter Toon has listed thirty-one different passages (not counting parallel passages) in the Gospels that contain warnings about Hell.[6] I have shown in a book I wrote on Hell that in these references Jesus used the message of Hell in an evangelistic setting to motivate people to repent (e.g., Mark 8:31–38), in a pastoral setting to motivate people to holiness (Mark 9:43–48), and in a missionary setting to motivate people to evangelism (Matthew 10:28).[7]

There is a medieval story of a man who in a dream saw a woman carrying a torch and a pitcher of water. The torch was used to burn the pleasures of Heaven and the pitcher to quench the flames of Hell. The story teaches that by eliminating the supposedly unworthy motives of desiring Heaven and fearing Hell, people could begin to love God for God's own sake.[8] Such sentiments are very common today also. But those are not Biblical sentiments! Given our tendency to sin we should be using every possible legitimate means to motivate people to live godly lives. And God in his wisdom chose to use the prospect of punishment as one such motivation. How dare we refuse to use it?

Just a few hours before I wrote these words a Christian from a solidly evangelical church told me that he has not heard Hell mentioned in the pulpit for a long time. Actually ministers who fail to do this are guilty of criminal negligence. It is like a meteorologist refusing to warn fishermen about a terrible storm that is coming because he does not want to give them such an unpleasant message!

The doctrine of judgment needs to be rediscovered in today's world. Today most people use *Hell* more as slang or as a swearword rather than as an awesome reality that should constantly act as a warning to them. Here Moses uses judgment as God's way of acting: "Your eyes have seen what the LORD did at Baal-peor, for the LORD your God destroyed from among you . . . " (4:3). What we need, then, is a proper understanding of God. We would do well to heed the advice of Paul: "Note then the kindness and the severity of God: severity toward those who have fallen, but God's kindness to you, provided you continue in his kindness. Otherwise you too will be cut off" (Romans 11:22).

Clinging to God and His Word (4:4–6a)

Clinging to God (4:4–6a)

The good news regarding this stage of the journey was that those listening to Moses' speech did not disobey God. Verse 4 says, "But you who held fast to the LORD your God are all alive today." The word translated "held fast," *dabeq* and its related word *dabaq*, carry the idea of clinging as in the case of the belt clinging to the skin (Jeremiah 13:11), the tongue sticking to the roof of the mouth (Psalm 22:15), and the husband leaving his father and mother and cleaving to his wife (Genesis 2:24). So we cling to God. Those who cling to God love him, depend on him, give him first place in their lives, and do not entertain things that displease him.

J. Oswald Sanders (1902–1992), in his wonderful book *Enjoying Intimacy with God*, talks of a timid Christian who said, "I think I love him because there are things I refrain from doing for no other reason than that he forbids them, while I do other things simply because he desires them." Sanders says that obedience is the test of whether we love God or not and refers to John 14:21, where Jesus says, "Whoever has my commandments and keeps them, he it is who loves me." Sanders says, "The key question is not, 'How do you feel?' but, 'Have you obeyed?'"[9]

Sometimes clinging to God is all we can do as we go through a crisis. Everything seems to be bleak, and it is hard to obey. But we persevere, knowing that God will not let us down. For example, a former good friend is slandering you and doing a lot of damage to your reputation. You know some sordid details about this person's life that he shared with you in confidence when you were good friends. If you spread those stories, this person would be discredited. But you just cling to God, knowing that he will vindicate you in his time. And you refuse to disobey him by hitting back at the person who is hitting you so hard.

Especially after the revelation of God in Christ, we know that love is the cement that makes us cling to God. Obeying God's Word is not just a duty—it is a result of our loving God. And our loving God is a result of his first loving us (1 John 4:19). We plead with God to let us love him so much that we will lose the love for those things that keep us from him.

Once More, Keep the Law (4:5, 6a)

Verse 5a describes the divine origin of the Law: "See, I have taught you statutes and rules, as the Lord my God commanded me." But soon after that Moses goes back to the main point he has been making in this passage. The Law was taught ". . . that you should do them in the land that you are entering to take possession of it. Keep them and do them . . . " (4:5b, 6a). In these two brief verses we find three verbs describing obedience to the Law. First, we are told that we are to "do" the Law (4:5b); we are also told that we must "keep them" (4:6a). Both these verbs are a translation of the same common word (appearing 2,254 times in the Old Testament), generally translated "do." The esv translates the third verb also as "do" (4:6a). But this is the word *shamar* meaning "pay careful attention to" that appeared in verse 2. The niv translation of verse 6a carries the idea better: "observe them carefully."

How often we are told to be careful about obedience! I believe this is because carelessness is so often the mother of sin.

- If we are careless about scrupulously keeping our daily time with God, we could get out of the habit and soon lose touch with God.
- We can get careless about the discipline of giving and end up not giving what we should to God.
- In our busyness we can get careless about spending quality time with our spouses and children. We can end up having serious problems in the family simply because we did not give the necessary time to them.

I think combating carelessness is the biggest battle I wage in my life. I often find that I am careless about the very things of which I should be most careful.

The Missionary Impact of Obedience (4:6b-8)

Wise and Understanding (4:6b)

The result of the Word-centered living prescribed above will be a missionary impact upon other peoples. They will recognize Israel as "a wise and understanding people." This brings us to the heart of Israel's special calling. As God told Abraham, out of his seed all of the nations of the world will be blessed (Genesis 12:3; 22:18). Through Israel others will come to understand the nature and ways of God. This mantle has been passed on to the church today. So this passage is very vital to us, too. Deuteronomy 4:6b says, ". . . for that will be your wisdom and your understanding in the sight of the peoples, who, when they hear all these statutes, will say, 'Surely this great nation is a wise and understanding people.'" The unusual phenomenon of a nation of law-abiding citizens will cause others to sit up and take note.

The Bible teaches that "the fear of the LORD is the beginning of knowledge" (Proverbs 1:7; cf. 9:10). So when we cling to God and his Word we become wise people. But usually the world does not recognize the wisdom of godly living. Usually people look up to a nation for its military might, wealth, and political power, not for its righteousness. Often people regard the righteous as good people perhaps, but ultimately as fools because they seem to forgo success because of righteousness. They see us taking up the cross, and they regard the cross as folly.

God Is with Us (4:7)

Moses goes on to give two more points that are actually reasons why outsiders will think Israel (and by application the church) is wise. First, they will see that God is with us: "For what great nation is there that has a god so near to it as the LORD our God is to us, whenever we call upon him?" (4:7). Because God is with us and is there for us whenever we call on him, they realize that though we may not have a lot of what the world thinks is necessary for a fulfilled life, we have peace and joy in our hearts. The happiest people in the world are not those who have no problems, but those who are not afraid of problems. We are not afraid of problems because we know that we can handle them with God's help and that God will turn every problem into something good.

Often people are attracted to God when they see him answer prayer. This is the most common way in which people of other faiths develop an interest in the gospel in Sri Lanka. This happens often through miraculous answers to prayer that open people's minds to give the gospel a hearing. The early church prayed for God to act with signs and wonders in the name of Christ (Acts 4:30). Other times this comes through less spectacular answers to prayer. A five-year-old Buddhist girl living in a remote village had a hole in her heart. Her situation seemed hopeless. We had a work in the village, and our worker told the girl's mother to come to the capital city Colombo to consult a specialist. We said we would look after her and prayed that God would heal her. The mother and daughter stayed in our home before and after the operation. We were desperately praying for her healing, for that would serve well to introduce God to the people of this unreached village.

One morning, a day or two before she went to the hospital, this little girl told her mother that Jesus had appeared to her in a dream and told her not to be afraid because he would look after her. She told her mother that she would like to become a follower of Jesus. The mother told her, "If that is what you want to do, you can do that."

She went for her operation, and we prayed desperately to God to heal the child! The operation was successful, and she went home a living testimony to the ability of God to look after her. Both she and her mother became Christians. How happy I was when I went to her village recently and saw that both of them are still very much committed to Christ more than twenty years after the operation.

Righteous Rules (4:8)

Next Moses says that the people will be impressed by the righteousness of the laws of Israel. "And what great nation is there, that has statutes and rules so righteous as all this law that I set before you today?" (4:8). There was a justice in the laws and their outworking that would impress the people. The extent to which the Old Testament went to ensure social justice is very impressive. They made sure that everyone in their community had a fair chance and that those who are particularly weak were given special help so they could be helped to progress in life. We see this in some of the passages in Deuteronomy that talk about justice to the poor (e.g., chapter 15).

The neighbors are going to be impressed by the justice behind the laws of the Israelites. They will be impressed by the way people respond to issues such as land disputes, economic relations, crime, the rights and needs of the poor and weak, and accusations brought against citizens. All people have a sense of fair play. When they see God's people as a righteous society, they will take note. Recently in Sri Lanka many poor people have come to Christ from other faiths. Several have told us that one of the things that attracted them to Christianity was that there was no class difference there. Everybody was treated equal. That was a powerful testimony in a nation where caste and class distinctions still continue.

Terrorists are usually people who have given up attempting to win what they regard as legitimate rights through legal means. After trying the legal method and failing, they have lost faith in the system, which they think is there to serve the privileged classes. They believe that the only means to get their rights will be violent revolution. We have had terrorist groups operating in Sri Lanka for many years. But I know of several situations where terrorists have respected and not interfered too much with Christians because they knew that we are truly committed to the rights of all the people.

I think one of the best ways to combat terrorism is righteous living. When people considering participation in a militant group see the church living out what the terrorist groups are trying to win through violence, they may decide that instead they will join the Jesus revolution of love and use that method to help the world and their people. A Hindu mother of a youth who had met Christ through Youth for Christ came for a gathering we organized for parents at which I spoke. Her elder son had joined the militants. She told our staff, "If you had come to our village a little earlier, my son would not have joined the militants." How important it is, in a world where millions of people are disillusioned with the injustice of the structures of society, to show that Christians are different. Jesus said, "Let your light shine before others, so that they may see your good works and give glory to your Father who is in heaven" (Matthew 5:16). May that be true of us.

Clinging to God's Acts (4:9–14)

Yet we could miss the opportunity of a missionary witness by not living out the wisdom of God. So Moses exhorts again about vigilance in our lives.

Take Care of Yourself (4:9a)

In verse 9 Moses goes back to his theme of being careful, saying, "Only take care, and keep your soul diligently." The Hebrew word *shamar,* meaning "be careful," that already appeared in verses 2 and 6 appears twice in this short expression of seven words in Hebrew. It could be translated "Only take care to take care of your soul diligently." We are to be careful about being careful! Actually in the Hebrew such repetition is a way to stress a point. Here it adds to the importance and seriousness of the pursuit. So it means something like "Be extremely careful to guard your souls" (McConville). If we are not alert to the possibility of carelessness we will unintentionally become careless. We are to be careful about our "soul." "Soul" (ESV and NASB) is *nephesh*, which refers to the real self—who we really are.

What Moses is saying here is well conveyed by Paul in his advice to his spiritual child Timothy: "Keep a close watch on yourself and on the teaching. Persist in this, for by so doing you will save both yourself and your hearers" (1 Timothy 4:16). This would, of course, involve a lot of self-examination to ensure that we are in the right place before God. So we would pray with David, "Search me, O God, and know my heart! Try me and know my thoughts! And see if there be any grievous way in me, and lead me in the way everlasting!" (Psalm 139:23, 24).

People with this attitude always want to learn from God. They are always open to correction. When they hear a message or read a book, they don't just say, "This is good for so and so." They say, "I needed to hear that."

Remember God's Acts (4:9b-14)

Moses next gives something very specific that they are to be careful about: ". . . lest you forget the things that your eyes have seen, and lest they depart from your heart all the days of your life" (4:9b). They might forget the history of God's redemption and provision. Other religions had idols and the like to remind them of their gods. The Israelites did not have those things. What they had was a history of God's great work among them. Moses says they saw these actions. But actually it was their parents who had seen them. But they were one with their parents, and thus it was as if they themselves had seen it.

The particular thing that God did that is mentioned here is the giving of the Law, along with the Ten Commandments, to Moses at Mount Horeb (4:10–14). Moses describes how it was given (4:10–13) and how important it is to their future preservation (4:10b). And then he says, "And the LORD commanded me at that time to teach you statutes and rules, that you might do them in the land that you are going over to possess" (4:14). Elsewhere also in Deuteronomy (4:15; 5:22) people are reminded of how the Law was given. The divine origin of Scripture was important for the people to remember because the Scriptures give a very countercultural message. It would seem foolish to follow such outmoded and unpopular laws—but not if those laws were given by the Creator and Lord of the universe who ultimately calls the shots relating to our lives and the lives of everybody on earth.

Others will look at idols and other touchable, visible things for security. Sometimes when problems come to Christians they panic and start going all over trying to find a solution for the problem. They may even go to shrines to other gods, to psychic counselors, or to astrologers. They want to grab onto something tangible to calm their anxiety. Moses said the Israelites "saw no form on the day that the LORD spoke to you at Horeb out of the midst of the fire" (4:15). Instead, what they had was the word of the Sovereign God. We see these other things prohibited in the word given to us by the Lord of the universe, and we stay clear of them, knowing that we would be fools to go against God.

Moses particularly mentions the importance of giving these stories to our children and grandchildren: "Make them known to your children and your children's children" (4:9c). Children learn truths best through stories. An important time in the life of any Christian family is when they recount the stories of God's dealings with humans. This may take the form of family devotions or simple conversations at home. Conversation about experiences that the family has had can become a very strong identity-buttressing event in the life of the children. They should have a sense that "This is our history, this is who we are, and it is beautiful." This will help them when they grow up and are tempted to do things that contradict the principles that form the Christian heritage of their family. Parents cannot hand over this task to Sunday schools and children's clubs.

The Jewish forms of family instruction were (and still are) very pleasant. Teaching times were happy times. That is what we should aim at doing with our children. I like to think of myself as a Bible teacher. But I have no hesitation to say that the most important Bible teacher in my life was my mother. She was a convert from Buddhism. I do not think she ever attended a class on how to study the Bible. But she told her five children the stories of the Bible when we were children. And from those we imbibed the Christian worldview, which all five of us continue to espouse.

Christians are people who give a place to God, to his Word, and to his acts in their lives. Our programs in our homes, our churches, and our special Christian groups should be fashioned to reflect that. And in our personal life we should always be asking, "Am I clinging close to God, his Word, and his acts"?

11

How to Prevent Idolatry

DEUTERONOMY 4:15-28

WE ARE STILL IN THE EXHORTATION following the historical review that ends Moses' first speech in Deuteronomy. Moses had urged the people to cling to God and the Law (4:1–14). Now he gives ways in which they can prevent idolatry. The issue of Christians becoming unfaithful and following paths opposed to God's way is a real problem today also. So this section of Deuteronomy is very relevant to us.

Remember the Divine Origin of the Law (4:15)

Using the now familiar word *shamar* (meaning "pay careful attention to"), Moses starts this paragraph by saying, "Therefore watch yourselves [literally, your souls] very carefully" (4:15). Leaders need to constantly warn themselves and others about the danger of drifting into unfaithfulness. Paul says, "Therefore let anyone who thinks that he stands take heed lest he fall" (1 Corinthians 10:12). This time we are asked to be alert to the possibility of falling into idolatry (Deuteronomy 4:16–19).

Moses goes on to give the reason why believers in God are particularly vulnerable to the danger of idolatry: "Since you saw no form on the day that the LORD spoke to you at Horeb out of the midst of the fire . . . " (4:15b). The expression "out of the midst of the fire" appears eleven times in Deuteronomy to describe how the Law was given.[1] For it to be repeated so many times, it must be important. We will look at this in some detail in our discussion of 4:32, 33.

When people feel weak and vulnerable, they could be tempted to look to something tangible, something they could see and touch, like an idol.

127

Believers could also get caught in that trap. The answer to this trap is a proper understanding of God's Word. It is the word of the Lord who "spoke . . . out of the midst of the fire." This word was given in an awesome way. That reminds them that this is the word of the almighty Creator and Lord of the universe. It would be wise not to clash with such force. Again we are reminded that the belief in the divine origin of the Bible helps give us an inclination to faithfully live in submission to the Word. The Word then is a tangible aid to faithfulness and a preventative to the danger of idolatry.

Idolatry Described (4:16–19)

Verses 16–19 describe the forms that idolatry takes and how one can fall into it. Moses says that to worship idols is to "act corruptly" (4:16). This verb has the idea of spoiling and even destroying. God intended us to live in blessed fellowship with him, with our consciences clear and our lives pure because we obey him. He intended us to be joyful because we have achieved the end for which we were made: enjoying intimacy with the God whom we love deeply. This beautiful plan is destroyed when idols and nature take the place of God in our lives. We become corrupted, spoiled.

Idols can take human forms. Moses says, "Beware lest you act corruptly by making a carved image for yourselves in the form of any figure, the likeness of male or female" (4:16). They can take animal forms: ". . . the likeness of any animal that is on the earth, the likeness of any winged bird that flies in the air, the likeness of anything that creeps on the ground, the likeness of any fish that is in the water under the earth" (4:17, 18). People can worship objects of nature: "And beware lest you raise your eyes to heaven, and when you see the sun and the moon and the stars, all the host of heaven, you be drawn away and bow down to them and serve them" (4:19a).

Describing the descent of the human race, Paul says that humans made images in the likeness of other creatures without worshiping the Creator. He says, "Claiming to be wise, they became fools, and exchanged the glory of the immortal God for images resembling mortal man and birds and animals and creeping things" (Romans 1:22, 23). Interestingly, this description of the corruption of humanity roughly parallels Moses' description of the possible descent into idolatry by the Israelites (Deuteronomy 4:16–18).

The order used by Moses and Paul to describe such unfaithfulness is the exact opposite of the order in which God created the world according to Genesis 1. Chris Wright thinks that probably the point is being made that "idolatry not only corrupts God's redemptive achievement for God's people, but perverts and turns upside-down the whole created order." This represents our basic attitude to idolatry and nature worship: it destroys what God intended for us. This is why when Paul went to Athens, "his spirit was provoked within him as he saw that the city was full of idols" (Acts 17:16). Actually the temples that caused such revulsion in him were beautiful works of art. But they took people away from enjoying the blessings God intended to give them as his children and made them enemies of God instead.

The last part of Deuteronomy 4:19 describes the possible objects of worship as "things that the LORD your God has allotted to all the peoples under the whole heaven." Moses is not saying here that God has allotted these things for them to worship. Rather he is saying that they have been allotted for all people to use for their benefit. Jesus said, "For he makes his sun rise on the evil and on the good, and sends rain on the just and on the unjust" (Matthew 5:45). The supreme Creator God has given us natural resources to use for our benefit, and we have made gods out of them and worshipped them! The folly to which people could descend is simply amazing, as they are "drawn away" or "enticed" (NIV) by idolatry. And folly is how Paul describes this descent of the human race: "their foolish hearts were darkened. Claiming to be wise, they became fools, and exchanged the glory of the immortal God for images . . . " (Romans 1:21b-23a).

The Biblical revulsion for idolatry is something we must never forget in our pluralistic age. Pluralism keeps all the different ideologies as more or less equals. But the Bible says that idolatry is repulsive to God. Therefore our attitude to it also should be one of revulsion. The Old Testament prophets expressed this revulsion with thunderous rebukes and threats. But when talking to the Athenians who did not have God's special revelation Paul "reasoned" with them about idolatry and the gospel of Christ (Acts 17:17–31). This gives a good guideline for dealing with idolatry. Within the church, we rebuke. Outside the church, we reason.

Today idolatry can take various forms. Sometimes the idol could be wealth, education, or prestige, if we pursue these at the cost of Biblical principles. Idolatry could be the unacceptable pleasure received through sex outside of marriage or through getting high on a chemical like a drug or alcohol. It could be our love for a person, which we will pursue even though that relationship is not sanctioned by God. Our idol could also be the security that we try to receive through getting a word from a psychic counselor, astrologer, or soothsayer.

We succumb to these idols in a similar way to the way people succumb to literal idols. When we lose our vital relationship with God through disobedience, the Bible's hold on us gets less and less. In the insecurity that results from losing our security in the eternal Word, we could shift to looking to another image for security.

- A Christian lady who had struggled with her husband's drug addiction for a long time went to a soothsayer to find out why her husband had fallen again. When she told us this, we were shocked. We realized that in her desperation and depression, when she could not find a tangible thing to do other than pray, she was lured into finding out from a soothsayer whether there was some evil spiritual influence that had caused him to fall again.
- A woman wants to get married and is discouraged about not being married yet and is upset about the way people keep asking her about this. In a weak moment she succumbs to the charms of an unbeliever who claims to love her and compromises her commitment by deciding to marry him.
- A salesperson who desperately needs to make a sale in order to keep his job succumbs to the temptation to be unfaithful to God by telling a lie about an item. He is able to sell the item, but he had to be unfaithful to God in order to do so.

These examples show how vulnerable Christians can be to unfaithfulness. In addition to a proper attitude toward the Word, our passage gives us more steps we can take to avoid idolatry.

Remember Your Redemption (4:20)

Moses' next step in motivating the Israelites to remain faithful is to remind them of their redemption. First he reminds them of what they were before their redemption: "But the LORD has taken you and brought you out of the iron furnace, out of Egypt . . . " (4:20a). "The iron furnace" probably recalls the way they suffered having to work in the burning heat of the day. How soon they forgot how much they'd suffered! Once during the journey when they had no meat to eat, they said, "Who will give us meat to eat? For it was better for us in Egypt" (Numbers 11:18). Another time they cried, "And why have you made us come up out of Egypt to bring us to this evil place? It is no place for grain or figs or vines or pomegranates, and there is no water to drink" (Numbers 20:5).

How much like us this is. When the going gets tough, we begin to complain against God and accuse him of not looking after us. We say things like, "I was better off before I committed my life to Christ." We were sinners destined for Hell, and now we have been given an eternal home in Heaven. And yet we say it was better for us before we came to Christ! We have forgotten the misery of unbelief and the destiny of unbelievers. This is why it is important for us to occasionally remember who we were before we were saved. Paul exhorts us, "Remember that you were at that time separated from Christ, alienated from the commonwealth of Israel and strangers to the covenants of promise, having no hope and without God in the world" (Ephesians 2:12).

After reminding the people of what their pre-redemption situation was like, Moses tells them what happened as a result of their redemption. He says, "But the LORD has taken you and brought you out of the iron furnace, out of Egypt, to be a people of his own inheritance, as you are this day" (Deuteronomy 4:20). After describing the pre-conversion state of the Ephesians Paul does a similar thing in the passage just quoted. He tells them what God has now made them into: "But now in Christ Jesus you who once were far off have been brought near by the blood of Christ" (Ephesians 2:13).

Moses' words "a people of his own inheritance" point to possibly the greatest blessing that the people of God enjoy: we are God's, and God is ours. Exodus 19:5 presents this truth by calling the people God's "treasured possession." The New Testament takes on this theme by using the language of being children of God (John 1:12; Romans 8:14–17; etc.). This theme appears in Deuteronomy also, though in a somewhat less direct way (1:31; 8:5; 14:1; 32:6). John was thrilled by this amazing truth. He said, "See what kind of love the Father has given to us, that we should be called children of God; and so we are" (1 John 3:1).

A lifetime would not be enough for us to fully understand the implications of this truth. We have experienced so much rejection during our lifetime that it is difficult for us to fully accept that God finds us so lovable. God loves us and treats us as his treasured inheritance, his own children. But we live like people permanently wounded by rejection. When something goes wrong, our insecurity and feelings of being rejected surface, and we act as if we cannot believe that God will look after us. At such times we are tempted to be unfaithful. When we keep clinging fervently to the twin truths of our past wretched state and our present glorious state, the temptation to unfaithfulness will lose its power. We reason that it would be a great folly to miss all the glorious blessings that are ours by right by moving away from God.

John Newton was a converted slave trader who became a great minister of the gospel and song-writer. He often referred to his conversion as "the day I first believed," and those words appear in his famous hymn "Amazing Grace." When he was dying he told those around him that he was "packed and sealed . . . and waiting for the post." These were his last words: "My memory is nearly gone. But I remember two things: that I am a great sinner . . . " He paused for breath, and then he said, "And that Christ—is a great Savior."[2] These are the two distinguishing marks of a believer.

Remember How God Punished the Leader (4:21, 22)

In his exhortation to encourage faithfulness, Moses next uses himself as a negative example. He says, "Furthermore, the LORD was angry with me because of you, and he swore that I should not cross the Jordan, and that I should not enter the good land that the LORD your God is giving you for an inheritance" (4:21). We have already discussed Moses' sin in our discussions on 1:37 and 3:23–26. He uses it here to tell the people that the holy God will not tolerate disobedience, even if it comes from a revered and beloved leader. So he says, with much sorrow, "For I must die in this land; I must not go over the Jordan. But you shall go over and take possession of that good land" (4:22).

We need to tell people and ourselves that Christians cannot play with sin. I find that sometimes I get careless and flirt close to overt disobedience without a terror of displeasing God. We must remember that Moses' sin was an outburst without controlling himself when the people behaved badly. That did not seem to be a very serious sin, especially because the people he led were acting in an annoying and unpleasant way. But God used Moses as an example, to show believers in the centuries to follow that he does not tolerate disobedience from his people.

It is interesting that Moses mentions this sin and its punishment several times (1:37; 3:23–26; 4:21, 22; cf. 34:4). He must really have been sad about not getting to go into the land because of his sin. But he uses his experience to help others stay away from sin. Here we see Moses' humility, and I think the way in which he used his failure gives us a reason why we find the description that he "was very meek, more than all people who were on the face of the earth" (Numbers 12:3). He did not hide his sin. He did not try to downplay it. He decided to use it to help others avoid sin.

How sad that when some Christians speak of the sins for which they were disciplined, they speak only of the unfairness of the discipline and of the wrong way people treated them during that time. Indeed, people often wrongly treat those disciplined, and these reactions to that are quite normal. But grace should finally win through so that they focus on their own sin and God's grace in forgiving them. Hebrews says, "For the moment all discipline seems painful rather than pleasant, but later it yields the peaceful fruit of righteousness to those who have been trained by it" (12:11). If people look back to their discipline only in a negative way, it may be a sign that they have not "been trained by it." Those who accept their sin and the discipline given for it are qualified to be used by God again after their sin.

Remember the Covenant (4:23)

Once again, in verse 23, our familiar word, *shamar*, meaning "pay careful attention to," appears. This time it is about being careful not to forget the covenant between the people and God: "Take care, lest you forget the covenant of the LORD your God, which he made with you, and make a carved image, the form of anything that the LORD your God has forbidden you." To give place to an idol would be to break the covenant relationship they had solemnly entered into with God.

Moses says that it was God who made this covenant with the people ("which he made with you"). That is the same with us today. Having a relationship with God is something that we do not deserve. But God graciously took the initiative and entered into a relationship with us by first gifting us with salvation and then covenanting to look after us and bless us. But some stipulations are an integral part of this covenant relationship. If we violate those stipulations we violate the covenant relationship with God.

In this verse Moses gives one way to avoid violating the stipulations: "Take care, lest you forget the covenant." How can we do this? One way the Israelites did this was by renewing the covenant frequently. This was done in Moab before the death of Moses (Deuteronomy 29:1). During Joshua's tenure as leader, covenant renewal was done after the crossing of the Jordan (Joshua 5:1–15), after a victory at Ai (Joshua 8:30–35), and before Joshua's death (Joshua 24:1–28).

Today too we can follow the principle of renewing the covenant both formally and informally.

- The Methodists have a Covenant Service, usually on the first Sunday of the year. It involves looking back to the past year with thanksgiving and confession and committing themselves to be faithful to God in the new year by a ritual of renewing the covenant. It climaxes with the following prayer:

  I am no longer my own but yours.
  Put me to what you will,
  rank me with whom you will;
  put me to doing,
  put me to suffering;
  let me be employed for you
  or laid aside for you,
  exalted for you
  or brought low for you;
  let me be full,
  let me be empty,
  let me have all things,

let me have nothing;
I freely and wholeheartedly yield all things
to your pleasure and disposal.
And now, glorious and blessed God,
Father, Son and Holy Spirit,
you are mine and I am yours.
So be it.
And the covenant now made on earth,
let it be ratified in heaven. Amen.

- In Youth for Christ in Sri Lanka we have a national convocation for our volunteers once every two years when we commit ourselves afresh to our call and to living lives worthy of that call. At the beginning of each year our different divisions have retreats for volunteers and staff at which commitment is renewed.
- I know of churches that have services of dedication for Sunday school teachers and officers of the church when their commitment to the task and to God is renewed.
- Special or even normal Sunday worship services often end with a call to rededication that could serve as a time to renew the covenant.
- Individuals also can have special days of such renewing of their covenant with God. One's birthday, New Year's Day, or the start of a new assignment or a new job could be good occasions to renew their covenant with God.
- Sometimes God may speak to us through circumstances such as a sermon, a book we read, or a process of confession after sin that will trigger a special act of renewing the covenant.

I suppose the basic attitude that lies behind all the suggestions given above is one that constantly recognizes that we are a people governed by a covenant. Our whole life is influenced by this covenant relationship. The attitude we are speaking of is well expressed in the following statement by Paul:

> For none of us lives to himself, and none of us dies to himself. For if we live, we live to the Lord, and if we die, we die to the Lord. So then, whether we live or whether we die, we are the Lord's. (Romans 14:7, 8)

Remember the Wrath of God (4:24)

After asking the people to take care not to forget the covenant, Moses reminds them of the wrath of God that they would face if they do forget: "For the LORD your God is a consuming fire, a jealous God" (4:24).

A Consuming Fire (4:24a)

The symbol of "consuming fire" is used here to communicate the idea of destructive punishment. The same expression is used of God in 9:3 when it says that he will destroy those who come up against Israel: "Know therefore today that he who goes over before you as a consuming fire is the LORD your God. He will destroy them and subdue them before you." Lest we think that this description of God should be discarded in the era of the new covenant, we must remember that Hebrews uses it in connection with the worship of Christians: ". . . let us offer to God acceptable worship, with reverence and awe, for our God is a consuming fire" (Hebrews 12:28b, 29).

So when people are tempted to break their covenant with God, we should remind them that God is a consuming fire. Though the desire to save ourselves from punishment does not look like a very noble motive, if it keeps us from committing a terrible sin we should gratefully use it, as the Bible does.

A Jealous God (4:24b)

I found God described as a jealous God thirty times in my ESV Bible. Five of these references are in Deuteronomy. In twenty of the thirty occurrences God's jealousy is said to be over the sin of Israel.[3] Once it is used of God's response to sin in the church (1 Corinthians 10:22). Seven times God is said to be jealous over what enemies did to Israel, the people he loves.[4] Three times God's jealousy is simply used to refer to his being against the nations (Nahum 1:2; Zephaniah 1:18; 3:8).

In Hebrew the word for jealousy is the same as the word for zeal. The word used in verse 24 has been described as "an adjective or title used exclusively of God, focusing on his desire for exclusive relationships."[5] God, who is zealous in his commitment to his covenant people, is also jealous to see them remain faithful to him. The sense here is that God's zeal for his people is such that he will not tolerate unfaithfulness or seeing his people dishonored.

This concept of exclusive commitment is difficult to understand in an age when commitment has gone out of fashion in society. Many people do not see even the highest of exclusive relationships of commitment—the marriage tie—as absolutely binding. Some people enter marriage with the idea that if it does not work they can always divorce. Even within marriage some find ideas like "open marriage," which permits casual spouse-swapping or affairs, acceptable. One day crowds cheer with great emotion a player who plays for their favorite football team. A few weeks later that same player plays for a rival team because he is part of a player trading process over which he himself does not have much control. Sadly, many see the marriage commitment in the same way. In the religious sphere the pluralistic mood has presented a model of religious life where people can pick and choose religious practices as they would commodities in a supermarket.

Today people may equate the jealousy of God with a bondage in which he holds us captive. However, Biblical Christians see his jealousy as an aspect of his love. Chris Wright says that "the fire of Yahweh as a jealous God is the fire of an exclusive commitment to his people that demands an exclusive commitment in return." Wright calls this "the fire of redeeming love that has brought them out of the fires of bondage (v. 20) and would therefore tolerate no rival."

Remember That God Could Punish the People (4:25–28)

In verses 21, 22 Moses referred to how he was punished for his rash deed. Now he says that the people or their descendants would be punished if they are unfaithful to God. First, Moses explains how they could be unfaithful: "When you father children and children's children, and have grown old in the land, if you act corruptly by making a carved image in the form of anything, and by doing what is evil in the sight of the LORD your God. . . . " Then he tells them how this affects God: ". . . so as to provoke him to anger" (4:25). Next, he describes the punishment for this sin: "I call heaven and earth to witness against you today, that you will soon utterly perish from the land that you are going over the Jordan to possess. You will not live long in it, but will be utterly destroyed" (4:26). He has just referred to the covenant, and these verses read like the curses of a covenant made in the ancient Near East. Typically those covenants ask the gods to be witnesses to the covenant. Here God turns to the creation ("heaven and earth") to serve as witness (cf. 30:19; 31:28; 32:1). They will attest that this warning was given to the people. This talk of witnesses to the covenant highlights the seriousness of breaking it.

After calling for witnesses Moses describes the punishment for unfaithfulness. First he says they will "disappear from the land" (NLT) they are going into: ". . . that you will soon utterly perish from the land that you are going over the Jordan to possess. You will not live long in it, but will be utterly destroyed" (4:26). Then he says that they will be scattered and become exiles: "And the LORD will scatter you among the peoples, and you will be left few in number among the nations where the LORD will drive you" (4:27). Finally he says that they will serve other lifeless gods: "And there you will serve gods of wood and stone, the work of human hands, that neither see, nor hear, nor eat, nor smell" (4:28). This is a situation where part of God's punishment is that of permitting the sinners to do what they want to do (see Romans 1:24, 26, 28). In this case what they want is to worship other gods. Moses reminds the people that this is a futile exercise since these are lifeless idols, the work of human hands.

How do we harmonize this with the ample teaching in the New Testament that God will forgive those who have sinned when they repent and turn to God? John is clear about this. He says, "If we confess our sins, he is faithful and just to forgive us our sins and to cleanse us from all unrighteousness. . . . My little children, I am writing these things to you so that you may not sin. But if anyone does sin, we have an advocate with the Father, Jesus Christ the righteous" (1 John 1:9; 2:1). There is no exception here. God can forgive believers who commit even the grossest sins. The Bible is clear that God's grace in Christ is greater than all our sin (Romans 5:20).

We must note that we are talking here about gross violations of the covenant such as idolatry. We are not talking about sins like that of Moses when he acted rashly and was chastised but not cut off from God. Gross violations of the covenant are so serious that they require serious disciplinary action. The destruction and defeat in war resulting in exile is something that God does. We will leave such decisions up to God. But we cannot dismiss this passage and wash our hands of the responsibility to do something when people break the covenant in this way. After all, the words about God's wrath that introduce the topic here (4:24) are repeated in the New Testament, as we saw above.

Today we give expression to the seriousness of violations of the covenant through church discipline (Matthew 18:15–18; 1 Corinthians 5:1–13; 1 Timothy 1:19, 20). Speaking about sins similar to the Old Testament violations of the covenant, Paul says, "But now I am writing to you not to associate with anyone who bears the name of brother if he is guilty of sexual immorality or greed, or is an idolater, reviler, drunkard, or swindler—not even to eat with such a one" (1 Corinthians 5:11).

If the person repents he is accepted by God immediately. So forgiveness is assured on the basis of the work of Christ. If the person does not repent, the church may need to drop that person from the membership of the church, which is what Jesus and Paul intend in the New Testament church discipline passages. Paul describes this as delivering the person to Satan (1 Corinthians 5:5; 1 Timothy 1:19, 20), which probably means taking off the protective covering that comes with the security of being part of God's covenant community. In both those instances Paul's aim is that the person repents and comes back to God after experiencing the pain of church discipline. Certainly in the New Testament there is always the opportunity for a person to repent this side of death.

Here then is a comprehensive guide on how to avoid unfaithfulness. All the points given have to do with being careful to remember the great truths that sustain us and with being careful to remain true to God's way of life. Carelessness is the mother of sin. If we are not careful we can fall into a trap of Satan without deliberately planning to do so.

12

Returning to God after Disobedience

DEUTERONOMY 4:29-31

JOHN NEWTON (1725–1807) worked on a slave trading ship and moved away from the faith his godly mother had taught him. Living and working in grossly sinful surroundings, he joined in the sin of the people around him. But in a terrible storm when his ship nearly sank he cried out to God and was converted. He often referred to this incident as "the day I first believed." But he did not give up his involvement in the slave trade. Gradually he went back to the practices of those around him and finally sank deep into his old life of sin. Then God reached out to him and brought him back to himself. He never seriously slid back to a sinful life again.

Newton later became one of England's great preachers and hymn-writers whose hymns "Amazing Grace" and "How Sweet the Name of Jesus Sounds" are greatly loved even today. He had a strong influence on Christian social reformer William Wilberforce and became a staunch supporter of the anti-slavery movement that Wilberforce spearheaded.[1] In the Bible, too, we have stories of people who were given a second chance and returned to God, after backsliding, to become his mighty instruments. David, Jonah, and Peter are prime examples. We ended the last study with Moses' prediction of punishment and exile for the Israelites if they become unfaithful to God. Here we will look at how an exiled people could return to God.

Returning after Experiencing the Misery of Sin (4:29, 30)

Deuteronomy 4:26 says that the people will "utterly perish" and "will be utterly destroyed" after they become unfaithful and follow idols. Then they

139

would be exiled to different nations (v. 27). In those nations they will become idolaters (v. 28). But the nation of Israel will not be totally eradicated; a few will remain, but they will continue to live sinful lives.

However, these people will one day come to their senses, says Moses, and will return to God: "But from there you will seek the LORD your God and you will find him, if you search after him with all your heart and with all your soul" (v. 29). However long they may have rebelled and however far away they may have drifted from God, it is never too late, never too far to return. The door of opportunity remains open as long as we live.

It is the misery of their life without God that prompts them to return to God. Moses goes on to say, "When you are in tribulation, and all these things come upon you in the latter days, you will return to the LORD your God and obey his voice" (v. 30). Having moved away from God, their lives have become miserable. Now they see the terribleness of their tribulation and, like the prodigal son in the far country, they "[come] to [their] senses" (Luke 15:17, NIV) and remember that in their father's home there are wonderful provisions while they languish in the place to which their sin has brought them.

I have spoken to many people who have described the misery they experienced during a time when they backslid. One told me that during that period he was unhappier than he was before giving his life to Christ. But often sin has such a tight hold on us that it keeps us from coming back to God. Thankfully, some see the folly of their choices and return to God.

Anticipating Forgiveness before Sinning

Is it wise to promise forgiveness to people before they sin, as Moses does here? They could give in to temptation knowing that God would ultimately forgive them. I once spoke to a young person who was determined to do something illegal. I told him that what he was attempting to do was displeasing to God. He told me that he knew it was wrong, but, he said, "God will have to have mercy on me and forgive me for doing it." Does our passage encourage people to sin by promising forgiveness in advance to repentant sinners? Within this passage are imbedded three truths that act as a corrective to such a misuse of the promise of forgiveness.

First, many Israelites who sinned in the way Moses predicted did not receive forgiveness. They were destroyed before they repented (4:26). There is no guarantee that people will be spared in order to have an opportunity to repent. It is therefore dangerous to dabble in sin!

Second, those who repent in this passage do so from the bitterness of their chastised state. They are suffering intensely from the consequences of their sin. If the punishment for sin is more serious than the pleasure it brings, then only a fool gives in to the temptation to sin. Those who went into an extramarital affair and then repented would testify to this. Yes, God and their loving spouses forgave them and restored the relationship. But they had to endure severe pain during the affair because of hurting their spouses and their God. Now they have deep regret over having done something so bad to their loved ones. They have the huge battle to win back trust and to restore the relationship to the warmth they once enjoyed. Some have found that even though the spouse accepted them, their children were not so generous. Besides, although God forgets, other humans do not, and those who fell into sin may have to live with the stigma of what they did until they die.

The consequences of sin are so bad that even though there is forgiveness, sinning is never worthwhile. Our greatest and most enduring joys and pains have to do with relationships. The pleasures of sin have to do with a shallow and perhaps intense gratification that disappears soon after the sinful act. So after the act we have to live with the misery of knowing we have done wrong and also knowing that we have violated the relationships that hold the key to our true happiness. So one reason we stay away from sin is that we are committed to happiness. We choose the enduring joys of a relationship with God and those we love over the fleeting pleasures of sin.

Of course, here we have talked only of the earthly consequences of sin. Far worse than those are the eternal consequences, which would make committing sin the height of folly.

Third, Moses' statement about how they repent sheds some light on the situation. He says, "But from there you will seek the LORD your God and you will find him, if you search after him with all your heart and with all your soul" (4:29). Will it be possible for those who have been so dishonest with God to truly seek the Lord with all their heart and all their soul? It is, but because of the deception they practiced when they went into sin, it will not be automatic.

Those who go into sin saying, "Later I will ask God to forgive me" will have to drastically change their outlook if they are to truly repent. They would have to repent of their outlook of presuming upon grace even more than their view of the sin they committed. That outlook is far more serious than the act they committed. It is an insult to God upon whose mercy the stability of the whole world rests. It is a deliberate attack upon the very thing that keeps us from being destroyed this very moment. We are people who should have been sent to Hell immediately. But because of God's mercy we have been spared. To abuse this mercy, then, is a very serious thing.

Yet there is forgiveness for all who sincerely repent, even those who deliberately abuse grace. Nobody really comes to God with motives that are 100 percent pure. Forgiveness is all of grace. Even the little repentance we have is possible because God enabled us to think that way. So even those who abuse grace by going into sin anticipating forgiveness could be sincere in their repentance and seek God with their whole heart. Grace is always greater than sin (Romans 5:20), even greater than the sin of deception and of presuming upon grace. God's love is so great that he overlooks the insult to him and forgives the one who sincerely repents. However, those who presume upon grace and go into sin may never be sincere in their repentance and therefore may never be able to be recipients of God's abundant grace.

The value of this promise of forgiveness is that it keeps us from giving up after we sin. When some people fall, they think their situation is so hopeless that they give up hope. Then, given the power of temptation, they go deeper into sin. So God, in his abundant love, takes the huge risk of promising sinners forgiveness even before they commit sin.

Seeking God Wholeheartedly (4:29)

We will now take a closer look at Moses' description of those who truly repent. He says, "But from there you will seek the LORD your God and you will find him, if you search after him with all your heart and with all your soul" (4:29). Many centuries later Jeremiah, speaking about restoration after exile, makes an almost identical statement: "You will seek me and find me, when you seek me with all your heart" (Jeremiah 29:13). In both these texts two synonyms describe the quest of the repentant sinner, translated "seek" and "search," which appear in consecutive parallel statements. Exodus 33 gives an important exposition of three ingredients that go into seeking the Lord. Verse 7 says, "Everyone who sought the LORD would go out to the tent of meeting, which was outside the camp." But included here was (1) mourning for sin and its consequences (Exodus 33:4), (2) worshipping God in fear (Exodus 33:10), and (3) a manifestation of the glory of God (Exodus 33:21–23).[2]

Here Moses says this seeking is to be done "with all your heart and with all your soul" (Deuteronomy 4:29). It has been my sad experience to see many Christians who never fully recover from a serious sin they committed. Some even commit the same sin again. Some never have "the joy of . . . salvation" restored (Psalm 51:12) and often become judgmental (which is a common result of living with unhealed guilt). Some never return to having full and open fellowship with other Christians. I believe that the primary reason for such incomplete healing after sin is that they did not seek God fully after the sin as the Bible prescribes. Such wholehearted seeking would include five features.

First, there would be a wholehearted acceptance of sin with mourning for it, as we saw from Exodus 33:4. Sometimes people confess sin partially, usually sharing only what is found out by others. Some confess so generally that they do not come to grips with what they have actually done. For example, they say things like, "I am sorry if I have done something wrong." Such people never know freedom from the guilt of sin because they never brought it to the surface so the blood of Jesus could cleanse it. First John 1:7, which affirms that "the blood of Jesus his Son cleanses us from all sin," first says, "If we walk in the light, as he is in the light . . . " The context of that verse shows that such walking in the light involves accepting responsibility for our sins and confessing them (1 John 1:5–10).

Second, there would be humility about one's sin that stops the person from pointing to the faults of others. Often people do this to reduce their humiliation when they are confronted about their own sins. They say something like, "I accept that I have sinned, but why doesn't anyone do something about all the other leaders who do similar things?" When we hear such a statement, we sadly conclude that there is no true repentance because there is no wholehearted acceptance of responsibility for one's sin. The process of repentance has been sidetracked by a peripheral issue. It is true that the sins of others may be serious. But this is not the time to focus on those; this is the time to wholeheartedly pursue forgiveness for one's own sin.

Third, there should be an involvement of the community in the repentance. In Old Testament times, repentance was usually an act where the community was involved. I do not think that we must go to the community each time we do wrong. But because Christian growth takes place in community, when there is serious sin, selected people within the community need to be called in to help bring healing. This would include confession to someone or many in the community, depending on the nature of the sin and the sphere in which its effects are felt. It would include submitting to whatever discipline the community prescribes and being accountable to someone in the community regarding one's behavior. That is, this person will give a regular report about his behavior in his weak area to an accountability partner.

Fourth, there would be total surrender to God that affirms that we will do or give to God whatever he requires. This is an aspect of searching for God with all our heart and soul (4:29). It is always a lack of total surrender to God that leads to sin. So we reverse the process that caused the sin. Our commitment to God may have been halfhearted. We may have been slack about keeping our daily time with God. We may have been making compromises in areas of our lives though not committing prominent sins. With the prominent sin the deficiency in our surrender comes to light. The process of returning to God includes a fresh commitment—a rededication—of our lives to God. Someone has said that our sins are handles by which God gets hold of us. We had been moving away from God, and the sin showed us how far away we were and made us return to God.

Fifth, there would be a fresh resolve to be totally obedient to all that God requires. Speaking of the people's return to God, Moses says ". . . you will return to the LORD your God and obey his voice" (4:30). Obedience after sin would include restitution—e.g., paying back money that has been taken in the wrong way or apologizing to those who have been hurt. It could include giving up a relationship, such as an indiscreet relationship with someone of the opposite sex. It could include giving up wrong practices such as imprecise financial reporting, lying on the job, and taking revenge.

Non-Christians often speak disparagingly of the Christian doctrine of forgiveness, saying that it opens the door to irresponsible behavior. This was one of Mahatma Gandhi's primary objections to the Christian doctrine of salvation through the work of Christ. The above discussion shows that when the Biblical doctrine is understood, there would be no place for such objections.

The Mercy of the Covenant-Keeping God (4:31)

In verse 31 Moses gives what is actually the most important factor in this whole restoration process: the mercy of the covenant-keeping God. He starts with the word "for," indicating that he is giving the reason for what he has just said about the people returning to God: "For the LORD your God is a merciful God. He will not leave you or destroy you or forget the covenant with your fathers that he swore to them" (4:31). The key to our return to God after sin is not any attitude of ours but the mercy of the covenant-keeping God, who is committed to us. He wants us to come back to him and will do everything within his principles of holy love to make that possible.

Christians who have walked with God for some time realize that if God's blessing were dependent on their performance, there would be no hope for them. The most important factor in our lives is the mercy of God. When we sin, it is God who takes the initiative to woo us back to himself. He does not say, "Let him repent, and I will show him mercy." That is how we often respond to those who hurt us. But God does not act in this way. Our verse says, "He will not leave you." The Hebrew word translated "leave" means "to leave alone, abandon, withdraw" when appearing in that grammatical form (*hiphil*). In other words, God takes the initiative in bringing us back.

God does not leave it up to us to drum up the strength to repent. While we don't have an inclination to repent, he takes the initiative and acts to soften our hard hearts so that we see the folly and terribleness of our action and become open to repenting. God often orchestrates situations to soften the person. I have heard stories of people receiving letters at a crucial time, going to church to avoid the snow and hearing a message that was just for them, hearing a song sung in the room next to them in the hospital, receiving a visit from a friend who ministered to them. That providence was used by God to break through into the backslidden Christian's life.

Our verse also says, "[God] will not . . . forget the covenant with your fathers that he swore to them." So often we forget that we are a people bound by a covenant, and we move away from God. But God never forgets his covenant with us. To say he is a faithful God is to say he will be faithful to his covenant with us. What security we have when we have a God like this! Elsewhere we find God saying, "Can a woman forget her nursing child, that she should have no compassion on the son of her womb? Even these may forget, yet I will not forget you" (Isaiah 49:15). As the father of the prodigal son waits eagerly over a long period ready to welcome the son when he returns home, God waits at the door for the return of his wayward child. As we saw, he even prompts him to return and gives him the strength to do that.

The Civil War in the United States of America came to an end after the Confederate Army was finally defeated. At that time President Abraham Lincoln was asked how he would treat the rebellious southerners. The question hinted at the desire to see the South severely punished. Lincoln, who sought to follow God's principles in his life, replied, "I will treat them as if they had never been away."[3] That's how God treats us when we return to him.

13

Believing and Obeying
the Bible

DEUTERONOMY 4:32–43

SUSANNA WESLEY IS REPUTED TO HAVE told her son John, "This book will keep you from sin; or sin will keep you from this book." Wesley followed the pattern set by his godly mother and gave the Bible a high place in his life and in the Methodist movement, which he founded. He liked to call the Methodists "Bible Christians." He said about himself, "Yea I am a Bible bigot. I follow it in all things great and small."[1] By "Bible bigot" he would have meant one who is obstinately devoted to the Bible and determined to be totally obedient to it.

One of the most important keys to fostering obedience among Christians is getting them into the Word. The church I belong to and the organization I work for minister primarily with people originally from other faiths. We have found that those who get into the Word, primarily by being part of a small group where the Word is studied, mature well in the Christian life. Those who do not get into the Word do not mature. If we hope to remain faithful to God, we must stay close to his Word and ensure that it has a daily influence upon our lives.

It should not surprise us then that Deuteronomy, which aims to prepare the people to live obediently in the promised land, has a lot to say about the importance of God's Word. When Jesus was tempted by Satan, all three times it was to the Word that he appealed to in his answers to Satan (Matthew 4:1–10; Luke 4:1–13). Significantly all three statements that Jesus made in response to Satan were from Deuteronomy.

A Book Like No Other (4:32, 33)

Having described how the people will return to God after a destructive period of exile (4:29–31), Moses goes back to the task of inspiring the people to obedience. He does so by showing that they have a unique revelation given by a unique God.

A Unique Revelation (4:32, 33a)

Verses 32, 33a present the uniqueness of God's revelation: "For ask now of the days that are past, which were before you, since the day that God created man on the earth, and ask from one end of heaven to the other, whether such a great thing as this has ever happened or was ever heard of. Did any people ever hear the voice of a god speaking out of the midst of the fire, as you have heard . . . ?" The fact that God spoke out of the midst of the fire made the revelation unique.

Many today view the Bible as just another book. This has become a more serious issue in the postmodern world where there has been an assault on the importance of truth. Books, and even words, are regarded with less value than before. Our passage has some keys as to why we believe the content of the Bible is desperately important to people today.

This passage claims that God's revelation is unique. Its uniqueness has to do with revelatory events that took place. In this case the event is "the voice of a god speaking out of the midst of the fire" (4:33). In miraculous ways God authenticated the revelation he was giving, so that the people would know that the truth communicated is unique. Similarly in the New Testament the events surrounding Jesus' birth, life, teaching, death, resurrection, and ascension authenticate the uniqueness of the words of the apostles and their representatives who wrote the Bible.[2]

The affirmation that God's revelation is absolute truth goes against the pluralistic mood of our day. Pluralists affirm that revelation is what people discover through their unique experience shaped as it is by culture and history. Absolute truth is unknowable. If there is an absolute God, he cannot be known fully, though different peoples have experienced some truth about him. And that is what is recorded in the Scriptures of the different religions. The *Bhagavad Gita* records what the Indians discovered, and the *Qur'an* records what the Arabs discovered. And such truth is subjective, that is, it is based on experience. In contrast, the Christian claims that the truth of the Scriptures was not simply discovered, it was disclosed by God. True, the Biblical writers experienced the truth, and in that sense it is subjective. But in those acts God was specifically revealing his truth to humanity. We place our faith upon those acts and those words through which God brought his redemption to his fallen humanity.

So what we find in the Bible is objective truth, truth that the Creator of the world gave to his creation. In that sense it is absolute. Not only is it a clear and specific revelation of the truth, it is the answer of the Creator of the world to the basic needs of his creation.

An Awesome Revelation (4:33)

The second theme emerging from the statement that God spoke from the midst of the fire is that the Scriptures are awesome. Sadly, the word *awesome*, which is so important to Christian spirituality, has become so popular today that our generation has a much diluted understanding of it. My dictionary defines awe as "an emotion variously combining dread, veneration, and wonder that is inspired by authority or by the sacred or sublime."[3] Realizing the supernatural nature of God's revelation should fill us with such awe.

Verse 33, which we quoted as demonstrating the uniqueness of Scripture, goes on to demonstrate its awesomeness also: "Did any people ever hear the voice of a god speaking out of the midst of the fire, as you have heard, *and still live?*" So awesome was the giving of the Law that it is a surprise that those who received it did not die. A little later Moses says, "The Lord spoke with you face to face at the mountain, out of the midst of the fire, while I stood between the Lord and you at that time, to declare to you the word of the Lord. *For you were afraid because of the fire*, and you did not go up into the mountain" (5:4, 5). The fire elicited fear in the hearts of the people. This theme is described in 5:24–26:

> And you said, "Behold, the Lord our God has shown us his glory and greatness, and we have heard his voice out of the midst of the fire. This day we have seen God speak with man, and man still live. Now therefore why should we die? For this great fire will consume us. If we hear the voice of the Lord our God any more, we shall die. For who is there of all flesh, that has heard the voice of the living God speaking out of the midst of fire as we have, and has still lived?"

The Muslims are known for revering their Scriptures, which they call the Holy Qur'an. In some church traditions the congregation stands when the Scriptures are read. Awe could make the Scriptures a distant and inaccessible book. We welcome the familiarity with Scripture and the sense that it is a living word that characterizes the evangelical movement. But I think we have lost too much in the process of familiarizing Scripture. There should be a sense of the wonder of the Word in the Christian, a sense of urgency to get to know what it teaches, and a sense of fear to disobey its instructions.

David says, "My heart stands in awe of [NIV, trembles at] your words" (Psalm 119:161). Elsewhere he says, "I bow down toward your holy temple and give thanks to your name for your steadfast love and your faithfulness, for you have exalted above all things your name and your word" (Psalm 138:2). The words of Mahatma Gandhi, who was not a Christian, are a strong indictment on the church: "You Christians have in your keeping a document with enough dynamite in it to blow the whole of civilization to bits, to turn society upside down, to bring peace to this war-torn world. But you read it as if it were just good literature, and nothing else."[4]

A God Like No Other (4:34–39)

We have talked of the uniqueness and awesomeness of the Word of God. But for that to be of any significance, the God who inspired the Word should also be unique and awesome. This is what Moses shows in verses 34–39. Deuteronomy mentions often that remembering what God has done in history is a motivation to obedience (e.g., see the discussions on 1:4–8; 3:1–7; 4:9–14). This point is made again in this passage. Here I will only summarize what Moses says in this passage. He makes several points over and over.

- God is absolutely unique:
  "... know therefore today, and lay it to your heart, that the Lord is God in heaven above and on the earth beneath; there is no other." (4:39)

- God's uniqueness is evidenced by the particular concern and love he has shown to the Israelites:
  "Or has any god ever attempted to go and take a nation for himself from the midst of another nation, by trials, by signs, by wonders, and by war, by a mighty hand and an outstretched arm, and by great deeds of terror, all of which the LORD your God did for you in Egypt before your eyes? To you it was shown, that you might know that the LORD is God; there is no other besides him." (4:34, 35)
  "And because he loved your fathers and chose their offspring after them and brought you out of Egypt with his own presence. . . ." (4:37a)

- This concern has been expressed through great and miraculous acts that the Israelites themselves saw:
  "... by trials, by signs, by wonders, and by war, by a mighty hand and an outstretched arm, and by great deeds of terror, all of which the LORD your God did for you in Egypt before your eyes?" (4:34)
  "... brought you out of Egypt with his own presence, by his great power, driving out before you nations greater and mightier than yourselves, to

bring you in, to give you their land for an inheritance, as it is this day."
(4:37b, 38)

- This God has spoken a word to the people that is both unique and awesome:
  "Out of heaven he let you hear his voice, that he might discipline you.
  And on earth he let you see his great fire, and you heard his words out of
  the midst of the fire." (4:36)

Moses' point is that this unique, awesome God is personally committed to
the Israelites and has expressed this commitment by acting as their deliverer
in awesome and powerful ways. This is another compelling reason for obeying the Word. This God is committed to us. He did not simply give us laws
and forget about us, which is often how we think of authority figures. He is
committed to us and is willing to even perform miracles to help us.

This truth of God's powerful and loving care for us is expressed by Paul
in Romans 8:32, which is one of the most important texts in the Bible to
motivate Christians to remain faithful to God: "He who did not spare his own
Son but gave him up for us all, how will he not also with him graciously give
us all things?" God is so committed to us that he even gave his own Son to
die for us. A mother may love her daughter so much that she flings herself
between her husband and her daughter when the husband in a drunken rage
comes to assault their daughter. But because he is physically stronger than
she, he brushes her aside and attacks his daughter. That mother had deep and
sacrificial love for her daughter, but she did not have power to overcome her
husband. God not only loves us, he is also almighty, and therefore no one,
however powerful, can overcome him. Surely, then, we can know without a
doubt that he will look after us. As Paul says just before making the statement
we just quoted, "If God is for us, who can be against us?" (Romans 8:31).

Christians sometimes choose to disobey God's commands because they
feel they cannot overcome the force of temptation and survive. The Bible tells
us that because God is for us and because he more powerful than all other
forces, we can overcome the temptation.

- A father is afraid of not being able to provide the needs of his family; so
  he tells a lie in order to make a sale. We tell him that he does not need to
  do that because "God will supply every need of yours according to his
  riches in glory in Christ Jesus" (Philippians 4:19).
- A single woman who wants to get married and is getting on in years gives
  up looking for a committed Christian and marries someone who does not
  share her commitment to Christ. We point her to the truth of Psalm 138:8:
  "The LORD will fulfill his purpose for me; your steadfast love, O LORD,

endures forever." Based on that we tell her that God knows what is best for her and will give her that in his time.

- A young Christian is afraid to obey the Great Commission to share the gospel with others because of the opposition she anticipates from opponents of the gospel. We remind her that when Christ was sending his disciples to preach the good news, he told them to anticipate opposition. But then he told them, "Do not fear those who kill the body but cannot kill the soul. Rather fear him who can destroy both soul and body in hell" (Matthew 10:28).

- For fear of rejection by his peers a young person does not take exception when all the others in his group are indulging in racist conversation. We tell him that Jesus says, "For whoever is ashamed of me and of my words in this adulterous and sinful generation, of him will the Son of Man also be ashamed when he comes in the glory of his Father with the holy angels" (Mark 8:38).

In each of the above scenarios the path we presented to overcome the temptation was derived from the Word. And each time what the Word taught was something about the nature of God. It showed that God was bigger than the circumstance and would help give the best solution to it. The Word introduces us to God, and a proper knowledge of God helps us live a life of obedience. What the above examples show is that the safest thing we can do is to entrust ourselves to God's care, and the most foolish thing we can do is to disobey him. His power cannot be matched and could either work for us if we are obedient to him or against us if we are disobedient. God's love also cannot be matched, and it is expressed in today's world in his care for the obedient.

Obedience Is the Way to Prosperity (4:40)

Up to this point in this section, Moses has made two key points. First, the Word of God is unique and awesome—it is the word of the great God to his people. Second, this God loves his people and is committed to their welfare to the point of intervening in great power on their behalf. It is no surprise to find that after such an exposition he challenges the people to a life of obedience and exclusive loyalty to God. This is the God who cares for them and has given them a clear word on how to live. "Therefore," says Moses, "you shall keep his statutes and his commandments, which I command you today, that it may go well with you and with your children after you, and that you may prolong your days in the land that the LORD your God is giving you for all time" (4:40). From what precedes we can imply that Moses is saying that obedience is the only proper response to the Biblical doctrine of God and Scripture. But here he is explicitly saying that obedience is the only way to true prosperity for us and for our children. It is also the key to a long life (on this see the discussion on 5:16b).

Moses does not use the word *prosperity* here. Instead he says that the result of obedience is that it will "go well with" the people. This is better than just physical prosperity. Many rich people are very unhappy, because physical prosperity alone will not truly satisfy us. What we need is to know that everything is going well for us. That is true prosperity. One of the huge challenges facing the church today is motivating Christians to be obedient to the Word when those around them live in ways so different from what is prescribed in the Bible. And some of them seem to be prospering more than we are! Our answer to this is that the way of obedience is the best way for us.

Yet the lure of earthly prosperity may take us away from God's path. This is why Paul says that we must have our attitude straight. In Romans 12:2 he says, "Do not be conformed to this world, but be transformed by the renewal of your mind." We must not think like others do. We must let God transform us by renewing our minds. But is this worth it? Paul goes on to give the result of having our minds transformed: ". . . that by testing you may discern what is the will of God, what is good and acceptable and perfect" (Romans 12:2b). When our minds are transformed, we will realize that God's will is the best possible thing for us. Moses is saying something similar. He is saying that the Word of God is the best thing for us, and if we obey it, the best things possible will happen to us.

Providing Refuge to the Vulnerable (4:41–43)

We have come to the end of Moses' first speech, which was primarily a recounting of the history of God's dealings with the Israelites up to the point at which they were (1:6—3:29) followed by an exhortation to obedience (4:1–40). What we get next is somewhat unexpected. It is a note about how Moses set apart three cities of refuge: "Then Moses set apart three cities in the east beyond the Jordan" (4:41). The cities are identified in verse 43: "Bezer in the wilderness on the tableland for the Reubenites, Ramoth in Gilead for the Gadites, and Golan in Bashan for the Manassites." These are for the two and a half tribes—Reuben, Gad, and Manasseh—that are going to settle east of the Jordan in regions already secured by the Israelites.

Verse 42 gives the purpose of these cities of refuge: ". . . that the manslayer might flee there, anyone who kills his neighbor unintentionally, without being at enmity with him in time past; he may flee to one of these cities and save his life." The phenomenon of setting up such is described in greater detail in 19:1–10, which also gives an example of how such a killing can occur: the axe head slips from the handle and strikes a neighbor. We will discuss this practice in greater detail in our discussion of that passage. The city of refuge idea lies behind provisions made today for people to seek asylum in a different country when they feel their lives are in danger.

Here we will note the significance of placing this discussion immediately following the long speech of Moses that describes the history of God's covenant relationship with the people and closes with a rousing call to obedience to the Word. The discussion on cities of refuge falls more under the category of social justice. Those who have experienced God's salvation and protection need to immediately be thinking about the protection of the weak and vulnerable. Here the issue is more a national than a personal one. So Christians who have been personally touched by God need to think of how structures could be set in place nationally so as to protect the weak and the vulnerable.

In the history of the church there are many examples of Christians who after enjoying a warm evangelical experience addressed national issues while maintaining a warm walk with the Lord and promoting evangelistic and revival-related causes. The preacher John Wesley (1703–1791), who was a master at personal spirituality, had an important part to play in ridding Britain of the labor abuses that took place after the Industrial Revolution. The politician William Wilberforce (1759–1833) won a long and bruising battle to rid the British Empire of slavery. A British aristocrat, the seventh Earl of Shaftesbury, Anthony Ashley Cooper (1801–1885), did much to improve the working and living conditions of laborers, the mentally ill, Catholics, and other vulnerable groups in nineteenth-century Britain. The Japanese Christian leader Toyohiko Kagawa (1888–1960) was an evangelist known for his deep spirituality. But he also worked incessantly to improve the conditions of Japan's slum-dwellers among whom he chose to live. We will discuss these examples in our discussion of 10:19 also.

We have a great heritage of Christian leaders who were passionate about the spiritual life and moved by the terrible destiny of people apart from Christ while at the same time being passionate about protection and provision for the weak and vulnerable in society.[5] When we apply the truths of Scripture, we must apply it to both to our personal and social lives. In 1989 I did two Bible expositions on Romans 5—8 at the Lausanne II Conference on World Evangelization in Manila. While there I received a letter of reprimand from someone attending the conference. She complained that all my applications of the Biblical text had to do with personal righteousness and that I neglected the need for social righteousness. I am grateful for that reprimand. Now I try to include both these categories when I apply the Biblical text to my life and also when I speak and write.

14

How to Think about the Law

DEUTERONOMY 4:44—5:6

SOME CHRISTIANS THINK THAT because we are under grace, the laws of Deuteronomy (and Exodus 20–40 and Leviticus) are not very helpful to Christians today. This is because these sections of Scripture devote so much space to expounding the Law of the Israelites, which they believe no longer applies to their lives. Paul, however, was convinced that "all Scripture is breathed out by God and profitable for teaching, for reproof, for correction, and for training in righteousness" (2 Timothy 3:16). The exposition of the Law would be included within that "all."

Approaching the Laws of Deuteronomy

Our approach to the Old Testament Law in this book is that all of it has relevance to us today. This is because, as Dennis Kinlaw says, "When God spoke from Mt. Sinai and gave the Israelites the Law, he was not presenting them with rules to be followed. He was revealing his character, his nature, and his will for them."[1] Chris Wright explains in his book *Old Testament Ethics for the People of God* that we must take into consideration the context of each of the laws and look to see what the objective behind that law in Israelite society was. Then we apply that objective to our context today.[2] Though the details of the Law and its implementation may differ from past times, the theological intention behind the Law is maintained.

For example, the punishments for adultery, for dishonoring God in worship, and for dishonoring parents may differ today from what they were in the Old Testament era. But the Old Testament laws on these sins tell us that Christians must abhor them today just as in Old Testament times. The food laws stipulating that certain foods should not be eaten (Deuteronomy 12:23–25; 14:3–21) may not be specifically relevant to us. But we will ask why such laws were made and whether there is something we can learn from them. Many stipulations on worship cannot be fully applied by us today. But we can ask why a worship leader had to offer a sacrifice for himself before leading the people in worship. We can ask what we can learn by the specific instructions given for the selection of people who will look after the maintenance of the places of worship and the musical aspects of worship. Surely all of this will help mold our attitudes toward worship today.

So we will look for the theological and moral principles behind the laws listed in Deuteronomy and attempt to apply them to our lives today.

Introduction to Moses' Second Address (4:44–49)

Deuteronomy 4:44 begins the second and longest address of Moses. It describes the laws or stipulations connected to the covenant (chapters 5–26), and it is followed by two chapters about ratifying the covenant (chapter 27) and the blessings and curses related to the covenant (chapter 28). But first there is an introduction (4:44–49), which an editor must have influenced because verse 47 speaks of the land "beyond the Jordan," which means the writer is looking at things from the perspective of one who has already crossed the Jordan. The crossing took place after Moses' death.

The introduction first says, "This is the law that Moses set before the people of Israel. These are the testimonies, the statutes, and the rules, which Moses spoke to the people of Israel when they came out of Egypt" (4:44, 45). "Law" here is *Torah*, which is "a general term for the whole law." "Testimonies," "statutes," and "rules" refer to the different "specific stipulations" of that law.[3] These two verses introduce what is going to follow.

Verse 46 tells where the sermon was given: ". . . beyond the Jordan in the valley opposite Beth-peor, in the land of Sihon the king of the Amorites, who lived at Heshbon, whom Moses and the people of Israel defeated when they came out of Egypt." This was also the place where the first speech was given (3:29). Next there is a summary of the victories won just prior to the time of the address and the geographical areas conquered (4:46b–49). These details are condensed from 3:8–17, where the conquest of the Transjordan areas was described. The victories God gave the Israelites are the basis of giving the covenant stipulations (or laws). This point will be made once more just before the Ten Commandments are listed (5:6).

What to Do with the Law (5:1)

Hear

Moses' second address begins with a concise statement on what to do with the Law: "And Moses summoned all Israel and said to them, 'Hear, O Israel, the statutes and the rules that I speak in your hearing today, and you shall learn them and be careful to do them'" (5:1). Moses summoned "all Israel" for this exposition of the Law. This is for all the people. When it comes to vocation, there are different callings to different people, with some giving some time and others (like the Levites) giving much more time to God's work and perhaps having more constraints on what they can and cannot do. But when it comes to obedience to the Law there are not two callings. All are called to be totally obedient.

Those in situations where complete obedience is difficult are not let off the hook. They need to grapple and ask how they can be totally obedient to God in their situation, and if they cannot be totally obedient they need to change their situation. In Sri Lanka some jobs cannot be done if you are unwilling to give bribes. I have come to the sad conclusion that even though there is a desperately urgent need to have Christians in all segments of society, it may be necessary for Christians to leave such jobs if it is impossible for them to do them without doing some things that displease God.

Moses says, "Hear, O Israel, the statutes and the rules that I speak in your hearing today" (5:1). There are at least twenty-three references to the people hearing the word of God in Deuteronomy, with eight in chapter 5.[4] The solemn formula, "Hear, O Israel" appears five times in Deuteronomy at the start of important sections (5:1; 6:4; 9:1; 20:3; 27:9). Hearing from God was very important to them as they did not have idols and other physical objects that can be seen to represent God. Though Yahweh cannot be seen, unlike other gods, he can be heard. It is sad that, unlike in earlier years, the Ten Commandments are not read often when Christians gather.

Learn and Obey

Next the Israelites are to "learn" the laws of the Lord (5:1b). Some people who have an almost magical view about how God speaks to them think that studying the Word carefully to ascertain the meaning of the text is unspiritual. This is not so with the living Word of God, which is living and active. During the orientation for new students at Fuller Seminary, the president of the seminary, Dr. David Hubbard, told us we must learn to view study as worship. One of the most learned New Testament Greek resources available today, *The New International Dictionary of New Testament Theology*, begins with the words of the famous British Biblical scholar Sir Edwin Hoskyns (1884–1937): "Bury yourself in a dictionary and come up in the presence of God."[5] We go to the study of the Word with a desire to be with and to be instructed by God who is both our loving Savior and our supreme Lord.

Those who hear without learning fall into several categories. Some hear from one ear and let it go out of the other ear. They are like the seed that fell on the road in the Parable of the Sower. We preachers face the great danger of taking the message in through our ears and then proclaiming it with our mouth without letting it truly go in and change our own behavior. Anne Bradstreet has said, "Many can speak well, but few can do well. We are better scholars in the theory than the practice part."[6]

Others hear the Word and are even deeply moved, but it does not affect their behavior. I have seen people moved to tears as a result of hearing God's Word proclaimed. But after some time they went back to their former life of disobedience. The message touched the emotions, but it did not influence the will so as to make the person move along the path of obedience. Many go to the Bible for an emotional high, some inspiring thought, or some promise they can claim to calm their troubled minds. Indeed, the Bible does often have this effect upon us. But we also go to the Bible as students wanting to learn how to live. Even deep study can be an experience of worship if we always go to the Scriptures with a desire to learn and obey.

After surveying the use of the Hebrew word translated "learn" (*lamad*) in the form that it is used here (*qal*), Eugene Merrill concludes that "the learning [described here] is clearly, then, more than academic—it must impact and change life."[7] So our verse says, ". . . you shall learn them and be careful to do them" (5:1c). Once more we encounter the familiar word *shamar*, which carries the meaning "pay careful attention to."[8] We saw how in 4:9 Moses asked the people to be careful to remember the great events of history. In 4:23 he spoke about being careful not to forget the covenant and end up making an image. Now God talks about being careful to "do" the commands. This same charge is presented again in 5:32 and 6:3.

A pastor's wife was introduced to someone as the wife of Dr. _____. Thinking her husband was a medical doctor she responded, "Where does he practice?" The lady responded, "Oh no, he doesn't practice; he preaches." Sadly, this is literally true in some instances. We had a pastor in Sri Lanka who would say to people, "Do as I say, not as I do." In some religious traditions in Asia, preachers are not bound to practice everything their scriptures teach. That is not so in Christianity. Here are some ways in which we can approach the task of obedience conscientiously.

- We take careful note of what makes us disobey and what leads to disobedience and plan how we will avoid those steps.
- We find ways to do some of the hard things the life of obedience includes.
- We constantly pray for strength to obey, especially mentioning our vulnerable areas.
- We remain accountable to fellow Christians we can trust and share about our behavior in our weak areas.
- The moment we fall into sin, we plead for forgiveness, naming the sin, asking God for strength not to fall again.

The Basis: A Covenant Relationship (5:2)

Verse 2 reminds them of their covenant relationship with God and of the day when that covenant was first made: "The LORD our God made a covenant with us in Horeb" (or Sinai; see the discussion on 1:2). We looked at the need to remember the covenant in our discussion of 4:23, but let me simply mention here that Christians can't go on acting any way they like. They are bound by a covenant.

In Deuteronomy the primary emphasis when talking about the covenant was obedience. With Abraham and the other patriarchs the emphasis was on the promises. Now many of those promises have been fulfilled, and with the conquest of Canaan the biggest one would be fulfilled. It is important to emphasize both obedience and the promises. But after seeing God do so much to fulfill those promises we must put our major emphasis on living how God wants us to live.

A Personal and a Corporate Experience (5:3–5)

Verses 3–5 describe the covenant-making process at Mount Horeb, a major aspect of which was God's speaking to the people. Verses 3, 4 may sound incorrect to us: "Not with our fathers did the LORD make this covenant, but with us, who are all of us here alive today. The LORD spoke with you face to face at the mountain, out of the midst of the fire." But they were not there at that time! Their ancestors were the ones who were there. But the ancestors also did not speak face-to-face with God. Deuteronomy 5:5 says it was Moses who went up the mountain and spoke with God, "for [they] were afraid because of the fire." This is a rhetorical device to highlight the corporate solidarity that the people had with their ancestors. The experience of the ancestors was so real to their children that it was as if they were there too. When Moses was speaking face-to-face with God, it was as if they were speaking because he was their representative. As the Afro-American song puts it, we were there when they crucified the Lord. We were part of the transaction Jesus made because he was dying for our sins.

Because they were there in that sense, it is a personal thing to them because of their solidarity with their ancestors and with Moses. The covenant was personal in application and corporate in scope. This is a key aspect of Biblical religion. We are individually responsible for our behavior. We must individually accept the covenant into our lives. As the old saying goes, "God has no grandchildren." The Law does not consist of an abstract set of principles but is a personal message from the God with whom we have a personal relationship. It was intended to become personally internalized in our lives so as to change the way we think and act. But as we live out the Law we are one with our community and share together in their experience. Through stories from the history of our spiritual ancestors parents need to give their children this sense that they are part of a larger body. But they must also teach their children that they are personally responsible for their actions.

The Foundation: God's Redemptive Acts (5:6)

The God Who Commands

With verse 6 we begin God's words of giving the Law. He starts in a way that is very typical for God when establishing or confirming a covenant relationship with his people. It appeals to God's saving acts. "I am the LORD your God, who brought you out of the land of Egypt, out of the house of slavery" (5:6). The way God is described, "I am the LORD your God," has a bearing on our approach to the Law. The Lord of the universe, our God, has given these commands to us. Today we may be afraid to follow God's Law for fear of displeasing our peers, our leaders, or wicked people. By following the Law we may forfeit some material or social benefits. But God is greater than all these people, and he rules history. The boy who has beside him a strongly built brother three years senior to him will not fear the bully one year senior to him in school. The knowledge that these are the commands of the Lord of the universe gives us courage to obey.

Law Follows Grace

Verse 6 also teaches us that the Law is founded upon God's saving acts. The commands are given after God "brought [them] out of the land of Egypt, out of the house of slavery" (5:6). The Old Testament is a story of God's redemptive history. God first saves us, and the laws are a consequence of that salvation. They help us continue in the life with which God has gifted us. In other religions the gods show people how to live, and that *way of life* is primary to the religion. In Biblical religion what is primary is the *way to life* through the salvation God gives. Often we hear people say that all religions teach basically the same thing: how to be good. Not Biblical religion! Biblical religion is founded upon God's acts of redemption. The Law flows from that. Law follows gospel.

This is true of the Old Testament also. God took the initiative to save the Israelites before giving them the Law. So the Law is contrasted with "the house of slavery" in verse 6. The Law is not intended to enslave but to enhance the liberated life. We often hear people say that in the Old Testament salvation is by works and in the New Testament salvation is by grace through faith. But actually grace was operating and primary all along in God's dealings with his people.

A Response of Love

When God appeals to us through the Decalogue, he does so as the one who loves us and has won our freedom. Since the coming of Christ this understanding has even deeper meaning as we now see God as the one who won our freedom by giving his own Son to be a sacrifice for our sins. Without this attitude we would not be able to see the Decalogue in the way the Bible intends us to see it. Our obedience to the commandments is an expression of our love for God. Deuteronomy 4:4–6 shows how love for God motivates our obedience to God's Word. Doing something for someone you deeply love is a delight.

One of the happiest memories I have in my life is that of taking my children to school when they were little children. It was a happy time of conversation. Now the children are grown up and quite independent. Now I wait to pounce upon any opportunity to drive them someplace. It may seem like a tough job for a busy person and like a sacrifice that I am making. Indeed, sometimes when I take them to different places, I am tired and under severe pressure with a lot of work to do. But for me as their father it is a way of expressing love. It is not a burden; it is a delight.

That is how the psalmists refer to the Law of God. Psalm 119 mentions delighting in God's Law ten times (in the ESV[9]). When we obey the Ten Commandments we are doing something we delight to do, for we are deeply in love with the God who gave us those commands and before doing so gave himself to rescue us from slavery. These commands don't bind us; they enable us to go on living in the liberty that the one who gave the commands won for us.

To sum up, our obedience to the Decalogue is a joyous response to the God who has loved and redeemed us. Because the Decalogue is a word from our loving Redeemer, it has a sweet sound to it. Like the psalmists we delight in it, just as I delight to hear the voice of my spouse over the phone when I am traveling in another country. This obedience is carried out within the context of a community of people who are similarly thrilled by the fact that God has had mercy on them.

Notes on the Ten Commandments

The Special Place They Have

It is clear from the references to the Ten Commandments in the Bible that they had a very special place in Biblical religion. They are sometimes referred to by a special name such as "the ten words," which is usually translated as "the Ten Commandments" (Exodus 34:28; Deuteronomy 4:13) or "the words" (Deuteronomy 5:22; 9:10). The word *Decalogue*, which is often used to refer to the Ten Commandments, comes from the Greek meaning "the ten words." This is the only material in the Bible inscribed on two tablets of stone by the finger of God (Exodus 24:12; Deuteronomy 5:22; 10:1–5). We will discuss the unique signature found at the end of the record of the Ten Commandments in 5:22 in our comments on that verse.

So the Jewish and Christian traditions are right in giving the Decalogue an exalted place. It is dangerous to say that some passages in Scripture are more inspired than others. Some people speak of the canon within the canon. As we noted earlier, Paul, speaking about the whole Old Testament, says, "All Scripture is breathed out by God and profitable for teaching, for reproof, for correction, and for training in righteousness" (2 Timothy 3:16). The importance of the Decalogue is that it is a summary presenting the basic principles that govern the whole Law. The rest of the laws of the Old Testament derive from the Decalogue.

Of course, the Ten Commandments were given into a specific historical situation, which is described in the Pentateuch. Therefore we will study it in the same way that we study the rest of the Law. We will look for theological principles behind each of the commands, and from those we will see how we can apply the command for today. Because the Decalogue consists of general guidelines that provide the base for the other laws, we can see that all of the commandments apply to us today.

Their Sequence

It has often been pointed out that the Decalogue can be divided into two parts. The first part, covering the first four commands, present vertical issues—that is, how we relate to God. The second part, covering the rest of the commands, present horizontal issues—that is, how we relate to other human beings. It is most significant that when Jesus gave his two great commandments, he also followed this sequence. Jesus' "great and first commandment" (Matthew 22:38) was, "You shall love the Lord your God with all your heart and with all your soul and with all your mind" (Matthew 22:37). His second one was, "You shall love your neighbor as yourself" (Matthew 22:39).

Chris Wright says that the sequence in which the commands appear in the Decalogue may suggest priority. The highest priority is relating to God. Next comes relating to other humans such as family members, the society in which we live, and our neighbors. Third comes property. It seems that today we have reversed this order. Today wealth is the most important value in life; then come people. And God is generally ignored.

Their Negative Orientation

While the Decalogue begins with a positive affirmation of God's deliverance, eight of the ten commands themselves are negative. The only positive ones are the fourth commandment about remembering the Sabbath and the fifth about honoring parents. But the fourth also is largely negative in prescribing that the people are not to work on the Sabbath. The positive salvation is what is most important in our lives. But we must remember there are many things that we do not do as redeemed people living in a fallen world. Therefore, the negatives are also very important.

But to those who love God and relish their salvation the negatives are not viewed as a burden. They are means to a glorious and strongly positive end. They help us to get closer and to remain close to the One who is the most important person in our lives and with whom we have a love relationship that is the most enjoyable thing in life. So these negative commands are a means to further liberation for us. They free us in order to achieve our goals, just as giving up heavy and cumbersome clothing frees a runner to run as fast as he can.

However, for those whose primary goal in life is not knowing and pleasing God, to those who are not secure in their enjoyment of salvation, these become burdens and apparent restrictions of freedom. Therefore today when someone, recalling the old version of the Ten Commandments, says, "Thou shalt not," it is usually with a negative connotation. But those who are really free are not those who have won the freedom to do this or that. It is rather those who are free not to do some things. They have come to the state where they do not need this or that for satisfaction. Therefore they can forgo anything, so long as that does not hinder their walk with God.[10]

- If an unemployed Christian has to lie to get a good job, she refuses to lie and chooses to forgo the comfort, status, and security of having a job because she knows that lying would displease God. True, having a job solves a lot of her problems, but having God with her enables her to live at peace amidst her problems.

- Someone has insulted a Christian's wife, and he feels he must get even by insulting the person who insulted his wife. In Sri Lanka many think this is necessary to preserve the honor of the family. But he is willing to go without that satisfaction and honor because God has asked us to leave those matters to him to settle. He has the deeper satisfaction of pleasing God though he misses the shallow and temporary satisfaction of defending the family honor according to a warped sense of values.

Several years ago I read a piece by F. W. Boreham who argued that the happiest people on earth are those who can enjoy winter sunshine—that is, those who can be happy even when things are gloomy. We can do that because the salvation God gives us is a pearl of great price that is so valuable that we would be willing to sell all that we have in order to acquire it. Giving up something so we can remain firm in the enjoyment of life with God is therefore not a big deal for a Christian.

Their Role in Determining the Nature of a Crime

Chris Wright, to whom I am indebted for most of what is in the sub-section below,[11] points out that the Decalogue "was a summary of certain fundamental kinds of behavior either required or prohibited on the authority of the God by whose grace and power Israel existed as a people." He says it was not a criminal law code because it does not give detailed specifications and penalties. The Decalogue gave the principles, and the laws worked out the details. Wright points out that all the laws with the death penalty can be related to the Decalogue. The death penalty showed how serious breaking the covenant was and how that affects the whole community.

Though all the crimes requiring the death penalty can be traced to the Decalogue, not all the commands in the Decalogue bring the death penalty. In fact, coveting does not bring with it any penalty at all. Yet the command about coveting is very important because "it shows that a person could be thought of as morally guilty before God without having committed an external, judicially punishable, offence." Wright shows how Jesus applied this principle to other commandments when he extended the understanding of murder to being angry with one's brother (Matthew 5:21–24) and adultery to "[looking] at a woman with lustful intent" (Matthew 5:27, 28).

15

Exclusive Loyalty to God

DEUTERONOMY 5:7–10

EVEN THOUGH THE ENGLISH OF THE King James Version is not as popular now as it was a few years ago, the words, "Thou shalt not," coming from that translation of the Bible, is still the dominant impression that comes to many English-speaking people when they think of the laws of God and of the Ten Commandments. Generally that does not leave us with a very positive impression of these commandments. The archaic language seems to typify how out-of-date they are. To many these laws are outdated, gloomy representations of a life they do not want to have anything to do with, a life of bondage from which they have been liberated.

The way the Ten Commandments begin suggests that another picture is truer to them: "I am the LORD your God, who brought you out of the land of Egypt, out of the house of slavery" (5:6). This is the Liberator speaking to the people he liberated! The people of India love the name Mohandas Karamchand Gandhi because of his great contribution to their freedom struggle. That is how African-Americans think about Martin Luther King Jr. and how most South Africans think about Nelson Mandela. Each of these names is associated with an attitude of affection. The Ten Commandments, or the Decalogue, are words from the Liberator to the people he liberated.

The First Commandment: No Other Gods (5:7)

The first two commandments call for exclusive loyalty to God. The first is, "You shall have no other gods before me" (5:7).

Before God

This wording "before me" can be somewhat misleading "because it suggests precedence in rank or importance" (McConville), as if God wants to be first in line! Literally it reads, "before my face." McConville renders it, "in my presence." Once the Philistines captured the ark of the covenant and brought it to Ashdod and kept it beside the image of Dagon in their temple. The next morning the image had fallen, facedown. They put it back, only to find that it had fallen again; and this time the hands and the head were separated from its trunk (1 Samuel 5). God was showing that there was not to be any other god in his presence. Chris Wright says this phrase can be translated "as rivals to me." The people of Israel are in a covenant relationship that involves exclusive and absolute loyalty to God.

Who Are These Gods?[1]

The phrase "other gods" appears sixty-four times in the Old Testament and is a technical description of the gods of other people (Craigie). There is some debate within the church about who these gods are. This has intensified with the rise of religious pluralism. Many pluralists say that people of all religions are worshiping the same God based on their incomplete understanding of God. Therefore they speak of "the Hindu understanding of God," "the Christian understanding of God," "the Sikh understanding of God," etc. The various scriptures of the different religions are said to reflect what a people have learned about the one God. A recent pluralist book accused those who said that non-Christians were worshipping different gods of un-Biblical polytheism.[2]

The Old Testament accepts the existence of other gods but presents Yahweh as being radically separate from them. The first commandment certainly buttresses this truth. The Bible uses three different categories to describe divine beings or non-beings other than Yahweh. First, sometimes the Bible speaks of those being worshiped by others as being "no gods": "They have made me jealous with what is no god; they have provoked me to anger with their idols" (Deuteronomy 32:21a). "Has a nation changed its gods, though they are no gods? But my people have changed their glory for that which does not profit" (Jeremiah 2:11). Galatians 4:8, 9 says that what it identifies as "elementary principles" (probably meaning demonic forces, *stoicheia*) "by nature are not gods." The designation of "no god" applies to both real and imaginary beings.

The second category, "other gods," appears not only in the Old Testament but in the New Testament also, and this is significant because the social environment in which the New Testament was written was clearly a pluralistic one. But Paul presents these gods as clearly different and unacceptable entities. "Therefore, as to the eating of food offered to idols, we know that 'an idol has no real existence,' and that 'there is no God but one.' For although there may be so-called gods in heaven or on earth—*as indeed there are many 'gods' and many 'lords'*—yet for us there is one God, the Father . . . " (1 Corinthians 8:4–6). Later, still speaking about food offered to idols, Paul calls the idols "demons": "I imply that what pagans sacrifice they offer to demons and not to God. I do not want you to be participants with demons" (1 Corinthians 10:20).

The third category of texts presents the people worshipping the same God as the God of the Bible. However, these texts say that their knowledge of God is inadequate and their worship is unacceptable to God. Paul told the Athenians that when he went through their city, "[he] found also an altar with this inscription, 'To the unknown god.'" Then, equating that with the God of the gospel, he said, "What therefore you worship as unknown, this I proclaim to you" (Acts 17:23). He does not say that their worship of the unknown God was acceptable to God. In fact, he asks them to repent and to accept the gospel (vv. 30, 31).

The God of the Muslims could be classed under this category, though some identify this god as a demon. Muslims clearly say they are worshipping the same God as the God of the Israelites as described in the Old Testament. But we know that their knowledge of God is inadequate and their worship is unacceptable. Therefore they need to hear and respond to the gospel of Christ.[3]

Actually this whole discussion shows us the urgency of evangelism. If this is what the Bible says about the gods that others worship, then it is desperately important for them to get to know the God of the Bible.

How Could They Change Gods?

How could a people who have experienced God's redemption in such a marvelous way exchange Yahweh for other gods? Here are some suggestions about how this could happen. When they go to the promised land they will need to learn farming from their neighbors, for that is something they don't know how to do. But the neighbors have a lot of religious ritual connected with their farming. They will need to leave those out of their farming practices. It would be easy to get dragged into performing these rituals as they seem to bring the divine so near in very tangible forms, unlike the God who speaks but cannot be seen. If the people are not having a vibrant relationship with God, if they are not spending time with God and the Word and thus not really hearing from God, they could get dragged into performing pagan rituals, such as making an offering, that seem to give them the satisfaction of doing something tangible.

This danger lurks in the shadows of our lives, too. As Christianity is a religion nurtured by vibrant communion with God through prayer, Bible reading, worship, fellowship, and obedience, when these means of God's communicating with us and blessing us are removed from our lives, it would be easy for us also to go after other gods. Having lost the security of a close walk with the almighty God we may, in a time of crisis, go to a psychic counselor, an astrologer, or a medicine man for guidance about what to do. Or we may go to someone who can make a charm or give a talisman or do an exorcism to solve a serious problem we are having.

Sometimes after praying to God over a problem for an extended period of time and not receiving a satisfying answer, a Christian may in desperation try something new and unfamiliar because a friend tells him that there is much power there. Just as people change doctors when the treatment prescribed by one doctor does not seem to be effective, Christians who are not firm in their commitment to Christ can get lured into going to a place that promises quick results.

Sometimes Christians who have moved away from a warm relationship with God might embrace a "non-religious" god like wealth, position, status, or an addiction and let that god have their primary allegiance. Lacking the security and fulfillment that comes from a close relationship with God, they look for more tangible forms of security and fulfillment. Philippians 3:19 talks about people whose "god is their belly."

The Bible is clear that nothing, absolutely nothing, must take the supreme place of God in the lives of believers. If they embrace other gods, they must be warned of dire consequences. The next commandment describes this. The climax of the rebellion of the first generation of Israelites who came with Moses from Egypt was when they worshipped the god Baal of Peor. There was a huge death toll after this that in effect resulted in the end of this whole first generation (Numbers 25:1–15). Deuteronomy 13:1–18 says that those who lead others astray to worship other gods will especially be punished with death.

Involvement in a Multi-Religious Society[4]

Today we face a somewhat different situation than that of the Israelites in the Old Testament since Israel was a theocracy and the governing of the nation was done according to God's principles. The Old Testament had the status of a national constitution in Israel. Most of us live under vastly different circumstances in multi-religious societies. We reside and work side by side with fellow citizens who are from other faiths.

Paul's ministry in Athens gives us some important keys to how we should respond in such situations. When Paul had stayed a short time in Athens, "his spirit was provoked within him as he saw that the city was full of idols" (Acts 17:16). He was really upset by the idolatry. This is the basic Biblical attitude toward idols. As we see idols and other indicators of idolatry all around us, we can get so used to them that they no longer shock us. People were created to live for God, and anything less than that is a terrible tragedy.

But Paul did not thunder against idols like an Old Testament prophet would have done in the theocratic state of Israel. He did not even express his anger. Instead "he reasoned [Greek: *dialegomai*] . . . in the marketplace every day with those who happened to be there" (Acts 17:17). He treated the people with respect, and he discussed the gospel with them. But he desired to see them leave these gods and follow the one true God. So when he went before the Areopagus, he argued for the futility of idolatry and the wisdom of the gospel (Acts 17:22–31).

The Christian shows respect for others while seeking to persuade them about the truth of the gospel. Therefore, if a person comes to Christ from a non-Christian family, we will need to discuss with that person the difference between respect for family and compromise of principles. The family may go to a temple as part of the family holiday. Being faithful to God at such a time does not necessarily mean that the Christian member should not join in the holiday. It means that he or she will not worship at the temple with the rest. Many family functions may have religious elements to them. The Christian will not join in these rituals. But he or she will work hard in doing things that do not involve the religious practices (cooking, cleaning up, washing the dishes, etc.). The principles Paul presented in his discussion on meat offered to idols in Romans 14 are helpful here. We are asked not to be judgmental about those who think differently than we do (14:1–4, 10–13). We are to grapple with the issue until we are convinced in our minds and are sure that what we are doing is for the honor of the Lord (14:5–9, 23). We are to avoid putting a stumbling block before other Christians, but rather to "pursue what makes for peace and for mutual upbuilding" and to ensure that God's work is not destroyed by our actions (14:13–23). We must "not, for the sake of food [or another such issue], destroy the work of God" (14:20).

The Second Commandment: No Images (5:8, 9a)

The second commandment is about images: "You shall not make for yourself a carved image, or any likeness of anything that is in heaven above, or that is on the earth beneath, or that is in the water under the earth. You shall not bow down to them or serve them" (5:8, 9a). There is a total ban on making images "in the likeness of anything" in all of creation. The first sentence in this commandment may suggest that art and sculpture are prohibited. But the second sentence shows that these prohibited images are made with a view to bowing down to them and serving them. As the first command talked about other gods and thus idols are included, it could be that what is meant in the second command is primarily representations in the form of images of the God of the Bible. So what the first command prohibits is having any other god, and what the second command prohibits is representing Yahweh by an image. I am using this interpretation in the following comments.

Chris Wright points out that the issue here is that "Yahweh is the *living* God, and any carved statue is necessarily lifeless. Something that can *do nothing* is no image of the God who can *do all things*."[5] We are always in danger of having too small a conception of God, and idols are among the worst ways of expressing that. What a contrast there is between lifelessness and life, between doing nothing and doing all things. Yet God cannot be seen by the human eye, and we can lose touch with God through unbelief, neglect, or disobedience. Then we will begin to doubt that he can do all things, and we may turn to something that is more tangible like an idol to represent God to us.

Peter Craigie helpfully points out that "the only manner in which God could be represented was by means of language." He says, "Language too is a means of imagery, but it is necessary in order to articulate the knowledge and experience of God." The advantage of language is that, unlike an image, we can always add to our conception of God. We know and acknowledge that language never tells the full picture. As our understanding of God keeps growing, we can use language to add what we learn. Even after that we can say that we know only a fraction of what can be known. It is no accident then that God revealed himself through the medium of language. It is imperative that we do all we can to maintain the place of importance that God gives to language in this postmodern age. Today deconstructionists are trying to take away from language the important role it has of being a bearer of vitally important truth. We need to consciously keep ourselves alert to the danger. One way to do this is to use words carefully so that people learn through experience to trust the words of Christians.

God's Response to Our Response (5:9b, 10)

Verses 9b, 10 give God's response to our response to the first two commandments. Both commandments seem to be included in the Jewish tradition. Later
Augustine, the Lutherans, and the Roman Catholics viewed what we call the
first two commands as a single command. In order to get Ten Commandments
they divide what we usually call the tenth command into two. God describes
his response in these verses.

A Jealous God (5:9b)

Verse 9b says, ". . . for I the LORD your God am a jealous God." God requires
exclusive loyalty, and no rivals are allowed. The Bible often compares
God's relationship with his covenant people with the relationship between a
husband and wife (see especially the book of Hosea). In a true relationship
between husband and wife, no other human can take the place of the spouse.
The record of the institution of marriage says the husband must leave his
father and mother and hold fast to his wife (Genesis 2:24). This statement
is so important that it is cited three times in the New Testament (Matthew
19:5; Mark 10:7; Ephesians 5:31). The Song of Solomon expresses the tie
between husband and wife, saying, "Set me as a seal upon your heart, as a
seal upon your arm, for love is strong as death, jealousy is fierce as the grave"
(Song 8:6).

Jay Kesler wrote that his married daughter told him, "I would be hurt
more deeply if I found out my husband had a strong friendship with another
woman, in which he discussed things with her that he couldn't or wouldn't
discuss with me, than I would be if I discovered he'd had a one-night stand."[6]
This comment was not intended to give legitimacy to one-night stands! But
I think it is significant that she expressed how extremely upset she would be
if she found out that another woman had won the heart of her husband to the
point of being the recipient of conversation that she alone deserved to have as
his spouse. Married love tolerates no rivals, and that is how it should be. The
concept of open marriage is a mockery of one of the most beautiful things in
life. A wife who does not care if her husband went with other women has a
weak, insecure, and superficial relationship with her husband. True love has
a right to be jealous. We were made for such exclusive commitment.

What security there is when we know that God jealously guards his relationship with us. We can be sure that he will look after us if he is so committed
to us. And when we know that he is the almighty Lord over the universe, our
security peaks! There can be no higher security than having the God who is
able to do anything he wants totally committed to us. But because he refuses

to force his will on us, he will not stop us if we want to be unfaithful. But at the same time he will keep providing ways of escape so that we will not fall into sin (1 Corinthians 10:13). The knowledge of his jealous love and the fact that he helps us find a way of escape when we are tempted give us the courage to hope that we, too, could be totally committed to him.

All this talk of a jealous God goes against the pluralistic mood of the day. Chris Wright says, "We have come to regard religion, like everything else, as a matter of 'consumer choice' which we have virtually deified for its own sake. We resent monopolies." So the idea of God being jealous may sound strange to some ears. However, as Wright puts it, ". . . the unique and incomparable, only living God makes necessarily exclusive claims and has the right to a monopoly on our love."

Visiting Iniquity (5:9c)

A jealous God will not tolerate unfaithfulness. So verse 9 describes God as ". . . visiting the iniquity of the fathers on the children to the third and fourth generation of those who hate me." Judgment awaits those who rebel against God and go after other gods. But why should the judgment go on "to the third and fourth generation"? If the children grow up in an environment where God is not respected, it is very likely that they will reject God just as their parents did. So they will be judged—not for their parents' sins but for their own. Usually the extended families in those days had three or four generations living together. Of course, there will be exceptions. The Bible is clear that no one who repents and turns to God will be rejected by God. Josiah was a righteous king who spearheaded a great religious revival in Judah. But his father Amon and grandfather Manasseh were wicked idolaters (2 Kings 21, 22).

Showing Covenant Love (5:10)

The statement of God's response to our response to the first two commandments does not end with judgment. As McConville says, "Mercy finally outweighs judgment." So after talking about visiting the iniquity of the sinful people, God describes himself as ". . . showing steadfast love to thousands of those who love me and keep my commandments" (5:10). The Hebrew word translated "steadfast love," *hesedh*, is a very important word that appears 238 times in the Old Testament. It is the word used for God's covenant love. It usually refers to God's faithfulness to his people in keeping with his covenant. The ESV and the NRSV usually translate it as "steadfast love," and the NIV (though not here) sometimes translates it as "unfailing love." The REB translates it here as "I keep faith." God is a faithful God who will remain true to his commitment to his covenant people.

The reason why God made this covenant with humans is not so that he might punish them, but so he might show them love. Love has the last word. He visits three or four generations with his punishment, but he visits "thousands" with his faithful love. "Thousands" here probably refers to "a thousand generations," which is how the NIV renders it. God woos his people back and lets them enjoy his love for thousands of generations.

God says that the blessing of *hesedh* is for "those who love me and keep my commandments." Loving obedience to a loving God could be considered as the dominant theme of Deuteronomy. As we see the picture of the nature of God in this passage, what else would be appropriate and wise for humans? May we never let Satan deceive us into thinking, even for a moment, that a life of disobedience is worth anything of value.

The Key: Trusting God

So the Ten Commandments begin with a call to exclusive loyalty to God. But as we saw in the earlier chapter and here, this is the God who has redeemed us and who has entered into a covenant with us, and his steadfast covenant love is a major ingredient of our relationship with him. We can be sure then that if we are faithful to God he will look after us.

Why is it then that so many within the Christian community seem to wilt when things are tough and temptation gets severe? They act as if God will not look after them, and they give in to idolatry. They do not exercise their faith; they do not trust God to look after them. The key is trusting God to do what is best for us. That is the theme of Hebrews 11. The heroes mentioned there believed God and refused to give up on his way when the going was tough. And it will be tough—that was the promise of God. But if we cling to God's promise to work things out for good, we will see victory and will be like these heroes.

Hudson Taylor says, "Want of trust is at the root of almost all our sins and all our weaknesses; and how shall we escape from it, but by looking at him, and observing his faithfulness? . . . All God's giants have been weak men, who did great things for God because they reckoned on God being with them."[7] The key is to trust God even when the going is tough. He has already acted to redeem us. Therefore now we can be "sure of this, that he who began a good work in [us] will bring it to completion at the day of Jesus Christ" (Philippians 1:6).

16

Honoring God's Name

DEUTERONOMY 5:11

WHEN WE THINK OF the attitude of honor to God prescribed in the third and fourth commandments, it is amazing that people speak of God in such a trivial way. It is quite clear that the attitude of reverence and awe that the Bible recommends for our approach to God (Hebrews 12:28) is very distant to that of many people today. One reason is that we have lost the sense of the awesomeness of God. So before we look at the next two commands, which have to do with honoring God, we will take a brief look at the honor of God in the Bible.

The Honor of God in the Bible

There are so many Biblical passages describing God's glory and greatness that it is difficult to know which ones to include. Let me mention a few that highlight the difference between God and humans. Two of these have to do with God as the Creator of the vast universe. David said:

> O LORD, our Lord,
>   how majestic is your name in all the earth!
> You have set your glory above the heavens. . . .
> When I look at your heavens, the work of your fingers,
>   the moon and the stars, which you have set in place,
> what is man that you are mindful of him,
>   and the son of man that you care for him? (Psalm 8:1, 3, 4)

Most of the book of Job is a rich drama with Job and his friends grappling with why he is suffering, even though Job claimed to be innocent. The book has a surprising climax, with God breaking into the drama and giving a powerful exposition of who he is:

> Where were you when I laid the foundation of the earth?
>   Tell me, if you have understanding.
> Who determined its measurements—surely you know!
>   Or who stretched the line upon it?
> On what were its bases sunk,
>   or who laid its cornerstone,
> when the morning stars sang together
>   and all the sons of God shouted for joy? (Job 38:4–7)

This monologue of God goes on in the same vein for another sixty-four verses (until Job 39:30)! Both these passages show the utter smallness of humans in comparison to God.

When great Biblical characters saw a glimpse of God's majesty and glory, they responded with severe shock. When Isaiah "saw the Lord sitting upon a throne, high and lifted up" (Isaiah 6:1), he cried, "Woe is me! For I am lost; for I am a man of unclean lips, and I dwell in the midst of a people of unclean lips; for my eyes have seen the King, the LORD of hosts!" (Isaiah 6:5). When Ezekiel had a glimpse of "the appearance of the likeness of the glory of the LORD," he "fell on [his] face" (Ezekiel 1:28). Three times we find Daniel falling to the ground facedown after seeing visions of God or heavenly beings (Daniel 8:17; 10:7–9, 15–17). John "fell at his feet as though dead" after seeing the heavenly Christ (Revelation 1:17). When faced with such Biblical evidence, we are not surprised to find the exhortation, ". . . let us offer to God acceptable worship, with reverence and awe, for our God is a consuming fire" (Hebrews 12:28, 29). We also find that the faithful are encouraged to tremble in the presence of God (Psalm 2:11; 96:9; 99:1; 114:7; Isaiah 66:5; see Philippians 2:12).

God's Name Is to Be Hallowed (5:11)

The third commandment reads, "You shall not take the name of the LORD your God in vain" (Deuteronomy 5:11a). In the Bible God's name represents who God is. We pray in the name of Christ because we know that God gives us the confidence to ask what we ask. By their actions humans, especially those who are known as God's people, can represent God in such a way that his name looks empty or worthless. This command literally translates as "You shall not lift up the name of Yahweh your God to emptiness or worthlessness." The representation of the glorious God as worthless is a terrible thing. The most important factor in creation is that God is glorious. All creation looks to the day when "the earth will be filled with the knowledge of the glory of the LORD as the waters cover the sea" (Habakkuk 2:14; see Isaiah 11:9). When people know who God is, they should see the value of responding to God and returning to the state that God intended for them when he created them (unless, blinded by unbelief, they refuse to see).

Therefore, those who follow God are called to lift high the name of God before the world. Paul presents our aim in life as follows: ". . . whether you eat or drink, or whatever you do, do all to the glory of God" (1 Corinthians 10:31; see Colossians 3:17). Whenever we pray the Lord's Prayer, we pray, "Hallowed ['honored'] be your name" (Matthew 6:9; Luke 11:2). Jesus prayed, "Father, glorify your name" (John 12:28). And the psalmists often tell us things like "Ascribe to the LORD the glory due his name" (Psalm 29:2a; 96:8a), ". . . sing the glory of his name; give to him glorious praise!" (Psalm 66:2), and "Bless the LORD, O my soul, and all that is within me, bless his holy name!" (Psalm 103:1; see also 72:19)

Dishonoring God in Worship

One of the primary applications of this command is in the context of worship. The word *worship* comes from the old English *weorth-scipe* or *worthship*, which carries the idea of expressing the worthiness of God. To worship God in a way that does not express his worthiness — his glory — is to take the name of the Lord in vain.

Haphazard Worship

Haphazard and low-quality worship dishonors God's name. So does worship that lacks a sincere desire to honor God (this does not apply only to those leading the worship). Sometimes we see people choosing the hymns for the worship service just before it starts. Sometimes the leader is choosing the songs while the service is going on! Sometimes when you hear the preacher rambling, you realize that he has not prepared his message adequately. Sadly, many people associate church with outmoded, boring, and low-quality programs — this is a great dishonor to God.

Three times in the Old Testament we are told to "worship the LORD in the splendor of holiness" (1 Chronicles 16:29; Psalm 29:2; 96:9). People must get a sense of the greatness of God when they come for worship. In my teenage years that is exactly how I felt on Sundays. An Irish minister, George Good, was our pastor. The hymns he had judiciously chosen, the prayers he prayed, and the way he preached all left us with the impression that we had been at something great. It made us proud, in a good way, to be Christians.

The Old Testament shows us that God intended for us to be well-prepared when we worship. There are several lists of musical instruments used in worship (2 Samuel 6:5; 1 Chronicles 13:8; 15:16, 28; Psalm 81:2, 3; 150:3–5). Similarly people were set apart to lead in worship and to participate in the music during worship (1 Chronicles 15:16–22). They needed to pick people with musical ability (1 Chronicles 15:22), and instructions were given about what they should do (2 Chronicles 5:12–14). So important was music to the people that 4,000 Levites were set apart for it (1 Chronicles 23:5).

At the start of worship at the tabernacle, Aaron's sons Nadab and Abihu were killed because they "offered unauthorized fire before the LORD, which he had not commanded them" (Leviticus 10:1). We are not sure exactly what their sin was. Robert Gordon suggests, "Perhaps the incense was burned at the wrong time, or the fire was not taken from the bronze altar (cf. 16:12), or some other breach of ritual was committed. Because verse 9 speaks of drunkenness it is a commonplace in Jewish tradition that Nadab and Abihu had acted under the influence of strong drink."[1] This incident tells us that God takes worship seriously, and we must, too. I often lead the worship until the sermon is given at our church. I find myself quite drained at the end of that, sometimes even more drained than after I preach. I think this is because of a deep desire to lead God's people to honor him in worship with the accompanying fear that something might happen that dishonors God.

Will this result in a constant fear of displeasing God that takes away the joy of life? This would be so if God is like an unpleasant father who is never satisfied with our "performance." But God is not like that. Micah 7:18 says, "He does not retain his anger forever, because he delights in steadfast love." God does not enjoy punishing us; he wants to love us. Not only does he love us, he delights in us (Psalm 35:27; 147:11; 149:4). We experience the freedom of being loved by God daily. That is the most important factor in our lives, even more important than our worship. We fail him often, but he loves us and yearns to forgive and restore us.

If we lead worship with a sincere and earnest heart, there would be no doubt that God would accept it with joy. Proverbs 15:8 says, "The sacrifice of the wicked is an abomination to the LORD, but the prayer of the upright is His delight" (NASB). Besides, the God we worship is the one we love and long to please. So when we try to worship in a way that honors God, we are fulfilling our heart's deep desire. Because we love God so much and he has brought us so much joy, we want others to see his glory. Worship becomes a means by which this desire is fulfilled.

Irreverent Worship

Another way to dishonor God during worship is by irreverent worship. Hebrews 12:28, 29 says, ". . . let us offer to God acceptable worship, with reverence and awe, for our God is a consuming fire." God cannot be seen; therefore it is very important that we create a suitable atmosphere to enable people to sense the presence of God. As it is so easy to get distracted during worship, we must work hard at helping people experience what can be described as the beauty of holiness.

We need to develop an atmosphere of quietness where people can worship with "reverence and awe." It would be good to help people meditate before the service begins by encouraging quietness before the service. Quietness helps us slow down so we can hear from God. Our activity and busyness can hinder this. Obligatory quietness in church helps us make the difficult transition from activity to listening to God. Habakkuk 2:20 says, "But the LORD is in his holy temple; let all the earth keep silence before him."

When people testify or speak in other ways in a worship service, we must encourage them to be careful with the way they use words. We are in the awesome presence of God. He wants to speak to us. So we will be humble when we speak. In the context of worship, Ecclesiastes warns us, "Be not rash with your mouth, nor let your heart be hasty to utter a word before God, for God is in heaven and you are on earth. Therefore let your words be few" (5:2).

In keeping with the principle of preserving the reverence of worship, some churches do not seat latecomers except at certain interlude times, usually not during singing, readings, and prayers. One of the most detestable things I heard that happened during a worship service in Sri Lanka was when the preacher got a call on his cell phone and answered it while the congregation waited! Even keeping our cell phones on silent mode during worship suggests that we cannot switch off from other things to concentrate fully on God for a brief period of worship. It may be an indication of busyness and a sign of seriously ill health, as we will see in the next study. Some people need to keep their phones on owing to exceptional reasons, but these are rare exceptions.

Unholy Worship

If God is worshipped in the beauty of holiness, the lives of those who lead worship and the way they lead should reflect his holiness. Unholiness in worship dishonors God's name. For example, if a brilliant musician who leads a major portion of the worship service needs to be disciplined for some serious sin, then he should be disciplined and not used for worship. This may result in a severe lowering of the quality of the music. But using that person would result in greater dishonor to Christ.

Sometimes God is dishonored by the presence of corporate unholiness in the church. God says, "Take away from me the noise of your songs; to the melody of your harps I will not listen. But let justice roll down like waters, and righteousness like an ever-flowing stream" (Amos 5:23, 24). If the poor are given a less significant place than the rich in contradiction to what is taught in James 2:1–7, we dishonor God through injustice. Even greater injustice is done when people from a certain race, caste, or class are made to feel unwelcome in a church.

In a Roman Catholic Church near my home a notice was posted a few months ago stating that there were going to be many weddings that month in the church. The church authorities promised to faithfully perform their services, but they asked the congregation also to cooperate by coming for the weddings in attire appropriate for worship. They assured the worshippers that if they are short of material, the church could provide them with cloth to cover their bodies! The way we dress must not take people's focus away from God.

Dishonoring God in Conversation

The first thought that comes to people when they hear this command is about how we can dishonor God through the literal use of the name of God in conversation.

When Taking Vows

If we use God's name when taking a vow or giving evidence at a court or inquiry and we tell lies, it is very serious. Our legal systems usually consider lying under oath or perjury to be a very serious crime. It threatens the stability of a nation when the legal system is not able to act properly. And perjury buckles the system. Imagine the seriousness when the oath is taken in God's name! A proclamation has been made that the person is a follower of God and that God is witness and attester of the statements to be made. To then lie is an open defiance of the authority and importance of God. It is a public proclamation that the person has no fear of dishonoring God. Christians must be very careful even when saying things like "God is my witness." Sometimes to assure people we are saying the truth we say, "I swear to God." That is too serious a statement to make in casual conversation.

Our commitment to truthfulness, of course, is bound up with our belief in the absolute faithfulness of God. He means what he says. With him "there is no variation or shadow due to change" (James 1:17). Hebrews 6:18 says

". . . it is impossible for God to lie"; and Paul says that God "never lies" (Titus 1:2). God means what he says, and so must we. Jesus said that it was unnecessary for us to take oaths. Instead, he said, "All you need to say is simply 'Yes' or 'No'" (Matthew 5:37, NIV). So God's follower "swears to his own hurt and does not change" (Psalm 15:4). They keep their promises even though they find after making the promise that it will hurt them to keep it.

When Using God's Name Trivially

Michael Moriarty has given three ways in which God's name can be misused trivially. He says it is "misused when it's used as a filler for absent syntax," such as when people say, "O God." It is "profaned when irreverently used as a divine exclamation" such as when people say, "Jesus" or "Christ." It is "debased when used as a curse word (damning something or someone)."[2] I hope we cringe when we hear things like this. They are so common that we may simply hear and not feel pain over the dishonor that such statements bring to God.

I think we Christians sometimes dishonor God when we glibly say things like "Praise the Lord" without really thinking about what we are saying. Sometimes we have heard of situations where people said, "Praise the Lord" in most inappropriate times, like when someone announces that his mother is sick!

Empty words while praying also come under this category. We should not mouth words that are considered appropriate for prayer if we do not mean them. Hamlet in Shakespeare's play said, "My words fly up, my thoughts remain below; words without thoughts never to heaven go."[3]

The Israelites took the idea of profaning God's name very seriously; so they did not pronounce the name of God—probably spelled Yahweh—in conversation. They usually substituted Yahweh with *adonay,* which is the word for *lord.* So in most of our modern English Bibles, when Yahweh appears in the Hebrew, we find "LORD" in capitals and small capitals. When *adonay* appears, it is rendered as "Lord" with the letters after the first letter in lowercase. Perhaps they went too far. But I think we have gone too far the other direction!

Dishonoring God in Behavior

Christians, especially leaders, can dishonor God through bad behavior. Here are some examples.

- Sincere Christians often associate the projects and ideas of a Christian leader with God's will. They participate in a project with the attitude that they are doing it for God. Later they find out that this does not seem to have been God's will after all. God's name is dishonored because God was associated with a project that was not his will and proved to be a failure or a disaster.

- Some leaders urge giving to God's work and use some of the funds to support lifestyles way above that of those who sacrificially gave to the work. Some projects are aimed more at enhancing the leader's reputation than God's name.

- Sometimes leaders push people to accept an idea saying it was God's will even though they were not sure about it. Examples include encouraging one to marry or not to marry a given person and urging someone to leave his job to join the church because he seems to have gifts that can be of great benefit to the church. Often I qualify the advice I give with something like, "This is what I think; I am not sure whether this is God's will." Even Paul did that in 1 Corinthians 7:12 when he said, "To the rest I say (I, not the Lord). . . ."

- False prophecy is very common today. Later Moses will speak of severe punishment for prophets whose prophecies are not fulfilled (Deuteronomy 18:20–22). This happens all the time today, and we seem to ignore it. It is a very serious thing to make prophecies as direct messages from God.

- We all know of wars between nations and conflicts between Christians within the church that are fought in the name of God. Sometimes both sides claim to have God on their side. We should be very careful about bringing God's name into our battles. It could help rouse support for the cause, but it could really hurt the much more important cause of Christ. This is especially true of political causes. As a visitor to the United States I sometimes feel very uneasy about issues that Christians are fighting for as being God's battles. Coming from another country where a different dynamic is at work, I wonder what makes a particular cause so Christian, especially when other Christians seem to oppose it. If we do this indiscriminately, the next generation might reject God because he was, in the minds of these people, on the wrong side.

The Consequences of Misusing God's Name (5:11b)

Our command ends with a rather strange statement: ". . . for the Lord will not hold him guiltless who takes his name in vain" (5:11b). This is a curious use of the double negative. It would have been much smoother to say, ". . . will hold him guilty." Perhaps the reason this double negative is given is because people can invoke God's name very piously and look innocent and godly even while they are taking the name of God in vain. People listen to them and think they are guiltless, but they are guilty. This command says they won't get away with it, even though they can fool a lot of people into thinking they are innocent. The doctrine of judgment brings a certain sobriety to our lives.

Because we stand liable to judgment for dishonoring God's name, we will be careful of the way we behave.

A few days ago I went to the courts because one of our volunteers had been arrested on suspicion of being a terrorist. He was at a bus stop after an early-morning YFC prayer meeting, and a terrorist suspect was at the same bus stop. So my friend was taken in, too. We were trying to get him out on bail, but we failed to do so. He had to spend over two weeks in prison. I felt the lawyer whom we had retained was not presenting our case well, and I wanted to intervene. But I realized I could not tamper with the form of the court procedures. If I did that, I would be guilty of contempt of court—a serious offense under the law. On that occasion I was reprimanded by a policeman because I walked into an area that was out of bounds to the public. I was impressed by how careful the people there were to follow proper procedure.

In the same way we who bear the name of a majestic and holy God on earth should be careful about profaning his name by our behavior.

17

Sabbath-Keeping

DEUTERONOMY 5:12-15

THE FOURTH COMMANDMENT is the one command of the ten that most Christians are somewhat reluctant to take too literally today. Yet it represents a practice that has had a marked influence upon the world. David Payne observes that "sacred days were common enough in the ancient world, but it seems probable that a weekly *Sabbath* was unique to Israel." Yet, as Payne points out, "The human value of such an institution is widely recognized in practical terms, in that most of the world now divides time into weeks." The world realized the value of the Sabbath principle that God instituted. However, our reflection on the Sabbath today needs to tempered by the cautious approach to it adopted in the New Testament.

Observe the Sabbath (5:12)

The basic command is, "Observe the Sabbath day, to keep it holy, as the LORD your God commanded you." The word "Sabbath" (Hebrew *šabbāt*) derives from the verb *šābat*, "to stop, cease, rest." Therefore rest—not working on that day—is a key aspect of this command, as we will see in verse 14.

The first word in the form of this command in Exodus is "remember." But in the Deuteronomy account the first word is *shamar*—a common word in Deuteronomy usually translated "be careful" (so HCSB). We must carefully ensure that we observe it.

I have found that the Sabbath command is the one I find easiest to break without many pangs of guilt. After all, work is a good thing. But not when you should be resting, says the Bible! I believe this is why this particular command has some special words to express the importance of keeping it. For example, this is the only command in the Decalogue that starts with *shamar*. The other commands start with "You shall" or "You shall not" (the fifth command begins with "Honor"). Only this command and the next go on to say "as the Lord your God commanded you." This command ends with the words, "Therefore the LORD your God commanded you to keep the Sabbath day" (5:15). These are obvious means of stressing the importance of obedience to this command. Exodus 31:15 says, "Whoever does any work on the Sabbath day shall be put to death."

Keep It Holy (5:12)

We are to "observe the Sabbath day, to keep it holy" Exodus 31:15 says, ". . . the seventh day is a Sabbath of solemn rest, holy to the LORD." It is a day that is different from other days because it is devoted to a special emphasis on God. This follows the principle of festival that is a key to the Biblical lifestyle. God provides for us every day, but there are festivals at harvesttimes to especially remind us that God is the one who provides for us every day. We are prone to take these basic things for granted; therefore we need special days with special emphases. Similarly by keeping the Sabbath day holy we remind ourselves that our lives belong to God and that every day is lived for God.

The command of God to Moses to remove his sandals because the place where he stands is holy ground in Exodus 3:5 gives us a hint on how to understand what holiness means in the context of the Sabbath day. As the *NIV Study Bible* notes explain, "The ground was not holy by nature but was made so by the divine presence (see, e.g., Gen. 2:3). Holiness involves being consecrated to the Lord's service and thus being separated from the commonplace."[1] While all of life is holy, the Sabbath becomes a special holy day on which we separate ourselves from our usual activities to devote ourselves to God.

The highest form of serving God is worship. It is not an accident that the popular words for worship in the Bible also have the idea of service (*abad* in the Old Testament and *latreia/latreuō, leitourgia/leitourgeō* in the New Testament). On the day we set apart for God we would like to render him the highest service we can offer. So when we worship God in community we keep it holy. Leviticus 23:3 calls the Sabbath "a holy convocation" (NIV: "a day of sacred assembly"), when people gather for worship.

At worship we meditate on God's goodness and praise him and thank him for it. We hear his Word read and preached, and we learn how to live in a way that is more pleasing to him. We present our petitions to him and intercede on behalf of others and thus affirm that we rely on him for protection, sustenance, and blessing. We respond to what we hear through fresh acts of commitment. So worship affirms the lordship of God over our lives, making it a most appropriate way to keep the Sabbath holy to the Lord.

Those of us who are in ministry find that Sunday is not a Sabbath day for us. In fact, it is one of our busiest work days in the week. So we worship God in community on the Lord's Day, and we have another day—our "day off"—when we get our Sabbath rest. Yet on that day too we can do some special things that affirm that we are a holy people separated to God. Usually my devotions on my "day off" are different from those on other days. On other days most of my prayer time is given to intercession; on my "day off" I try to spend most of my prayer time praising God, usually through hymns. We must all find ways to make our Sabbath a special day of honoring God.

We will see that the comments of Jesus and Paul on the Sabbath should make us cautious about insisting on strict rules for Sabbath-keeping for everyone. Because of this, different Christians will come up with different ideas of what it means to honor the Sabbath and keep it holy. Some would decide that they should not participate in competitive sports on the Lord's Day. This is what the Scottish Christian Eric Liddell (1902–1945) decided. He was a brilliant sportsman who represented Scotland in rugby and Britain in track and whose Sabbath principles and the resulting challenges became the subject of the popular film *Chariots of Fire*. His pet event was the 100 meters dash, and he was considered a possible contender for the Gold Medal at the 1924 Paris Olympic Games.

But Liddell found out that a preliminary round for the 100 meters event was on a Sunday. To the dismay of the British people he decided he would not run in this, his favorite event. Instead he switched to the very different 400 meters event and the 200 meters. He was not considered a good prospect for either event, especially the 400 meters. But he was selected for both those events. This is how a British newspaper reported about his chances: "It is unfortunate that E. H. Liddell's religious scruples will not permit of him running on Sunday, which rules him out of the short sprint, for I am not at all confident regarding his prospects in the 400 meters."[2]

Liddell won a Bronze Medal in the 200 meters. As he was leaving his quarters on the day of the semi-finals and the finals of the 400 meters, one of the British team masseurs pressed a folded note into his hand. Eric thanked him and added, "I'll read it when I get to the stadium." What it said was, "It says in the Old Book, 'Him that honours me, I will honour.' Wishing you the best of success always." His biographer writes, "Eric had never doubted his decision not to run on Sunday, but the barbed comments about his disloyalty and selfishness in putting his personal religious beliefs above the national interest had always hurt. It came as a great encouragement to know that someone shared his conviction, and to be reminded that the honor God gave, whatever form it might take, was all that really mattered."[3]

Liddell went on to win the Gold Medal in the 400 meters, five meters ahead of his nearest rival. He also broke the world record. The next year he went to China as a missionary, where he ultimately died of a brain tumor in a Japanese internment camp in 1945. At that camp he became a father to numerous youths who were separated from their parents. One of these young people was my friend the late James Hudson Taylor IV, former general director of Overseas Missionary Fellowship, who would speak warmly of the influence Liddell had upon his life.

A Day of Rest (5:12–15)

How Can Christians Rest Today?

What the word "Sabbath"—which derives from the verb meaning "to stop, cease, rest"— implied is explicitly stated in verses 13, 14: "Six days you shall labor and do all your work, but the seventh day is a Sabbath to the LORD your God. On it you shall not do any work, you or your son or your daughter or your male servant or your female servant. . . ." This command has resulted in some legalistic attitudes, and consequently some Christians have rejected it as not being relevant to us today, especially in view of some negative comments found in the New Testament. We will apply this law as we do the others in Deuteronomy. We will look for the reason behind the law and apply it to today. We will also take into consideration the New Testament comments on this law.

Jesus' comments about the Sabbath should cause us to be cautious about being too stringent in applying this law. He said that some of the things the Israelites of his day considered as work should be done on the Sabbath because of humanitarian concerns. Examples are picking heads of grain, rubbing them in their hands, and eating when one is hungry (Matthew 12:1–8), healing the sick (Matthew 12:10–13; Luke 13:10–17), picking up one's mat and walking home with it after being healed (John 5:5–15), and rescuing a sheep that had fallen into a pit by lifting it out (Matthew 12:11, 12). As Walter Liefeld comments, "Ceremonial rites (being only a means to an end) must give way to a higher moral law" (on Matthew 12:1–8). It is good to have rules for resting on the Sabbath, but when confronted by urgent human need we may suspend those rules because of the moral law of love. This is the way I have approached my "day off." My colleagues know that on that day no routine issues should be brought up. But they also know that if there is an emergency, I am happy to chip in with whatever help I can give.

Paul seems to be even more negative than Jesus about what he saw of Sabbath observance in his day. He says, ". . . let no one pass judgment on you . . . with regard to a festival or a new moon or a Sabbath" (Colossians 2:16). This verse sums up his attitude to the Sabbath. The Old Testament regulations about the Sabbath are no longer binding for Christians. To "observe days and months and seasons and years" was equivalent to returning to slavery (Galatians 4:9, 10). What I learn from Paul is that we must be careful about making binding rules about the Sabbath and thrusting them on all Christians.

Though the Old Testament Sabbath regulations may not be binding on us, there is a principle behind the Sabbath idea that is an important part of living a godly life. Jesus was not disputing the Sabbath principle. He was attacking the legalistic way in which it was applied by the Jewish people in his day, so that humanitarian concerns were not given due weight. We need to take a day of rest, and God seems to think that doing that one day in seven is the ideal thing. We can look at this day in a positive light—especially because it is given as a positive command unlike most of the other commands. Philip Graham Ryken's explanation is helpful: ". . . it is a day for relaxation and recuperation, a day to step back from life's ordinary routines in order to rediscover God's goodness and grace."[4]

As work often keeps us from giving as much time as we would like to give to our families, the Sabbath day could be a special family day when family love is given special opportunities to express itself. Going to church together as a family, perhaps having a special meal, just spending time chatting or doing some recreational activity all help us to be freed from the rigors of work in order to enjoy rest and recuperation as a family.

On my "day off" I do errands for my family and for my aging mother, I take my wife to places she would like to go but cannot because she does not drive, and I try to do some repairs around the house if that is necessary (though sometimes the items are worse off after the repair than before!). I find that all of these activities are a refreshing change from the pressures and demands of ministry.

If we keep breaking the Sabbath law, then we are calling into question the wisdom of God's Word. We are communicating a message that God's Word is not relevant to today's life. This is one of the most serious errors a Christian can make, because the Word is our authority for all faith and practice. Only in emergency situations, when the moral law of love demands it, should we do typical work on the Sabbath. But if we have emergencies on every Sabbath day, then something is wrong. Our understanding of work and rest is seriously flawed.

Rest for Those under Our Care (5:14b)

This command specifically states that all who come under our care must also experience Sabbath rest: "On it you shall not do any work, you or your son or your daughter or your male servant or your female servant, or your ox or your donkey or any of your livestock, or the sojourner who is within your gates, that your male servant and your female servant may rest as well as you" (5:14b). Those last few words, "that your male servant and your female servant may rest as well as you," are not found in the Exodus version of the fourth command. Deuteronomy has a special emphasis on social justice, so this extra emphasis is not surprising.

Scholars tell us that this level of concern for animals and slaves is unique in ancient Near Eastern literature. This radical feature of Biblical religion is still relevant to us. In Sri Lanka many people do not give their domestic aides a "day off." That is not permissible for Christians. Harold Macmillan, who was Prime Minister of Britain from 1957 to 1963, is said to have described the Sabbath law as the first and greatest worker protection act in history.[5]

Christians are always people who are concerned for all of life. Proverbs 12:10 says, "Whoever is righteous has regard for the life of his beast." The Royal Society for the Prevention of Cruelty to Animals was founded in England in 1824 by Arthur Broome, an Anglican clergyman, with the aid of the great evangelical leader and social reformer William Wilberforce and his friends.[6] In several countries Christians, though a minority, have been in the forefront of advocating humane ways to slaughter animals.

When people are touched by God, they are touched by a respect for God's creation. So they extend kindness to animals and certainly to all people who work under them. So honoring God on the Sabbath has a vertical and a horizontal aspect. It is a day dedicated unto the Lord, but also it is good for society, and therefore care is taken to ensure that humans and beasts of labor have a Sabbath.

Remembering Deliverance from Slavery (5:15)

In Exodus the reason for the Sabbath is that God rested after seven days (Exodus 20:11). Here the reason is that it reminds the people of their redemption and the covenant that accompanied it: "You shall remember that you were a slave in the land of Egypt, and the LORD your God brought you out from there with a mighty hand and an outstretched arm. Therefore the LORD your God commanded you to keep the Sabbath day" (Deuteronomy 5:15). The Sabbath is a sign of the covenant, as Exodus 31:13, 16 show: ". . . you shall keep my Sabbaths, for this is a sign between me and you throughout your generations . . . . Therefore the people of Israel shall keep the Sabbath, observing the Sabbath throughout their generations, as a covenant forever." As God's covenant people whom he redeemed, they depend daily upon him for everything. A great way to affirm the rest they have because of redemption is to do nothing on the Sabbath. For doing nothing is a sign that they are totally dependent on God's grace.

Rest and Restlessness

The first two commands talked about idolatry. The fourth implies another type of idolatry: work. To keep the Sabbath is to celebrate God's work on our behalf by resting and to affirm that God is the one whose work ultimately matters. The core of the sin of Adam and Eve was that they chose to depend on their work rather than on God's work for salvation. Many of their descendants end up looking to work to give them the fulfillment that God (who works for us) alone can give. Those who find too much fulfillment from work find it difficult to rest and celebrate God's work for them by not working. Work is a form of idolatry for such people.

The noted French mathematician and inventor Blaise Pascal (1623–1662) has some insightful comments on this in his brilliant unfinished apology for the Christian faith, which was published after his death under the title *Pensées* (meaning "Thoughts"). He says that a basic feature of life is that all people seek happiness, and he goes on to describe how people who are not happy try to overcome that lack. He says they need distractions to help them forget their unhappiness.

One such distraction is busy activity. "In busyness we have a narcotic to keep us from brooding and take our minds off these things" (that is, our unhappy lot). Pascal says, "That is why the pleasures of solitude are considered incomprehensible." He goes on to say that "those who are naturally conscious of what they avoid, avoid rest like the plague."[7] They would do anything to be kept busy. This provides the context for his famous words, "I have often felt that the sole cause of man's unhappiness is that he does not know how to stay quietly in his own room."[8]

In a less severe way, believers who have not learned to rest in God need work to keep them from seeing the emptiness of their lives. They go on working without rest, first, because they have not come to understand the beauty of trusting totally in the God who works for them, and, second, because they are afraid of silence, for silence forces them to face up to who they really are. Those who do not take Sabbath rest should ask whether there is something seriously wrong in their lives. Are they getting from work the satisfaction they should be getting from God? "Much of our busy activity is little more than a cheap anesthetic to deaden the pain of an empty life" (attributed to various Christian spokesmen).

Sadly, many stop the mad rush of their workaholism only after something drastic happens. They suffer from serious burnout, or they are laid low for an extended period through sickness or through physical injury as a result of an accident. They fall into a serious and prominent sin or face a huge failure in their life. Now brought to the end of their resources, they have nowhere to look but up to God, and, praise God, they find him to be adequate to meet their needs. These problems are disciplines brought by God to win back the love of people who have turned elsewhere for affirmation, as is taught in Hebrews 12:3–11.

Some who do not take their Sabbath rest get burned out long before retirement age. At midlife, with a body and mind that have been abused, they find they have little strength or motivation to go on. Wayne Clark has said, "Neglected Sabbaths collect compound interest after the age of forty."[9] Sadly, I have seen this too often. People who show so much potential in their thirties are shadows of their old self when they come to their fifties. Lacking the motivation and drive they had in their younger days, they go through the motions of their work and are angry, uninspiring, and unhappy. Others do not want to be like these people. Those who are in Christian ministry move to another type of work that does not require spiritual vitality, for their vitality has been long gone.

This is a common phenomenon in youth work. I live in fear that those working for the organization I had the privilege of leading for many years, Youth for Christ, will not finish well because they were not disciplined in their lifestyle in their younger days. Let us learn the primary lesson of the first four commandments: God is most important; he alone is the one who consumes our passion; for his glory alone will we live.

From the Sabbath to the Lord's Day

A word would be in order as to why most Christians have substituted the Lord's Day for the Jewish Sabbath. There is ample evidence in the New Testament that the resurrection is the cornerstone of the Christian gospel.[10] This event occurred on the first day of the week. When events are mentioned in the record of Christ's post-resurrection appearances, they always occurred on Sundays (Matthew 28:1–9; Luke 24:1, 13–34; John 20:19–23). The day of Pentecost, when the Holy Spirit came down to the church, again was a Sunday (Acts 2).

Quite early in the history of the church most Christians shifted their holy day from Saturday to Sunday. While we do not know the exact time for sure, we know that the trend was already evident in New Testament times. In Romans 14:5 Paul, after stating that different Christians regard special days differently, says, "Each one should be fully convinced in his own mind." And he says in Colossians 2:16, 17, "Therefore let no one pass judgment on you in questions of food and drink, or with regard to a festival or a new moon or a Sabbath. These are a shadow of the things to come, but the substance belongs to Christ." These verses indicate that the strict Jewish understanding of the Sabbath was dying down.

There are indications that Christians were beginning to consider Sunday as their day of worship even during the New Testament era. Paul met with the church in Troas on the first day of the week at what seems to have been a regular gathering (Acts 20:7). John, explaining how he received the visions recorded in the book of Revelation, says, "I was in the Spirit on the Lord's day" (Revelation 1:10). As G. E. Ladd points out, "It is . . . likely that we see here the emerging language referring to the Lord's Day as the Christian's distinctive day of religious devotion."[11]

When Paul asked the Corinthian church to put something aside for poorer Christians and store it up "on the first day of every week" (1 Corinthians 16:2), he was probably asking them to set aside funds at home for this offering rather than bring it to church. That is what the wording suggests. "Yet," as Craig Blomberg points out, "even if the Corinthians did not bring their monies to a weekly worship service, the fact that this storing was to take place on Sunday strongly suggests that the first day of the week, not the seventh . . . had already become the most special day of the week for these Christians."[12]

Early in the second century AD, Ignatius of Antioch said, "Those who followed ancient customs [that is, the Israelites] have come to a new hope, no longer celebrating the Sabbath but observing the Lord's Day, the day on which our life sprang up through Christ."[13]

Payne points out that one reason why the Christian church decided to change its holy day may be because "by Christian times, the Jewish Sabbath had attracted a multitude of rules." He says, "Most of the commandments are negatives, but this one is positive— 'Observe the Sabbath day'—and there is something basically wrong when it is turned into a day of prohibitions."

In the early church, worship and not rest from work was the priority in the observance of the Lord's Day. Sunday was a workday in the countries where most of the earliest Christians lived, and so they met for worship either early in the morning before going for work or in the evening after work.[14] In

Israel Christians would have had the Sabbath as their day of rest and Sunday as their day of worship.

Christians in Muslim countries have a similar situation today, as the day of rest there is Friday. We had a similar situation for some years in Sri Lanka when the weekly holiday was decided based on the lunar calendar, and Sunday was usually a workday. We met for worship on Sunday but had "Sunday school" on the weekly holiday.

All this points to the fact that the Old Testament regulations about the Sabbath were distinctly Jewish laws that others do not need to slavishly follow in cultures where ceasing from work on the Jewish Sabbath is not possible. The principle of a day of rest and of worship, however, is a key to the Biblical lifestyle. And in certain places the day of rest and the day of worship were different. Even in countries where Sunday is the day of the weekly holiday, church workers have to have their day of rest on a day other than Sunday because Sunday is often the day of the week they work the hardest.

The key, then, is to ensure that we have a day of rest and a day of worship. Ideally both these functions are observed on the same day. But even if that is not possible, the need for setting apart a day for rest and a day for worship remains. We can use our creativity to see how we can best fulfill these two Biblical mandates.

18

Honoring Parents

DEUTERONOMY 5:16

JESUS SAID THAT the Law and the Prophets depended on two commands—loving God with all our heart, soul, and mind and loving our neighbor as ourselves (Matthew 22:37–40). The first four commands of the Decalogue had to do with loving God, and the rest have to do with loving our neighbor. The sequence in which the commands are given represents the two priorities of Christian behavior. It begins on the vertical plane with our relationship with God, and it flows onto the horizontal plane to our relationship with people and things here on earth. We cannot have one without the other.

The Importance of Honoring Parents (5:16)

It is significant that this most basic statement about human relationships should begin with relationships within the family unit. As the old saying goes, "Charity begins at home." The fifth command states, "Honor your father and your mother, as the LORD your God commanded you, that your days may be long, and that it may go well with you in the land that the LORD your God is giving you" (5:16). The command is cited several times in the New Testament (Matthew 15:3; Mark 7:10; 10:19; Luke 18:20; Ephesians 6:1–3; see Colossians 3:20). Another list of miscellaneous laws in Leviticus 19 begins with the words, "You shall be holy, for I the LORD your God am holy. Every one of you shall revere his mother and his father, and you shall keep my Sabbaths: I am the LORD your God" (vv. 2, 3). "Many Jewish writers believed that honoring one's parents was the most important commandment."[1]

The important place given to honoring parents in the Bible suggests that this practice is a basic ingredient of a healthy society. When children do not respect their parents, something is seriously wrong. So Paul stipulates that an overseer "must manage his own household well, with all dignity keeping his children submissive" (1 Timothy 3:4). Dignified submission of children to parents is a key to a healthy Christian home. The absence of this is very serious. Later Moses says, "Cursed be anyone who dishonors his father or his mother" (Deuteronomy 27:16).

Why is honoring parents so important? Submission and honor are an important part of the liberated life. One of the basic results of the fall, which Paul describes as "not see[ing] fit to acknowledge God," is children being "disobedient to parents" (Romans 1:28–30). One of the best ways to describe the rebellion against God that lies at the heart of the fall is that people do "not honor him as God or give thanks to him" (Romans 1:21). Human relationships are intended to mirror our relationship with God. Therefore Paul tells wives: ". . . submit to your own husbands, *as to the Lord*" (Ephesians 5:22; see also 5:24). He tells slaves: ". . . obey your earthly masters with fear and trembling, with a sincere heart, *as you would Christ*" (Ephesians 6:5). Similarly, we relate to our earthly fathers with respect and love, just as we must relate to our heavenly Father with respect and love. If we fail to do that we perpetuate the attitude that lies at the heart of the most serious defect in fallen humanity: the refusal to honor God.

Godly people then are skilled in showing honor. So in church life we are to "outdo one another in showing honor" (Romans 12:10; see Philippians 2:29; 1 Peter 2:17). In social life, we are to "pay to all what is owed to them: . . . respect to whom respect is owed, honor to whom honor is owed" (Romans 13:7). Slaves honor their masters (1 Timothy 6:1). Husbands honor their wives (1 Peter 3:7). Christians honor national rulers (1 Peter 2:17). It is especially important to honor those who are older than we are. Leviticus 19:32 places respect for elders alongside fearing the Lord: "You shall stand up before the gray head and honor the face of an old man, and you shall fear your God: I am the LORD."

Parents also need to act in a way that makes them worthy of honor. They need to earn respect through teaching their children, and they must not abuse their authority. So Paul says, "Fathers, do not provoke your children to anger, but bring them up in the discipline and instruction of the Lord" (Ephesians 6:4; see also Colossians 3:21). The Old Testament often talks about the responsibility of parents to teach their children (Deuteronomy 6:7; 11:19; Proverbs 1:8; 6:20) and to discipline them (Proverbs 23:13; 29:17). When parents fail in these duties, their children find it difficult to honor them. This in turn results in a stunted personality that is reluctant to give honor to humans or to God.

Two Challenges

In the ancient Near East the family was the basic unit of society, and if the family was attacked, the whole fabric of society was in danger of disintegrating.[2] Today too, for several reasons, the family is under fire. Therefore, this command should receive new prominence in contemporary Christian thinking. I want to highlight two huge challenges facing the church—one has become urgent especially in affluent Westernized cultures and the other in poorer cultures.

Attack on Authority

The first challenge we are facing is that there has been a revolt against the idea of respecting authority and elders especially, but not exclusively, in the West. Philip Ryken refers to an analysis of the 1960s by Annie Gottlieb, which she describes as "the generation that destroyed the American family." She says, "We might not have been able to tear down the state, but the family was closer. We could get our hands on it." She goes on, "We believed that the family was the foundation of the state, as well as the collective state of mind. . . . We truly believed that the family had to be torn apart to free love, which alone could heal the damage done when the atom was split to release energy. And the first step was to tear ourselves free from our parents."[3]

Perhaps the older generation was partly to blame for this dismantling of the fabric of society. Perhaps the reaction of the sixties was a reaction to some wrong attitudes of the earlier generation, such as a conservatism that had no heart and had little interest in the aspirations of the poor and oppressed. Certainly many of us in the so-called Two-Thirds World can identify with the protests against unilateral decisions and initiatives by richer countries that have a major impact on the poorer nations and against things like the idea of Western superiority. But what they replaced this with seems to be worse than the thing against which they protested.

Today people are reluctant to stick to relationships that they think are threats to their freedom to do what they want and feel like doing. So commitment is seen as passé. The loss of faith in the value of objective truth has resulted in people finding it difficult to stomach the applying of binding principles that determine faith and action. In this environment Biblical preaching and exhortation has gone out of fashion. Ways of disciplining children, which were normal in Biblical times, are regarded today as abusive treatment of children. In such an environment we should not be surprised that people are finding it difficult to obey and honor their parents and to express that honor in costly commitment to their welfare. People do not act with this type of commitment because they feel like doing it. Often, especially with elderly parents, they may not feel like doing it. They do these things because they believe this is the right thing to do. Of course, at the heart of such commitment is love, too.

Yet humans cannot violate the Biblical lifestyle and expect to experience the freedom they seek. Their quest for liberation or personal fulfillment only serves to enslave them to the shackles of unfulfillment. We were made in the image of a God who is a person and whose character is holy love. God's holiness calls for respect, and his love and the fact that he is a person invite us to intimacy. The Biblical ideal of parenthood is patterned after our relationship with God as Father. It is characterized by the beautiful mingling of respect with intimacy and sacrificial concern. That is the relationship that truly satisfies the deep yearnings of our hearts. We were made to honor and respect what is exalted and to relish intimacy with and sacrifice for loving persons. The perfection of such a relationship can be achieved only with God. But the relationship with godly parents can be a fitting shadow of that. May God help Christians to restore this model.

Vocational Ambitions of Parents

Another serious threat to the Biblical model of parent-child relationships is the neglect of children especially because of the vocational ambitions of parents. This is seen in affluent circles when parents are so busy in their professions that their children are neglected. But the extreme form is seen in poorer nations where, in a desperate attempt to free a family from the grinding poverty they face, parents, especially mothers, leave home to work abroad.

In several poorer countries today millions of children's mothers have decided to go abroad to work because they believed they could find no other way to free their families from hopeless poverty. Our ministry works with many of these children. They are brought up by grandparents or by other relatives. Often their fathers waste the money that mothers send home on liquor and sexual sin. Many such children, lacking the security of alert supervision by loving and firm parents, have adopted destructive lifestyles. Many end up addicted to drugs or pornography. Some children drop out of school and become delinquents.

One of the saddest things we see is young girls who seem to be doing so well in their Christian life but suddenly run away with a young man, often a person with serious problem—a drug addict, for example. Starved of the affection of parents, they do not have the strength to overcome the immediate gratification that comes from the attention this person gives them. And they live the rest of their lives regretting their rash decision to move in with this person.

When I go to countries where such parents work, I try to help those ministering among them. It is heartbreaking after preaching to pray with these people whose hearts are broken over their choices. Some mothers have told me that their children do not want them to return home as they know that then their supply of funds and gifts would be gone. Many say that their children do not regard them as their mothers. Some speak of husbands who have taken on another woman.

I have decided that I will continue to try hard to dissuade married people from leaving their families and going abroad. But we must not blind ourselves to the reality of poverty in today's world. Those who are hopelessly poor need outside help to be freed from poverty. The structures of society need to be adjusted so that some may not have such an unfair disadvantage. As Deuteronomy 15:11 tells us, ". . . there will never cease to be poor in the land. Therefore I command you, 'You shall open wide your hand to your brother, to the needy and to the poor, in your land.'" Christians will always need to keep in mind situations where poverty drives the parents to live lives that harm their children.

I would like to give a word of caution to all parents about the dangers of their careers causing them to have less influence upon their children than is healthy for them. While we cannot make rules here, I usually give the advice that Norman Wright gives to couples preparing for marriage: "One personal conviction that I try to get across is that it's very important when children are in the preschool years for the mother to be the one who is responsible for training, guiding them and nurturing them. After the children are old enough to go to school, then the wife might find it beneficial to be employed."[4] Again, qualifying what I say with the caution about making inflexible rules, I would suggest that if mothers of small children absolutely must work, they should look for part-time work rather than full-time jobs.

Hope for Neglected Children

Yet I must also give a word of encouragement to children whose parents have not had time for them. Indeed they may be deprived in some ways and may have to struggle with the scars of that neglect as long as they live. But God's grace can help them overcome these obstacles so that they become great people. Gaius Davies, a leading psychiatrist in London, has written a book entitled *Genius, Grief and Grace* in which he shows that some of the greatest heroes in Christian history were people who had psychological deficiencies but were nevertheless used mightily because of the grace of God.[5] One such person was Anthony Ashley Cooper, better known as the Earl of Shaftesbury (1801–1885), who achieved much in the political sphere on behalf of the poor, the weak, abused children, and the insane. He was also active in several evangelical causes. His parents were wealthy and influential socialites who had little time for their son. But the maid who looked after him led him to Christ and was the person whom he considered to be the closest friend he ever had. Even as an adult he was often depressed and was sometimes difficult to get along with, but he achieved an enormous amount of good for the kingdom of God.

I have seen some people become effective leaders in spite of having come from dysfunctional family backgrounds. They have not let their deprivation cause too much damage. These people were able to overcome this by accepting that they have a problem, by being teachable, and by making adjustments so that their weaknesses are compensated for. They were willing to get help, to work on their weaknesses, and to get others to do what they cannot do well.

Often they learned the principle of affectionate respect and honor by having spiritual parents whom they could genuinely love and honor. Most importantly, they learned to respect and relate affectionately with God through the influence of these spiritual parents. These parents helped them gain a sense of self-worth that opened them up to receive the much greater self-worth that God gives.

How to Honor Parents (5:16a)

There are many ways in which parents can be honored today.

Obeying Parents

The most obvious way to honor parents is by obeying them. Paul uses the fifth commandment to teach about the parent-child relationship (Ephesians 6:2, 3). But before quoting this he says, "Children, obey your parents in the Lord, for this is right" (v. 1). Elsewhere Paul says, "Children, obey your parents in everything, for this pleases the Lord" (Colossians 3:20). The phrase "in everything" should perhaps be understood as referring to everything that you can do as a Christian that is not contrary to the Word of God. This could be one implication of the expression, "obey your parents *in the Lord*" in the Ephesians passage. We obey as if we were obeying the Lord Jesus himself. Another implication of obeying "in the Lord" is that we obey our parents whether they are Christians or not, for when we obey we do so as if we were obeying the Lord. So these two verses seem to imply that we are to obey non-

Christian parents always unless what they say contradicts the clear teaching of Christ.

As most of the young people reached through our Youth for Christ ministry are from non-Christian families, we often face situations where we have to counsel young people about how they can honor their parents. Our advice to them generally is that they obey their parents even when those parents may seem unreasonable so long as they are not explicitly disobeying God by doing so. Florence Nightingale did not begin her life's work till she was over thirty because her mother bitterly opposed her becoming a nurse.[6] Though she had a late start, she certainly made up for lost time and became a hero through what she did as a nurse.

It is true that Jesus said that he came to bring a sword that causes divisions in families (Matthew 10:34–39). But that refers to situations where we have to make a choice between following Christ and obeying parents. These statements of Christ have been used in such a way as to trigger unnecessary ruptures in families and persecution that could have been avoided. In our youth work we always try to prevent ruptures in relationships within a family unless that is absolutely necessary (for example, when family members are keeping the young person from following Christ). Even after a rupture takes place, we will do our utmost to restore the broken relationship.

Samuel Ganesh was a Brahmin, the highest caste in the Hindu system, and a vehement opponent of Christianity. When he heard that a Christian (YFC) open-air meeting was going on in his hometown, Chennai in South India, he took his gang of militant Hindu youths and went to disrupt the meeting. There he heard the gospel and was dramatically converted to Christ the same day. His parents disowned him and refused to have anything to do with him for several years. Ganesh became an evangelist who communicates the gospel powerfully, especially to Hindu audiences, using his vast knowledge of the Hindu scriptures to show that what they are looking for only Christ can give.

Some years after Ganesh's conversion his father died. In keeping with Brahmin custom, he began to send regular financial support to his widowed mother. She received the money but refused to establish contact with him. After six long years of this she reached out to him. When this happened, Ganesh expressed more and more willingness to take on responsibility for his mother's welfare. Today she is proud of his concern for her, and a door has been opened for a Christian witness to the whole family.[7]

Our parents may reject us because of our Christian commitment. But they are still our parents. So we will honor them "in the Lord"—that is, as if we were doing it for Jesus.

Respecting Parents

Respecting parents is another way we can honor them. God says, "Every one of you shall revere his mother and his father . . . I am the LORD your God" (Leviticus 19:3). The Levites were asked to proclaim to the people, "Cursed be anyone who dishonors his father or his mother" (Deuteronomy 27:16). Proverbs 30:17 says, "The eye that mocks a father and scorns to obey a mother will be picked out by the ravens of the valley and eaten by the vultures." Today children often speak rudely to their parents. That is something that is not acceptable for Christians. Indeed at home, when we are not acting a part, our bad moods often find expression in disrespectful talk. But we must learn to be able to express our moods without hurting others and without being disrespectful.

It is particularly important to respect parents when they are old. So we are told, "Listen to your father who gave you life, and do not despise your mother when she is old" (Proverbs 23:22). Often when parents are old they do things that their children find annoying. Sometimes they may need to be restrained through a rebuke or some other drastic method. Often they need to be directed just as we direct children. But though their actions may annoy us and though we may need to be firm in insisting on some things with them, we must always do so with the respect that is due to parents.

Caring for Parents

While Jesus was on the cross bearing the sins of the world and experiencing the greatest suffering that a human ever endured, he asked John to look after his mother (John 19:26, 27). No work is more important than what Jesus did to save the world. And no work we do is too important to warrant the neglect of parents. We see in Mark 7:10–13 that when Jesus used the fifth command to present the responsibility to look after parents, he showed how ridiculous it is for people to claim they are giving things for God's work and in that way avoid their responsibilities toward their parents.

In a passage about caring for widows, Paul says, "But if a widow has children or grandchildren, let them first learn to show godliness to their own household and to make some return to their parents, for this is pleasing in the sight of God" (1 Timothy 5:4). Here caring for parents and grandparents is given as evidence of the godliness of a person. A few verses later Paul becomes somewhat caustic and says, "But if anyone does not provide for his relatives, and especially for members of his household, he has denied the faith and is worse than an unbeliever" (v. 8).

Paul says that to care for widows is "to make some return to [our] parents" (1 Timothy 5:4). As Adam Clarke puts it, "Your parents supported and nourished you when you were young and helpless; *you* ought therefore to support *them* when they are old and destitute."[8] In both cases there is helplessness. Often aged parents behave like children. Then why is it that children don't look after aged parents with the same enthusiasm that these parents looked after them when they were children? Indeed, older parents can be quite difficult. When they become old they can get quite demanding and stubborn. Sometimes their condition is such that they require a lot of care. But infants are like that, too.

Perhaps one reason for the difference in the way helpless parents and helpless infants are treated is that the infants were rich with potential, and the parents found their identity in helping those infants reach that potential. Elderly parents do not look like people with much potential, and in our marketing-oriented culture, going through a lot of trouble for such people is often considered a waste of time. So often children try to see how they can avoid the nuisance associated with looking after aged parents.

Christians follow another ethic. One of the main teachings of the great love passage—1 Corinthians 12:31—14:1—is that love is not just a means to an end; it is an end in itself.[9] For Christians the primary motivation for loving is not the prospect of the results that love produces. It is that love is part of our lifestyle. We love because we want to love. Our reward is having the privilege of loving. And if we have loved we have been successful. Parental love is part of the Christian lifestyle. So we do it whether those for whom we care are able to respond to that love or not.

I believe this kind of love is one of the most radical features of Christianity. It has a lot to say to people today who are suffering from severe insecurity because the idea of costly commitment has been abandoned. Insecurity is one of the sad consequences of the disposable relationships that have become so normal in society today. People give up friends, churches, jobs, girlfriends and boyfriends, and even spouses when they become a nuisance. They do not know the security that comes at the end of serious threats to a relationship that, after a heavy struggle, remains intact. They are afraid to fully give themselves to a relationship because they do not know when they will have to end it. If you do not give yourself fully to a relationship, you will not enjoy it fully, either.

Braced by the joy of the Lord that gives us the strength to face hardship without losing our peace, we embrace the suffering and pain that go with our commitments. Christians often do things they may not necessarily like to do. They are not emotional cripples who want to do only what they like to do. They are skilled in taking up their cross daily (Luke 9:23) and in giving their bodies as living sacrifices (Romans 12:1). They know that their joy is not taken away by hardship, but that it can be taken away by disobedience. Because our primary source of fulfillment—God—is not put off by the pain, and because the primary expression of that fulfillment—the joy of the Lord—can coexist with pain, we are able to go on without becoming disillusioned.

What a contrast this life of joy is to the guilt that people live with over not caring for their loved ones and to the unhappiness that is the inevitable result of a self-centered life.

The Reward of Honoring Parents (5:16b)

After stating the fifth command Moses gives a promise of a reward for honoring parents: ". . . that your days may be long, and that it may go well with you in the land that the LORD your God is giving you." How can we apply this today? We have said that though the Law was specifically given to Israel, it was given by God whose nature does not change. Therefore even from laws specifically given to Israel we can glean abiding principles that reflect the mind of God. The reference to the land here must clearly be confined to Israel.

Paul quotes this reward in Ephesians, and that can help us apply this promise for today: "' . . . that it may go well with you and that you may live long in the land'" (Ephesians 6:3). Though "the land" refers to Canaan in its original context, the prospect of long life ("in the land") is mentioned here too. But the word used could better be translated "earth," in which case for us it is a promise for long life on earth. As A. Skevington Wood points out "the prospect of longevity is not held out elsewhere in the New Testament as part of the Christian hope."[10] In fact, in the five other times in the New Testament that the command to honor parents appears this promise of long life is not found.

This New Testament promise has been interpreted in different ways. First, some take this promise of long life as referring to the community and not the individual.[11] Second, some think that those who honor their parents will generally literally live long, though "in some cases God's providence orders otherwise."[12] Third, some spiritualize the reference to long life and make it to refer to eternal life. But that seems unlikely as the promise is that "they may live long *in the land*." Fourth, some think the focus should be on the phrase "that it may go well with you" and that Paul means that such "children will live to prove that their true welfare . . . depends on God."[13]

I am drawn to this fourth interpretation. I think that what Paul is saying is that children who honor their parents will receive God's blessing. God will work things out for them, and they will not lack anything they need. Just as the

Israelites interpreted God's blessing in terms of a long life, we will interpret it in terms of a full life where God leads and provides all that we need. Included here could be the second interpretation—a long life as a general rule, along with exceptions that were found in the Old Testament, too.

Whatever the exact meaning of Paul's interpretation of the blessing of keeping the fifth commandment may be, the general message is clear: God will bless those who honor their parents. The other side of this coin is also true: if we do not honor our parents, we should not expect God to bless us.

19

The Sanctity of Life

DEUTERONOMY 5:17

COMMANDS SIX TO TEN in the Decalogue remind us that we are people who live under restraint, especially with things that do not belong to us. The prohibition of murder tells us that we cannot do as we like when it comes to the life of another. The prohibition of adultery calls for restraint in our relationships with members of the opposite sex. The prohibitions of stealing and coveting call for restraint with things that do not belong to us. And the prohibition of false witness calls for us to be restrained in what we say because of a commitment to truth. We are seeing huge challenges today in each area covered by these commands.

What Kind of Killing Is Intended, and What Is Not

The newer translations correctly render the sixth command as, "You shall not murder" (5:17), using the word "murder" rather than "kill" as in the older translations. The Hebrew Bible has eight words for killing, of which the most common is *harag*, and that is a more general word for killing. The word used here is *rasah*, which has more the idea of "murder." "It describes any form of unlawful or unauthorized killing" (Wright). This word can be used for manslaughter, that is, accidental killings. But for that there are separate laws, and cities of refuge were built to protect those who accidentally killed someone from their avengers (4:41, 42; 19:1–13).

The reason for this command is that humans are made in the image of God (Genesis 1:27). "Whoever sheds the blood of man, by man shall his blood be shed, for God made man in his own image" (Genesis 9:6). Only God has the authority to take a life. Sometimes, however, God delegates that authority to humans to exercise on his behalf. Speaking about Roman authorities, Paul says, ". . . for he is God's servant for your good. But if you do wrong, be afraid, for he does not bear the sword in vain. For he is the servant of God, an avenger who carries out God's wrath on the wrongdoer" (Romans 13:4; see 1 Peter 2:14). Scholars are agreed that included in the meaning of the word "sword" here is capital punishment.[1] If a person does a crime against another that is punishable with death, the aggrieved parties are not to take the law into their own hands. They are to follow the judicial procedures prescribed in the Bible. Paul says, "Beloved, never avenge yourselves, but leave it to the wrath of God, for it is written, 'Vengeance is mine, I will repay, says the Lord'" (Romans 12:19). In doing this God often uses the national authorities and other citizens as agents of justice.

God also sanctioned wars in which people were killed. This raises several troublesome questions, some of which are addressed in our treatment of Deuteronomy 7 and 20. The wars of Deuteronomy were unique. Clearly then the sixth commandment cannot be used to abolish the death penalty and to advocate pacifism. Those who want to argue for these positions will need to look elsewhere in the Scriptures for backing.

Even though the Bible does not comment much on the morality of suicide, the early Christians, especially Augustine in his book *City of God*, held that suicide was akin to murder and thus condemned it. Such an attitude certainly goes with the premise that life can be terminated only by God.[2] The same could be said about abortion-on-demand, by which a person takes the life of an unborn child, usually for matters of convenience.

Euthanasia is becoming legal in some countries and states. This is "the act . . . of killing or permitting the death of hopelessly sick or injured individuals . . . in a relatively painless way for reasons of mercy."[3] This, too, is not acceptable to Christians because it advocates human sovereignty in terminating life. There are situations where brain-dead people are kept alive through artificial life-support systems. Here withdrawal of these supports may be permissible. As Michael Moriarty says, "There is no moral obligation to prolong the process of dying through the use of artificial means if it only prolongs suffering. The moral duty is to prolong life, not to use artificial means to prolong the process of death. . . . It is not morally wrong to allow the person to die."[4]

I had intended to say at the start of this chapter that the command on murder is one command in the Decalogue that most people agree with today. But as I proceeded with my study I realized that I could not say this, as murder in different forms is advocated by supposedly "civilized" people today. The Bible affirms that the right to terminate life is God's alone. To some humans, like judges, God may give limited authority (based on his principles) to represent him in doing this. But there, too, they must follow his guidelines. Today the term *pro-choice* has become popular. That is an expression of human rebellion against God's lordship over creation. Humans do not have the choice of terminating human life.

Terrorism and Combating It: Murdering for a Cause

In recent times we are seeing more and more examples of people getting frustrated over their failure to achieve their goals through the usual means acceptable to civil society and resorting to murder as a means of shocking people into listening to their cry. This is very serious because often the causes are just and the people resorting to terrorism have tried hard to achieve their goals through legal means but found no favorable response from the authorities. But this means does not justify their supposedly just ends.

I think all Christians will condemn the night clubs with their loose moral culture that are found in Bali. Bali's population is predominantly non-Muslim, though it is part of Indonesia, whose population is predominantly Muslim. However, murder through bombs is not the way to overcome the scourge of loose morals that tourists practice in many Asian countries.

Christians will agree that nudist and semi-nudist beaches should not be found in any country. But authorities in the Muslim country of Egypt turn a blind eye to this because tourism helps the economy so much. Those who have tried to protest against this have not succeeded. But that is not a reason for placing bombs in tourist hotels on the shores of the Red Sea.

We can say the same thing about bombing abortion clinics. Though we abhor abortion and view it as the murder of innocent children, we do not condone murderous attacks on those who perform abortions.

Often terrorists are agitating for legitimate rights. After finding that the authorities are not interested in giving them these rights, they resort to terrorist tactics to get a hearing or to win their rights. Therefore, those whom some call "terrorists" are called "freedom fighters" by others. Sadly, some legitimate rights have been won only after terrorist activity forced the authorities to give concessions to aggrieved parties. This has led some to conclude that terrorism was necessary in order to win the rights of people.

This shows how important it is for Christians to speak up against and do something about the injustices that ultimately help breed terrorism. It has long been held that the evangelical revival under John Wesley helped Britain avoid a French-style revolution, because it sought to win the rights of the downtrodden through other means. This claim is being disputed today, and some feel that the influence of Methodism is not as large as earlier claimed.[5] However, we know for sure that Wesley "pioneered or participated in most of the good causes of his day: legal and prison reform, the abolition of slavery, civil rights, and popular education."[6]

In Sri Lanka we see many people who in their bitterness against those of the other race angrily leave the country or join militant movements. But we have also seen members of the majority community who truly listen to those of the minority community and take risks in order to help them and be with them during their tough times. Then their bitterness based on ethnicity is severely challenged, and there is a chance that they will not adopt extreme measures to achieve the rights of their people.

It is important for Muslims to know that Christians are strongly opposed to radically selfish individualism, the lack of respect for elders, the lack of care for elderly parents, and sexual promiscuity. They see these coming to their cultures with such force from the West, and they seem helpless to counteract their influence. Sadly, they associate these things with Christianity. They must know that Christians, too, deplore them. This could act as a deterrent to people with moderate views joining militant groups. It is hard to wipe out terrorism once it is entrenched in a nation. This is why our focus should be on dealing with the causes that drive people into becoming terrorists.

Some governments have resorted to using groups doing extrajudicial killings to tackle the problem of terrorism and other difficult problems. God gave the right to execute criminals only to legitimate government authorities. If governments begin to use such paramilitary groups to do what they find difficult to do, they are creating a culture where people get used to killing enemies indiscriminately. Related to this is the growing use of the underworld by supposedly respectable people to get things done—such as receiving protection or eliminating enemies. Even some politicians who present a clean public image are using this means. This is a dangerous trend that can result in the legitimizing of the underworld as a parallel power alongside the legal structures.

Genocide

One of the worst forms of killing is when groups, including elected governments, eliminate large numbers of civilians because they belong to the "wrong" ethnic, social, political, or religious group. This is called genocide, and it has taken place far too many times in the past 100 years.

- The first great genocide of the twentieth century was the massacre of over one million Armenians under the Ottoman Empire. Some Turkish authors are trying to highlight this these days, resulting in their being branded as traitors.

- When the power and control of the brutal Russian dictator Joseph Stalin was threatened, he began what came to be known as "the Great Purge." No one knows exactly how many were killed, but estimates of those arrested and executed from 1936 to 1938 run between 1.5 and 7 million.
- Then we had the Holocaust under Adolf Hitler during the Second World War (1939–1945), which resulted in the extermination of 5.6 to 5.9 million Jews by the Nazis.
- The Khmer Rouge, headed by the guerrilla commander Pol Pot, ruled Cambodia from 1975 to 1979. This regime killed about 1.7 million Cambodians who were considered a threat to the government in what became known as "the Killing Fields."
- In the mid-1990s during clashes between the Hutus and the Tutsis in Rwanda between 500,000 and one million Rwandans were killed. Sadly, both the Tutsis and the Hutus claim to be Christians. Today there are Christian clergymen among those being tried in the war tribunal looking into what happened.
- The former Yugoslavia also saw tens of thousands of deaths, and it was there that the expression *ethnic cleansing* gained prominence. Fortunately, the international community did well to intervene fairly early in the genocide process there. Tens of thousands of international peacekeeping forces came to help restore peace.

It should sober us to note that all these genocides took place in the "civilized" twentieth century. It shows how hatred can drive people to commit unimaginable atrocities. In most of the genocides of the twentieth century, the rest of the world permitted it to happen until it was very late. Perhaps this is because leaders were reluctant to get involved in the internal affairs of other nations. Whatever the reason, the scandal of it must not be downplayed.

Emotions That Lead to Murder

The Bible gives rich insight into what triggers murderous intentions in people in several of the murder stories and comments about murder it records.

- In the first murder Cain's *jealousy* over God's accepting Abel's sacrifice and not his led him to kill Abel (Genesis 4:1–16).
- Lamech killed a young man as an act of *revenge* for wounding him (Genesis 4:23).
- Jacob's sons Simeon and Levi killed the men of Shechem because one of them had defiled their sister Dinah (Genesis 34:1–31). Absalom killed his half-brother Amnon for the same reason—he defiled Absalom's sister Tamar (2 Samuel 13). These were cases of defending the *family honor* that had been offended.

- Pharaoh ordered that the male children of the Israelites should be killed for *national security*, so that their growing population could be kept in check (Exodus 1:8–22).
- Moses killed an Egyptian out of rage when "he saw an Egyptian beating a Hebrew, one of his people" (Exodus 2:11, 12). Here it was *ethnic loyalty* confronting injustice to one's own people.
- Ehud, seeking *freedom from oppression*, killed Eglon, king of Moab, who had oppressed the Israelites for eighteen long years (Judges 3:12–26).
- Abimelech killed seventy people from a royal family who were a *threat to his royal ambitions* (Judges 9:5–56).
- Joab stabbed Abner to *avenge the death of his brother* (2 Samuel 3:24–27).
- David had the Uriah the Hittite killed because of his *lustful desires* for Uriah's wife Bathsheba (2 Samuel 11).
- Ahab was a rich king whose *greed* for a vineyard belonging to Naboth caused his wife Jezebel to have Naboth killed so he could acquire the vineyard (1 Kings 21:1–16).
- Proverbs talks of the *greed of robbers* who kill in order to get material things from the people they kill (Proverbs 1:10–19).
- Herod the Great killed boys in the Bethlehem area because he feared *a threat to his rule* through a child who had been born there (Matthew 2:13–18).
- Herodias had Herod the tetrarch behead the bold prophet John the Baptist because he disapproved of the adulterous relationship between them (Matthew 14:3–12). It was a case of *wicked people angry at being confronted* by righteous servants of God.

What an amazing list this is! Almost every conceivable trigger for murder is found in this list of murders. It shows what a relevant book the Bible is!

The only kind of murderer found today that I did not see in the Bible is the psychotic serial killer. This may have been because such are usually found in highly individualistic cultures where the family unit is not so binding and where it is possible for a person to become so separate from the rest of society that he or she can act in such a highly individualistic way. That was not the culture of societies in Biblical times.

Jesus on the Root Causes

When Jesus commented on this command, he implied that giving in to the motive without committing murder can be as serious as the act itself. He said:

> You have heard that it was said to those of old, "You shall not murder; and whoever murders will be liable to judgment." But I say to you that everyone who is angry with his brother will be liable to judgment; whoever insults his brother will be liable to the council; and whoever says, "You fool!" will be liable to the hell of fire. (Matthew 5:21, 22)

Often people in prison for murder seem unlikely to have done such a thing. They may be mild-mannered people whom others considered to be decent citizens. But they let anger against someone grow in their heart until it became a consuming passion. It ruled them to the point of making them do something that seemed so uncharacteristic of them. Paul warns, "Be angry and do not sin; do not let the sun go down on your anger" (Ephesians 4:26). There is a need for urgency when it comes to battling anger. It is indeed a battle—I have found that it is one of the most serious battles in my life. But I know that if I do not conquer here, I am going to become crippled spiritually. Someone has said, "He who angers you controls you."

The Trivialization of Murder

Before we pass on to the next command, I need to add that we are living at a time when murder has become so commonplace that we are in danger of not being horrified by it. Pope John Paul II has called our culture a "culture of death." Philip Ryken reports that "according to the American Psychological Association by the time the average child finishes elementary school, he or she will have watched eight thousand televised murders and a hundred thousand acts of on-screen violence."

Ryken also points out that "movies are not just getting more violent; they are also treating violence as a form of humorous entertainment."[7] He says, "We are teaching our children how to kill, and we should not be surprised when they do."[8] We should make sure that murder and violence continue to be things that horrify us. That will act as a deterrent to us when we are tempted to respond to provocation violently. Many murders today are not premeditated acts. They are the result of a gut reaction of one who was provoked and had not taught himself to be warned when provoked like that.

20

The Sanctity of Marriage

DEUTERONOMY 5:18

AMONG THE TEN COMMANDMENTS perhaps the law that we see treated with least respect in the media is the law prohibiting adultery. It is amazing how sex outside marriage has become such a trivial thing. And considering how powerful the media is today, it should not surprise us that this peddling of adultery has influenced people's behavior, too. Statistics are showing that this is indeed the case, even within the church.

In conservative Asian societies there is no public official encouraging of adultery, and it is still looked upon as a grave sin. However, in secret there is a lot of adultery taking place, especially as we find ourselves suddenly exposed to a barrage of morally loose and pornographic films coming from the West.

The Seriousness of Adultery in the Bible

The seventh command says, "And you shall not commit adultery" (5:18). In the Old Testament the word *adultery* does not cover all forms of sexual sin. It refers to sexual intercourse in which at least one person is married (or betrothed).[1] Other forms of sexual sin are discussed in Deuteronomy 22. The punishment for adultery in the Old Testament is death (Leviticus 20:10–12; Deuteronomy 22:22–25). Whereas in the ancient Near East adultery was considered a sin only against the other partner in the marriage, in the Bible it is regarded as a sin against God, as both Joseph and David have stated (Genesis 39:9; Psalm 51:4). Nathan, declaring God's word to David about the king's adultery, said, ". . . you have despised me and have taken the wife of Uriah the Hittite to be your wife" (2 Samuel 12:10).

It Violates the Covenant Principle of Commitment

Peter Craigie points out that "the reason why adultery is singled out for attention in the Decalogue is because adultery, more than other illicit behavior, has to do with unfaithfulness in a relationship of commitment." Later the idolatry and religious apostasy of Israel were described as adultery (Isaiah 57:3; Jeremiah 3:8, 9; Ezekiel 23:43; Hosea 2:2). That is, the marriage tie mirrors the tie between God and his people. It has to do with that all-important aspect of human life: binding commitment to God and to spouse.

The seriousness of adultery lay in the fact that the family was an absolutely vital aspect of the covenant relationship of God with the community of Israel. So much of God's will for his people is achieved through the family. The Bible takes the principle of commitment that lies behind God's covenant relationship with humans and the covenant relationship between a man and his wife very seriously. To violate that principle is to violate the way God works with humans. This is a serious crime.[2] Earlier God included honoring parents in the Ten Commandments as that, too, is a part of this God-and-family tie included in the covenant with Israel.

Our Bodies Are Linked with Christ

In 1 Corinthians 6:12–20 Paul presents another strong reason why adultery is so serious. It is based on the fact that there is a very close tie between Christ and our bodies. He emphasizes this point through four statements in this one paragraph: "The body is not meant for sexual immorality, but for the Lord, and the Lord for the body" (v. 13b); "Your bodies are members of Christ" (v. 15b); "he who is joined to the Lord becomes one spirit with him" (v. 17); "your body is a temple of the Holy Spirit within you" (v. 19b). Because of this union between Christ and our bodies, Paul says, "So glorify God in your body" (v. 20b).

Sexual relations make two bodies into one, says Paul, quoting the oft-quoted words from the institution of marriage in Genesis 2:24: "The two will become one flesh." Relations between man and wife are an aspect of our relationship with Christ, and therefore it is part of the body being one with Christ. But if one commits adultery, the body belonging to Christ becomes one with someone in a way that violates the oneness with Christ. Paul says, ". . . do you not know that he who is joined to a prostitute becomes one body with her?" (1 Corinthians 6:16). The person has rejected Christ and has replaced him with a prostitute.

Paul says that the damage done through adultery is more serious than other sins done with the body: "Every other sin a person commits is outside the body, but the sexually immoral person sins against his own body" (1 Corinthians 6:18b). Other sins such as drunkenness are also sins against the body. But adultery does this in a unique way in that the body becomes one in the fullest sense with another person when it should be one only with Christ. And Christ detests this oneness through adultery.

All this would not make sense if we did not grasp fully that the believer's body is one with Christ. Say the principal of a school is in the front seat of a vehicle while a student of the school drives that vehicle. What if the student screams obscenities at other drivers while driving and breaks all the road rules? What an insult to the principal that would be! Adultery heaps a greater insult on Christ, which can only be committed by kicking Christ out of the car (our body)!

Adultery Reaps Terrible Earthly Consequences

David was told, ". . . the sword shall never depart from your house, because you have despised me [the Lord] and have taken the wife of Uriah the Hittite to be your wife" (2 Samuel 12:10). And that is what happened to David. His relationship with the Lord was restored, and (I believe) so was "the joy of . . . salvation" for which he asked in his heartfelt psalm of penitence (Psalm 51:12). But his family history after the adultery was one of serious strife.

This is so today, too. The spouse is deeply hurt and lives with a wound all her life. Children not only live with the wound—they often live with anger and shame over what their parent did. Though God forgets when he forgives our sins, people often don't. And that could be a scar on the person's reputation. Then there is the other person involved in the adulterous act. That person is usually wounded deeply. A pastor committed adultery with a young girl but was subsequently restored to his wife and his ministry following genuine repentance. But he found out many years later that the girl had become a prostitute.

Adultery Reaps Terrible Eternal Consequences

The Bible often uses the threat of eternal consequences when appealing to people to abstain from adultery. Paul says, "Put to death therefore what is earthly in you: sexual immorality, impurity, passion, evil desire, and covetousness, which is idolatry" (Colossians 3:5). Immediately after that he says, "On account of these the wrath of God is coming" (v. 6). Again writing to the Corinthians he says, "We must not indulge in sexual immorality as some of them did, and twenty-three thousand fell in a single day" (1 Corinthians

10:8). Earlier he had said that "the sexually immoral. . . . will [not] inherit the kingdom of God" (1 Corinthians 6:9, 10).

Adultery Hurts the Church

Finally, there is the effect that adultery has on the church or organization, especially when it is committed by a leader. People are confused and discouraged. They reason, "If he can't make it, what hope is there for us?" There is disillusionment over and anger against the leadership as the members feel they have been let down. When the leadership proceeds to discipline the wrongdoer or fails to do so adequately, the unity breaks as the members usually divide into groups—some agree with the action taken and some don't. I have never seen a disciplinary process for adultery that has gone smoothly. It always leaves behind a lot of hurt and angry people.

Using a word used for fleeing from danger, Paul says, "Flee from sexual immorality" (1 Corinthians 6:18a). We are to avoid it like the plague. We are to run away from it like running away from a forest fire or a wild animal waiting to devour us. It is absolutely dangerous. When we are tempted, we must run away from it in terror. A friend of mine in the ministry asked his former senior pastor who had fallen into adulterous sin what he would say by way of advice to younger ministers after what happened to him. He simply said, "Don't do it!"

Today's Casual Attitude toward Adultery

The attitude of abhorrence of adultery in the Bible sharply contrasts with the casual attitude toward adultery today. Research has demonstrated that sex is not a biological necessity, so abstinence does not harm people.[3] But today sex is considered almost a necessary aspect of adult life. The extent to which sex outside marriage has become acceptable in society is illustrated by an episode involving an Australian teenage boy who was dying of cancer. He was a virgin, and some people felt that he should experience having sexual intercourse with a woman before he died. So after a lot of controversy the authorities gave permission for him to have time alone with a woman for this purpose. What a contrast to this was a biography of the Bible teacher John Stott that I read recently. Stott was single, and the book talked about his having to deny sexual desires because of his singleness. But there was no sense of regret. Rather there was immense joy for the full life God had given him.[4]

Just today I read in the newspapers that interrogators had offered a prostitute to a detained terrorist suspect in return for information. He is said to have felt insulted at such an offer because of his strong Muslim beliefs. Western

Christians must know that the militant Muslims believe they are fighting God's battle to prevent the invasion of Western values into the Islamic community. One of these values that they detest is the casual attitude toward sex, even in official circles.

The media report, as something quite normal, that famous people (many of them heroes to our youth) are living together though they are not married to each other. Philip Ryken quotes some research that shows that "with all the encounters and innuendoes, the average American views sexual material more than ten thousand times a year."[5] Ryken says that "by a ratio of more than ten to one, the couplings on television involve sex outside of marriage." One TV producer explained the reason for this by saying, "Married or celibate characters aren't much fun."[6] A famous Indian actress when interviewed by *The Times of India* said, "Monogamy is weird. One is boring."[7] Novels also thrive on adultery.

In this environment Christians can lose their sense of horror over adultery. Then when temptation hits them with great force, they might not have the moral strength to resist it. Statistics seem to show that this has indeed started to happen in today's church. Often the sins common in society find expression in the church, too. The most serious sexual sin that appears in the New Testament came from the church in Corinth, a city well known for sexual license. But Paul did not give the slightest hint of condoning it. He told them that adulterers "will [not] inherit the kingdom of God" (1 Corinthians 6:9, 10). He rebuked the Corinthian church for not taking severe steps against a member who had committed sexual sin (1 Corinthians 5).

As in the Old Testament, Paul used the threat of punishment for sin as a deterrent to adultery (1 Corinthians 6:9, 10; 10:8; Colossians 3:5, 6). If the church was more faithful in warning its members of this reality, I believe people would be more cautious about extramarital sex. One of the first thoughts that came to me when I read about the dying Australian boy and his sexual experience was the words of Paul that adulterers "will [not] inherit the kingdom of God" (1 Corinthians 6:9, 10). This was certainly not a good way to prepare that youth for death! If the church had been more vocal about its belief in the consequences of adultery, perhaps the authorities would have been more cautious about permitting that youth to have sex with a woman.

Adultery Is a Statement of Discontent over What God Gives

When the prophet Nathan confronted David about his adultery, he implied that the adultery was a statement of his dissatisfaction with all the blessings God had showered on him. "Thus says the LORD, the God of Israel, 'I anointed you king over Israel, and I delivered you out of the hand of Saul. And I gave you your master's house and your master's wives into your arms and gave you the house of Israel and of Judah. And if this were too little, I would add to you as much more'" (2 Samuel 12:7, 8). Nathan viewed this as despising the word of the Lord. "Why have you despised the word of the LORD, to do what is evil in his sight?" (v. 9).

Whenever Christians break God's laws, they are declaring that God is unable to satisfy them, and therefore they are forced to disobey God. God is perfectly capable of giving people "life . . . to the full" (John 10:10, NIV). So those who follow God can be satisfied with life whether they are married or single, widowed or divorced. Those who seek satisfaction through adultery have been trapped into thinking that they need extramarital sex in order to live a satisfied life. That is a lie!

To seek satisfaction from things that violate God's Law is a form of idolatry. We trusted in God because we believed that he would fulfill our deepest yearnings. Those who commit adultery are saying that extramarital sex can give satisfaction that God cannot give. This is the same as replacing God with an idol. Paul shows that there is a close connection between idolatry and sexual sin in Romans 1:25–27 and Colossians 3:5.

God promises to satisfy us so that we can say with Paul, "Not that I am speaking of being in need, for I have learned in whatever situation I am to be content" (Philippians 4:11). While Paul was talking here about economic need, the principle applies to all situations. We must pursue this contentment and joy that God gives us.

Single Christians may miss some of the joys of marriage, but God's promise of a full life (John 10:10) applies to them, too. They need to seek that fullness through enjoying God and the friends, families, and "children" from the Christian community whom God will give them. The church must ensure that singles have opportunities to receive these blessings. My wife has some single women friends who are fine Christians. Sometimes when they are sick, they come and stay at our home, so they can receive the "family care" they need at that time. But even if the church fails them, God can give them a fulfilled life. They do not need to resort to adultery for satisfaction.

Married people need to pursue the joy that God wishes for them to have from him and through their spouses. This will mean that they will carefully nurture their marriages, so that being with their spouses becomes a delightful experience. George Muller said, "I never saw my beloved wife, at any time when I met her unexpectedly in Bristol, without being delighted to do so."[8] Martin Luther said, "There is no more lovely, friendly or charming relationship, communion or company, than a good marriage."[9]

Giving priority to our marriage relationships is one of the best deterrents to adultery. Paul said this about the need for married couples to have regular sexual relationships: "Do not deprive one another, except perhaps by agreement for a limited time, that you may devote yourselves to prayer; but then come together again, so that Satan may not tempt you because of your lack of self-control" (1 Corinthians 7:5). We know that some people who work very hard and do not give sufficient time to their home have fallen into adultery, often with people in their workplace. Sadly, this has happened to many Christian workers. Hermas, who was probably an early second century church father, said, "Guard your chastity. . . . If you always remember your own wife, you will never sin."[10] This is something we must be careful to do. If we get careless about nurturing our marriages, it is very easy to fall into the traps of Satan.

I have heard of Christian men who have told women who are not their spouses that their wives do not satisfy them and therefore they would like a special relationship with these women. Usually this is a lie. But even if it is not a lie, an unhappy marriage is *never* an excuse for an affair. God is able to give a fulfilled life even to those in unhappy marriages. Besides, an affair will never give this person the satisfaction he or she seeks. You cannot rebel against God and expect to be satisfied. People in adulterous relationships do not go into them because their marriages are unhappy; they go into them because they have been disobedient to God and his laws by succumbing to temptation.

Jesus Goes to the Root Causes

In his Sermon on the Mount Jesus went to the root cause of adultery by saying, "But I say to you that everyone who looks at a woman with lustful intent has already committed adultery with her in his heart" (Matthew 5:28). In today's world where the idea of women looking at men lustfully is being aggressively peddled in the media, we should, in the application of this verse, include the possibility of women lusting after men, too. Earlier we had lists of the most beautiful women and the most handsome men in the world. Now lists of the sexiest women and men are more popular. The idea is that you can enjoy their sexuality, which the Bible confines to the marriage tie. The Bible says, "Don't look at a woman lustfully"; the world says, "That is your right!"

Next Jesus shows how serious sexual purity is by recommending drastic action to overcome temptation and avert judgment for sexual sin, saying, "If your right eye causes you to sin, tear it out and throw it away. For it is better that you lose one of your members than that your whole body be thrown into hell. And if your right hand causes you to sin, cut it off and throw it away. For it is better that you lose one of your members than that your whole body go into hell" (Matthew 5:29, 30). When we get sexual satisfaction through looking at someone who is not our spouse, we are committing adultery. This is such a serious thing and its consequences so dangerous that it would be better to be without something considered essential like an eye or hand if that is what it takes to stay away from it.

No one falls into adultery suddenly. There has been a process of compromise of which the physical act is the climax. The compromise involved sins of the mind where illicit pleasure was obtained from things or persons from whom we are not permitted to get sexual pleasure.

The media is bombarding us with the message that we have a right to find sexual satisfaction from people besides our spouses. So we are constantly exposed to sexually stimulating images in advertising. The idea is that given the plethora of messages people are exposed to in this media age, the advertisers can attract our attention by giving us a sexually stimulating image. And they rarely fail to get the desired response from the viewer. The fashion world is peddling its wares by using blatant sexuality. The sexiness of the sexiest men and women in our polls are presented not only to their spouses but to the general public.

In this atmosphere, is it possible to not commit adultery in the heart? I have found 1 John 1:7—2:2 very helpful. John says that there is no excuse for a Christian to sin: "My little children, I am writing these things to you so that you may not sin" (2:1a). We must never condone looking at a member of the opposite sex lustfully. Even though "everyone" may do it, Christians have no license to do so. But, sadly, many Christians do yield to this temptation. John goes on to say that God has made provision for that: "But if anyone does sin, we have an advocate with the Father, Jesus Christ the righteous. He is the propitiation for our sins" (2:1b, 2a).

How can we avail of God's provision for our sins? John says, "If we confess our sins, he is faithful and just to forgive us our sins and to cleanse us from all unrighteousness" (1 John 1:9). We must confess the sin. The word "confess" is the translation of the Greek word *homologeō*, which translated literally means "to say the same thing." We face up squarely to the seriousness of our sin, and we confess what we did, agreeing with God. We tell God that we looked at this person lustfully and that we are sorry for it and wish not to do so again. This way we bring to the surface exactly what we did without diminishing the seriousness of it. Once it has been brought to the surface, "the blood of Jesus his Son cleanses us from all sin" (1 John 1:7b).

Satan does not like us to recover like this from our sin. Therefore he tries to convince us that it is useless, that we'll never make it to purity. This paralyzes us spiritually, and we live defeated lives. Having given up the fight we do not strive toward the wonderful things God has planned for us. Instead, we may go deeper and deeper into impurity. We must show people how great grace is and warn them of Satan's attempts to make them ineffective by keeping them from availing themselves of God's grace.

We must be constantly aware of the real possibility of falling into the traps laid out for us by the media and by actual people of the other sex (especially those who have dressed indiscreetly). And if we fall into the trap, we must face up squarely to the fact that we have sinned against God. We won't say something like, "What could I do considering that I am exposed to these images constantly?" If there is no total confession of our wrong, along with a decisive repudiation of the act, we will live with the guilt of the action and also with some vestiges of the sin still in our system. This makes us vulnerable to further sin.

If we keep on giving in to the temptation to look lustfully, our minds will be so impure that, given the proper conditions, it could result in a physical act of adultery. In my youth I heard the story of a respectable Sunday school superintendent committing a sexual sin against a minor. Everyone was shocked by what had happened. When someone visited him in prison, he found out that this person had been reading pornographic books privately at night after his family had gone to sleep. Suddenly a situation arose that tallied with his fantasies, and he could not resist the temptation to put into practice what had been going through his mind. We know how much more vulnerable we are today than when this incident took place because of the easy access to pornography on the Internet.

In view of the above dangers it would be wise for all Christians to have at least one person to whom they are accountable. Ideally they should have an accountability group. This seems to be implied in 1 John 1:7 where, before saying that the blood of Christ cleanses us from sin, John says, "But if we walk in the light, as he is in the light, we have fellowship with one another." The context is talking about confession of sin, and therefore we could interpret the walking in the light that opens the door to fellowship as referring to being honest about our sins. Personally I cannot underestimate the immense role my accountability partners have played in my battle for holiness.

Sex is a part of life in which we are all vulnerable to temptation. Therefore it is imperative that we always remain on guard against the enemy. It is dangerous for anyone to think that he is above temptation in this area. Some who talk in this way may be lying. A preacher friend of mine was staying in a hotel when he began to face great temptation. This was before the time when free communication with one's spouse was possible through mobile phones. In desperation he looked up the Yellow Pages and found a pastor from his denomination and called him and told him of his struggle. The pastor suggested that this was not a problem. A few weeks later my friend found out that this pastor had to leave the ministry because of an adulterous affair.

One of Sri Lanka's great Christian leaders, Dr. Colton Wickramaratne, tells how he met the elder statesman of the worldwide Pentecostal movement, David du Plessis, when du Plessis was in his eighties. Dr. Colton asked him at what age a man could consider himself freed from sexual temptation. The old warrior of God responded, "Don't ask me, I am too young to answer that question."

21

Respect for Property and Truth

DEUTERONOMY 5:19, 20

A CHILD WROTE A LETTER to a Christian magazine saying that though he was taught in Sunday school that honesty pays, all around him he sees evidence to the contrary. He asked whether anyone could demonstrate to him how honesty pays, so that he would know that it is worthwhile being honest.[1] The eighth and ninth commandments have to do with honesty.

The Prohibition of Stealing (5:19)

Kinds of Stealing in the Bible

The eighth command crisply states a prohibition with no reasons or explanations given: "And you shall not steal" (5:19). Several words are used in the Bible for stealing. The verb used here (*ganab*) "can be used of stealing property," but "the command is much broader in its focus. Issues such as kidnapping (cf. Deut 24:7) as well as stealing intangibles (dignity, self-respect, freedom, rights) are all important. The word is also used for stealing in the sense of cheating."[2]

Usually we associate stealing with the type of people we call robbers. These are people who break into homes, pick pockets, or hijack vehicles. Usually such are not common within the Christian community. But there are other kinds of stealing in which even Christians indulge. Cheating on taxes is found among some Christians who do not disclose real values or earnings. When I was selling a portion of the land beside our home, the real estate agent simply could not understand why I wanted to write the exact price of the sale in the deed and thus have to pay the full tax on capital gains. He told me about various famous people he had done business with who did not do that. I had

225

to finally convince him by saying that my God would be displeased. When one particular Christian in Sri Lanka purchased land and insisted on the exact amount being put on the deed, the seller (a church member) increased his price so that his loss through additional taxes paid by making a full disclosure would be covered!

Christians often take days off saying they are sick when they are not sick. In some countries medical doctors sometimes give false certificates confirming that these people were sick. One hotel in North America "reported in its first year of business having to replace thirty-eight thousand spoons, eighteen thousand tiles, three hundred and fifty-five coffee pots . . . and one hundred Bibles!"[3] Recently stories have emerged of corporate fraud in once respected corporations and of auditing firms that have permitted such to go on without confronting them. It seems as if everyone is doing this today. But this has been a problem from the earliest times. Martin Luther said, "If we look at mankind in all its conditions, it is nothing but a vast, wide stable full of great thieves."[4]

Another word used for stealing (*gazal*) appears in connection with exploiting the poor: "Do not rob [NIV, exploit] the poor, because he is poor" (Proverbs 22:22). That same word is used of rulers and judges who deprive the poor of justice: "Woe to those who decree iniquitous decrees, and the writers who keep writing oppression, to turn aside the needy from justice and to rob the poor of my people of their right" (Isaiah 10:1, 2). The Biblical understanding of a robber includes officials who are responsible for the poor not receiving justice.

In a robbery-related passage we see how God detests exploiting people in helpless situations for personal gain at their expense. Ezekiel says a righteous person "does not oppress anyone, but restores to the debtor his pledge, commits no robbery, gives his bread to the hungry and covers the naked with a garment, does not lend at interest or take any profit, withholds his hand from injustice, executes true justice between man and man" (Ezekiel 18:7, 8). Some people have become rich by pouncing on vulnerable people and using their weakness to acquire wealth. A trusted relative gets an old widow to transfer large sums of money to his account, stating that it is for expenses incurred in handling her affairs. In Sri Lanka poor people who would not be able to get loans from a bank get loans for emergencies from moneylenders who charge exorbitant interest. All such people are robbers.

Using a different Hebrew word (*qaba'*) Malachi 3:8 says that those who do not give their tithes are robbing God. I have heard people who do not tithe or give anything close to what they can and should give to God's work speak eloquently about the dishonesty that is found within the church. But according to Malachi they too would be considered robbers because of their failure to give as they should.

No Death Penalty for Stealing

It is interesting that unlike the other commands there is no death penalty for stealing other than man-stealing, kidnapping (Deuteronomy 24:7). Chris Wright says that the refusal to have the death penalty for stealing, unlike the other commands, "reflects a scale of values in which human life is of immeasurably higher value than property." Wright points out that in the law codes of the ancient Near East "there was a wide range of penalties, including mutilation and death, for different kinds of theft." Yet theft is severely condemned in the Bible. Several times it is presented as an example of serious sin. The law about stealing is included in summary statements listing three or four commands (Mark 10:19; Romans 2:21; 13:9). Thieves are included in the list of the wicked who will not enter the kingdom of God (1 Corinthians 6:9, 10). Jeremiah speaks of the disgrace of a thief when caught (Jeremiah 2:26). And we are warned about being "companions of thieves" (Proverbs 29:24; Isaiah 1:23).

Wright says that in the ancient Near East, the social rank of the victim would determine the extent of the penalty. In some of these laws those of a higher rank could pay a penalty and avoid more severe punishments. The Old Testament, on the other hand, does not have any extra leniency toward the rich. What we find instead is some special consideration for the poor who steal: "People do not despise a thief if he steals to satisfy his appetite when he is hungry, but if he is caught, he will pay sevenfold; he will give all the goods of his house" (Proverbs 6:30, 31; see Proverbs 30:7–9). The sin is not condoned, and the punishment is meted out, but there is some special consideration for those who are in abject poverty.

How Our Concept of God Influences Attitudes toward Stealing and Lying

Several times in Deuteronomy we see how our concept of God has a huge effect on our behavior. This is particularly relevant in our discussion on the prohibitions on stealing and on false witness, which is the subject of the ninth commandment. Except among the Christians, Muslims, and Jews, the ideas regarding the divine in Asia and much of the world today is very different from the Biblical idea of God as one who is holy and to whom humans are personally accountable, a God who wants to relate to us in every aspect of life as our loving Lord and who will judge us for what we do on earth.

Some people have a polytheistic understanding of the divine, and they go to different gods for help regarding the different needs in which these gods specialize. None of these gods demand total commitment or accountability for one's personal life. Rather, they demand certain ceremonial things so that they may bless the person. Demands include things like abstaining from meat for a given period or offering sacrifices to the god.

Also growing rapidly in the West is the pantheistic idea of God that is found in most forms of Hinduism and in the New Age movements. Here everything is God. Humans, animals, chairs, and tables are all manifestations of God. God may be expressed as an individual god, but that individual god is part of the absolute God who is unknowable. Again there is no concept of a personal God having specific plans for us and making demands upon us.[5]

So while there are good rules in a land, they do not have a big influence in determining behavior. If one breaks a law, that is not a big deal as long as that person doesn't get caught or doesn't cause much harm to others. Therefore, there aren't the old constraints against stealing and lying. A friend of mine, living in an Asian country where road rules were routinely disregarded by drivers, asked a person who was questioning him about Christianity, "At a traffic light, when the light is red, what influences you more to stop—the law of the land or the policeman?" Without hesitation he said it was the policeman. When there is no fear of getting caught and punished, many people have no restraint when it comes to breaking the law.

The structures of Western society were built on a worldview that holds that there is a personal and holy God to whom we are accountable. Therefore, a lot of things depend on trust. It was assumed that people will not steal from a supermarket. As the former belief about God is being rapidly replaced by a pantheistic view of the divine we can expect to see some big changes in the behavior of people. The millions of dollars spent on security systems and the millions of dollars lost because of stealing bear testimony to the breakdown of the system of trust. We should not expect people to be honest anymore.

This shows how important it is for us to teach people about the nature of God. They must know that "it is a fearful thing to fall into the hands of the living God" (Hebrews 10:31). Their actions need to be motivated by the prospect of facing God's judgment someday. Ecclesiastes, after reflecting on the meaninglessness of life, concludes the book by saying that what gives meaning to life is that "God will bring every deed into judgment, with every secret thing, whether good or evil" (Ecclesiastes 12:14). Paul says ". . . we must all appear before the judgment seat of Christ, so that each one may receive what is due for what he has done in the body, whether good or evil. Therefore, knowing the fear of the Lord, we persuade others" (2 Corinthians 5:10, 11a). The prospect of judgment motivated him to the ministry of persuasion. Judgment has a similar deterrent on stealing.

Why It Is Not Worth Stealing and Lying

Because stealing and lying are so commonplace in today's world, a word is in order about why it is not worth acting in this way. The first point has already been stated above. We will be judged for our actions. Therefore, we play safe by not stealing and lying, for at the judgment we will be sorry if we did.

Second, God made us in his image, and when we act contrary to that image we lose our fulfillment. In a discourse in which Jesus was speaking about slavery to sin, he said, "You will know the truth, and the truth will set you free. . . . So if the Son sets you free, you will be free indeed" (John 8:32, 36). To know freedom and fulfillment, we must come to the one who made us. Sin will give us temporary satisfaction, but it will leave us restless and unhappy. In our comments on 2:24, 25 we quoted the American preacher Henry Clay Morrison who said, "God never fixed me up so that I cannot sin; he fixed me up so that I cannot sin and enjoy it."

My wife and I know a person who steals and lies a lot though she claims to be a Christian. She is one of the jolliest people I have met. She seems to be so happy and has a carefree attitude toward life, even though she faces a lot of problems. This puzzled me until we visited her one day when she was screaming at one of her children and using very bad language. She had lost control of herself in her anger. Then I realized that underneath the facade of happiness there was no peace and joy. Sinning leaves our conscience guilty.

A third reason is our belief that God will look after us. At a time of great need, when there is a huge possibility of advancement through lying or stealing, we could be tempted to reason that we must meet our needs and that is the only way to do it. But to yield to that is equivalent to saying that God cannot look after us by his methods, and therefore we need to resort to Satan's methods to meet our needs. We must trust God to look after us, and he will. In fact, we will have some tremendous testimonies of God's provision in times of great need. Not only are we provided for, life becomes an exciting adventure. David said, "I have been young, and now am old, yet I have not seen the righteous forsaken or his children begging for bread" (Psalm 37:25).

Forgiveness and Restoration after Stealing

There is a great tradition of forgiveness for robbers in the Scriptures. Paul says, "Let the thief no longer steal, but rather let him labor, doing honest work with his own hands, so that he may have something to share with anyone in need" (Ephesians 4:28). The person who was once a robber is now a hardworking person who gives to others without grabbing from others. I will never forget the shock I got when a student at our drug rehabilitation center described to me how he formerly got money to support his drug habit by robbing houses during the night. I thought, *This is the type of person I would get mad about and regard as a nuisance in society. Now he has become my brother in Christ.* Today he is a beloved volunteer in our ministry, running a small vegetable stand. Four days before writing this I returned from a five-day preaching tour during which he was with me as a traveling companion.

Along with the promise of forgiveness for robbery is also the call to pay back what was stolen along with something added to the original thing stolen as a penalty (Exodus 22:1–4; Leviticus 6:2–5). In Old Testament times only after restitution was made was the person permitted to approach the Lord with a guilt offering (Leviticus 6:6). This would be included under what John the Baptist called "fruit in keeping with repentance" (Matthew 3:8). This was so important that if he failed to pay back he must be sold as a slave until the amount of the theft had been earned for restitution (Exodus 22:3).

There was a young man whom God used powerfully to bring other youths from totally unreached backgrounds to Christ. Some of those he reached are now in vocational Christian ministry. But he had a weakness with which he battled: a lack of discipline in handling money. Sadly, because of a problem related to this he began to backslide and finally even stopped going to church. Then I heard that he had come back to Christ and had gone forward at the end of a service to make a public expression of rededicating his life to Christ.

I met him a few days later and was thrilled to see how warmly he spoke of the things of God. He was back in fellowship with Christians and well on the way to recovering his usefulness in the kingdom of God. I told him that he should, however, pay back some funds that he owed a Christian organization. He agreed that he should, but I saw that he was not eager to follow through with that. So there was a block to fully walking in the light so he could have fellowship with God's people (1 John 1:7). This young man never paid back the money, and he never recovered fully. He became an alcoholic, his marriage broke down, and he finally died, probably through suicide, while he was in his mid-thirties.

The Prohibition of False Witness (5:20)

The Primary Meaning of the Command

The ninth commandment states, "And you shall not bear false witness against your neighbor" (5:20). Lying is prohibited in the Bible, as, for example,

Leviticus 19:11 shows: "You shall not steal; you shall not deal falsely; you shall not lie to one another." This command, however, looks at the most serious kind of lying: perjury or lying under oath in a court of law. When people do wrong, it is serious. But when people make a mockery of the legal system of a land, it is extremely serious. The courts are one of the key institutions aiding in a nation's restraining evil and promoting good. When corruption enters that process, the nation is on very dangerous footing. Indeed, judges do make mistakes. But deliberate deception at this forum is absolutely unacceptable. This is why even today perjury is considered such a serious crime.

The seriousness of the crime of perjury is evidenced by the fact that those who commit it will suffer the same punishment that the victim would have suffered if he or she had been condemned (Deuteronomy 19:16–19). Moses says this is done so that "the rest shall hear and fear, and shall never again commit any such evil among you" (Deuteronomy 19:20). Moses does not leave room for leniency with false witnesses: "Your eye shall not pity. It shall be life for life, eye for eye, tooth for tooth, hand for hand, foot for foot" (Deuteronomy 19:21). Clearly, then, false witness is a very serious sin.

Wider Applications of the Command

While the ninth commandment refers primarily to the law courts, its intention is fulfilled today when we extend it to apply to other kinds of false witness, too. This is because Israel was a theocracy, and all its legal procedures were included in the Law. There was no separation of church and state there. Today many such procedures would take place within the church. Therefore, we could extend this law to include the prohibition of making formal or even informal accusations about people within the church and also in society at large.

We need to be very careful about accusing other Christians of wrongdoing. John Wesley counsels that if we are sure that someone has done something wrong, we should talk about it only if it is "necessary to mention it just then, for the glory of God, the safety or good of some other person, or for the benefit of him that hath done amiss." Wesley then cites how damaging inappropriate talk of people's wrongdoing can be: "O beware of this! *It is scattering abroad arrows, fire-brands, and death*" (italics his).[6]

It is sad but true that even though grace is much greater than sin in the Christian approach to life, talking about the sins of others is a favorite Christian pastime. If you speak evil of others, you can be sure of an attentive audience. And we all like it when people listen to us speak! So we find ourselves saying negative things we have heard about people without being sure they are true. Even if they are true, we often repeat these things to those who do not need to know. This seems to be a besetting sin of the evangelical movement.

Once a wrong story has been repeated, it is very difficult to erase it. Usually by the time we realize that it is wrong or that we should not have repeated it where or when we did, the story has gone to many others. Often with each repetition new features are added to it. Once a few days after my mother returned from the hospital after an operation, my father got a sympathy card over her death from a Sri Lankan living abroad! My mother is very much alive today, though my father died several years ago. The stories of her illness had expanded considerably as it went from person to person.

This is an area where all Christians can fail. Even esteemed and godly Christian leaders are sometimes guilty. The great evangelical politician the Earl of Shaftesbury (1801–1885) performed a great service for the poor and vulnerable in society by helping enact laws that would protect them and give them their rights. But he, too, was vulnerable. "He announced that, after much study, he was convinced that the Salvation Army was the antichrist. Then an admirer of the Earl announced that in his own studies, he learned that the 'number' of William Booth's [founder of the Salvation Army] name added up to 666!"[7]

If we realize that we have spoken out of turn, we must do all we can to erase the effects of our words. This is very difficult to do completely. But it is the least we can do. Sometimes Christians have to live the rest of their life with the stigma of people thinking that they have committed a sin that they did not commit. Without realizing it, the person who gossiped has done something very wicked.

Safeguards to Prevent Errors of Judgment

Deuteronomy presents some safeguards to prevent people from being the victims of false witnesses. It says there must be more than one witness to the crime: "A single witness shall not suffice against a person for any crime or for any wrong in connection with any offense that he has committed. Only on the evidence of two witnesses or of three witnesses shall a charge be established" (19:15; see 1 Timothy 5:19). Then Moses says, "The judges shall inquire diligently" (Deuteronomy 19:18). This will be discussed in our study of that passage. We cannot conduct these things hurriedly. We must make sure that wrong has actually been done and what exactly has been done.

Lying and the Nature of God

Three times the Bible says that it is impossible for God to lie (Numbers 23:19; Titus 1:2; Hebrews 6:18). Our conversation must reflect this faithfulness of

God. Therefore, those who take "an oath in the land shall swear by the God of truth" (Isaiah 65:16). Among the "six things that the LORD hates" are "a lying tongue" and "a false witness who breathes out lies" (Proverbs 6:16–19). "Lying lips are an abomination to the LORD, but those who act faithfully are his delight" (Proverbs 12:22). It is not surprising then that being truthful is an essential feature of the life of God's community. Just as we trust God's word, we must be able to trust the words of God's people. Paul said, "Therefore, having put away falsehood, let each one of you speak the truth with his neighbor, for we are members one of another" (Ephesians 4:25).

Yet this is not in keeping with the shame culture that is characteristic of Asia and is growing in other parts of the world too. People often tell lies to avoid unpleasantness or losing face. So when a plumber is told to come the next day to repair something, he agrees to do so without being sure that he can do it. The wife and children know for sure that a husband/father who is denying wrongdoing has actually done the thing he is denying. But they choose not to talk about it because doing so would cause a more serious problem—loss of face for the head of the family. It is almost an accepted fact that a politician or athlete will initially deny some wrongdoing, hoping the issue will stop at that. People usually forgive the leader for lying and forget the matter.

In this context it is very difficult to pursue the procedure outlined in Matthew 18:15–20 of what to do when a brother sins against us. Jesus says that we must first go to the person alone. If that fails, we are to go with one or two others. Finally, we are to go to the church. This is an area where we need to teach the people to be countercultural. However, we also need to be sensitive to the culture. Where public confrontation is not culturally appropriate, this is to be done only as the last resort, as the procedure outlined by Jesus indicates. When we do confront people of whom we are expected to be respectful according to the culture, we should do so respectfully. Paul tells Timothy, "Do not rebuke an older man but encourage him as you would a father" (1 Timothy 5:1). The verb translated "encourage" here, *parakaleō*, can also mean "to ask for something earnestly and with propriety."[8] This seems to be the meaning here. We are to respectfully confront elders against whom there have been allegations of wrongdoing.

So Christians are to constantly pray the prayer of the psalmist: "Deliver me, O LORD, from lying lips, from a deceitful tongue" (Psalm 120:2).

22

Covetousness versus Contentment

DEUTERONOMY 5:21

THE LAST OF THE TEN COMMANDMENTS prohibits covetousness. It is different from the rest because it moves from actions to the attitude that lies behind actions. Those who break it are usually not found out, and thus not prosecuted, unless the attitude triggers an illegal action. But this is in keeping with the teaching of Deuteronomy, which presents a religion of the heart as we shall see in our discussion of 6:5. Indeed, the new covenant perfected the religion of the heart, and the prophets anticipated this perfection of heart religion in their prophecies about the new covenant (Jeremiah 31:31–34; Ezekiel 36:26, 27). But heart religion was already a part of Old Testament experience.

This emphasis harmonizes with the teaching of Jesus in relation to the Law. Explaining his statement that he came to fulfill the Law and not to abolish it (Matthew 5:17–20), he said that our focus should be on anger more than on murder (Matthew 5:21–26), on lust more than on adultery (Matthew 5:27–30), on speaking the truth more than on taking oaths (Matthew 5:33–37). Jesus was saying here that we should concentrate on the inner motivations that cause people to break the Law.

Coveting Persons, Property, and Possessions (5:21)

This last command states, "And you shall not covet your neighbor's wife. And you shall not desire your neighbor's house, his field, or his male servant, or his female servant, his ox, or his donkey, or anything that is your neighbor's"

(5:21). Craigie points to the comprehensiveness of the command in that it covers persons, possessions, and property.

Coveting Persons

The person particularly mentioned is one's "neighbor's wife." Servants are also mentioned, but in the culture of that time that would fall more in the category of possessions. I want to consider an extreme situation involving coveting one's neighbor's wife that some people even regard as acceptable according to their value system. This is the situation where there are extreme conditions that hinder satisfaction in the marriage. The couple may be desperately unhappy, or one person may be a very disagreeable partner with whom it is very difficult to live; they may be sexually incompatible owing to physical or psychological causes resulting in sexual relations being nonexistent. In such times many in our society think that coveting another is acceptable.

How could Christians stay away from coveting someone else if they are unhappily married? First, whether we are happily married or not, sin is never acceptable. Desiring someone else is sin against our holy God, and Christians must stay away from sin. It is as simple as that! The media proclaims lists of the sexiest women and sexiest men in the world that in effect state that we have a right to desire such women or men. But as Jesus stated, looking at a woman to lust after her is adultery (Matthew 5:28).

Second, we do not need to do this because God is able to give us a completely full life amidst human deprivation. Jesus came to this world to give us abundant life (John 10:10), and that life is available to us whether we are married, single, unhappily married, divorced, or widowed. Being satisfied in him makes it unnecessary for us to sin in order to find satisfaction.

Third, Christians adhere to the principle of binding commitment to spouses, which they vow to keep at the wedding service. When we make such commitments, we stick to them however difficult the circumstances. Here we mirror God who has patience with us in spite of all our sin. Like Hosea, we cling to our spouses despite all their weaknesses.

Fourth, even in an unhappy marriage God can do something beautiful that serves a greater purpose than the suffering people can ever imagine. Hosea must never have thought that God was going to use his terrible experience with an unfaithful wife to help millions of people after him to understand the immensity of God's love. Unhappily married Christians will steadfastly cling to the fact that God will look after them and help turn their misery into something good. This in turn helps them overcome the temptation to look lustfully at another person.

Coveting Property

Next, the command says, "And you shall not desire your neighbor's house, his field . . . " I think it is amazing how many Christians throw away their Christian principles when it comes to their desires for property. Siblings end up as enemies over the dividing of family property. People end up trying to exploit close relatives who trust them for help regarding their affairs and end up grabbing what is not rightly theirs.

I suppose a major reason for this kind of desire is the sense that house and property have a feel of permanence. We like to think that we have something of permanent value on earth that will give us some security and peace of mind. This is not necessarily a bad thing. However, it becomes bad when we are jealous of others who have better property than we do and when we desire such in a way that we will compromise our principles. How alien to this is the attitude described in Hebrews 13:13, 14: "Therefore let us go to him outside the camp and bear the reproach he endured. For here we have no lasting city, but we seek the city that is to come."

Another way in which this desire expresses itself is in competitive fashioning of houses and other property. A certain ornate type of gate became popular in an area in Sri Lanka. It is interesting to see how so many homes in this area have installed such gates. It is clear that there is an attempt by some to have gates that are more ornate and thus more expensive-looking than the gates of others. When I visited a certain country I was told that the bishops there compete with each other for owning the most luxurious vehicle.

The Bible tells the story of King Ahab, who obviously had enough land to be the most secure person in Israel and also would not have had any rivals to his grandeur. Yet he coveted Naboth's vineyard, which was next to his palace. When Naboth said he could not give up his ancestral property, "Ahab went into his house vexed and sullen. . . . And he lay down on his bed and turned away his face and would eat no food" (1 Kings 21:4). His wife Jezebel solved the problem by having Naboth killed. How could a person who had so much still feel upset when a person refused him one small vineyard? That is the discontentment of a person with a lust for property.

Coveting Possessions

After prohibiting the coveting of persons and property, the command goes on to list the possessions of others: "And you shall not covet your neighbor's . . . male servant, or his female servant, his ox, or his donkey, or anything that is your neighbor's" (5:21). These were indicators of wealth and prestige in those days. The equivalent of these today are things like vehicles, mobile phones, computers, and clothes. An incredible amount of money is being spent today by Christians who want to keep up with the latest fads in these areas.

It is amazing that after all of God's blessings to us we should crave for things that we have no right to have. A Christian I know in an Asian country had a pastor as his immediate neighbor. It soon became evident to my friend that this pastor was an unhappy man. My friend subsequently left the area. But before he left he was very grieved to lose his beloved pet. Several months later imagine his shock when his niece told him that she went to this pastor's house and saw her uncle's pet. It was called by the same name that my friend called it. The pastor had stolen it and hidden it inside the house until my friend left the area.

Ever since I heard this story, I have kept asking myself how a pastor could do a thing like this. Something must be seriously wrong for a pastor to do something so un-Christian. In all the examples of coveting persons, property, and possessions there was one common factor: discontentment. The opposite of covetousness is contentment.

Covetousness Is the Lack of Contentment

So the main reason people covet is that they are not content with what they have, or actually with who they are. Let me first say that there is a kind of discontent that is pleasing to God. This is the discontent of wanting all of God. The Bible describes this as hungering and thirsting after righteousness (Matthew 5:6), as the soul panting, fainting, and thirsting after God (Psalm 42:1, 2; 63:1), and as "straining forward to what lies ahead" and "press[ing] on toward the goal" (Philippians 3:13, 14). Then there is the discontent of wanting to do one's best for God. Paul tells Timothy to "devote" himself to diligence in the practice of ministry "so that all may see [his] progress" (1 Timothy 4:13–16).

While we have this divinely inspired discontent that is a key to progress in life, we also have the satisfaction of having the water of which Christ spoke: ". . . whoever drinks of the water that I will give him will never be thirsty forever [ESV margin]. The water that I will give him will become in him a spring of water welling up to eternal life" (John 4:14). The deep discontent of not having found the purpose for life is gone. We have discovered the way to true fulfillment and meaning. The world's hunger is gone, and we are joyous people. When we have this life in us, we are able to say with Paul, "I have learned in whatever situation I am to be content. I know how to be brought low, and I know how to abound. In any and every circumstance, I have learned the secret of facing plenty and hunger, abundance and need" (Philippians 4:11b, 12). Those words were written from a Roman prison!

Such people are truly rich. Paul says, ". . . there is great gain in godliness with contentment" (1 Timothy 6:6). Their satisfaction does not depend on whether they have things but on the fact that God is for them—a feature that is not influenced by the presence or absence of any earthly thing. A man told his wife, "One day we will be rich and be able to buy a lot of things." The wife replied, "We are already rich. Perhaps one day we will be able to buy a lot of things."

When John Wesley encountered a poor servant at Oxford University who was a radiant Christian, he became "convinced . . . that there was something in religion that he had not grasped." This janitor possessed only one coat and had not had anything to eat that day. Though he had tasted only water, he was full of thanks to God. Wesley asked him, "You thank God when you have nothing to wear, nothing to eat, and no bed to lie upon. What else do you thank him for?" He replied, "I thank him that he has given me life and being, and a heart to love him, and a desire to serve him."[1] This man is an example of following what Hebrews 13:5 teaches: "Keep your life free from love of money, and be content with what you have, for he has said, 'I will never leave you nor forsake you.'" Jesus is enough to bring us deep joy. And as we shall see below, that is a key to the life of contentment.

It is when we give too much value to earthly things that we become discontent and start coveting. We may legitimately desire to have some earthly things as Christians, but they are not a big deal to us. Their absence does not take away our joy. And we are not upset by the fact that others have something we like that we don't have. If we get upset we will covet those things and lose our joy. We may even use wrong means to get those things.

Contentment in a World of Greed

Surely the words of Jesus, "Take care, and be on your guard against all covetousness, for one's life does not consist in the abundance of his possessions" (Luke 12:15), are very pertinent today. Greed has become respectable in today's society. When I was a seminary student in the USA I remember seeing a gold Rolls-Royce in the Los Angeles International Airport with a license plate saying "GREED." This was in the 1970s when owning a Rolls-Royce was the ultimate status symbol. Today this trend has reached its zenith with people on TV showing shameless delight over the prospect of receiving material things and also immense anger and disappointment when they are deprived of them.

When faced with the prospect of quick money people do not "take care" as Jesus warned, and they are trapped into losing the little they have by investing in scams. The regularity with which we hear of people being duped by such scams is significant. Paul warned, ". . . those who desire to be rich fall into temptation, into a snare, into many senseless and harmful desires that plunge people into ruin and destruction. For the love of money is a root of all kinds of evils. It is through this craving that some have wandered away from the faith and pierced themselves with many pangs" (1 Timothy 6:9, 10).

Yet the advertising industry seeks to convince us that we absolutely must purchase their wares if we are to be content. Most of these things are unnecessary for us. Luxuries have become necessities within a few months of their introduction to the market. A good example of this is the way people convince themselves that they absolutely must purchase the newest brand of mobile phone because the new features would enable them to become "so much more effective" in life. The words of Jeremiah in a different context are pertinent to us today: "The heart is deceitful above all things, and desperately sick; who can understand it?" (Jeremiah 17:9).

One of the most prestigious international banks in Sri Lanka advertises what they call "lifestyle loans" with the slogan, "Don't ask, 'Why?' Ask, 'Why not?'" If you want a new set of furniture, the question to ask is not, "Why should I buy this?" but "Why shouldn't I buy this, considering that the bank is willing to give me a loan?" The credit culture makes it possible to purchase things even when we do not have money. And sometimes the advertising industry uses covetousness as a means of getting people to buy what they push. Today I was watching some cricket on TV, and I noticed how the motivation used in advertising a brand of cars was envy. Envy is considered an appropriate reason to purchase a vehicle!

I realized afresh the seriousness of the way our market-driven culture has affected us when I talked to a Christian leader from the former East Germany. She said that the church there is struggling to survive with the new freedoms they have. When facing persecution under Communist rule, Christians experienced vibrant community life because they desperately needed each other. Now there is no persecution, and everyone is in a mad rush to become wealthy. This lady told me that God made us to live in community, but he did not make us to pursue wealth. In pursuing wealth people have lost one of life's most precious values: community life. We can become so engrossed in our greed that we forget other more valuable things. In the Parable of the Sower, Jesus described how "the cares of the world and the deceitfulness of riches and the desires for other things enter in and choke the word" (Mark 4:19).

The most graphic story I heard of how greed can get hold of people and control their lives is connected with the estate of Henrietta Garrett of the USA who died at the age of eighty-one, leaving no will and a $17-million estate.

She had only one relative (a second cousin) and very few friends. Yet 2,600 people attempted to prove a relationship and lay claim to her fortune. These people came from forty-seven states in the USA and twenty-nine other countries and were represented by more than 3,000 lawyers.

The things these people did to stake a claim to the estate are astounding. Some committed perjury, some faked family records, and others changed their own names, altered data in church Bibles, and made up tales of illegitimacy. As a result twelve were fined, ten received jail sentences, two committed suicide, and three were murdered.[2] Before we dismiss this story as an extreme case that does not apply to our lives, let me say that I have seen greed cause people to do some things that one would have thought were totally out of character for them. People can become slaves to desire.

Of course, the Bible does not teach that money itself is evil. It is "the love of money" that is evil. When discussing with a friend the values of the simple life, especially in view of the problem of poverty in the world today, he directed me to 1 Timothy 6:17: "As for the rich in this present age, charge them not to be haughty, nor to set their hopes on the uncertainty of riches, but on God, who *richly provides us with everything to enjoy.*" My friend's focus was on the last part of the verse. It is not wrong to enjoy possessions. This verse warns us about falling into the error of some of the false teachers in Paul's time who advocated an ascetic lifestyle because they viewed all earthly things as evil. Paul countered that teaching earlier in the epistle, saying, "For everything created by God is good, and nothing is to be rejected if it is received with thanksgiving, for it is made holy by the word of God and prayer" (1 Timothy 4:4, 5).

The above two texts show us that we can enjoy wealth and what it brings. But we must always remember that wealth is not a big deal. It is uncertain, says Paul; so we must set our hopes on God rather than on wealth.

Overcoming Covetousness through Redeemed Desires

How do we overcome covetousness? The Christian answer to this question is not simply a negative path of prohibition as could be implied by the tenth command itself. Some of the passages we cited above give us clues to how we can do this. Essentially it is all about having the right desires. In Christianity we do not indulge desire, like the sinful hedonist; we don't deny desire, like the ascetic; we redeem desire. We surrender it to God and let him give it back to us so that we can pursue those things that please God and bring joy to our life. But that is the topic of another study!

23

A Conversation between God, Moses, and the People

DEUTERONOMY 5:22–33

AFTER CLIMBING THE LOFTY HEIGHTS of God's revelation, the Ten Commandments, we come to a tender passage talking about the people's very human response to receiving this message and God's response to them. Like the rest of the Bible, this passage brings the lofty truths of God right down to the human level. The conversation between God, Moses, and the people shows a people who are very human with the weaknesses attached to that and a God who understands their feelings and yearns for them with the love of a father.

God's Awesome Word (5:22–27)

The Awesome Giving of the Decalogue (5:22)

Our passage begins with a statement that has been described as the signature at the end of the Decalogue: "These words the LORD spoke to all your assembly at the mountain out of the midst of the fire, the cloud, and the thick darkness, with a loud voice; and he added no more. And he wrote them on two tablets of stone and gave them to me" (5:22). We have already seen how the uniqueness and awesomeness of God's revelation is expressed in statements about God speaking "out of the fire," "out of the cloud," etc. (see the discussions on 4:15 and 4:33). Most of the stipulations of the covenant—such as what is recorded in the rest of this second speech of Deuteronomy (6:1—28:68)—were given to Moses when he was alone with God. But these words were spoken aloud in a most awesome way so that all the people could hear. This caused the people to be very afraid and to marvel that they were not killed (5:24–26).

The signature also says that God "added no more." Of course, God did give the details of the Law later. But the special word, the Decalogue, is now complete. This statement of completion also gives a sense of finality to the Decalogue. As we have said in our discussion of 4:2, the idea of not adding to (and subtracting from) the Word of God includes the idea of having it as our sole authority, of living under it. There was a practice in the church, which is fast dying out, of memorizing the Ten Commandments. Considering how important they are, I believe this is a practice we should bring back to the church.

After giving the Ten Commandments for all to hear, God "wrote them on two tablets of stone and gave them to [Moses]" (5:22b). Scholars suggest that "the use of two tablets probably indicates that Moses was given two copies, not that some of the commandments were on one tablet and some on the other."[1] Stone tablets used in those days were usually large enough for one tablet to hold all of the commandments.

Let me reiterate here that the Bible presents an awesome approach to God's revelation that is missing in the attitude of present-day Christians toward the Bible. We would do well to ask ourselves what this awesomeness should do to the way we handle God's Word. Thoughts that come to me are:

- care in studying it, so that we can understand what it truly means;
- care in obeying what it says;
- conscientious preparation before communicating its truth to others, so that it will be accurately and effectively communicated;
- not claiming Scriptural authority for ideas if we are not certain they are clearly taught in the Scriptures;
- care in not using Scripture to make wild conjectures that may not be implied by what the text says;
- not rejecting things in the Bible that we find difficult to accept.

This and the previous point are covered in Revelation 22:18, 19: "I warn everyone who hears the words of the prophecy of this book: if anyone adds to them, God will add to him the plagues described in this book, and if anyone takes away from the words of the book of this prophecy, God will take away his share in the tree of life and in the holy city, which are described in this book."

In addition we should:

- exercise caution in making statements that might undermine its authority, though that practice is fashionable in some circles;

- humbly admit our inability to solve some problems associated with the Word, such as apparent contradictions and errors, rather than saying that what it says is wrong;
- avoid flippant talk on things related to what is found in the Bible.

I think the Muslims put us to shame here. They treat the Qur'an with so much respect. Of course, they approach it almost like a magical book, whereas for us the Bible is pulsating with life. But we can learn a lesson or two from their approach to their holy book. Once I was in a church in Pakistan seated on the platform before preaching, and during a prayer a leader came up to me and gently asked me to pick up my Bible, which I had kept on the floor. The Christians there had learned to treat the Word with respect.

The People's Response (5:23–27)

Next, Moses describes the people's response to the awesome way in which the Decalogue was given. First, they come to Moses: "And as soon as you heard the voice out of the midst of the darkness, while the mountain was burning with fire, you came near to me, all the heads of your tribes, and your elders" (5:23). What they say is quite strange, but I suppose understandable, considering that they had just witnessed something frightfully amazing.

They first express their sense of relief that they had seen God's glory and had not been killed: "Behold, the LORD our God has shown us his glory and greatness, and we have heard his voice out of the midst of the fire. This day we have seen God speak with man and man still live" (5:24). Many Israelites thought that to see God would mean certain death. When Samson's father Manoah realized that he had encountered God, he told his wife, "We shall surely die, for we have seen God" (Judges 13:22). They fear that more of this would result in their deaths: "Now therefore why should we die? For this great fire will consume us. If we hear the voice of the LORD our God any more, we shall die" (Deuteronomy 5:25). And why? Because no one hears God's voice and lives. "For who is there of all flesh, that has heard the voice of the living God speaking out of the midst of fire as we have, and has still lived?" (5:26).

Obviously they think that Moses is not an ordinary human being, so they say, "Go near and hear all that the LORD our God will say and speak to us all that the LORD our God will speak to you, and we will hear and do it" (5:27). They want Moses as their mediator. Job also expressed the need for a mediator: "For he is not a man, as I am, that I might answer him, that we should come to trial together. There is no arbiter between us, who might lay his hand on us both" (Job 9:32, 33). Here Moses becomes a type of Christ. And Christ becomes the perfect Mediator between God and humans: "For there is one

God, and there is one mediator between God and men, the man Christ Jesus" (1 Timothy 2:5). Unlike during Moses' time, we have Jesus with us always and so have direct access to God through Christ. Hebrews talks about this and twice uses the word "confidence" or "boldness" about our approach to God's throne (Hebrews 4:16; 10:19–22). The fear that the Israelites expressed has been replaced by boldness in Christ.

Though they do not want another such frightening experience of being exposed to the awesome revelation of God, they promise to keep the covenant stipulations. They say, ". . . and we will hear and do it" (Deuteronomy 5:27b). The ensuing record shows that God accepts their words. Yet we are faced with the sad story of how these same people who saw the awesomeness of God and promised to obey him later flagrantly violated this covenant. How much more amazing that today we do the same thing as these Israelites did. We have a fuller revelation of the nature of God than they had. Yet we continue to disobey God, even after receiving his salvation. Ultimately, then, the secret of holiness is not knowledge alone. Indeed, that is vital, but as God wishes in verse 29, what we need most is "a mind . . . to fear [God] and to keep all [his] commandments." Let us then look at God's response to the words of these people.

God's Yearning Love (5:28–30)

Accepting Them with Their Weaknesses (5:28, 30)

We are not certain how correct the response of the Israelites to God's awesome act of revelation was. God sees beyond the external and senses a desire for obedience. Did they not say regarding the commands of God, "We will hear and do it" (5:27b)? These people had rebelled so many times, but God accepts their word and tells Moses, "I have heard the words of this people, which they have spoken to you. They are right in all that they have spoken. . . . Go and say to them, 'Return to your tents'" (5:28, 30).

Here God is like an understanding and loving father. As the psalmist says, "The LORD is like a father to his children, tender and compassionate to those who fear him. For he understands how weak we are; he remembers we are only dust" (Psalm 103:13, 14, NLT). This is what gives us hope when we are overwhelmed by our failures and weaknesses. We go to God and cry to him, telling him that despite our terrible shortcomings we still love him and want to serve him, and he accepts us and heals us and gives us a bright future.

We have found that this attitude is a key to perseverance with drug addicts. Some who had been drug-free for a time and then went back to drugs came back to God, sincerely desiring to return to the path of discipleship. They may fall again, but we will not give up on them. Those who work with such people testify to how people have come back to God for good after ten or fifteen falls. If they are willing to humble themselves before God, there is always hope for them. As for Israel, they dabbled with idolatry for centuries, but after returning from their final exile they never went back to worshipping idols.

God's Yearning for Souls (5:29)

Verse 29 gives us a rich picture of the tender and yearning compassion of our loving heavenly Father. This is the all-knowing God speaking. God knows these people will soon rebel against him and forfeit the chance to enter the land. But for now he accepts their word, and he expresses his deep yearning for their souls: "Oh, that they would always have hearts like this, that they might fear me and obey all my commands! If they did, they and their descendants would prosper forever" (5:29, NLT).

We see a similar sentiment being expressed by Jesus as he approaches the beloved city of God, Jerusalem, for the last time, this time to be crucified by the people there. Luke says, "And when he drew near and saw the city, he wept over it, saying, 'Would that you, even you, had known on this day the things that make for peace! But now they are hidden from your eyes'" (Luke 19:41, 42). Earlier he had lamented, "O Jerusalem, Jerusalem, the city that kills the prophets and stones those who are sent to it! How often would I have gathered your children together as a hen gathers her brood under her wings, and you would not!" (Luke 13:34). Because they would not, they too would suffer like the generation that left Egypt with Moses. Within four decades of Jesus' words, Jerusalem fell, its glorious temple was burned and leveled to the ground, and most of the city was destroyed.

Today, too, we can sense that God yearns for people to turn to him. While some people impatiently wait for the rapture in order to escape the tribulation, God delays his promised wrapping up of history, yearning for people to come to him. Peter says, "The Lord is not slow to fulfill his promise as some count slowness, but is patient toward you, not wishing that any should perish, but that all should reach repentance" (2 Peter 3:9). This was the sentiment of Paul, too, when he cried, "I have great sorrow and unceasing anguish in my heart. For I could wish that I myself were accursed and cut off from Christ for the sake of my brothers, my kinsmen according to the flesh" (Romans 9:2, 3).

The heroic missionary to the Muslims in India and Iran and a brilliant Bible translator, Henry Martyn (1781–1812), expressed this sentiment well when he said, "The spirit of Christ is the spirit of missions, and the nearer we get to him the more intensely missionary must we become." Shortly after his arrival in Calcutta he wrote in his diary, "Let me burn out for thee." He once viewed a worship ceremony at a Hindu temple. He saw the worshippers prostrating themselves before the images and striking the ground with their foreheads. Martyn wrote, "This excited more horror in me than I can well express." Then he described his response to this horror: "I thought that if I had words I would preach to the multitudes all day if I lost my life for it."[2] He suffered much because of his call and died in his early thirties. But he left an incalculable legacy that has influenced hundreds of thousands of people. Today he is considered one of most heroic figures in the history of the church. Martyn had imbibed the spirit of God's yearning for people

God's Requirement: Fear God and Obey (5:29, 32, 33)
Being Careful to Obey (5:32, 33)

Verse 29 reveals what God wishes for the people to do: "Oh that they had such a mind as this always, to fear me and to keep all my commandments." Verses 32, 33 explain this in even greater detail with a call to be meticulous in keeping the Law and the promise of blessing for doing so:

> You shall be careful therefore to do as the LORD your God has commanded you. You shall not turn aside to the right hand or to the left. You shall walk in all the way that the LORD your God has commanded you, that you may live, and that it may go well with you, and that you may live long in the land that you shall possess.

We have looked at this topic in our discussions of 4:2, 5, 6 and 5:1. The word *shamar,* which appears sixty-five times in Deuteronomy, appears here too, translated as "be careful" (5:32). It is significant that in this book focusing on obedience to God there are so many exhortations about being careful to obey. Certainly in my life I have seen that most of the times I have stumbled, it has been because I was not careful. I have come to understand certain things about the life of holiness, and I know that if I become slack in an area I can begin to slide on a slippery slope that leads to sin. If I am not careful to avoid those steps, I will live to regret it. We cannot be careless when it comes to the life of holiness.

Moses warns about a way we can be careless: ". . . turn[ing] aside to the right hand or to the left." Small forays into enemy territory can lead to major sins. Once we turn aside a bit, we give Satan a foothold and he can then lead us along dangerous paths. Almost no Christian begins an illicit affair saying, "I want to have an affair with this person." Usually it starts in what seems like a healthy relationship. Then there is a temptation to break a rule, usually saying that this is an exception to the rule. From there the slide is quick.

The Fear of the Lord and Obedience (5:29)

Verse 29 brings up an important topic, which also appeared in 4:10: the fear of the Lord. God says, "Oh that they had such a mind as this always, to fear me and to keep all my commandments, that it might go well with them and with their descendants forever!" (5:29). *Fearing God* is the characteristic term for describing Old Testament religion, somewhat like *belief* in the New Testament. One dictionary article describes the fear of God as the "religion of God's people."[3] It is not confined to the Old Testament. An angel in Revelation, who is described as "flying . . . with an eternal gospel to proclaim to those who dwell on earth, to every nation and tribe and language and people," gave a message that includes the fear of God: "Fear God and give him glory, because the hour of his judgment has come, and worship him who made heaven and earth, the sea and the springs of water" (Revelation 14:6, 7).

That the fear of the Lord should be a key theme in the Old Testament should not surprise us because the Old Testament focused a lot on the majesty and holiness of God, and fear is the natural response to such. However, the fear of the Lord in the Bible is liberating; it is not something that binds us with terror. So the Bible describes it as "a fountain of life" (Proverbs 14:27). Essentially this is because of who God is. The fear of the Lord comes from knowing that God rewards those who obey him and punishes those who disobey him. Far from binding us, it opens the door to true freedom. When *the fear of the Lord* is used in this sense it is almost synonymous with *belief.* We entrust ourselves to God and his way, believing what the Scriptures teach about him.

So while one aspect of the fear of the Lord is terror of punishment, the moment we turn from sin to the way of God, the terror is replaced by the joy of living with and for God. So we can cry out with David, "Oh, how abundant is your goodness, which you have stored up for those who fear you" (Psalm 31:19). A financier made ten million dollars by dealing dishonestly with checks. He eventually gave himself up and said, "I'm glad it's over; I've been in prison for fifteen years. Now I'm free." Stanley Jones, commenting on this said, "He was 'free' to go to jail!"[4] When he submitted himself to the police to receive the punishment for his crimes, he felt a freedom he had never known before. How much more free are those who come to God and find that Christ has fully paid for their sins! Indeed, God hates and punishes our sins. But he has also made a way of salvation for us. What folly then to not fear the God who is both Judge and Savior.

There are thirteen references to fearing God in Deuteronomy,[5] and in eleven of those references the fear of God is connected with God's Word, as in the verse we are looking at. Deuteronomy 4:10 says, "Gather the people to me, that I may let them hear my words, *so that they may learn to fear me* all the days that they live on the earth, and that they may teach their children so." In nine of the thirteen passages mentioning fearing God, the need to obey the commands or words of the law is also mentioned, as is the case in our verse (5:29).[6] This cluster of texts presents a triad of hearing the Word, fearing God, and keeping his commands. If you hear the Word of God, you will learn to fear God. And if you fear God you will keep his commandments. One who fears God and desires to please him will regularly seek his guidance through learning from the Word.

I used to lead a Bible study with two new believers. One had been a terrible alcoholic though he was still young and the other a drug addict. After a few months the drug addict went back to drugs. I told the sad news to the other believer. His first response was to say, "He has lost the fear of God."

When people speak of the fear of the divine today, it means something very different than what we mean. Today in the East and the West people go to various gods and occult forces for help, especially for power—power over anxiety about the future (soothsayers), power over enemies (charms), power over our bodies and minds (Transcendental Meditation), power over sickness (psychic healing), and power for challenges people face such as business ventures and exams (temples of gods who help with such). Practices that were common earlier in animistic tribal cultures and in Eastern religions have now become mainstream practices in the West, also.

This fear of the divine and seeking to appease supernatural forces is very different from the Biblical fear of God. The former views the divine in a somewhat utilitarian manner. In order to get something from the divine forces, you follow some ritual, such as making certain offerings or abstaining from eating beef. There is no question of giving one's whole life to these gods. The God of the Bible is personal, and his nature is holy love. He wants to enter into a love relationship with us in which we accept his principles of holiness. This calls for total dedication—so different from the piecemeal commitment to the gods that is popular today.

It is important for us to bear in mind this vastly different understanding of the nature of God among people today. An extra effort must be taken in order to make people understand that the God of the Bible is a personal God whose nature is holy love and that he desires a love relationship with us that encompasses all we do and is characterized by holiness.

The difference in devotion to God and to the spiritual forces popular today is expressed in God's wish that they have "such a mind as this always" (5:29). The word translated "mind" has been defined as "heart; by extension: the inner person, self, the seat of thought and emotion."[7] We are talking about having a life that is dedicated totally to pleasing God every moment. We don't take leave from God. Often we are not with our fellow believers and at such times we may slip into a life of disobedience. For example, we may join in a racist or sexually charged conversation in the office. Though our Christian friends are not there, God is with us always. And he is the one we fear displeasing. So our inner being daily seeks only those things that please God.

God's Spokesman (5:31)

After acceding to the people's request to be spared the awesome experience of receiving God's revelation, God affirms that Moses will continue to be the mediator through whom God will speak to the people: "But you, stand here by me, and I will tell you the whole commandment and the statutes and the rules that you shall teach them, that they may do them in the land that I am giving them to possess" (5:31). God agrees to the people's request and makes Moses the mediator between the people and God.

Do we need such a mediator today? We saw above that Jesus has become the perfect mediator between God and humans. We also know that we have a completed Bible that is sufficient revelation for faith and practice. The Bible is accessible to all Christians, and all may use it and grow to maturity. It is clear then that the need for a mediator exactly like Moses does not exist. But we have always needed people who "teach" God's ways so that the people may "do them." So Moses' job was not only receiving the word; he also had to teach it. God says, "I will tell you the whole commandment and the statutes and the rules that you shall teach them, that they may do them in the land that I am giving them to possess" (5:31). People need to be fed the Word so they can learn how to obey it in the places where they live and work. Three times in Deuteronomy there are instructions to gather and teach the people so they will fear God and obey his commandments (4:10; 6:1, 2; 31:12, 13).

In view of the high place that teaching takes in a leader's activities, it is no surprise that in Paul's list of qualifications for leadership in 1 Timothy, the only ability-related qualification is that a leader should be able to teach (1 Timothy 3:2). The rest of the qualities concern reputation, character, behavior, and family life. I think the list of qualifications asked for today in most churches would sadly be very different from that of Paul.

A gangster who came to Christ was once met by his friends who were dismayed by the change in his life. They yearned to get him back to their fold, and they thought they might succeed if they could get him to lose his temper—in his pre-conversion days he could get quite violent when he got angry. They began to annoy him, and he was beginning to lose his temper. In desperation he prayed to God, "Lord, give me five minutes' leave. I will attend to some business and come back to you." Today's passage, coming as it does immediately following the Ten Commandments, shows us that we have no option to take leave from the path of obedience, even for five minutes.

24

How Fear and Love
Can Make Us Holy

DEUTERONOMY 6:1–5

DEUTERONOMY 6:1–9 IS PART OF Moses' expounding of the Law. But this passage talks about how the Law can truly enter our minds so that it will influence our actions. The idea of objective truths like the teachings of the Bible influencing our behavior has come under much fire. The challenge of having the Word transform people into holy individuals is so great today that I will devote two whole chapters to this short passage.

The Postmodern Challenge

Today many people are saying that what ultimately determines one's actions is not what one believes intellectually but what one feels at the gut level. This attitude has grown during the postmodern era when we are seeing a devaluing of objective truth. People are said to have been tyrannized and their freedom restricted by objective truths (truths arising from outside of us) during the modern era. Examples of objective truths that are said to have tyrannized us are scientific laws, religious dogma, productivity targets, and sales figures to which people were forced to submit. In reaction people have forged what has been called an "instinctually stimulated generation" where "people prefer to feel than to think."[1]

In this environment books are going out of fashion, and statistics are showing that in many economically "developed" and "developing" nations people are reading less and less. The Bible also has taken a beating, with many Christian leaders saying that what we have come to know as Bible teaching is not relevant to today's generation. The Bible reading habits of the average Christian today is nothing like the disciplined "quiet time" habits of Christians of earlier generations. Some Christians are even claiming that we should not aim at such standards in this postmodern generation.

I do not think that we must ignore the postmodern emphases. I believe postmodernism has highlighted features of human nature that the modern era may have neglected but that the Bible regards as important. The Bible has a very important place for subjective experience, and there are Christian movements today that, while seeking to be Biblical, have given a high place to the subjective side of life. The most successful of these is the charismatic movement, which many analysts view as a postmodern movement, though its origins were earlier than the postmodern era. It has attracted many millions of people in every part of the globe. And many growing charismatic groups have a good mix of emphasis on both the subjective and the objective aspects of Christianity.

However, some Christians who have tried to be relevant to postmodern people have left out chunks of the whole counsel of God. They have taken a path that has greatly reduced the authority of Scripture for daily life and that has diluted the gospel by discounting some key aspects of Biblical truth. Some are not doing much Bible teaching, saying that people are not interested in that. I believe that Deuteronomy 6:1–9 has much to say that will help us navigate our lives and ministries in the postmodern era. It challenges us to stick to the orthodox attitude of submission to the Scriptures, and it also challenges us to find new ways of communicating Scripture, as our discussion on creative, sensual communication (6:8, 9) will show.

The Bible says that objective truth does influence action. David said, "I have stored up your word in my heart, that I might not sin against you" (Psalm 119:11). The use of heart (*leb*) here suggests that more than mere intellectual knowledge is involved in hiding the Word. Our passage gives a good description of how the Word can truly influence one's behavior. It says that fear for God (Deuteronomy 6:2) and love for God with all our heart, soul, and strength become the basis of all we do (6:5). Both fear and love have an objective side (they are based on facts) and a subjective side (they involve our emotions and our feelings). Similarly, love is an emotion that gives us a gut feeling of wanting to please the one we love.

The Word Is Given for Obedience (6:1)

Verses 1–3 traverse territory that we have already covered in this book. First we are introduced to the topic of chapter 6. It is about obeying God's commands: "Now this is the commandment, the statutes and the rules that the LORD your God commanded me to teach you, that you may do them in the land to which you are going over, to possess it" (6:1). In the Hebrew (as in the ESV but not in the NIV) the first of the three words describing the Law, "commandment" (*mitsevah*), is singular. Probably this is intended to be taken in a more general way to refer to the whole Law, as Keil and Delitzsch suggest, or to the principle underlying the whole Law, as Peter Craigie suggests. In that case the next two plural words refer to the details of the Law. The word translated "statutes" (*choq*) means "prescription, a clear communication of what someone should do."[2] "Rules" (*mishepat*) means "regulation, prescription, specification."[3]

Moses says that the Law was given by God to Moses so that he would teach them to the people and so that they "may do them in the land." The end of the giving of the Law is obedience. Today people are not accustomed to taking the rules and the like seriously enough to obey them fully. Individuals respect the holy book of their religion and believe that what it says is true. They will fight to ensure that it is revered. But that is because of their commitment to their tradition that shapes their identity, not because of their desire to obey all that is taught in the holy book.

Therefore, some people may battle the legalization of homosexual marriage because it challenges the Judeo-Christian roots on which their society has been founded (a cause well worth fighting for). But they will also commit adultery in their personal lives. They do not want the teachings of the Bible discarded, but they do not feel bad about not obeying those teachings in their personal lives.

To use another example, the Bible is very clear that lying is wrong. Psalm 101:7 says, "No one who practices deceit shall dwell in my house; no one who utters lies shall continue before my eyes." Yet many Christians in Sri Lanka lie quite unashamedly. Recently a church member obtained a forged passport in order to go abroad. She came to her pastor and told him what she was going to do and asked him to prophesy as to whether she would get caught when she went through immigration. He "inquired of the Lord" and said she would not get caught. But she did get caught and ended up in prison. Her husband then blamed the pastor for making a false prophecy! This is an extreme case of a common scenario in the church today. People have become attracted by the power of God to meet their need and so become Christians. But they have not understood that becoming a Christian involves obeying the Bible.

This is not a problem confined to Asia. Christian young people in the West know in their heads that sex outside of marriage is identified as sin in the Bible. But daily the media bombard them with the idea that sexual relations are normal and necessary for a healthy life, even for singles. This message is presented so attractively that it has a huge impact on Christian people; often this impact is greater than the impact of the Bible to which the Christians are not exposed in such a powerful manner. Therefore sex outside of marriage is common among Christians in the West. Somehow there seems to be the idea that truth is not absolutely binding.

There is a trend away from holding to absolutes today. Therefore we need to present truths in the Bible from the context of absoluteness in which they are found in the Bible. So in the Old Testament adultery is punishable with death. That suggests that it is absolutely serious. But many Christians today have dropped judgment from their worldview and have lost the sense of the absolute seriousness of holiness.

Transformation through Fear (6:2, 3)

A key aspect of living under the absoluteness of God's Word is having the fear of the Lord. In 6:2 Moses describes the result of his giving the laws and the people obeying them: ". . . that you may fear the LORD your God, you and your son and your son's son, by keeping all his statutes and his commandments, which I command you, all the days of your life, and that your days may be long" (6:2). Keeping the commandments is an expression of fearing the Lord. We have looked at the meaning and significance of fearing the Lord in our discussion of 5:29.

Fear is an emotion, a gut feeling, caused by objective truths that are too obvious to ignore. The objective truth of the sight of an unchained tiger close to you will spark a gut feeling that will stimulate immediate action to get to a safe place. So in the Bible objective truths cause subjective feelings that motivate action. It is not a question of either subjective or objective; rather it is a question of both the objective and the subjective.

When warning the disciples not to give up evangelism because of persecution Jesus said, "And do not fear those who kill the body but cannot kill the soul. Rather fear him who can destroy both soul and body in hell" (Matthew 10:28). Fear may not be the noblest motive for obedience, but it is a wise motive. Wise people avoid dangerous situations that are certain to harm them.

Today we are faced with the challenge of communicating truths that elicit fear in people, such as the doctrine of judgment. After the Asian tsunami there has been a lot of talk of early warning systems. People must be warned of impending catastrophes. Judgment is such a catastrophe for those who are not ready for it. Yet people do not like to hear this message today. Francis Schaeffer explained that people have built a roof over their heads to shield them from the powerful rays of the unpleasant truths that confront them—such as the existence of a holy God to whom humans are accountable (see the discussion on 8:18–20). That way they can live with some comfort by not being exposed to uncomfortable truths. Schaeffer says our job is to "take the roof off."

Verse 3 presents the need to be careful to obey the laws and the blessings that accrue from such obedience: "Hear therefore, O Israel, and be careful to do them, that it may go well with you, and that you may multiply greatly, as the LORD, the God of your fathers, has promised you, in a land flowing with milk and honey." These are familiar themes in Deuteronomy. We have looked at hearing and obeying in our discussion on 5:1, at being careful to obey in our discussion on 4:2–6, and at the rewards of obedience in our discussion on 2:32–33.

Transformation through Love: the *Shema* (6:4, 5)

Verses 4, 5 record what has become the key confession of the Jews. It is called the *Shema*, which comes from the Hebrew word for "hear," with which it begins. Moses says, "Hear, O Israel: The LORD our God, the LORD is one. You shall love the LORD your God with all your heart and with all your soul and with all your might."

Personal and Propositional Revelation

The people are addressed six times in Deuteronomy with the words, "Hear, O Israel" (5:1; 6:3, 4; 9:1; 20:3; 27:9). Chris Wright says, "It is . . . a constant reminder that Israel is a people summoned by God to hear God's Word. They were not merely spectators at a divine 'show,' but recipients of the divine revelation in words. They were to *hear* the truth and respond to it." Wright says that this goes against the common idea today that religious truth is personal, not propositional—that is, "the view that God does not reveal timeless truths propositionally, but simply acts in love and leaves to each individual his or her own interpretative conclusions as we respond in personal relationship to him and to one another."

This "postmodern hermeneutic" reflects the postmodern discounting of the value of objective truth. It is right in bringing in the personal aspect of God's revelation. Verse 5 shows that God's Word is to be obeyed out of a personal relationship with him. Wright says, "Such reductionist views of revelation ignore the reality that truth in human experience is *both propositional and personal* and deny the biblical emphasis on both. Deuteronomy 6:4–5 is one whole sentence; nothing could be more 'propositional' than 6:4 and nothing more 'personal' than 6:5." When we read the Scriptures we learn truths about God, and we also deepen our personal relationship with him. Both our intellect and our emotions are involved in this process.

Faced with the charge from postmodernists that Christianity does not fully satisfy human yearning for subjective spirituality, when we look to the Scriptures we find that the Bible was not defective. It was our understanding of the Bible and our practice of Biblical religion that was defective. Every generation has the challenge to be fully Biblical. Usually the church of every generation misses some vital aspect of Christianity. Sometimes people outside the church discover the need for stressing that. Christians will discover that what these people are looking for is satisfied only through Biblical religion. The challenge from outside may help the church rediscover a treasure that it had buried and neglected.

The Only God (6:4)

Because there is no verb in the Hebrew in this verse, it can be translated in many different ways, as the footnotes to most English Bibles indicate. We will follow the rendering in the ESV and the NIV: "The LORD our God, the LORD is one." This could mean one or more of several ideas. It could mean that Yahweh is incomparable. Or it could mean that Yahweh is united in his will and purpose—what Wright describes as the integrity of God. More probably it means that Yahweh is the only God, not only for Israel but for the whole universe. Therefore Israel must have no other God. This phrase could also mean that God is a unity—one and not many. I think that the idea of God being the one and only is what is being communicated here.

Again Chris Wright has helpful words for us. He points out that Baal, the name for the Canaanite gods, was a very general name. The "term 'Baal' could be applied to various divine powers. The Canaanites could never have said, 'Baal is one,' or even comprehended the idea of such a statement." Wright summarizes the teaching of this text as follows:

> Our text is asserting, quite distinctively from the surrounding polytheistic religions, that Yahweh is God, Yahweh is our God, and Yahweh is one God. He is a singular God, with his own integrity, character, will and purpose; one God whom we are to worship.[4]

We have looked into this theme in detail in our discussion of the first two commandments of the Decalogue (5:6–10). In this pluralistic era this is a truth that needs to be specially emphasized, explained, and defended.

Loving God with Our Whole Being (6:5)

In verse 5 we have what Jesus called "the great and first commandment" (Matthew 22:36–38; see also Mark 12:28–30). It is a command to love God completely: "You shall love the LORD your God with all your heart and with all your soul and with all your might."

It is precarious to try to develop a theology of the parts or faculties of a human being based on the call to love God with heart, soul, and might. Earl Kalland helpfully comments that this verse "is not a study in faculty psychology. It is rather a gathering of terms to indicate the totality of a person's commitment of self in the purest and noblest intentions of trust and obedience toward God." "Might" (in some translations, "strength") does not usually appear in the Old Testament along with "heart" and "soul." That is further evidence to believe that the Bible does not clearly present the human being as being made up of three faculties—heart, soul, and strength. Besides Jesus added a fourth word—"mind"—to "heart," "soul," and "strength" in Mark 12:30. However, it would be good to know what the Israelites meant when they used these words.

Though today we see the heart as the seat of emotions, in Biblical times "heart" (*lebab*) referred to what we today would call the mind. Chris Wright says, "The heart was the organ of the will. It was where you made decisions and choices." The "soul" (*nephesh*) referred to "the inner person, you as you know yourself to be." Wright explains that the phrase "with all your strength," translated literally, means "with your very muchness." As Wright says, "There are no limits on loving God. You can never say you have loved him enough."[5]

But can you command such heart love? To answer that question we must first look at what loving God means in the Bible. First, it is not a love that we create out of nothing. Its source is the love with which God has loved us. As John said, "We love because he first loved us" (1 John 4:19). He acts to save us because he loves us (Romans 5:8) and also fills us with his love (Romans 5:5). A change takes place within us that is brought about by the Holy Spirit. He gives us new life, and our eyes are open to see the beauty of God. John Piper puts it like this: "You do not merely decide to love him. Something changes inside of you, and as a result he becomes compellingly attractive. His glory—his beauty—compels your admiration and delight. He becomes your supreme treasure. You love him."[6]

We respond to this revelation of the beauty of God by loving him back. But in doing that, the love we use is the love that God puts in us. Paul said, ". . . the love of Christ controls us" (2 Corinthians 5:14). How this expresses itself was discussed in our treatment of 4:4–6 when we expounded on what it means to cling to God.

Yet we cannot do justice to such love from God without loving God with our whole being. The great English hymn-writer Isaac Watts (1674–1748) put it well in his beloved hymn, "When I Survey the Wondrous Cross." He ends this hymn with the words, "Love so amazing, so divine, demands my soul, my life, my all." Anything short of total loyalty would bring in things that eat into our love relationship with God and spoil it. God is Lord of the universe. He made everything there is for his glory. So if there is anything in life that we do not surrender to God's will, we violate the true nature of that thing. Such an action is destined to result in our being unfulfilled.

So when God asks us to love him with our whole being, he has our own welfare in mind. We can regard the command to love God with our whole being as actually a command for us to be fully human, to be what we are made to be. It is like a command to someone who loves the beach to take a few days off to rest by the beach in order to recover from exhaustion. Or it is like a command to a hungry person to eat a delicious meal. Once we have experienced God's love and know what a wonderful thing it is, a command to total love would not be viewed as a burdensome obligation. It would be viewed as an invitation to self-actualization—to freedom, joy, and finding ourselves.

But why does God have to command this? We need to be nudged in this direction through commands because we have a nature that is tainted by sin. Satan and the world's values work on this sinful nature of ours to attempt to get us to follow a sinful path that will destroy our relationship with God. We are tempted to keep small areas of our lives from God, and even though they are very small they will eat into our commitment and ruin our life. So in some ways the call to love God with our whole being is a call to total dedication. But for us total dedication is much more than obedience to some rules. It has to do with a relationship with God that oozes with love. To be totally dedicated to God is to be madly in love with him.

The passages I used above in explaining our understanding of loving God are from the New Testament. But the idea that we love because God first loved us and that our obedience is a response to that is not confined to the New Testament. These are very important themes in Deuteronomy, too. In our introduction to the Ten Commandments we said that the foundation for our obedience is the redemptive acts of God (5:6) and that our obedience is a loving response to the one who loved us. Explicit statements to love God appear at least eight times in Deuteronomy.[7] Deuteronomy has a lot to say about obedience, but this obedience springs from love. This is why I have subtitled this book *Loving Obedience to a Loving God*. The call to love we are now considering comes in a passage whose main theme is obeying the commandments. Genuine love for God results in obedience. Jesus often talked of the connection between loving God and obedience (John 14:15, 23; 15:14). John even defined love in terms of keeping God's commands: "For this is the love of God, that we keep his commandments" (1 John 5:3a).

A visiting preacher arrived early at the church he was preaching at. He struck up a conversation with a member of the congregation. This member told the preacher that he loved God so much that he was willing to die for him. The preacher noticed the gusto with which this member sang the hymns and was very impressed by him. In his sermon the preacher mentioned what an inspiration it had been for him to come to this church and meet such dedicated members who were willing to die for Christ. Other members of the congregation, however, knew that despite the profession of love for Christ this member was extremely disobedient to Christ in his family life, at his workplace, and even at church. His profession of love had a hollow ring to it because it was not backed by obedience.

May our obedience to God be sincere and genuine!

25

How the Word Can Make Us Holy

DEUTERONOMY 6:6–9

ONE OF THE GREATEST CHALLENGES facing the church today is how to get the Word into the hearts and minds of people. People forget most of what they hear in a sermon. They receive so much more information and ideas packaged in very attractive and impacting ways from the world around them. Do we have any hope of success in getting people to grasp and digest the truths of the Word? Deuteronomy 6:6–9 gives us clues on how we can meet this challenge.

Internalize the Word (6:6)

In verse 6 Moses presents what one's relationship with the Word should be: "And these words that I command you today shall be on your heart." The word translated "heart" (*lebab*) refers to what we would call the mind, the organ of the will where decisions and choices are made. This verse is saying that the person's thinking and behavior is markedly affected by the Word. We are calling this the internalizing of the Word. John Wesley liked to call the Methodists "Bible Christians." That is what Moses wanted the Israelites to be. David said, "I have stored up your word in my heart, that I might not sin against you" (Psalm 119:11).

In the previous chapter we saw how a person can be oriented in a direction that makes it possible for the Word to do its work. This orientation comes when we fear and love the Lord. That gives us the gut feelings that motivate us to respond to the truths learned in the Word. We saw that getting people to obey the Word is a huge challenge today. For this the Word must go into the heart.

Teach the Word (6:7a)

Verse 7 first says, "You shall teach them diligently to your children." "Teach them diligently" is the translation of a single word that means "repeat," and this is reflected in the NLT rendering: "Repeat them again and again to your children." The truths of God's Word might not go into the mind and transform our lives after one hearing. Therefore they need to be repeated often, and the primary place where this takes place in the lives of children is the home.

The advertising industry has understood the importance of repetition in helping children to acquire truth. Raymond McHenry reports that "researchers in San Diego monitored ninety-five hours of weekday afternoon and Saturday morning television shows targeted at children. The two-month study revealed children are exposed to twenty-one commercials an hour."[1] This is a case of persistent and repetitive instruction. I have no doubt that the most influential Bible teacher in my life has been my mother. I believe that my other four siblings, all of whom love and serve the Lord, would testify to the same thing. My mother was a convert from Buddhism in her teenage years. I do not think she ever had a course on how to study the Bible. But she learned to read the Bible cover to cover. She faithfully gathered us together on most mornings and went through the Bible, Old Testament and New Testament, with us. What we learned there gave us the worldview that enabled us to evaluate what the world around us confronted us with. My wife did the same thing with our children. She went through an excellent children's resource, *The Picture Bible*, with our children.[2] After they were able to read, they themselves went through it.

According to the Bible, teaching is not solely a mother's task. Proverbs often speaks of the value of a father's instruction (1:8; 4:1; 6:20; 13:1; 15:5). Proverbs 1:8 says, "Hear, my son, your father's instruction, and forsake not your mother's teaching." Considering that this follows the pattern of Hebrew poetry we need to be careful about making too much of the difference between a "father's instruction" and a "mother's teaching." But the word translated "instruction" often takes the meaning of correction, chastisement, or discipline.[3] It is used in connection with the type of teaching found in Wisdom Literature, like Proverbs. The word translated "teaching" is "*torah*" (literally "direction"), which is used for the Law.[4] Possibly the mother did the more systematic teaching that takes place in a routine manner, while the father's instruction focused more on the application of Biblical truth to situations in the lives of the children, including their disciplining. Both father and mother should be involved in the teaching of the children. The teaching is to be done "diligently," which, again, has the idea of repeating. This is not an occasional thing that parents do; it is a regular part of the life of the family. "Train up a child in the way he should go; even when he is old he will not depart from it" (Proverbs 22:6).

The teaching function should be extended to the church too, especially in places where most of the members have not had the privilege of growing up in Christian homes. The church provides spiritual parents to those who don't have earthly parents to perform that task. This can be done through the Sunday school, church Bible studies, and Sunday worship.

Discuss the Word (6:7b)

Second, Deuteronomy 6:7b says that the Scriptures should be the constant topic of conversation among the faithful in their day-to-day lives: "You . . . shall talk of them when you sit in your house, and when you walk by the way, and when you lie down, and when you rise." The picture we have is of constant input into the lives of children.

Word-Centered Conversation

Different aspects of family life are included. They are to talk about the Word when they "sit in [their] house." Mealtime in the home is an ideal time for such conversation. Similarly, having meals with our spiritual children can provide us with a wonderful opportunity to communicate the truths of God to them. In the Gospels (especially Luke) and Acts a very important place is given to meals, and some of Jesus' teaching took place during these meals. Mealtimes usually have an atmosphere of informality and warmth that is well suited to foster discussion.

In many cultures today "walk[ing] by the way" would need to be substituted by "driving in the family vehicle." This is a wonderful time for good conversation, when there is no TV, no phone calls, and no Internet (though competition can come from car radios, Walkmans, MP3s, and iPods).

This principle can be extended to our ministry with those whom we disciple. Paul virtually conducted a traveling Bible school with his many traveling companions whom he mentored. In my days in seminary I belonged to a discipleship group with my professor, Dr. Robert Coleman, who became a spiritual father to me. He would take the members of our group with him when he went on ministry assignments. We had some memorable conversations in his large station wagon during those trips. Some of my happiest memories of travel have been when I traveled with young Youth for Christ staff and volunteers and had wonderful opportunities to chat with them about the things of God.

They are then told to talk about the Law "when you lie down, and when you rise." They are to think about God at the start and the end of the day. That will help us to be godly all through the day. By doing so we affirm that all of life is under God's lordship and that God is with us. Therefore we do not need to fear because God will look after us. We often disobey because we lose our trust in God to see us through a situation. The messages of the world overcome the influence of the Word of God. The best way to counteract this is to constantly be exposed to the Word.

In Old Testament times when the people were not bombarded through the media by as many un-Biblical messages as we are today, so much more time was spent discussing the Word than today. Considering the volume and content of what we are exposed to these days, we should be spending more time than the people in Old Testament times counteracting the anti-Christian messages that we encounter. Clearly, this is an area that needs urgent attention.

So the Word is to be the topic of discussion in ordinary conversation. This can happen in different ways. Today we do a lot of sharing of testimonies in conversation, which is indeed a good thing. But so is what I might call Word-directed testimony, when we talk about what we learned from the Bible. Then we can discuss passages we find difficult to understand. We can discuss difficult issues we face and see what the Word has to say about them. When we see a movie or a program on TV or an advertisement, we can evaluate it using criteria from the Word as our benchmark. Because we seek to be Word-directed in everything we do, we discuss what the Word has to say about each situation we face.

Sadly, in today's world family discussion has gone out of vogue. Writing in 1970 in an article entitled "The High Price of TV," Joseph Bayly quotes Dr. Graham Blaine, the chief psychiatrist in the student health service at Harvard University, as saying that "the most serious problem of TV is not poor programming, but that it has destroyed the average family's exchange of views and information at the evening meal. People are anxious to get to their favorite program, he says, and so they hurry to finish eating." Bayly says, "What happened during the day, the little things, and bigger matters are never discussed."[5]

There is a great joy that comes from just chatting about the things of God with others who love Christ. For example, C. S. Lewis goes into raptures as he talks about this in his book *The Four Loves*.[6] In a letter he says, "Is any pleasure on earth as great as a circle of Christian friends by a fire?"[7] Some of the most pleasant memories I have of Christian ministry are occasions when I just sat with colleagues—either my peers or younger staff and volunteers—simply chatting about the things of God. During my accountability group meeting a lot of the time is spent discussing issues we face in personal, church, and national life from a Biblical perspective. I sometimes let our team and committee meetings drag on with conversations beyond the plain business to time spent on relaxed Word-influenced conversation. Some of the happiest times in the life of a family are at the dinner table, when the washing up waits while they talk about the things that matter most in life.

In today's world the Internet has provided a meaningful way of conversation to a lot of people, as the word *chat*, used for Internet communication, indicates. I know that my son has good discussions about the things of the Lord with his friends by chatting over the Internet. Both of my children have asked me questions over the Internet that have provided me with what to me is a thrilling opportunity to enter into serious discussion with them.

Small Group Bible Studies

The small group Bible study combines both the teaching and discussing aspects of handling the Word. It is one of the most important means to fostering spiritual growth. Here people are not only confronted with the Word but are also forced to apply it to their lives at home, at school, at work, on the playground, and in the neighborhood. The small group Bible study gives the participants an opportunity to see how the belief that the Word is authoritative for daily life works out in practice. They see how the Bible speaks to daily life, and they become skilled in looking at everything they face in life from the perspective of what the Bible teaches. They develop what Harry Blamires called "the Christian mind."[8]

My observation both in our Youth for Christ ministry and in our church has been that all the people converted from other faiths whose lives and behaviors have been genuinely transformed have been part of a small group that studied the Word and applied it to daily life. The Bible study helped them learn the way Biblical Christians live.

We must restore the small group Bible study in the life of the church. Today there is a fresh emphasis on small groups in the church. People call them by different names—cell groups, house churches, house fellowships, house groups, G-12 groups, living unit groups, class meetings, etc. However, in many groups today insufficient time is given for Bible study. Usually there is a time of music-oriented praise, a time for sharing testimonies and presenting and praying for needs, and a small devotional to round off the meeting. The participants do not really get an opportunity to grapple with the Word.

Communicate It Creatively, Sensually (6:8, 9)

Deuteronomy 6:8, 9 present creative uses of symbolic visual aids to communicate the Word and to help people to be constantly aware of it. As these ways involve the senses, I am describing it as sensual communication. First, Moses talks of armbands and headbands: "You shall bind them as a sign on your hand, and they shall be as frontlets between your eyes" (6:8). Then he talks about inscriptions at the entrance to house and property: "You shall write them on the doorposts of your house and on your gates" (6:9).

There is some question among scholars as to whether these verses were intended to be followed literally or metaphorically. I believe that they were to be used literally because this type of thing was regularly practiced in the ancient Near East at that time. Israel's neighbors used it in a superstitious way, just like people use good luck charms and talismans today. But in the Bible it is used as a reminder of covenant identity and the covenant responsibility to obey God's Word. It is interesting how the Bible invests holy meanings to practices that pagans used for their religious rituals and redeems them for God's glory. Today we are sometimes afraid to do this because of the pagan connotations attached to these practices. Indeed we must be careful when we venture into these areas. But in the Bible there is such a passion to communicate God's truth that whatever means is able to break through to people's hearts is used so long as it does not harm the receiver of the message.

Artists use God-given abilities to express themselves. Sometimes pagan artists produce beautiful art that sadly communicates a wrong message. We can use the same art form, which is familiar to the people, to communicate the Christian gospel. A passion to communicate God's truth should cause us to use our creativity in finding the best ways to communicate the message. When our Youth for Christ ministry decided to concentrate on non-Christians who have no contact with the church, we had to relearn our music and drama from non-Christian teachers because the styles used by those we were trying to reach were very different from those used by Christians.

Moses lived in a pre-literate society in which people did not read much. At that time sensual ways of communication—that is, those that use the five senses (sight, smell, sound, touch, and taste)—came to the fore. Today many societies could be called post-literate, as people are reading less and less. So we, too, may need to make a fresh effort to look for ways that use the five senses as in Old Testament times. Sensual ways of communication were very important in Old Testament religion. Here are some examples:

- Incense, which was seen as bringing joy in everyday life in Biblical times (Proverbs 27:9), was used in the temple partly perhaps to counteract the smell from the animal sacrifices but mainly because Orientals loved sweet odors.⁹ It gave a sweet-smelling pleasantness to worship. Incense also symbolized the ascending prayers of God's people (Psalm 141:2; Revelation 8:3–5).

- Festival meals were fashioned so as to communicate specific truths, and certain things were eaten simply because of their symbolic value. Bitter herbs were eaten during the Passover to symbolize the bitterness of the slavery from which the people were delivered (Exodus 1:14; 12:8; Numbers 9:11). Unleavened bread, which was bread prepared in haste, was also eaten at the Passover to remind the people of their hurried exit from Egypt and also of the pilgrim character of their lives (Exodus 12:11, 20, 34, 39).
- Actually the festivals, which played a very important part in Jewish life, were educational events. As A. W. Morton explains, "Through participation in the festivals, the children would learn their meaning, and in this way the festivals became a part of life indelibly etched upon their minds. The festivals were unique opportunities for teaching the young the great truths of the Jewish faith. They provided a dramatic, vivid and intrinsically interesting way of teaching."¹⁰
- We know that the prophets acted out their message so that it would make a graphic impact upon the people. This was particularly seen in the acted parables of Isaiah, Jeremiah, and Ezekiel. For example, God asked Jeremiah to buy a linen waistcloth and cause it to be spoiled even before its first wash, to show how the Lord would spoil the pride of Judah (Jeremiah 13:1–11).
- Different musical instruments communicated different messages to the people. The trumpet, for example, was sometimes used in music, but more often it was used to proclaim a message through its loudness. It was used as a summons to battle (Jeremiah 4:19) and to proclaim victory in battle (1 Samuel 13:3). In the context of worship, trumpets along with cymbals were used to accompany exuberant praise (1 Chronicles 15:28).

Always, however, truth is primary. What we want is to get the unchanging message out to people. Sometimes people get so engrossed in the art form that the message gets neglected, and all the time is spent perfecting the art form without much interest in getting the Word across to people's hearts.¹¹

There have been abuses of the symbolic in history. The Protestant Reformation was a reaction to these abuses. The symbols assumed a magical quality, and people began to give to the symbol the place that should go to what the symbol symbolized. That happens when religiosity takes the place of a living faith. Deuteronomy 6 presents a corrective to this by the call in verse 5 to love the Lord with our whole being. If that love is there, the symbols will serve as *aids to* devotion. Without it they will become *objects of* devotion.

Adam Clarke, writing about 200 years ago, saw this as an example of God's accommodation to human weakness: "God, who knows how slow of heart we are to understand, graciously orders us to make use of every help, and through the means of things sensible [or sensual], to rise to things spiritual." We are to use creativity in helping people remember the truth. We need to keep in mind that visual creative means of communicating truth leave one with a much greater likelihood of internalizing the truth and remembering it. We do this a lot with children, but we seem to think that adults do not need such things. Perhaps this is indicative of the overly rational orientation that Protestantism developed over the centuries.

The Protestant church still has several symbolic items in its life that have been derived directly from the Scriptures—like the Lord's Supper and baptism. To these we could add symbolic items that help us remember the Word of God. Calligraphy with Scripture verses on our walls was common at one time. I was encouraged when young people began to wear bands with the letters WWJD, from the motto, "What would Jesus do?" While things like this could become meaningless fads, I believe many use them out of a sincere desire to be obedient to God.

Banners in church buildings can be used to help highlight important truths. When Kent Hughes preached through a book at College Church in Wheaton, Illinois, a banner hung in the sanctuary that represented the message of that book. Those banners provided the covers for many of the books of the Preaching the Word series, of which this book is a part.

When I am struggling with applying a Scriptural truth in my life, I sometimes have that truth prominently displayed near my desk or where I pray. When I took a sabbatical to write a commentary on Acts, I pasted, right in front of my computer, a card with a sketch of the head of Christ and the words, "Seek his face continually" (Psalm 105:4 NASB). I needed to remind myself that in my pursuit of excellence I must not neglect my pursuit of God.

A young Youth for Christ trainee told me that when he wears a YFC T-shirt he is always alert to make sure he is on his best behavior because he does not want to give a bad name to YFC by what he does. The symbol identifies him as a Christian and challenges him to live up to his profession. In the same discussion another young person told me that it is such a shame to see singers on TV wearing large crosses round their neck but dressed in indecent attire and singing songs with terrible lyrics. Symbols can be used well or can be abused. But if the focus of our lives is on loving God with our whole being (Deuteronomy 6:5), then the stage is set for symbols as aids to devotion.

We need to also consider the communication of Scripture through means such as the dramatic reading of Scripture, film, and drama. The phenomenal success of the *Jesus* film (distributed by Campus Crusade for Christ) and of

Mel Gibson's *The Passion of the Christ* attests to the value of using these types of media for communicating the message of the Bible.

I have often used the dramatic reading of Scripture during expository preaching and can attest to the effectiveness of this medium. For example, in our evangelistic camps, which introduce the Christian message to non-Christian youth, I am often asked to speak on the fall. I usually give an expository message on the story of the fall of Adam and Eve in Genesis 3. I use a team with individuals representing the different characters in the story and a narrator and have them read dramatically the part I am about to expound. I think it helps to keep the attention of the hearers and to get the message across.

The influence of the media is such that culture is once again moving to what we might call a visual-oriented direction. People are not reading as much as they used to. People did not read much in the time of Moses also, but for very different reasons. It is possible that many Israelites were not literate during Moses' time.[12] Certainly most people did not have access to books. Today, too, people are most used to receiving information through sensual means. So the use of symbols and other sensual means has become a necessity in today's world.

26

How to Avoid the Pitfalls of Prosperity

DEUTERONOMY 6:10–25

IT IS SIGNIFICANT that in Moses' basic description of faithfulness (6:1–25) there is a long section about the pitfalls of prosperity. Though there is much preaching today about the prospects and promise of prosperity, the Biblical focus on material possessions was more on warning people about its dangers. Jesus said, "How difficult it is for those who have wealth to enter the kingdom of God! For it is easier for a camel to go through the eye of a needle than for a rich person to enter the kingdom of God" (Luke 18:24, 25). As Erwin Lutzer, pastor of the Moody Church in Chicago, has said, "Few people have the spiritual resources needed to be both wealthy and godly."[1]

Our passage also has much to say on this topic. The value of this passage is that it gives specific ways in which we can avoid the traps that the prosperous face.

Maintain the Grace Perspective (6:10–12)

In Deuteronomy 6:10–25 Moses knows that the people might forget God after they acquire all the wealth of the promised land. He first puts the emphasis on grace, which is one of the most important themes of Deuteronomy.[2] He begins by showing that by giving the land to the people, God is fulfilling a promise made centuries earlier: "And when the LORD your God brings you into the land that he swore to your fathers, to Abraham, to Isaac, and to Jacob, to give you—with great and good cities that you did not build . . . "

(6:10a). This covers a period of about 650 years. The newly rich (which is what Moses' hearers were soon going to become) could get blinded by their temporary prosperity and lose the long view of a God who works in history to keep his promises. This could result in their compromising their principles for temporary gain. Their sudden wealth could cause greed and confidence in themselves, resulting in their disregarding God and his commands. That would be folly, for they would be putting their trust in a very unstable entity unlike the God of the ages.

Verses 10b, 11 describe the land they are going to receive, and in the process they present two themes that again accentuate God's grace to the people, as the following table shows:

Figure 26.1: Divine Grace in Receiving the Land

	The Greatness of the Land	The Blessing Was Not Earned
6:10b	. . . with great and good cities	. . . that you did not build
6:11a	. . . houses full of all good things	. . . that you did not fill
6:11b	. . . cisterns	. . . that you did not dig
6:11c	. . . vineyards and olive trees	. . . that you did not plant

The repetition of "that you did not" is clearly intended to show the people that they were not to take the credit for their successes. This in turn would have an effect on the people that would result in their ultimate good.

Then Moses warns them about the possibility of forgetting God's grace: ". . . when you eat and are full, then take care lest you forget the LORD, who brought you out of the land of Egypt, out of the house of slavery" (6:11, 12). Once more we encounter the Hebrew word *shamar*, meaning "pay careful attention to," which comes so many times in Deuteronomy. This time the people are asked to be careful not to forget the Lord who redeemed them from such a terrible state. It is easy to take the credit for our successes when things are going well for us. Others notice our success and speak about it, and without deflecting the honor from ourselves to God, we enjoy the honor so much that we do not want to miss the opportunity of being the object of envy and admiration (see the discussion on 8:11–18; 9:4–6).

Proverbs 16:18 says, "Pride goes before destruction, and a haughty spirit before a fall." In our work with drug addicts, when we see someone who has been off drugs and professed faith in Christ getting proud, we get really concerned. They become very critical of other Christians. They act as if they are proud of the way they have faced life with all its problems and somehow made it without resorting to the hypocrisy of church folks who have an appearance of godliness but whose lives are a sham. These are signs that they have begun to trust in themselves for success. Soon they face problems, and they do not have the strength to overcome them. They feel insecure and angry. And to numb their feelings they go back to drugs.

A similar thing happens with the prosperous. They take the credit for their success. Thus they lose the security of belonging to God and of having him as their refuge and strength. They look to earthly success for security. They lose the perspective of Isaiah 26:3: "You keep him in perfect peace whose mind is stayed on you, because he trusts in you." They begin to look for other things to fill up their emptiness and restlessness. They acquire more trappings of success like bigger and more expensive cars and property. Their desire for affirmation becomes like a lust. Their desire to be admired by people of the other sex or to prove their sexual virility drags them into affairs. In their insecurity they take on other gods like money, success, or fame. They may turn to alcohol in order to numb the sense of restlessness in them. Now that they don't hear God's voice, they go to astrologers or soothsayers, hoping those persons might give them a message that calms their fears. Their lust for prosperity causes them to rebel against God's laws, and they end up lying to make a sale or underpaying and exploiting their employees.

How can we maintain the grace perspective in our lives? Verse 12 suggests that it would be good for us to remember who we were before God redeemed us. They are asked to "take care lest [they] forget the LORD." But the Lord is described as the one "who brought [them] out of the land of Egypt, out of the house of slavery." Remembering our past without God with a view to giving God all the honor for our life is an important Christian discipline. In Ephesians 2:11, 12, using the word "remember" twice, Paul describes the hopeless situation his readers were in before they came to Christ. But these two verses are surrounded by statements that talk about grace. The next verse says, "But now in Christ Jesus you who once were far off have been brought near by the blood of Christ" (v. 13). We see a similar sequence in the first paragraph of that chapter also. In verses 1–3 Paul describes the pre-conversion state of his readers. Then, beginning with the words "But God, being rich in mercy, because of the great love with which he loved us," he expounds the nature of salvation (2:4–10).

Remembering the radical change that took place when we were redeemed keeps us humble. Humility makes us dependent, and dependence keeps us in touch with God's power. This ensures that our life will be characterized by security and strength in the face of temptation.

Follow a God-Fearing Lifestyle (6:13–15)

Deuteronomy 6:13 is the verse that Jesus used to respond to Satan when the devil asked him to worship him (Matthew 4:10; Luke 4:8). It gives three key points in what we may call a God-fearing lifestyle. First Moses says, "It is the Lord your God you shall fear" (6:13a). We have already studied what it means to fear the Lord (see the discussion on 5:29). The significance of its appearance here is that it implies that prosperity should not make a person arrogant. Some prosperous people are very arrogant. They don't care how they treat their employees because they feel they have so much authority they can do what they like. In certain cultures the rich and powerful are immune to prosecution or can make themselves immune by paying a bribe. This adds to their arrogance.

Those who fear God see the folly of arrogance because they know how powerful God is and that God opposes the proud. Twice in the New Testament we find the following quotation of Proverbs 3:34 from the Greek version of the Old Testament (the Septuagint): "God opposes the proud, but gives grace to the humble" (James 4:6; 1 Peter 5:5). Not only is humility the right way, it is also the safest way to live! Having a conflict with God would be a lost cause!

Deuteronomy 6:13b gives the second feature of the God-fearing lifestyle: "Him you shall serve." Chris Wright alerts us to the fact that the same Hebrew root appears in verses 12 and 13. Verse 12 has the noun "slavery" (*ebed*), referring to the enslavement of the Israelites in Egypt. Verse 13 has the corresponding verb "serve" (*abad*), referring to the fact that the liberated Israelites were to serve God in their new land. The bondage of being slaves of the Egyptians is replaced by the freedom of being slaves of God. But we are slaves all the same. Happy slaves, but not proud slaves. People who are so thrilled with the privilege of serving God that they have no interest in pushing themselves forward.

How beautiful it is to see people who have succeeded in life but who are God-fearing and therefore humble and whose lives are consumed with serving God. Sometimes you do not realize they are so famous because in their humility they do not flaunt their success. This is the impression I got when, as a young preacher, I met some of the great giants of the church like evangelist Billy Graham, Bible translator Kenneth Taylor, and Bible expositor and influential thinker John Stott. They seemed to be eager to encourage this unknown preacher from Sri Lanka and did not have any desire to show how great they were. I have seen some wealthy lay Christians, too, who have this

perspective—unassuming servants of God whom we would have not identified as wealthy and influential unless someone had told us.

I have always admired Senator Mark Hatfield, who was a fine Christian
and a U.S. Senator from Oregon for many years. He had a long and distinguished career in politics. Howard Hendricks tells about an incident that
took place when he spoke at an early-morning father-son breakfast at the
Fourth Presbyterian Church in Washington, DC Many prominent and not so
prominent people were there. He said, "After I had finished speaking and the
meeting was dismissed, I looked over to my right, and there was Senator Mark
Hatfield, stacking chairs and picking up napkins that had fallen on the floor."
Hendricks comments, "Ladies and gentlemen, if you are impressed that you
are a United States senator, you don't stack chairs and pick up napkins."
Hendricks says that people who are impressed by their success "do not serve.
[They] live to be served."[3]

The third feature of the God-fearing lifestyle reads, ". . . and by his name
you shall swear" (6:13c). Peter Craigie explains, "The context suggests that
the reference of these words is to the oath of allegiance to God as the Lord of
the covenant; because he had liberated his people from Egypt, they committed
themselves solemnly to him in obedience and love." So the next verse says,
"You shall not go after other gods, the gods of the peoples who are around
you" (6:14). The word translated "swear" in verse 13 appears two other times
in our passage (6:10, 18). There the swearing is done by God, and he swears
to give them the land and will do so soon. Now God asks the people, to whom
he has been faithful, to be faithful to him.

The history of Israel shows that after they came into the land and began
to enjoy the benefits of the land, they became careless with their commitment
to God and followed other gods also. All our power and advancement and the
sense of independence and control that accompanies it should not cause us
to forget that we are under solemn oath to serve God only. Jesus knew that
prosperity and wealth can become gods and can keep us from giving God the
place he must have. So he warned, "No one can serve two masters, for either
he will hate the one and love the other, or he will be devoted to the one and
despise the other. You cannot serve God and money" (Matthew 6:24).

Verse 15 reminds the people that God will not tolerate such unfaithfulness: ". . . for the LORD your God in your midst is a jealous God—lest the
anger of the LORD your God be kindled against you, and he destroy you from
off the face of the earth." This is one of four times in Deuteronomy where God
is described as a jealous God (4:24; 5:9; 6:15; 32:21). And each time God is
said to be jealous because his place of supreme lordship has been replaced
by another god. Our verse says that if the Israelites are unfaithful and follow

another God, he will act in his jealousy and "destroy [them] from off the face of the earth." These are strong words.

Such warnings as we see in this verse are appropriate today, too—especially with the prosperous who are so confident that they do not feel a need for God. I spoke once at a meeting on the prodigal son. I fielded questions after I had spoken, and a successful businessman commented on my talk with some disdain. He seemed to say that the loving God I spoke about was good for weak people who needed a crutch to help them stand. He, on the other hand, was a self-made person. He was able to come to the top without God and did not seem to be interested in him now.

I went from that meeting troubled. I wondered how could we reach people like this with the gospel. Then when studying how God got through to Nebuchadnezzar when he was very confident and brutally cruel (Daniel 4), I realized that part of the answer was to show this man that God is the powerful judge and ruler of the world. Powerful people respect power. They know that they need to respond carefully when confronted by people or forces more powerful than themselves. God is the ultimate in terms of power. And we would do well to make that known to those who have no time for God in their prosperous lives.

Have Sanctified Ambitions (6:16–19)

Testing God (6:16)

Now Moses talks about the ambitions that the people should have. Verse 16 was also quoted by Jesus to Satan, this time when the devil asked Jesus to throw himself down from the pinnacle of the temple in order to demonstrate that he is the Son of God (Matthew 4:7; Luke 4:12). Moses tells the people, "You shall not put the LORD your God to the test, as you tested him at Massah" (6:16). In Massah "the people quarreled with Moses and said, 'Give us water to drink.' And Moses said to them, 'Why do you quarrel with me? Why do you test the LORD?'" (Exodus 17:2). The people responded by scolding Moses for bringing them out of Egypt to die of thirst in the wilderness (v. 3). "So Moses cried to the LORD, 'What shall I do with this people? They are almost ready to stone me'" (v. 4). Then God provided water for the people.

Moses renamed the place Massah, meaning "testing" because "they tested the LORD by saying, 'Is the LORD among us or not?'" (v. 7). They had pushed God into giving them water. Moses was not pleased because they had demanded water from God. It was a case of uncrucified desire. Describing this era in Israel's history Psalm 78:18 says, "They tested God in their heart by demanding the food they craved." The word "craved" points to desire that is out of control. So *Massah* speaks of wrong ambition—ambition that has gone out of control. Ambition pursues what is wrong even if the person knows that what he or she is aiming at is wrong.

This type of ambition can be seen when we launch out on a project that will bring us earthly success but that displeases God. I know of Christian entrepreneurs who enter into partnerships with those who do not care for God or for principles of integrity. The prospects of making quick money are so great that they suppress those red flags of doubt about their methods that crop up during the negotiation phase. They get themselves into a business that does a lot of illegal things and later find it difficult to extricate themselves from the project.

Diligent Obedience (6:17)

Next Moses describes the ambition of obedience to the Word: "You shall diligently keep the commandments of the LORD your God, and his testimonies and his statutes, which he has commanded you" (6:17). The familiar word *shamar*, which appeared in verse 12, appears twice here, yielding the translation, "You shall diligently keep." We are talking about people who are so eager to do the will of God that they will study the Word and always ask what the Bible says about what they are thinking of doing. This is like the people in Charles Sheldon's book *In His Steps* who asked, "What would Jesus do?" in every situation of life. It revolutionized their lives. We have expounded on this theme several times in this book (see the discussions on 4:2, 5, 6; 5:32, 33).

Psalm 119:4 describes what our verse says: "You have commanded your precepts to be kept diligently." Then it gives a prayer that should be in the hearts of those who want to do this: "Oh that my ways may be steadfast in keeping your statutes!" (v. 5). The Bible is a book that is not only to be studied but should be studied primarily with the intention of obedience. As Oswald Chambers said, "Never try to explain God until you have obeyed Him. The only bit of God we understand is the bit we have obeyed."[4]

Good Character (6:18a)

Next Moses focuses on what's right and good: "And you shall do what is right and good in the sight of the LORD" (6:18a). The word translated "right" (*yashar*) has been defined as "straight (not crooked or twisted); by extension, something morally straight: right, upright, innocent."[5] The word translated "good" (*tob*) is a very common word in the Bible, appearing 458 times in the Old Testament, and has been defined as "good, pleasing, desirable; goodness; this can refer to quality as well as to moral goodness."[6] Both these words have to do more with actions coming from what I would describe as integrity and good, honorable, and moral character rather than from strict adherence to the Law as in the previous verse.

People with these characteristics are those whom we consider great persons from the Christian perspective, for in Christianity greatness has more to do with character, which reaps eternal rewards, than with earthly success and fame, which often does not even last our lifetime. We are talking about people who have a steadfast desire to do what pleases God and believe that God will honor their action with his blessing, as verse 18 explains. Such people, who refuse to use opportunities for cheap gain and who will do what is right and good whatever the cost may be, are so hard to find today.

David was a man of integrity. He refused to kill Saul when he had the chance even though Saul had attempted to kill him so often. He knew that he had been anointed as Israel's future king. His faithful followers found it difficult to understand why he was not hitting this man who had hurt him so badly. Our loyal friends often cannot understand the generous attitude shown to those who have hurt us. But David persuaded them by explaining "to his men, 'The LORD forbid that I should do this thing to my lord, the LORD's anointed, to put out my hand against him, seeing he is the LORD's anointed'" (1 Samuel 24:6).

Let's look at some contemporary examples of such honorable behavior.

- When someone slanders us, we are greatly tempted to tell others some bad things we know about that person. But we won't, even though refraining may look like a big disadvantage for us in our battle with this person.
- If we are competing with another person for a position or would like a position or responsibility that another person has, we will never use tactics to discredit that person, we will never lie to move forward, we will never deny damaging things that this person tells about us that are true. We may explain, but we will not deny.
- When someone leaves our church or organization and says a lot of bad things about us, we will not slander that person. We may give our explanation about the accusations that this person makes, but we will not slander him. If he is in need of a job we will do all we can within our principles to help him.
- If we have to do something because we promised to do it on our word of honor, we will do it however disadvantageous that may be for us. Psalm 15:4 says the one who dwells on God's holy hill ". . . swears to his own hurt and does not change."
- In the sharing of family assets we will give the needier one (like a sister who is married to an alcoholic and is struggling financially) a lion's share and deprive ourselves of what is our legal right. How sad that Christ's

name has been dishonored so much recently by Christian siblings fighting over family wealth.

Sadly, today evangelicals do not have a good name in society. They are known as people who are so committed to what they think is right that they do not care about others. The perception is that they are selfish. Waitresses don't like to work on Sundays as many Christians come for meals after church but do not tip well. Or perhaps some people give high tips as a way of flirting. May we tip as a way of showing appreciation for good service. We must preach and teach more about Christian character in our churches and homes so that Christians will soon become known as those who truly live humble, gentle, just, fair, and servant-like lives in the world.

The Rewards of Righteousness (6:18b, 19)

Deuteronomy 6:18, 19 say that God will bless the righteous so ". . . that it may go well with you, and that you may go in and take possession of the good land that the LORD swore to give to your fathers by thrusting out all your enemies from before you, as the LORD has promised." Believing that God rewards righteousness is an essential motivation for doing good in a world where goodness has gone out of fashion. People do underhanded things, act without integrity, and look for quick but un-Biblical solutions to their problems because they think it is not worth being right and good in today's society. But the Bible clearly tells us that God does reward handsomely. Though we may not see the reward immediately it is as sure as the rising of the sun in the morning, because God is a faithful God.

The Biblical doctrine of rewards is a key aspect of godly motivation for obedience. We don't do what is right only because it is correct to do that. Many people have rejected righteousness because they think it is not worth being righteous. The Bible says that righteousness brings wonderful rewards and that the failure of unrighteousness brings terrible punishment.

The doctrine of rewards is also one of the keys to overcoming bitterness in our lives. So many Christians are angry about how they have suffered even though they were righteous. Bitterness takes away their joy and makes the life of righteousness look like it is not worthwhile. Psalm 73 begins with the psalmist struggling with the fact that the righteous are suffering while the wicked are prospering (vv. 1–14). But when he decided to look at things from God's perspective by going to his sanctuary, his whole perspective changed (vv. 15–17). He "understood their final destiny" (v. 17, NIV). His bitterness vanished, and he began to reflect on the terrible end of these people and his folly in being upset about them (vv. 18–22). The rest of the Psalm is a vibrant hymn of praise to God (vv. 23–28).

Teach the Children about Their Heritage (6:20–25)

Next Moses envisages a time when the children, who did not go through the experiences of deliverance and conquest when the Law was given, question their parents about the meaning of the laws: "When your son asks you in time to come, 'What is the meaning of the testimonies and the statutes and the rules that the LORD our God has commanded you?' . . . " (6:20). Notice that they say the laws were commanded to the parents. They want to know why they also should obey them. Sometimes amidst the prosperity of a family the children may not see the appropriateness of some of the family values, especially because they were not involved in the process by which the family forged those values. Parents who came to Christ from non-Christian backgrounds in their youth must be alert to this phenomenon. Young people tend to rebel against and to question the value of accepted norms. When the parents did this, they rejected their parents' values and embraced Christianity. Accepting Christianity was an expression of their youthful questioning of the status quo. Their children, however, grew up in an environment where Christianity was the status quo. This calls for alertness on the part of the parents so that they can contend for the truth in such a way that the children will be convinced.

The Israelite children would have wondered why their values are so different from other children. Certainly today's Christian youths often ask why they have to be different from the rest, especially when peer pressure makes that a difficult thing to do. Moses commands the parents to explain these things to their children. Conversation about religious matters was a common feature of an Israelite home. Today many prosperous parents are too busy to do this. They are so busy maintaining their prosperity levels that they have no time to even listen to their children. They buy a lot of things for the children that money can buy. But they do not give their children the principles needed to use those things properly. Children of famous people often complain that their famous parent did not have time for them. Talking to children is an important part of the Christian lifestyle, as we saw in our discussion on 6:7.

Moses asks the parents to tell their children the story of the redemption of the people:

> . . . then you shall say to your son, "We were Pharaoh's slaves in Egypt. And the LORD brought us out of Egypt with a mighty hand. And the LORD showed signs and wonders, great and grievous, against Egypt and against Pharaoh and all his household, before our eyes. And he brought us out from

there, that he might bring us in and give us the land that he swore to give to our fathers." (6:21–23)

To us today this would apply as telling the children the family history, especially the history of God's dealings with the family (we looked at this in our discussion on 5:3–5).

Verses 24 and 25 show that, using the history of the nation, the parents should demonstrate the value and appropriateness of the commands. The parents are to tell the children, "And the LORD commanded us to do all these statutes, to fear the LORD our God, for our good always, that he might preserve us alive, as we are this day. And it will be righteousness for us, if we are careful to do all this commandment before the LORD our God, as he has commanded us" (6:24, 25). This is one of the most important challenges facing parents today. They need to talk to their children so that they may be able to say that God's laws are for their righteousness and for their good always.

The world is giving another message. There is a message coming from society that extramarital sex is appropriate. People who do not join this trend are considered to be deprived and abnormal. We need to show our children not only why extramarital sexual abstinence is righteous but also why it is "for our good always." We must convince them that Christian sexual ethics give us the wisest, the most fulfilling, and the most joyous life.

We have similar challenges with showing the goodness of the Christian alternative to many of the common ideas that are peddled in the circles in which our children move. Here are some of these ideas:

- *Spend your money on yourself to buy the latest gadgets and clothes.* This would make it difficult to give sacrificially to alleviate the suffering of the poor, which is an essential Christian discipline that we must get our children into from the time they are young.
- *It is impossible to be successful without telling lies in today's world, so why not tell a lie or two and save ourselves a lot of trouble and inconvenience?*
- *It is necessary to take revenge on those who insult our family because the refusal to do so is considered a failure to protect the family's honor.*

Our passage is a very sobering one. It reminds us of the dangers of prosperity. Moses will have more to say about this topic beyond this chapter. Deuteronomy 8 addresses the issue with more warnings on the dangers of prosperity. We should take this very seriously, for the danger is real, and God thinks it is important to remind us of it in the Bible. As Haddon Robinson has said, "For every verse in the Bible that tells us the benefits of wealth, there are ten that tell us the danger of wealth."[7]

27

Show Them No Mercy[1]

DEUTERONOMY 7:1–26

DEUTERONOMY 7 GIVES God's instructions for fighting the Canaanites and gives some orders that would startle people today because they seem to be repulsive to modern sensibilities. Some use these to demonstrate the inappropriateness of Old Testament ethics for today. Others use the same instructions to justify severe actions against their enemies that seem to contradict other passages of Scripture. We must seek to understand what this passage intends to say and what principles we can apply for today. In our approach to Deuteronomy, every passage has something to teach us, though we may not apply the passage today exactly as prescribed in the book.

A Never-to-Be-Repeated Type of War

Deuteronomy speaks of two types of war. Chapter 20 explains the difference between them. Deuteronomy 20:10–15 describes what we may call ordinary wars, that is, wars against cities outside the territory promised to Israel. Usually accepted principles of warfare are given for such wars. Deuteronomy 20:16–18 describes what we may call *herem* wars (we will explain the meaning of *herem* below). These are wars with people who live in the lands promised to Israel. Here some special rules apply.

The principles of warfare explained in chapter 7 are for never-to-be-repeated *herem* wars, fought to occupy the promised land. Therefore, we must be careful about applying this passage to wars fought today. Certainly they cannot be used in order to back the idea of ethnic cleansing. The giving of a certain geographical area to the people who were going to be the bearers of God's revelation to the whole world is so unique that we should be very careful about applying this passage to the issue of land and ethnicity in other cases. This is an urgent issue today as the phenomenon of ethnic cleansing has resulted in the killing of hundreds of thousands of people in recent decades.

Devotion to Complete Destruction (7:1–5, 16, 25, 26)

Herem (7:1, 2)

Verse 1 states that what is given in this chapter relates to nations whose land Israel is going to take possession of and occupy: "When the LORD your God brings you into the land that you are entering *to take possession of it*, and clears away many nations before you, the Hittites, the Girgashites, the Amorites, the Canaanites, the Perizzites, the Hivites, and the Jebusites, seven nations more numerous and mightier than yourselves . . . " Verse 2 is the command to totally destroy these people: ". . . and when the LORD your God gives them over to you, and you defeat them, then you must devote them to complete destruction. You shall make no covenant with them and show no mercy to them" (7:2).

The expression "devote . . . to complete destruction" is a translation of the same verb (*haram*) used twice next to each other. The noun of this is *herem*, and today that is used as a technical term to describe this type of "holy war." It basically means something like "ban," in this case "ban from common use." It often takes the idea of being completely devoted to God either for his service or for total destruction. Hence the ESV translation, ". . . devote them to complete destruction." The use of the verb twice here gives more force to it.

The *herem* concept here is that captured people and the spoils of war are kept away from the Israelites and given totally into the hands of God. They cannot be used by people. Therefore, they must be totally destroyed. The next verse commands the people not to intermarry with these people. This, of course, suggests that the destruction was not going to be total.

They Could Ensnare and Cause Destruction (7:3–5, 16, 25, 26)

A reason for the total ban is given several times in this passage: these people and their practices could ensnare Israel and lead them astray. So intermarriage is prohibited because religious compromise would result when people marry those who serve other gods: "You shall not intermarry with them, giving your daughters to their sons or taking their daughters for your sons, for they would turn away your sons from following me, to serve other gods" (7:3, 4a). The result for Israel would be tragic: "Then the anger of the LORD would be kindled against you, and he would destroy you quickly" (7:4b). Because of this there is special mention of the destruction of the objects of religious devotion of these people: "But thus shall you deal with them: you shall break down their altars and dash in pieces their pillars and chop down their Asherim and burn their carved images with fire" (7:5). "The Asherim were cult objects thought to have been wooden poles representing the goddess Asherah."[2]

Verse 16 says that the people are also to be destroyed: "And you shall consume all the peoples that the LORD your God will give over to you. Your eye shall not pity them, neither shall you serve their gods." The reason for this is, ". . . for that would be a snare to you." Verse 25 talks about destroying images and not taking the silver and gold of the people: "The carved images of their gods you shall burn with fire. You shall not covet the silver or the gold that is on them or take it for yourselves, lest you be ensnared by it, for it is an abomination to the LORD your God."

Serious consequences would result if Israel were to get ensnared. Verse 4 says, "Then the anger of the LORD would be kindled against you, and he would destroy you quickly." Verse 26a is even more vivid: "And you shall not bring an abominable thing into your house and become devoted to destruction like it." If a person takes a thing that has been devoted to destruction, that person also becomes devoted to destruction. So Moses says, "You shall utterly detest and abhor it, for it is devoted to destruction" (7:26b).

We Too Must Totally Avoid Some Things

Though we cannot directly apply all the teachings here, there is a principle that we can glean from this call to totally destroy: We must give no space to things that could ensnare us and lead us to sin. We are sent into the world by Christ (John 17:15–18) to be like salt and light (Matthew 5:13–16). Therefore we are going to be geographically close to some things in society that can lure us into sin. Some of these things are very appealing and even addictive. Therefore we have to deal with such things with severe revulsion and get no satisfaction from them.

Because we are surrounded by sinful things, we could lose this hatred for them and treat them as if they are harmless. I think of things like sexually explicit images that come in from the media. These can easily ensnare people and lead to addiction to pornography. Because sexuality is so commonly exploited by the media and we are constantly exposed to this, it could be easy for us men to get used to looking at women lustfully and thinking nothing about it despite Jesus' strong words about it (Matthew 5:28). Those who can get easily lured into sin here need to have some strict guidelines to help them overcome this. They should be accountable to someone to ensure that they do not get careless in following the guidelines. I chose the topic of sex because I believe sex has been elevated to a godlike status. The devotion of many to sex is one of the most common forms of idolatry today. Paul used a word from the battlefield for fleeing from an army when he said, "Flee youthful passions" (2 Timothy 2:22). There can be no negotiation with sin.

But what about idols? Should we destroy the idols that we see in our societies today? Here the difference between Israel, a theocracy, and a multi-religious society like what we have today must be borne in mind. When Paul went to the city of Athens, "he was greatly distressed to see that the city was full of idols" (Acts 17:16, NIV). But he did not destroy the idols. Instead, he argued against them and pointed to their futility (Acts 17:22–31). Similarly we need to argue for the Christian message in our multi-religious societies. Paul did not physically destroy idols in Athens; he did so spiritually and intellectually through the use of persuasion. Elsewhere he said, "We destroy arguments and every lofty opinion raised against the knowledge of God, and take every thought captive to obey Christ" (2 Corinthians 10:5).

However, if people start idol worship in the church, we must adopt a more insistent tone because the church is by its "constitution" governed by God's specific guidelines in the Scriptures, just like ancient Israel. This is why when Paul found out about false teaching in Galatia, he did not adopt the irenic approach that he adopted in Athens. He thundered angrily against the false teaching and the false teachers.

The two specifics mentioned in Deuteronomy 7, not directly related to worship, that the Israelites are to avoid are significant because they are areas in which people still stumble often. The first is intermarriage with people from other nations (7:3, 4). Next to one's relationship with God, marriage is the closest relationship a human being can have. This is God's intention (Genesis 2:24). If you cannot share the most important factor in your life (God) with the person you are going to become one with, something will have to be compromised in order to survive. Usually it is one's faith that is compromised.

It is true that the New Testament gives guidelines to believers about how to relate to unbelieving spouses. This advice generally was for those who became believers after they were married. Always the great aim there is to see the unbelieving spouse converted. God will help a Christian who has married an unbeliever to make the best of the situation, if he or she seeks God's help. But that does not give us any license to go into marriage with an unbeliever. In light of this it is a surprise to me to see how in the West (where singles date single members of the opposite sex) Christians speak so little about the dangers of dating unbelievers.

The second non-cultic thing the Israelites are asked to stay away from is the silver and gold of these people (7:25). It is possible that what is meant here is silver and gold once used for idols. But the important point here is that the prospect of material treasure could cause one to compromise one's principles. Money, like sex, has the ability to control our emotions and blind us to the dangers of the paths along which it can lead us. Achan did exactly this after one of the wars that were fought for the land. When questioned by Joshua, he said, ". . . I saw among the spoil a beautiful cloak from Shinar, and 200 shekels of silver, and a bar of gold weighing 50 shekels, then I coveted them and took them" (Joshua 7:21).

We need always to be alert to the danger of falling into sin over material possessions. How many Christians have ruined their spiritual lives and their testimonies because of greed for possessions! Christian ministries raise money using unethical methods. Siblings fight among each other for family wealth. People exploit others and make money unethically. Some underpay their employees. Some manipulate helpless widows into giving them large sums of money. Some resort to dishonest methods, such as lying, to make a sale. Some borrow money that they can't pay back and get into a huge bondage because of that. We must be very careful about the way we handle possessions.

The Unique Place of Israel (7:6–24)

Is God's Special Concern for the Israelites Unfair? (7:6–8, 26)

Our passage not only says that Israel could get ensnared by their neighbors' sins and thus be punished; it also implies that Israel simply must not be destroyed because they are God's chosen race: "For you are a people holy to the LORD your God. The LORD your God has chosen you to be a people for his treasured possession, out of all the peoples who are on the face of the earth" (7:6). The cause for this special concern for Israel was not their numerical size; it was God's love and promise to their fathers:

> It was not because you were more in number than any other people that the LORD set his love on you and chose you, for you were the fewest of all peoples, but it is because the LORD loves you and is keeping the oath that he swore to your fathers, that the LORD has brought you out with a mighty hand and redeemed you from the house of slavery, from the hand of Pharaoh king of Egypt. (7:7, 8)

Later Moses would say that it was not the righteousness of Israel that caused God to give them this land; it was the wickedness of the people (9:4–6). Kalland points out that the Pentateuch does not say much about why Israel of all nations was chosen. Its focus is on God's love rather than any human qualifications. We know from the promises made to Abraham that God's faithfulness has something to do with Abraham's call (Genesis 22:18). But, more importantly, five times in Genesis God gives the promise to bless all the nations of the world through his seed (Genesis 12:3; 18:18; 22:18; 26:4; 28:14). The whole world would benefit from the revelation of the Law culminating in the appearing of the Messiah himself through Israel. Therefore, this nation needed to be protected. This is like one of those situations where a surgeon needs to take away a cancerous organ in order to prevent the destruction of the whole body.

Though our passage seems to suggest that God loves Israel and hates the nations—that there is an unfair favoritism of Israel—his concern for the nations is not abandoned here. So that all the nations may be ultimately blessed, Israel needed to be protected in order that it could mediate the revelation that God was going to give to the whole world. Thus God needed to purge Canaan of the wicked people who lived there who could have ensnared Israel and led them astray.

If Israel disobeyed the covenant, they too would be punished. Verse 26 says that the same fate will await them if they become like these nations: "And you shall not bring an abominable thing into your house and become devoted to destruction like it." This is also implied in the section below, which shows that the blessings of God will be theirs only if they remain faithful to the covenant. So this is not a case of unfair favoritism. We will see below that the Canaanites were guilty of gross wickedness. So their destruction was also a punishment for dangerous sin.

The Covenant Blessings Are for a Faithful People (7:9–15)

Moses tells the people about God's faithfulness to his covenant: "Know therefore that the LORD your God is God, the faithful God who keeps covenant and steadfast love with those who love him and keep his commandments, to a thousand generations" (7:9). This does not imply unconditional endorsement of all they do. So he warns, ". . . and repays to their face those who hate him, by destroying them. He will not be slack with one who hates him. He will repay him to his face" (7:10). God is committed to those who love him and punishes those who hate him; so Moses says, "You shall therefore be careful to do the commandment and the statutes and the rules that I command you today" (7:11).

We will not go into a detailed exposition of 7:9–15 as we studied similar themes in our exposition of Deuteronomy 4. But note that even today the promises of God to Israel are for a righteous nation. We must not blindly support the actions of the Israeli government in decisions that it may make that may deprive the Palestinians of their legitimate rights. The perception among Muslims that Christians do this is a major obstacle to evangelizing them, which is a cause much more important than the agenda of any nation.

Once more Moses says that if they remain faithful to the covenant, God will also remain faithful to it: "And because you listen to these rules and keep and do them, the Lord your God will keep with you the covenant and the steadfast love that he swore to your fathers" (7:12). Then he proceeds to explain the blessings that will come to them when they are obedient:

> He will love you, bless you, and multiply you. He will also bless the fruit of your womb and the fruit of your ground, your grain and your wine and your oil, the increase of your herds and the young of your flock, in the land that he swore to your fathers to give you. You shall be blessed above all peoples. There shall not be male or female barren among you or among your livestock. And the Lord will take away from you all sickness, and none of the evil diseases of Egypt, which you knew, will he inflict on you, but he will lay them on all who hate you. (7:13–15)

The Promise of Victory in the Battles for the Land (7:17–24)

After the warnings about being ensnared by the customs of the people and exhortations to remain faithful and a promise of blessing in the land (7:1–16), Moses goes to talk about how God will give them victory in battle (7:17–24). The principles enumerated here have been commented on in our discussions of Deuteronomy 1, 2. Therefore here we will only briefly list and summarize what Moses said.

- Don't be afraid of the greatness of these nations and think that you cannot dispossess them. Think instead of what God did in delivering you from Egypt with all the miracles he performed. What God did to Egypt, he will do to all the peoples of whom you are afraid (7:17–19).
- God says he will send hornets among these enemies. Hornets were large, virulent insects common in Canaan (7:20). This is probably talking about the sense of fear, panic, or discouragement that the Canaanites would have (11:25).
- God's presence with them should take away their fear: "You shall not be in dread of them, for the Lord your God is in your midst, a great and awesome God" (7:21).
- The conquest would take time. The enemies will be driven out only gradually. Otherwise there will be too many wild beasts in the land (7:22).
- But victory will surely come ultimately: "But the Lord your God will give them over to you and throw them into great confusion, until they are destroyed" (7:23).
- All the kings will be given into their hands, so that all opponents will be finally destroyed (7:24).

A Case of Judgment for Gross Wickedness

Later Moses tells the people, "Not because of your righteousness or the uprightness of your heart are you going in to possess their land, but because of the wickedness of these nations the LORD your God is driving them out from before you" (9:5). The conquest of Canaan was not a case of some innocent people being destroyed in order to give a favored people a land. The people in Canaan were grossly unrighteous.

In another passage warning the people about being ensnared into adopting Canaanite practices, Moses says that those pagan nations have gone to the extent of burning their children in the fire as sacrifices to their gods (Deuteronomy 12:30, 31). In Leviticus 18:25 God says, ". . . and the land became unclean, so that I punished its iniquity, and the land vomited out its inhabitants" (see also Leviticus 20:22–24). Chris Wright comments on this verse: "This speaks of something that is not merely an 'abomination,' to God, but also repulsive and disgusting, so much so that he can no longer 'stomach it.'"[3]

When God promised the land of Canaan to Abraham, he also said that it was his descendants who would take full possession of the land. This is because they were not yet ripe for judgment: "And they shall come back here in the fourth generation, for the iniquity of the Amorites is not yet complete" (Genesis 15:16). By the time of Moses the unrighteousness had peaked, and the time was ripe for judgment. So part of the reason for their total destruction is that this was God's judgment for their gross unrighteousness. Two reasons, then, dovetailed so as to make the destruction of these nations a righteous act: Israel needed this land, and those living in it were grossly wicked and ripe for judgment.

I think all of us are troubled by passages like Deuteronomy 7. However, some find them impossible to understand because the doctrine of judgment is not a major factor influencing their thinking and behavior. One reason for this is that God does not usually judge today as he did in Old Testament times. The Old Testament times were special revelatory eras when God clearly showed his principles to the people. One of those principles is that sin will be punished. Right at the beginning of the life of the church, God acted to judge Ananias and Sapphira so that the Christians would know that God has not changed his attitude of antipathy toward sin (Acts 5:1–11).

Though the New Testament mentions only a few occasions of physical judgments in history, it speaks a lot about the eschatological judgment at the end of time. Paul, while exhorting the people to love those who harm them and not take revenge, says that vengeance belongs to God who will repay

(Romans 12:14–21). Jesus is the one who spoke most about Hell in the New Testament. God's nature has not changed since Old Testament times. These difficult passages in the Old Testament remind us that God is holy and that one day all who do not know Christ will appear before God's judgment seat (Revelation 20:11, 12) and we who do know Christ will have to stand before the awesome judgment seat of Christ (2 Corinthians 5:10, 11).

The Unadorned Realism of Old Testament War Records

Peter Craigie, in his book *The Problem of War in the Old Testament*, comments on the value of the stark representation of war in the Old Testament. This is not the focus that is found often in contemporary reporting on war. Today writers on war often focus on the heroism of a few soldiers that comes to the fore during a war. Craigie describes how the common approach to war held by most Christian denominations — called the just war theory — can tend to take away our focus from the horrors of war. Ambrose and Augustine first wrote about this in the fourth and fifth centuries. "According to the Just War theory, there were certain rules of conduct which were to be observed in war; there was to be no unnecessary violence, no needless destruction, no looting, no large-scale massacre of populations, and no acts of vengeance or reprisal."[4] Craigie agrees that the spirit of such legislation is admirable and foreshadows the later Geneva Convention, which was a "series of international agreements that created the International Red Cross and developed humanitarian law intended to protect wounded combatants and civilians during times of war or other conflicts."[5]

However, Craigie points out that focus on the heroism and the just war features in a war can mask the horror of it. He agrees that sometimes a state cannot avoid being involved in a war. But he says, "If war is to be waged at all, it must be done thoroughly. There are no half measures in war; it is not a game to be played casually."[6] Even if a war is won, usually there is a lot of death. Craigie says, "Warfare by definition involves ruthlessness and killing." An American general during the Civil War, William Sherman (1820–1891), said, "War is hell."[7]

The Old Testament does not skirt this issue. It presents a realistic view of war. Craigie says this may be a safer guide to the nature of war than the just war theories, which perhaps unintentionally tend to focus so much on fairness in war that the horrors of war may not receive the prominence they should receive. He says that while "our novelists, historians and film-makers all too often glorify war, they lack the honesty of some Old Testament writers." Craigie forthrightly says, "If we read the ruthless laws of war in the Old

Testament and express pious shock, we are deceiving ourselves. War is a manifestation of violence to achieve a purpose."[8]

The Bible has always been a realistic book. It presents an unadorned picture of life, and the horrors of war are presented accurately. So if we are considering whether to go to war, the Bible will be a reliable guide. Unlike the romanticized picture of it presented in the media and the theories of war, the Bible depicts war as a stark reality that includes brutal killing. A sensitive person reading the Scriptures would realize how important it is to attempt to achieve the desired end without resorting to war. So these descriptions of war in the Old Testament act as a deterrent rather than an encouragement to war.

Radical Individual Pacifism

The Bible gives two different approaches to the use of force by individuals and by the state. It is clear from the Old Testament that nations are permitted to engage in war for self-defense. Both the Old Testament and the New Testament give permission for the state to use force and punish people on behalf of God (see Romans 13:1–7). However, both Testaments teach what G. P. Hugenberger describes as a radical individual pacifism, because the right to take life has not been entrusted to individuals acting on their own.[9]

Deuteronomy teaches that vengeance is God's, and he will repay (32:35). Romans quotes this text in the context of loving enemies (12:19). The Old Testament teaches us not hate our enemies (Leviticus 19:17, 18) and to do kind deeds to them (Exodus 23:4, 5; see 2 Kings 6:22; Psalm 35:12–14). This is the teaching of the New Testament also (Matthew 5:44; Luke 6:27, 35). David, the warrior king, refused to attack and take revenge, when he could have in his personal conflicts with Saul, even though his associates thought these were God-given opportunities to attack the king (1 Samuel 24, 26).

When Peter cut the ear of the high priest's servant, "Jesus said, 'No more of this!' And he touched his ear and healed him" (Luke 22:51). On this occasion he told Peter, "Put your sword back into its place. For all who take the sword will perish by the sword" (Matthew 26:52). Later Peter wrote, "For to this [suffering] you have been called, because Christ also suffered for you, leaving you an example, so that you might follow in his steps. . . . When he was reviled, he did not revile in return; when he suffered, he did not threaten, but continued entrusting himself to him who judges justly" (1 Peter 2:21, 23).

We also know that the kingdom of God is going to grow and be defended not by the use of force but by messengers of the kingdom working with people until they are persuaded of the truths of the gospel and undergo a transformation of the heart. Such changes in people cannot be won through the use of force.

Let's summarize some of the principles we have expounded in this study:

- Because the *herem* wars are unique, never-to-be-repeated events, we need to exercise extra caution when applying this chapter to daily life.
- We need to be alert to the temptation to yield to things that are harmful to our Christian life and not negotiate with them. We must have nothing to do with them. We need to use special care when it comes to the choice of one's marriage partner and the acquiring of material possessions.
- The three causes for the total destruction of the Canaanites were 1) judgment for their gross unrighteousness, 2) the need to give Israel their land, and 3) the need to prevent God's people from being ensnared by the sins of the Canaanites.
- Through the preservation of Israel the whole world would ultimately be blessed.
- Israel, too, would be punished if she was unfaithful.
- The description of war in Deuteronomy is helpful because it is unadorned and presents war in all its horror, unlike much thinking and reporting about war today.
- Though the Bible permits the state to sometimes resort to the use of force in carrying out its responsibilities, it also teaches that the lifestyle of the believer must be characterized by a radical individual pacifism. Christians seek to bring about change through persuasion, not force.

28

How Not to Forget God

DEUTERONOMY 8:1–20

ONE OF THE MOST PAINFUL THINGS those of us in youth ministry face is seeing young people who were on fire for the Lord gradually lose that fire as they get older to become lukewarm Christians or sometimes to even abandon the faith altogether. One of the encouragements of youth ministry is to see some of these people who fell away coming back to God some years later. We can all lose our spiritual glow, so we must be on guard against this. Paul exhorted, "Never be lacking in zeal, but keep your spiritual fervor, serving the Lord" (Romans 12:11, NIV).

Moses addresses this problem in Deuteronomy 8. He uses the figure of forgetting God to describe the danger we face (8:11, 14, 19). He gives several principles that will help us avoid this pitfall. He has given almost all these principles before, but it is so easy to fall that he repeats them several times in Deuteronomy.

Be Careful to Obey (8:1, 6, 11)

The charge to be careful to obey may be the charge given most often in Deuteronomy. It appears in 8:1, 6, and 11. As is often the case, there is the promise of prosperity for the obedient. Verse 1 says, "The whole commandment that I command you today you shall be careful [*shamar*] to do, that you may live and multiply, and go in and possess the land that the LORD swore to give to your fathers." They are to be careful to do "the whole commandment." Many Christians never experience the victory, joy, and provision that the Bible speaks of because they have kept a few areas of disobedience in their lives. A friend of mine went abroad to work and changed jobs illegally because he could make more money that way. He called me from abroad and told me that what he did was wrong. At the end of the conversation he said, "Pray for me." But he had no intention of righting his wrong. I should have told him, "Don't expect God to bless you if you live in disobedience." Sadly, all I said was, "OK." The word *shamar* that is used here is a familiar word, appearing sixty-five times in Deuteronomy and meaning "pay careful attention to."

The charge is given in verse 6 also: "So you shall keep the commandments of the LORD your God by walking in his ways and by fearing him." This verse gives the heart attitude needed for obedience (fearing God) and the practical working out of that attitude (walking in his ways). If we revere God, we will live lives of daily obedience. These themes have already been discussed.[1] The charge appears again in verse 11: "Take care lest you forget the LORD your God by not keeping his commandments and his rules and his statutes, which I command you today." This time disobedience is said to cause us to forget God. People who do not obey God forget him. They may preach in God's name, they may go from meeting to meeting seeking a blessing, and they may be consistent in presenting prayer requests for God's help in their lives. They may remember to give large offerings regularly for religious causes. But if they are not obedient to God, that is the same as forgetting God. Their religious behavior is that of those whom Paul describes as "having the appearance of godliness, but denying its power" (2 Timothy 3:5).

Remember Times of Discipline (8:2–6)

Moses then explains that the difficult forty-year period of wandering in the dreary wilderness was a time that God used to show many important truths to the people that would help them remain faithful. It was a discipline time necessitated by the sins of the people. The sovereign Lord worked through this situation to extract great good from it. It was the rebellion of the people following the incident of the twelve spies that necessitated this discipline. But we know that after that, the people returned to being faithful to God (2:1–3), giving God an opportunity to bless them. Moses said, "Know then in your heart that, as a man disciplines his son, the LORD your God disciplines you" (8:5).

Humbling (8:2, 3)

Verses 2–6 tell us that the whole journey was one of leading and provision by God (see the discussion on 2:1–23). First, Moses says it was a time of humbling: "And you shall remember the whole way that the LORD your God has led you these forty years in the wilderness, that he might humble you" (8:2a). That God used the wilderness wanderings to humble them is mentioned three times in this chapter (8:2, 3, 16). The humbling is closely related to the disciplining process. Deuteronomy 8:3 explains that God "humbled [them] and let [them] hunger and fed [them] with manna."

Discipline helps produce humility by taking away the human props of which we are sometimes proud. Then as helpless people we have to trust in God alone. Last night I was working on trying to restore information on my computer until 4 A.M. I had lost everything on the computer during a trip to the war-torn north part of Sri Lanka. It must have been erased when it went through a powerful security X-ray scan. I was reloading using my backups, but some of my backups did not install. I lost many years of photos. I do a lot of study while traveling, and my key reference works are in the computer. My computer was one of my sources of pride and security. When studying this passage I realized that God had permitted this crash so that he could wean me of finding security in the wrong things. Having lost confidence in earthly props of which I could be proud, I am driven to trust in God alone. I hope that will produce humility.

Testing (8:2)

The wilderness experience was also a test: ". . . testing you to know what was in your heart, whether you would keep his commandments or not" (8:2; see v. 16). Chris Wright points out that the Israelites thought they were testing God at Massah when they demanded water from God (see 6:16), but God was testing them. God wanted them to demonstrate their commitment to him through obedience.

E. Stanley Jones, American missionary to India, used to say that circumstances don't make a person, they reveal a person. Of course, in the process, as happens when metals are tested, they are refined. As James said, ". . . the testing of your faith produces steadfastness" (James 1:3). Testing does the work of both revealing and refining. Difficult circumstances will reveal whether people follow God with all their heart. If they followed him just to get some temporal blessings, the difficult circumstances could reveal their counterfeit faith as they move away from God, or it could refine their mixed-motive faith and help them develop a more genuine faith.

We sometimes have two candidates for one leadership slot. Both seem to be equally qualified, but finally one has to be left out and the other appointed. Sometimes the person who is left out reacts very angrily and causes serious unrest in the community because of his anger. That person did not come through the trial well. The selection process was a test that revealed that the person was not qualified for leadership. Others accept this disappointment as a learning experience. They go to God and grapple with God and their disappointment. And they finally come out better people, refined by the test of failure.

Hunger (8:3a)

Next Moses talks about another learning tool that God used: hunger. He says, "And he humbled you and let you hunger." God is preparing them to live with plenty. But prosperity brings with it many dangers (see the discussion on 6:10–25). One way to prepare people for prosperity is to send them through an experience where they have nothing. When they have nothing, they are forced to look to God, and they rediscover the most important thing in life—faith in God. They will see that even though they do not have all that they want, they are happy. They will find that God gives them just what they need each day, sometimes miraculously. This experience makes them realize that the greatest wealth is one's relationship with God. Then earthly wealth loses its lure, and they are able to handle the temptations that come with wealth.

Prosperity makes us act as if we don't need God. Adam Clarke says, "God knows [the perils of prosperity] well; and therefore, in his love to man, makes comparative poverty, and frequent affliction his general lot." After quoting David's statement, "Before I was afflicted, I went astray," Clarke says, "And had it not been for poverty and affliction, as instruments in the hands of God's grace, multitudes of souls now happy in heaven would have been wretched in hell."[2] This is what God does to the Israelites. He brings them to the end of themselves, so that they would acknowledge their helplessness. Then they can look to him and avail themselves of his help, and that, in turn, will give them an attitude that makes obedience to the commands possible. This is why Martin Luther said that affliction was the best book in his library.

Provision (8:3, 4)

After God allowed the Israelites to be hungry, he provided for their need in a miraculous way. So Moses goes on to give the reason for letting them go hungry: "[God] humbled you and let you hunger and fed you with manna, which you did not know, nor did your fathers know" (8:3a). Not only did he provide manna, he also miraculously preserved their clothes and feet as they went through the rough terrain of the wilderness: "Your clothing did not wear out on you and your foot did not swell these forty years" (8:4). The experience of being in need not only teaches us to depend on God—it also opens the door for God's marvelous provision. How often I have seen this in my life! I wonder, *Why is God letting me go through such frustrating times?* Much later I realize that God had done things through that time way above anything I had dreamed.

A popular Christian song some years ago by Andre Crouch proclaimed this message well:

I thank God for the mountains and I thank him for the valleys,
I thank him for the storms he bought me through;
For if I'd never had a problem I wouldn't know that he could solve them,
I'd never know what faith in God could do.
Through it all, through it all,
O I've learned to trust in Jesus, I've learned to trust in God;
Through it all, through it all,
I've learned to depend upon his Word.[3]

Moses goes on to give God's purpose in giving them this unusual food called "manna, which [they] did not know, nor did [their] fathers know." It was so that "he might make [them] know that man does not live by bread alone, but man lives by every word that comes from the mouth of the LORD" (8:3b). These words were spoken by Jesus to Satan when the devil asked him to turn stones into bread (Matthew 4:4). Many Christians think these words teach that Jesus did not need physical food because he had spiritual food at that time. But the context in Deuteronomy shows that this is not the meaning, for it describes how God gave them physical food and how through that provision they were going to learn that "man does not live by bread alone." What he means is that God and his words are "more basic to Israelite existence than food."[4] The words from God's mouth include the life-giving word that gave us physical life and spiritual life through salvation in the past. It includes the commands that tell us how to live in the present and the promises that assure us of security and success in the future. Food is important. But even more important than food is obeying God's Word always. We can trust God to provide all our needs, including food. Jesus said, "Seek first the kingdom of God and his righteousness, and all these things will be added to you" (Matthew 6:33).

Discipline (8:5)

Next Moses describes this experience as a disciplining, similar to the discipline that a parent does to a child: "Know then in your heart that, as a man disciplines his son, the LORD your God disciplines you" (8:5). This is a theme that occurs often in the Bible. Proverbs 3:11, 12 give the principle with a little more detail: "My son, do not despise the LORD's discipline or be weary of his reproof, for the LORD reproves him whom he loves, as a father the son in whom he delights" (see also Hebrews 12:5, 6).

According to one understanding of discipline, all our hardships can be called disciplines of God. But we should take this passage as referring specifically to discipline for sin, because Moses is talking about the wilderness wanderings, which were because of the sin of the people. But the point here is that even periods of discipline for sin can be used to achieve a good purpose under God.

Once there was a tedious administrative task that needed to be done. The result of this work would produce much good for the kingdom of God. We chose a man who was under discipline to do this administrative job. If he were doing his usual ministry, he would not have had time to do this tedious administrative job. But during his discipline time he did this as he was not permitted to do public ministry. The result was that immense good was done for the kingdom, and thousands of people were blessed (many more than he would bless through his regular ministry). It was a painful time for him, as discipline is always "painful" (Hebrews 12:11). But it was a time that God used to do much good in him and through him.

Obedience (8:6)

The result of the discipline is that the people are equipped with the strength and ability needed for obedience. So Moses says, "So you shall keep the commandments of the LORD your God by walking in his ways and by fearing him" (8:6). Someone has said that our sins are handles by which God gets ahold of us. Often people who are living away from an intimate relationship with God are not committing any huge sin that reveals their serious condition. Then they commit a sin that is very unbecoming for a believer. It reveals the real state of their spiritual life. Then they turn to God for help. The subsequent course of action, including repentance and discipline, helps them return to becoming totally dependent on God. With dependence comes the grace that strengthens us for obedience. This verse gives two ways in which "we keep the commandments": the action of "walking in his ways" and the attitude of "fearing him."

Praise God for His Blessings (8:7–10)

After explaining the purpose of the discipline, Moses then talks about the beauty of the land they are going to inherit. Verses 7–10 provide an extended reflection on this beauty, leading to a statement of praise to God.

Moses first describes the ample water resources and the rich vegetation of the land:

> For the LORD your God is bringing you into a good land, a land of brooks of water, of fountains and springs, flowing out in the valleys and hills, a land of wheat and barley, of vines and fig trees and pomegranates, a land of olive trees and honey. (8:7, 8)

Then he says that with such plenty they will have no shortage of food and metal substances, so that they are going to be fully satisfied: ". . . a land in which you will eat bread without scarcity, in which you will lack nothing, a land whose stones are iron, and out of whose hills you can dig copper. And you shall eat and be full" (8:9, 10a).

Such meditation on the goodness of the land prompts Moses to say, ". . . and you shall bless [praise, NIV] the LORD your God for the good land he has given you" (8:10b). When we take time to meditate on the good that God has done for us, we will end up praising him. The trouble with us is that we do not stop to meditate on God's goodness. It takes time to do this, and, given our busy lives, we can easily overlook it. Taking time to praise God for his goodness is one of the necessary disciplines of the Christian life. I have found that I can go for days without really stopping to have a good time for praise. I have my time with God, but I spend all the time studying the Word and interceding in prayer. Not giving time for praise can seriously warp my Christian life. Therefore I need to separate times for praise. I find the hymnbook to be a helpful resource for such a time. Hymns help me realize what God has done for me, and they often express what is in my heart better than I can.

The prosperous are particularly vulnerable to the trap of not giving time to meditate on God's goodness. They get busy protecting their wealth and their status and trying to gain more. They have neither the time nor the inclination to stop and meditate on the goodness of the Lord. When they are prosperous they can think they achieved the prosperity through their own strength. Verse 17 warns, "Beware lest you say in your heart, 'My power and the might of my hand have gotten me this wealth.'" This means that their approach to life is inconsistent with an attitude of praise. Praise gives all the credit to God, but now they have started taking credit for their success.

A certain Christian woman was married to an unbeliever who was wealthy and successful in his career. She always praised God when something good happened to their family. This annoyed her husband who felt that he should receive some of the credit for the blessing. He felt cheated of the recognition that he thought he deserved. Those who think they deserve praise for their achievements will never be happy. Some people may praise them, but others will not. Furthermore, they often focus so much attention on those who did not praise them that they cannot fully enjoy the praise they get.

When the prosperous praise God genuinely, they confirm the fact that they are totally dependent on God. Dependence opens the door to grace. And with grace comes the strength to obey.

Beware of Prosperity (8:11–20)

Pride (8:11–17)

Verses 11–17 warn about the dangers of prosperity. This passage first says, as we saw earlier, that they could forget God through disobedience: "Take care lest you forget the LORD your God by not keeping his commandments and his rules and his statutes, which I command you today" (8:11). The trigger for this forgetting God is material prosperity: ". . . lest, when you have eaten and are full and have built good houses and live in them, and when your herds and flocks multiply and your silver and gold is multiplied and all that you have is multiplied . . . " (8:12, 13). They will get proud in their prosperity: ". . . then your heart be lifted up, and you forget the LORD your God" (8:14a). We enjoy the status that comes with our wealth, and we think that we deserve it (on the dangers of pride see the discussion on 6:10–12).

In verses 12, 13 Moses is describing how people living in the lap of luxury take credit for their prosperity. In such situations it is easy to forget their tough situation before God intervened and helped them. So Moses reminds them of the deliverance that God gave them. He describes God as the one "who brought you out of the land of Egypt, out of the house of slavery, who led you through the great and terrifying wilderness, with its fiery serpents and scorpions and thirsty ground where there was no water, who brought you water out of the flinty rock, who fed you in the wilderness with manna that your fathers did not know" (8:14b–16a).

Then he says that they went through these unusual experiences for a reason. It was so "that he might humble you and test you, to do you good in the end" (8:16b). He is reminding them that God is sovereign over their lives. Even though they are feeling very proud of their success, they are actually little people in comparison to God's greatness, and their destinies depend on his mercy. Therefore they are to be careful about taking credit for their successes. "Beware lest you say in your heart, 'My power and the might of my hand have gotten me this wealth'" (8:17).

One of the most exhilarating experiences I have had in my forays into Western music was singing in the Asbury Seminary choir when they performed *The Creation* by Franz Joseph Haydn (1732–1809). There is a memorable place in this oratorio where the following words are sung: "And God said, 'Let there be light.' And there was light." The words, timing, volume, and melody blend beautifully to communicate a powerful message. When Haydn was an old man, he was brought on a stretcher to hear a performance of *The Creation* in Vienna. When the chorus sang, "And there was light," the audience burst into applause. Haydn lifted up his trembling hands and said, "Not from me. It all comes from Above."[5]

Judgment (8:18–20)

Our passage teaches that when the Israelites lose the sense of being under God, God will become their adversary. That is a terribly dangerous situation in which to be. They are a people whose success depends on the covenant that God made with them. So Moses tells them that acknowledging that God is the source of their wealth is necessary for God to continue to look after them according to his covenant. "You shall remember the LORD your God, for it is he who gives you power to get wealth, that he may confirm his covenant that he swore to your fathers, as it is this day" (8:18). Indeed, they did do some work toward achieving this wealth, but God was the one who gave them the "power to get wealth."

Those who bask in the glory of self-congratulation must be confronted with the judgment that such arrogant denial of God merits. So Moses solemnly warns, "And if you forget the LORD your God and go after other gods and serve them and worship them, I solemnly warn you today that you shall surely perish. Like the nations that the LORD makes to perish before you, so shall you perish, because you would not obey the voice of the LORD your God" (8:19, 20). The prosperous respect power, and while they may dismiss God's love as being for the weak, they can be made to consider the power of God, as Nebuchadnezzar did. God had spoken to him several times, but he would not listen. One day, a year after he had been warned by God through Daniel, while walking on the roof of his royal palace he said something similar to the words that Moses said the arrogant Israelites would say (8:17): "Is not this great Babylon, which I have built by my mighty power as a royal residence and for the glory of my majesty?" (Daniel 4:30). While he was saying those words, judgment came upon him, and he was reduced to being like an animal. Fortunately for Nebuchadnezzar, he got an opportunity to repent, and he was restored to his former glory.

How amazing that those who rebel against God continue in their rebellion in spite of many warnings from God. It may be a severe heart attack that brings them close to death's door. They call for the pastor to come and pray. They seem to want to return to God. But when they are better, they continue along their former path, putting the pursuit of wealth and status in place of God. What can we do with such people? We can pray earnestly for a breakthrough in their life. We can use whatever opportunities we have to urge them to come back to God. Another thing we must try to do is to warn them about judgment, just as Moses did in our passage and as Daniel did with Nebuchadnezzar. I wrote a book on the doctrine of Hell several years ago.[6] When it became known that I was writing this book, many people volunteered the information that it was the doctrine of Hell that triggered the process that resulted in their conversion. A wise person would heed a warning of danger.

Yet many people today have tried to trivialize Hell, and they try to make light of the prospect of a coming judgment. *Hell* has become a swear word that people use very casually. They act confident and joke about spiritual things to put on a show of not being too worried about their spiritual destiny. But they cannot totally eradicate the fear of judgment.

As I said earlier, Francis Schaeffer used to say that people build a roof over their heads to prevent themselves from facing the rays of truth that confront them. The prospect of judgment is one of those things that should terrify them. But they try to live as if it is not a reality with which to reckon. They may do this through a carefree attitude. They may bring intellectual arguments against belief. They may try to show that only what happens on earth really matters. But deep down there is a sense in every person that sin ought to be punished. Paul, speaking of rebellious humans, says, "Though they know God's decree that those who practice such things deserve to die, they not only do them but give approval to those who practice them" (Romans 1:32). Schaeffer says that our calling as witnesses to the truth is to take off this roof that blocks the rays of truth from hitting them.

Deuteronomy 8 shows us that the great danger of prosperity is that it can cause people to take the credit for their success, which will lead them to forget God. It also shows that God sends deprivations that will push them back to trusting in him. When such deprivations come, may we not fight them but take them as gifts of God aimed at bringing us back to the things that matter most in life.

29

God Wins in Spite of Us

DEUTERONOMY 9:1–8

THIS PASSAGE COMES in the middle of Moses's second and longest speech in a section that gives several exhortations on life as a covenant people. Deuteronomy 9:1—10:11 forms a unit in which Moses warns the people about the possibility of unfaithfulness based on their past failures.

God's Plan to Defeat Powerful Enemies (9:1–4)

Two Ways of Looking at Challenges (9:1–3a)

In verses 1, 2 Moses tells the people that they are to cross the Jordan and take over the Canaanite nations. He describes those peoples as "nations greater and mightier than yourselves, cities great and fortified up to heaven, a people great and tall, the sons of the Anakim, whom you know, and of whom you have heard it said, 'Who can stand before the sons of Anak?'" The power of the nations and their people are highlighted. These verses have a lot in common with 1:28, but there the greatness of these peoples is highlighted as an excuse for not going out to battle them. Here the same truth is used to remind the people that the God who goes out with them to battle is greater than these enemy forces. So the next verse says, "Know therefore today that he who goes over before you as a consuming fire is the LORD your God. He will destroy them and subdue them before you. So you shall drive them out and make them perish quickly, as the LORD has promised you" (9:3).

In chapter 1 the challenge is an excuse for giving up the battle. In chapter 9 the same challenge is an occasion to prove God's ability. Some when faced with a huge challenge begin to grumble as if to say that God has forsaken or failed them. They throw in the towel even before the battle begins. As leaders our task is to do what Moses often did: to help boost the people's faith by challenging them to persevere, believing in God's power without giving up. Others say that if God has permitted such a huge challenge it is because he has planned a great victory. The challenge spurs them to be more determined, so they work with greater intensity until the battle is won.

These two reactions are seen when Christians face problems in marriage or when a project they started, believing it is of God, encounters major problems. One group gives up, while the other keeps believing that it is God's will for them to persevere until victory comes. Countless couples who are now enjoying a relatively happy home life will testify to God's sufficient grace carrying them through tough years in their marriages as they strove to make the marriage succeed amidst much conflict. Most great leaders who have succeeded in tough tasks will, if asked, talk of huge challenges they faced before success came. They refused to give up because they knew that God was greater than the challenges.

In verse 3 Moses tells the people that the Lord their God "goes over before [them] as a consuming fire" to "destroy" and "subdue" their enemies just as he has "promised." We have already discussed how God was described as "a consuming fire" in 4:24. But there the figure was used to say that he will punish Israel if they follow idols. Here it is used when describing God's ability to destroy and subdue the enemies of Israel. Note how the same quality of God's wrath is used to describe God's punishment of those who identify as his people and of those who don't.

The way the figure of God as a consuming fire is used here can be a great source of encouragement to us. We often encounter huge enemies that seem to stop us from experiencing what we know clearly to be God's will for us. It may be the fiery darts of Satan coming in the form of temptation or discouragement; it may be a human enemy; it may be what seems to be an obstacle that we cannot surmount. We must not lose heart. Our God goes before us as a consuming fire that will destroy and subdue all hindrances to his plans. The power of the enemy may seem to be much greater than our own, and we may seem dwarfed by this huge giant. But we can trust in God's ability and concentrate on obedience, knowing that the key that opens the door to his ability is our obedience. Let's not be afraid of our enemies!

It's God's Victory, Not Ours (9:3b–6a)

Not Because of Our Righteousness 9:3b–6

In verse 3 Moses says that the battle is won by God: "He will destroy them and subdue them before you." But God uses the people as his instruments:

"So you shall drive them out and make them perish quickly." Their part is to obey. Earlier when God asked them to go and take the land, they refused, and as a result they had to wander in the wilderness for thirty-eight years. This time, however, they will obey. But they might become proud and take the credit for the victory. So Moses says, "Do not say in your heart, after the LORD your God has thrust them out before you, 'It is because of my righteousness that the LORD has brought me in to possess this land,' whereas it is because of the wickedness of these nations that the LORD is driving them out before you" (9:4). Many contemporary commentators think that the quote marks indicating what the people could say should end at the end of this verse.[1] That is, Moses sees the possibility of the Israelites saying that they won this victory because God thought they were righteous and the Canaanites were wicked. Verse 5 says, ". . . because of the wickedness of these nations the LORD your God is driving them out from before you." They would be right about the wickedness of the Canaanites but wrong about their own righteousness being the cause of the conquest.

Three times (in verses 4, 5, and 6) Moses states that it is not because of their righteousness that the victory will come. The repetition highlights the fact that this is the most important point in these three verses. How often we try to show that we deserve the blessings we have received. People boast unashamedly in the media, and it is not usually considered inappropriate. Even in Christian settings people seem to think they deserve to get the credit for some achievement of theirs. Some would preface a boastful statement with the words "I am humbled" as if they were giving the credit to God. Some even plan, or get others to plan, felicitation ceremonies to honor themselves over some victory. I wish more people would rise up against these and show that these are inappropriate and a waste of time.

The Bible has a very high place for ceremonies and songs celebrating God's victories. But there all the glory should go to God (see, e.g., Exodus 15:1–21; Judges 5; Psalm 47; Jonah 2). Testimony must have an important place in Christian community life, but our experiences need to be shared in a way that will bring all the glory to God. The great Scottish pastor-theologian James Denney (1856–1917) had framed in his church vestry the words, "No man can bear witness to Christ and to himself at the same time. No man can give the impression that he himself is clever and that Christ is mighty to save."[2] In 1992 an interviewer asked Billy Graham, "What do you want people to say about you when you're gone?" He responded by saying, "I don't want people to say anything about me. I want them to talk about my Savior. The only thing I want to hear is Jesus saying, 'Well done, my good and faithful servant.' But I'm not sure I'm going to hear that."[3]

Many testimonies we hear today draw attention more to the testifier than to God. A more Christian way to testify would be to show how helpless and desperately needy we were or how we messed up a situation and how God in his mercy intervened and saw us through. The thrust of verses 6, 7 is that it is *not because of* their righteousness but *in spite of* their stubbornness that God will give them victory.

Those who focus on their qualifications for service will never be happy people. Deep down they know that they don't deserve the honors they receive because their lives do not match up to God's standard of righteousness. So they cannot fully enjoy those honors. Because they are looking for honor on earth, they will feel cheated when not recognized. They will see the victories of others as threats to their position, and so they cannot enjoy the blessings God gives through others in the body. What freedom there is when you live with an ambition to deflect all glory to God! When God gets any glory we are thrilled because we are one with him. So we do get glory from victories. But it is the reflected glory that we share over our heavenly Father's victories. Besides, when you recognize that you don't deserve honor, everything you get becomes a bonus. Instead of being angry at not being recognized, we rejoice that we were given all these bonus blessings from God.

Because of His Promise (9:5)

In addition to the wickedness of the nations, verse 5 ends with another reason for God's granting the people victory: ". . . and that he may confirm the word that the LORD swore to your fathers, to Abraham, to Isaac, and to Jacob." The key to the victory is that it has gone toward accomplishing God's purpose for the history of the world. He has revealed some things about that history, and based on that revelation we set the course for our lives and work. This gives us confidence as we seek to serve God. The obstacles are huge, and sometimes we seem to be laboring with no results in sight. But God is working out his purposes, and our work is a building block used in the constructing of his kingdom.

I write this at a time when Christians doing evangelism in Sri Lanka are living with much uncertainty and fear. Following several months of physical attacks on Christians, legislation has been sent to parliament that could outlaw much of what we do. We have great concern and some trepidation. But deep down there is an excitement at the thought that God is going to use this crisis to do something wonderful in our land. Evangelism is God's agenda. We must not be surprised if we suffer for doing it. In fact, the Bible promises that this will happen (John 15:20; 2 Timothy 3:12). If we are faithful to our task, we will find out someday that the apparent defeats were actually means used by God to take his work forward.

It is a great thrill to be used in the cause of the kingdom of God, which is moving toward the day when it will rule the whole the universe. Isaiah says, "How beautiful upon the mountains are the feet of him who brings good news, who publishes peace, who brings good news of happiness, who publishes salvation, who says to Zion, 'Your God reigns'" (Isaiah 52:7). The world may not recognize this, but we know that it is true. This is a source of great joy to us (see 1 Timothy 1:12–17). The joy of thanksgiving for God's grace in using us in so significant a work is the best alternative there is to self-glorying. It surpasses by far the satisfaction that earthly glory brings.

Remember Past Stubbornness (9:6b–8)

Why We Must Remember (9:6b, 7)

After saying that God is not giving them the land because of their righteousness, Moses said, ". . . for you are a stubborn people" (9:6b). "Stubborn" (9:6, 13) is usually translated "stiff-necked" (the two Hebrew words used here literally mean "hard of neck"). Eugene Merrill describes its use here as meaning "unwillingness to submit to the yoke of God's sovereignty (cf. Exodus 32:9; 33:3, 5; 34:9; Isaiah 48:4)." Often this is what leads to disobedience. We refuse to accept that God knows best and rebel against what happens to us. We lose "joy and peace in believing" (Romans 15:13). We try alternative paths to fulfill our aims: we lie, we take revenge, we go to another, we betray our friends, or we marry an unbeliever. We reason that because God is not doing a good job looking after us, we must use other methods. Then Moses said, "Remember and do not forget how you provoked the LORD your God to wrath in the wilderness. From the day you came out of the land of Egypt until you came to this place, you have been rebellious against the LORD" (Deuteronomy 9:7).

Moses says, "From the day you came out of the land of Egypt until you came to this place, you have been rebellious against the LORD" (9:7b). Then he goes on to describe a specific instance of this rebellion: the golden calf incident (9:8–21). Sadly, many of us who serve the Lord have a similar testimony. We cannot say that God used us primarily because of our obedience. We can list a catalog of sins and shortcomings that would disqualify us from being used by God. But God has still used us. That does not mean we forget our failures. Note how emphatic Moses' words about remembering their past sins are in verse 7: "Remember and do not forget . . . " Verse 6 starts with, "Know, therefore . . . "

Why is it so important to remember our past failures? Doesn't Paul speak about "forgetting what lies behind and straining forward to what lies ahead" (Philippians 3:13)? Paul is speaking about forgetting those things that hinder our forward march. Most probably he means resting on our past achievements and becoming complacent, thinking that we have "arrived." It could also mean depression over past failures and sorrows. Moses is talking about something else. Their past sins revealed weak areas in their lives. They need to be watchful in those areas and not take risks by putting themselves into situations that make them vulnerable to temptation. So they must remember these past failings.

A recently recovered alcoholic or drug user must stay clear of situations where he would be tempted to consume "just a little." This step could take him along a path that soon gets him back to his addictive behavior. One who was addicted to pornography must not expose himself to even "borderline" websites, TV programs, films, or literature that could open the door to his return to addictive behavior. One with a history of overworking and neglecting her family must be constantly alert to this danger because she could get so engrossed in work that she ends up neglecting the family without realizing it. We remember so that we won't get careless about obedience, especially in our weak areas.

God Is Provoked (9:7, 8)

Both verses 7 and 8 say that the people "provoked the Lord to wrath." Verse 8 goes on, "and the LORD was so angry with you that he was ready to destroy you." There was a move in the last century connected with scholars like C. H. Dodd to separate wrath from the nature of God. These scholars argued that though the Old Testament presents God's wrath as part of his nature, in the New Testament wrath is an impersonal force of cause and effect in response to sin and is not part of God's nature. This would make it much like the karmic force in Eastern religions by which individuals accrue good and bad merit respectively according to their thoughts and actions. This determines what they will be and encounter in their next life. However, it can be amply demonstrated that both in the New and Old Testaments wrath is very much a part of God's nature.[4]

It has been said that there are more references to the wrath and anger of God in the Bible than to the love of God. Possibly this is because wrath is a topic we would easily ignore, because it is not a pleasant topic about which to think or talk. We must heed the advice of Paul: "Note then the kindness and the severity of God: severity toward those who have fallen, but God's kindness to you, provided you continue in his kindness. Otherwise you too will be cut off" (Romans 11:22).

There is very little teaching on the wrath of God in the church today. The effects of this are disastrous. We cannot fully understand the meaning of salvation until we understand God's wrath over our sin that Christ took upon himself at the cross. How can we understand what it means to be saved if we do not know what we are saved from? Salvation can become merely a plus that comes to our life and makes it more meaningful rather than a transformation from death to life, from eternal damnation to eternal salvation. Without a proper understanding of wrath we would not know how to have the healthy fear of God that is essential for healthy Christian living and worship. Hebrews 12:28, 29 says, "Therefore let us be grateful for receiving a kingdom that cannot be shaken, and thus let us offer to God acceptable worship, with reverence and awe, for our God is a consuming fire" (see also Philippians 2:12; Hebrews 10:31).

The result of this neglect is the carelessness about sin, holiness, and discipline that we see among Christians today. If we saw sin as something that provokes Almighty God to anger, we would be more careful about living holy lives. Horror of sin would motivate us to flee from it, even though the majority of our contemporaries embrace it with relish. Our evangelism would also be affected. The Bible teaches that sin and unbelief arouse God's wrath (Romans 1:18–32). That would spur us to evangelism so that we could "save others by snatching them out of the fire" (Jude 23).

So let us look at life through the lens of God's working in this world. We can join him and march along his victorious way, or we can disobey to our peril.

30

A Rebellious People and
a Praying Leader

DEUTERONOMY 9:9–24

IN DEUTERONOMY 9:4–6 Moses asserts that the Israelites will conquer the land not because of their righteousness but because of the wickedness of the people of the nations and because of God's action in fulfilling his promises. To buttress this point he states that the Israelites had been a stubborn and rebellious people (9:6, 7). The previous study ended with the introduction of an event in Horeb, or Mount Sinai, that is given as an example of the rebelliousness of the people (9:8). Now we will look at Moses' description of that event and its aftermath. In the process we get a model of how to lead a people after they have sinned. In this passage we see Moses as a high priest, representing God to the people and the people to God.

The Leader Receives God's Word (9:9, 10)

Moses begins the story by describing his first visit to the mountain (9:9–12). Here he is equipped so he can represent God to the people. He is given two tablets of stone "written with the finger of God" (9:10). Moses says these are "the tablets of the covenant that the LORD made with you" (9:9), and that "on them were all the words that the LORD had spoken with you on the mountain" (9:10). Deuteronomy 10:4 explains that the tablets contained the Ten Commandments. The Ten Commandments were a unique summary of the Law and were a complete unit. So we interpret "all the words" in verse 10 as referring to all the words of the Ten Commandments.

During the forty days and forty nights that Moses spent on the mountain, he "neither ate bread nor drank water" (9:9). During this time of fasting, God gave him the Law that would become a key block of God's unique revelation to humanity. I am assuming that Moses also spent time praying during these forty days. Now that we have a complete Bible we are not bearers of normative revelation to the people of God like Moses was. But we, especially those of us in leadership positions, often mediate God's message to his people. Parents do this with their children. Preachers lead their people into an understanding of God's ways and plan for their lives and for the community to which they belong. Because the world's way of thinking is so different from God's way of thinking, it is vitally important that the leaders of God's people orient their minds to God's way of thinking. The only way we can do this is by lingering in the presence of God in prayer and with his Word, like Moses did.

Sometimes we need to give special extended periods to seeking God's face—possibly with fasting—especially because the world's ways and rush could affect us so much that it takes some effort to wean us from its influence. It is especially important to spend special time at the start of a major project or before an important event when God's leadership and the leader's anointing are desperately needed. When we are in close communion with God there is a greater chance that our decisions, our initiatives, and our reactions to situations will be close to God's way of thinking. When counseling people and praying for them, we must be in tune with God. Generally before I preach or teach or counsel or pray with a person, and also during this activity, I ask God to guide me to say the right thing. Usually these are desperate pleas for help, which I believe God hears and answers. But it is even more important for us to be in tune with God through unhurried times with him. In fact, if we are not in tune with him we may not even be in a mood to pray those emergency prayers.

As the church is an institution in society, we can adopt methods of leadership that are proven to be effective in society and see significant growth and what looks like success. But because God's thoughts and ways are so different from the thoughts and ways of the world (Isaiah 55:8, 9), what looks like success in the world could be failure in God's sight. This is why it is so dangerous when Christian leaders do not spend extended times with God. They could lead God's people away from God! Current statistics of the behavior and lifestyles of Christians suggests that something is wrong in the program of the church. We don't seem to be able to nurture godly people in the church! Could it be that our programs are attracting people to church but not to the ways of God?

Our leadership must flow from intimate communion with God. I would say that this is the most important part of the schedule of any Christian, especially a Christian leader. When the great British Baptist preacher Charles

Spurgeon (1834–1892) was asked the secret of his success, he replied, "Knee work! Knee work."[1] My father made his commitment to Christ under the preaching of American missionary E. Stanley Jones, when he was a university student in Sri Lanka. Jones had a brilliant and amazingly deep evangelistic and preaching ministry until he was in his late eighties. My homiletics teacher Donald Demaray once gave him a ride after a meeting and asked him what the secret of his effectiveness was. Jones was embarrassed by the question and did not answer at first. Then just before he got out of the car he said, "Prayer."

Some days when my time with God has been rushed I sense the pressure of the world hitting me. I try to take off and spend some special time with God and his Word at home or in some other quiet place. This is because I know that if I am out of touch with God I could easily do and say things that are not in keeping with God's will. I sometimes sing a simple song by William Longstaff titled "Take Time to Be Holy" in my devotional time because it reminds us that we must prioritize the pursuit of holiness and that a key to this is giving time to be with God. One verse in this song says:

> Take time to be holy, the world rushes on;
> Spend much time in secret with Jesus alone.
> By looking to Jesus, like him thou shalt be;
> Thy friends in thy conduct his likeness shall see.

Lingering for extended periods seeking God's face does not come naturally to me. This has been a major battle for me in more than forty-eight years as a committed Christian and thirty-five years as a "full-time" minister. I find that I take to work more naturally than lingering in the presence of God! But this is a battle I have kept on fighting all these years, I hope with some success. We may not take to being alone with God so naturally, but the theology we derive from the Bible informs us of its importance. Then we would pray as an act of obedience to the God we love. Someone has said the secret of prayer is praying. We may not feel like doing it, but we do it!

The Leader Confronts the People's Rebellion (9:12–16, 21–24)

Moses' reaction to the idolatry gives us a good picture of how a real mediator between God and humans acts when the people sin. To the people he talks about God's wrath and to God he talks about the people's need.

Confronting the Sin of the People (9:12–17, 21)

After Moses' time of receiving the Law is complete, God asks him to "go down quickly" to the people because they have "turned aside quickly out of the way" of God (9:12). God tells Moses that he plans to destroy the people: "I have seen this people, and behold, it is a stubborn people. Let me alone, that I may destroy them and blot out their name from under heaven" (9:13, 14a). Moses may have started to plead on behalf of the people as soon as he heard about their apostasy, resulting in God's saying, "Let me alone." Then God says that he will punish the people because of what they did and that the destruction of the people will result in personal gain for Moses: "And I will make of you a nation mightier and greater than they" (9:14b). Moses does not even consider that prospect. Exodus records a plea to God to have mercy on the people (Exodus 32:11–13), which Moses prayed after God told him about the apostasy.

This passage is helpful to us today because even under the new covenant, some people turn away from God when they are free from the influence of their godly leaders. How did Moses handle the sin of the people? He went down and saw the golden calf and immediately expressed his disapproval of it (9:15, 16). Then he "took hold of the two tablets and threw them out of [his] two hands and broke them before [their] eyes" (9:17). Clearly Moses was provoked to anger by the sin of the people. The tablets were symbols of the covenant relationship between God and the Israelites. The breaking of the tablets signified the breaking of the covenant relationship. Earlier we talked about how Moses took on the stress of the people (1:9–13). Now we see him expressing his anger over the people's behavior. In the previous study we said that wrath is an essential part of God's nature. As representatives of God we too should express anger when confronted with the people's sin.

Moses expresses God's wrath by burning the golden calf with fire: "Then I took the sinful thing, the calf that you had made, and burned it with fire and crushed it, grinding it very small, until it was as fine as dust. And I threw the dust of it into the brook that ran down from the mountain" (9:21). In Biblical times gold was "taken as the representation of the most valuable of man's material possessions (cf. Psalm 19:10; 1 Peter 1:7)."[2] So what was destroyed must have been worth a lot. Today we may be tempted to sell the gold or to melt it to make something legitimate out of it. But it was polluted and could distract people from God, so it needed to be renounced totally.

It is necessary for us to renounce everything associated to things that held us in sinful bondage. When my roommate in university came to Christ, he wore an expensive gold talisman around his waist. He had obtained it for protection from evil influences. I remember how he came in one day to our room and announced that he had thrown the talisman into a rice field. He could have had it melted and made use of or sold the gold. But he needed to sever all contacts with it. Similarly, a repentant user of pornography needs to burn (not sell or give away) the books and videos that once held him in bondage. A woman who ends an affair needs to get rid of everything associated with it such as photos, letters, and gifts.

Corporate Solidarity (9:16, 17)

Earlier we saw Moses' solidarity with the people when he identified with their sin even though *he* had not sinned. The idea of corporate solidarity is taken a step further in verses 16, 17 when Moses speaks to the people in the second person when talking about the sins of their parents. None of the generation that sinned at Horeb remained, but Moses says, "And I looked, and behold, *you* had sinned against the LORD your God. *You* had made *yourselves* a golden calf. *You* had turned aside quickly from the way that the LORD had commanded *you*" (9:16). Is this fair? This comes from the Biblical idea of corporate solidarity by which individuals are viewed very much in connection with the community to which they belong. So they identify with their parents' sin as if it were their own (for more on corporate solidarity see the discussion on 5:3–5).

This is an aspect of Biblical religion that has become neglected, especially in the West, with the rise of individualism. Christians pay so much attention to the individual aspects of conversion and Christian living that they miss out on the Biblical insistence that Christianity is lived out in community. We forget, for example, that most of the passages in the New Testament about living the Christian life are in the plural. This is a fact that is often not noticed in the English because in English, words like "you" and "your" can be singular or plural.

In our passage the children are made to identify with the sins of the parents. This is something that Christians must take into account, especially when they relate to groups in which the idea of corporate solidarity is still very strong. And that is the way it is in most of the non-Western world. So in the last century when Japanese Christians met with other Asian Christians at conferences, it was quite common to see them enact some formal rituals of apologizing to the people and seeking their forgiveness for the atrocities the Japanese committed in their nations about fifty years earlier. I am sure that none of those people personally had anything to do with those actions. But they knew it was their duty to apologize for the sins of the Japanese imperialists. The result was a sense of healing and new openings for true fellowship between the Japanese and other Asians, such as the Chinese and the Koreans.

In 1983 in Sri Lanka, the people of my Sinhala race went on the rampage and committed many atrocities against the Tamil people. Bishop Lakshman

Wickremasinghe, who was an esteemed Anglican bishop and from the Sinhala race, was not in Sri Lanka during the riots. When he landed in Sri Lanka, the first thing he said was, "We have sinned." He took responsibility for the sin of his people. During those riots and afterward, my wife and I kept several Tamils in our home either for their safety or because their houses had been burned. Some of them would heatedly express their anger to me about what the people of my race had done. They were deeply hurt, and sometimes their anger was directed at me. I felt it was my privilege to take on that burden on behalf of my people and, by giving them an opportunity to share their pain and anger, hopefully be an agent of healing in their lives.

Today Native Americans and Afro-Americans may accuse the Caucasian people of North America of being responsible for the drunkenness and lack of motivation and initiative that is rampant in their communities. These are communities in which corporate solidarity is stronger than in the Caucasian community. Some would say there are ample opportunities for them to thrive if they only work hard. But the blows to their identity received in history may act as a deterrent to a majority of them being motivated enough to make use of these opportunities. An attitude of humble penitence for the sins of the forefathers would be much more appropriate in this environment.

In the Middle Ages the Muslim empires were generally more tolerant of the Christians than the Christians were of the Muslims. This plus things like the awful history of the Crusades and the recent attacks on morality coming through Western media that are threatening the very fabric of Muslim society has left many bitter feelings about Christians among Muslims. When they accuse us of such injustice and immorality, it would be good for us to accept responsibility in a humble and apologetic manner and try to show that true Christians today are also enraged by these same things.

More Instances of Rebellion (9:22–24)

In the middle of the narrative about the golden calf incident, Moses slips in four more instances of the rebelliousness of the people. He simply states the places where three of them occurred— Taberah (Numbers 11:3), Massah (Exodus 17:7), and Kibroth-hattaavah (Numbers 11:34)—and says that in these places they "provoked the LORD to wrath" (Deuteronomy 9:22). A little more space is devoted to the incident in Kadesh-barnea, where they refused to go up and possess the land after the spies brought their report of the land (9:23). This incident had figured in Moses' first speech (see Deuteronomy 1). After this Moses presents his indictment against the people: "You have been rebellious against the LORD from the day that I knew you" (9:24). Our passage shows that despite such rebellions, Moses did not give up on the people he was called to lead.

The Leader Intercedes for the People (9:18–20)

Taking on the Pain of the People

Note God's words: ". . . your people whom you have brought from Egypt have acted corruptly" (9:12). Moses was not there when they rebelled, and he had absolutely no part in their rebellion. In fact they were always rebelling against Moses also. But God describes them as "*your* people whom *you* have brought from Egypt." Would he want to associate himself so closely with the people at this time?

God gives him another proposal in verse 14: "Let me alone, that I may destroy them and blot out their name from under heaven. And I will make of you a nation mightier and greater than they." Because of their rebellion Moses had complained against them often. Now God was offering him a way out of the problem. There could be a new nation to bear God's name with Moses as the father of the nation. What an honor that would be! It is like a pastor who is really frustrated with his congregation because they are behaving so badly. They have rejected his authority and have taken on practices that he specifically prohibited. Something in him tells him he deserves a better congregation. And just at that time he gets the opportunity to be senior pastor of a large thriving congregation. What would he do? I think most Christian leaders would take the new offer!

But Moses was like the Good Shepherd who died for the sheep without forsaking them when the wolves came (John 10:11–15). The word *pastor* is the Latin word for "shepherd." Pastors are people who die for their sheep! Moses did something like that. I do not know how he managed without dying the first time he spent forty days without food and water. But now he goes back to the mountain for another grueling forty-day fast to intercede for the people (9:18). He did not want to be the father of "a nation mightier and greater than they" (9:14). He wanted to see his people saved. He was like the Scottish reformer John Knox (1514–1572) who cried, "Give me Scotland or I die." Today many will just change churches or groups when they face severe disappointment. In fact, we have made things really simple. When we ask people to commit to a small group, we also give a time limitation. How convenient! And yet how hard it is to learn Christian commitment in such an environment!

Moses and the great Biblical leaders were passionately committed to their people. The English word *passion* comes from the Latin word *passio* meaning "suffering." A sure test of commitment to a group is the willingness to suffer for them. After a long list of his sufferings for the gospel Paul said, "And, apart from other things, there is the daily pressure on me of my anxiety for all the churches. Who is weak, and I am not weak? Who is made to fall, and I am not indignant?" (2 Corinthians 11:28, 29).

We may call Paul a basket case in need of psychological counseling for taking on such stress! But the weeping prophet Jeremiah did the same (see Jeremiah 9, 15), and so did the righteous man Daniel as they thought about their people. Daniel even confessed the sin of the people in the first person, as if the people's sin was his own sin (see Daniel 9). Nehemiah was, like Daniel, also successful in a foreign country, but when he heard bad news from the home country, he wept, fasted, prayed, and confessed in the first person for days. Even his master the king noticed that his face was sad (see Nehemiah 1, 2). I fear that today if a pastor came to church on Sunday with such a face, he might lose his job!

I think we have developed a worldly understanding of joy that cannot coexist with the stress of concern for people. But if we have the joy of the Lord, that will give us the strength to face the stress. This is why, before commanding his disciples to love one another by giving their lives for each other, Jesus told them that he was giving them his joy and that with his joy their joy would be full (John 15:11–13).

Humble, Earnest, Persevering Intercession (9:18, 19a)

Moses had just returned from the mountain after forty days of fasting. There he was equipped to represent God before the people. And now he goes up again for another forty-day fast (9:18). This time he goes to represent the people before God. As their priest he will intercede for them. The people, and even their high priest Aaron, had become restless during Moses' absence and had done something terrible. It was a crisis time. We would have expected Moses to stay with the people to get them back onto the right path. I suppose today most people would advise a leader in this type of situation to stay back for the sake of his own physical health and for the overall health of the people. But at this time more important than all of this was the need to go to God and plead for his mercy on the people. So Moses took the risk of leaving the people under the care of the leaders who had just failed so badly, and he went away to be with God. Often when we think of solutions to problems, the importance of our actions is overrated, while the importance of pleading with God in prayer is underrated.

The Bible is clear that the prayer life of leaders has a huge impact on those they lead. Abraham reasoned with God on behalf of Sodom, and Lot and his family were saved because of that (Genesis 18, 19). When Joshua led the people in a war against the Amalekites, Moses prayed, with Aaron and Hur helping to hold his hands up, until the battle was won (Exodus 17:8–13). Samuel thought that he would "sin against the LORD by ceasing to pray for" the people of Israel (1 Samuel 12:23). The longest subject of the longest recorded prayer of Jesus was his praying for his disciples, which covers seventeen of the twenty-six verses (John 17:6–19, 24–26). The only time Jesus spoke about his prayer life outside a prayer was when he said that he prayed for Peter (Luke 22:31, 32). Paul mentions praying for his recipients in ten of his thirteen letters. Prayer is so powerful that Paul viewed Epaphras as "always wrestling in prayer for [the Colossians]" even though he was not with them (Colossians 4:12, NIV).

Twice Moses "lay prostrate [or fell down, NASB] before the LORD . . . forty days and forty nights" (Deuteronomy 9:18, 25). Prostration expresses two things. First, it expresses *humility*. Moses had not sinned on this occasion, but he takes a humble posture. Humility is the only possible way that flawed human beings can approach the almighty and holy God. Even the perfect beings in Heaven "fall down before him" and "cast their crowns before the throne" (Revelation 4:10). So after our people have sinned, we too go to God with humility even though we are not the ones who sinned. We represent the people and are responsible for them; so we go to God like desperately hungry beggars pleading for mercy for our people.

Second, prostration expresses *earnestness*. This is a desperate situation that calls for desperate prayer. In two key places Luke uses the Greek word *ektenos* or "earnest" to describe prayer. One was the earnest prayer of Jesus in the garden of Gethsemane (Luke 22:44), and the other was the earnest prayer of the church for Peter when he was in prison (Acts 12:5). *Ektenos* literally means "stretched out." Earnest prayer is symbolized by hands stretched out to God in fervent supplication. This is wholehearted, urgent pleading to God.

The English preacher Samuel Chadwick has said, "Intensity is a law of prayer. . . . There are blessings of the kingdom that are only yielded to the violence of the vehement soul."[3] He gives several examples of this type of earnest prayer from the Bible: "Abraham pleading for Sodom, Jacob wrestling in the stillness of the night, Moses standing in the breach, Hannah intoxicated with sorrow, David heartbroken with remorse and grief."[4] Such prayer when used in intercession comes out of a passionate commitment to the people such as we talked about earlier.

About seventeen years ago we faced what I consider to be the biggest crisis in my time as Director of Youth for Christ (YFC) in Sri Lanka. Our method of operation had always included leaders debating long and hard on contentious issues until they came to agreement. This time we could not agree. And there were many angry people within the YFC family. Unused to working in a situation where there was such serious division among the leaders, all I could do was to go to God in sheer desperation. I would spend long hours seated helplessly in my room. I was unable to articulate my prayers too well, but I was aware of the fact that I was in the presence of God and was seeking his help. I think all of us, including me, made many mistakes during that crisis. But God saw us through and enabled us to work toward a resolution without relationships being permanently broken.

During this crisis I learned that prayer is one way to lead a movement. Prayer is one of the keys to leadership development also, as the examples from the prayer lives of Jesus and Paul cited above would suggest. I would say it is the most important key, though I cannot back that from Scripture. I believe that the most important thing I do for the people I lead is to pray for them (though I do not think I have done that as conscientiously as I should). For this reason praying for YFC is the first point on my job description. I have seen that the best leadership developers in our ministry are people of prayer. Growth in leadership is all a matter of grace, and prayer mediates grace to the lives of others.

Moses' extended period of forty days of prayer reminds us of the importance of what we may call prevailing prayer. This is the type of prayer in which a person perseveres in prayer for an extended period of time until the desired result comes. Jesus told the parable of the unjust judge and the persevering widow to encourage such prayer. Luke prefaces the parable by saying, "And he told them a parable to the effect that they ought always to pray and not lose heart" (Luke 18:1). This is how the disciples responded when Jesus "ordered them not to depart from Jerusalem, but to wait for the promise of the Father" (Acts 1:4). After Christ's ascension the disciples "with one accord were devoting themselves to prayer" (Acts 1:14).

In November 1844 George Muller began to pray for the conversion of five individuals. He says, "I prayed every day without one single intermission, whether sick or in health, on the land or on the sea, and whatever the pressure of my engagements might be." After eighteen months of such praying the first of the five was converted. Five years after this the second came to Christ, and the third after a further six years. Mueller said that he had been praying for thirty-six years for the other two and that they still remained unconverted. His biographer says that one of those two "became a Christian before Mueller's death and the other a few years later."[5]

Today we often find people addressing a situation by pronouncing

Christ's victory over that situation. This may be an appropriate practice in certain situations. But I fear that it has become more popular than the more important practice of persevering prayer. Perhaps this is a symptom of an impatient age that looks for instant solutions for every problem. Sometimes before a deep work of God is done, it needs to be preceded by patient, believing perseverance in prayer to God. We persevere not to overcome God's reluctance to answer but to battle those forces of evil that bind people and situations and prevent them from receiving God's blessings. Immediately after Paul mentions the armor of God he says, ". . . praying at all times in the Spirit, with all prayer and supplication. To that end keep alert with all perseverance, making supplication for all the saints . . . " (Ephesians 6:18). Such prayer is a form of spiritual warfare.

In this era of specialization we are seeing people who are known as specialists in prayer. We can thank God that at a time when a feature in the Christian life grows dim, God raises individuals to specially call the church back to that feature. However, all Christian leaders need to be specialists in prayer. We thank God for the specialists we have and hope that their message will find a fertile soil in the hearts of Christian leaders.

The Power of Intercession (9:19b, 20)

Moses then explains how serious the situation was: "For I was afraid of the anger and hot displeasure that the LORD bore against you, so that he was ready to destroy you" (9:19a). Yet Moses' intervention served to change things. He says, "But the LORD listened to me that time also" (9:19b). Exodus 32:14 explains, "And the LORD relented from the disaster that he had spoken of bringing on his people." Deuteronomy 9:20 implies that God didn't "destroy" Aaron as he had planned because of the prayers of Moses for Aaron. James 5:16b says, "The prayer of a righteous person has great power as it is working."

It is a mystery that the sovereign God would change his course of action in response to the prayers of righteous people. But that is the way he has chosen to work. And we have the great privilege of influencing the course of history through our prayers.

31

Powerful Prayer

DEUTERONOMY 9:25—10:11

IN MUCH OF CHAPTER 9 Moses has been explaining the golden calf incident at Horeb in a way that did not strictly follow chronological order. After talking about how he spent forty days and nights on the mountain fasting and praying and how God heard his prayer and spared the people, he backtracks a bit and describes the prayer he prayed (9:25–29) and then proceeds to describe the change of fortune resulting in the progress that the Israelites enjoyed after the prayer (10:1–11).

A Leader's Prayer (9:25–29)

Arguing with God

Verse 25 expresses again (see 9:18, 19) the serious crisis that faced the people and the submissive and earnest praying of Moses: "So I lay prostrate before the LORD for these forty days and forty nights, because the LORD had said he would destroy you." Verses 26–29 record the prayer of Moses, which sounds like an argument Moses had with God. Like a lawyer, Moses reasons with God as to why he should not destroy the Israelites.

Wesley Duewel in his wonderful book *Mighty Prevailing Prayer* has a chapter entitled "Holy Pleading and Argument Before God." He says:

> This holy argument with God is not done in a negative complaining spirit. It is an expression not of a critical heart but of a heart burning with love for God, for his name, and for his glory. This holy debate with God is a passionate presentation to God of the many reasons why it will be in harmony with his nature, his righteous government, and the history of his holy interventions on behalf of his people.[1]

Abraham argues like this with God over the destruction of Sodom (Genesis 18:22–33), which like Moses' prayer has a combination of both boldness and humility before God (see Genesis 18:27). We see Abraham arguing and God conceding points based on his requests, until a way is found for Lot and his family to be saved. As we said in the last chapter, it is a mystery that the sovereign Lord of the universe chooses to act in this way, but it indicates that our prayers do carry weight in God's scheme of things. And J. I. Packer gives another reason why God acts in this way. From insights gained from the writings of Bishop J. C. Ryle, John Owen, John Calvin, and P. T. Forsyth, he says, "God may actually resist us when we pray in order that we in turn may resist and overcome his resistance and so be led to deeper dependence on him and greater enrichment from him at the end of the day."[2] In other words, God lets us debate him for our own good and for the deepening of our faith.

They Are God's People (9:26, 29)

The main argument Moses makes in his prayer is that the Israelites are God's people. The ESV has Moses using the words "you" and "your" twelve times in this short prayer of four verses (9:26–29). Verses 26 and 29 are typical: "O Lord GOD, do not destroy *your* people and *your* heritage, whom *you* have redeemed through *your* greatness, whom *you* have brought out of Egypt with a mighty hand. . . . For they are *your* people and *your* heritage, whom *you* brought out by *your* great power and by *your* outstretched arm." Daniel prayed a similar prayer for Israel that he concluded with the words, "O Lord, hear; O Lord, forgive. O Lord, pay attention and act. Delay not, for *your own* sake, O my God, because *your* city and *your* people are called by *your name*" (Daniel 9:19). Twice in his prayer Moses refers to the Israelites as "your people and your heritage" (Deuteronomy 9:26, 29). His point is that God must protect the Israelites because they belong to God; they are God's covenant people. God's honor is at stake here. Defeat for God's people is an affront to the glory of God.

Jesus expressed the attitude we are describing when he cleansed the temple. After recording the incident, John comments, "His disciples remembered that it was written, 'Zeal for your house will consume me'" (John 2:17). The verb "consume" is in the future tense, but in Psalm 69:9, the source of that quote, it is in the past tense. Some scholars believe that the change to the future tense was because the disciples felt that "zeal for the temple will destroy Jesus and bring his death."[3] Jesus was willing to sacrifice his life to take away the dishonor that came to the name of the Lord God through his temple being misused.

The honor of God's name is one of the motivations that drive us in our prayers for and commitment to the church. We may be utterly disillusioned with the church, and in this era where lasting commitments are so out of fashion, we will be strongly tempted to leave our churches when something happens there that infuriates or hurts us. But this is God's church. We cannot leave the church so easily, for it bears the name of God on earth. We will identify ourselves with God's people and seek to bring about change so that the church will better reflect the nature of God.

Henry Martyn (1781–1812) was one of the most heroic figures in missionary history. After graduating at the top of his class in mathematics and receiving the coveted Wrangler award, he shunned the prospect of prosperity in England and went to India as a missionary to Muslims. After translating the New Testament and the Book of Common Prayer into the Hindustani language he went to Persia (now Iran) and translated the Bible into the Persian language. Once when he was in Persia a Muslim friend told him about an incident that is supposed to have taken place during the Crusades. He said, "Prince Abbas Mirza killed so many Christians that Christ from the fourth heaven took hold of [Muhammad's] skirt to entreat him to desist."

Martyn says, "I was cut to the soul at this blasphemy." The friend, observing his distress, asked him what was so offensive about what he had said. Martyn replied, "I could not endure existence if Jesus was not glorified; it would be hell to me if he was thus to be always dishonoured." The astonished visitor asked him, "Why?" Martyn said, "If anyone pluck out your eyes, there is no telling *why* you feel pain—it is feeling. It is because I am one with Christ that I am so dreadfully wounded."[4] He had a passionate commitment to the honor of God's name.

They Are a Redeemed People (9:26, 29)

Twice in this prayer Moses appeals to the fact that the Israelites have been redeemed by God: ". . . whom you have redeemed through your greatness, whom you have brought out of Egypt with a mighty hand" (9:26; see also 9:29). Their redemption, accompanied by great miraculous acts of God, would be rendered meaningless if they were destroyed now. Destroying them after this is like throwing away something very costly. What a terrible waste this would be!

This is the same thing we can appeal to when praying for the church. Speaking to leaders from the church at Ephesus Paul says, "Pay careful attention to yourselves and to all the flock, in which the Holy Spirit has made you overseers, to care for the church of God, which he obtained with his own blood" (Acts 20:28). We can pray to God to consider the huge price

Jesus paid to save the church so as to prevent that price from being rendered meaningless.

When we apply this after Calvary and realize that Christ died for all, then we look at people with eyes tinted by the gospel. We see people as those for whom Christ died. A great price has been paid for their redemption. What a tragedy it would be for such a person to be lost. I think the most meaningful Christmas day I ever had was a few years ago when one of my colleagues was in prison falsely accused of being a terrorist. He was released after fifteen months without any charges being brought against him. He had a great ministry there, and many people met Christ in the prison. On Christmas day I went with a team from Youth for Christ to take a Christmas meal for everyone in the prison (about 700 meals). All the prisoners there had either been convicted or were awaiting trial for terrorism. What joy we had when people came and told us that they thank God they came to prison because there they met Christ.

There I was introduced to a person who I was told was the mastermind of the bombing of our Joint Operations Command (JOC) building (the equivalent of the Pentagon in the USA). I remember that bombing very well because I heard it go off. When I asked someone where the bomb had exploded, he said, "At Royal College." That is the school where my little son was studying. His school was next to the JOC building, and so my informant thought that the bomb had gone off in the school. It was the scariest day of my life. I got on my motorcycle and rode as close to the school as they would let me go. Then I ran the rest of the way. What a relief it was when I found my son. All he had was a cut on his cheek from something that had fallen from the roof.

And now I was face-to-face with the person who was the mastermind of the whole thing. And all I could think of was that he was a person for whom Christ died. My colleague had told me that he was considering the gospel. When such a great price has been paid for people's redemption, their redemption becomes the most important thing about them. Have they been redeemed or have they not?

They Are a People Undergirded by Promises (9:27)

Moses now follows another path in his appeal to God. He asks God not to regard the stubbornness of the people but rather to regard the promises made to their forefathers: "Remember your servants, Abraham, Isaac, and Jacob. Do not regard the stubbornness of this people, or their wickedness or their sin" (9:27). Always the promises of God are greater than the sins of people. True, there are promises that include judgment for stubbornness, and we must not neglect those. But because the Bible says, ". . . where sin increased, grace abounded all the more" (Romans 5:20), we can appeal to grace to overcome their sinfulness.

We can invoke the covenant promises to plead for God's mercy, so that he can do what he promised to do for the church. Moses did this, invoking the promises made to the fathers of the Jewish nation. This is most interesting considering that God was offering Moses the opportunity to be the father of a new nation (9:14). But he would have none of it. He appeals to God to consider the real fathers of the nation. We can apply this to praying for revival or healing of our churches, our families, or our organizations. We can see how the promises give us boldness to believe and thus earnestly ask God to act. We pray, "Lord, you promised to give us all these blessings, but we don't presently enjoy them. Please give these blessings to us."

There was a great revival in the Hebrides Islands in the North of Scotland in the mid-twentieth century, the effects of which are said to still be evident. This revival has been linked to the earnest prayer of two sisters named Miss Smith and of a group of seven young men in a church. The latter group covenanted to meet three nights a week in a barn to pray for revival. They committed themselves to pray in keeping with Isaiah 62:6, 7 (NIV): "I have posted watchmen on your walls, Jerusalem; they will never be silent day or night. You who call on the LORD, give yourselves no rest, and give him no rest till he establishes Jerusalem and makes her the praise of the earth." They believed God had a plan for their islands, and they decided to storm the gates of Heaven—to give God no rest—until that plan was realized. One day as they prayed one of them led them in an act of confession and consecration. Heaven broke loose, and the revival that began with that small group spread to the whole island and then to many of the other islands.[5]

In our drug rehabilitation ministry we have seen some people come through and continue strong with the Lord. But we have seen others fall away. Some leave our rehab center confident that they are going to live a drug-free life. But after some time they are back on drugs and come them back to the center. We have seen many such failures. Yet one of the things that keep us motivated is the possibility of grace. Grace is greater than all sin, even addiction. The promise of God is sure. There can be victory. Braced with our confidence in the promises of God we persevere in this work.

Their Defeat Will Bring Shame to God (9:28)

Next, Moses goes back to his theme of God's honor. In the first and last verses of the prayer he reminds God that the Israelites are God's people (9:26, 29). In verse 28 he says that the destruction of these people will bring shame to God:

". . . lest the land from which you brought us say, 'Because the LORD was not able to bring them into the land that he promised them, and because he hated them, he has brought them out to put them to death in the wilderness'" (9:28).

The most awesome thing in the world—its greatest wealth and its reason to exist—is the glory of God. The biggest tragedy in the world is that so much of it does not recognize this glory. The great climax to which history is moving is the day when "the earth shall be full of the knowledge of the LORD as the waters cover the sea" (Isaiah 11:9). Therefore, the greatest ambition that drives us is enhancing the honor of God on earth. When that honor is diminished, it is a tragedy beyond comparison. Moses says that the destruction of the Israelites will be such an event. So he asks God to spare the people so that the Egyptians would not interpret that action in a way that is dishonoring to God.

How important it is for us to maintain this perspective of jealousy for the honor of God's name. When a good project that goes against the stream of worldliness by upholding God's principles is allowed to go under for lack of support, God is dishonored, because people say that it is not worthwhile or possible to follow God's principles in this world. So out of our commitment to the honor of God's name we should support the project at personal cost to ourselves to keep it from going under. When Christians go to courts against each other or battle each other in public the world laughs at us, and God is dishonored. Paul says it is better for us to suffer a personal loss than be a cause for the biggest tragedy to happen—for God to be dishonored by our fighting for a legitimate cause of ours (1 Corinthians 6:5–7).

This is why we cannot keep silent when we see things that dishonor God in church and society. Jealousy for God's honor banishes apathy. So when we see things that need to be confronted, rather than just ignoring them, we ask God what we should be doing about these things.

So we see that though Moses' prayer was specifically for God to have mercy on the Israelites, the underlying theme was the glory of God. Their destruction would dishonor God for four reasons:

1. They are God's own people (9:26, 29).
2. He had redeemed them before, and that redemption would be rendered meaningless by their destruction (9:26, 29).
3. The promises God made to their forefathers would be rendered meaningless by it (9:27).
4. It could cause people to say shameful things about God's motives for saving his people (9:28).

May our lives be similarly burdened by the vision of the glory of God so that all we do and all we ask of God may be motivated by this passion.

Progress after Intercession (10:1–11)

Deuteronomy 10:1–11 gives a summary of what happened after and as a result of Moses' prayer. The fortunes of God's people changed, and they began to move forward and progress again.

The Covenant Is Renewed (10:1–5)

First, God renews his covenant relationship with the people. He tells Moses, "Cut for yourself two tablets of stone like the first, and come up to me on the mountain and make an ark of wood" (10:1). On the tablets God would write the Ten Commandments, which were what was written on the previous tablets (10:2–4). A wooden ark was to house the tablets (10:5). In this very brief summary of a complex process Moses says that he made the ark (10:3). It was Bezalel who actually made it (Exodus 37:1). Moses initiated and directed the process; therefore Moses' claim is legitimate in such a brief summary.

Next, Moses says, "Then I turned and came down from the mountain and put the tablets in the ark that I had made. And there they are, as the LORD commanded me" (Deuteronomy 10:5). The account in Exodus shows that this whole process took a lot of time. What we have here is a summary that highlights the fact that the covenant was renewed. All this leads up to verse 12 where God tells the people what is required of them: a heart religion that majors on obedience.

J. A. Thompson explains, "The requirement that the covenant document was to be housed in the ark is a reflection of secular practice in the ancient Near East. It was normal to lodge copies of the treaty document in the sanctuaries of contracting parties, where they were under the surveillance of the deities who would guarantee the treaty, and, in case of a breach of treaty, would visit the party with judgment."[6] This is another case where Biblical religion uses some of the practices used by people in the society in which it is found without assimilating the system behind those practices. Here the ark and the tablets are used as visual reminders to the people that they are a covenant people whose lives are controlled by a treaty made with God.

Our passage implies that there was an act of renewal of the covenant in connection with the bringing of the second set of tablets by Moses. The account in Exodus 34 clearly describes what happened. The tablets and the ark were symbolic of the covenant and the path of obedience that it includes. I believe there is still a place for such acts of corporate renewal of our commitment to God along with some ritual or symbolic reminders of what that commitment means. When the people do not experience a vital relationship with God, these rituals and symbols become a substitute for heart religion and are sometimes considered a means to salvation. Evangelicals who are alert to the dangers of the misuse of corporate rituals and symbols can go to the extreme of neglecting them altogether, an equally dangerous error.

Deuteronomy 10 has a beautiful combination of the symbolic and ritual aspect and the heart-religion aspect of the life of faith. Verses 1–5 present the symbolic, with the ark and the tablets that will be a constant reminder to the people of the covenant. Verses 12–22 talk about a religion of the heart in response to the love of God. Even the New Testament has a place for symbolic rituals enacted in community such as the Lord's Supper and baptism.

We could also follow Moses' precedent of renewing the covenant after sin by having services of repentance or rededication. If we find that we have moved from our primary call, a service of recommitment to the call could signal a new phase in the life of our group. If we find that apathy and sin have entered our group, we could have acts of community confession and rededication, especially after what we now call revival meetings. The restoration of a Christian who has been disciplined could be accompanied by a service of restoration. The same could be done with a couple whose marriage had gone through tough times and who are now ready to start afresh with God's help. Sometimes these services will be done with the whole congregation or group. Sometimes only those in an inner circle need to be involved in it. These events could be preceded by a period of fasting that affirms our serious intent to follow God's will over our personal desires.

The Journey Is Resumed (10:6, 7)

Verses 6–9 are in the third person and may be an explanatory addition rather than a part of Moses' speech. For this reason many translations have this section as a parenthesis. With the covenant renewed and the people's relationship with God restored, they are able to restart their onward journey (10:6a). In "Moserah . . . Aaron died, and there he was buried" (10:6b). He, too, would have been restored to a relationship with God in answer to Moses' prayer for him (9:20), and therefore he probably dies of natural causes rather than as a punishment from God. "His son Eleazar ministered as priest in his place" (10:6c). After Aaron's burial, they proceed further in the journey.

There are some differences in the details of the account here and the parallel account in Numbers 33. The Numbers account presents itself as an itinerary, whereas in Deuteronomy what we have is a very brief summary statement. So we should go to Numbers for details about the itinerary. The locations of most of the places mentioned here have not been identified with certainty. The purpose of these verses in Deuteronomy is to state the fact that they started journeying after the terrible golden calf episode. Names of places are mentioned but probably without much attention being paid to the chronological order in which the places were visited. This happens sometimes in the Bible, such as in the record of the temptations of Christ in Matthew and Luke where the order of the second and third temptations is reversed.

Levites Are Set Apart (10:8, 9)

Verses 8, 9 include a note about the Levites being set apart for God's work. Four things are said about them. We will look at two of these in our discussion on 18:1–8. These are the call "to stand before the LORD to minister to him" (10:8c) and the rule that "Levi has no portion or inheritance with his brothers" because "the LORD is his inheritance" (10:9). The other two things are the duties of the Levites "to carry the ark of the covenant of the LORD" and "to bless in his name" (10:8b, d).

The task of carrying the ark was entrusted to the Kohathites, who were a non-priestly family of Levites (see Numbers 3, 4). That task was needed during the journeys of the people, and they carried it on their shoulders. The Kohathites were also responsible for the care of the tabernacle and all the services pertaining to it (Numbers 3:27–32). This was very important work in the Old Testament and needed to be done with meticulous care. Therefore considerable space is given in the Old Testament to describing this work.

There would not be a direct equivalent of this work today because we do not have a Tabernacle or as sacred an object as the ark of the covenant. But when we remember that these were the visible reminders of God's presence with the people, we could say that the equivalent of the Kohathites today are those whose service has to do with special occasions and places that show the presence of God. Included here would be getting the sanctuary prepared for worship so that it is a place that gives people an environment conducive to worshipping God "in spirit and truth" (John 4:24) and "with reverence and awe" (Hebrews 12:28). This includes architects, interior decorators, janitors, those responsible for maintenance, and those who arrange chairs and flowers. Some of us are not alert to these aesthetic things (I am notoriously weak here). We need people who love God's worship, who are aware of his holiness and love, and who are committed to beauty and order to help prepare our places of worship for use. And considering the space given to this type of thing in the Bible, we need to emphasize that this is an important aspect of the service the church renders to God.

The other Levite responsibility is "to bless [people] in [God's] name" (10:8d). This is a privilege that Christians, especially leaders, have. Mary

Evans explains that "to bless somebody is to express a hope or prayer that good, desirable things will happen to that person."[7] There are several blessings mentioned as having been given to people in both the Old and New Testaments. Sometimes blessings are pronounced on individuals and other times to whole groups.[8] The most famous Biblical blessing was the Aaronic blessing, which we still use: "The LORD bless you and keep you; the LORD make his face to shine upon you and be gracious to you; the LORD lift up his countenance upon you and give you peace" (Numbers 6:24–26). God usually mediates his blessings through others, and one of the ways he does this is through Christians pronouncing blessings on others. This is something that all Christians can do, and leaders have a particular privilege and responsibility to do this.

The most common way blessings are pronounced today is through the benedictions that are said before the gathered people of God leave. Today the leader often substitutes "us" for "you" as the object of the blessing. This misses something of the Biblical significance of God's blessing as being mediated by God's representative to another. Sometimes the gathering is asked to say the blessing to each other. In such a blessing this significance would be retained if we pronounced the blessing in the second person rather than the first—that is, by saying "bless you" to each other rather than "bless us."

We need to rediscover something of the sense of the importance of simple statements like "God bless you." When we want to communicate a loving desire for good to a person and there is not much time to do it, the best way to express our wish briefly is to say, "God bless you." It is an expression of love and of desiring the best for the person. Let's restore the practice of blessing people in God's name among Christians today!

Moses' Powerful Prayer (10:10, 11)

Before going into a further exhortation to holiness that begins at verse 12, Moses summarizes what happened after the people's sin. This shows the power of Moses' praying. He says, "I myself stayed on the mountain, as at the first time, forty days and forty nights, and the LORD listened to me that time also. The LORD was unwilling to destroy you" (10:10). There is a clear link implied here between Moses' prayer and God's unwillingness to destroy the people. They are ready now to proceed on their journey. So Moses says, "And the LORD said to me, 'Arise, go on your journey at the head of the people, so that they may go in and possess the land, which I swore to their fathers to give them'" (10:11). Moses' prayer was powerful.

Over the years I have felt that one of the best motivations to prayer that I have had in my personal life has been a theology of prayer that not only says it is necessary but also that it is powerful. Often I may not feel like praying. Often it is difficult to make extended time for prayer. But my theology—my mind—informs my will that this is the secret of effectiveness in life and ministry. This conviction helps me overcome my laziness and my inclination to activity rather than contemplation, and it drives me to prayer. James says, "The prayer of a righteous person has great power as it is working" (James 5:16).

32

A Vision of God
Fosters Heart Religion

DEUTERONOMY 10:12–22

THE DAY MY SON first rode his bicycle to school was an important milestone in our family. Our roads are not very safe for bicycles. So I gave him several instructions, and then I did the journey with him, he on his bicycle and me on mine. Before the first day he went alone, I repeated certain safety tips to him several times. I knew that if these were drilled into his mind right at the start, there was a good chance that he would be a safe rider and, later, a safe driver, too.

Moses was like this. Before he left his people, he drilled into them the keys to a life that pleases God.

Repeating the Basic Calls to Devotion (10:12, 13)

Five Keys to Faithfulness (10:12, 13a)

Deuteronomy 10:12–22 is a summary of the teaching of Deuteronomy. Many themes already discussed in Deuteronomy are brought up again here. Deuteronomy 10:12, 13 answers the basic question, "And now, Israel, what does the LORD your God require of you . . . ?" (10:12a). Sometimes people ask me questions like "What is the one thing you would like to tell a youth worker?" or "What is the single most helpful thing you have learned during your years of ministry?" This statement of Moses has that feel. It describes the greatest way to live.

After the buildup about the importance of what follows (10:12a), Moses simply restates some very basic things in 10:12a, 13. These two verses have five segments of a life that is faithful to God. First, we are to "fear the LORD [our] God" (10:12b). There are some things church members would be afraid to do when their pastor is around or that schoolchildren would be afraid to do when their principal is around. But God is always present wherever we are. That should make us even more careful in our behavior than when a pastor or principal is around. Why don't we act in keeping with this unassailable logic? We don't have the fear of God. The Bible says of the wicked, "There is no fear of God before their eyes" (Psalm 36:1; Romans 3:18). God is right there before them, but they choose not to see him. And by not seeing him, they lose their fear of God. Sadly, that could be said of us, too. Calvin describes the fear of the Lord as "a bridle to restrain our wickedness."[1] We must keep asking God to help us always keep his fear before our eyes.

Second, we are "to walk in all his ways" (10:12c). To be faithful to God is to live according to God's way. There is a distinct lifestyle that marks out a Biblical person. We love our neighbors; we show special consideration for the poor and the helpless; we shun corruption and impure talk; we speak up for justice and oppose the exploitation of vulnerable people; and we are consistent in the practice of devotional exercises and of regular participation in corporate worship. A faithful person would be upset at the thought of not acting in this way.

Third, we are to "love him" (10:12d). To us love is first an attitude and then a command. But it is not enough to fall in love. After that, love must be nurtured through the exercise of the will. This is why we are commanded to love. We give those we love a special place in our lives. We nurture our love for our spouses by spending time with them, by sharing what is in our hearts, by giving time to meditate on their virtues, and by seeking to know what they like and need and doing all we can to give them what they like and need. We approach our love for God with similar devotion.

Fourth, Moses says, ". . . serve the LORD your God with all your heart and with all your soul" (10:12e). Paul exhorts us, "So, whether you eat or drink, or whatever you do, do all to the glory of God" (1 Corinthians 10:31). Everything we do is done for God, and we must do it with all our heart and soul. We work hard whether people are watching or not and even if all the others are taking it easy. When we care for the needy, not expecting an earthly reward, we do it well as if we are doing it for God, remembering Christ's statement at the judgment that we did it to him (Matthew 25:40).

Fifth, we are "to keep the commandments and statutes of the LORD" (10:13a). The Hebrew word translated "keep" is the familiar word *shamar*, usually translated "be careful" and meaning "to pay close attention to some-thing." This is a call to diligent awareness of the possibility of falling and diligent pursuit of the path of obedience. Carelessness is the mother of sin, especially in the areas of our weaknesses. If we have rules about TV-watching and Internet surfing, we must be careful to keep them without making little compromises that lead to big sins. If we have rules about how we do our daily devotions, we must daily take those rules into reckoning so that we can ensure that we spend adequate time daily in the Word and in prayer.

Repeating the Key Points

While it is not surprising to find themes found in other passages repeated here, it is surprising to note the number of times they are repeated in Deuteronomy. The need to fear God is mentioned fourteen times in Deuteronomy.[2] The call to walk in all his ways appears ten times in Deuteronomy.[3] The call to love God appears eight times.[4] And the call to serve the LORD appears six times.[5] The idea of serving God with the heart appears three times (10:12; 11:13; 28:47). And the idea that this is a religion that is practiced with all our heart appears at least twenty-two times.[6] The word translated "keep," *shamar*, appears sixty-five times in Deuteronomy.[7]

Why is it necessary to keep repeating the same thing over and over? Jesus did this with the Great Commission just before his death and after his resurrection. We have seven statements of the Great Commission in the Gospels and Acts, of which six are given during and after the last week of Christ's life.[8] Obviously, Jesus wanted to burn into the minds of the apostles the priority of this commission. We constantly face the temptation to neglect this commission and to concentrate on those who have already been saved. But the constant repetition confronts us with its priority, and we are compelled to go to the unreached and pay the price of doing so.

Placing a value constantly before people is particularly important when we have a weakness or tendency to neglect or be careless about that value. A hymn by Robert Robinson (1735–1790), "Come, Thou Fount of Every Blessing," puts it this way: "Prone to wander, Lord, I feel it, prone to leave the God I love." It is easy to overlook the things we have learned about being faithful to God, especially in our weak areas. It is easy to get careless and to lose the vigilant attitude toward the life of obedience that Deuteronomy advocates. Therefore, repetition is necessary.

The Commands Are for Our Good (10:13b)

Verse 13 ends by describing the commands as being "for your good." God's way is the best for us. Doing anything else will be as foolish an act as that of Esau who exchanged his birthright for a stew that his brother Jacob had cooked (Genesis 25:29–34). He satisfied his immediate hunger but lived to regret his folly. It never pays to sin because God wants only our good, and anything contrary to his will is not good for us. As Paul puts it "the will of God . . . is good and acceptable and perfect" (Romans 12:2b).

People may think that we are making big sacrifices to follow Christ. But ultimately it is no sacrifice, because this is the best possible path we could follow. Paul said, ". . . godliness is of value in every way, as it holds promise for the present life and also for the life to come" (1 Timothy 4:8). The obedient are the only ones who really have the best of both worlds. We have the peace and joy of the Lord in this life, and we have glory in the next.

In verses 14–19 we find what Wright describes as "two matching triplets" (10:14–16 and 10:17–19). Each triplet contains a description, first, of who God is; and second, of something surprising that he has done; and third, of Israel's appropriate response to who God is and what he has done. We will look at each triplet separately.

Election by the Supreme LORD Calls for Circumcised Hearts (10:14–16)

Description of God: Owner of Everything (10:14)

First Moses says, "Behold, to the LORD your God belong heaven and the heaven of heavens, the earth with all that is in it." Everything in the universe as we know it and beyond that ("the heaven of heavens") belongs to him. If we think of the most powerful ruler who ever lived, his authority would be an insignificant dot in comparison to that of God. Here is Isaiah's vivid description of the greatness of God.

> Behold, the nations are like a drop from a bucket,
>   and are accounted as the dust on the scales;
>   behold, he takes up the coastlands like fine dust.
> Lebanon would not suffice for fuel,
>   nor are its beasts enough for a burnt offering.
> All the nations are as nothing before him,
>   they are accounted by him as less than nothing and emptiness.
> To whom then will you liken God,
>   or what likeness compare with him? . . .
> It is he who sits above the circle of the earth,
>   and its inhabitants are like grasshoppers;
> who stretches out the heavens like a curtain,
>   and spreads them like a tent to dwell in;
> who brings princes to nothing,
>   and makes the rulers of the earth as emptiness.
> Scarcely are they planted, scarcely sown,
>   scarcely has their stem taken root in the earth,
> when he blows on them, and they wither,

and the tempest carries them off like stubble.
To whom then will you compare me,
    that I should be like him? says the Holy One. (Isaiah 40:15–18, 22–25)

His Surprising Action: Election (10:15)

Next Moses presents the amazing truth that this God, who is the owner of everything, elected the Jewish nation and its people to be recipients of his love: "Yet the LORD set his heart in love on your fathers and chose their off-spring after them, you above all peoples, as you are this day" (10:15). Note the tenderness with which this election is mentioned: ". . . [he] set his heart in love." We do not know why they were chosen. Certainly it was not because of any intrinsic qualification that they had, as we saw in our discussion on 9:4–6. Election will always remain a mystery. But it is also a glorious reality.

The wonder of election also applies to the new Israel—the church. We did nothing to merit salvation, but he chose to love us and make us his own children. We must never lose the sense of the sheer wonder of this. The beloved singer of the Billy Graham evangelistic team, George Beverly Shea, wrote a beautiful song about this, and its chorus goes like this:

The wonder of it all; the wonder of it all—
Just to think that God loves me!
The wonder of it all; the wonder of it all—
Just to think that God loves me!

This God does more than call us to himself. I found seven places where the Bible states that God delights in or takes pleasure in us,[9] once that he delights in our welfare (Psalm 35:27), and three times that he delights in loving and blessing us (Deuteronomy 28:63; 30:9; Micah 7:18). So there are eleven references to the glorious truth that God delights in us. Those basking in the glory of being delighted in by God would naturally find that God is their source of greatest delight (Nehemiah 1:11; Psalm 37:4; Isaiah 58:2, 14).

The Appropriate Response: Heart Circumcision (10:16)

Today the doctrine of election has received a bad name because some people, resting secure in their place in God's family, have neglected the pursuit of holiness. Some present the idea of the carnal Christian—one who, though saved, is not living a godly life—almost as a legitimate form of Christianity. They forget that the Bible addresses those who call themselves Christians with severe warnings about the possibility of falling away. Peter says, "Therefore, brothers, be all the more diligent to make your calling and election sure, for if you practice these qualities you will never fall" (2 Peter 1:10). The privilege of election brings with it the responsibility to live a holy life. So Paul urges the Ephesians, ". . . walk in a manner worthy of the calling to which you have been called" (Ephesians 4:1).

In Deuteronomy 10:16 Moses presents as the essential implication of election the genuine working out of our faith: "Circumcise therefore the foreskin of your heart, and be no longer stubborn." In the earlier verse Moses had talked about how God called the fathers of Israel (the patriarchs). The first patriarch, Abraham, was asked to practice the rite of circumcision as an external sign of loyalty to the covenant (Genesis 17:9–14). Here Moses says that this outward ritual is useless if not backed by an inner change of life. He calls them to "circumcise . . . the foreskin of [their] heart[s]." An uncircumcised ear hears imperfectly because it is covered (Jeremiah 6:10). Similarly, with a circumcised heart, that which hinders obedience is cut away, and the heart is free to be "pliable and amenable to the direction of God" (Thompson). Moses goes on to give the opposite of a circumcised heart when he says, ". . . and be no longer stubborn" (literally, "stiff-necked").

Moses is asking the people to have soft hearts toward God and his Word—hearts that God can mold into his image like a potter molds a lump of clay. This would be accomplished fully in the era of the new covenant when the Spirit would be more real in the experience of the people. Ezekiel, speaking about the new covenant, says, "And I will give them one heart, and a new spirit I will put within them. I will remove the heart of stone from their flesh and give them a heart of flesh, that they may walk in my statutes and keep my rules and obey them. And they shall be my people, and I will be their God" (Ezekiel 11:19, 20; see Ezekiel 36:26, 27).

Charles Wesley (1707–1788) described the circumcised heart like this:

O for a heart to praise my God,
A heart from sin set free,
A heart that always feels Thy blood
So freely shed for me.
A heart resigned, submissive, meek,
My great Redeemer's throne,
Where only Christ is heard to speak,
Where Jesus reigns alone.
A humble, lowly, contrite heart,
Believing true and clean,
Which neither life nor death can part
From that which dwells within.

Wesley and Moses are speaking about a heart that God can easily penetrate with his message. Essentially this comes from a love for God that over-

comes the love for things that our sinful nature prompts us to do. People with
such a heart are willing to stand corrected when they do something wrong.
Their passionate love for God shudders at the thought of even a moment without the smile of God's approval. Such will abstain from doing what displeases
God even though they may want to do that. And they will eagerly do what
God wants them to do even though at first they did not want to do that. This
is what it means to not be stubborn or stiff-necked.

The Justice of the Awesome God Calls for Care for the Needy (10:17–19)

Description of God: Awesome Lord (10:17)

It has been said that the nature of God can be summarized by the expression
holy love. These are said to be two sides of the same coin. We see this combination of holiness and love in this passage. The first triplet focused on God's
electing love (10:14–16). Our hearts are warmed by this display of love, and
through that we are motivated to total devotion to the One who loves us. The
focus in the second triplet (10:17–19) is on the holiness of God. It presents the
lordship of the mighty God, and the desired response is one of awe resulting
in motivation to obedience from noting the justice of God.

Verse 17a talks of God's great power as Lord over all: "For the LORD
your God is God of gods and Lord of lords, the great, the mighty, and the
awesome God." The word translated "mighty" is used of warriors. The next
word, "awesome," has become popular today. Unfortunately the way it is
used is very different from the way it is used in the Bible. Today it is used
to mean something like "wonderful" or "amazing" or "tremendous." But the
Hebrew word translated "awesome" is defined as "to be awesome, be dread-
ful, be feared."[10] Most often it is translated in the Bible as "to fear." A recent
encyclopedia of Bible words comments, "There is no instance in the OT or
NT where . . . 'awesome' could not be translated 'fearsome.'"[11]

I think the way *awesome* is used today opens us to the danger of losing
the Biblical idea of awesomeness. This passage is saying that because God is
so great and mighty, we should be terrified. Of course, as Hebrews says twice,
because he has opened a way for us to be his children through the work of
Christ, we can boldly approach his throne of grace (Hebrews 4:16; 10:19).
But Hebrews also says, ". . . let us offer to God acceptable worship, with reverence and awe, for our God is a consuming fire" (Hebrews 12:28, 29) and
"it is a fearful thing to fall into the hands of the living God" (Hebrews 10:31).
The thrust of Deuteronomy 10:17, then, is that God is mighty and fearsome.

His Surprising Action: Justice to the Weak (10:17b, 18)

Moses follows the description of the awesomeness of God with a description of his acts. Here the acts have to do with justice. First, we are told he "is not partial and takes no bribe" (10:17b). God is so immovable that he cannot be influenced to change his principles of justice based on people's status or background (he is impartial) or on so-called favors people do for him (he cannot be bribed). Today unscrupulous businesspeople often go to shrines and churches and make generous contributions to try to bribe their way out of the consequences of their dishonesty. But God cannot be bribed. Neither will he act differently according to the background or status of people. God is a just God.

Next, Moses says that God "executes justice for the fatherless and the widow" (10:18a). People today exploit the weak in society and think they can get away with it. But God is on the side of the needy, and those who try to fight him by being unjust to the weak are going to suffer some dire consequences. Moses says that God "loves the sojourner, giving him food and clothing" (10:18b). Sojourners are people who do not have the government machinery working for them because they are outsiders. Refugees and immigrants can be considered as today's equivalent of sojourners. We know that people often exploit refugees and immigrants by underpaying them for work they do. This is particularly true of illegal immigrants. Christians should never condone people going to another country illegally. Neither should we condone the exploitation of illegal immigrants by underpaying them. Moses is implying that if we are unjust toward the weak in society, we will have to face God's fearsome justice.

The Appropriate Response: Concern for the Weak (10:19)

After talking about God's awesome justice and his solidarity with the weak, Moses tells the people that they, too, must express solidarity with the weak: "Love the sojourner, therefore, for you were sojourners in the land of Egypt" (10:19). Note how he reminds the Israelites that they were sojourners in Egypt. Just as God liberated them when they were slaves there, they must now work for the liberation of those who are weak and oppressed.

The combination of election and justice in this passage is enormously significant. In the history of the church we have seen people who emphasized the great privileges of election but ignored the responsibility to ensure justice to the weak. Perhaps they unconsciously became so taken up by the privileges of election that they blinded their eyes to the needs of the downtrodden, who are also loved by God. They may even have thanked God that they are not in that wretched state because of God's electing grace. Moses' point is that once we are saved we need to do all we can to lift up those who are down. It seems that some did not know that it was a terrible sin in God's sight to allow some to be treated as inferior. We dare not smugly sit on our laurels and ignore the cry of the poor.

In the history of the church Bible-believing Christians, who have emphasized the importance of salvation, have often been guilty of tolerating injustice. Evangelical Christians were among those who opposed the dismantling of the institution of slavery in the West and of apartheid in South Africa. In Asia the caste and class system is still very strong, and many Christians have accepted this status quo and allowed those considered as coming from a low caste or class to be deprived of the rights they should have.

Thankfully there were evangelicals who, out of Biblical convictions, fought against both slavery and apartheid. Missionary explorer David Livingstone (1813–1873) was not only horrified by the lostness of the people in the interior of Africa, he was also horrified by the trade in humans as slaves. So he was determined to open routes to the interior so that missionaries would come in with the gospel and traders would come in with legitimate trade that would make the trade of humans unnecessary. One writer says, "It has been said that he not only discovered Africa, but the African too. Largely due to his reports, it was not long before slavery was made illegal throughout the civilized world."[12]

Parliamentarian William Wilberforce (1759–1833) was the main force in getting slavery outlawed in the British Empire—a battle that he waged for over twenty years. He was a convinced evangelical and had the support of a group of wealthy evangelicals who formed the Clapham Sect, to which he belonged. Wilberforce also valued the gift of personal salvation greatly and tried in his personal dealings to share the gospel whenever possible. Others can be mentioned such as the Earl of Shaftesbury, Anthony Ashley Cooper (1801–1885), John Wesley (1703–1791) and the early Methodists, and the Japanese mass evangelist and social reformer Toyohiko Kagawa (1888–1960).

Our triplets, then, give us two important responses to God. First, because of the amazing love that caused the Lord of creation to save us, we must be totally devoted to him. Second, because the mighty and thus fearsome God is committed to the needy, we must be committed to them too. If not we will face the wrath of the holy God. God's love is not the only thing that prompts devotion to God. But it is an important trigger. Similarly, God's awesome power is not the only thing to motivate us to care for the poor and needy. But it is certainly one of the motivations. When it comes to the possibility of arousing the wrath of God, it is better to be safe than sorry. In other words, it would be better to care for the poor rather than neglect them and face God's wrath. A wise man of Athens was asked when injustice would be abolished. He said, "When those who are not wronged feel as indignant as those who are."[13]

Another Call to Commitment (10:20–22)

The chapter ends with another call to commitment from Moses. The order here is reversed with the exhortation to action coming before the description of who God is and what he has done. But, as before, here too what drives our action is the nature and works of God. Moses exhorts, "You shall fear the LORD your God. You shall serve him and hold fast to him, and by his name you shall swear" (10:20). These exhortations were discussed in our treatment of 6:13–15 and elsewhere.

Moses backs this exhortation by saying something about God's nature: "He is your praise. He is your God" (10:21a). We are familiar with the statement, "He is your God." But the statement about God being our praise is new. What a beautiful way to refer to God, and how characteristic of the life of faith this is! Our thoughts about God trigger praise all the time, so that we can refer to him as "[our] praise."

John Wesley had many disappointments in life including rejection by the church he loved so dearly and a failed marriage because of his wife's leaving him. But he would have agreed with the designation of God as "[our] praise." A few weeks before his death he wrote to a friend, "I am half blind and half lame, but by the help of God I creep on still." The day before he died he asked for pen and ink, but he could no longer write. A lady who was at his side said, "Let me write for you, sir; tell me what you would say." He replied, "Nothing, but that God is with us." That afternoon Wesley got up and to the astonishment of all there broke out in the words of a hymn by Isaac Watts:

> I'll praise my Maker while I've breath,
> And when my voice is lost in death,
> Praise shall employ my nobler powers;
> My days of praise shall ne'er be past,
> While life, and thought, and being last,
> Or immortality endures.
> Happy the man whose hopes rely
> On Israel's God: he made the sky,
> And earth, and seas, with all their train;
> His truth for ever stands secure,
> He saves th' oppressed, he feeds the poor,
> And none shall find his promise vain.

A little later he gathered his strength once more and cried out, "The best of all, God is with us!" Throughout that night he kept repeating the words from Watts's hymn, "I'll praise; I'll praise." The following morning he said, "Farewell!" and died.[14]

Finally, Moses recounts God's acts on behalf of the people: ". . . who has done for you these great and terrifying things that your eyes have seen. Your fathers went down to Egypt seventy persons, and now the LORD your God has made you as numerous as the stars of heaven" (10:21b, 22). Moses never tires of reminding the people of the great things God has done. This needs to be the thought that always dominates our thinking. God has done great things for us. These acts of God elicit both praise and commitment. Because God is so great and has been so good to us, let us be totally devoted to him.

33

Seven Motivations to Obedience

DEUTERONOMY 11:1–32

DEUTERONOMY 11 brings us to the end of a major section of the book (5:1 – 11:32) with exhortations that give the basic principles and responses to the Law. Early in this section were the Ten Commandments (5:6–21). Then there were numerous exhortations on what a life of obedience to the Law means. In Deuteronomy 12 Moses will present the detailed stipulations of the Law. Before he gets to that he gives something like a summary of the exhortations he has made in the preceding chapters. It is a fitting way to end this section. Essentially this chapter is another exhortation to give priority to obedience.

Almost everything said in this chapter has already been presented earlier on. This tells us again that we need to be reminded about the battle for obedience because it is so easy for us to get careless and slide into disobedience. In the previous study we referred to Robert Robinson's hymn "Come, Thou Fount of Every Blessing," in which are found the words: "Prone to wander, Lord, I feel it, prone to leave the God I love." Most of us have grown up with some attitudes that do not please God. Often these attitudes are considered acceptable in the society around us. Therefore, given the fact that our natural sinful orientation is not totally eradicated, we could easily stray into sin if we are not careful. So we need to be constantly reminded to be careful. It is not surprising then that the familiar word *shamar*, which appears sixty-five times in Deuteronomy and essentially means "pay careful attention to,"[1] is found four times in this chapter (11:1, 8, 16, 32).

This passage gives seven motivations to obedience. But before each motivation is given, there is a description of what obedience looks like.

God's Mighty Works of Discipline (11:1–7)

Obedience

The first statement on obedience is almost a summary of the main thrust of the book: "You shall therefore love the LORD your God and keep his charge, his statutes, his rules, and his commandments always" (11:1). Love is presented alongside and distinct from obedience here. But verse 13 includes love as an aspect of obedience (on love, see discussions on 6:1–5; 10:12, 13; 11:13).

Motivation

The motivation for obedience presented here is "the discipline of the LORD your God, his greatness, his mighty hand and his outstretched arm, his signs and his deeds . . . " (11:2b, 3a). Moses goes on to list these mighty works of God as the events surrounding the exodus (11:3b), the destruction of the Egyptian army that pursued the Israelites to the Red Sea (11:4), and how God dealt with the Israelites during their journey to this point (11:5, 6). There is a particular reference to what is generally called Korah's rebellion when Korah, Dathan, Abiram, and some others rebelled against Moses and Aaron and God destroyed them (Numbers 16:1–35). Interestingly, Korah's name is not mentioned here.

So we have three instances of God's discipline—two when he showed his power against the Egyptians and once when he punished the Israelites. Twice Moses asks them to "consider" these mighty works of God: "And consider today (since I am not speaking to your children who have not known or seen it), consider the discipline of the LORD your God" (11:2). The word translated "consider" is the common word *yada'*, which occurs 873 times in the Old Testament and usually takes the meanings "to know, recognize, understand; to have sexual relations."[2] The NIV and several other translations render this word as "remember" here. John Wesley comments that what is intended here is, "acknowledge and consider it with diligence and thankfulness." This idea is accented when after reciting the incidents of discipline Moses says, "For your eyes have seen all the great work of the LORD that he did" (11:7). Verses 2, 5, and 7 point out that they saw these incidents.

We have the responsibility to conscientiously remember God's mighty acts of discipline. Usually when we think of God's "greatness, his mighty hand and his outstretched arm, his signs and his deeds" (11:2b, 3a) we think of acts of deliverance that encourage us to "pray for a miracle." We don't usually think of his acts of discipline. But doing so is a very important part of the life of obedience. God's acts of discipline warn us of the consequences of disobedience and urge us along the path of obedience. Many parents don't tell the unpleasant stories of judgment in the Old Testament to their physical and spiritual children. If we miss getting a good dose of this key aspect of the Biblical revelation, we are going to miss a key aspect of the Christian worldview. We will be spiritually stunted and more vulnerable to temptation.

Moses says: ". . . since I am not speaking to your children who have not known or seen it" (11:2). These are things that had happened during their own lifetime. In the same way we must recount and remember the disciplines of God that we saw happening during our own lifetime. They should be part of our conversation, and they should constantly be a warning to us. We usually do not talk about these things because they are unpleasant. But if we do, when we face temptation to do some similar thing, a message will come to us saying, "The last time this was done there were terrible consequences." The warning could help us abstain.

The Hope of Conquest and Occupying a Good Land (11:8–12)
Obedience
The second call to obedience is, "You shall therefore keep the whole commandment that I command you today" (11:8a). Notice how what is to be kept is described as "the whole commandment." This is singular in the Hebrew, referring to the whole Law as a unit (the NIV has it as plural—"all the commands"). It is something you take on *in toto*. Matthew's Great Commission has the same idea when Jesus says, "Go . . . teaching them to observe all that I have commanded you" (Matthew 28:19, 20). Paul's description of nine essential Christian character traits is subsumed under a single expression, "the fruit [singular] of the Spirit" (Galatians 5:22, 23). Christians cannot pick and choose what fruit they will have in their life. There is only one fruit, and it includes all the characteristics.

If we hold back on obeying Christ in one or two areas, we "give the devil a foothold" (Ephesians 4:27, NIV). Satan will hammer away at that, seeking to totally destroy us. Recently some famous Christian leaders have suddenly been exposed after committing some scandalous sin. While the exposure was sudden, the fall was not. They had entertained an area of compromise. They had stopped battling it and had not shared about it with those to whom they were accountable. It remained hidden for a while, until Satan with a masterstroke led the leader to do something that brought it all out into the open. Most of us have one or two areas that we have trouble fully yielding to God. Those areas could cause havoc in our lives.

Motivation

The motivation to obedience here has several features. First, Moses says that when they keep the whole commandment, they will "be strong, and go in and take possession of the land that you are going over to possess" (11:8c). Obedience in every area gives strength for conquest. Soldiers sometimes are known for being obedient in their military duties but wildly sinful in their personal behavior. That scenario does not work for those hoping for God's blessings. When we obey, we are confident about God's ability to see us through the challenges of life. This is a strong motivation to launch out in faith in an exploit for God.

Not only is there going to be conquest of the land, but Moses goes on to say, ". . . and that you may live long in the land that the LORD swore to your fathers to give to them and to their offspring" (11:9a). We have looked at how we can apply the promise of long life in the land in our discussion on 5:16. Here we will say that whatever it meant then, today it means security and a bright future for the obedient. This is accented in Moses description of the land as "a land flowing with milk and honey" (11:9b).

He goes on to say that this land is much better than Egypt, to which Dathan and Abiram wanted to go back in the rebellion mentioned in verse 6. They even called Egypt "a land flowing with milk and honey" (Numbers 16:13). Moses says that Egypt had to be cultivated through difficult irrigation schemes: "For the land that you are entering to take possession of it is not like the land of Egypt, from which you have come, where you sowed your seed and irrigated it, like a garden of vegetables" (Deuteronomy 11:10). Most of Egypt, except the Nile delta, was and still is arid desert. Cultivation required irrigation, and the Israelites worked painfully hard as slaves to keep this irrigation system working. By contrast the promised land would have sufficient rain, and that would be evidence of God's care of them all year: "But the land that you are going over to possess is a land of hills and valleys, which drinks water by the rain from heaven, a land that the LORD your God cares for. The eyes of the LORD your God are always upon it, from the beginning of the year to the end of the year" (11:11, 12).

Isn't it strange that these Israelites would ever think of going back to Egypt considering all that they had suffered there? How could they have thought of such a thing? Waiting periods are tough. Though they always had the presence of God, it was taking a long time for God's promise to give them the land to be fulfilled. In our impatience we can forget the horror of our life before we met Christ and complain that God is not looking after us. Some even complain that things were better before they came to Christ. They forget that before they came to Christ they had no meaningful direction in life, no peace in their hearts, and they were headed for Hell. Paul tells us to remember our past life because it gives perspective to the present. He says, "Remember that you were at that time separated from Christ, alienated from the commonwealth of Israel and strangers to the covenants of promise, having no hope and without God in the world" (Ephesians 2:12). These things are so easy to forget.

If you are in an in-between time and it looks like God is slow to act on your behalf, it would be good for you to remember your past and take into account the fact that our God is a God who keeps his promises.

The Promise of Daily Provision (11:13–15)

Obedience

The call to obedience in verse 13 adds a new feature, service: "And if you will indeed obey my commandments that I command you today, to love the LORD your God, and to serve him with all your heart and with all your soul . . . " The three features mentioned here—obedience, love, and service—make a combination that comprehensively describes the walk of faith. First Moses says, ". . . obey my commandments that I command you today" (11:13a). Then the specific aspects of obedience are mentioned here. The first is love. Moses says, ". . . obey my commandments . . . to love the LORD your God" (11:13b). In our discussion of 6:5 we looked at the question of whether it is appropriate to command people to love God. We said that God commands us to do what is best for us, to be fully human. We were made to love God. If our whole life were consumed only with a meticulous attempt to obey every command, we would be gloomy people. There is no beauty in duty when it is done only as a duty. This is why some duty-conscious people are not very pleasant to be around. The phrase "goody-goody" is used to describe a righteous though boring and unpleasant person.

When I was in university I had a friend who lived a rather wild life. I also knew a young woman from a very conservative background who lived a very sheltered life of obedience to her very strict parents. The young woman once told me that she was really envious of his carefree life and his being able to do whatever he wanted to do, even though much of that she would classify as sin. She was obedient, but she was in bondage and clearly not enjoying life. Our obedience springs out of love for God. This love is the most wonderful thing in our life. It is the source of our deepest joys. When we love God we want to obey God, not just because it is our duty, but because it is our joy to please the one we love.

The second aspect of obedience is "to serve him with all your heart and with all your soul" (11:13c). We must serve God wholeheartedly. In our discussion on the call to serve God in 6:13 we said that the verb used for serving (*abad*) is related to the idea of slavery or servanthood. We are talking about a wholehearted commitment to God that extends itself in service because of an ambition to see God's name honored. So as our service to God we visit sick workmates in the hospital; we practice hard at songs that the choir sings at worship on Sunday; we open our homes for single persons to stay a few days because they are sick and have no family nearby; we battle long and hard through prayer, conversation, and concern to restore a backsliding Christian; we help needy people financially; we wash up and care for an invalid neighbor when the usual help does not come; we take responsibility for the nurture of a new Christian; and if we get a call from God, we give up a promising career in business to come into vocational Christian service.

We do not do this grudgingly. Moses says, "Serve him with all your heart and with all your soul." If we do this work grudgingly we actually bring dishonor to God. People would look at us and end up with bad thoughts about the God we serve. Some serve as if they are doing God and the church a great favor. If they are not appreciated or honored for their service, they get angry. Christian service is not some huge sacrifice we condescend to make to help the needy. It is a great honor that we do not deserve. We are unworthy sinners called to represent the Lord of the universe, even though we don't deserve it. And we think we are making some big sacrifice!

This wrong attitude to service influences the value system of many Christians. Too many parents prefer to have their children give time for sports or some school activity that will bring them earthly honors and think their children are wasting their time when they do Christian ministry on the school campus. They think their children must secure a good future for themselves; after they are established in life, then they could give time to church work. These parents are sadly mistaken. Our passage goes on to say that serving God is the best way to secure a good future for ourselves.

Motivation

Verses 14, 15 say that when the people obey God by loving and serving him, ". . . he will give the rain for your land in its season, the early rain and the later rain, that you may gather in your grain and your wine and your oil. And he will give grass in your fields for your livestock, and you shall eat and be full." Our needs will be met! True, we may not be very wealthy. But we have the assurance that God will look after us. And we live each day in the peace of knowing this. Our security is not dependent on market forces or weather patterns. It depends on the God who rules the universe and who has promised to look after us. Because of that, we are actually very rich—we have the peace and satisfaction that earthly riches cannot give.

Of course, we will have times when we feel that it was not worth our while serving God. We will have times when supplies seem to be dwindling with little prospect of fresh provisions. But we trust God. We reckon that we believe in the same God as the one of whom David said, "I have been young, and now am old, yet I have not seen the righteous forsaken or his children begging for bread" (Psalm 37:25). Often at the last moment God supplies our need, and we marvel and are thrilled over what has happened. Life is one long adventure with God for those who have placed their trust in him. The unfaithful rich may have all that money can buy, but they will never know the thrill of having the Lord of creation supplying their needs.

I have seen people who rejected a life of service because they wanted to progress in society. Some refused vocational Christian ministry because of the poor financial remuneration. Some moved away from difficult or low-paying vocations that they originally went into out of a sense of call from God. Some of these people are unhappy today. Some have had very unhappy marital experiences. Some have children who are acting in a way that will land them in eternal Hell unless they repent. Some struggle with a sense of not being fulfilled despite their material and social success.

One of the greatest blessings of obeying, loving, and serving God is the knowledge that he looks after us and that we do not need to fear the future. We may have lean periods, but we can always testify, "My God will supply every need of [ours] according to his riches in glory in Christ Jesus" (Philippians 4:19).

The Prospect of Wrath and No Provision (11:16, 17)

Obedience

The next call to obedience takes the form of a warning about unfaithfulness: "Take care lest your heart be deceived, and you turn aside and serve other gods and worship them" (11:16). We have already seen many places where Moses warned against idolatry. What is significant here is that it talks about the people turning aside from God's way after the heart is deceived. When there is no rain and they lose their trust in God, they could be deceived and try going for help to one of the gods that the Canaanites say provides rain. They know that the Canaanites do some rituals to get their rain god to help them. As prayer does not seem to have worked, they decide to try these rituals.

They have been deceived into disobedience. In the next verse Moses warns that the result of such an action would be God's stopping the rain from coming to them.

People can do things like this today also. I know of friends who have persuaded a committed Christian woman who wants to get married but has not found a believing partner to give up the wait and marry an unbeliever, assuring her that she can gradually bring him to faith. Men watch harmful things in the media, saying that they need to be educated about what others are watching. Such deceived disobedience can be tragic.

Motivation

Next Moses seeks to motivate people to remain faithful by warning them of the wrath of God if they disobey. ". . . then the anger of the Lord will be kindled against you, and he will shut up the heavens, so that there will be no rain, and the land will yield no fruit, and you will perish quickly off the good land that the Lord is giving you" (11:17). Earlier, rain and fruit were promised for obedience (11:14). Now he says that disobedience will result in no rain and no fruit. The reason for this barrenness is the anger of the Lord being kindled against the ungodly.

Will we experience God's wrath if we disobey him today? In connection with abuses of the Lord's Supper in Corinth, Paul says, "For anyone who eats and drinks without discerning the body eats and drinks judgment on himself" (1 Corinthians 11:29). God did not punish people on earth for sin in this life only in Old Testament times. This is something that happened in New Testament times also. So Paul says, "That is why many of you are weak and ill, and some have died" (1 Corinthians 11:30). We know that Ananias and Sapphira were killed immediately after they lied about their gift to the church (Acts 5:1–11).

I have seen this in my own life. When I have disobeyed God I have sometimes clearly sensed that God's hand has left me. Sometimes this is seen in the way nothing seems to go right. Sometimes it is seen in the form of sickness. There is the sense that God's wonderful providing, protecting, and strengthening presence has left me, and I am now under the wrath of God.

The last assertion of the paragraph we are looking at is powerful: ". . . and you will perish quickly off the good land that the Lord is giving you" (11:17). Here is God giving them a "good land." But they reject God in favor of another way. They say that this other god would look after them better or satisfy them better. Every act of disobedience is a statement that God does not truly satisfy us. Sometimes we do this unconsciously, as when a Christian turns to pornography for pleasure or when a Christian in a desperate situation tells a lie or steals something to get out of the mess in which he finds himself. Sometimes it is done consciously as when a Christian says she has waited long enough for God to provide a Christian spouse, but because he has not done so she will marry a non-Christian who has expressed interest in her.

Again we turn to Philippians 4:19: "And my God will supply every need of yours according to his riches in glory in Christ Jesus." If we believe this we will see the folly of trying another method for fulfilling our needs and desires.

The Prospect of Rich and Long-Lasting Blessing (11:18–21)

Obedience

The next call to obedience is actually a call to take the Word of God seriously. All the affirmations made in verses 18–20 have already been made in this book (6:6–9), though there are slight changes in the wording. It is a call to remember the Word and teach it to children and use aids to remember it.

The experience of many Christians would attest to the value of repeating this command. I know some who pored over the Scriptures when they were new Christians but are not doing so anymore. Some settle for a quick daily devotional reading. Others read little or nothing of the Bible as a daily habit. I often face challenges in this area. Daily I need to make a conscious effort to really get into the Word without depending on a quick spiritual injection through a rushed time with God.

The Word is particularly needed as we do not have many tangible things such as talismans, idols, and specific predictions of soothsayers to remind us of God. The forces of temptation and testing can be very severe. When we go through a trying time it is easy to go to one of these quick-fix agents for support, reassurance, and guidance. But we do have something very powerful and tangible: the Scriptures, which we view as God's infallible Word to us. There we have clear instructions of what we are to do and not do. So though we cannot see God with our physical eyes, we can hear him speak through the Scriptures. And what we hear helps us stay obedient.

Motivation

Next Moses gives the consequence of holding fast to God's Word: ". . . that your days and the days of your children may be multiplied in the land that the LORD swore to your fathers to give them, as long as the heavens are above the earth" (11:21). The promise of long life is given as a reward for honoring parents in the fifth commandment (5:16), and we have attempted to discuss the meaning of that promise in our discussion of this commandment. After looking at different ways in which this promise is looked at, we concluded that whatever its exact meaning to the people at that time, for us today it implies that God's rich blessings will come to us. Those who live by the Word will not ever lack God's blessings in their lives, right to the end of their lives.

The Prospect of Conquest and Security (11:22–25)

Obedience

The next description of obedience also repeats some familiar themes. It describes obedience as four actions. First, Moses says, "For if you will be careful to do all this commandment that I command you to do . . . " (11:22a). Again we are told to follow the whole commandment. The familiar word *shamar*, "be careful to do," on which we have commented often (see the discussions on 4:2; 5:32, 33; 6:17; 10:12, 13) appears here again.

Second, Moses says, ". . . loving the LORD your God" (11:22b), which has also been discussed earlier (see the discussions on 4:4–6a; 6:5; 11:13). This reminds us that the life of obedience is not some dreary duty to perform; it is a labor of love. The third description of obedience is related to the first: ". . . walking in all his ways" (11:22c). This, too, is a common theme in Deuteronomy, appearing ten times in the book.[3] It reminds us that that obedience is a daily step-by-step process of doing only what God wants us to do (see the discussion on 10:12). The fourth description is related to the second, pointing to the heart attitude of devotion to God: ". . . holding fast to him" (11:22d).

Motivation

Moses mentions three-pronged motivation to obedience in verses 23–25, all of which are presented as rewards for obedience. The first is the defeat of enemy nations: "then the LORD will drive out all these nations before you, and you will dispossess nations greater and mightier than yourselves" (11:23). Second, there is the promise of conquest of the lands they are to inherit: "Every place on which the sole of your foot treads shall be yours. Your territory shall be from the wilderness to the Lebanon and from the River, the river Euphrates, to the western sea" (11:24). The third prong is security through a fear of them that God implants in their enemies: "No one shall be able to stand against you. The LORD your God will lay the fear of you and the dread of you on all the land that you shall tread, as he promised you" (11:25). This promise, which was also given in 2:25, was fulfilled. Rahab told the two spies whom she hid, "I know that the LORD has given you the land, and that the fear of you has fallen upon us, and that all the inhabitants of the land melt away before you" (Joshua 2:9). The Israelites would have been afraid of the Canaanites. But what happened was that the Canaanites were afraid of the Israelites because they knew that God was with them.

Do our enemies always fear us like this? Sometimes they do, for they know there is something powerful about Christianity and our God. Often their show of hostile confidence is really a mask to hide this fear. But sometimes people may not know enough about our God to be afraid. What we do know is that God goes before us always (Deuteronomy 31:3) and that if God is for us, no one can stand against us (Romans 8:31). Therefore, we have no valid reason to be afraid. Once an envoy from the Pope threatened Martin Luther with what would follow if he persisted in his course. He warned Luther that in the end he would be deserted by all his supporters. "Where will you be then?" demanded the envoy. "Then as now," Luther answered, "in the hands of God."[4]

The knowledge that God's power is sufficient to protect us is a great incentive to obedience. The forces that could cause us to leave God's path may look very powerful, but we know that God is more powerful. The only thing we should fear is disobedience.

The Prospect of Blessing and Curse (11:26–32)

We said that Deuteronomy 11 is a summary of chapters 5—10. The last section of chapter 11 (vv. 26–32) is a summary of 11:1–25 and also an introduction to the details of the Law that will be described in chapters 12—26.

Obedience

Obedience is described in three forms here. First, there is the typical positive call: ". . . the blessing, if you obey the commandments of the LORD your God, which I command you today" (11:27). Second, there is a negative warning: ". . . and the curse, if you do not obey the commandments of the LORD your God, but turn aside from the way that I am commanding you today, to go after other gods that you have not known" (11:28). Third, there is another typical positive call: "you shall be careful to do all the statutes and the rules that I am setting before you today" (11:32). This third call has two key features that have been repeated several times in Deuteronomy. First, they must be "careful to do." Second, they must "be careful to do *all* the statutes and the rules." There are no exemptions (see the discussion on 11:8). All of God's Law is important; we must not give the devil a foothold by neglecting any area.

The three statements present oft-repeated points except for the statement, ". . . to go after other gods that you have not known" (11:28b). This will appear three more times in Deuteronomy (13:2, 13; 29:26; see Jeremiah 7:9).

This verb "know" (*yadah*) "often connotes a more intimate relationship than mere intellectual acquaintance (9:24 . . .)."[5] It was used of sexual relations (Genesis 4:17, 25). God had done so much for them; he had nurtured them and delivered them powerfully. They regarded him as their God. Now, after all they have experienced, will they forsake him? Malachi 2:13–16 says that a man who leaves the wife of his youth, with whom he experienced the ups and downs of building a family, will bring a curse upon himself (unanswered prayers). In the same way, people can leave the Lord with whom they have experienced so much.

How could people do that? J. Allan Petersen has written a book on extra-marital affairs called *The Myth of Greener Grass*.[6] We can believe this myth in our relationships with God, too. When the way of God becomes a threat to our way of life, when other ways come with temptations that are difficult to resist, when we are disappointed that God has not given us something we have asked for, we can be attracted to other gods and try them out. Ignoring all the past blessings God gave us, we opt for another god.

Motivation

The motivation here is presented as the choice between a blessing and a curse. "See, I am setting before you today a blessing and a curse: the blessing, if you obey the commandments of the LORD your God, which I command you today, and the curse, if you do not obey the commandments of the LORD your God . . . " (11:26–28a). Deuteronomy 12:1 — 26:19 will give the details of the way they are to accept or reject. They have to make a decision, and the options are given in stark contrast. It is a choice between life and death, security and disaster, and blessing and curse. To be cursed means to forfeit God's blessings and protection and to have to face the consequences of their rebellion against God.

Do we place this stark contrast between blessing and curse before people? Do we realize that when we invite people to follow Christ we are dealing with such a serious issue? We are not simply asking people to add Christ into their life because that will be helpful to them. We are telling them that if they do not accept the gospel they will perish. Often parents get so much more upset when their child gets sick or fails an exam or fails at a job than over the fact that this child has rejected the gospel. Temporary loss seems to be more serious than eternal destruction.

I was once talking to a Christian leader about a certain family. He told me that all but one member of this family have been very successful in their jobs. The one member who has not been successful is a person suffering from serious schizophrenia. But this person is a devoted Christian. The leader told me that even though all the other members of this family seem to be successful and living wholesome lives, the only one going to Heaven from that family might be the person suffering from serious mental illness.

Next Moses tells them that when they arrive in the land they must designate two mountains as symbols of the blessing and the curse: "And when the LORD your God brings you into the land that you are entering to take possession of it, you shall set the blessing on Mount Gerizim and the curse on Mount Ebal" (11:29). He then presents their geographical location (11:30). As Chris Wright points out, these two mountains "are more visible and durable than anything sculpted by hand." Two mountains are certainly huge symbols to choose to remind people of blessing and curse. It is another pointer to us about the importance of presenting clearly to people what is at stake when it comes to obedience to God's Word.

Obedience to God is serious business! But that is not all. Obedience is always worthwhile, and disobedience is never worthwhile. People will disobey for pleasure or for meeting some need. But the pleasure will soon turn to pain, and the provision will soon turn into a curse.

34

Worshipping God's Way

DEUTERONOMY 12:1-32

CHAPTERS 5—11 GAVE the Ten Commandments followed by exhortations to faithfulness and descriptions of the consequences of obedience and disobedience. With chapter 12 we start part two of Moses second speech (12—26), where the specific laws are going to be explained in some detail so that the people will know what it means to live like a covenant community. The first verse is like a heading for the whole section: "These are the statutes and rules that you shall be careful to do in the land that the LORD, the God of your fathers, has given you to possess, all the days that you live on the earth" (12:1). As these laws are given to a theocratic state, where God is the ruler and the word of God is the national constitution, many of the laws cannot be directly applied by us today. But because each law is a reflection of the mind of God, we can glean principles that are relevant to all of God's people in every generation.

There is what Chris Wright calls a sandwich structure in chapter 12 that gives us the key to understanding what the chapter is about. On the front end, verses 2–4 say that all vestiges of Canaanite worship must be destroyed. On the back end verses 29–32 say that they must have nothing to do with any form of Canaanite worship. Verses 4 and 31a say the same thing: "You shall not worship the LORD your God in that way"; or putting it more literally, "You shall not act like this toward the LORD your God" (NASB). The key to this passage is that because the Israelites are God's holy people, they are to be different from the Canaanites.

Destroy Other Places of Worship (12:2–4)

Moses first commands that all places of Canaanite worship should be destroyed when they go into the promised land. "You shall surely destroy all the places where the nations whom you shall dispossess served their gods, on the high mountains and on the hills and under every green tree" (12:2). Then he elaborates on this: "You shall tear down their altars and dash in pieces their pillars and burn their Asherim with fire. You shall chop down the carved images of their gods and destroy their name out of that place" (12:3). Deuteronomy 7:5 says something similar, and in our study of that passage we said that as we live in multi-religious societies and not in theocracies like Israel today, we do not have to destroy the idols of people of other faiths but should demonstrate through persuasion that there is no valid case for idols. However, when idols and the like appear within the church, then total physical destruction is necessary.

There is a new feature in 12:3 that is not found in 7:5: ". . . and destroy their name out of that place." This is paralleled in verse 5, which says that God will choose a place of worship for all the people "to put his name and make his habitation there." So there is going to be a clear-cut name change. The Israelites could call on only one name. There is something absolute about that name. Today what this means for Christians is that there is no place for a religious pluralism, which says that all religions are more or less equal in the religious marketplace.

- Some say that each religion presents different expressions of the same God discovered through the unique experiences of the people who birthed the religion. Some, referring to the various religions of the world, say that just as there are different paths to the summit of a mountain, all religions lead to the same summit though using different paths. Our text would imply that all such ideas are abhorrent to God.
- When people become Christians they have to renounce their dependence on other gods. Today in Asia we find some "Christians" who claim to follow Christ but also maintain devotion to the powerful miracle-working "god-man" Sai Baba. Several years ago when the Youth for Christ magazine in Sri Lanka ran a piece exposing Sai Baba, one of his "Christian" devotees told me, "Wouldn't it be better for you to be safe than sorry and not broach this topic at all? What if he is a god? Then you would be found to be going against God." When we speak against false gods we *are* playing safe, because the Bible teaches that it is dangerous to displease almighty God!
- There was a dance to the Hindu god Shiva in the local cathedral at the opening ceremony of an international Christian conference in Sri Lanka. The reasoning seemed to be that Hindus and Christians are worshipping the same God; so a dance to Shiva would be appropriate if it were offered

to the Christian God, too. Some horrified members asked for a recon-
secration of the cathedral, which had been defiled by this act. I believe
they were right in expressing their outrage. Sadly, the issue was quietly
allowed to fade away from the church's view with no action taken. Such
a response would not have been allowed by Moses.

Worship in God's Chosen Place (12:5–14)

Only Where God Chooses (12:5)

The next few verses focus on the fact that they must worship in the place of
God's choosing (12:5–14). Verse 5 introduces the concept: "But you shall
seek the place that the LORD your God will choose out of all your tribes to
put his name and make his habitation there. There you shall go. . . ." Three
things are said about this place.

First, it is "the place that the LORD your God will choose out of all your
tribes" (12:5). This is the most important point in this verse. God decides
the best way for them to worship. When they want something done and God
does not seem to be acting quickly enough, they can lose their security in
God, get impatient, and go to some other god or try some new technique to
look for relief. When Moses delayed coming from the mountain, the people
made a golden calf and worshipped it (Exodus 32:1–6; cf. Deuteronomy
9:7–12). When Saul was at war at against the Philistines at Gilgal and Samuel
delayed coming, resulting in the people getting impatient, he himself offered
sacrifices. The result was that Samuel told Saul that the throne was going to
be given to another (1 Samuel 13:7–14). On another occasion after Samuel's
death, again when he was battling the Philistines, Saul consulted a medium in
Endor outside Israel (because he had forced all fortune-tellers and mediums
to leave his kingdom!). This was so he could receive a word from Samuel
(1 Samuel 28). This time God seems to have used the occasion to tell Saul of
the doom that awaited him.

Some "Christians" today do things similar to what Saul did. They resort
to astrology or tarot cards to know their future. They go to mediums to speak
to their dead loved ones. They use *feng shui* or geomancy to locate suitable
building sites and to aid in the design and construction of office towers, hotels,
restaurants, and shopping centers. Newspapers and magazines all over the
world devote space to these practices nowadays.

Second, Moses says about this place that the Lord will "put his name
. . . there" (12:5b). The idea is that the name of the Lord is exclusive. There
were many gods with different names in Canaan. Once their shrines have
been destroyed, there will only be God's place of worship with only his
name. We are reminded how much this grates against the pluralistic mood

of the day. Popular author Deepak Chopra, the Indian medical doctor who has done much to popularize New Age thought in the West, says, "Christ-consciousness, God-consciousness, Buddha-consciousness—it's all the same thing. Rather than 'love thy neighbor,' this consciousness says, 'You and I are the same beings.'"[1] There is a growing tolerance toward other beliefs that advocates an attitude of respect and esteem for others and includes refusing to reject the validity of their worship and gods. Biblical Christians urgently need to ask how they can be winsome witnesses without arrogance who respect individuals and are servants of others while holding to the absolute uniqueness and exclusiveness of the gospel.

Third, Moses says that "God will . . . make his habitation" in the place that he chooses. This must refer to the presence of the tabernacle and the ark of the covenant. There will be different central places of worship over time until they settle on Jerusalem, but when they move to a new place the tabernacle and the ark would move to the new place. Now Christ has come and declared that there will no longer be a centralized place of worship of God but that the key to worshipping him is doing so "in spirit and truth" (John 4:21–24). We have now become God's temple because the Holy Spirit dwells in us (2 Corinthians 6:16; Ephesians 2:14–22). Talking about the geographical location of the tabernacle and the ark seems not to be relevant to us. However, the principle of God's holiness and the awe that should accompany worship that was powerfully demonstrated in the worship at the tabernacle still remains unchanged. In the New Testament we read, ". . . let us offer to God acceptable worship, with reverence and awe, for our God is a consuming fire" (Hebrews 12:28, 29). This is language reminiscent of tabernacle worship.

As God's temple we must be morally pure. In a passage on sexual immorality in the church Paul says, "Or do you not know that your body is a temple of the Holy Spirit within you, whom you have from God? You are not your own, for you were bought with a price. So glorify God in your body" (1 Corinthians 6:19, 20). As we are the temple of God, all of our life is one act of worship. And that worship needs to be "in spirit and truth" (John 4:24). As Donald Guthrie puts it, "God desires worshippers who are in tune with him."[2]

Bringing Offerings with Joy (12:6, 7, 11, 12)

Various kinds of offerings are to be brought to God's chosen place of worship: ". . . and there you shall bring your burnt offerings and your sacrifices, your tithes and the contribution that you present, your vow offerings, your freewill offerings, and the firstborn of your herd and of your flock" (12:6).

- The "burnt offerings" were fully burnt and offered to God.

- The term "sacrifices," when used alongside burnt offerings, usually refers to offerings that were not totally burned. The fat was "burned as the Lord's portion and the remaining parts [went] to the priests and the offerer" (Craigie).
- Several other offerings are to be brought into the place of worship. "Tithes" consist of a tenth of produce of the land or livestock (see the discussion on 14:22–29).
- The "contribution" mentioned next seems to refer to "holy gifts given to priests."[3]
- Then there were "vow offerings," which are gifts given in fulfillment of vows made earlier.
- Just as God freely showed his love toward the people, they in turn respond with "freewill offerings"—offerings given voluntarily.
- Finally, they are to bring "the firstborn of your herd and of your flock" (see the discussion on 15:19–23). An allowance was made to pay a ransom (usually a little higher than the cost) and redeem these animals (Exodus 13:11–16).

Some of the offerings were for forgiveness, while others were expressions of gratitude to God. Giving, then, is an important part of worship. The giving is not something done grudgingly. It is to be accompanied by joy as verse 7 says: ". . . there you shall eat before the LORD your God, and you shall rejoice, you and your households, in all that you undertake, in which the LORD your God has blessed you." The importance of joy is underlined by the fact that it is referred to twice more in this chapter in connection with the meals accompanying sacrifices and offerings (12:12, 18). Giving is one of the happiest things about Christianity. There is great joy in divesting ourselves of earthly encumbrances by giving to the needy and for God's work. Paul says, "Each one must give as he has decided in his heart, not reluctantly or under compulsion, for God loves a cheerful giver" (2 Corinthians 9:7).

The joy is of a communal nature and is part of the worship life of the people. We are reminded of the time when Ezra gathered the people together and began to explain the Law to them. They began to cry. What happened after that is very significant. First Nehemiah, Ezra, and the Levites tell the people, "This day is holy to the LORD your God; do not mourn or weep." Then Nehemiah speaks: "Go your way. Eat the fat and drink sweet wine and send portions to anyone who has nothing ready, for this day is holy to our Lord. And do not be grieved, for the joy of the LORD is your strength." Then "the Levites calmed all the people, saying, 'Be quiet, for this day is holy; do not be grieved'" (Nehemiah 8:9–11). The holiness of the day demanded joy and feasting and the sharing of food with the needy. The background of the eating is that a portion of what is given to God is consumed by the giver. They are to share in the blessing of the gift they give to God.

How important it is for us to recover this idea of the joy of community worship, of making offerings and of holy banqueting with God's people. This is seen in Acts, which says about the first Christians, "And day by day, attending the temple together and breaking bread in their homes, they received their food with glad and generous hearts" (2:46). The great Old and New Testament festivals celebrating redemption—particularly the Passover and the Lord's Supper—included eating in community. The Old Testament feasts were happy times when people got together and enjoyed fellowship and praise and expressed it in song and dance. The early church used to have love feasts (also known as *agapē*) where Christians would get together and share testimonies and food. The tradition of having potluck meals that is found in some churches does have good Scriptural backing. One scholar has named the first group of believers "the Lukan banquet community."[4]

It is so important for our children to think of worship, church, and religion as sources of joy. They should know that when they come to church they come to meet and enjoy friendship with good people. They should think of our favorite festival, Christmas, as a time when the church and families enjoy themselves. Sadly, for many children Christmas is a time when the push to perform at celebrations at home and at Christmas programs in church cause a lot of tension and disharmony. I know of people who have left a church because their child was not given the part they felt she should have been given in the Christmas drama! To such the words of Nehemiah are surely relevant as he tells the people to go home and enjoy without weeping. The problem for many at Christmas, however, is a tense atmosphere at home during Christmas that is much worse than weeping.

The second call to rejoice in verse 12 elaborates on what is meant by the "households" in verse 7, with whom the meal is to be eaten: "And you shall rejoice before the LORD your God, you and your sons and your daughters, your male servants and your female servants, and the Levite that is within your towns, since he has no portion or inheritance with you." Servants are included in the household celebration. Servants were included in the Biblical household and therefore participated in family events. All who come under our roof, whether servants or strangers, become our responsibility. We must see that they join in when the family is happy. In keeping with another important Jewish practice, this verse says that the Levites, who are not given an inheritance in terms of land, should be looked after.

Not Our Way (12:8–14)

Verses 8–14 repeat what has been said in verses 4–7. Some say this is because these sections came from different sources and were left separate when an editor compiled it. But as Chris Wright points out, this kind of repetition is helpful when one is teaching. Actually repetition is a key strategy in Deuteronomy.

The particular stress in this version of these instructions is that when it comes to worship we are not to do things any way we want. Things are going to change when they come to the promised land. Moses says, "You shall not do according to all that we are doing here today, everyone doing whatever is right in his own eyes, for you have not as yet come to the rest and to the inheritance that the LORD your God is giving you" (12:8, 9). This is similar to what happens in pioneering situations. The people had not yet come to the land, so the rules for long-term effectiveness in the land had not been established. Therefore, the people did as they saw fit. This works for a time, but soon there is need for more solid and permanent structures. People who were active in pioneering situations often get angry, thinking that their wings have been clipped or that they are not being trusted because they cannot do what they have been doing before. But rules and restrictions are necessary for healthy passing down of the practices and principles that govern an organization.

Verses 10–12 repeat, more elaborately than before, what they must do when they come to the place God has chosen for worship. Then again there is a stress on not worshiping any way we like, but the way God likes. Verse 8 talked about "everyone doing whatever is right in his own eyes." Verse 13 says, "Take care that you do not offer your burnt offerings at any place that you see." The way out of this is to go to "the place that the LORD will choose . . . and . . . do all that I am commanding you" (12:14).

The focus in verse 14 is on submission to God's will at all times. The sphere in which this is applied is worship. Worship and the arts are closely intertwined. Biblical religion from Old Testament times has been in the forefront of artistic expression, especially in the field of music. Yet a key to success in the arts is creativity. Creativity, of course, is a very important value to Christians who believe they have been made in the image of the Creator God. Yet creative people must approach worship with the ambition of helping people worship God as God would have them worship. Sometimes they may not be able to do something they want to do because it will not have the desired effect of aiding the people in worship. That is hard for creative people, but they must learn submission, so that the goal of all worship is honoring God and helping people to worship aright.

New Freedom to Enjoy Eating Meat (12:15–28)

The next section is about eating meat. Again we have two parallel passages, the second (12:20–28) elaborating somewhat on the first (12:15–19). According to the regulations described in Leviticus 17, meat from the kinds of animals used for sacrifices, like sheep and cattle, could be eaten only during meals in connection with the sacrificial ritual. And only those who were ceremonially clean could eat this meat. Hunted animals like the deer and the gazelle could be consumed at any time by ceremonially clean and unclean people. This was because during the wilderness travels there weren't many cattle and sheep, and also because everyone was near to the tabernacle where the sacrifices were offered.

When they go to the promised land, all people will not be near the place of sacrifice. As there will be opportunity to have large herds of cattle and flocks of sheep, there won't be a shortage of sacrificial animals. So the restrictions are removed: "However, you may slaughter and eat meat within any of your towns, as much as you desire, according to the blessing of the LORD your God that he has given you. The unclean and the clean may eat of it, as of the gazelle and as of the deer" (12:15). The parallel version of this is more elaborate and says this is necessary when "the place that the LORD your God will choose to put his name there is too far from you" (12:21).

The first fourteen verses of chapter 12 brought in some restrictions that were necessary for proper worship in the promised land. The next section is not about restrictions but about the removal of restrictions because of practical considerations. The laws of the Old Testament are given for practical reasons and are not just restrictions of people's freedom so that they learn the discipline of obedience. This section bears in mind people who crave for meat and does not condemn their craving but shows them ways to satisfy these cravings. "When the LORD your God enlarges your territory, as he has promised you, and you say, 'I will eat meat,' because you crave meat, you may eat meat whenever you desire" (12:20).

This chapter shows us that the Old Testament Law is not some dreary list of dos and don'ts but is a way to lead people to the full enjoyment of life with God and with each other. Desire is not something to deny; it is something to surrender to God so that he will redeem it and will help us enjoy fulfilling it in his way. And this is the path to fullest enjoyment because it was God who created our capacity to desire and to enjoy.

This passage also gives some restrictions that moderate the enjoyment of the people.

- They must not compromise their giving to God in their enjoyment: "You may not eat within your towns the tithe of your grain or of your wine or of your oil, or the firstborn of your herd or of your flock, or any of your vow offerings that you vow, or your freewill offerings or the contribution that you present, but you shall eat them before the LORD your God in the place that the LORD your God will choose . . . " (12:17, 18a; see also 12:26, 27). Yet this restriction does not involve a loss of joy. In connection with the sacrificial meal Moses goes on to say, "And you shall rejoice before the LORD your God in all that you undertake" (12:18b).
- Enjoyment must not be selfish, so that in the midst of it we forget the needs of others. Giving to others is a basic expenditure for God's people. Therefore they must ensure that the Levites are well looked after: "Take care that you do not neglect the Levite as long as you live in your land" (12:19).
- Just as with sacrifices, blood must not be consumed when eating meat in an ordinary meal: "Only you shall not eat the blood; you shall pour it out on the earth like water" (12:16; see also 12:27b). Eugene Merrill explains, "The idea seems to be that blood, as the very essence of life, must be returned to the earth from which the Creator at the beginning had brought it forth (cf. Genesis 1:24; 2:19; 3:23; 4:10–11; Deuteronomy 15:23)."

Commenting on the pouring out of blood even in normal (non-religious) meals, Merrill observes, "In a sense, then, even profane slaughter had overtones of worship and holiness and was subject to cultic regulation." Biblical religion is truly holistic. We don't put worship and pleasurable experiences into different compartments. Just as our worship is done as an expression of our devotion to God, so are our feasting and partying and playing. We don't break God's principles in any of these areas—in fact, we enjoy them fully with God as our companion. The peace or *shalom* that God gives us involves a harmony of all aspects of life. When our conscience does not contradict our pleasure we have pure pleasure.

But that is not all. If our lives were happy only for the moment we have pleasure, that pleasure is clouded by the knowledge deep down that the future is uncertain. But this is not so when we follow God's prescription for life. Twice in this section Moses says that when we follow God the future is secure. Verse 28 says, "Be careful to obey all these words that I command you, that it may go well with you and with your children after you forever, when you do what is good and right in the sight of the LORD your God" (see also 12:25).

So Biblical religion is holistic not only in the way it gives us *shalom* in every area of life in the present; it is holistic with regard to time too. There is a provision for past sins as they are submerged in the sea of God's forgetfulness so that we are freed from that nagging feeling of guilt that makes us feel bad about ourselves. The present, too, is bright with God's *shalom*—what Jesus called abundant life (John 10:10). And the future is as bright as the promises of the God who holds the future.

Do Not Even Learn (12:29–32)

Verses 29–31 bring us back to the theme that forms the framework of this chapter: the dangers of foreign religions. They talk of what could happen after the nations of Canaan have been cut off and the Israelites go and "dwell in their land" (12:29). Moses says, "take care that you be not ensnared to follow them, after they have been destroyed before you" (12:30a). Once more we see the familiar word "take care" (*shamar*), which Moses uses six times in this chapter and sixty-five times in Deuteronomy. In all but one of those sixty-five references the word was used in connection with care to be taken in the life of obedience (see the discussions on 4:2; 5:32, 33; 6:17; 10:12, 13). We need to be very careful in matters relating to areas where we are especially vulnerable to temptation. And conformity to the world in worship is one of them, meriting six warnings to be careful in this chapter.

Moses goes on to give a particular way the people are to be careful: ". . . and that you do not inquire about their gods, saying, 'How did these nations serve their gods?—that I also may do the same'" (12:30b). In this age when we have access to unlimited amounts of knowledge at the click of a button there is a message here that is relevant to us. Indeed, we need to learn as much as we can, and some of the helpful learning we get will be from non-Christian sources. Of course, the material that we glean from these helpful sources needs to be sent through the sieve of the Christian worldview. For example, medical students can learn much from a textbook on obstetrics, but they would reject what the book says about abortion.

There are some sources of knowledge, however, to which we must not go with an attitude of learning. They are so dangerous that following them will send us along the path to destruction. Today we need to know about other religions just as Daniel (Daniel 1:4) and Paul (Acts 17:28) did. We do this for information, not in order to learn how to live. But at a time when a person is in desperate need of guidance and God seems to be silent in responding to her prayers, someone may tell her that she would be able to find an answer through a source such as a spiritualist counselor or an astrologer or one who talks to the dead. I have seen Christians do this at times when they are desperate. This passage tells us that this is terribly dangerous. We should be careful about reading too much about sexual behavior because sometimes it may be more for sexual pleasure than for learning. This is also relevant to new Christians being exposed to teaching from sub-Christian cults. The teaching is presented with "Biblical proof," and the new believer does not know how to counteract it. At such times it would be better to insulate the new believer from exposure to people from these cults.

The availability of unlimited knowledge today does not mean that we should access all of it. Exposure to some things will harm us, and it would be best to stay away from them completely. I think this is particularly relevant regarding much that can be found on the Internet and cable television. Some information can harm us. And some information has to do with areas of vulnerability to us, such as sexually stimulating material. It would be best to stay away from these totally, for even brief contact could trap us into a path that results in damaging exposure to filthy material. Talking about sexually implicit material is very relevant in a discussion of other gods and worship, because sex has become a god that is worshipped with more dedication than the gods of the religions people claim to follow. A similar case could be made for the danger of watching violence on TV.

Verse 31 gives us one reason why total destruction of the Canaanites was necessary. Moses says, "You shall not worship the LORD your God in that way, for every abominable thing that the LORD hates they have done for their gods. . . ." As Peter Craigie explains, "They were not dealt with harshly simply at the Lord's whim, nor out of sheer political necessity, but because their lifestyle, as reflected in their religion, had become repugnant to God, the creator of all men."

Moses goes on to give an example of their abominable religious behavior: ". . . for they even burn their sons and their daughters in the fire to their gods" (12:31b). How ironic that twice in Israel's history this abominable practice raised its ugly head (2 Kings 21:6; 2 Chronicles 28:3). Today God would respond with similar wrath to the human sacrifices being offered as part of satanic worship. We, too, should reflect God's horror at such acts. While many may be tolerant about these things, according to the pluralistic mood of the day, we need to oppose them in ways appropriate to our legal systems.

The right to take the life of a human belongs to God alone. He hands over some limited authority to use the sword to earthly governing authorities (Romans 13:1–4), but that is in order to punish wrongdoing. No human has the right to sacrifice a son. How amazing then that God exercised his right to do this when he offered his Son as a sacrifice for our sins!

The chapter ends with Moses calling for obedience to all that God commands without adding or taking away from it (12:32; see the discussion on 4:2). Ultimately this is the message of much of the book: be faithful to the revealed word of God in the Law.

35

Encountering Occult Power

DEUTERONOMY 13:1–18

THE TEMPTATION TO FOLLOW other gods may have seemed a theoretical one without much relevance to Western Christians until a few decades ago. Now, however, in magazines and newspapers and on TV there are several opportunities to harness the power of what we could call other gods to receive some "blessing" that we seek. Our passage deals with this same issue. But the attitude of Moses toward these other powers may seem startling in our age of tolerance.

False Prophets and Dreamers with Real Power (13:1–3)

Moses first speaks about "a prophet or a dreamer of dreams [who] arises among you and gives you a sign or a wonder, and the sign or wonder that he tells you comes to pass" (13:1, 2a). "Dreams were one of the standard means for receiving messages from a god in the ancient Near East."[1] Moses is talking about false prophets and dreamers who will perform miraculous signs and wonders! Is this possible? Jesus warned that in the last days "false christs and false prophets will arise and perform signs and wonders, to lead astray, if possible, the elect" (Mark 13:22). The Bible acknowledges that other forces and gods have supernatural powers. It even says that believers are constantly fighting with such forces (Ephesians 6:12).

Moses says that though these prophets and dreamers may have power to give us something that we are looking for, they are dangerous because they take us away from trusting in the one true God to trusting in other gods. He says that the prophet or dreamer will say, "'Let us go after other gods,' which you have not known, 'and let us serve them'" (13:2b). We have looked at the danger of going after gods "you have not known" in our discussion on 11:28.

The danger from similar sources of power today cannot be exaggerated. People are impatient and accustomed to controlling their lives by using the various conveniences readily available. Therefore, they are unused to grappling with uncertainly about what will happen to them and to waiting patiently for God to act in solving their problem or giving them the guidance they need. A tarot card reader, palm reader, astrologer, psychic counselor, or medicine man could give the answer to the problem instantly. And sometimes they give the desired answer! Christians lacking the faith to wait patiently for God's deliverance could in their desperation go to such a person.

Besides, today when people think about religion and spirituality they generally think about things that have to do with power and control rather than with the holy nature of God. So people meditate and do yoga exercises to have control of their mind and body. They go to a temple or shrine to get help from a god in a specific area such as success in their career or studies or business. They go to a palm reader to have some control over their lives by knowing something about the future. Many Christians today view Christ as the answer to their problems rather than as the absolute and sole Lord of their whole life (an attitude they should have moved beyond early in their Christian walk). In this environment we can see how people could be lured into going to powerful prophets of other gods.

Moses tells the people, "You shall not listen to the words of that prophet or that dreamer of dreams" (13:3a). Shouldn't we know some things about these false prophets? Indeed, we all need some knowledge about the way these people operate. But that is different from listening to messages they give us. These can have a marked effect on us. As astrology and palmistry are very popular in Sri Lanka, I have read a lot about these practices. But to date I have not allowed anyone to read my palm or prepare a horoscope for me, even though this is something that people often do in relaxed social settings in Sri Lanka. When people playfully ask to read my palm I politely decline. Once my roommate in university read my palm without my knowledge, but I did not permit him to tell me what he found out. The reason for this "total ban" is that this knowledge can affect us. It tends to affect our attitudes, actions, and plans. It comes through a source hostile to God. Even if what it says is correct, this is knowledge that God has chosen not to give us through legitimate means. Having such knowledge will only harm us.

We can be at peace believing that the almighty God who is sovereign over the affairs of history holds not only the future but also our hands and that he is committed to our welfare. In times of uncertainty and trouble we will cling to him in faith, believing that in his time he will surely use even the present gloomy situation to enact his good purpose for us (Romans 8:28). We do not need to know what God chooses not to reveal to us. What we do need to know is that God is committed to our welfare and will never forsake us.

A reason is given as to why God permits the Israelites to be exposed to these false prophets and dreamers: "For the LORD your God is testing you, to know whether you love the LORD your God with all your heart and with all your soul" (13:3b). Does God not know what is in our hearts? In the Bible the testing of believers serves to confirm whether "their actions would tally with their profession."[2] It is a necessary step in the process of growth in discipleship. It confirms to us "whether [we] love the LORD [our] God with all [our] heart and with all [our] soul." The test reveals whether we are genuine in our commitment. When a test reveals that there is a lack in our commitment, we can take remedial action to ensure that we truly love the Lord wholeheartedly. Someone has said that our sins are handles by which the Lord gets ahold of us. When we realize that we have failed a test by sinning, then God has a way to work in us to bring us fully to himself.

What Total Dedication Is Like (13:4)

Verse 4 gives us several qualities of the totally dedicated persons described in verse 3 as loving the Lord "with all [their] heart and with all [their] soul." These qualities appear often in Deuteronomy, and we have discussed some of them elsewhere. So we will discuss these qualities only briefly, focusing on how each quality relates to the life of faithfulness and how they combine to give a comprehensive description of it. The repetition in Deuteronomy of matters relating to practicing the life of holiness is surely significant. This is so urgent and so easily neglected that it was necessary for it to be repeated several times. About 1,400 out of 2,005 verses in Paul's letters have to do with the life of holiness. Clearly this must always be a front-burner issue in the program of the church.

First, Moses says, "You shall walk after [or follow, NIV] the LORD your God." The way to avoid following wrong paths is to follow God. This describes an attitude of obedience, when the person wants to do God's will. Next, Moses says that the people must "fear him." This presents the other side of the desire to do God's will—an attitude of reverence and awe toward God that produces a healthy fear of displeasing him.

The next two qualities are the practical outworking of these two attitudes: they are to "keep his commandments and obey his voice." A general attitude of commitment is not enough. We must know the will of God and do it in day-to-day life. Practically today this works out to knowing God's Word and obeying it meticulously. The word translated "keep" is the familiar word *shamar* that appears about sixty-five times in Deuteronomy and essentially means "be careful." I can say without any hesitation that when I do something that displeases God, every time at the root of it is my carelessness about being scrupulous about the choices I make. Now this may come out of a lack of dedication to God. But that expresses itself in carelessness.

Then Moses says, ". . . you shall serve him." Here we have the standard word *abad*, meaning "service" or "work" or sometimes "worship," which appears 261 times in the Old Testament (on servanthood see the discussion on 6:13 and 11:13). The life of obedience is not a static, purposeless adherence to rules given by a God who acts like a policeman or enforcer of discipline. The life of holiness is one of serving the Lord of creation and participating in fulfilling his glorious agenda for this world. This invests us with significance and worth. We cannot serve God while we live ungodly lives. One who is a vessel fit for the Master's use must be purified from what is dishonorable, flee youthful passions, and follow after the way of righteousness (2 Timothy 2:21, 22). That is what is described in the earlier qualities. One who is careful to obey God can be used in his service.

The last point Moses gives is, "hold fast to him." Two closely related Hebrew words (*dabeq* and *dabaq*, meaning "clinging" or "holding fast to"), appear five times in Deuteronomy and refer to clinging to God or his word (4:4; 10:20; 11:22; 13:4; 30:20). We looked at this in our discussion of Deuteronomy 4:4. We said that this word can be used for the belt clinging to the skin (Jeremiah 13:11) and the husband leaving his father and mother and being united to his wife (Genesis 2:24). In some ways this summarizes all the qualities given above. We are weak and vulnerable to temptation and can easily fall into sin if we try to live in our own strength. So in desperation we cling to God—getting our strength, identity, wisdom, and directions for life from him. We are careful to always let God be so important to us that we will do only what pleases him. Like children who are well aware of their dependence on their parents for provision and protection, we cling to our heavenly Father, humbly submitting to him and seeking his help.

Punishment for Those Who Lead Others Astray (13:5)

After warning the people to have nothing to do with those who lead them astray, Moses goes on to an extended discussion on the punishment to be meted out to them. First he says, "But that prophet or that dreamer of dreams shall be put to death" (13:5a). The punishment is so severe because in the theocratic state of Israel this would be equivalent to treason. Moses says that the person is to be put to death "because he has taught rebellion against the LORD your God" (13:5b). This would not transfer exactly to our present societies, which are not theocracies. However, in keeping with our approach to the Law in Deuteronomy (see the discussion on 4:44—5:6) we need to ask what principles we can apply from this stipulation of punishment. What we can apply is the thought that we cannot tolerate people in our churches who deliberately try to take us away from the worship of God as prescribed in his Word. Today what we can do is to expel them from the church. Paul did this with Hymenaeus and Alexander, about whom he said, ". . . whom I have handed over to Satan that they may learn not to blaspheme" (1 Timothy 1:20).

Moses says that the God against whom the people rebelled "brought [them] out of the land of Egypt and redeemed [them] out of the house of slavery" (Deuteronomy 13:5c). When God gave the first commandment, he presented the exodus as its preamble (5:6). Now Moses uses the exodus again when warning the people about breaking the first commandment.[3] The equivalent event for us is our redemption through the death and resurrection of Christ. The appeal here is not simply to a debtor's ethic by which we are challenged to be faithful out of an indebtedness to live for Christ because he has done so much for us. Rather we are being directed to a fresh understanding of the seriousness of apostasy.

Hebrews 6:4–6 describes how serious a thing it is for one who has tasted God's salvation to fall away. It says that "they are crucifying once again the Son of God to their own harm and holding him up to contempt." They have become like those who crucified Christ by rejecting him, but they are worse because unlike those people they had tasted of the Lord's grace. And Hebrews says this action holds Christ up to public shame.

The repeated use of the exodus story in Deuteronomy to motivate people to faithfulness shows how important it is to lead Christians to live constantly under the perspective of grace. Just as the Israelites were constantly reminded that they were slaves redeemed by grace, Christians need to be constantly reminded that they are sinners saved by grace. Then when we face huge problems, the force of temptation to unfaithfulness will be greatly reduced as we realize that God has saved us from a much more serious problem— eternal damnation. In light of that, our huge problem is not huge at all. Then we would realize that it is sheer folly to give up the God who has saved us from eternal damnation because we are having a problem of a much lesser magnitude.

In our church we have a lady from a Buddhist background who was suffering from demon possession when she first came to us. She had spent a lot of money going to various exorcists to overcome this problem. We prayed with her over a period of a few months before she was fully healed. The most obvious evidence of her healing and conversion to Christ was the brightness on her face. But she continued to have serious problems even after her conversion owing to her husband's addiction to drugs. She would often share her desperate plight with us and ask for prayer. She has been a Christian now for several years, and her husband is still enslaved to drugs. Yet she never gave up her commitment to Christ. Something she always says before sharing her need for prayer gives us the clue to her faithfulness. She prefaces every prayer request by praising God for saving her from sin! When you always have that blessing before you, the power of the temptation to turn away from God when lesser blessings are denied is greatly reduced.

Verse 5 ends with the statement, "So you shall purge the evil from your midst." This statement appears ten times in Deuteronomy referring to exercising the death sentence on wrongdoers.[4] Once it is said that they are to purge evil from their midst "so that it may be well with" them (19:13). God cannot bless his people when they tolerate such serious sin in their midst. We find this concept difficult to understand because we live in a highly individualistic society where the Biblical idea of corporate solidarity is missing. In the Bible the faithful live out their lives in community. So when there is serious sin from one segment of the community, the other segments cannot say, "This is not our business," and ignore it. When Daniel saw the state of his nation, though he was a righteous person, he confessed sin using the first person saying, "We have sinned" (Daniel 9:5, 6). Applying this today, when there is serious sin in the body, such as an unmarried couple living together, the church will need to ensure that the guilty persons do not participate in the celebration of the Lord's Supper until they repent. They cannot avoid taking up the responsibility by saying that it is none of their business.

When Paul calls for the expulsion of a man who was having sexual relations with his father's wife, he quotes this statement about purging evil from Deuteronomy (1 Corinthians 5:13). How alien this type of thinking is to us today. When someone who is seriously causing harm to the church is disciplined today Christians often say things like, "Is there no forgiveness in Christianity?" or, "Is not the church a hospital for sick people rather than a hotel for whole people?" Indeed, there is always a welcome to sinners in the body of Christ. But those who claim to be believers and lead others away from the way of God belong to a completely different category. They are dangerous to the church and must be disciplined.

When Loved Ones Are the Wrongdoers (13:6–11)

After prescribing the punishment for those who lead people to worship other gods, Moses says that exceptions should not be made if the wrongdoers are family members and friends. He mentions the closest people one can have: "your brother, the son of your mother, or your son or your daughter or the wife you embrace or your friend who is as your own soul" (13:6). The command is not only that we do "not yield to . . . or listen to" their enticements (13:8a). Moses also says, ". . . nor shall your eye pity him, nor shall you spare him" (13:8b). Christians often relax strict rules of discipline when family members are the wrongdoers. Sometimes we do not make the sin known out of loyalty to the person. So Moses says, ". . . nor shall you conceal him" (13:8c). How painful it is when we have to turn in a family member or a close friend. But commitment to God and his honor should make us do it.

Verse 9 is almost too painful to read. The one who reports the crime needs to take responsibility for the punishment against his loved one.[5] Therefore Moses says, "Your hand shall be first against him to put him to death" (13:9b). Yet he is not going to have to carry out this responsibility alone, for Moses goes on to say that others will share in it: ". . . and afterward the hand of all the people" (13:9c). Generally the whole community was involved in execution by stoning because "every citizen was required to take a hand in purging the community of evil (Deuteronomy 17:5; 20:27; Leviticus 24:14; Joshua 7:25)."[6] The community was involved in doing what we now look to legal and prison authorities to do for the community.

We tend to see the punishment talked about in the Old Testament as being vindictive in contrast to the New Testament ethic that asks us to love our enemies. But the Old Testament also teaches us to love our enemies (see also Exodus 23:4, 5; 2 Kings 6:22; 2 Chronicles 28:15; Proverbs 25:21, 22). The Old and New Testaments both teach the dual doctrines of punishment for sin and love for enemies. Jesus also said this.

The reason given for the punishment has a lot of relevance to us today: "You shall stone him to death with stones, because he sought to draw you away from the LORD your God, who brought you out of the land of Egypt, out of the house of slavery" (13:10). Nothing on earth is as important as one's relationship with God. Anything that acts as a deterrent to one's relationship with God must be attacked like a dangerous poison. This is why Jesus said about those who bring temptation to sin to others, "It would be better for him if a millstone were hung around his neck and he were cast into the sea than that he should cause one of these little ones to sin" (Luke 17:2).

Next, Moses gives the consequence of the punishment meted out to a blasphemous loved one: "And all Israel shall hear and fear and never again do any such wickedness as this among you" (13:11). The punishment would give rise to a fear of sinning among God's people. When Ananias and Sapphira died as a result of lying about their gift to the church, twice we are told that "great fear came upon all who heard of it" (Acts 5:5, 11). Paul says, "As for those [elders] who persist in sin, rebuke them in the presence of all" (1 Timothy 5:20). Why? ". . . so that the rest may stand in fear." When God's people deal with sin as something deadly serious, people develop a fear of sinning. By punishing an unrepentant blasphemer we save others from falling into the same error.

When Wrongdoers Are in Another City (13:12–18)

The principle of rooting out those who encourage the worship of other gods is extended to cities other than one's own. Moses addresses this issue next: "If you hear in one of your cities, which the LORD your God is giving you to dwell there, that certain worthless fellows have gone out among you and have drawn away the inhabitants of their city, saying, 'Let us go and serve other gods,' which you have not known . . . " (13:12, 13). Moses says that they must first "inquire and make search and ask diligently" (13:14a). Disciplinary procedures call for the hard work of ensuring that all the facts are known. It is a terrible thing to condemn an innocent person. Sometimes Christian leaders are quick to attribute a demonic influence to things that have natural causes. This is a trap we must be careful to avoid. The lure of the esteem that comes with battling demonic forces could cause us to attribute things to demons too quickly.

Once there is proof that there has been a worship of other gods, the principle of *herem* or devotion to total destruction, discussed in our study on Deuteronomy 7, comes into operation (13:15). Usually this principle was applied to pagan cities that could have led Israel astray. This time it applied to a Jewish city that became apostate. As Chris Wright points out, this "law illustrates the precise opposite of the divine favoritism that Deuteronomy is sometimes accused of."

The various *herem* regulations, such as completely destroying the people and livestock (13:15) and totally destroying by fire everything in the city (13:16), are made to apply here, too. Moses warns, "None of the devoted things shall stick to your hand" (13:17). Raiders can't simply attack a town on the pretext that it is apostate and carry off its wealth! Nothing is to be left for humans to use in any way. Here, too, the destroyed beings and things are presented to God as an offering: "You shall gather all its spoil into the midst of its open square and burn the city and all its spoil with fire, as a whole burnt offering to the LORD your God. It shall be a heap forever. It shall not be built again" (13:16). The punishment described in this passage was inflicted upon the city of Gibeah later in Israel's history (Judges 19, 20).[7]

When the offending city has been punished, God's wrath will be appeased. The result is : ". . . the LORD may turn from the fierceness of his anger and show you mercy and have compassion on you and multiply you, as he swore to your fathers" (13:17b). We can do nothing to deserve his mercy. But without repentance and the fruit of repentance we forfeit the mercy, because that represents an attitude of rebellion against God. So Moses goes on to say that the mercy is conditional upon human obedience: ". . . if you obey the voice of the LORD your God, keeping all his commandments that I am commanding you today, and doing what is right in the sight of the LORD your God" (13:18).

If a church or prominent Christian, with which we have no official contact, is doing something dangerously wrong, should we poke our fingers into that affair? I must confess that my immediate response to this is to say, "Don't get involved." But we belong to the one body of Christ. We are organically connected to every part of the body. As Indian church leader Sam Kamaleson once said at the Urbana Student Missions Conference, the church "is not an organization but a supernatural organism: She feels, she throbs with vitality. In other words, when the church in the United States is pinched, the church in India must say, 'Ah, that hurts!'"[8] Unfortunately, evangelical Christians are deficient here. We have little understanding of the body of Christ, and when we do take it seriously we apply the idea primarily to the local church rather than to the universal church.

The material in this chapter goes against the grain of popular thinking today, even among Christians. I will conclude this chapter with an extended quote from Chris Wright's excellent commentary on Deuteronomy:

> C. S. Lewis once said that if we no longer feel comfortable with the cursing psalms, for example, it is not because of our greater, "Christian" sensitivity, but because of our appalling moral apathy. We no longer feel the passion of the psalmist that God should deal with evil and evildoers and vindicate God's own moral order in the world. We respond to idolatrous, blasphemous evil not with a curse, but a shrug, and then we have the gall to claim morally higher ground than ancient Israel. Similarly, if we can no longer identify with the scale of priorities and values that under-gird Deuteronomy 13, it is manifestly not because we have acquired a greater appreciation of the value of human life, but because we have lost any sense of the awful majesty of God's reality.

36

We Will Be Different from Others

DEUTERONOMY 14:1–21

AFTER THE STRONG PROHIBITION of having anything to do with occult powers, Moses goes on to show how the distinctiveness of the Israelites in relation to surrounding peoples is demonstrated in some expressions of their religious life (14:1–21). The discussion below will show that the primary purpose for these rules, some of which seem strange to us, is that of helping the Israelites to remember that they are a people who are different from others because they are God's people. Our discussion of this passage will major on what we can learn that will help us to be a people for God who are different from others.

We Are a People Holy to the LORD (14:1, 2, 21)

The uniqueness of Israel is expressed is 14:1 where Moses says, "You are the sons of the LORD your God." In 14:2 Moses says, "For you are a people holy to the LORD your God, and the LORD has chosen you to be a people for his treasured possession, out of all the peoples who are on the face of the earth." The order of words in the Hebrew of both these sentences is significant. They begin by stating, "Sons you are . . . " and "a holy people you are. . . ." This emphasizes their unique identity. The same words as in verse 2 were used in 7:6, the passage that commands the Israelites to utterly destroy the nations they overthrow in their conquest of the promised land. Moses ends this discussion of prohibited things by saying, "For you are a people holy to the LORD your God" (14:21c).

Three things mark out the people as different from others. The first is *adoption*: they are God's children (14:1). The most important thing about them is that they belong to God as a child belongs to a father. Earlier in 1:31 and 8:5 the fact that they were God's children was used to demonstrate, as Chris Wright says, "God's action for Israel, in care and discipline." He initiated a covenant with them, and he has so far kept that covenant in an amazing way, giving them all they needed, sometimes through miraculous provision. "Here, however, the stress is on the other side of the parent-child relationship, namely the duty of the child to obey the parent's will" (Wright).

As people who belong to God, their behavior needs to be different from that of others, and chapter 14 gives some behaviors that mark them out from their neighbors. Many conform to the world because they feel that this is the way to acceptance by others and thus to significance. They are looking for a sense of belonging. But there is a much more powerful influence on them—the sense of belonging to God as his children. If they grasp this, they will realize that it is not necessary for them to sin in order to belong. In fact, sin would be below their dignity as God's children.

One of our greatest challenges in discipling Christians is helping them understand and revel in their adoption by God. One of the saddest experiences we have in youth ministry has to do with young people, especially girls, who come from terribly dysfunctional backgrounds. They meet the Lord and seem to be growing well in the faith. Suddenly a young man who is not a Christian and is sometimes very mixed up (a drug addict, for example) shows them some affection and attention, and they give up the faith in order to have a relationship with that person. Sometimes they run away with the person. Often within a few days they regret the decision they made. But the attention that the person showed seems to have filled the void that was created by the lack of care at home. How we wish that they would have understood more fully the security of being children of God before this happened.

This is why we should do all we can—through faithful teaching of the Word, through personal care and counsel and vibrant community life—to let Christians understand as soon as possible the glorious implications of being children of God. Our aim should be to see them having the same exhilaration over adoption that John had when he exclaimed, "See what kind of love the Father has given to us, that we should be called children of God; and so we are" (1 John 3:1). Then the lure of deceptive signs of concern from others that lead to sin will be greatly reduced.

The second thing that marks out the Israelites is *sanctification or holiness*, which is stated twice in this passage. Verse 2 says, "For you are a people holy to the LORD your God" (see v. 21c). We are separated for God and his service. This presents another aspect of our identity. We are under a new ownership, and in this we find meaning and purpose. If we sin we lose our way and our peace, for we are not being what we were meant to be. So Paul says that the peace of God guards us (Philippians 4:7) and rules in our hearts (Colossians 3:15). Peace helps keep us holy, for the loss of it would alert us to the dangerous situation we are in.

I once heard the beloved preacher Howard Hendricks tell a story about how he was on a flight that was greatly delayed. Most of the passengers were angry, and they spoke rudely to the flight attendants who in turn spoke rudely to the passengers. But one flight attendant was polite through all of the stress of this flight. At the end of the flight Dr. Hendricks spoke to this flight attendant and asked for her name because he wanted to write to American Airlines about her excellent performance under pressure. She responded, "But I don't work for American Airlines, I work for God!" She was God's person, and everything she did was determined by this identity.

The third thing that marks out the Israelites is *election*[1]: ". . . and the LORD has chosen you to be a people for his treasured possession, out of all the peoples who are on the face of the earth" (14:2b). They did not deserve salvation. It was a free, unmerited gift given by God to an unworthy people. But election did not involve only a change of status; it involved becoming God's treasured possession. I am writing this while traveling abroad. I miss my wife terribly. But as I was praying for her this morning, I was filled with joy over the truth that I am her treasured possession and she is mine. How much more precious is the privilege of being God's treasured possession!

We do not know why God chose us and showered his mercy on us. But we know that he did. And now we are his, and he is ours. As his treasured possession we are invested with rich value and significance. What folly it would be to compromise our commitment in order to succeed and gain acceptance in a world that is so unreliable. But people do this. Therefore, we constantly need to remind ourselves of our position in Christ. This gives us security by assuring us that God is greater than all the forces that can harm us and that God delights to give us all we need. Such security is a springboard for the joy and peace of salvation, which is the greatest treasure we have on earth. John Wesley said, "O what a pearl of so great a price is the lowest degree of the peace of God." Even if we have to sacrifice earthly treasures in order to secure this, it is a treasure that surpasses by far in value all that we lose.

Using several Old Testament concepts Peter says, "But you are a chosen race, a royal priesthood, a holy nation, a people for his own possession [a peculiar people, KJV], that you may proclaim the excellencies of him who called you out of darkness into his marvelous light. Once you were not a people, but now you are God's people; once you had not received mercy, but now you have received mercy" (1 Peter 2:9, 10). Being this is not easy because we would stick out as different and "peculiar." But what Peter says are necessary aspects of our identity help us to be obedient to God. Peter's statement is found within a passage urging Christians to live holy lives in a world where others are not doing so (1 Peter 2:1–10).

The sense of belonging is a very important aspect of one's identity and of the security and significance that one feels. Cults exploit this by challenging people to exclusiveness in return for the security of belonging to a supposedly warm and caring community. May we do all we can to lead people to the joy of belonging to God and his people, which will give them the strength to be faithful to him in a world that is hostile to his ways.

Our Ways of Mourning Are Different (14:1b)

The first command found in this passage has to do with rituals that Israel's neighbors practiced when someone died. Referring to such practices Moses says, "You shall not cut yourselves or make any baldness on your foreheads for the dead" (14:1b). J. A. Thompson observes that even today the practice of mutilating the body in honor of the dead persists in some countries such as New Guinea. Thompson feels that this prohibition was made "because they hinted at some conformity to pagan practices and also because Israel had a respect for the body as God's creation which was not to be disfigured or mis-used (cf. Leviticus 19:27)."

All cultures have such rituals, and there is a close connection between religion and the way people mourn for and honor their dead. In most non-Western cultures funerals are an extremely important aspect of community life, usually with neighbors, relatives, and friends getting involved in the arrangements. Protestant Christianity does not have many elaborate mourn-ing rituals, and, especially in the West, funerals are somewhat sanitized with few public expressions of mourning. As an outsider I have felt that this is a weakness because people miss the opportunity of mourning for and honoring adequately their departed loved ones. The lack of this could make the recov-ery process much harder. In the Bible several acceptable mourning rituals gave people an opportunity to express their sorrow over the passing of their loved ones.

Christians today have a challenge not envisaged in the law in Deuteronomy. We live in multi-religious societies, and many Christians come from non-Christian families who have specific mourning rituals. My wife has shared the gospel with a dear friend who is a Hindu who accepts that the gospel is the truth and the best way. But she held back from becoming a Christian because she says she does not want to dishonor the family by not doing the Hindu funerary rituals. Sadly, she has stopped going to church.

The advice we have given to converts to Christ from other faiths has been to do all they can during funerals without isolating themselves from the family at the time of death. For example, they should not worship the monks who come for the almsgiving meal in memory of the dead person. But they can help in the preparation of the meal, the washing up of the dishes, and the cleaning of the house.

Because funerals are an extremely important part of the life of a community, it is imperative that Christians find ways to bury their dead that help express grief and adequately honor the dead person. The Israelites had such procedures. They did not do some of the things their neighbors did. But there was weeping, tearing of clothes, and wearing of sackcloth (Genesis 37:34). Mourning ceremonies could last for between seven (Genesis 50:10) and thirty days (Deuteronomy 34:8). Sometimes poetic laments were composed for the occasion (2 Samuel 1:17; 2 Chronicles 35:25). Sometimes people were summoned to come and mourn over the dead (Amos 5:16). Jeremiah asked skillful people to come to wail over the dead (Jeremiah 9:17–20), suggesting a class of professional mourners, which we could replace today with a choir. People would fast after someone died (1 Samuel 31:13; 2 Samuel 1:12; 3:35).[2] Luke reports that "devout men buried Stephen and made great lamentation over him" (Acts 8:2).

By having rituals that give adequate expression to our response to the death of a person, we avoid giving the impression that we have dishonored the dead. But most important for Christians would be the task of presenting the hope of the resurrection, which is the most glorious thing about the death of a Christian. A hearing is won by adequate ritual, and this could open the door to a powerful witness to the gospel by appropriately presenting the good news of Christ's victory over death.

We Don't Do Some Things Others Do (14:3–21b)

Deuteronomy 14:3–21b has to do with clean and unclean food and has puzzled students of the Word because it is difficult to understand the reason why some foods are designated as clean and others as unclean. The section begins with a general statement: "You shall not eat any abomination" (14:3; "detestable thing," NIV). This is a "term that suggests anything that is repulsive to and abhorred by God or even man."[3] Before we discuss the issue of what makes some foods unclean and others clean, we will do an overview of the instructions given in verses 4–21.

Clean Land Animals

Reason for acceptance: ". . . parts the hoof and has the hoof cloven in two and chews the cud" (14:6). **Accepted animals**: ". . . the ox, the sheep, the goat, the deer, the gazelle, the roebuck, the wild goat, the ibex, the antelope, and the mountain sheep" (14:4, 5).

Unclean Land Animals

Reason for rejection: ". . . chew the cud or have the hoof cloven . . . but do not part the hoof" (14:7). **Rejected animals:** ". . . the camel, the hare, and the rock badger" (14:7). **Reason for rejection:** ". . . it parts the hoof but does not chew the cud" (14:8). **Rejected animal:** pig (14:8).

Clean Fish

Reason for acceptance: ". . . whatever has fins and scales" (14:9). **Accepted fish:** ". . . all that are in the waters" that have fins and scales (14:9).

Unclean Fish

Reason for rejection: ". . . whatever does not have fins and scales" (14:10). **Rejected fish:** All the fish that fall into that category (14:10).

Clean Creatures of the Air

Reason for acceptance: "clean" (14:11, 20). No other reason is given. **Accepted creatures:** "all clean birds" (14:11); "all clean winged things" (14:20).

Unclean Creatures of the Air

Reason for rejection: No reason is given. *Rejected creatures*: ". . . the eagle, the bearded vulture, the black vulture, the kite, the falcon of any kind; every raven of any kind; the ostrich, the nighthawk, the sea gull, the hawk of any kind; the little owl and the short-eared owl, the barn owl and the tawny owl, the carrion vulture and the cormorant, the stork, the heron of any kind; the hoopoe and the bat" (14:12–18). **Reason for rejection:** "unclean" (14:19). No other reason is given. **Rejected creatures:** "all winged insects" (14:19).

In some of the above cases of prohibited animals we can find a rationale for their designation as unclean. For example, vultures (14:12) are scavengers who eat animals that die naturally, and eating such is prohibited in verse 21. This could apply to the birds of prey also (14:12–16).[4] Some of these unclean animals had associations with Canaanite religions. Some interpreters have claimed that the unclean foods were regarded as unfit to eat mainly for health reasons. While that may be true for some of the prohibited animals, it does not seem to be the case for most of these animals. For example, the Israelites are given permission to give or sell some of these meats to neighboring nations (14:21). In 14:7 the NIV offers an interpretation by adding "ceremonially" before unclean, even though that is not in the Hebrew text. According to this interpretation, the uncleanness has to do with the religious regulations of the Israelites.

God allowed the eating of some of these foods later in his encounter with Peter in Joppa, which shows that some of these animals were not harmful to health. When Peter, as a Jew, expressed reluctance to eat this food he was told, "What God has made clean, do not call common" (Acts 11:9). This gives us a clue as to what made these foods clean and unclean. They are such because God regarded them to be such.

A similar conclusion can be drawn from Deuteronomy 14:21a, b: "You shall not eat anything that has died naturally. You may give it to the sojourner who is within your towns, that he may eat it, or you may sell it to a foreigner." The reason for prohibiting the eating of the flesh of animals that have died naturally must not primarily have been nutritional because this same flesh could be given to sojourners and foreigners who were not part of the covenant community. Moses goes on to give the real reason for the prohibitions: "For you are a people holy to the LORD your God" (14:21c). Israelites were not permitted to eat blood, so the blood was poured out before the flesh was cooked (12:23–25). This was one of their covenant regulations relating to ritual cleansing. Such food was not kosher.

We must remember that the overriding theme of this passage is that Israel is a people holy to God, separated from the rest of the nations because they had a unique covenant relationship with God (14:1, 2, 21). God, because of his sovereign will, called Israel to be holy even though they had no intrinsic qualifications of their own for this. For these holy people he determined that some foods were acceptable and others were not—not because they are intrinsically good and bad but because that is what he willed for his chosen people.

That God dispensed of this distinction between foods in the new covenant is evidenced in his command to Peter to eat such food (Acts 11:7–9). This is more explicitly stated in Mark 7:14–23 where Jesus says that what counts is not what goes into the mouth but what comes out of the heart. Mark adds a comment to this discussion saying, "Thus he declared all foods clean" (Mark 7:19b).

Though we do not follow these dietary laws, there are some lessons we can learn from this Old Testament practice. First, we learn that holiness encompasses all of life, even what we eat. We must consider eating as something we do for God. Paul said, "So, whether you eat or drink, or whatever you do, do all to the glory of God" (1 Corinthians 10:31). Excessive spending on food, eating unhealthy food, overeating, and gluttony are practices that go against the Christian ethic and so are sins against God.

Second, we said above that these food laws were given to Israel to remind them of the fact that God had graciously called them to himself so they would be thankful and also so they would not conform to the lifestyle of their neighboring nations. These implications of God's call—thanksgiving and nonconformity to the world—are relevant to Christians, too. Gordon Wenham points out, "Though the Christian is so much more privileged than ancient Israel, it is easy to take for granted the grace that has been given him and fail to acknowledge it. The ancient food laws were designed to curb such forgetfulness."[5]

We also can do things to help us remember God's grace in electing us and making us a people holy to him. The Lord's Supper plays this role admirably. Like many of the food regulations, a scientific study will not reveal any particular significance in bread and wine. But spiritually it reminds us of the grace that made us who we are and what Christ did to make that possible. Similarly, each time someone is baptized, we can remind ourselves of this grace and of our position in Christ. The food laws then remind us of the need to take special steps to help us live in keeping with our unique call and identity.

Unacceptable Additions to Acceptable Practices (14:21d)

The last part of verse 21 has a puzzling command: "You shall not boil a young goat in its mother's milk." This command appears twice in Exodus in festival contexts (23:19; 34:26). In Deuteronomy, too, it comes just before a festival-related passage. It seems to have been something that the neighboring nations practiced and that the Israelites were tempted to practice, especially at feast time.[6] This prohibition may have been given to demonstrate that the people are to be different from others. But it may also "reflect the principle that what is designed to give life [milk] should not become a means of death."[7]

This was a case of the prohibition of unacceptable additions to acceptable practices during festivals. I can see some applications of this to the lives of Christians today.

- Celebrating Christmas is a good opportunity to honor Christ. But we can add unacceptable practices to it like unhealthy revelry, extravagant spending, and competitive gift buying. These are practices acquired from the world around us.

- When laying the foundation stone for a new building, the contractors may want to follow the superstitions normal in society like burying valuables that are supposed to ward off danger and bring good luck. We must explain to the contractor that we do not believe in such things and do Christian things in their place like praying and dedicating the construction process to God.
- We find parents of a Christian bride or groom who do not know the Lord wanting to have the wedding at a time in line with astrological approval. The couple needs to firmly disapprove of this.

Sometimes the problems we have today may be more complex than in Old Testament times because we live and work with people of different religions. In such situations we need to pray for guidance, carefully study the issues, discuss with other Christians, and come up with Biblically-based responses to non-Christian practices.

The Need to Affirm Our Identity as Christians

The key to this whole passage is the need to affirm our identity as Christians. We need to always remember and our friends and family members need to know that our identity as Christians brings with it some principles that mark us out as different from the world. Unlike the theocratic nation of Israel, where violations of the covenant were dealt with severely, in multi-religious societies we should politely explain our convictions, especially when the religious practices of people are involved. If we do not make our stand clear, we may end up compromising our principles.

I was the only Protestant Christian in the school of science where I studied in university. We had about four Roman Catholics in all the classes at the school. The rest were Buddhists and Muslims. During the first few days in college, my fellow-students got to know that I was a Christian because I refused to do a few of the things that the senior students asked me to do as a freshman. Giving freshmen a hard time during the first few weeks of the year is a common practice in our universities. I did all the humiliating things they asked me to do, except those things that compromised my faith. I had to explain that I could not do those things "because my God will not be pleased." The news spread that there was a devout Christian in the school.

Soon my friends found out that I do not enjoy obscene jokes and that this, too, was because of my faith. Later when someone made a very funny but obscene joke, sometimes I could not help laughing. Then my friends would remind me that I am not permitted to laugh at such jokes because of my principles. The fact that they knew about my principles right at the start of my college career greatly helped me stick to them.

Christians are different from others in many of their practices, and that is because of their identity as adopted, sanctified, and called people of God. Peter said, "But you are a chosen race, a royal priesthood, a holy nation, a people for his own possession, that you may proclaim the excellencies of him who called you out of darkness into his marvelous light" (1 Peter 2:9).

37

Giving to God

DEUTERONOMY 14:22–29; 15:19–23

A CLERGYMAN WROTE a wealthy and influential businessman, requesting a subscription to a worthy charity. He promptly received a curt refusal that ended by saying, "As far as I can see, this Christian business is just one continuous give, give, give." After a brief interval the clergyman answered, "I wish to thank you for the best definition of the Christian life that I have yet heard."[1]

Giving is a topic that appears several times in the Pentateuch, and Deuteronomy has its fair share of passages on the subject. It is a major theme of the section of Deuteronomy that we are presently going through (chapters 12–26), appearing in chapters 12, 14, 15, 16, 18, and 26. Apart from the special offerings that are given at special events and for special reasons like thanksgiving and forgiveness, Deuteronomy speaks of four kinds of regular offerings: the annual tithe, the tithe that is given once every three years, and the offering of firstborn livestock and of firstfruits. The two passages we are looking at here describe all but the firstfruits offering, which will be examined in our discussion on 26:1–11.

The Annual Tithe (14:22–27)

Using a technique that is often used in this section of Deuteronomy, Moses first gives the law in a brief statement and then expounds it further. He first talks about the annual tithe: "You shall tithe all the yield of your seed that comes from the field year by year" (14:22). *Tithe* is the old English word for "tenth" and has now become part of Judeo-Christian English vocabulary. Next Moses says, "And before the LORD your God, in the place that he will choose, to make his name dwell there, you shall eat the tithe of your grain, of your wine, and of your oil, and the firstborn of your herd and flock, that you may learn to fear the LORD your God always" (14:23). A tithe of grain, wine, and oil is asked for. Included in the list is the firstborn of the herd and flock, which will be the topic of a later paragraph (15:19–23). In those days currency was hardly used, and things were bought and sold in kind. In an agricultural economy earnings were generally measured by the yield of the field and livestock.

The more basic teachings about tithing are given in the more formal sections of the Law in Leviticus (27:30–33) and Numbers (18:21–32). What we have here is a sermonic summary. As we saw in our discussion of Deuteronomy 12:6–12, the tithe was to be eaten along with the family in the place that God would choose (14:23a). Presumably only some of it was consumed, and the rest was given to the Levites who served in the central place of worship.

Money comes into play when the place of worship is so far away that it would be difficult to take their produce and livestock to the central sanctuary (14:24). "Then," says Moses, "you shall turn it into money and bind up the money in your hand and go to the place that the LORD your God chooses and spend the money for whatever you desire—oxen or sheep or wine or strong drink, whatever your appetite craves" (14:25, 26a). As we saw in 12:6, 7 and 12:11, 12, they are asked to eat what they like to eat and to do so as families with joy: "And you shall eat there before the LORD your God and rejoice, you and your household" (14:26b).

Next Moses again tells the people not to forget the Levites in their towns: "And you shall not neglect the Levite who is within your towns, for he has no portion or inheritance with you" (14:27; see 12:19 and also 12:12, 18). The tithe given once in three years is especially for Levites and needy people in their community (14:28, 29).

Tithing Helps Us Fear God (14:23b)

Tithing achieves some important ends. As David Payne points out, "Tithing had two values: (1) it represented a gift to God, recognizing that farm produce and livestock came from him—indeed, a tithe was a token of repayment to him; (2) it provided a large part of the resources needed to maintain temples and temple personnel, such as priests and Levites."

In our passage Moses mentions another important purpose of tithing: ". . . that you may learn to fear the LORD your God always" (14:23b). Fearing God in the Old Testament is the basic response to God and is almost equivalent to what the New Testament calls belief. The discipline of tithing confirms and establishes one's commitment to God. We can begin to neglect

God's lordship over our lives as we get engrossed in the things of this world. But being in the habit of giving a tithe of everything we earn reminds us and affirms that God is most important to us.

Sam Houston (1793–1863) was an American statesman and military commander who led the fight for Texas independence from Mexico and later its admission into the United States. The city of Houston is named in his honor.[2] He was led to Christ by George W. Baines, the great-grandfather of President Lyndon Johnson. After his conversion Houston "was a changed man, no longer coarse and belligerent, but peaceful and content." Those who knew him were very surprised when he was baptized. After his baptism he offered to pay half the local minister's salary. "When someone asked him why, he said, 'My pocketbook was baptized too.'"[3] Giving is a good sign that a person has truly been converted.

A Christian leader once told Randy Alcorn, "As I reflect on my growth as a Christian across the years, the second most important gift of grace I have received has been the discipline of tithing. The first was the surrender of my will to Jesus Christ." He went on to say of himself and his wife, "The Lord got our hearts when we began to tithe."[4] Tithing is a sign of submission to God, and it keeps us spiritually active and therefore alert.

Joy as a Means to Fearing God (14:26)

In an earlier discussion (on 12:6, 7, 11, 12) we looked at the significance of the fact that a part of the offerings is to be eaten as part of the family joy. This is repeated here too. If God's chosen place to make the offering is too far to take an offering with them, they are to convert the offering into cash. Moses tells them, ". . . and spend the money for whatever you desire—oxen or sheep or wine or strong drink, whatever your appetite craves. And you shall eat there before the LORD your God and rejoice, you and your household" (14:26).

Earlier Moses said that the offering would help them fear the Lord (14:23). Now he is saying that one way in which they learn to fear the Lord is by enjoying an offering meal with the family, eating things for which they crave. On this Chris Wright comments, "Inculcating the fear of God could be achieved during a family party just as much as during family prayers." This reminds us again that happiness is very much a part of the holy life. There is a seamless connection between devotion, the fear of God, prayer, and celebration. When the prayer before the meal is a genuine proclamation of thanks to God for his provision, those who are there will realize that it is indeed worthwhile fearing the God who is no one's debtor.

Christian parents would do well to ensure that their children see this connection. On the one hand, grace before meals is not a formality that must be done away with quickly so people can give themselves to the main business — eating. On the other hand, prayers before meals should not be so long that they cause some to long for the "Amen" so they can go ahead and eat. In the early years of Asbury Theological Seminary, my alma mater, a visiting preacher was asked to say grace before breakfast. He went on and on. After some time the founding president of the seminary, Henry Clay Morrison, got up and said, "Let's have our breakfast while our brother has his morning devotions."

Should Christians Tithe?

Tithing is a part of the Old Testament Law. And our approach to the Law has been that all of it has principles for us to follow though we do not need to observe all the practices prescribed in it. As Brian K. Morley points out, "Nowhere does the NT require Christians to tithe in the sense of giving 10%. Therefore there is a debate in the church about whether Christians need to be required to give away 10% of their income." Morley says that the New Testament "reiterate[s] many things associated with tithing" in the Old Testament.

> . . . those who minister are entitled to receive support (1 Cor. 9:14); the poor and needy should be cared for (1 Cor. 16:1; Gal. 2:10); those who give can trust God, as the source of all that is given (2 Cor. 9:10), to supply their needs (2 Cor. 9:8; Phil. 4:19); and giving should be done joyously (2 Cor. 9:7).[5]

Charles Feinberg points out that "for several centuries in the Early Church there was no support of the clergy by a systematic giving of a tithe." He says, "Rather, freedom in Christian giving was emphasized." However, "In time the tithe came to be regarded generally after the pattern in the Jewish synagogue."[6] It would be good to take seriously the sayings about tithing in the Old Testament and out of them derive principles for our own giving. The Old Testament tells us that the tithe belongs to God (Leviticus 27:30) and that those who do not tithe are robbing God (Malachi 3:8–10).

The church father Augustine (354–430) said, "Tithes are required as a matter of debt, and he who has been unwilling to give them has been guilty of robbery. Whoever, therefore, desires to secure a reward for himself . . . let him render tithes, and out of the nine parts let him seek to give alms."[7] Augustine makes a distinction between tithes and additional almsgiving to needy people. Earlier Irenaeus, who flourished in the latter part of the second century, said, "The Jews were constrained to a regular payment of tithes; Christians, who have liberty, assign all their possessions to the Lord, bestowing freely not the lesser portions of their property, since they have the hope of greater things."[8] Irenaeus seems to be saying that the tenth is the lower portion, the minimum standard, which Christians should try to exceed. This has been the attitude of many Christians over the years. James Lewis Kraft was the founder of the food products company that bears his name. He used to say, "I don't believe in tithing . . . but it's a good place to start."[9]

Sadly, many Christians today do not take tithing seriously. George Barna's research group has found that the more money a person makes, the less likely he or she is to tithe.[10] Studies done by the Gallup organization, presumably in North America, show that those who attend weekly church services give 3.45 percent of their income annually, whereas those who do not go to church give between 1.1 and 1.4 percent. Other studies show that giving is declining among Christians.[11]

Money is certainly not the most important factor in the work of God's kingdom. But there can be no doubt that so much more could be done if Christians gave more generously. All over the world vocational Christian workers feel they are underpaid, even though the New Testament is strong on the fact that they should be paid adequately (1 Corinthians 9:3–11; 1 Timothy 5:17, 18). Paul even says, "Let the elders who rule well be considered worthy of double honor, especially those who labor in preaching and teaching" (1 Timothy 5:17). This would not be the problem it is today if God's people gave as they should.

I believe that in view of the strong teaching in the Old Testament on tithing and in the New Testament on giving, and in view of the great needs in the church and the world, it would be wise for Christians to adopt tithing as a principle for their lives along with gifts given above the tithe as offerings, especially to the needy. I am reluctant, however, to make this an absolute rule, though I see it as essential in the Christian life. Giving generously is the basic Christian rule.

The Tithe at the End of Three Years (14:28, 29)

Moses goes on to say that there is a different kind of tithe once every three years: "At the end of every three years you shall bring out all the tithe of your produce in the same year and lay it up within your towns. And the Levite, because he has no portion or inheritance with you, and the sojourner, the fatherless, and the widow, who are within your towns, shall come and eat and be filled, that the LORD your God may bless you in all the work of your hands that you do" (14:28, 29). Does this mean that there are two separate tithes in the third year or that there is only one tithe that is used for local needs rather than being given at the central place of worship? Scholars line up on both sides, as it is difficult to decide from the Biblical evidence. I think only one tithe is given at the end of the third year, but I am not going to press for that view as we cannot be certain.

The Levites, who do not own land, would not have an income once the local shrines are closed and the central sanctuary is set up. Therefore, provision is made from these tithes for their needs and also for the needs of foreigners, who do not receive the regular help given to members of the community, and of the fatherless and the widows. We must find who are the equivalents of these people today and ensure that they, too, are included in our giving. Giving to the needy will be the major focus of our next study (on 15:1–18).

Tithes to the Storehouse

Some insist that the teaching about tithes and separate offerings and also the teaching in Malachi 3:6–15 on bringing tithes to the storehouse implies that one's full tithe should be paid to the local church (the storehouse) and that the gifts to the poor and other groups should be above and beyond the tithe. The fact that the poor are included in the triennial tithe would suggest that it is not necessary to insist on that storehouse principle. However, as we are taking principles of tithing from the Old Testament Law and not following the exact Old Testament practices of tithing, I believe that the principle of storehouse tithing could be legitimately held by individual churches who agree that is what they will recommend to their members. To insist that all believers follow this practice would be unwarranted. However, to members of churches that follow the practice of insisting on a tenth being given to the local church, my advice is to submit to the church's policy. These are small things about which we do not need to be quarrelling, especially because there is no explicit teaching about it in the New Testament.

God Blesses Those Who Give (14:29b)

Moses ends this section by stating a consequence of giving: ". . . that the LORD your God may bless you in all the work of your hands that you do" (14:29b). The consistent teaching of the Bible is that God is no one's debtor. When we give to his causes, he blesses us with more than what we give him. Malachi 3:10 says, "Bring the full tithe into the storehouse, that there may be food in my house. And thereby put me to the test, says the LORD of hosts, if I will not open the windows of heaven for you and pour down for you a blessing until there is no more need." In a passage where Paul urges the Corinthians to give, he says,

> The point is this: whoever sows sparingly will also reap sparingly, and whoever sows bountifully will also reap bountifully. . . . And God is able to make all grace abound to you, so that having all sufficiency in all things at all times, you may abound in every good work. . . . He who supplies seed to the sower and bread for food will supply and multiply your seed for sowing and increase the harvest of your righteousness. You will be enriched in every way to be generous in every way, which through us will produce thanksgiving to God. (2 Corinthians 9:6, 8, 10, 11)

This does not mean that we give for selfish reasons, or that we can motivate others to give purely so they can get more by giving. What it does mean is that Biblical giving actually serves our best interests. God knows how to look after us if we obey him. If we disobey by holding back on our giving, we miss that blessing. The promise of blessing for giving reminds us that Biblical giving is a wise thing to do.

Sometimes we are not certain whether we should give something away. At such a time because we fear God we decide that it is better to be safe than sorry when it comes to obedience. That is, it is better to lose something we like because God *may* want us to give it away than to cling to it when we are not fully sure whether it is God's will that we give it away. Those who have learned to give Biblically will testify to wonderful experiences of God's provision. Often people give at great cost and wonder how they will make ends meet because they gave so much. And they find that that God provides their every need. The result is great joy at God's provision. Life becomes an exciting adventure.

Just as tithing helps us fear God (14:23), the refusal to tithe could be considered as a sign of not fearing God. Sometimes people claim to fear and love God, but their devotion to God does not go down to their pocketbook. They are going to miss out on some of life's great adventures. Not only do they fail to experience God's provision, they also lose their security in Christ. Knowing that they have not fully given themselves to God, they cannot freely expect God to look after them. They play safe by not giving, but they end up losing their sense of safety, of being undergirded by the everlasting arms of God (33:27).

Indian Christian leader and evangelist Sam Kamaleson tells the story of a girl who had some very tasty candy that her brother wanted. He asked her to give the candy to her, but she refused. Finally they struck a deal in which the brother promised to give her all the marbles that were in his pocket if the sister would give him all her candy. The brother put his hand into the pocket and, through touch, was able to locate his favorite blue marble. He kept that aside and gave all but that marble to his sister, though he had promised to give all the marbles. In return the sister gave him all her candy. When she did so, he immediately asked her, "Did you give me all your candy?" Not having given all his marbles, that brother did not have the confidence that his sister would give him all her candy. It is like that with our relationship with God. If we hold back on something, we will not live in trust. When problems come, we panic and behave as if God is not able to help us. One of the greatest blessings of giving is the sense of security and the peace that comes from knowing that the sovereign and almighty God will look after us.

Dedication of the Firstborn (15:19–23)

Next Moses teaches about caring for the needy during the sabbatical year (15:1–18). This will be the focus of our next study. Following that he talks about the dedication of firstborn males of their herds and flocks: "All the firstborn males that are born of your herd and flock you shall dedicate to the LORD your God. You shall do no work with the firstborn of your herd, nor shear the firstborn of your flock" (15:19). Moses must have had a very good reason for placing this immediately after the releasing of slaves and canceling debts in the sabbatical year.[12] But we are going to look at it along with the discussion on tithing, which like this one is a regular gift that applies to the whole community.

It Is for God Only (15:19b)

As is often the case in Deuteronomy, the basic law that we quoted above (15:19a) is first stated and then is expounded in the following verses. First, they are not to use the firstborn for their personal ends: "You shall do no work with the firstborn of your herd, nor shear the firstborn of your flock" (15:19b). Here we see the Biblical teaching about being careful to single out our giving and keep it only for God. The idea seems to be that setting apart the firstborn is a way of acknowledging that God is Lord of our lives. Some say they do not give to God's work because they are not sure how the funds will be used. In the Bible you give to God's work because that is a necessary discipline that acknowledges God's supremacy and rule over our lives.

Applying this today would mean that we are not to keep designated gifts for a time and put it in a bank to earn interest or use it on some project with the plan to give it later on to God. Paul warned that ". . . the love of money is a root of all kinds of evils. It is through this craving that some have wandered away from the faith and pierced themselves with many pangs" (1 Timothy 6:10). Money is an area where we are so vulnerable to a fall that we should be very careful about the way we use it. The safest way is clear-cut decision-making.

If we know that an amount of money is to be given out, then, whatever our needs, we play it safe and give it. Giving is viewed as a basic expenditure and not as something we decide on after we have spent our income and found out how much we have remaining. Such action helps us develop alertness to issues that have to do with money. We learn not to touch money or anything else that belongs to God because it is an offering.

Blemished Offerings Prohibited (15:20–23)

Next Moses says that the offering should be presented and eaten at the central sanctuary: "You shall eat it, you and your household, before the LORD your God year by year at the place that the LORD will choose" (15:20). We have looked at this in the discussion on 12:5. Moses also says that blemished offerings should not be given: "But if it has any blemish, if it is lame or blind or has any serious blemish whatever, you shall not sacrifice it to the LORD your God" (15:21).

Malachi vividly describes the seriousness of giving blemished gifts to God:

> A son honors his father, and a servant his master. If then I am a father, where is my honor? And if I am a master, where is my fear? says the LORD of hosts to you, O priests, who despise my name. But you say, "How have we despised your name?" By offering polluted food upon my altar. But you say, "How have we polluted you?" By saying that the LORD's table may be despised. When you offer blind animals in sacrifice, is that not evil? And when you offer those that are lame or sick, is that not evil? (Malachi 1:6–8a).

To offer blemished gifts is to despise God. The Malachi text goes on to give an analogy from everyday life: "Present that to your governor; will he accept you or show you favor? says the LORD of hosts" (1:8b). To put it in today's language, "What sort of idiot would give a gift of rancid cake to the CEO of his company? How minute in significance is a CEO in comparison to the Lord of the universe!" Yet that is what we often do. Our offerings are not offerings; they are crumbs from our plates.

Some people give only what they can't use, such as clothes that the user has outgrown or that have gone out of fashion. Such gifts are not wrong per se, but they should not be regarded as offerings. They are convenient ways of getting rid of our waste. Sometimes people give damaged and low-quality things that cannot be used by them. Some people have even sent used tea bags in missionary care packages. After the tsunami we saw an outpouring of generosity of people from within and from outside the country. Most of the gifts were lovingly and sacrificially given. But if we gave away some of the gifts we would be insulting the recipient.

The command not to bring a blemished offering is another way of teaching us to fear the Lord, as we saw in our discussion of 14:23. We are constantly tempted to give God second place. The command to be very careful to give the best to God reminds us that we must give *only* our best to God. It places before us the supremacy of God and the total devotion that should characterize our relationship with him. By getting used to giving God only the best, we develop an attitude to life that says God is most important. By giving something other than the best we insult God and entrench ourselves in our rebellion against him.

Moses goes on to say that the meat of blemished animals may be consumed like normal meat: "You shall eat it within your towns. The unclean and the clean alike may eat it, as though it were a gazelle or a deer" (15:22). Once again there is the prohibition of consuming the blood of the killed animal: "Only you shall not eat its blood; you shall pour it out on the ground like water" (15:23). We dealt with this in our discussion on 12:16.

Andrew Fuller (1754–1815) was a Baptist theologian who had a big influence on the Baptist Missionary Society and on William Carey. One day he asked a friend for a gift for missions. The friend said, "Well, Andrew, I'll give you five pounds, seeing it is you." Fuller replied, "No, I can't take anything for this cause, seeing that it is for me that you are doing it." Feeling rebuked, the man hesitated for a moment and said, "Andrew, you are right, here are ten pounds seeing that it is for the Lord Jesus Christ!"[13] Without doubt, regular giving is a serious aspect of the life of obedience. Holy people give wholeheartedly as if they are giving to God. Let's get serious about giving!

38

Special Consideration for the Poor

DEUTERONOMY 15:1–18

"OUR EARL'S GONE! God A'mighty knows he loved us, and we loved him. We shan't see his likes again!" Those words were spoken by a poor laborer, in tattered clothes, with only a piece of crepe sewed onto his sleeve as a sign of mourning, as he watched the coffin of Anthony Ashley-Cooper, the seventh Earl of Shaftesbury, being carried out of Westminster Abbey.[1] The Earl of Shaftesbury (1801–1885) was an evangelical social reformer who was responsible for enacting important legislation in Britain that brought relief to the poor, the oppressed, and the insane. That poor laborer knew that he had loved them and worked for them even though he had come from an aristocratic background.

If Christians take what the Bible says about poverty seriously, the poor would view Christians the way they viewed Shaftesbury. Sadly, today the poor generally regard evangelical Christians as being distant from them, unaware of their problems, and opposed to legislation aimed at giving them relief. Deuteronomy 15 gives us important teachings about our approach to the poor and needy. It had a marked impact on my life and ministry when I studied it for my devotions about thirty-three years ago. The needy people mentioned here are the poor and slaves. Today we could add to that list people such as the mentally and physically handicapped and insane, the terminally ill including those suffering from AIDS, and orphans and the aged who have no family to care for them.

Releasing and Setting Apart

Deuteronomy 15 gives laws about releasing people from debts during the sabbatical year (15:1–11), releasing slaves after six years (15:12–18), and setting apart firstborn males from the flock (15:19–23). At first these laws may seem to be quite unrelated to our lives in the twenty-first century. Therefore, it is easy to read this passage as a record of how a group of ancient people lived that is of some academic interest but with little practical relevance to us today. But that has not been our approach to the laws of Deuteronomy. We believe that there are principles in these laws that should influence our behavior today as they give us a window into the mind of their Creator. The importance of this chapter is evidenced by the fact that this chapter has the words "you shall" used in an imperative sense twenty-three times in the ESV. Other statements such as "take care," "strictly obey," and "be careful" appear five times, emphasizing the importance of obedience to the laws given here.

The sabbatical idea was originally derived from God's resting on the seventh day after completing his creation of the world (Exodus 20:8–11). This became the model for human life, resting one day in seven. The Jewish law extended this idea to other spheres also. One way this was done was through the practice of sabbatical release. Exodus talks about the sabbatical year being a year of release for the land: ". . . the seventh year you shall let it rest and lie fallow, that the poor of your people may eat; and what they leave the beasts of the field may eat" (23:11). The sabbatical year idea is used for the release from debts with an additional note on generous giving (Deuteronomy 15:1–11) and the release from slavery (15:12–18).

Releasing Debts and Generous Giving (15:1–11)

There is some disagreement among scholars about what exactly is being prescribed here regarding the release from debts. Verse 1 says, "At the end of every seven years you shall grant a release." Verse 2 explains what that means: "And this is the manner of the release: every creditor shall release what he has lent to his neighbor. He shall not exact it of his neighbor, his brother, because the LORD's release has been proclaimed." Three interpretations are commonly given for what exactly this release meant.

The first interpretation, implied in the NIV and ESV renderings of verse 2, is that a complete release from the debt is intended. I favor this interpretation, because this is the interpretation that harmonizes with verse 9, which talks about not refusing to give loans when the sabbatical year is near as then the lender would lose a lot. Verse 9 would make most sense if the lender loses the loan rather than the things suggested by the other two interpretations. The second interpretation is that the release has to do with the pledge that was given with the loan. The REB translation of verse 2 implies this: "Everyone who holds a pledge shall return the pledge to the person indebted to him." Often that pledge was the borrower's land or another essential item that provided him with his source of income. Giving back the pledge would help the borrower get back on his or her feet. The third interpretation is that the borrower is released from the repayment of debt just for the duration of the sabbatical year.

Whatever the exact meaning is, what we see here is that release is given to the borrower. Often it is crippling debts that keep people poor and give them no chance of getting ahead however hard they try. This law is aimed at giving them that chance.

We should distinguish between the loans spoken of here and modern-day business loans. As Donald Kraybill explains in his book *The Upside-Down Kingdom*, "Since Israel had an agricultural economy, debts were mostly charitable loans to needy persons, not commercial ones."[2] Verse 3, talking about commercial-type loans, says that the lender may exact payment for loans given to foreigners, unlike what was given to a brother or fellow Israelite. The foreigners who lived with the Israelites would have been traders. The sabbatical law is to help struggling poor people, not to let businesspeople off the hook when it comes to paying their loans.

This passage teaches five important principles that should govern our response to human need.

Principle One: We Are in Solidarity with Our Brothers and Sisters (15:2, 3)

Verse 2 first uses the word "neighbor" when referring to the person who is to be released of a loan. Then in verses 2, 3 the word "brother" is used for the neighbor and is contrasted with "foreigner." The words "brother" and "brothers" appear seven times in 15:1–12. The Israelites did not have a particular responsibility to look after foreign traders, but they had to work hard to ensure that ". . . there will be no poor among" their own people (15:4)—that is, those toward whom they had a particular responsibility. Later Moses becomes more wide-ranging in his application by saying that the Israelites must help all their brothers who become poor (15:7–11). We are to treat our neighbors as our brothers, which means that we have a special responsibility toward them. In Leviticus 19:18 God commands, "You shall love your neighbor as yourself." That statement is quoted eight times in the New Testament.[3]

Applying this passage today, we would include the new Israel, or the church, as those for whom we are to primarily care. Paul says ". . . let us do good to everyone, and especially to those who are of the household of faith" (Galatians 6:10). Paul's statement implies that we would, secondarily, include those in the community and nation to which we belong.

The idea that the needs of people in our community are our responsibility sounds strange in our individualistic culture. Today we are taught that individuals are responsible for their financial dealings and that we do not need to pry into the affairs of other people. This is an area where the Biblical lifestyle is very different from that of those around us. This challenges us to be a prophetic presence in this world, pointing people to the value of radical commitment to others. While Christian community solidarity makes us different from those around us, it can be a very attractive feature of the gospel, especially in a world where people are struggling so much with loneliness. In the early years of the Christian church, outsiders were very impressed by the way the Christians cared for each other. The early church father Tertullian (c. 160/170–c. 215/220) wrote, "It is our care of the helpless, our practice of loving kindness that brands us in the eyes of many of our opponents. 'Only look,' they say, 'look how they love one another!'"[4]

This solidarity with our brothers and sisters comes from an attitude toward personal possessions that, according to Acts, was a key to the sharing of possessions that took place in the early church. Acts 4:32b says, ". . . no one said that any of the things that belonged to him was his own, but they had everything in common." The result was that "there was not a needy person among them" (Acts 4:34a). We cannot say that about our churches today. We need a new approach to wealth that looks at it as something that we do not absolutely own. So when a member of the family is in need, we immediately ask whether God is telling us to give the needy person something of what God has given us. Russian Christian philosopher Nikolai Berdyaev (1874–1948), is reported to have said, "Bread for myself is a material problem. Bread for my neighbor is a spiritual problem."

Principle Two: We Are Urgently Commanded to Help the Poor (15:4, 5, 9)
Verse 4 describes the ideal situation if God's plan is carried out without hindrance from the ravages of human sin and its consequences: "But there will be no poor among you; for the LORD will bless you in the land that the LORD your God is giving you for an inheritance to possess." But things did not work out this way, because the Israelites did not abide by the words of verse 5: ". . . if only you will strictly obey the voice of the LORD your God, being careful to do all this commandment that I command you today."

Knowing that they will not fully obey, a few verses later Moses mentions what the actual situation will be: "For there will never cease to be poor in the land" (15:11). However, even though the utopia without any poverty described in verse 4 is unattainable because of human sin, this passage presents the next best approach: those who have must give to those who do not have. Verse 5 presents the seriousness of obedience to God's command: ". . . if only you will strictly obey the voice of the LORD your God, being careful to do all this commandment that I command you today." The command spoken of here is giving to the needy.

The wording of verse 5 is very strong in the Hebrew. They are to "*strictly obey*" God's voice, "*being careful to do all this commandment.*" "Strictly obey" is the rendering of an interesting Hebrew rhetorical device that Chris Wright describes as "stylistically emphatic." When a command or promise comes with two forms of the same verb one after the other in Hebrew (that is, if a command has an infinitive plus an imperative), it means that strong emphasis is being made. For example, the literal rendering of what the ESV translates as "strictly obey" is "to obey you shall obey." The same verb is used twice next to each other to press home the point. Wright points out, "There is a greater density of this emphatic construction than any other chapter in the book." Later in verses 8, 10 the same stylistic emphatic rhetorical device is used to encourage generosity.

We sometimes think that helping the poor among us is an option, a great favor that we are under no obligation to do. The urgent commands to give to the needy show that this is not an option in the Bible. Later Moses says that if they refuse to help their poor brother, he will "cry to the LORD against you, and you [will] be guilty of sin" (15:9). In Jesus' parable of the sheep and the goats, Jesus says, "Depart from me, you cursed, into the eternal fire prepared for the devil and his angels. For I was hungry and you gave me no food, I was thirsty and you gave me no drink, I was a stranger and you did not welcome me, naked and you did not clothe me, sick and in prison and you did not visit me" (Matthew 25:41–43). His reply to their question about when they missed this opportunity to serve is, ". . . as you did not do it to one of the least of these, you did not do it to me" (v. 45). Not to help the least significant brother (see v. 40) is like refusing to help Jesus, a serious crime meriting eternal punishment! We know that doing good works is not the primary criterion for salvation—faith is. But those with real faith do these works. Not doing them is evidence of the absence of real faith.

The early church fathers understood this. John Chrysostom (c. 344/354–407), who is considered one of the greatest preachers in the church's history, viewed the failure to give to the poor as a kind of robbery: "Not giving to the poor of what one has is to commit robbery against them and to attempt against their very life, for we must remember that what we withhold is not ours, but theirs."[5] Chrysostom's contemporary, Augustine Aurelius of Hippo (354–430), one of the greatest theologians in the church's history, said that much of what the rich have is superfluous. But what is superfluous to them is necessary to the poor. He said, "Not to give to the needy what is superfluous is akin to fraud."[6]

Principle Three: God Will Bless Those Who Help the Poor (15:6, 10)

Not only does Moses view the refusal to give to the needy as a punishable offense, he also views giving to the poor as a means of blessing. Verses 4, 5 had already implied that obedience will bring blessing to the people. Verse 6 elaborates on this promise: "For the LORD your God will bless you, as he promised you, and you shall lend to many nations, but you shall not borrow, and you shall rule over many nations, but they shall not rule over you." Verse 10 presents the promise of blessing for individuals who give generously to the needy: "You shall give to him freely, and your heart shall not be grudging when you give to him, because for this the LORD your God will bless you in all your work and in all that you undertake." Jesus highlighted this truth when he said, "It is more blessed to give than to receive" (Acts 20:35).

When we consider the above points—namely, the urgent calls to obedience, the threat of punishment for disobedience, and the promise of blessing for obedience—together, we can conclude that when it comes to obedience, it is better to be safe than to be sorry. We must be wise in the way we use our resources. It is better to play safe by giving to the needy than to be sorry because by not giving we displeased God and missed his blessing and merited his punishment.

Clearly the prospect of blessing is a key motivation to generosity. It is true that the prospect of blessing for giving has been misused to raise funds by manipulating people unscrupulously. But it is undeniable that the Bible presents the prospect of blessing as part of the rationale for giving. Perhaps the most vivid reference is Proverbs 19:17: "Whoever is generous to the poor lends to the LORD, and he will repay him for his deed." This message is found in many other texts as well.[7] We are logical beings. When we spend our money, we like to know that the investment we make will yield good results. The Bible says that obedience to God is the securest and most profitable investment one can make on earth. God's people who have learned to give generously will testify to some wonderful blessings that God gave them. Sometimes the greatest thrill is to see God provide when we decide to make what looks like a sacrificial gift. I have experienced this many times in my life, and I can testify that giving is one of the thrills of the Christian life.

The distinctive contribution of the New Testament to the issue of reward for generosity is that the greatest reward will be in Heaven. In the parable of the sheep and the goats, the King says to those on his right, "Come, you who are blessed by my Father, inherit the kingdom prepared for you from the foundation of the world" (Matthew 25:34). This great blessing is a reward for generosity toward the King (Matthew 25:35, 36; see also Luke 6:30–36; 12:33, 34). When the surprised recipients of the reward ask the King when they did these things to him, the King tells them, "Truly, I say to you, as you did it to one of the least of these my brothers, you did it to me" (Matthew 25:40). We are often tempted to give special attention to supposedly significant people and to neglect supposedly poor people. Jesus' parable says that when we help supposedly insignificant people we are helping the Judge of all the earth.

Principle Four: What We Have Is from God (15:7, 14)

Twice in this passage a key aspect of the Biblical approach to resources appears. Verse 7 introduces a section on helping the poor and says that these poor will be "within your land that the LORD your God is giving you." This land is a gift from God. In verse 14 when talking about generosity to slaves who are being freed, Moses says, "As the LORD your God has blessed you, you shall give to him [your brother]." Both times the resources of the people are presented as having come from God. Leviticus 25:23 presents the implication of this fact explicitly: "The land shall not be sold in perpetuity, for the land is mine. For you are strangers and sojourners with me." The idea is that the land belongs to God, and we are actually only stewards of his resources. In David's famous prayer when the people brought offerings for the temple he planned to build, he said, ". . . all things come from you, and of your own have we given you" (1 Chronicles 29:14). God is the giver of our resources, and what we give actually already belongs to God.

Far from being a dampener of satisfaction, the realization that we do not own anything is the springboard to great liberation and joy. I have seen wealthy people who are unhappy because they are bound by their wealth. It is tragic to see them preoccupied with how they can protect their riches and prevent others from exploiting them. A loss becomes a terrible tragedy. If and when they give to others, they do so grudgingly, often out of a sense of duty rather than pleasure. If our primary ambition in life is to glorify God, and if giving to others is a means to glorify God, then when we give we are actually fulfilling a personal ambition. We don't see the giving as losing money; we see it as a pleasurable action that gives us great joy. In our entertainment-oriented world people know what it is to pay for pleasure. Our giving is such a payment.

This is why the Bible speaks about the joy of giving. Paul says, "Each one must give as he has decided in his heart, not reluctantly or under compulsion, for God loves a cheerful giver" (2 Corinthians 9:7). Proverbs 14:21 says, "Happy are those who are kind to the poor" (NRSV; see Psalm 41:1). Francis of Assisi was known for the joy with which he gave to the poor. If he saw a poor person without warm clothing in the winter, he would gladly remove his cloak and give it to that person while he suffered in the cold with joy! The example of the Macedonians, who were not wealthy, gives an example of the joy of eager giving: "For they gave according to their means, as I can testify, and beyond their means, of their own accord, begging us earnestly for the favor of taking part in the relief of the saints" (2 Corinthians 8:3, 4). When you look at giving from this perspective, what is termed sacrificial giving is not a sacrifice at all.

Principle Five: We Must Be Generous (15:7–11)

After speaking specifically about people who had taken loans, Moses moves to a more general discussion on the poor among the Israelites. He commands generosity toward the poor in verses 7–11. We see a powerful case made for being generous here. Usually generosity would be considered an optional extra to one's life. But here it is commanded with utmost seriousness through the use of strong and vivid language.

The stylistically emphatic Hebrew rhetorical device that we described in our discussion on 15:5 appears in verses 8, 10. They are translated as ". . . but you shall open your hand to him and lend him sufficient for his need, whatever it may be" and "You shall give to him freely." The Hebrew style used in both these verses shows that the truth presented is being specially emphasized. So these are urgent commands.

Moses uses different figures to describe generosity or the lack of it. The first is the hardened heart. He urges against the lack of generosity, saying, ". . . you shall not harden your heart" (15:7); "Take care lest there be an unworthy thought in your heart" (15:9); ". . . your heart shall not be grudging" (15:10). He also uses figures of the closed hand and grudging eye when advising against the lack of generosity: "You shall not . . . shut your hand against your poor brother" (15:7); "Take care lest . . . your eye look grudgingly on your poor brother" (15:9). To describe generosity he uses the figure of the open hand: ". . . you shall open your hand to him" (15:8); "You shall open wide your hand to your brother" (15:11). That adds up to seven expressions with figurative language to describe generosity or its lack. Moses is trying to press home the importance of generosity.

Moses says we are not to harden our hearts (15:7). That is, we need to have a soft heart that is open to feeling the needs of the poor. Then he also says that our hearts should not be "grudging" (15:9–10). That is, our hearts should be open to giving to others. The idea communicated by the open heart is further emphasized by the figure of the hand that is wide open to give to the needy (15:7, 8, 11). Some people who have a soft heart and are moved even to tears by the needs of people may not have an open hand that gives from what they have to meet those needs. Our emotions must influence our wills, so that when we are moved with compassion we respond with constructive action to alleviate the suffering.

Jesus also used some vivid language to command generosity. He said, "And if anyone would sue you and take your tunic, let him have your cloak as well. And if anyone forces you to go one mile, go with him two miles. Give to the one who begs from you, and do not refuse the one who would borrow from you" (Matthew 5:40–42). We go beyond what is expected of us when giving to the needy.

Today many people feel that we have won a victory when we can get away with giving less than what was asked of us. After reading a tract on how to respond to poverty, I decided that I will not bargain with the poor when I buy something from them or hire them to do something for me. Sometimes they quote a price that takes into account that the one who pays will bargain. But if I think this person is very needy, unless the figure asked for is ridiculously high I will not bargain with the person—often much to his or her surprise. Extending this principle a little further, if I feel that the poor person has done a good job, I sometimes overpay him or her, giving more than what was asked for.

Of course we must not be foolish in our generosity. Other Scriptures speak against laziness,[8] dishonesty,[9] and lying.[10] And we must not tolerate such. Verse 8 says, ". . . you shall open your hand to him and lend him *sufficient for his need*, whatever it may be." We must ask what a person's need really is. We may be wise not to give money to an alcoholic or drug addict who is hungry because he would probably use it to buy the chemical on which he is dependent. Instead, we may give his wife some provisions for the home.

I have a friend who was constantly in debt. I sometimes tried to help him pay his debts. Once I told an accountant friend about his situation, and he told me that he would like to meet with my friend and his wife. They met several times for extended discussions and exercises relating to how he should budget his funds. Though he was at first reluctant to meet the accountant, he later testified to the marvelous way in which his financial practices turned around and he learned to live a responsible life. If I had kept giving him funds to overcome his immediate need, I would probably not have helped him.

Sometimes we may be called to help a person find a way to earn money. This may mean paying for him or her to get training in some field and perhaps even helping the person with some start-up funds for a new enterprise. Giving funds is much quicker and easier than finding out why the needy persons are in the situation they are in and helping them find ways to come out of it, but the latter option is much more effective.

There are, then, complex situations calling for wisdom on the part of the giver. However, when it comes to giving it would be better, as we said before, to be safe and give rather than to be sorry for not giving. Eleanor of Austria (1655–1720) said, "I cannot know the real poor from the false; but God can, and he lets his sun shine alike on the wicked and on the just."[11]

Verse 11a shows that God's people should always be thinking about their responsibility toward the poor because "there will never cease to be poor in the land." This statement was used by Jesus to answer the charge that the woman who anointed his feet should have used the cost of it to help the poor (Matthew 26:11; Mark 14:7; John 12:8). Some Christians take Jesus' words to mean that because the problem of poverty will never be completely solved we should give priority to worship over social justice. The context of the statement in Deuteronomy shows that this interpretation of Jesus' use of it is wrong. Just after the statement that we have the poor always with us, Moses says, "Therefore I command you, 'You shall open wide your hand to your brother, to the needy and to the poor, in your land" (Deuteronomy 15:11b). This is a strong command to be generous to the poor. Jesus used 15:11a to tell them that they can always help the poor, while they cannot always anoint Christ for burial.

Others may concentrate on making more and more money and then spending it on themselves or saving it prudently. We will follow John Wesley's prescription in his famous sermon on "The Use of Money," of which the main outline was:

> Gain all you can;
> Save [or economize] all you can; and
> Give all you can.[12]

Releasing Slaves (15:12–18)

After describing the kindness that needs to be shown to the poor, Moses describes the kindness that needs to be shown to slaves. A similar passage is found in Exodus. There it is found at the start of what is known as the Book of the Covenant (Exodus 21 — 23), which comes shortly after the giving of the Ten Commandments. The first part of this book is a long list of laws dealing with various aspects of everyday life (21:1 — 22:20), and the first of these laws relates to the freeing of slaves. Many Christians today do not associate the way they treat the maid, the gardener, or the employee who works for them as a primary aspect of their Christian life. But in the Bible this aspect of life is so important that it comes right at the start of the rules for daily life in Exodus.

There seem to have been two types of slaves in Israel in the Old Testament era (see Leviticus 25:44–46). The first are foreign slaves who have been sold to the owner. The second are fellow Israelites who will not usually be permanent slaves. Our passage speaks about the second group. These are possibly people who got into financial difficulties and sold themselves (possibly to their creditors) as a way of surviving the emergency. Moses says that such slaves must be released seven years after they were taken on: "If your brother, a Hebrew man or a Hebrew woman, is sold to you [sells himself, ESV margin], he shall serve you six years, and in the seventh year you shall let him go free from you" (Deuteronomy 15:12). Here the years are counted beginning with the time the enslavement took place, unlike the sabbatical year that came according to the regular calendar.

The released slave is to leave with generous gifts from his or her master: "And when you let him go free from you, you shall not let him go empty-handed. You shall furnish him liberally out of your flock, out of your threshing floor, and out of your winepress" (15:13, 14a). The law in Exodus 21:1–6 does not specify such generous giving. It only prescribes the freeing of slaves. Moses here tells the people that they must go beyond the Law in their generosity to their departing slave.

When someone leaves us we tend to give that person the least possible terminal benefits, as the welfare of that person is no longer going to be our responsibility. Often our giving to our employees is motivated by the desire to keep the person happy so that he or she will work hard. But that is not the Biblical way. God's people care for others, even for those who are going to be released from being their responsibility. They want the best for them. If we are truly committed to those who work for us, we would want to see them happy and secure after they leave us, too.

Some of our staff leave us after several years of service, usually sensing that their time in a youth organization is over. My desire and prayer for them is that when they leave they will go to a better job. This is not easy because of the severe unemployment problems in Sri Lanka. So even while they work for us, we may encourage them to get the type of training that would help them if they leave us. When they leave we do all we can to ensure that they have a good job. If possible, we use our influence as leaders to try and find a good place for them.

Sometimes those who leave do not leave very happily. Sometimes they may even leave scolding the leadership. My thinking on this is that they are the ones who are vulnerable and uncertain about their future at this time, not us. Therefore, we must do all we can to help them have a secure future. Our commitment to their welfare does not end because they are upset with us and hurt us through harsh words. This commitment may cause us to go out of our way to help the person leaving. For example, sometimes we cannot use organizational funds, so we may need to look for funds elsewhere to help them. Some may abuse this kindness. But in the long run the environment created by such care gives the staff workers the motivation to be committed to the organization. That would make these "sacrifices" profitable to the organization.

The last part of verse 14 says that what they give the released slave is out of what God blessed them with: "As the LORD your God has blessed you, you shall give to him." This was a case of profit sharing with slaves! This shows the radical nature of Biblical religion. Christians are truly concerned for everyone they lead, and that concern expresses itself in sharing blessings with those viewed by society as being at the bottom of the social ladder.

Verse 15 gives us a reason why we should be generous to slaves: "You shall remember that you were a slave in the land of Egypt, and the LORD your God redeemed you; therefore I command you this today." Redeemed people seek to redeem others through generosity. Our redemption may not have been redemption from physical slavery. But it was something even more serious: redemption from slavery to sin. Now that we have been redeemed from such a great need we are to help others in need.

Sometimes we spiritualize our understanding of Christianity so much that we do not extend it to the physical and material areas of life. So even though we may be willing to preach the gospel of redemption to the poor, we may not be willing to do something to help alleviate their poverty. Sometimes Christian employers, who are willing to have prayer meetings in their establishments and to share Christ with all, including the poor, are not similarly generous in the way they pay and reward their workers for their service. In Christianity those who have experienced God's generosity in redemption are generous both in sharing the message of redemption and in helping needy people with material assistance. God gave us what we do not deserve, which gives us the strength to give others what we may sometimes think they do not deserve.

Sometimes a slave may want to remain in the master's service even after the six years. Moses says this is "because he loves you and your household, since he is well-off with you" (15:16). This attitude is what we should aim at seeing in all those who work for us. Indeed they may leave because of better prospects elsewhere. But while they stay with us may they love us and know they are well-off with us.

There is a procedure to initiate with these slaves who want to serve all their life with their master: "then you shall take an awl, and put it through his ear into the door, and he shall be your slave forever" (15:17a). An awl is a pointed tool for marking surfaces or piercing small holes. In the Old Testament "entrance ways are sacred and legally significant spots." The procedure is to "bring him to his master's doorway and then symbolically attach the slave to that place by driving an awl through his earlobe into the doorpost. It is possible that a ring was then placed on the ear to mark him as a perpetual slave."[13] Moses adds, "And to your female slave you shall do the same" (15:17b).

Verse 18 gives two reasons why this act of generosity to slaves is not some great act of generosity about which one can boast. First, Moses points out how cheap this person's labor had been: "It shall not seem hard to you when you let him go free from you, for at half the cost of a hired servant he has served you six years." There's down-to-earth common sense here! Next, Moses presents the promise of blessing for generosity: "So the LORD your God will bless you in all that you do." When we help the poor we are not making a huge sacrifice: we are giving what God has given us and through that opening the door for God's blessings upon us. It is not foolish to be generous. The great folly is to miss out on God's blessings by clinging to what we mistakenly think we own. When we follow God's ways of generosity we know that God is pleased and will bless us, so we are happy—happy to be conduits of his love and to be traveling along the path of blessing. What do we want—boasting or happiness? I will choose happiness any day!

God's people, then, should consider looking after those who work for them as one of their most important responsibilities. That should enter into their understanding of Christianity, morality, and holiness. Godly people care for their employees!

Going Beyond Strict Justice

This passage shows us that we must not always enforce inflexible legal procedures with thoroughgoing strictness. The extreme helplessness of some people may cause us to make special allowances in our dealings with them. The law is often depicted by a blindfolded woman who is holding up a pair of scales. The blindfolding refers to the absence of favoritism or prejudice; the law is not changed according to the person. The scales refer to the impartiality with which all are treated. But this passage shows that in Biblical justice all are not treated in the same way.

Those who are economically needy, who would be crushed by the law of repaying debts, are given release from debts. The Old Testament ensured this by the principle of sabbatical release. We, too, need to find ways to ensure that the economically needy are not destroyed by trying to pay back loans. We should think of people's needs without strictly enforcing the law and making demands on people that will destroy them. I believe this has some bearing on the crippling burden of national debt under which many of our poorer nations labor. Moses' sermon here goes beyond the law of Exodus and prescribes that freed slaves are given a special boost to get started along the path of economic self-sufficiency.

Christians go beyond the law to help the needy. At the heart of all this is generosity. God has been generous to us, and now we are generous to others.

39

Pilgrimage Festivals

DEUTERONOMY 16:1–17

THE ANNUAL FEASTS played a very important role in the Jewish calendar. They were occasions of great joy and of affirming truths that bonded the community together. This was one of the things that enhanced the community solidarity that is a characteristic of the people of God in the Bible. Deuteronomy 16 describes the three major annual festivals of ancient Israel. Technically, there were four feasts, as the first was divided into two, as we shall see below. All three of them were pilgrimage festivals in those days. That is, in order to celebrate them, the people had to go to the place where God chose to have his central sanctuary. After the temple was built, this place became Jerusalem. The records of the ministries of Jesus and Paul show that they also went to Jerusalem intending to observe the festivals. In keeping with the sermonic style of Deuteronomy, what we have here is a summary of what is described in greater detail elsewhere in the Pentateuch (Exodus 12; Leviticus 23).

Feasts of the Passover and Unleavened Bread (16:1–8)

The Procedure (16:1–8)

Verses 1–8 give as a unit what are actually two separate festivals. That is how they are presented in Leviticus 23:5–8. First, Moses gives the date and the reason for the Passover Festival: "Observe the month of Abib and keep the Passover to the LORD your God, for in the month of Abib the LORD your God brought you out of Egypt by night" (Deuteronomy 16:1). Abib is the first month of the religious calendar of Israel, and it falls on today's March-April period. The Passover was observed to remember how God had brought them out of Egypt by night. The English word *Passover* comes from the Hebrew noun *pesach* meaning "pass over" or "spare." The Greek word used in the New Testament is *pascha*, which is a transliteration of the Aramaic word for the Passover celebration. From that we get the phrase "paschal lamb." Paul says, "Christ, our *pascha* [translated "Passover Lamb"], has been sacrificed" (1 Corinthians 5:7b). Passover recalls how the angel of death spared the people of Israel just before the exodus.

Moses then describes the sacrifice to be offered and the location where it was to be offered: "And you shall offer the Passover sacrifice to the LORD your God, from the flock or the herd, at the place that the LORD will choose, to make his name dwell there" (Deuteronomy 16:2). The sacrifice is to be made at the same time that the people came out of Egypt: ". . . you shall offer the Passover sacrifice, in the evening at sunset, at the time you came out of Egypt" (16:6). They are to "cook it and eat it at the place that the LORD your God will choose" (16:7a).

Two things will remind them of the haste with which they left Egypt. Verse 4 says, "No leaven shall be seen with you in all your territory for seven days, nor shall any of the flesh that you sacrifice on the evening of the first day remain all night until morning." Leavened bread takes time to rise. So all yeast was taken away from the home as a symbol of the rushed departure from Egypt. Today parents hide leavened bread in different places at home so the children can compete with each other to find the pieces. It is one of the creative ways in which children are made to participate in the festival ritual and also learn the truths that lie behind it.

The second thing reminding the people of the haste with which they left was that flesh sacrificed should not be kept until morning. The reason for this rule was probably not to prevent the flesh from becoming rancid. Roast meat could be kept overnight without spoiling. More probably this was because leaving "any until the morning suggests time-consuming preparation of breakfast." It would have been fatal if they delayed their departure.[1]

The location where the festival is observed—the central sanctuary—was a very important issue, and therefore it is brought up six times in chapter 16 (vv. 2, 6, 7, 11, 15, 16). This sacrifice in the central sanctuary replaced the sacrifice that was made at home when the blood was applied to the doorposts. We discussed the importance of the central sanctuary in our comments on 12:5. First, this shows that it is God who decides the best way for us to worship. Second, the focus on the name of God points to the exclusiveness of the God of Israel. No other gods are to be tolerated. Third, holiness and awe in worship were required because God makes his habitation there. With the destruction of the Jerusalem temple in AD 70 the Passover began to be observed at home and in local synagogues.

The next seven days following the Passover sacrifice became known as the Feast of Unleavened Bread: "Seven days you shall eat it with unleavened bread, the bread of affliction—for you came out of the land of Egypt in haste—that all the days of your life you may remember the day when you came out of the land of Egypt" (16:3b). Note that the bread is called "the bread of affliction." This was to remind them of what they suffered under the Egyptians. Exodus and Numbers show that this sense was enhanced by the use of "bitter herbs" along with the unleavened bread (Exodus 12:8; Numbers 9:11). On the seventh day there is to be a national gathering for worship: "For six days you shall eat unleavened bread, and on the seventh day there shall be a solemn assembly to the LORD your God. You shall do no work on it" (Deuteronomy 16:8).

The Need to Remember (16:3)

The primary reason for the Passover festival is ". . . that all the days of your life you may remember the day when you came out of the land of Egypt" (16:3). They were a community whose existence was based on certain events in their history, a history that we now call redemptive history. Through the festival the individuals will develop the Biblical worldview of which the event remembered is a key ingredient. The Biblical approach to life is based on events that were the building blocks that God used to achieve his plan of redemption. This is even more marked in Christianity with what happened through the birth, life, ministry, death, resurrection, and ascension of the Lord Jesus Christ. It is as we give these events an important place in our thinking and know how they fit within God's plan of salvation that we will grow to be mature Christians.

Christians can remember two things that could be considered equivalents to what the Passover festival remembered. First, just as the Israelites remembered God's acting to redeem them from slavery in Egypt, we can remember how God acted to redeem us from bondage to sin. This is done whenever we take Communion and also can be done even more dramatically during Holy Week—our equivalent of the Passover week—when we recall how "Christ, our Passover Lamb, has been sacrificed" (1 Corinthians 5:7).

Second, just as the use of bitter herbs and "the bread of affliction" (Deuteronomy 16:3) reminded the Israelites of their bitter experience of slavery, we need to remind ourselves regularly of the bitterness of lostness. Paul exhorted:

> Therefore remember that at one time you Gentiles in the flesh, called 'the uncircumcision' by what is called the circumcision, which is made in the flesh by hands—remember that you were at that time separated from Christ,

alienated from the commonwealth of Israel and strangers to the covenants of promise, having no hope and without God in the world. (Ephesians 2:11, 12)

This opens the door for us to exult in the glory of our conversion. So Paul goes on to say, "But now in Christ Jesus you who once were far off have been brought near by the blood of Christ" (Ephesians 2:13). To remember this, it would help to frequently retell one's testimony and to praise God for it.

When we realize that God rescued us from a certain eternity in Hell, perhaps we would not be so prone to complaining that God does not look after us when we face disappointments. God rescued us when we were headed for Hell and sent us on our way to a glorious future in Heaven. How can we say that God is not watching over us!

Sadly, however, Christians today, especially evangelical Christians, do not give a very high place to the pivotal events that undergird our faith. We revolted against a church that emphasized the Christian calendar with dry ritual lacking the vibrancy that should characterize Christianity. After all, we said, Christianity is an experiential religion. We discovered the vibrancy of a personal relationship with God and were so taken up with this that we neglected the great events and doctrines of the Bible that form the basis of that experience. This will surely stunt our growth and leave us ultimately impoverished spiritually.

This malady is particularly fostered by an approach to religion that looks at experience as the most important factor in religion and often looks at doctrine as an impediment to freedom. This approach to religion is growing today all over the world. Thinking about events that took place long ago seems to be a waste of time. When we do this we will end up with a religion that misses some key ingredients of Biblical Christianity.

One of the ways we can remedy this situation is to communicate the great doctrines of Biblical religion through the creative use of festivals. The festivals of the Bible were enjoyable times when not only was truth communicated through creative means but the people really enjoyed themselves in community. This is a great way for Christians to imbibe the Biblical worldview. So Christians can use festivals in the Christian calendar to good effect. Here is a basic list of such festivals: Holy Week (especially Thursday and Friday), Easter Sunday, Ascension, Pentecost, and, of course, Christmas.

The Feast of Weeks or Pentecost (16:9–12)

The Date and Place (16:9, 11)

The Feast of Weeks was a harvest festival. The description here is very brief: "You shall count seven weeks. Begin to count the seven weeks from the time the sickle is first put to the standing grain" (16:9), that is, the start of the wheat harvest. The date on which it is held is somewhat imprecise in Deuteronomy. This is clearer in Leviticus where there is a more comprehensive description of this festival: "You shall count seven full weeks from the day after the Sabbath, from the day that you brought the sheaf of the wave offering. You shall count fifty days to the day after the seventh Sabbath. Then you shall present a grain offering of new grain to the LORD" (Leviticus 23:15, 16). From the fifty days came the Greek name *pentēcostē*, meaning fiftieth. Incidentally, the counting of the fifty days began with the day following the Passover.

As with the other two pilgrimage festivals described in this chapter, this one too is observed "at the place that the LORD your God will choose, to make his name dwell there" (16:11b). The significance of that was discussed above.

Freewill Offerings (16:10–12)

The primary task at this festival is to give a freewill offering in proportion to God's blessing. Verse 10 says, "Then you shall keep the Feast of Weeks to the LORD your God with the tribute of a freewill offering from your hand, which you shall give as the LORD your God blesses you." That it is a harvest festival is confirmed in Exodus 23:16: "You shall keep the Feast of Harvest, of the firstfruits of your labor, of what you sow in the field." The Leviticus passage shows that most of it goes for the Levites (Leviticus 23:20).

The term "freewill" shows that the offering is given willingly without any rules regarding how much one should give. This suggests that it is distinct from the tithe which is definitely one-tenth of what one earns. The word translated "tribute" by the ESV (also NAS, AMPLIFIED, ASV) is a rare word that has the idea of sufficiency.[2] How the offering becomes sufficient is given in the following point: ". . . as the LORD your God blesses you." This is mentioned again in verses 15 and 17.

That the offering is in proportion to the blessings of God to us reminds us that when we give, we are simply giving a portion of what he gave us. We are reminded here also that what we have are primarily gifts of grace from God and not the result of our hard work. That takes away pride from the giver. True, these gifts will help in the upkeep of God's work. But that does not mean they are obligated to us. We are all ultimately obligated to God. When we give to God, we are simply discharging a responsibility entrusted to us. As David said, "But who am I, and what is my people, that we should be able thus to offer willingly? For all things come from you, and of your own have we given you" (1 Chronicles 29:14).

After that statement David recalls the past history of Israel, which gives evidence of God's great grace: "For we are strangers before you and sojourners, as all our fathers were. Our days on the earth are like a shadow, and there is no abiding" (1 Chronicles 29:15). Moses does something similar at the end of the discussion on this feast: "You shall remember that you were a slave in Egypt; and you shall be careful to observe these statutes" (Deuteronomy 16:12). When they give to God, they are to remember that God has marvelously provided for them despite their unworthiness. They are so happy about God's provision that they give joyfully. So Moses says in verse 11, "And you shall rejoice before the LORD your God." Even stronger language for joy is used in the next paragraph (16:14, 15).

The sense of receiving God's blessing despite our unworthiness also helps foster humility in the those who make an offering. They give happily not as big shots helping people who are of a lower status to them but as fellow unworthy recipients of God's grace. I work for Youth for Christ, which depends on donations for its subsistence. The Lord has blessed us with many donors both from among the rich and the poor. I have encountered a few rich donors who have given with what looked to me like an attitude of condescension. But the vast majority of richer donors have given their gifts with what looked like humility and joy over the privilege of partnering in the work of God's kingdom.

Because the giving is to be in proportion to what one has been given by God, some who give small gifts may in fact be giving huge donations by God's standards. Jesus highlighted this with his comment on the "two small copper coins, which make a penny" that the widow gave at the temple (Mark 12:42). He said, "Truly, I say to you, this poor widow has put in more than all those who are contributing to the offering box. For they all contributed out of their abundance, but she out of her poverty has put in everything she had, all she had to live on" (Mark 12:43, 44). When the offering was being counted after a youth gathering, the counters found a picture of a teenage girl. They assumed this was a practical joke, probably by a boy, until they saw what was written on the other side of the photo: "I have nothing to give, but I give myself."[3]

On the other hand, others should be giving much more than they give even if that was already a substantial amount. Once after a pastor had made an appeal for a worthy cause, a woman came up to him and handed him a check for fifty dollars and asked him whether her gift was satisfactory. The pastor replied, "If it represents you." After a time of thinking she asked for the check to be returned to her. When she came with a check of 5,000 dollars and asked the same question, the pastor again answered, "If it represents you."

Again she took back the check. A few days later she came with a check for 50,000 dollars. As she placed it in the pastor's hand, she said, "After earnest, prayerful thought, I have come to the conclusion that this gift does represent me and I am happy to give it."[4]

Celebrating with the Needy (16:11, 14)

Both the Feast of Weeks and the Feast of Booths are to be celebrated with a wider circle than one's own family. Verse 11 says, "And you shall rejoice before the LORD your God, you and your son and your daughter, your male servant and your female servant, the Levite who is within your towns, the sojourner, the fatherless, and the widow who are among you" (see also 16:14). The term "sojourner" is used in the Bible for those we would describe as "resident aliens"—foreigners who have settled in the land. The King James Version rendering, "stranger," is therefore misleading. Also included in the festival celebration are people whom the hosts would consider as being of a lower class and therefore who would usually not be included in celebratory meals with the family: ". . . your male servant and your female servant." Then there were "the fatherless" and "the widow," who were needy people. There was economic disparity in Israel, but no class difference was tolerated among the people of God. We must do things to ease the burdens of the poor and needy, as we saw in our study on 15:1–18, but we must never treat them as in any way inferior or not equal to us.

Chris Wright points out that Jesus also directed us to invite the needy to our banquets: "When you give a dinner or a banquet, do not invite your friends or your brothers or your relatives or rich neighbors, lest they also invite you in return and you be repaid. But when you give a feast, invite the poor, the crip-pled, the lame, the blind, and you will be blessed, because they cannot repay you. For you will be repaid at the resurrection of the just" (Luke 14:12–14). If Jesus really meant this, then this is an area where Christians today are very disobedient to Christ. This is certainly the case with Christians in Sri Lanka.

This command of Christ and the instructions for the Jewish feasts should influence who we invite for our weddings and Christmas dinners. We should include servants and the poor people we help; and they should be sitting at the table with us as equals.

Following this direction is not as easy as it may seem at first. There's an awkwardness that comes when people who are culturally different from us join in a family event. Some who are not used to this equality do not know what to do with it, and they could exploit the situation in inappropriate ways. Some who discover the Christian doctrine of equality do not realize that this does not negate the Christian practice of respect for elders and leaders. Some may not do their work properly as they do not feel so afraid of their Christian employers anymore. These problems may be the price that we pay for fostering the type of community described in the Bible. And this especially happened in the early years of change in the Christian community. Yet it would be better for us to be exploited by the needy than to be guilty of not treating them as the Bible says we should. To be sinned against is better than to sin against another!

As we seek to foster equality we will learn how to do these things wisely. Then there is a good chance of both the rich and the poor benefiting from the exercise. But the learning process may go on for a considerable period of time. During that time we may need to bear the cross of being humiliated because people we were bold to treat as equals abused our trust in them.

It must be noted that religious festivals the world over are associated with giving to the needy. In many religions the motivation is the earning of merit through giving to the needy. The distinctive feature of Biblical festivals is that we give out of gratitude to what God has given to us; in fact, even what we give are things that God has given us. We give humbly, not like great benefactors. We give with a joyful heart of gratitude to the God who has helped us even though we did not deserve it. Often in religious festivals when the rich give to the poor they give as superior people helping inferior people. As Christians we identify with those we help by having them over to share a meal with us as our equals.

The Feast of Booths or Tabernacles (16:13–15)

Linking Agricultural Festivals to Redemptive History

The Feast of Booths or Tabernacles is a seven-day harvest festival to be celebrated at the central sanctuary like the other feasts mentioned in this chapter. Moses says, "You shall keep the Feast of Booths seven days, when you have gathered in the produce from your threshing floor and your winepress" (16:13). This is the final harvest held at the end of the agricultural year, around September, before the rains come. As with the Feast of Weeks, the families are to include the needy in their celebrations: "You shall rejoice in your feast, you and your son and your daughter, your male servant and your female servant, the Levite, the sojourner, the fatherless, and the widow who are within your towns" (16:14).

The feast's name probably comes from the fact that they are to dwell in booths during this festival. This was an act intended to remind them of how they dwelled in booths when they came out of Egypt. Leviticus 23:42, 43 says, "You shall dwell in booths for seven days. All native Israelites shall dwell in booths, that your generations may know that I made the people of Israel dwell in booths when I brought them out of the land of Egypt: I am the LORD your God." This follows the Israelite practice of relating the festivals of their agricultural year to events in their redemptive history. A similar thing happens with the feast of Pentecost when, even though it is a harvest festival, Moses tells the people, "You shall remember that you were a slave in Egypt" (Deuteronomy 16:12). Chris Wright says, "It is regrettable that Christian harvest festivals largely ignore this powerful combination of the redemptive-historical with the creation-providential traditions of our biblical faith."

I find this to be very relevant to our situation in Sri Lanka, where this combination can make two important contributions to the life of the church. First, harvest festivals are an important aspect of our culture. In such an environment it would be important for us to affirm that it is the God who created the world who is responsible for the harvest. A harvest festival, with its symbolic representations of God's providence, can be a very helpful way to communicate this truth to our people and through that to help them learn to trust in the providence of God.

Secondly, in our experience-oriented cultures today, because most people initially come to Christ to meet a personal need, it is possible for them not to give the place of centrality that the Bible gives to the objective redemptive events that won our salvation. We should be using every means possible to remind people of the centrality of Christ's work in winning our salvation. The experience-oriented harvest festival could be a good way to help our people imbibe the objective truths about Christ's work. Like the Israelites, we should be looking for creative ways to make links between daily life and the central themes of the Bible.

Altogether Joyful (16:15)

Three times in the description of the Feast of Weeks and of Booths there is reference to joy in the way they celebrate (16:11, 14, 15). The third time they are asked (or commanded) to be "altogether joyful" (16:15c). There is a stress on the completeness of the joy here. And this joy is "because the LORD your God will bless you in all your produce and in all the work of your hands" (16:15b). Those who are conscious of God's grace being the key to their lives will be joyful people. And their joy will be unmixed because they are conscious that God is altogether satisfying. If you think you deserve the blessings you received, then you will automatically desire others to know that you deserve it. And others will never adequately recognize your achievements and blessings. So there will be a disappointment that dampens all experiences of joy.

When God is most important to you and you are deeply in love with him, and when you realize that he keeps blessing you, then you can have unalloyed joy. This is the kind of joy that can withstand even painful experiences. Before Jesus went to the most painful death ever, and already knowing something about the extent of pain, he told his disciples, "These things I have spoken to you, that my joy may be in you, and that your joy may be full" (John 15:11). He had complete joy while facing the greatest suffering any human ever experienced.

People with such joy would be looking for opportunities to express that joy. We would look for ways to celebrate our joy over God's goodness, especially in our family life. Festivals become one of these. In a festival we enjoy by rejoicing in worship especially through music and song, by being together as a community, and by enjoying special meals. We must try to bring this into the annual calendars of our families. The mood we are thinking about is expressed well in a description of some other Biblical feasts:

> Sing aloud to God our strength;
>   shout for joy to the God of Jacob!
> Raise a song; sound the tambourine,
>   the sweet lyre with the harp.
> Blow the trumpet at the new moon,
>   at the full moon, on our feast day. (Psalm 81:1–3)

This shows that music, being the language of joy, would figure prominently during festivals, as we see in the above verses. Music is an excellent avenue to express joy. The great composer Joseph Haydn (1732–1809) was once asked why his church music was so cheerful. He replied, "When I think upon God, my heart is so full of joy that the notes dance and leap, as it were, from my pen, and since God has given me a cheerful heart it will be pardoned me that I serve Him with a cheerful spirit."[5]

When I think of Haydn I immediately think of an exhilarating experience I had singing his famous work *The Creation* while a student in seminary. It was difficult music, and we had to work very hard at achieving some level of quality. But the overarching memory I have of that is of the sheer joy of praising God with such wonderful music. Now sometimes we think of such performances as burdensome attempts to show off our talents. That has ruined the joy of many of our festival celebrations. Not only does it become a prideful performance, but people also get competitive as they vie for the most prominent roles in the musical or dramatic production.

We must work hard at keeping our musical and other performances at Christmas, Easter, and such festivals as extremely joyful times. May our children remember festivals as times of enjoyment. May they know that when they want to enjoy being in community they don't have to join sinful people, they can do it with Christians. This is a very important aspect of the Christian upbringing of children.

Sadly, our festivals and such special events in church are often marred by conflicts over the way the things are done. Some get angry that their children were overlooked for the most important parts. Some get angry that their opinions about how the program should have been run were not taken seriously. So in some Christian communities these special days are not celebrations but occasions for conflict. One of the main reasons for this is that many do not know the joy of the Lord in the church today. They are angry with life. A joyful Christian would overlook small errors if that would help the people remain joyful. This is not a big deal. The big deal is for the church to honor God by rejoicing in him at the event that celebrates his goodness.

Vertical and Horizontal Giving (16:16, 17)

The last paragraph of our section summarizes what has been said in the preceding fifteen verses:

> Three times a year all your males shall appear before the LORD your God at the place that he will choose: at the Feast of Unleavened Bread, at the Feast of Weeks, and at the Feast of Booths. They shall not appear before the LORD empty-handed. Every man shall give as he is able, according to the blessing of the LORD your God that he has given you. (16:16, 17)

One new truth is mentioned here. Before saying that people should give according to how God has blessed them (16:17), Moses says, "They shall not appear before the LORD empty-handed" (16:16b). Wright points out that in 15:13 the same word is used regarding the release of slaves: "And when you let him go free from you, you shall not let him go empty-handed." Just as we don't come to God empty-handed, we don't send the needy away empty-handed. When God blesses us, we give to God and to the needy. Giving has a horizontal and a vertical aspect.

Festivals Enhance Community Solidarity

One of the great values of these three pilgrimage festivals was that they enhanced the sense of community solidarity that is a key aspect of Biblical religion. David Payne reminds us that it is well known that the annual pilgrimage of Muslims to Mecca creates a great sense of joy and brotherhood.

In some ways the solidarity of the Muslims is closer to Biblical religion than is the radical individualism of many Christians. In fact, among the things that Muslims fear as Western culture permeates the world is that their children will give up this solidarity and become culturally individualistic. The church needs to show Muslims that we, too, are in agreement with their concerns regarding these issues. (Other such issues are the export of pornography, the devaluing of the lifelong nature of the marriage tie, and the neglect of the duty to care for parents in their old age.)

In a Biblical community the actions of an individual affect the whole community. Leaders confess the sins of the community as if they themselves had sinned (see, for example, Daniel 9:3–20). Confession is often made to the community (James 5:16). The community is involved in major decisions that people make—such as the choice of one's job or one's spouse.

All this comes from the sense that our identity is wrapped up in the community of God's people. In the Christian church this tie should be even closer than in Israel because Christians are one in Christ in an even closer tie as the body of Christ. But in evangelical Christianity this sense of solidarity and accountability to the community is woefully lacking. Possibly the radical individualism of society has influenced Christians, also. Possibly our reaction to Roman Catholicism, with its emphasis on salvation through the church, caused us to emphasize individual salvation to the exclusion of the primacy of community solidarity in Christianity.

So we must develop events that help restore the sense of community among Christians. They must feel that they belong to a community in such an intimate way that they cannot think of life apart from the whole community. A modern-day equivalent of the pilgrimage festival will help in this. The large Christian music festivals today have some features of the pilgrimage festivals, but what you have there are people of roughly the same age group and culture who come because of the program, not because this is a time when "our community gathers."

We need creative people to work on developing festivals where the whole Christian community can get together to celebrate the things that unite us in Christ. This calls for hard work. The detailed instructions given in the Old Testament on how to conduct these festivals show us that the Bible is very serious about planning these events in such a way that all will benefit from them. In Sri Lanka we occasionally have bilingual or trilingual services when those who usually worship in different languages get together for common worship experiences. I have found that such services are extremely difficult to organize. It takes many hours of creative thinking, meditation, and consultation to develop a good program. We have to ensure that each group can fully participate and that the experience is not boring. Sadly, most such services in Sri Lanka are terribly boring. Sometimes one group gets upset because they feel left out.

So we leaders have a big challenge before us. We have to find theologically meaningful and experientially enjoyable ways in which people of all groups in the body can celebrate together. By doing so they will discover afresh the value of belonging to a body in which we are all joined together to form a unit and where our actions affect the others and their actions affect us.

40

Principles of Leadership and Justice

DEUTERONOMY 16:18—17:13

THE HEALTH AND EFFECTIVENESS OF any good nation or church or group depends to a great extent on its leaders. So the Bible speaks a lot about leadership. A lot of space is given in the prophetic books to denounce the sins of the leaders. Jesus was harsh with the leaders who led people astray and were bad examples. But all this was after the Bible had also given principles that should characterize leaders. The next section of Moses' speech (16:18—18:22) is about the different classes of leaders who will be found in Israel.

How to Be a Good Judicial Officer (16:18–20)

In 1:16–18 Moses described how he instructed the judges during the wilderness years. The judges seem to have been appointed to represent different tribes. In chapter 16 Moses gives instructions on appointing judges after they enter the promised land. Here, too, the judges are chosen according to tribes, but now the town where they will serve also is a factor in making the appointment: "You shall appoint judges and officers in all your towns that the LORD your God is giving you, according to your tribes" (16:18a). "Officers" are also mentioned. These could be another class of judicial officer as the only function mentioned for both groups is judging. Possibly they were subordinate to the judges. On the other hand, these two terms, "judges" and "officers," could refer to the same group of people.[1]

Moses says the judges and officers "shall judge the people with righteous judgment" (16:18b). We saw in our discussion of 1:16 that "righteous judgment" means presenting the best solution to the problem so that it is in line with all of God's nature as holy love. Therefore, it considers both the merits of the case and human compassion.

Next, judges and officers are told, "You shall not pervert [or distort, NASB, NRSV] justice" (16:19a). Bribery is one of the terrible ways in which justice is perverted. Perverting justice is a serious thing. When those who are the custodians of the law act in ways that make people think the law will not protect them, they are hitting at the very heart of what makes a society stable and healthy. The law protects the nation by rewarding those who do good and punishing those who do evil (Romans 13:3, 4). Therefore, those who enforce the law are a key ingredient to the health of a nation. This is why contempt of court is dealt with so severely in the law. The honor and esteem in which the court is held must be protected, and this is why those who dishonor the court must be severely punished.

The next quality, "You shall not show partiality" (16:19b), was also mentioned in 1:17. In our discussion of that verse we said that when judges act partially by favoring the rich, the powerful, and their friends, those without influence and power end up resenting the law because it reminds them of their weakness. Both these qualities are required of judges in today's society, too. Earthly judges represent God in judging humans. Paul said that even a non-Christian judge "is the servant of God, an avenger who carries out God's wrath on the wrongdoer" (Romans 13:4). The nature of God that lies behind his laws should resonate with all people who are committed to justice, as humans are all made in the image of God. Therefore, what the Bible says about the character of judges and officers should be applicable to all judges and officers, even if they do not acknowledge God's lordship over their lives.

Next, Moses says, ". . . and you shall not accept a bribe, for a bribe blinds the eyes of the wise and subverts the cause of the righteous" (Deuteronomy 16:19c). Moses earlier spoke of "the great, the mighty, and the awesome God, who is not partial and takes no bribe" (10:17). Proverbs 17:23 says, "The wicked accepts a bribe in secret to pervert the ways of justice." Deuteronomy 16:19 gives two damaging effects of bribes. First, it "blinds the eyes of the wise" (see also Exodus 23:8; 1 Samuel 12:3). I'm sure you have seen how people who are usually very sensible in the way they act become erratic when dealing with someone who has given them substantial gifts. Sadly, recent history has shown that even judges can be bought. Sometimes leaders do things that are not good for the organization, the church, or the nation to satisfy people who give them some monetary gratuity. The bribe blinds them so that they are forced to satisfy the donor rather than doing what is right.

My father worked for the Inland Revenue (tax) Department in Sri Lanka (the equivalent of the IRS in the USA) for over thirty years, ending his career as its Commissioner. He had given us children instructions never to take a gift that anyone brought home. My father did not want to let gifts color his judgment. Sadly, often when it comes to awarding contracts and purchasing items, the judgment of the official concerned is colored by the prospect of personal financial gain. In a certain country the defense establishment purchased some equipment that did not really protect military personnel rather than buying the better product because of the commission that the corrupt official received. They were more committed to getting illegal money than to ensuring the safety of those who risk their lives for the country on the battlefield.

Second, bribery ". . . subverts the cause of the righteous" (16:19). Some translations render this "perverts" (NASB) or "twists" (NIV). Whatever the exact meaning, this statement says that bribes harm the righteous, the people whom God has sworn to protect. Thus bribery causes one to go against God—a dangerous way to live.

There is an epidemic of dishonesty in the world today. Larry Wolters says, "A commentary of the times is that the word honesty is now preceded by old-fashioned."[2] Interestingly Sir Thomas Fuller (1608–1661) saw this problem in the seventeenth century also. He said, "Honesty is a fine jewel, but much out of fashion."[3] The commonness of bribery today is matched by the frequency of mentions to it in the Bible. I found twenty-eight references in twenty-four sections. In addition to the themes already mentioned and to general descriptions of bribery, the Bible speaks of hating bribes (Exodus 18:21; Proverbs 15:27) and of severe punishment for those who take bribes (Deuteronomy 27:25; Job 15:34).

Recently I attended a seminar for representatives from the different religions in Sri Lanka on the role that religion can play in combating corruption. There a Christian layman bemoaned the fact that he has almost never heard dishonesty being denounced from the Christian pulpit. May we not be guilty of failing to address so serious an issue.

Moses is emphatic when he repeats the term "justice" in verse 20: "Justice, and only justice [literally, justice, justice], you shall follow, that you may live and inherit the land that the LORD your God is giving you." The repetition of "justice" points to the urgency of the task. Commitment to justice is a key concern of the people of God, because God is a God of justice. In recent times evangelicals have been known for their commitment to evangelism and personal morality. And this is as it should be, for the Bible gives a high place to both these activities. But we must also be committed to justice. In our personal lives and as a group we should seek to ensure that all people are treated fairly and that none are deprived of their rights.

When systems of government make it difficult for the poor to progress in life or to receive the best possible support in legal matters, Biblical Christians should do all they can to see that these injustices are removed. Because of our silence on these matters sometimes evangelical Christians have themselves been guilty of exploiting their employees and other injustices. They may not, for example, see the glaring contradiction involved in testifying to the love of God through the provision of personal needs while at the same time not giving their employees a proper wage.

How to Deal with Forbidden Forms of Worship (16:21—17:7)

Sacred and Secular: Part of a Whole

In the middle of this discussion on national leadership and justice we unexpectedly find a section on forbidden forms of worship. Some think this section was not part of the original text of Deuteronomy and was added later on. Yet this mingling of "sacred" and "secular" law is in keeping with the approach to life in the Old Testament because both were integral parts of a whole. In terms of our justice systems this is not so anymore, as we do not live in a theocracy as the Israelites did. But in terms of our personal lives these two must always be regarded as a whole. We are devoted to the values of the kingdom of God and must apply them in society, church, home, and private life.

Before going to seminary my son was a schoolteacher and boarding master in a church-related school. Once the students in his boarding dormitory were accused of doing something that my son was sure they did not do. A senior teacher sharply reprimanded the students for this offense that they were alleged to have committed. Privately my son met the teacher and, speaking up in their defense, asked him whether he was sure they had done this. The teacher got very angry and scolded my son and told him that he should concentrate on teaching the Bible and not try to be a schoolteacher. The idea was that discipline in a school and Biblical principles do not harmonize and that at any one time you should practice one and not the other. Not so in the Bible! Religious law and social law are both derived from the unchanging God "with whom there is no variation or shadow due to change" (James 1:17).

Reminders of Prohibitions (16:21—17:1)

Next are two prohibitions that have already been brought up in this same long second address of Moses. First, Moses talks about Asherim (the plural of Asherah) and pillars: "You shall not plant any tree as an Asherah beside the altar of the LORD your God that you shall make. And you shall not set up a pillar, which the LORD your God hates" (16:21, 22). An Asherah was a representation (often a wooden pole or a living tree) of a goddess by that name, possibly a fertility goddess. The "pillar" or "sacred stone" (NIV) symbolized a male deity, possibly Baal. Moses says, ". . . the LORD your God hates" these pillars.

These two objects of Canaanite worship were among the things the Israelites had already been asked to completely destroy when they entered the promised land (7:5; 12:3). The subsequent history of Israel shows how pathetically they failed to keep these instructions. Clearly, in the first two millennia of Israel's history this was one of their weak areas. Therefore, the Bible does not take for granted that instructions given once will be obeyed for the rest of one's life. In areas of vulnerability constant repetition is necessary.

Today many Christians may not be tempted to go after typical religious deities. But many will be tempted to succumb to the worship of other gods.

- We need to warn people constantly about the god of materialism, just as the Bible warns us about the dangers of "the love of money" (1 Timothy 6:10; Hebrews 13:5), about "the deceitfulness of riches" (Mark 4:19), and about "how difficult it will be for those who have wealth to enter the kingdom of God" (Mark 10:23–31).
- Many Christians are vulnerable to succumbing to the god of activism that prevents them from spending time with God. I have found that simply asking Christians regularly how they are doing with their devotions is very effective in "stirring up one another" (Hebrews 10:24) to faithfulness in this area.
- Worldwide, one of the most prominent gods today is sinful sexuality. Society keeps bombarding us with the idea that we can find sexual satisfaction from those who are not our spouses. As sexuality is such a powerful force it is easy for Christians to succumb to wrong uses of it, despite sincere previous resolutions to keep themselves pure. Constant reminders and the probing questions of accountability partners will go a long way in helping Christians to remain sexually pure.

The next wrong practice that Moses warns the people about is bringing blemished offerings: "You shall not sacrifice to the LORD your God an ox or a sheep in which is a blemish, any defect whatever, for that is an abomination to the LORD your God" (17:1). We looked at this in our discussion of 15:20–23. The repetition suggests that this was a common practice, just as not giving God the best is common today.

Those Who Break the Covenant (17:2–7)

Next, Moses goes to describe how those who break the covenant by worshipping other deities are to be dealt with.

Transgressing the covenant is evil (17:2, 3). The sin that is described here is called transgressing the covenant:

> If there is found among you, within any of your towns that the LORD your God is giving you, a man or woman who does what is evil in the sight of the LORD your God, in transgressing his covenant, and has gone and served other gods and worshiped them, or the sun or the moon or any of the host of heaven, which I have forbidden . . . . (17:2, 3)

Not only are other gods mentioned as objects of worship, also mentioned are "the sun," "the moon," and "any of the host of heaven." The worship of celestial bodies was popular in the ancient Near East, and the Israelites continued to resort to it up to the era of the prophets (2 Kings 21:1–7; 23:4, 5; Jeremiah 19:13).[4]

We have looked into the nature of this sin in our treatment of the first and second commandment of the Decalogue. Here I wish to highlight that this sin is described as doing "evil in the sight of the LORD your God." Usually when we talk of evil people we do not include the worship of idols. But this is a case of rebellion against God, for these practices are "forbidden" by God. The Bible views those who commit religious sins like this one as evil. This sin is described here as an "abomination" (17:4); that is, something that causes disgust. Deuteronomy 7:25 says, ". . . it is an abomination to the LORD your God." Deuteronomy 29:17 describes idols as "detestable things." Several times this is described as spiritual adultery (Deuteronomy 31:16; Judges 2:17; Hosea 1:2).

We must, of course, note that today we do not need to refer to non-Christians who worship idols as evil. They do not know the truth of the gospel. As Paul did in Athens, we will need to argue for the futility of worshipping idols and call them to repentance (Acts 17:22–31). But when Christians resort to idolatry it must be viewed with utmost seriousness and should be denounced with the same severity that the Old Testament does. As we have often said in this book, even today Christians may resort to worship of other gods when they feel that their needs are not being met by the God of the Bible.

What a contrast were the three young men Shadrach, Meshach, and Abednego. They would rather die than worship an idol. But their refusal to worship the image that King Nebuchadnezzar made resulted in God's miraculous deliverance and great glory coming to his name (Daniel 3).

A careful and serious investigation (17:4–7). Often when Christians hear that a fellow Christian has been worshipping another god or committing a serious sin, they adopt a "that is none of my business" approach. That is not the approach advocated in this passage. Moses says that if such a thing happens, ". . . and it is told you and you hear of it, then you shall inquire diligently"(17:4a). If the result yields that "it is true and certain that such an abomination has been done in Israel" (17:4b), the offending person is to be punished. Should Christians act in this way? Most of us have seen angry people who are always finding fault with others and always looking to see where there is sin in the body and pursuing the wrongdoer until he or she is punished. We are usually repelled by such behavior. Our primary focus is always on grace, for ultimately it is the availability of grace that enables us to be obedient to God. But when serious sins such as idolatry and adultery surface in the body, we must act decisively against that.

Many of us find this a hard principle to follow, as we do not enjoy being accusers of fellow Christians. But if we are faithful servants of God who are jealous for the honor of his name, we know we have no choice but to diligently pursue such cases. Paul severely rebuked the Corinthians for their slowness to respond when incest occurred within the church and charged them to immediately act to discipline the offending person (1 Corinthians 5). Despite such strong evidence for it in the Bible, I have become involved in such disciplinary matters very reluctantly. It is so painful and unpleasant. Sometimes it is really hard to find the truth. But this is a responsibility a leader cannot shirk.

Deuteronomy 17:6 says that we should be at pains to find out that those accused of guilt are really guilty: "On the evidence of two witnesses or of three witnesses the one who is to die shall be put to death; a person shall not be put to death on the evidence of one witness" (17:6). We can make a mistake and convict people who are not guilty of wrongdoing. So there must be corroborating evidence from more than one witness. This principle of using more than one witness is carried over into the New Testament, also (Matthew 18:16; 2 Corinthians 13:1; 1 Timothy 5:19).

Because of the need to be sure, in some churches and organizations disciplinary inquiries drag on too long. This causes some to get impatient and accuse the leaders. The law functions both to punish the guilty and protect the innocent. Vindictive people who unjustly slander innocent persons must not be allowed to cause harm to the innocent. Indeed, some guilty persons may get away because there wasn't sufficient evidence. But that is a price worth paying to ensure that the innocent are protected.

We see that this process was not a secret one. The people in general knew what was happening. Moses says, "You shall bring out to your gates that man or woman who has done this evil thing" (17:5). "The city gate is the open space where all public business is carried on."[5] It is implied that there is a public trial. There is no place in the Bible for witch hunts in which people are arrested and secretly tried and condemned without sufficient evidence. The evidence must be corroborated by more than one witness, and the people need to know that a proper process was followed.

The process is so serious that "the hand of the witnesses shall be first against him to put him to death, and afterward the hand of all the people" (17:7). The witness takes a lead in the execution of the criminal. Chris Wright explains, ". . . this ruling must have had a strong psychological deterrent effect against frivolous or false accusation in local communities where the accuser and the accused would be acquaintances." Being a witness is an awesome responsibility. If witnesses make the accusation, they must also take part in inflicting the punishment. If what they said was not true, not only were they guilty of perjury, they were also guilty of the murder of an innocent person. Similarly today, Christians must not be permitted to simply go about making accusations about a person without taking responsibility for the accusation.

All the points in this section show what a serious thing making accusations against another is. It is a responsibility we should not shirk. And it is also a responsibility that must be carried out with utmost care and commitment to the truth.

Capital punishment (17:5, 7). Stoning (17:5) does not seem to have been used as a means of capital punishment outside Israel. Stoning seems to have been "chosen as a form of execution because it was communal. No one person was responsible for the death of the condemned criminal, but in the case of public offenses (apostasy, blasphemy, sorcery, stealing from the *herem*) every citizen was required to take a hand in purging the community of evil (see Deuteronomy 17:5; Leviticus 20:27; 24:14; Joshua 7:25)."[6]

This has something to teach us about disciplining Christians in the church today. While we may not have public trials, the congregation needs to be involved in the discipline process. One of the hardest verses in the New Testament for me is 1 Timothy 5:20: "As for those [elders] who persist in sin, rebuke them in the presence of all, so that the rest may stand in fear." If a leader is disciplined, the congregation needs to know why he was disciplined. We like to hush up the process and quietly have the leader submit to the discipline. But that is not the method advocated by Paul.

While the debate rages on as to whether capital punishment should be enacted today, we can safely say that we do not have a warrant to execute idolaters today. Our nations are not theocracies like ancient Israel, and we ensure freedom of religion for all the people. I do not believe the burning of heretics that took place in earlier times was justifiable. However, the principle of severe punishment for serious sin still applies today. Paul said that the person guilty of incest in Corinth should be handed over to Satan (1 Corinthians 5:5). A similar fate befell the blasphemers Hymenaeus and Alexander (1

Timothy 1:19). Handing over to Satan means expulsion from the church. The church is God's domain, and those in it enjoy his protection. To hand one over to Satan is to cause the person to be released from God's protective hand into Satan's territory.

This paragraph ends by describing what happens as a result of the execution of the wrongdoer: "So you shall purge the evil from your midst" (17:7b). This idea of purging evil through punishment appears nine times in Deuteronomy.[7] One cannot live in sin and expect to remain in the church. The church is a pure bride of Christ, and Christ cannot dwell alongside a rebellious people. The church will always welcome sinners from outside its borders, as Christ did when he was on earth. But if members of the church commit serious sins they must be sent out at least until they repent and give up their rebellious acts.

Respect for the Decision of the Higher Court (17:8–13)

Some cases are too complex for the local courts to handle: "If any case arises requiring decision between one kind of homicide and another, one kind of legal right and another, or one kind of assault and another, any case within your towns that is too difficult for you . . . " (17:8a, b). Because they are too difficult, Moses says, ". . . then you shall arise and go up to the place that the LORD your God will choose" (17:8c). This place is probably where the central sanctuary is (see the discussion on 12:5; 16:1–8). Here the priests and the judge get involved. Deuteronomy 17:9 says, "And you shall come to the Levitical priests and to the judge who is in office in those days, and you shall consult them, and they shall declare to you the decision." While this verse speaks of priests in the plural, verse 12 refers to "the priest" in the singular. So while priests may be involved in the process, the final decision belongs to the chief judge and the high priest.

The decision made by this highest court has to be meticulously carried out:

> Then you shall do according to what they declare to you from that place that the LORD will choose. And you shall be careful to do according to all that they direct you. According to the instructions that they give you, and according to the decision which they pronounce to you, you shall do. You shall not turn aside from the verdict that they declare to you, either to the right hand or to the left. (17:10, 11)

Similar terms were used to describe obedience to the Law. The familiar Hebrew word *shamar*, meaning "be careful to do," which is used so often with regard to obeying the Law, appears here, also. So does the charge not to turn to the left or the right, which appears three times in connection with obedience to the Law (5:32; 17:20; 28:14). Not only is it important for people to keep the Law, they must learn to submit to and obey the verdicts of the custodians of the Law. This is because these custodians are God's agents needed for maintaining the stability and peace and honor of the state. We saw earlier how Paul viewed even non-Christian judges as having such a function (Romans 13:4). If the verdicts are not carried out, that is similar to challenging the constitution of the nation—a serious crime.

The person who refuses to obey the verdict is to be severely punished: "The man who acts presumptuously by not obeying the priest who stands to minister there before the LORD your God, or the judge, that man shall die. So you shall purge the evil from Israel" (17:12). Elsewhere the expression "purge evil" is used for putting to death prophets or dreamers who lead the people to follow other gods (13:1–5) and those who have committed a variety of serious sins, such as premeditated murder (19:11–13), false witness (19:15–21), and sexual sin (22:13–24). Now it is used for those who do not obey the verdict of the courts.

Moses describes the person who violates the verdict of the court as one who "acts presumptuously" (17:12). The NIV translates this as "anyone who shows contempt for the judge or for the priest." This carries the idea of contempt of court, which in any legal system is a serious crime. J. A. Thompson says, "The root [of the word translated "presumptuously"] means 'to boil up' and suggests an angry rejection of the decision." I am reminded of those who angrily create chaos in the group when leaders make a decision that goes against them. This is very common in churches and organizations. Indeed they can express their dissatisfaction in the proper time and place. But they must obey the verdict until it is overturned. To rise up in rebellion indicates that anger over the decision has blinded the persons so that in order to retrieve their lost standing they will act in ways that are detrimental to the group.

What if the person strongly believes that the highest court has made an erroneous decision? The law of the land is that because this is the decision of the court, they have to comply and face the consequences. However, they may use legitimate and available means to prove their innocence.

Respecting the decisions of the leadership is necessary for Christian organizations, also. If the leaders are clearly acting in an unjust manner, then one may need to follow whatever measures are available to bring about a change in the way the leaders behave or to see the leaders replaced. But generally they must obey the leadership as long as they do not have to sin in order to do that. This is how we advise young Christians in our ministry regarding the things their non-Christian parents ask them to do. Of course, they should first try all possible means to explain their viewpoint and raise objections if they have them. Hebrews 13:17 describes the ideal relationship between leaders and the others: "Obey your leaders and submit to them, for they are keeping watch over your souls, as those who will have to give an account." Respecting and obeying leaders is an aspect of Christian character.

Deuteronomy 17:13 presents the effect that capital punishment has on the people: "And all the people shall hear and fear and not act presumptuously again." Similar results are seen when church leaders are disciplined. "As for [elders] who persist in sin, rebuke them in the presence of all, so that the rest may stand in fear" (1 Timothy 5:20; see Acts 5:5, 11). In our discussion of Deuteronomy 4:3 we discussed the role that the fear of punishment plays in motivating people to obedience. To fear punishment is not the same as living constantly with a morbid fear. Fear of punishment causes us to turn from the way of sin. But when we do so we turn to the way of the God who loves us and gives us freedom, joy, and peace. The fear is forgotten as we bask in the sheer joy of walking in the ways of the Lord.

41

How to Be a Good King

DEUTERONOMY 17:14–20

MOSES ANTICIPATES THE TIME when the people are going to ask for a king, so they will be like the other nations: "When you come to the land that the LORD your God is giving you, and you possess it and dwell in it and then say, 'I will set a king over me, like all the nations that are around me . . . ' (17:14). Originally God was to be the King of Israel, and the judges and priests were to perform the functions of a king on the human side on behalf of God. But Moses knew that one day they would want a human king, and he gives the nation guidelines for the appointing of one.

Some have said that the material we find here must be dated to the period of the kings of Israel and attributed to Moses by the writer/editor of Deuteronomy, because the things warned about here are exactly what happened in their history. That conclusion is not necessary. Moses grew up in a king's palace in Egypt, and he would have seen firsthand all the dangers associated with being a monarch. He would also have had a chance to interact with kings during his journeys. Besides, God can inspire prophets to warn people about things that could happen in the future.

Desiring to Be Like Neighboring Nations (17:14, 15)

Structures Can Change after a Time (17:14)

Like Israel, movements today will, after they outgrow their original structure, also need to develop new structures. Yet when forging these new structures and positions we must ensure that Biblical principles are not broken. Our passage gives several of those principles. For example, in several nations the law requires that in religious and voluntary organizations there can be no

447

full-time workers or only a minority of them on the board. Therefore, they have to select "lay" board members. But in doing so they must follow the Biblical principles demanded of leaders, such as spiritual maturity, Christian character, esteem in the community, and exemplary family life (1 Timothy 3:1–7). Many churches and organizations have come into serious problems because they appointed to their boards people with financial and social clout but without the spiritual requirements for Christian leadership.

God Concedes to the Request (17:15)

The wording here might suggest that the king was given to Israel as a concession. As Chris Wright says, "This section . . . is permissive rather than prescriptive legislation. It does not command monarchy but allows for it." Yet the wording suggests that God will willingly grant the request for a king: ". . . you may indeed set a king over you whom the LORD your God will choose" (17:15a). When they did actually ask for a king, we see that Samuel permitted it though he was displeased by the request (1 Samuel 8:5–7). This seems to be a case of God's permitting something as a concession, taking into account human frailty, like his permitting the Israelites to send the twelve spies (see the discussion on Deuteronomy 1:22–25).

There are two stipulations regarding the choice. First, Moses says, the king had to be the person "whom the LORD your God will choose" (17:15a). Always in the selection of leaders our great desire is to find out who the Lord chooses for the job. Interestingly God's choice of many of Israel's great leaders, such as Moses, Gideon, David, Jeremiah, and Isaiah, was not expected, and sometimes the chosen one did not think he was suited for the job. In the appointment of the first two kings of Israel God's choice was revealed through his prophet Samuel. Today we have numerous Scriptural guidelines to help us find God's choice, and also we have the opportunity to pray and ask God to lead.

Second, Moses says, "One from among your brothers you shall set as king over you. You may not put a foreigner over you, who is not your brother" (17:15b). This would primarily be because a foreigner who is not a follower of the LORD God of Israel could not lead a theocracy. Later we will see that the fact that he is "your brother" also has some significance.

Lusting for War Power, Women, and Wealth (17:16, 17, 20)

Even the king chosen by God must be careful about the three big symbols of power among kings at that time: war power, women, and wealth. King Solomon started off as a wise king who did not even ask for wealth when he was presented with a choice from God. But with time he abused his power and became a prey to these three dangers (1 Kings 10:26—11:8). How true the adage is that power corrupts and absolute power corrupts absolutely. History has shown how people who start as good leaders end up doing terrible things after a time in power. The power brings with it the possibility of meeting desires that others cannot easily meet. The easy availability of things we desire can lure us into abusing our authority to get them. Therefore, leaders need to have some checks in place to ensure that this does not happen. Our passage speaks about some of these things.

Increasing Military Power (17:16)

"Only he must not acquire many horses for himself or cause the people to return to Egypt in order to acquire many horses, since the LORD has said to you, 'You shall never return that way again'" (17:16). The primary use of horses in those days was for war. Therefore "the acquisition of large numbers of these animals implies either an aggressive foreign policy or a monarch who wishes to impress his people and his neighbors with his wealth and power."[1] Going back to Egypt would suggest an alliance in which Israel depends on Egypt for military supplies. Such alliances proved to be disastrous later in Israel's history and were condemned by the prophets (Isaiah 31:1–3; Micah 5:10).

Several times in the history of this nation God acted on their behalf to demonstrate that they should depend on him and not on earthly indicators of security. A good example is how Gideon routed the powerful Midianite army of 135,000 with only 300 men (Judges 7:1—8:21). Later Moses would talk about reducing soldiers in the army (Deuteronomy 20:5–8). David said, "Some trust in chariots and some in horses, but we trust in the name of the LORD our God" (Psalm 20:7). When a king amasses the trappings of military power he can get into a false confidence in his abilities and launch into military exercises that are unnecessary—which will drain the kingdom and even result in military defeats. But most dangerous is the possibility of ceasing to humbly trust in God by trusting in military power.

All people have insecurities. And sometimes the thirst behind these insecurities is temporarily lessened by external trappings of power. When the power is there, many like to wield it and do so unnecessarily to have the thrill of a further ego boost through defeating another. So when a king has too much military power he might desire to conquer other nations and bring them under his reign. And he could wage war against those countries resulting in several unnecessary abuses of and pain to people. This has happened throughout history, a recent example being the expansionism of the Nazi regime under Hitler.

Christians leaders are also vulnerable to the temptation to use the power they have to fulfill earthly desires that do not please God. Christian institutions are sometimes launched just to fulfill the leader's desire for more power and prestige. In the end we will see that such labors have brought no eternal fruit. Even if these leaders make it to Heaven, their work will be seen to be worthless (1 Corinthians 3:13–15).

Too Many Wives (17:17a)

Next Moses says, "And he shall not acquire many wives for himself, lest his heart turn away" (17:17a). It is beyond the scope of this book to look into the puzzling issue of why polygamy was permitted in Old Testament times, even though it violated God's plan for marriage implied in many places in the Old Testament (e.g., Genesis 2:23, 24) and explicitly stated in the New Testament (e.g., Matthew 19:9; Ephesians 5:23). Gleason Archer says, "As we examine the scriptural record, we come to the realization that every case of polygamy or concubinage amounted to a failure to follow God's original model and plan."[2] It seems to have been a practice common among neighboring countries that was tolerated in Israel until the people fully understood that it was against God's plan for marriage. We must also bear in mind that polygamy was not widely practiced in Israel. It was only the wealthy (for example, kings) who could afford it. In fact, it was a sign of wealth in those days.

Moses gives a reason why a king should not take many wives: ". . . lest his heart turn away" (17:17b). Marriage was used as a tool of diplomacy in the ancient Near East, and kings would give their "daughters to cement alliances and establish treaties with his neighboring kingdoms."[3] Though there may be political advantages to such marriages, the sad case of Solomon's wives introducing the worship of other gods shows the peril of this course of action for Jewish kings (1 Kings 11:4–8).

The same principle applies for the marriages of Christians. We have heard how God has sometimes mercifully brought unbelieving spouses to himself after they married unbelievers. But these acts of God's mercy are not the norm. Often the Christian who marries a non-Christian is either led away to a life of compromise or to relative inactivity in God's service. And how sad it would be if we cannot share the most precious thing in our lives—our relationship with God—with the most precious person in our lives—our spouses. Those who are already married to unbelievers can take heart that now that they are married, God desires for them to be united and will help them. Those who are single should shun such a marriage as something that is against God's will.

In the ancient world taking on many wives was a symbol of power. Today we often find powerful people having sexual relations with people who are not their spouses. This is more common among men, though recently it seems to be growing among women, also. Leaders are sometimes insecure people who have partially overcome their insecurity by climbing to the top in their fields. This could be in business, politics, religion, entertainment, sports, or some other sphere. But success does not eradicate the insecurity. One way some male leaders overcome their insecurity is through sexual conquests.

A leader finds a woman attractive and desires her. This happens to a lot of people, but they give up dreaming of this "conquest" when they know it will be impossible to "get" the woman. But leaders are often able to get the person they want, and the conquest gives temporary relief to their insecurity. This is why sometimes we find men having affairs with women who are, by the world's warped standards, less sexually attractive than their wives. People ask, "Why did he fall for her when he had such a beautiful wife?" It is because this affair had more to do with filling the emptiness of insecurity than with looking for sexual and romantic satisfaction.

As most of us suffer from some sort of insecurity, it is important for us to be aware of this trap and to avoid falling into it. We also need to seek our security from legitimate means. Primarily this should come from our relationship with God and secondarily from those to whom we are committed, such as our spouses and the members of the group to which we belong.

Excessive Treasures (17:17c)

The king is then given another caution: ". . . nor shall he acquire for himself excessive silver and gold." Treasures also are related to power and leadership, which bring new opportunities to make a fortune. Here what is intended could be "overtaxing the people simply to fill the royal treasury."[4] Archaeologists have discovered rooms in palaces that were treasuries (places to keep these treasures).

Acquiring large amounts of wealth and desiring to do so bring with it many dangers. First, the persons will tend to depend more on their ability than on God. This is why Jesus said it is so hard for rich people to enter the kingdom (Luke 18:18–30). They are so focused on maintaining the "security" that money brings that they neglect finding their security in God. So they resist the idea of a God who calls them to bow down in childlike trust before him. Wealth gives them a wrong sense of power and self-sufficiency.

Second, many who get the taste of the empty satisfaction that wealth brings find themselves lusting for more wealth. And that causes them to go against their principles to acquire more. They are not satisfied with what they have, even if they have a lot. Mammon is a brutal taskmaster—it makes slaves of humans and drives them into an insatiable quest for more. A famous cricketer who was known to be a committed Christian was implicated in a match-fixing scandal. His Christianity resurfaced, and he confessed to having taken money to influence the outcomes of some international games. When asked about how he could have done this, he said that he loved cricket and God, but he found that he loved money even more. So we have politicians who are very rich but amass more fortunes by taking bribes. We have wealthy doctors who neglect their families and become hasty in examining their patients so they can have more (too many) patients and make more money.

Third, the desire for more wealth can blind people to the dangers of foolish investments that promise quick gain. In Sri Lanka many people have lost all their savings by investing in finance companies that promised huge interest (as high as 30–35 percent) but went bankrupt. When kings do things like this, whole countries suffer. When leaders of churches and organizations do this, the group they lead suffers. Recently some Christian organizations lost large amounts of money by investing in organizations that promised to bring huge gains.

Fourth, the desire for more wealth can cause people to exploit or hurt others in their quest for it. So kings tax the people more than they should. Businesspeople underpay their workers. Householders underpay their domestic helpers. People underpay their workers because weak people cannot find a way to push them to make fair payment. I think one of the worst expressions of this sin is when people dupe a trusting relative, such as an elderly widow, in order to acquire for themselves wealth belonging to that person.

Christian leaders are vulnerable to all these dangers. How sad that we have heard so many stories of Christian leaders who took money from poor but generous people to live ostentatious lives! How easy it is to take money trustingly given for "our work" and use it for ourselves. How easy it is to have high expense accounts by staying and eating at places that our donors themselves could never afford to enter.

Staying Close to the Word (17:18, 19a)

After presenting three things that the king should not do, Moses gives two positive things that he must do. The first has to do with the Word of God: "And when he sits on the throne of his kingdom, he shall write for himself in a book a copy of this law, approved by the Levitical priests. And it shall be with him, and he shall read in it all the days of his life" (17:18, 19a). The original scroll of the Law was kept in the sanctuary under the care of the priests. The language in the ESV, NIV, and many other translations suggest that the king himself was to write a copy of the Law for himself. The wording could also yield the interpretation that the king was to get others to do the writing for him (NRSV). If the ESV and other translations are correct, then the writing itself would have helped drive home into the king's mind the importance of what the Law contains.

Notice that the Law is to "be with him." The Bible is the companion of the leader, and like a good Jew he is to "read in it all the days of his life." Daily he must go to it for a word from his Master. We saw the importance of this in our discussions on 6:1–5 and 6:6–9. It is particularly important for kings and Christian leaders to stay close to the Bible as their job is to lead people to God's ways. So they must know God's ways, and the best way to gain this knowledge is from the Scriptures. Christians who are leaders in non-ecclesiastical organizations also need to stay close to the Bible because they are Christians first, and their Christianity influences all they do in their leadership role.

A senior minister in the Sri Lankan Cabinet presided at a recent national awards ceremony because the President could not attend. He is a staunch Buddhist, and there were some monks among the honorees. The cabinet minister surprised everyone by being very critical of politicians in Sri Lanka in his speech. He faulted them for being unprincipled and selfish. Then he told the story about Abraham Lincoln who was traveling in a train. Someone in his compartment heard some groans coming from his cabin, and he peeped in to see what was happening. He saw Lincoln on his knees, with an open Bible in front of him, reading it and praying. The minister said that is the kind of leader Sri Lanka needs—people who are driven by their religious principles.

If religious principles come from the Creator of the world, they should be considered indispensable for a meaningful life in any society. Lincoln said, "In regard to this great book, I have but to say, it is the best gift God has given to man. . . . But for it we could not know right from wrong. All things most desirable for man's welfare, here and hereafter, are to be found portrayed in it."[5] George Washington said, "It is impossible to rightly govern the world without God and the Bible."[6]

The Old Testament gives detailed descriptions of the responsibilities given to people who are appointed to different tasks in Israel. In light of this, isn't it interesting that the only positive responsibility mentioned in this list for the king of Israel is that he must stay close to the Word of God? In the life of a leader the primary need is always to know what God's will is and to do it. Therefore, leaders must know what the Bible teaches and become skilled in applying it to the challenges they face. Their lives must be saturated in the Word, and that should show in their leadership.

Learning Attitudes That Make Leaders Teachable (17:19b, 20)

Learning to Fear the Lord (17:19b)

Moses says that the Word will do two things to the king. First, it teaches him to fear the Lord. After saying that the king should stay close to the Word, Moses says ". . . that he may learn to fear the LORD his God by keeping all the words of this law and these statutes, and doing them" (17:19b). This is done in several ways.

- When we spend time in the Word we are affirming that God is indeed our Master whom we want to follow in all we do. Attitudes grow with practice. Reading the Word comes from a humble desire to learn from and obey God, which is an aspect of fearing God. The more we read the Bible, the more this attitude is fostered in us.
- When we read the Bible we see where we fall short, and we are warned about the danger of wrong ways we may be taking or are about to take. David said about the laws in the Bible, ". . . by them is your servant warned" (Psalm 19:11). There were key times in Israel's history when the reading of the Word triggered spectacular repentance. This happened to King Josiah when the Book of the Law was read to him (2 Kings 22:9–13) and when Ezra read the Law to the people (Nehemiah 8). Repentance is an expression of fearing God.
- The Bible reminds us of judgment, which in turn should create within us a fear of displeasing God.
- The consequence of the three functions of the Word just mentioned is that we are helped to be obedient to God. David said, "I have stored up your word in my heart, that I might not sin against you" (Psalm 119:11). Obedience to God is the best evidence that we truly fear him.

Essentially, then, the Bible helps create in us the humble attitude that is the key to fearing God. David, the great king of Israel, was a humble man. This must surely have been enhanced by his reverence for the Word. He said, ". . . my heart stands in awe of your words" (Psalm 119:161).

Accountability (17:20)

The second thing that Moses says the Word will do to the king is given in verse 20a: ". . . that his heart may not be lifted up above his brothers, and that he may not turn aside from the commandment, either to the right hand or to the left." As the Word humbles us constantly, we will not fall into the trap into which many leaders fall. They think they are superior to others who live and work with them. Moses talks of a situation that can arise when the king's "heart may . . . be lifted up above his brothers, and . . . he . . . turn[s] aside from the commandment. . . ." Leaders can become "a law unto themselves." Many leaders today are like this. People treat them as kings and keep a distance from them. If they have some of the more spectacular gifts, such as the ability to prophesy or heal, people treat them as they would a holy man in many religious traditions—someone who is separated from the people because of his supposed spiritual superiority.

When leaders elevate themselves above their brothers and sisters, they lose an important source of help along the path of obedience. Leaders need others who will be their brothers and sisters and help them along in their personal lives. It is easy for leaders to come to a state when they are distant from others in the group because they have been elevated to leadership. Sadly, in some Christian groups leaders have distanced themselves from their colleagues and sometimes only let their family members and a few cronies know about their personal transactions. These stand to gain by their abuse of power and to lose greatly by the exposure of these abuses. Therefore, family members and cronies will not usually "betray" leaders by exposing their abuses of their position.

It is imperative that leaders submit themselves to being accountable to others. They will need to voluntarily do this because often others will not require this of them. Friends see the folly of some of our actions that we may not see when we are blinded by desire. They would advise us against such actions. This function was particularly performed by the prophets of Israel. It has been said that David and Josiah were good kings because they had prophets and priests to warn and instruct them. Leaders can fall into the trap of having people around them who only tell positive things to them and of eliminating people who frankly tell the truth when they feel the leader is doing something wrong.

Many leaders who have fallen into sexual and financial sin have said that during the time they fell they were not accountable to anyone for their personal behavior. Leadership had elevated them above others and left them without others who could comfort and confront them. Dr. Waylon B. Moore refers to a survey where "200 ministers revealed they had committed adultery. Talking with each one, it was discovered they had four things in common:

- They never believed they would be guilty of adultery.
- Each had regular contact in his ministry with an attractive lady.
- None were in an accountability group.

• Each had little or no regular Quiet Time for personal feeding and confession."[7]

The value of friends is not only in confronting us with what is wrong but also in comforting us when we are hurt. Leaders will face many blows in life that could make them bitter and cynical. The comfort of God is the best antidote for this. But often God's comfort is mediated by friends.

Proverbs and Ecclesiastes have some interesting things to say about advice, rebuke, flattery, and comfort that all wise leaders should heed:

• "Whoever loves discipline loves knowledge, but he who hates reproof is stupid" (Proverbs 12:1).
• "The way of a fool is right in his own eyes, but a wise man listens to advice" (Proverbs 12:15).
• "The ear that listens to life-giving reproof will dwell among the wise. Whoever ignores instruction despises himself, but he who listens to reproof gains intelligence" (Proverbs 15:31, 32).
• "Cease to hear instruction, my son, and you will stray from the words of knowledge" (Proverbs 19:27).
• "Better is open rebuke than hidden love. Faithful are the wounds of a friend; profuse are the kisses of an enemy" (Proverbs 27:5, 6).
• "A man who flatters his neighbor spreads a net for his feet" (Proverbs 29:5).
• "Whoever rebukes a man will afterward find more favor than he who flatters with his tongue" (Proverbs 28:23).
• "Two are better than one, because they have a good reward for their toil [fruitfulness]. For if they fall, one will lift up his fellow. But woe to him who is alone when he falls and has not another to lift him up! Again, if two lie together, they keep warm, but how can one keep warm alone [comfort and encouragement]? And though a man might prevail against one who is alone, two will withstand him—a threefold cord is not quickly broken [strength]" (Ecclesiastes 4:9–12).

If you are a leader, make sure you have friends. And if you are not, do all you can to ensure that your leaders have friends!

42

Priests and Prophets:
The Good, the Bad, the Best,
and the False

DEUTERONOMY 18:1–22

WE NEED ALL THE HELP WE CAN GET in the challenge of being faithful to God. There are crucial decisions to take and big mistakes that we can make. So we need to constantly grapple to know what's best for us. Today we have the Scriptures as our ultimate guide in all these things, but we know that even today God uses people whom he sets apart as his representatives to speak to us. Deuteronomy 18 presents four kinds of people who stake a claim to be representatives of God: good, bad, best, and false.

It is easy to make mistakes in our relationships with leaders. It is possible not to care for them properly, to be misled by them, to not recognize those who are God's chosen representatives, and to follow those who are not God's representatives. Therefore, the Bible gives us a lot of instructions about leaders. Our passage presents some of these instructions.

The Good: Care for Them (18:1–8)

The Duty to Care for God's Servants

First, we have eight verses devoted not to the duties but to the welfare of the priests, and the duty spoken of is the duty of the general population to look after their priests. This is relevant to us today, too. We must care for those who minister among us. These verses are about "the Levitical priests, all the tribe of Levi . . . " (18:1a). Verse 3 refers only to "priests" and verses 6,

7 to "Levites." All the priests of Israel were Levites, but not all the Levites were priests. But all the Levites were sanctuary personnel, in that they had responsibilities related to the priestly functions within the sanctuary of God. So Moses is referring to all the Levites here. I suppose today we could apply this passage by seeing the ordained clergy as being equivalent to priests and seeing other church workers (such as administrative and support staff and parachurch workers) as being equivalent to Levites.

Offerings to the Lord to Go to God's Servants (18:1–4)

Verses 1a, 2a say, "The Levitical priests, all the tribe of Levi, shall have no portion or inheritance with Israel. . . . They shall have no inheritance among their brothers." The word "inheritance" here is used in the sense of "tribal territory."[1] The Levites were not permitted the private ownership of lands. Forty-eight towns with surrounding pasturelands were reserved for the Levites (Numbers 35:1–8; Joshua 21:41, 42).

Two other factors are presented as their inheritance. First, Moses says, "They shall eat the LORD's food offerings as their inheritance" (18:1b); and second, ". . . the LORD is their inheritance, as he promised them" (18:2b). About the food offerings, Moses says, "And this shall be the priests' due from the people, from those offering a sacrifice, whether an ox or a sheep: they shall give to the priest the shoulder and the two cheeks and the stomach. The firstfruits of your grain, of your wine and of your oil, and the first fleece of your sheep, you shall give him" (18:3, 4). They are given a portion of the sacrifices and the firstfruits (see the discussion on 26:1–15).

The words "the priests' *due* from the people" (18:3) suggest that supplying the needs of priests was similar to a legal obligation expected by God from the faithful. Some Christian workers have unscrupulously exploited the Biblical teaching about the obligation to give and the blessings of doing so to get very rich, much richer than the people who sacrificially give to their ministry. Because of such abuses it is always good for those in ministry to have strict guidelines set by others than themselves about how they should be remunerated. The practice in the Bible of giving instructions regarding provisions for Levites is a good precedent to follow.

Moses' wording is very significant: "They shall eat the LORD's food offerings as their inheritance . . . the LORD is their inheritance, as he promised them" (18:1b, 2b). What is given to the Lord is for them, as the Lord is their inheritance. If they are not looked after, that means that the people have not given God what is his due. To neglect caring for God's servants is to neglect giving to God. In fact, Malachi views the failure to pay tithes as robbing God

(Malachi 3:8–10). It is true that the New Testament does not have such clear guidelines for giving as in the Old Testament. But the principles are given. And one of them is that those who minister must be cared for. Paul said, "Let the elders who rule well be considered worthy of double honor, especially those who labor in preaching and teaching. For the Scripture says, 'You shall not muzzle an ox when it treads out the grain,' and, 'The laborer deserves his wages'" (1 Timothy 5:17, 18; see also Luke 10:7; 1 Corinthians 9:9, 10).

The abuses by some of monies given for God's work should not be an excuse for not adequately caring for those in the ministry. Exploiting the greater freedom from regulations in the New Testament, some Christians have given much less than they should to God's work, not even giving a tithe of their earnings. Consequently, many of God's servants are underpaid. A fairly wealthy Christian leader once in conversation with me tried to justify underpaying Christian workers, stating that the ministry involves sacrifice and therefore people in ministry should not expect to be well paid.

If we justify ministers' being underpaid, what do we do with the statement that "the Lord is their inheritance, as he promised them" (18:2)? Has the Lord forsaken his servant who put his trust in him? Today there are children of Christian workers who are angry with the church and sometimes angry with God because their parents were treated so badly by the church. Some ministers have moved away from the call that they felt they had clearly received from God because they could not survive financially and provide for their families. Others have persevered amidst great hardship.

We must remember that in this fallen world the theology of suffering and the theology of God's providence often intersect in our experience. God's faithful servants often have to live with what looks like less than ideal situations because of the sin of others and because the general consequences of sin are enmeshed with life in this fallen world. But the church should never be guilty of deliberately underpaying her workers.

This passage teaches that the money given to ministers is God's money. Those who give it are to do so as if they were giving to God. Those who receive it should spend it as if it belongs to God. Indeed, all the money in the world belongs to God. So every financial transaction in which we engage must be done as if the money was God's (which it is). While we are careful with all funds, we have to be extra-careful with money that has been designated as belonging to God. Just as the failure to give God his due is viewed in the Bible as robbing God, the failure to use God's funds responsibly could be viewed as defrauding God. This means that Christian workers need to be very careful how they use their personal finances, realizing that their salaries come from money belonging to God in a special way. And how much more careful must we be with funds belonging to the church or a Christian organization—funds that have been given as to God.

The Lord Is Their Inheritance (18:2)

The statement that "the LORD is their inheritance" derives from the fact that the tithes and offerings given by the people was God's inheritance. A portion of that went to God's servants, and the fact that they serve God ensured that they have an inheritance via what is given to God. So the primary idea here is that what they receive comes out of the tithes and offerings given to God.

Note how God associates himself with his servants so closely. When the people rob God and do not give their tithes to him, the servants of God suffer because of the insult hurled at God. But that does not prevent God from being with these servants. While God has chosen to work through people and permits the sins of people to sometimes affect his faithful servants, he never leaves these servants alone and uncared for. David said, "For my father and my mother have forsaken me, but the LORD will take me in" (Psalm 27:10).

After listing the many earthly honors and privileges he had to give up for the sake of Christ, Paul said:

> But whatever gain I had, I counted as loss for the sake of Christ. Indeed, I count everything as loss because of the surpassing worth of knowing Christ Jesus my Lord. For his sake I have suffered the loss of all things and count them as rubbish, in order that I may gain Christ and be found in him. (Philippians 3:7–9a)

James Orr, commenting on Deuteronomy 18:2, says, "In possessing God, the believer possesses all things."[2] This is why despite the hardships we have, we cannot really say that we have sacrificed by coming into the ministry. Someone commented to David Livingstone about the sacrifices he had made because of his work for God. He is reported to have replied, "Sacrifice? The only sacrifice is to live outside the will of God." When he was asked what kept him going amidst so much hardship and sickness, he said always ringing in his ears were the words of Jesus, "Lo, I am with you always, even unto the end of the world" (Matthew 28:20, KJV).

When we have Jesus, we have a treasure more satisfying than all earthly treasures. With Christ we have a peace and joy that more than compensates for all earthly deprivation. The Old Testament heroes did not experience this to the fullest extent as they did not have the full blessings of the new covenant. But they persevered in faith. Hebrews 11:39, 40 says of them, "And all these, though commended through their faith, did not receive what was promised, since God had provided something better for us, that apart from us they should not be made perfect." They persevered with so little. May we who have so much more than they did be motivated to persevere amidst whatever hardship we may endure along the way.

The Privilege of Being God's Representative (18:5–8)

The rest of this paragraph presents the privilege associated with the call of the Levites. Verse 5a says, "For the LORD your God has chosen him out of all your tribes. . . ." They have been chosen by the Lord of all creation for a special task. There is a mystery as to why God chooses those whom he chooses to be his special vessels on earth. Certainly it is not because of any innate greatness on their part. Paul says:

> For consider your calling, brothers: not many of you were wise according to worldly standards, not many were powerful, not many were of noble birth. But God chose what is foolish in the world to shame the wise; God chose what is weak in the world to shame the strong; God chose what is low and despised in the world, even things that are not, to bring to nothing things that are, so that no human being might boast in the presence of God (1 Corinthians 1:26–29).

We cannot boast about our own achievements. One who does that is fully out of line in terms of God's way of thinking. But we can rejoice that God has chosen us and has given us such a high privilege.

Deuteronomy 18:5 goes on to say that the Levite was chosen "to stand and minister in the name of the LORD, him and his sons for all time." This theme is repeated twice with slight modifications in verse 7: ". . . and ministers in the name of the LORD his God, like all his fellow Levites who stand to minister there before the LORD." They are to "minister" in his name and "stand" before him. They are to represent God before the rest of the people. And they represent the people before God. They lead the people of God in worshipping God through thanksgiving and praise (1 Chronicles 16:4; Psalm 135:1, 2) and through offering the sacrifices (Exodus 30:20). They are also responsible for caring for the place of worship (Numbers 1:50; 3:31).

What an honor this is! True, they do not possess symbols of earthly success, but they have something far more important—they have the privilege of being on a special assignment for the eternal Lord of creation whose kingdom will have no end.

One would wish that parents of children who opt for Christian service would understand this. Sometimes we hear of parents getting very angry that after spending so much money on their education their children went into professions that do not pay well. The parents of many missionaries were not happy about their children's decision to become missionaries. I know that some of the missionaries who came to Sri Lanka in the last two centuries gave up prospects of brilliant careers in their home countries to come into sheer deprivation in our nation. But if they had not come to our nation, we would still be in sin headed for Hell. Parents think their investment in their children's education was a waste. But it is not a waste. The education prepared their children for a high calling. My first degree was in biology, and I know that it did much to prepare me for Christian ministry. It gave me the discipline of looking for adequate evidence before accepting or proclaiming any affirmations. It gave me some credibility in evangelism among Buddhist youths, many of whom believe science has disproved the existence of God. It opened the door for me to go directly into the ministry God gave me.

True, there is not much earthly reward in terms of salary received, but there is a great heavenly reward and the earthly reward of knowing that we are doing something extremely significant. Psychologists tell us that those who believe that what they are doing is significant will be happy people. And all this is in addition to the joy of living with and for God. These make the servant of Christ a very wealthy person!

Verses 6–8 talk about Levites living in the towns. They would have served as religious professionals, performing sacrifices and instructing the people in the Law.[3] They may come to the place of the central sanctuary on "a temporary tour of duty,"[4] and those who come need to be supplied with their needs according to the procedures just outlined. When God's servants come to our cities for some work or when missionaries come home on furlough, we must make sure they are cared for. In our ministry when those working in less urban areas come to the city, they get quite frustrated because the city workers are so busy that they have no time to look into the needs of these colleagues who are visiting the city. But when we go to their smaller towns, they treat us like royalty! We needed to devise systems to ensure that workers are cared for.

The Bad: Have Nothing to Do with Them (18:9–14)

Next, Moses goes back to a theme that he had already tackled in chapter 13. There he talked about people who led others to follow false gods through performing signs and wonders. In 12:2–4 he talked about the need to destroy places used for the worship of other gods. Here he speaks primarily of practices that the Israelites would be tempted to try out in order to get some supernatural guidance. We looked at many of the principles of dealing with such in our studies on chapters 12, 13. So our discussion here will be brief.

Verses 10–12 give a comprehensive list of the practices that are condemned. Moses says in verse 10, "There shall not be found among you any-one" who performs these acts.

- The first is "anyone who burns his son or his daughter as an offering. . . ." Here the child is given as an offering to a god in order to gain a victory or, more probably in this context, some specific guidance.
- The next three have to do with the use of different methods to seek divine wisdom ("anyone who practices divination"), to predict the future ("tells fortunes"), and to give an explanation of why certain events are taking place ("interprets omens").
- Then there are two methods that have to do with the use of magic with the intention of influencing events or persons by the use of supernatural methods: ". . . or a sorcerer or a charmer." People can use these methods to help others or more often to harm them.
- The next three have to do with communicating with others in order to bring a message: ". . . a medium [who communicates information from non-physical beings such as spirits, demons, and false deities] or a nec-romancer [who communicates with the dead in order to get guidance or some other help; 'spiritist,' NASB, NIV] or one who inquires of the dead."

Many of these practices are quite common today. I have seen programs on TV where people allegedly spoke to the dead or gave advice to others using supposedly supernatural means. Many popular magazines and newspapers in the East and the West have a section devoted to astrology. Psychic counselors are getting more and more popular. The most famous Biblical example of this is when King Saul, who was in a desperate situation, consulted a witch at Endor (1 Samuel 28:7–14). I know of Christians who, desperate for some guidance in a crisis situation, have gone for help to astrologers or palmists or others using such means.

The Bible is clear that we should have nothing to do with these things. Three times our passage refers to these practices as abominable: ". . . you shall not learn to follow the abominable practices of those nations . . . for whoever does these things is an abomination to the LORD. And because of these abominations the LORD your God is driving them out before you" (18:9, 12). That last statement says that one reason God commanded the Israelites to completely destroy the Canaanite people was that they indulged in these abominable practices. These activities were so harmful to humanity that the nation through whom God's message of salvation to humanity was to be communicated needed to be protected from being contaminated by them.

The word "abominable" shows that these actions are totally evil and repul-sive to God and his people. Yet, that is not the attitude toward these actions in contemporary society. In our discussions on chapters 7 and 12 we pointed out that today we live in multi-religious societies and not in theocracies like

Israel. Therefore, we cannot forcefully destroy these practices that people of other faiths regard as helpful and good. But we can use arguments to persuade people about their futility. Paul said, "We destroy arguments and every lofty opinion raised against the knowledge of God, and take every thought captive to obey Christ" (2 Corinthians 10:5). We must warn Christians severely about the dangers of these practices, as Moses does in this passage.

After the stern warning in Deuteronomy 18:12, Moses says, "You shall be blameless before the LORD your God" (v. 13). The word translated "blameless" refers to a life that, in keeping with the covenant God made with Israel, is totally devoted to God without anything coming in between the person and God. The moment we begin to compromise and entertain things that displease God in our lives, we dishonor our relationship with God with a halfhearted commitment that is very dangerous. Yet all around us we may see others succumbing to the lure of these things that could drag us away from God. Moses warns, ". . . for these nations, which you are about to dispossess, listen to fortune-tellers and to diviners" (18:14a). But God's people are prohibited from involvement: "But as for you, the LORD your God has not allowed you to do this" (18:14b). The teaching is unambiguously clear. We must have nothing to do with these things.

Christians who have been involved in these practices before or after they became Christians may need some spiritual therapy or deliverance to free them from the insidious hold that occult forces can have on them. We should be alert to this possibility and counsel those whom we know have had such backgrounds to seek some special help to be delivered from any vestiges of these influences that Satan can use to cause havoc in their lives.[5]

The Best: Listen to Him (18:15–19)

The Prophet Described

Next Moses talks of a new prophet like Moses himself. The original application of this would be to the prophetic line that followed Moses in the history of Israel. He says, "The LORD your God will raise up for you a prophet like me from among you, from your brothers" (18:15a; also 18:18a). Note that this prophet is going to be appointed neither because of birth to a certain family nor because of election or appointment by humans to the task. God will raise up prophets for his service by directly calling them. The prophet is to be "like [Moses]." The Israelites needed to hear from God, but they could not handle the strain of a direct encounter with God. So they "desired of the LORD [their] God at Horeb on the day of the assembly, [and] said, 'Let me not hear again the voice of the LORD my God or see this great fire any more, lest I die'" (18:16). The Lord agreed: "They are right in what they have spoken" (18:17).

His answer was, "I will raise up for them a prophet like you from among their brothers. And I will put my words in his mouth, and he shall speak to them all that I command him" (18:18).

The Israelites did not have idols. But they had what they knew to be direct words from God. This gave them the security of living under the authority of the Lord of the universe. But they couldn't stand the strain of the awesome experience of exposing themselves to God's direct revelation. Therefore, they asked Moses to do that for them. The prophets continued this tradition of hearing directly from God and communicating it to the people. And it is this prophetic function that is predicted in our passage: "And I will put my words in his mouth, and he shall speak to them all that I command him" (18:18b). Today we have those words of God, which are "profitable for teaching, for reproof, for correction, and for training in righteousness," in the Bible, which we recognize as "breathed out by God" (2 Timothy 3:16).

When we preach and teach today, we expound or exposit the Word of God that has been given to us through the prophets and apostles in the Scriptures. What we say is not the Word of God in the sense that the prophets communicated it. We may be prophetic in that we reflect the thrust of the teaching of the prophets in what we say. But prophecy is communicated only by those who have been called to give the gift of prophecy. Though the need for the gift of prophecy is reduced because now we have a complete Bible that we recognize as God's Word, we know from the New Testament that this gift is still given even in the era of the church.

The people are responsible to listen to the prophet: ". . . it is to him you shall listen. . . . And whoever will not listen to my words that he shall speak in my name, I myself will require it of him" (18:15b, 19). Applying this to our day, it is a big mistake to ignore the Scriptures. People may not be interested in listening to the Bible. Then we have the task of making the message interesting just like the prophets did with their acted messages and other creative means of communication. People may not like to hear what the Bible says, but that was true of the message of the prophets, too. Most of them were very unpopular during their lifetime. But they faithfully shared God's message, and suffered for it. May we do so, also.

What the Bible teaches, we would do well to listen to actively in the sense of accepting it and obeying it. If the Bible says that homosexual practice and heterosexual sex outside marriage are wrong, we must accept that and seek the most prudent way to communicate this truth in a world that has rejected that idea. If the Bible says that Christ is the only way to salvation, we must accept that and its implications such as seeking to bring all people to accept this gospel—a view that is totally out of step with the pluralistic mood of our day.

But the consequence of ignoring Scriptural truths is much more serious than the adverse effects of upholding them in a hostile world. God says, "And whoever will not listen to my words that he shall speak in my name, I myself will require it of him" (18:19). This is a threat of judgment. I believe it is appropriate for us to place before people the prospect of judgment for refusing to obey what the Bible teaches—especially in view of the arrogant disregard with which many so-called Christians reject what it teaches on several issues today. Vance Havner has said, "There is a comfortable attitude about Jesus Christ in our churches today, and it is our greatest peril. After all, we are not judged so much by how many sins we have committed but by how much light we have rejected."[6]

Is This the Messiah?

The immediate question that arises in Christians when they read this prediction about a prophet like Moses is whether this is a prediction about the Messiah. The natural way to interpret this passage is to refer to the line of prophets God sent to the Israelites after Moses, even though only one prophet is mentioned. The Israelites needed to hear from God, and Moses was telling them that God would send his prophets to give them his word. Verse 20 speaks of a false prophet of Israel as opposed to the good one mentioned in verses 15–19, suggesting that the good one refers to the good prophets of Israel.

However, during the 400-year intertestamental period, when no prophet arose among the Israelites, the idea began to grow that this passage was indeed talking about a single prophet who was to come. By the first century this prophecy was being given a messianic interpretation by numerous groups. So the people asked John the Baptist, "Are you the Prophet?" and John answered "No" (John 1:21). Twice the people identified Jesus as "the Prophet" (John 6:14; 7:40). Jesus himself may have been referring to this passage when he said, "If you believed Moses, you would believe me; for he wrote of me" (John 5:46). Peter and Stephen took our passage as a prediction about Jesus (Acts 3:22, 23; 7:37).

This seems to be another case of a prophecy that has near and far fulfillments. Some Old Testament prophecies have more than one fulfillment, some fairly near to the date of the prophecy and others later on. The classic case of this is the prediction about the abomination of desolation. This appeared first in Daniel (9:27; 11:31; 12:11) and was commonly believed to have been fulfilled with the desecration of the temple under the Syrian king Antiochus Epiphanes in 165 BC But Jesus used it to refer to the coming desecration and destruction of the temple (Matthew 24:15; Mark 13:14), which took place in

AD 70. Paul seems to carry this message even further to refer to "the man of lawlessness" (or abomination) we call the Antichrist (2 Thessalonians 2:3). In the same way the prophets fulfilled incompletely what Christ fulfilled completely.

In the Bible we have the phenomenon known as typology where a historical figure, event, or institution (called the type) foreshadows a later more marked manifestation (the antitype) of what the figure, event, or institution represents. The sacrificing of Isaac was a type of the perfect sacrifice of Jesus. In Hebrews 5—7 the King of Salem, Melchizedek, from Genesis 14 is a type of Christ who is the antitype. Similarly, Walter Kaiser suggests that it is possible to take each prophet as being a type of the final prophet who was to appear.[7]

There is a sense in which only Christ fulfills the prophecy about the prophet like Moses perfectly. God says that Moses is different from the other prophets: "Hear my words: If there is a prophet among you, I the LORD make myself known to him in a vision; I speak with him in a dream. Not so with my servant Moses. He is faithful in all my house. With him I speak mouth to mouth, clearly, and not in riddles, and he beholds the form of the LORD" (Numbers 12:6–8). Only Jesus had such intimate connection with God after Moses. And Jesus surpassed Moses in being the perfect embodiment of everything good about a prophet that Moses represented.

So we conclude that while this prophecy is initially fulfilled in the form of the Old Testament prophets, it is finally and perfectly fulfilled only in Jesus.

The False: Don't Fear Them (18:20–22)

False Prophecy and the Punishment for It (18:20)

Verse 20 says, "But the prophet who presumes to speak a word in my name that I have not commanded him to speak, or who speaks in the name of other gods, that same prophet shall die." In the second section of this chapter (on 18:9–14) we discussed the bad prophet—the one "who speaks in the name of other gods." In verses 20–22 we have described what is commonly called the false prophet, one "who presumes to speak a word in [God's] name that [he has] not commanded him to speak." Sixteen passages from the Old Testament and the New Testament refer to this kind of false prophet, indicating that despite this prohibition false prophets remained a serious problem for God's people.[8]

Prophets are different from preachers in that they give direct messages from God. This is shown by familiar formulas such as "Thus says the Lord," which appears over 400 times in the Bible, and "The word of the Lord came to," which appears about 100 times. Today we have the Scriptures in which are recorded those messages given by God that he deemed profitable to us (2 Timothy 3:16). We also still have people who prophesy a direct word from God to a situation, a person, or a group, as the New Testament amply bears witness.[9] I have personally encountered some such prophecies that have done specific good to God's people, giving them what has proved to be direction from God.

But it is also possible for people to say things that did not come directly from God and claim that they are prophecies. This is what is condemned here as being presumptuous. The word translated "presumes" means "to act arrogantly, be contemptuous."[10] False prophecy is arrogant because it disregards God's exclusive right to tell us what is absolutely binding on our lives. False prophets act with enormous arrogance by saying that something is from God that actually is from their own minds. Moses says of such, ". . . that same prophet shall die" (18:20). The harshest punishment possible is decreed for this because it is grave sin. Unlike in the theocratic nation of Israel, today we do not exact the death penalty for sins that are of a religious nature, such as false prophecy. Instead, we do things such as excommunication and discipline if such sins surface in the church. With false prophecy we would probably ban the person from further prophesying after repentance and require public confession if it was a public prophecy.

How to Test a Prophecy (18:21, 22a)

Moses goes on to explain how to tell whether or not a prophecy is authentic: "And if you say in your heart, 'How may we know the word that the LORD has not spoken?' — when a prophet speaks in the name of the LORD, if the word does not come to pass or come true, that is a word that the LORD has not spoken; the prophet has spoken it presumptuously" (18:21, 22a). Jeremiah 28:9 says, "As for the prophet who prophesies peace, when the word of that prophet comes to pass, then it will be known that the LORD has truly sent the prophet." This test of authenticity applies only to predictive prophecies. In Deuteronomy 13:1, 2 Moses says that the predictions of evil prophets also can come to pass. So there are other criteria for authenticity of prophets. Jeremiah 29:23 connects false prophecy with bad character. First Corinthians 14:29–34 speaks of procedural criteria for the exercise of the gift of prophecy. But the criterion given here in Deuteronomy is the fulfillment of the prophecy.

I did an Internet search under the topic "False Prophets." I heard and watched very famous preachers giving prophecies. One famous preacher prophesied that Fidel Castro would get sick and die in the 1990s and that

"Cuba will be visited of God" after his death. In 2011 Castro is still alive. In another clip, recorded sometime in 2000, this same preacher prefaced his comments with the words "I prophesy." He said that before the Syrian President Hafez al-Assad died, he would sign a peace treaty with Israel brokered by President Clinton. This would result in a huge world revival and in an increase in miraculous signs and prosperity. Several times during this statement he said that he was prophesying. Once he said, "I am not preaching, I am prophesying." He said that those who sow now will reap during the coming prosperity. Then, as a means of sowing, he urged his viewers to get to the phone and make a pledge (I presume) of a financial contribution to his ministry. Assad died that year, but no treaty was signed. This preacher is as popular as ever today.[11]

People love to hear exotic messages that make them feel good because they get a sense of being in touch with the supernatural. Sometimes the prophecy tells of some good thing that is going to happen. Sometimes it predicts a bad thing such as a catastrophe. But it feels good to have heard from God, to be in the center of God's powerful working among his people. In such situations prophecies could unwittingly become a means of giving Christians a kind of spiritual entertainment. Sadly, a lot of sincere Christians, who seriously desire to please God, fall into the trap of believing these false prophecies because the people who give them are respected and admired leaders in the church. When the prophecies do not come to pass, either they are conveniently forgotten or the prophet is forgiven for his lapse. But the Bible takes this as something far more serious.

One reason why false prophecy is so serious is that sincere people believe it despite the skepticism of unbelievers. They believe the prophecy because they believe in the supernatural. What if time after time statements claiming to be prophecies are not fulfilled? Soon skepticism could grow even among sincere Christians, and the door could open for a new era of liberalism in the church. When the things we accept because of our belief in the supernatural are proved to be a sham, some could conclude that belief in the supernatural itself is a sham. This buttresses what our passage says about taking a serious view of false prophecy without conveniently ignoring the issue.

Don't Be Afraid of False Prophets (18:22b)

Moses wraps us his comments on false prophets by saying, "You need not be afraid of him" (18:22b). This suggests that the real prophet must be feared. What is this fear? It is not the fear that some have for leaders because they are tyrannical, harsh, or demanding. It is the fear that one has for the representative of the God we fear. This God is holy, and it is a fearful thing to fall into his hands (Hebrews 10:31). Our fear is the fear of sinning, of doing things that go against the Word of God. As God's prophets proclaim that Word, we fear them in that sense. So the wicked, powerful, and brutal kings Ahab and Herod feared Elijah and John the Baptist respectively. We don't need to have such fear for people who do not act under the authority of the Lord of all creation.

One day when I was in my early teens I was extremely angry with my brother and had on a terrible face. Just at that time my pastor, the Rev. George Good, walked into our house. My angry face suddenly was transformed into an angelically gentle face. My pastor was a very godly man in whom I saw a lot of the nature of Christ. The sight of him made me so ashamed of my anger that my face automatically changed its appearance. A quick temper was a serious sin in my life before I committed my life to Christ in my teens and for a few years after that, too. I believe this incident had a part to play in the spiritual struggle that culminated in my looking to Christ for salvation. Since then I have never forgotten the impact that my pastor had—he was a mild-mannered and gentle individual, but I was afraid of sinning in his presence.

May our holiness be a source of fear for people. May our behavior challenge the sinful lifestyle of people who are living away from God. May our words be backed by an authenticity that causes people to fear to disregard them. This comes not by asserting our authority or by showing off our strength. It comes from people's sensing that we have come from the presence of God with his anointing. As for false prophets, they may seem to be powerful and influential, but we have no need to fear them.

The situation regarding the people who presented themselves as God's representatives in the early history of Israel was not much different from that which we have today. Today, too, we have the good, the bad, the best, and the false. Because our relationship with God is the most important thing in our lives, we must be very careful about what we do with those who claim to represent God. Those who are legitimate must be cared for, listened to, obeyed, and feared. The illegitimate ones must be roundly condemned and avoided.

43

Legal Protection for the Vulnerable

DEUTERONOMY 19:1–21

A JUST NATION MUST BOTH punish wrongdoers and protect the innocent. The Bible shows a concern for both these functions. And this is well illustrated in Deuteronomy 19. Moses gives guidelines for developing legal procedures to ensure that this is done. The particular emphasis here is on those who are vulnerable to undeserved punishment

Cities of Refuge for Involuntary Manslaughter (19:1–10)

Make Provision for the Vulnerable

The first vulnerable person mentioned is called a "manslayer" (19:3, 4, 6). Manslaughter has been defined as "the unlawful killing of a human being without express or implied malice."[1] Here's how Moses describes the situation: "If anyone kills his neighbor unintentionally without having hated him in the past . . . " (19:4b). The particular type of manslaughter described here is what is today called involuntary manslaughter. This is distinguished from voluntary manslaughter, which is "an unintentional killing of sudden heat or passion resulting from a provocation that palliated the offense, as when the person killed had grossly insulted, wronged, or quarreled with the slayer."[2] Involuntary manslaughter, on the other hand, takes place through negligence or through an accident. Moses gives an example of this kind of manslaughter: ". . . as when someone goes into the forest with his neighbor to cut wood, and his hand swings the axe to cut down a tree, and the head slips from the handle and strikes his neighbor so that he dies" (19:5a).

Once they take occupation of the land (19:1), Moses tells the people, ". . . you shall set apart three cities for yourselves in the land that the LORD your God is giving you to possess. You shall measure the distances and divide into three parts the area of the land that the LORD your God gives you as a possession, so that any manslayer can flee to them" (19:2, 3). Three cities have already been set apart by Moses in the land east of the Jordan (4:41–43). The cities mentioned here are in the land that they will occupy after crossing the Jordan. The land was regionally divided "into three parts," and cities were put in such a way that the whole population had a city within fleeing distance. If the city is not nearby, "the avenger of blood in hot anger [will] pursue the manslayer and overtake him, because the way is long, and strike him fatally, though the man did not deserve to die, since he had not hated his neighbor in the past" (19:6).

Note that Moses says, "If anyone kills his neighbor unintentionally without having hated him in the past" (19:4). Today we see a lot of staged "accidents." A person gets a vehicle to bang into the car of someone he wants to harm or silence. Brakes are tampered with; electrical shorts are engineered. This is the stuff out of which mystery novels are made. And it happens often and is effective in eliminating or silencing people. So Moses says we have to ensure that there had been no bad history between the two people.

Verse 6 talks of "the avenger of blood in hot anger [pursuing] the manslayer." Theoretically he should not be angry because it was an accident. But because these things happen in today's world, we must make provision for less ideal human reactions to them. The Bible, being a very practical book, makes provision to protect people who face uncontrolled rage over unintended hurt. The literal rendering of the Hebrew, which the ESV renders as "in hot anger" and the NIV translates as "in a rage," is "while his heart was hot" (ASV). The implication is that this rage might subside. But the initial shock of the death could trigger an extreme reaction. Provision is being made for those initial reactions.

Provision is made for this situation right at the start of their life in their new land. In the same way we need to have systems in place that enable the vulnerable to seek justice, especially when powerful people seem to be targeting them. If we do not have such a system in place, we need to set it up the moment the need is seen. Usually this happens when a situation arises that highlights the vulnerability of a person. For example, when there has been abuse of an employee by his or her supervisor, that person may not have any way to express the complaint unless a grievance procedure is in place. Procedures need to be in place and known by everyone so that those who are vulnerable to being treated unjustly have a way of recourse.

Moses once more presents the prospect of conquest in verse 8: "And if the LORD your God enlarges your territory, as he has sworn to your fathers, and gives you all the land that he promised to give to your fathers . . . " This time he adds that this blessing is contingent upon their obedience: ". . . provided you are careful to keep all this commandment, which I command you today, by loving the LORD your God and by walking ever in his ways" (19:9a). This is a common theme in Deuteronomy. Then he says that they should add three more cities if needed to ensure the safety of manslayers: ". . . then you shall add three other cities to these three, lest innocent blood be shed in your land that the LORD your God is giving you for an inheritance" (19:9b, 10a).

This paragraph ends with an ominous warning about not making provision for the adequate protection of manslayers, so that "innocent blood is shed in your land . . . and so the guilt of bloodshed be upon you" (19:10). When weak and innocent people suffer because their society has not made provision for their safety, the whole society shares in the guilt of the harm done.

Today, with the terrorist threat, those belonging to the same ethnic or religious group as the terrorists become automatic terrorist suspects. One of the sad results of the war on terror is racial profiling—when people of a race are treated with suspicion simply because of their race. Sadly, what happens then is that sometimes those who are opposed to terrorism are tempted to join the terrorists or at least to support them because of what they suffer at the hands of the law enforcement authorities. We must rise up in protest against this racial profiling.

The problem is a complex one because people can exploit Christians' trust in them to gain an entrance into societies and then perform the tasks assigned to them by the militant groups. Recently in Sri Lanka a pastor was found with a suicide bomb kit. He had gained the trust of the Christians and became a pastor of a thoroughly evangelical church while he was actually working for the terrorists. He attended a church camp that was held at the camp site run by our sister organization. This made the camp site a suspicious place, resulting in about 150 police personnel suddenly swooping in on the place while an evangelistic camp was being held and conducting a thorough search operation. Fortunately the police personnel acted politely during this operation.

The fact that the problems are complex does not condone the treatment of innocent people as if they were criminals. We had a staff worker who was in prison without charges for fifteen months. He was born in a town that had produced a lot of terrorists. The fact that the sovereign God used him to lead many to Christ in the prison and to have an amazing ministry there does not take away from the injustice of the situation. We have to be very careful to ensure that the way our war on terror is conducted does not provoke moderate peace-loving people to side with the terrorist option.

We must keep our eyes and ears open to finding out about the needs of the weak so that they are treated justly. Probably the leaders may not have occasion to observe them much. Then they should have others within the group who act as their eyes and ears. And the moment a shortcoming surfaces, immediate steps must be taken to remedy it. We usually delay, often stating practical and economic reasons for the delay. In God's sight such a delay is not tolerated.

A Widely Applicable Divine Principle

The principle of showing sympathy to a person who is responsible for such a deadly serious act as causing the death of a person accidentally is part of God's Law and thus represents God's way of thinking. Therefore, we could extend what lies behind this law and apply the principle to other situations also, for example, when a driver knocks down and kills a person, but he was not breaking a law or driving recklessly or under the influence of alcohol. The well-known American Baptist preacher George W. Truett (1867–1944) accidentally shot his friend J. C. Arnold, chief of police of Dallas, on a hunting trip when he was a relatively young preacher. The cause of death was listed as a heart attack, but Truett blamed himself for the death of his friend. Deeply depressed, Truett decided to leave the ministry, even though the shot was accidental. But the prayers of many, plus a vision of seeing Jesus vividly standing beside him, saying, "Be not afraid, George. You are my man from now on," pulled him through his doldrums. His biographer says his life took on a new sense of soberness and grief after that incident.[3]

This is part of the frustration that we face because we live in a fallen world, as Paul explained in Romans 8:18–24. He says, "The creation was subjected to futility [NIV, frustration]" as a result of the fall (Romans 8:20). Ecclesiastes expounds this idea in great depth. All of us have to face this frustration on earth, and one of the hardest things is when others suffer because of things we did unintentionally to them.

The Asylum Principle

It is the teaching of this passage that lies behind the asylum principle that is common today. *Asylum* is the word used today for giving refuge and protection to people who feel unfairly exposed to danger. Biblical Christians have God's heart of concern for those who fear that the law will not give them a fair chance. So throughout history churches have been open to accepting people who flee to them seeking asylum. Some seek asylum in a nation or an embassy of a nation on the grounds that their lives are in danger.

This principle could be extended to other situations as well. When the Nazis were exterminating the Jews, many so-called "righteous Gentiles" offered them refuge or helped them escape at great risk. In Sri Lanka, where there were racial riots, those in the majority community often hid vulnerable people in their homes. My wife and I have done this several times. My brother, Duleep, who is a pastor would go through the mob wearing his clerical collar, rescue people from places of danger, and bring them to his church. The mob had to spare him because of his profession! Many churches were transformed into refugee camps. The church must always be a haven for genuine asylum seekers.

False Asylum Seekers (19:11–13)

When there is a facility to help needy people, there will always be people not qualified to receive help who will abuse it. Then, as now, there were genuine asylum seekers and false ones. Moses says that those who committed premeditated murder will also try to find refuge in the cities of refuge: "But if anyone hates his neighbor and lies in wait for him and attacks him and strikes him fatally so that he dies, and he flees into one of these cities . . . " (19:11). The murder was premeditated; in today's legal language it would be called murder in the first degree. It thus earns the maximum sentence.

The elders of the murderer's city are responsible for bringing the person back from the city of refuge: ". . . then the elders of his city shall send and take him from there" (19:12a). Probably they also acted as magistrates and judged the case, for they are the ones who hand over the wrongdoer to the family members. Moses calls the receiving person "the avenger of blood": ". . . the elders of his city shall . . . hand him over to the avenger of blood, so that he may die" (19:12b). The sentence for premeditated murder is capital punishment.

In 17:7 Moses, speaking of the result of executing a wrongdoer, says, "So you purge the evil from your midst." Here capital punishment achieves a slightly different result. Moses says, "You shall purge the guilt of innocent blood from Israel, so that it may be well with you" (19:13). When a community permits an innocent person to be murdered, the whole community bears the guilt of that action. Until the murderer is punished, the community as a whole bears the guilt, and it will not go well with the community as it has broken God's Law.

When evildoers are not punished in a nation, the nation is committing a grave wrong that affects the whole community. Indeed, Christians forgive their enemies, but crime dishonors a nation; it lowers its stability and makes it a debtor with a debt that can be paid only by the wrongdoer being punished. Today in Sri Lanka we see corruption and violence going on unabated. The media highlight it for a few days, and sometimes those who report it are harassed and even killed. Then after a few days in the limelight, the crime is conveniently forgotten. This is not good for a nation. Therefore, the just need to do all they can to ensure that evildoers are punished. The failure to punish them makes the country into a guilty nation, a bad nation.

Verses 1–13 show us that among the key responsibilities of any society, especially of its law enforcement officers, are protecting the innocent and punishing the guilty. A society that fails to do either of these is a sick society. And God's people should do all they can to ensure that health is restored in the societies in which they live.

Annexing Land Belonging to Others (19:14)

The next vulnerable person to be protected is the person who is subject to the unscrupulous annexing of land by another. Moses says, "You shall not move your neighbor's landmark, which the men of old have set, in the inheritance that you will hold in the land that the LORD your God is giving you to possess (19:14)". God had apportioned land equitably to all the families of the nation. The landmark was usually a boundary stone. Because God had apportioned land according to an equitable system based on a formula of his choosing, "to move boundary stones and thus appropriate territory unlawfully was a crime of theft against God."[4] Of course, with time people sold their ancestral land. The boundaries were not going to last forever. Yet the history of this nation showed that greedy landowners used different unscrupulous methods to annex land belonging to the poor. Most of the references to this sin in the Old Testament are to the strong annexing land from the weak. So this, too, is a law to protect the vulnerable.

Later Moses asks the Levites to proclaim, "Cursed be anyone who moves his neighbor's landmark," to which the people are to respond with a hearty, "Amen" (27:17). Hosea said, "The princes of Judah have become like those who move the landmark; upon them I will pour out my wrath like water" (Hosea 5:10). Elijah is sent to King Ahab, after Queen Jezebel had Naboth killed and Ahab annexed Naboth's vineyard, with the message of a curse to Ahab and Jezebel for their crime (1 Kings 21:1–24). Proverbs 23:10, 11 warns that God will appear on behalf of those against whom this crime is committed:

"Do not move an ancient landmark or enter the fields of the fatherless, for their Redeemer is strong; he will plead their cause against you."

Despite all of this teaching in the Bible, this happens all the time. I know of a pastor who moved his boundary to annex a few square feet of land because of an inconvenience he had in his land. I know of a wealthy elder brother who took most of the family wealth, leaving his sister who was widowed early in life with very little. Many grownup siblings are angry with each other because they could not divide the family estate in a way that pleased everyone. Many are sad because they did not contest a greedy sibling who unfairly took what should have been theirs. It is amazing how many Christians throw away their Christian principles when it comes to property. They try to annex land that is not theirs even though the annexing is done unfairly. They stay on in rented houses even though their landlord really needs them to leave. People who seem to be very kind and devoted to God suddenly turn wicked when there is the prospect of gaining property. Let us heed the warning of God. He hates such actions, and those who do it are cursed!

Prevention of Victimization through False Witness (19:15–21)

More Than One Witness Required (19:15, 16)

Next, Moses presents some safeguards to prevent people from being the victims of false witnesses. We know that while the points here apply primarily to the theocratic nation of Israel, it can apply also to life in the body of Christ. When a person does not own up to an alleged sin, witnesses are needed. But Moses says that one witness is not sufficient. "A single witness shall not suffice against a person for any crime or for any wrong in connection with any offense that he has committed. Only on the evidence of two witnesses or of three witnesses shall a charge be established" (19:15). One reason for requiring more than one witness is the problem of having malicious witnesses. Moses says, "If a malicious witness arises to accuse a person of wrongdoing . . . " (19:16).

It is dangerous to have an unrepentant sinner among us. But it is also dangerous to make a righteous person the victim of a malicious person who makes false accusations about him or her. The law says that people can be convicted of a charge only if it can be demonstrated "beyond reasonable doubt" that the person is guilty. Sometimes the judge knows that a person is guilty, but he is acquitted because it cannot be proved beyond reasonable doubt. That is the risk one has to take in order to avoid being influenced by false accusations. In a Christian group, the leaders, after much prayer, have to leave it in the hands of the sovereign God to help them in a situation where sin is not proved.

However, if an accusation has been made, and there is at least a little sense that the person may be guilty, it might be necessary to ensure that this person is not kept in a position that would make him vulnerable to temptation in the area in which he was accused. For example, we must ensure that a person accused of child abuse is never left alone with children. If a man was accused of taking unnecessary liberties with young women, we need to ensure that his job does not require him to be alone with young women.

Diligent Inquiry (19:17, 18)

Moses says that when an accusation has been made, "then both parties to the dispute shall appear before the LORD, before the priests and the judges who are in office in those days" (19:17). Note how first it is said that they must bring the accuser and the accused before the Lord, and then it says that they appear before the priests and judges. The human authorities are acting on behalf of God. This can be directly applied to Christian groups, where those inquiring into the matter are actually representing God. Paul says that in a sense earthly rulers also are acting on behalf of God when they reward the good and punish wrongdoers (Romans 13:1–5). This shows what an awesome responsibility judging a case is.

Next Moses says, "The judges shall inquire diligently, and if the witness is a false witness and has accused his brother falsely . . . " (Deuteronomy 19:18). We cannot conduct these things hurriedly. We must make sure that wrong has actually been done, and what exactly has been done. I have found that in cases requiring discipline, sometimes people get impatient with the pace in which the process takes place. I have often had to tell people that even though they are convinced that the person has done wrong, we have to take precautionary measures and follow the process set down by the church to ensure that no injustice is done. Sometimes taking our time helps us think reflectively over the situation and come up with a wise and compassionate response.

Sudden decisions are sometimes flawed because those administering discipline have not fully considered all the factors that need to be considered. Sometimes a guilty person goes scot-free because the leaders were not willing to pay the price that a full inquiry requires. For the same reason, a false accusation may be upheld without a thoroughgoing inquiry. Of course, sometimes these processes are allowed to drag on too long (for example, the committee is unable to find a suitable date to meet). Because this is an urgent situation we cannot sit on it for too long.

When sin appears in society or a church or a Christian organization, it results in an enormous drain of resources. Usually most groups are short of leaders, and the few leaders there have to make a special effort to devote themselves to ensuring that a just decision is made over the wrong act. But that is part of the cost of being a responsible society, church, or organization. Sin is serious, and it should not be taken lightly; but those who are not guilty should not be accused wrongfully.

When False Accusations Are Accepted

Sadly, incorrect decisions are made in both church and society. These can be very damaging to the accused person. Though false condemnation is a really bad thing, those who are falsely accused must remember that great people of God have been falsely accused throughout the ages. They did it to our own Lord in a court of law (Matthew 26:59–61) and to some of his great servants such as Stephen (Acts 6:11–13) and Paul (Acts 16:20, 21; 17:5–7; 24:5; 25:7, 8).

It is particularly painful when the slander comes from within the church. This happened to Paul. But he did not give up on the church because of that. He believed in the unity of the body of Christ; he defended himself, so the unity of the body would be restored. This is why we have a lengthy defense of his ministry in some epistles like 2 Corinthians and Galatians.

Yet there is a limit to which we will go to vindicate our name. From prison Paul wrote that some "proclaim Christ out of rivalry, not sincerely but thinking to afflict me in my imprisonment." I am sure this must have hurt him greatly, but he says, "What then? Only that in every way, whether in pretense or in truth, Christ is proclaimed, and in that I rejoice" (Philippians 1:17, 18). We will, for the sake of unity and the honor of God, do all we can to clear wrong stories. Beyond that we will place the matter in God's hands and go on serving him, knowing that if we are faithful to him, even this will be finally turned into something good, and God will vindicate us in his time.

When William Booth's son Bramwell showed him an article attacking his father in the newspapers, the father said, "Bramwell, fifty years hence it will matter very little indeed how these people treated us; it will matter a great deal how we dealt with the work of God."[5] Our job is to be faithful, anticipating the Lord's "well done." Jesus said, "Blessed are you when others revile you and persecute you and utter all kinds of evil against you falsely on my account. Rejoice and be glad, for your reward is great in heaven, for so they persecuted the prophets who were before you" (Matthew 5:11, 12).

Punishment for False Witnesses (19:18b-20)

If it is established that "the witness is a false witness and has accused his brother falsely" (19:18b), he is to receive the same punishment that his victim would have received if he was guilty of that of which he was accused: ". . . then you shall do to him as he had meant to do to his brother" (19:19a). There's a huge warning here about making accusations against another. This is serious business—not something to be launched into without serious thought. I do not think we see this instruction of Moses being followed much today. He is saying that a person who falsely accused another of murder or adultery must be given the punishment given to a murderer or an adulterer. Of course, strictly speaking, Moses is talking here about perjury—that is, lying under oath in a legal setting. But this gives us a sense of how abhorrent all false witness is to God.

False witness seems to be one of the besetting sins of the evangelical movement. We spread stories about people based on hearsay or conclusions that we have drawn without insufficient evidence. Some Christians' approach to others is governed by their anger with the world. Possibly because of hurts they have received, they look at others as being bad and look for bad things to say about them. It may be a personality weakness, but we cannot excuse it, for the damage done is huge. We must warn them that they are treading on very dangerous ground.

Moses goes on to give the result of punishing the false witness: "So you shall purge the evil from your midst" (19:19b). False witness is a blot of evil in a society or group. It ruins harmonious fellowship; it makes the group unrighteous and unclean because it is a serious sin. Punishing the false witness purifies the group.

The punishment also has a deterrent effect on others. Verse 20 says, "And the rest shall hear and fear, and shall never again commit any such evil among you." Fear is often the result of punishment among God's people (Acts 5:5, 11; 1 Timothy 5:20). This is one way in which punishment or discipline purifies a society or church. It discourages a repetition of the sin. People who are accustomed to making accusations about others, and who enjoy doing so, would be provoked to ask, "What if I'm wrong?" Punishment brings a sense of urgency to the process of making accusations.

The Law of Retaliation (19:21)

Finally, Moses gives what is now known as *lex talionis* or the law of retaliation: "Your eye shall not pity. It shall be life for life, eye for eye, tooth for tooth, hand for hand, foot for foot" (19:21). The statement in this verse does two things. On the one hand, it leaves us with no room for overlooking this offense. On the other hand, it gives the maximum sentence. If one tooth was involved, only one tooth is required, not two! It is possible to overpunish a convicted person.

We tend to contrast *lex talionis* with Christ's statement in the Sermon on the Mount: "You have heard that it was said, 'An eye for an eye and a tooth for a tooth.' But I say to you, Do not resist the one who is evil. But if anyone slaps you on the right cheek, turn to him the other also" (Matthew 5:38, 39). Here Jesus seems to be abrogating the *lex talionis* principle. But we must remember that in the Sermon on the Mount Jesus is talking about personal revenge, not about legal systems. We need to forgive those who hurt us for our own healing from the hurts they inflict. We leave the repaying part to God to handle.

Paul's teaching on this topic includes three themes: blessing those who hurt us, leaving God to repay, and overcoming the hurt inflicted on us. He says, "Beloved, never avenge yourselves, but leave it to the wrath of God, for it is written, 'Vengeance is mine, I will repay, says the Lord.' To the contrary, 'if your enemy is hungry, feed him; if he is thirsty, give him something to drink; for by so doing you will heap burning coals on his head'" (Romans 12:19–21). In the next chapter Paul says that a government authority "is the servant of God, an avenger who carries out God's wrath on the wrongdoer" (Romans 13:4b). Deuteronomy 19:21 deals with the law of the land, not personal revenge. It is necessary for wrong to be punished in order to maintain the stability and justice in any country.

Conclusion: God's Commitment to Just National Structures

This study has focused on what we might call structural change. However committed to the needy we are, sometimes there are structural problems that would leave people vulnerable to disadvantages. This chapter has shown us that God wishes to have structures in society—and, by implication, in the church—that protect the vulnerable. Therefore, we should all be concerned for this, too. Every society in every age has its vulnerable people. We need to be alert to discover who these are and to be committed to ensuring that they are treated justly.

God may call some to go into professions that help bring about structural change in society. People in politics can help formulate legislation that ensures that justice is meted out to all. There is a glorious line of Biblical people who did this, such as Queen Esther (not strictly a politician) and William Wilberforce. Others could use their standing in society or the organizations they represent to push for reform—for example, Martin Luther King Jr. Journalists could publicize the injustices suffered by the vulnerable and the way guilty people go scot-free. Lawyers could defend the vulnerable, and police officers can ensure that the law is justly enforced. Let us pray that God will continue to raise up people who will go into these professions.

Let us also pray that churches and Christian groups would be known as places with a deep and consistent commitment to justice in all their dealings.

44

Rules for Warfare

DEUTERONOMY 20:1–20

PREPARING FOR WAR is necessary for any nation. God needed to give rules for the conduct of war for the new nation of Israel. When we go to war we do not discard Biblical principles. Military personnel cannot separate their religious life from their military life. For Christians, military life is part of their religious life. To us today this passage can play a dual role. It gives guidelines for the conduct of war, but it also gives guidelines on how we should face other battles that we face. The Christian life is often described using battle language (2 Corinthians 10:3, 4; Ephesians 6:10–18; 1 Timothy 6:12; 2 Timothy 4:7). We can learn something about God's approach to the battles we encounter in life by looking at his rules for war given in Deuteronomy 20.

Fighting a More Powerful Enemy (20:1)

The Bigness of the Opposition

Moses is aware that the enemies the Israelites face are, humanly speaking, more powerful than they are. He says, "When you go out to war against your enemies, and see horses and chariots and an army larger than your own, you shall not be afraid of them, for the LORD your God is with you, who brought you up out of the land of Egypt" (20:1). Horses and chariots were the pride of the great ancient Near-Eastern armies. They could produce a severe sense of inferiority among the Israelites who had no opportunity to acquire such resources during their wilderness wanderings.

In our personal and corporate lives we all face situations when we seem to be weak in comparison to the challenge we face. Organizations and churches face financial crises, battles with government officials and policies, internal dissent, insufficient personnel to carry out essential tasks, and organized opposition such as persecution or slander. Individuals face the opposition of jealous colleagues who have become their rivals, persecution from family members who do not follow Christ, slander by opponents of the unpopular stands they have taken, and a host of other hostile situations.

If we focus our attention primarily on the bigness of the opposition, we would lose heart and give up the project because of the odds that are stacked up against us. But here Moses gives some other things on which the people can focus.

Faith Is Strengthened by Experience

The people were not asked to exercise blind faith. Moses says, ". . . for the LORD your God is with you, who brought you up out of the land of Egypt" (20:1). God has acted on their behalf in history, and these actions of God give powerful testimony to his ability to help the people face any challenge, however big it may be. They have history on their side. As Peter Craigie says, "The strength of their God was not simply a matter of faith, but a matter of experience."

As slaves they overcame the mighty Egyptians by the strength of God. Consider that seemingly insignificant band of persecuted Christians in the first century, attacked by Jews and Gentiles, used by the Emperor Nero as scapegoats to take the blame for the great fires of Rome. Yet within three centuries Rome had bowed its knee to Christ without the use of any weapons of war by the Christians.

Deuteronomy often speaks of the inspiration of history for the life of faith. This is why church history and biography are so important. My ministry over the past thirty-five years in Youth for Christ and in our church has primarily been with first-generation Christians. They are often told that they belong to an insignificant, powerless, and despised minority in our country. They are told that they have forsaken the religion their people have followed for millennia for a new religion that has no good credentials in our nation. Because of that I use many illustrations from church history when preaching and teaching. Our people need to know that they are part of a glorious stream of history orchestrated by the Creator of the world.

Today there is skepticism in many circles about the value of history. People are more concerned about what is happening now. However, that could lead to great insecurity, especially among Christians. Our history gives us guidelines and hope as we look to the future. It is an important part of our identity. Neglecting it could result in a people who are unsure about themselves, lacking the stability needed to face the challenges of life.

God Is with Us: Immanuel

The key, of course, is that the God of history is the Lord our God and is with us. In the Hebrew, "God" here is *elohim*, the plural of *el*, and "with" is *im*. These two words are key roots for the word *Immanuel*. The idea of God being with his people to save them was coming into prominence. Later Isaiah would say, "Behold, the virgin shall conceive and bear a son, and shall call his name Immanuel" (Isaiah 7:14). And still later Matthew would write about the birth of Jesus: "'Behold, the virgin shall conceive and bear a son, and they shall call his name Immanuel' (which means, God with us)" (Matthew 1:23).

John G. Paton, a Scottish missionary to the New Hebrides Islands in the South Pacific (now called Vanuatu), was a heroic figure in missionary history. His first wife died as a result of problems developed during childbirth. Seventeen days later the child also died. This all happened very early in his missionary career, and he had no one to comfort him. He even had to dig the graves for his wife and child. But he says about that difficult time, "I was never altogether forsaken. The ever merciful God sustained me to lay the precious dust of my loved ones in the same quiet grave. But for Jesus, and the fellowship he vouchsafed me there, I must have gone mad and died beside that lonely grave!"[1] Even though, humanly speaking, he was all alone, Jesus was there giving him sufficient grace. That grace was sufficient for him to stay on among those people to reap a great harvest for the kingdom.

David said, "Some trust in chariots and some in horses, but we trust in the name of the LORD our God. They collapse and fall, but we rise and stand upright" (Psalm 20:7, 8). Our security is in God. We trust him and move forward to do what we know is his will. It is so easy for us to see our primary security as from earthly things. Because of the huge battle involved in coming to financial stability and prosperity, even Christians can make the securing of such earthly treasures their main aim in life. Then their primary sources of security are their wealth and property, their job and their bank balance. Some have no joy if they are deprived in those areas.

In over three decades of directing Youth for Christ I have seen some amazing provisions of finances for huge projects that we launched into with faith—not knowing where the money would come from, but knowing that God wanted us to do these things. Somehow the funds came, often at the very last moment. Now we have started budgeting; so we have to anticipate the income for the year ahead of us. It is easy to lose that sense of daring faith when we get organized like this. The budgeting is a necessary exercise, but we must never lose that sense of being small people doing big things for a great God. Hudson Taylor used to say that our life is a hand-to-mouth existence — from God's hand to our mouth! It is normal then for God's followers to feel small and insignificant in this world. That is because the world does not bring God into their thinking.

Religious Leaders Encourage Faith (20:2–4)

The next piece of advice has to do with the role of priests in the battles. It is the role of encouragement to go forward to victory trusting in God without losing heart. "And when you draw near to the battle, the priest shall come forward and speak to the people and shall say to them, 'Hear, O Israel, today you are drawing near for battle against your enemies: let not your heart faint. Do not fear or panic or be in dread of them, for the LORD your God is he who goes with you to fight for you against your enemies, to give you the victory'" (20:2–4). The people needed to be reminded that this was God's war. Priests often accompanied the Israelite army in wars, often carrying the ark of the covenant, which symbolized God's presence. When Jericho fell, seven priests went ahead blowing trumpets followed by the ark of the covenant (Joshua 6).

The priests were not experts at war, but they knew the ways of God. So they could apply God's truth to the challenge the people faced. Today, too, Christian leaders need to be with those they lead when they face a big challenge. Youth workers can visit young people before a big exam to pray for them and encourage them. Pastors can be with members before a job interview or a difficult confrontation. Drug rehab workers can advise and go to court when those they work with go on trial. About thirty years ago I took to the court a gang member who had come to our ministry at a time when he was a murder suspect. With such murders often the victim's relatives assassinate the suspects when they are brought to the court. To say that I was scared would be an understatement. But this person never forgot that I had gone with him to the court. He subsequently became a Christian, and all his children, who are now adults, went through Youth for Christ in their youth. A few weeks ago I met him, and he told me how he is trying to witness to his former fellow gang members.

The leader's task is to encourage faith when people are afraid. This is what the priest's speech does. The themes of fear and faith have been discussed earlier, especially in our study of 1:19–33. There we saw the implications of one of the affirmations made in that passage (1:30) that is found in this passage, too (20:4): God fights for us. In terms of a speech to encourage people, there are some key concepts here.

- There is an implicit *admission that the enemy is powerful*: ". . . let not your heart faint. Do not fear or panic or be in dread of them" (20:3b).
- The statement quoted above is an *exhortation not to be afraid*.
- There is *encouragement coming from the fact that God is with them* and is fighting for them: ". . . for the LORD your God is he who goes with you to fight for you against your enemies" (20:4a).
- The *hope of victory is presented*: ". . . to give you the victory" (20:4b).

People facing opposition or hardships are often tempted to move away from God's ways as they try to solve their problems. They are overwhelmed by the problems and see no light at the end of the tunnel. The leader's job is to direct them to look beyond the temporary reality, which may be all they see at that time, to the long-term reality of God's ultimate triumph over every situation. Their outlook changes, and they are encouraged to go on. Leaders can do this by giving a talk to a group of people or a personal word to an individual. I have always considered the talks that I give to the leaders and volunteers of the Youth for Christ ministry at our camps and convocations as among the most important things I do. Thus I am able to challenge the key members of our team to faithfulness to our call.

Sir Winston Churchill was one of the most heroic figures of the twentieth century. He was Prime Minister of the United Kingdom during the Second World War. His inspiring speeches broadcast over the radio were credited as a decisive influence for good during those difficult years. His most famous was a brief speech given to the House of Commons on May 13, 1940, three days after he assumed office. It is quite similar in scope to the talk that the priests are asked to give in Deuteronomy. Here is an excerpt:

> . . . I say to the House, as I have said to ministers who have joined this government, I have nothing to offer but blood, toil, tears and sweat. We have before us an ordeal of the most grievous kind. We have before us many, many long months of struggle and of suffering.
>
> You ask, what is our policy? I say: It is to wage war, by land, sea, and air. War with all our might and with all the strength that God has given us, and to wage war against a monstrous tyranny never surpassed in the dark and lamentable catalogue of human crime. That is our policy.
>
> You ask, What is our aim? I can answer in one word: It is victory. Victory at all costs—victory in spite of all terrors—victory, however long and hard the road may be, for without victory, there is no survival.
>
> Let that be realized. No survival for the British Empire, no survival for all that the British Empire has stood for, no survival for the urge, the impulse of the ages, that mankind shall move forward towards its goal.

> I take up my task with buoyancy and hope. I feel sure that our cause
> will not be suffered to fail among men. I feel entitled at this juncture, at
> this time, to claim the aid of all and to say, "Come, then, let us go forward
> together with our united strength."[2]

When some leaders address their people, they miss the visionary motivation that is seen in Churchill's speech. They remind them of the rules of the group and the duties they are responsible to perform. They rebuke them for their shortcomings and give instructions about how things need to be done. All this is necessary, but without visionary motivation to move forward in God's power to do the wonderful things God has called them to do, they will lose their motivation. As people get bogged down in their particular corners doing their little things, they can lose sight of the grand vision that the little things they do contribute toward achieving. The leader's job is to place this grand vision before the people and to spur them on to do great things for God.

Trimming Scarce Resources (20:5–8)

Verses 5–8 may seem strange to many people. After the rousing call to arms there is a deliberate trimming of the troops! After talking about the fact that the enemy army is greater than their army, the officers (possibly representing the different tribes — see 1:15) are to work on reducing the size of the Israelite army. Because this is the Lord's battle, size is not a problem. Unsuitable soldiers would be a problem, for they might fail to carry out God's wishes; so they must be excluded.

Allowance for Domestic Responsibilities (20:5–7)

First, those who have built new houses are mentioned. "Then the officers shall speak to the people, saying, 'Is there any man who has built a new house and has not dedicated it? Let him go back to his house, lest he die in the battle and another man dedicate it'" (20:5). Next come vine-growers: "And is there any man who has planted a vineyard and has not enjoyed its fruit? Let him go back to his house, lest he die in the battle and another man enjoy its fruit" (20:6). Then there is one who engaged to be married (actually already registered, using our terminology) but is not yet living with his wife: "And is there any man who has betrothed a wife and has not taken her? Let him go back to his house, lest he die in the battle and another man take her" (20:7).

Clearly domestic responsibilities are important to God. Actually not only does this paragraph speak of responsibility, it talks about enjoyment of family matters. The person who planted a new vineyard should be able to "enjoy its fruit." The person betrothed should go to his wife. Later we are told that this

freedom from war is for a whole year: "He shall be free at home one year. . . ."
And why? ". . . to be happy with his wife whom he has taken" (24:5).

Sometimes in the business world and even in the church the goals of an organization are so important that people are expected to neglect their families in order to contribute to fulfilling those goals. Many great pioneers blazed new trails for the gospel but left behind a trail of unhappy spouses and children. Some of these hurt children have written books about their pain. Some of these pioneers themselves have confessed at the end of their lives that they were wrong to neglect their families.

In our goal-oriented society we need to remember that for a Christian a happy home where each one does his or her part and love each other is an important goal. This idea may not be easy to sustain in a society where many measure success by standards that are different than Christian standards. One of the saddest aspects of our ministry with poorer youths in Youth for Christ in Sri Lanka has been seeing the many youths whose lives have been badly scarred as a result of their mothers leaving them with relatives and going abroad as housemaids to earn money for the family. That seemed to be the only way they could get out of grinding poverty. But the children end up insecure, often thirsting for attention and seeking it in the wrong way. Some are abused by relatives. A large percentage of those who come to our drug rehabilitation program have experienced their mothers' living abroad during their childhood.

Parents know of these terrible results. We have tried to advise Christians not to go abroad for employment alone after getting married. But the prospect of economic advancement is so great that they are willing to take the risk. When we are so engrossed in one field of activity (which may in itself be a good field), it is easy to forget other important areas of our life. The urgent displaces the important until the important is totally ignored.

This is a selfish world where many people try to get away with doing the minimum amount of work. Will this strong emphasis on family responsibilities result in many shirking their duties elsewhere? We are finding that this is getting to be a bigger problem with the newer generation of workers than before. We have come to realize that we need more measurable indicators of the work one did (such as reports) than before, to ensure that people do their work properly. We must teach people that working hard is a Christian trait. And we must also teach them that as Christians they must care for their families while they work hard at their jobs and ministries. In fact, that may be their cross. It is easy to do one or the other. Doing both is the challenge.

I have seen situations where our leaders were insensitive to the needs of the spouses of some of our young male staff early in their married life and insisted that they should come for a YFC event when they wanted to be at home with their spouse on a special day such as a birthday. They obeyed, but the wife was wounded, and the wounds kept surfacing, often for many years, in times of crisis. Sometimes when the spouse is not excited about the ministry, people may even leave their call and go to something else to please their spouse, even though they know this was not their original call.

Perhaps we need to say a word about statements of Jesus that suggest that if we do not follow instantly when he calls us because of family responsibilities, we are not worthy of being his disciples. We saw this with the three men who refused the invitation to the banquet because they had bought a field, purchased five yoke of oxen, or married a wife (Luke 14:18–20). Then there was the would-be follower of Jesus who wanted to bury his father and the other who wanted to say good-bye to his family before coming to follow Christ (Luke 9:59–61). In each case their reason was rejected by Christ.

These passages have to do with discipleship, not with family responsibility. Jesus must be the sole Lord of our lives. As he said:

> Whoever loves father or mother *more than me* is not worthy of me, and whoever loves son or daughter *more than me* is not worthy of me. And whoever does not take his cross and follow me is not worthy of me. Whoever finds his life will lose it, and whoever loses his life for my sake will find it. (Matthew 10:37–39)

But Jesus also said that we must care for our families. He condemned those who tried to overcome their responsibilities to their parents by using a loophole in the Law (Matthew 15:3–6). Paul said, "But if anyone does not provide for his relatives, and especially for members of his household, he has denied the faith and is worse than an unbeliever" (1 Timothy 5:8). We care for our family as part of being believers. However, if the family gets in the way of our being faithful to Christ, then Christ has to be chosen over the family.

Allowance for Natural Timidity (20:8)

Next, Moses says that those who are timid should not join the army to go to battle: "And the officers shall speak further to the people, and say, 'Is there any man who is fearful and fainthearted? Let him go back to his house, lest he make the heart of his fellows melt like his own'" (20:8). People who are totally committed to God may be fearful and fainthearted with regard to certain challenges. They should be given other work to do. God knows our weaknesses; he will not ask us to do things for which we are not suited.

Sometimes God will surprise us by giving us amazing ability to face certain challenges that seem beyond us. But generally he will call us in keeping with our giftedness. I had a colleague who fearlessly served God in the war zone in Sri Lanka for fifteen years and did a heroic ministry there. But if he is responsible for organizing a big program he is a bundle of nerves. I had another colleague who thrived with big programs and bravely blazed some new daring trails for the gospel. But he was very scared about going to the war zone. The Bible is aware of human frailty and makes allowance for that. This is why patience is such an important Christian virtue.

Moses gives a reason for not including the fearful and fainthearted person: "Let him go back to his house, lest he make the heart of his fellows melt like his own" (20:8b). A fearful person, a grumbler, or one who does not agree with the basic plan can affect the morale of the whole group. A group needs to discuss the issues with dissenters and work hard to get unity. This can be a very time-consuming activity. But it is well worth it. Those who once disagreed may join in despite personal reservations because they are part of the group and their ideas were thoroughly considered. They might even end up the most enthusiastic workers.

We must always leave room for people to talk about their problems and fears. But a person with an overwhelmingly negative attitude can ruin a group. Negativity can be a ragingly infectious disease. There will always be weaknesses even in the best of groups under the best leaders. We must learn to work with the weaknesses. But a negative person can focus so much on the negative aspects that everyone in the group also suddenly focuses on the negative. The result is that the urgency and excitement over doing something significant can leave the group.

Often people are not motivated because they are in the wrong place, which is what this verse is actually saying. In Youth for Christ we have found that some of our volunteers who met Christ in our ministry lose their excitement over youth ministry after a time. They have passed the age of enjoying the crazy things we do with teenagers. They cannot stand the loud music that the youth love. They communicate the message that the YFC program needs to graduate to something more "serious" and "mature." It is not YFC that needs to graduate but those people. Though they met Christ in our ministry, the time is ripe for them to devote themselves to another kind of ministry.

God will provide the right people to do his work. We should not push unsuitable people to do work that they are not suited to do. When we lack people, we trust God to send the right people, do all we can to compensate, and leave the rest to God. But we do not force unwilling and unsuitable people to stay. Everything we do should be what God calls us to do. If someone is not called for something, we should not push that person to do that work.

God Works with Small Groups

Working with a small group to overcome big challenges is something God has done often. This is what happened with Gideon whose army, soon to battle powerful enemies, was reduced to a mere 300 men (Judges 7, 8). David is an example of this as he challenges Goliath. He asks, "For who is this uncircumcised Philistine, that he should defy the armies of the living God?" (1 Samuel 17:26). He volunteers, and when they try to put Saul's armor on him, he finds he cannot use it (1 Samuel 17:38, 39). So he goes with five smooth stones and a sling. Goliath fumes, "Am I a dog, that you come to me with sticks?" and curses David by his gods (17:43). Then come David's memorable words:

> You come to me with a sword and with a spear and with a javelin, but I come to you in the name of the LORD of hosts, the God of the armies of Israel, whom you have defied. This day the LORD will deliver you into my hand, and I will strike you down and cut off your head. And I will give the dead bodies of the host of the Philistines this day to the birds of the air and to the wild beasts of the earth, that all the earth may know that there is a God in Israel, and that all this assembly may know that the LORD saves not with sword and spear. For the battle is the LORD's, and he will give you into our hand. (1 Samuel 17:45–47)

In the discussion on Deuteronomy 5:7–10, we quoted a statement from Hudson Taylor: "All God's giants have been weak men, who did great things for God because they reckoned on God being with them."[3] This is a theme that appears often in the Bible. God assured Zerubbabel, "Not by might, nor by power, but by my Spirit, says the LORD of hosts" (Zechariah 4:6). Paul said, "But we have this treasure in jars of clay, to show that the surpassing power belongs to God and not to us" (2 Corinthians 4:7). Again he said, "God chose what is foolish in the world to shame the wise; God chose what is weak in the world to shame the strong; God chose what is low and despised in the world, even things that are not, to bring to nothing things that are, so that no human being might boast in the presence of God" (1 Corinthians 1:27–29).

Specific War Rules (20:9–20)

The next few verses are so specific to Israel's wars that we will not make many applications from them to our life in the present. After the officers have spoken about who should be excluded from the army before a battle, Moses says, ". . . commanders shall be appointed at the head of the people" (20:9). These "commanders" were probably heads of army units.

Verses 10–15 describe wars with "cities that are very far from" the Israelites that they will not inhabit (20:15). Moses says, "When you draw near to a city to fight against it, offer terms of peace to it" (20:10). The assumption is that these cities will be defeated if they enter into battle. So this offer of peace is actually "the terms of a vassal treaty" (Craigie). This helps us understand the somewhat puzzling next verse: "And if it responds to you peaceably and it opens to you, then all the people who are found in it shall do forced labor for you and shall serve you" (20:11). Craigie explains, "If the city accepted the terms, it would open its gates to the Israelites, as a symbol of surrender and to grant the Israelites access to the city; the inhabitants would become vassals and would serve Israel." This is a humane response in comparison to what was done in those days. Often vassals were subjected to great humiliation and brutality.[4]

If this offer of peace is not accepted, the Israelites are to besiege the city (20:12). After God gives this city into their hand, they are to "put all its males to the sword" (20:13). This was standard practice in wars at that time. So was the practice of taking plunder: "but the women and the little ones, the livestock, and everything else in the city, all its spoil, you shall take as plunder for yourselves. And you shall enjoy the spoil of your enemies, which the LORD your God has given you" (20:14). This enjoyment of the plunder, however, did not include the raping of women, which was, and sadly still is, common in war. Deuteronomy 21:10–14 presents a procedure for the respectful treatment of women who have been captured.

The Geneva Conventions were formulated in the last century to deal with treatment of prisoners of war and non-combatants. Long before that, Deuteronomy presents a convention that is markedly different from the inhumane treatment of such people by most military powers of the time.

Verses 16–18 are about the treatment of nations in lands that are going to be occupied by Israel. What we have here is a summary of chapter 7. Everything that breathes in those lands is to be completely destroyed. We have discussed this difficult concept in our study of chapter 7.

The chapter closes with a note about the treatment of trees. It was the practice of military powers in those days, and sometimes even now, to destroy all the trees in battle areas. That should not be done, says Moses (20:19). Instead, they can use the edible fruit of the trees and perhaps cut down trees not used for food if necessary to "build siegeworks against the city" (20:20). Moses asks, "Are the trees in the field human, that they should be besieged by you?" (20:19c). The battles in a war are against human opponents, not against morally neutral nature. Trees must be protected because they have an important God-given role to play in the health of creation.

Long before the development of "green theology," Deuteronomy advocated the conservation of trees, even though military powers of the time showed no concern for this. This problem persists today. J. A. Thompson says, "Had this law been observed by invaders throughout the centuries Palestine today would not be so denuded of trees." Christians today should have nothing to do with the illicit felling of trees that takes place and should not encourage that by purchasing furniture made from wood from these trees. They should also support legislation that promotes the protection of the forests that are so important for a healthy land. This is an urgent problem in the developing world.

So all our battles should be done using God's principles. We've all heard the statement that all is fair in love and war. Christians reject that idea for love and also for war!

45

Respect for Life and Land

DEUTERONOMY 21:1–23

CHAPTERS 21—25 have a miscellaneous selection of laws that are difficult to classify topically in the order in which they appear. Laws from different spheres of life are placed next to each other. It is difficult to come up with titles for the expositions on these chapters. For chapter 21 I am following David Payne who sees the theme of respect for life and land permeating the chapter. People are important, and so is the land. Therefore, we must not permit people or the land to be defiled. And if defilement has taken place, steps must be taken to purge the land or the people of it.

Atonement for Unsolved Murders (21:1–9)

The Proceedings (21:1–8)

The first section in this chapter has to do with a procedure to deal with unsolved murders committed outside city limits: "If in the land that the LORD your God is giving you to possess someone is found slain, lying in the open country, and it is not known who killed him . . . " (21:1). Presumably, efforts must be taken to investigate the murder before it is agreed that they do not know who the murderer is. However, the land has been polluted by a crime, and though the people are not individually responsible for the murder, the community bears the responsibility for this death. So a procedure is put in place to make atonement for the crime, that is, "to eliminate the bloodguilt created by the crime."[1]

First, the national officials act: ". . . your elders and your judges shall come out, and they shall measure the distance to the surrounding cities" (21:2). Their job is to find the closest city to the place where the body is found. After that the local authorities of that city enter the scene: "And the elders of the city that is nearest to the slain man shall take a heifer that has never been worked and that has not pulled in a yoke" (21:3). The heifer, which has not been contaminated by humans, will be taken to a valley and water that is similarly uncontaminated: "And the elders of that city shall bring the heifer down to a valley with running water, which is neither plowed nor sown" (21:4a). This would make the conditions ideal for a sacrifice, but what is offered is not a blood sacrifice. The animal is killed in a different way: ". . . and shall break the heifer's neck there in the valley" (21:4b). This reenacts the murder.[2]

Next "the priests, the sons of Levi, shall come forward, for the LORD your God has chosen them to minister to him and to bless in the name of the LORD, and by their word every dispute and every assault shall be settled" (21:5). Their three-pronged role is portrayed well here. First, they lead public worship, including the offering of sacrifices: "God has chosen them to minister to him." Second, they pronounce blessings: ". . . to bless in the name of the LORD." Third, they have a judicial role: ". . . and by their word every dispute and every assault shall be settled." They are God's representatives to the people and the people's representatives to God.

The elders of the city also come representing the people: "And all the elders of that city nearest to the slain man shall wash their hands over the heifer whose neck was broken in the valley, and they shall testify, 'Our hands did not shed this blood, nor did our eyes see it shed'" (21:6, 7). They wash their hands in "a public ritual of declaring innocence,"[3] just like Pilate tried to do in the trial of Jesus (Matthew 27:24). In a solemn ceremony such as when an oath is taken, they declare that they really did not know who had done the crime. There has been no cover-up.

Purging the Land of Blood Guilt (21:8, 9)

While they were themselves not guilty of the crime, the community had to shoulder the responsibility for it since it had happened among their people. There was guilt in their midst that needed to be purged. So they pray for atonement, that is, for forgiveness and reparation for the crime: "Accept atonement, O LORD, for your people Israel, whom you have redeemed, and do not set the guilt of innocent blood in the midst of your people Israel, so that their blood guilt be atoned for" (21:8). The act is viewed as a purging of the land of blood guilt: "So you shall purge the guilt of innocent blood from your midst, when you do what is right in the sight of the LORD" (21:9).

In neighboring nations magical and superstitious rites were done under similar circumstances to ward off bad luck from an unsolved murder. In the Bible the issue is purging the guilt of innocent blood from the people. The fact that they did not know who did it did not take away their responsibility because of the Biblical understanding of community solidarity, which is a strong emphasis in Deuteronomy (see our discussions on 5:3–5; 9:16, 17; 15:2, 3).

This passage shows us how important it is for a nation to deal adequately with crime. Crime dishonors a nation; it makes it guilty and unclean. To ignore it would be to degrade the nation, thus proclaiming that in this nation goodness is not good, important, and valued and that evil is not evil. An individual act of evil harms some people and as such is an act against the society. But the ignoring of an act of evil is a serious violation of what is good in a society. It says that justice is not important. It leaves the society filthy and vulnerable to serious aberrations of justice. So in a sense ignoring a crime may be more serious than the crime itself.

The Seriousness of Taking a Life

All national legal systems agree, at least in theory, that all murder is serious because it takes the life of a human being. Our passage emphasizes this fact in no uncertain terms by affirming that if a life is taken, something must be done to purge the society of blood-guilt even if the murderer is not found. Nothing is said about the person who has been killed. He may have been a good person or a bad person. But that is beside the point. Murder is not permitted. We remember the terrifying words of God to Cain after he killed Abel: "What have you done? The voice of your brother's blood is crying to me from the ground" (Genesis 4:10). If a nation permits capital punishment, as Israel did, then the verdict must be arrived at and the sentence carried out only after a diligent inquiry involving the testimony of sufficient credible witnesses (see our discussion on Deuteronomy 19:15–21).

How scandalous it is that life is so cheap in our supposedly sophisticated and advanced world today! "Undesirable" humans are eliminated, and only a few people rise up in protest. Perhaps the most shocking fact is the millions of unborn children who are eliminated through abortion annually. I looked at some websites for reasons why women have abortions. Here's one statement based on studies from the famed pro-choice Guttmacher Institute: "The vast majority of abortions are elective. Women generally decide to have an abortion because of economic or other personal reasons. Approximately ten to fifteen thousand abortions terminate pregnancies which resulted from rape or incest each year. This is on the order of 1% of all abortions."[4] Here's something from a publication of the Guttmacher Institute itself: "The reasons women give for having an abortion underscore their understanding of the responsibilities of parenthood and family life. Three-fourths of women cite concern for or responsibility to other individuals; three-fourths say they cannot afford a child; three-fourths say that having a baby would interfere with work, school or the ability to care for dependents; and half say they do not want to be a single parent or are having problems with their husband or partner."[5] A pro-life website compiling statistics from pro-choice publications reports, "1% of all abortions occur because of rape or incest; 6% of abortions occur because of potential health problems regarding either the mother or child, and 93% of all abortions occur for social reasons (i.e., the child is unwanted or inconvenient)."[6]

Extrajudicial killings have become commonplace in many places today. In some countries law enforcement authorities eliminate street children. In my part of the world some underworld figures are eliminated by the police because they find it impossible to bring them to justice. Other underworld people do favors for influential politicians, and when they are arrested the politicians apply pressure for their release. Many police personnel oblige, knowing there would be severe consequences if they refuse. Political enemies are killed by paramilitary groups supporting governments. So are human rights activists and journalists. This is wrong! It pollutes a nation with blood-guilt, it silences voices needed for the health of a nation, and it leads a nation to moral degradation. Martin Luther King Jr. made this famous statement in his Nobel Peace Prize lecture:

> Violence as a way of achieving racial justice is both impractical and immoral. I am not unmindful of the fact that violence often brings about momentary results. Nations have frequently won their independence in battle. But in spite of temporary victories, violence never brings permanent peace. It solves no social problem: it merely creates new and more complicated ones. Violence is impractical because it is a descending spiral ending in destruction for all. It is immoral because it seeks to humiliate the opponent rather than win his understanding: it seeks to annihilate rather than convert. Violence is immoral because it thrives on hatred rather than love. It destroys community and makes brotherhood impossible. It leaves society in monologue rather than dialogue. Violence ends up defeating itself. It creates bitterness in the survivors and brutality in the destroyers.[7]

Christians must raise their voices whenever the value of human life is cheapened.

Respect for Captured Women (21:10–14)

Treat the Woman with Respect

When we first read the next section, it looks like Moses is advocating the ill-treatment of captured women. But the intent of these instructions is exactly the opposite. This law is written in the interests of captive women and seeks to restrict the power of victorious soldiers.[8] Moses describes a familiar scenario: "When you go out to war against your enemies, and the Lord your God gives them into your hand and you take them captive, and you see among the captives a beautiful woman, and you desire to take her to be your wife . . . " (21:10, 11).

After a war captives were taken and brought back to the victorious nation. But this paragraph is about what happens when a soldier falls in love with a woman and wishes to marry her. First, the woman needed to be adopted into Israelite society.[9] This is what is meant by what Moses says next: ". . . and you bring her home to your house, she shall shave her head and pare her nails. And she shall take off the clothes in which she was captured and shall remain in your house" (21:12, 13a). Perhaps this is how we can reconcile this passage with Ezra 10:18–44 where intermarriage with people of other nations is severely condemned and dealt with in the harshest terms. Moses is not encouraging religious intermarriage here, though he approves interracial marriage as long as the person becomes a follower of God, like the Israelites.

The taking of a wife must not be an impulsive action of lust. Moses says, ". . . and shall remain in your house and lament her father and her mother a full month. After that you may go in to her and be her husband, and she shall be your wife" (21:13b, c). She must be allowed to mourn for the deaths in her family. Only after that can they truly become man and wife. This is not what we see happening today. Male soldiers rape women at will all over the world. Soldiers have power, and there is a close connection between physical power and giving in to lust. When soldiers know they have the power to abuse a women to satisfy their lusts, they find the opportunity irresistible. This kind of behavior is roundly condemned by decent society everywhere today, even though it still happens frequently. But in those days there was no such talk about the human rights of captive women. Moses' recommendation here is a revolutionary departure from prevailing practice. Captive women who are "taken" (21:10) by men must be treated just as if they were respectable women in their own nation.

What if they do not want to go with this man? We are not told what happens in such a situation, possibly because it rarely happened in those days. Women generally complied when a man was proposed to them. Actually, the proposal would have first been made to the parents of the woman. It could well be that if the woman absolutely refused to marry the man she was given the freedom to free herself from this marriage. But we are not told anything about that here. What we are told is that the woman must be treated with dignity. Thankfully in most parts of the world today the woman has a say in the choice of a husband. This development could be traced in part to the dignity that the gospel gave to women by treating them as equal in status to men.

Next, Moses envisages a situation where the man changes his mind: "But if you no longer delight in her, you shall let her go where she wants. But you shall not sell her for money, nor shall you treat her as a slave, since you have humiliated her" (21:14). Again the concern is for the woman. The man could not take advantage of her and sell her as a slave. Instead he must release her as a free woman to decide what she will do with her life. Chris Wright summarizes the teaching of this paragraph: ". . . the physical and emotional needs of the woman in her utter vulnerability are given moral and legal priority over the desires and claims of the man in his victorious strength."

The Abuse of Power Today

Whenever we are in a situation where we have power over someone, we face the strong temptation to abuse that power. All of us could have the tendency to abuse power in order to feed our egos and overcome our insecurities. The exploitation of a helpless person who is at our mercy does something to boost (only temporarily) our sense of importance and significance.

Many years ago I read the terrible story of a Nazi concentration camp (I think it was Treblinka). One of the most brutal Nazi officers there was an ordained Christian minister. He lost his self-control in the environment of abusing power and lost his soul in the process.

Earlier we mentioned John Newton, a former slave trader who became an Anglican priest and campaigner against the slave trade, best known for his hymn "Amazing Grace." He viewed the day of his first commitment to Christ as "the hour I first believed." But he did not at first give up his involvement in slave trading ships after becoming a Christian. There was a short period after his conversion when he went back to the sins of his old life. When confronted with the environment of men abusing helpless women, he joined the others and was involved in terrible abuse himself. Thankfully he moved away from this life completely and became a great instrument for God in Britain.[10]

Some Christian men have been known to exploit the vulnerability of women subordinates. They make off-color jokes in their presence. They make provocative statements of a sexual nature. They touch them where they should not. And some even go into more overt physical acts of a sexual nature.

Recently we have seen many examples of politicians with much power who have exploited young female interns sexually. Sadly, some interns comply either in their search for affection or pleasure or in the hope that this may increase their chances of vocational advancement.

All of us have insecurities that can take the form of abusing power because that makes us feel good for a moment. We must remember three things when confronted with the possibility of abusing power in a way that degrades another. First, we must remember that the abuse of power is wrong and shameful. Second, we must remember that such abuse only serves to increase rather than decrease our sense of insecurity, for we are rebelling against that which gives us real security—our standing before God. Third, we must strive to fully apprehend our security in the identity and significance that we have as princes and princesses of the Heavenly King. Given our natural insecurities it will take more than a lifetime to fully possess this treasure. Only in Heaven will we be fully rid of our insecurities. In the meantime we will pursue the joy of living under the smile of the Creator of the universe.

Fairness in Handing Down One's Inheritance (21:15–17)

The next law represents the respect a husband with more than one wife must show to the wife he dislikes and to her son. We showed in our discussion on 17:17 that while there is a concession to polygamy in the Old Testament, it is not presented as the ideal and that in fact usually it is mentioned in terms of the problems associated with it, as is the case here. The problem addressed in this paragraph arises when "a man has two wives, the one loved and the other unloved, and both the loved and the unloved have borne him children, and if the firstborn son belongs to the unloved . . . " (21:15).

In many parts of the ancient Near East the firstborn son received a double share of his father's property,[11] though the Bible gives some exceptions to this rule—such as Isaac and Ishmael and Jacob and Esau. Moses says:

> Then on the day when he assigns his possessions as an inheritance to his sons, he may not treat the son of the loved as the firstborn in preference to the son of the unloved, who is the firstborn, but he shall acknowledge the firstborn, the son of the unloved, by giving him a double portion of all that he has, for he is the firstfruits of his strength. The right of the firstborn is his. (21:16, 17)

Craigie points out that the extreme situation of a husband loving one wife and hating (that is what the Hebrew word means) the other is presented here "in order to anticipate thereby all potential situations, many of which might be expected to be less acute."

This law is given to guard against letting natural inclinations and emotional feelings get the better of us in dealing with the rights of people. We may feel like doing some things to some people because we like them, and thereby we could deprive others of their legitimate rights. As one commentator wrote, "Justice must not bend to personal like or dislike. Amid divided affections and divided authority, God and not caprice must rule."[12] This shows us why it is good always to have principles behind the things we do, especially when it comes to giving to others. We are bound by what James Orr calls "the duty of doing always what is right, whatever the bent of our private inclinations."[13]

This applies to other kinds of leadership too. Leaders like some and dislike others. But they cannot take their personal inclinations into account when recognizing and rewarding people for their services. When leaders act rightly in this regard, a certain stability and security comes to the group. Though there may be some temporary hurt, the people will realize that this group operates on principles, not on the likes and the dislikes of the leaders.

Protecting the Land from Rebellious Sons (21:18–21)

The next command would surprise many today. It has to do with "a man [who] has a stubborn and rebellious son who will not obey the voice of his father or the voice of his mother, and, though they discipline him, will not listen to them" (21:18). If the earlier command had to do with parents respecting the rights of a son, this one has to do with sons respecting the honor of his parents. Honoring parents is such an important aspect of the covenant community that one of the Ten Commandments is about it (5:16). Notice that the son referred to here has been warned and disciplined, but he continues to be stubborn and rebellious.

They have tried everything; but now he is a threat to society, so they must go to the state authorities to see what can be done: ". . . then his father and his mother shall take hold of him and bring him out to the elders of his city at the gate of the place where he lives, and they shall say to the elders of his city, 'This our son is stubborn and rebellious; he will not obey our voice; he is a glutton and a drunkard'" (21:19, 20). The city gate was the civic center of the city where public business was done. Clearly this is not a simple case of a "naughty boy" with whom the parents are frustrated. He has become a threat to society. He has violated one of the key features of the covenant lifestyle that go into making a stable society—respect for parents. Implied here is that he has also broken the laws of the land. We see later that the death penalty is decreed, which was done only for very serious wrongs. This is why verse 21 describes the act as purging evil from their midst. After trying to do all they can, the parents realize that they have to take the painful step of handing their son over to the authorities.

Moses' account does not go into all the details of what happens. But verse 21a says, "Then all the men of the city shall stone him to death with stones." Before that step is taken there would have been a careful examination of the case. In our studies of chapters 17 and 19 we saw how diligent inquiries are conducted to ensure that justice is served. But if the elders agree that the country has been seriously polluted by this person's behavior, then he must be put to death. Moses says of this action, "So you shall purge the evil from your midst" (21:21b). The result is: ". . . and all Israel shall hear, and fear" (21:21c). We have often discussed how fear of sin and its consequences is a key to a healthy lifestyle (see the discussions on 5:29; 6:2, 3; 10:12, 13). A healthy, happy community has a fear of sin and its consequences.

Chris Wright informs us that there is no account in the Bible of this law being applied and a son being put to death for disobedience. This does not mean it never happened. But if it did happen it must have been very rare. The law must have served as a deterrent to serious disobedience! Walter Kaiser, in his comment on this passage, points out that "for each crime demanding capital punishment (except premeditated murder) there was a substitution or ransom that could be offered (Numbers 35:31). Thus, while the penalty marked the seriousness of the crime, the offer of a ransom would mitigate some of the severity in the actual sentencing."[14] Were ransoms offered in place of death for a disobedient son? We are not told, but it is possible that this happened.

Today the instances of parents handing over their sons to the police are rare, though in our work with drug addicts this happens fairly often. Today parents, especially mothers, are coerced by their rebellious children not only to not punish them but also to steal or beg in order to supply what they want for their addiction to drugs or alcohol. Difficult as it may seem, the parents may need to hand over their children to the authorities so that the harm they do could be forcibly stopped. This passage teaches that if sons are a serious threat to society, then parents have the responsibility to ensure that something is done to prevent the harm that they might do.

Not Defiling the Land with the Body of a Cursed Man (21:22, 23)

The next law concerns the body of an executed criminal: "And if a man has committed a crime punishable by death and he is put to death, and you hang him on a tree, his body shall not remain all night on the tree, but you shall bury him the same day" (21:22, 23a). Criminals were usually executed by stoning. While the Biblical law does not seem to prescribe the practice of hanging the bodies of executed criminals, it was common in the ancient Near East, possibly because of the deterrent value of such a public display. But the hanged body needed to be buried soon, perhaps as soon as the deterring function has been accomplished. The reason for the quick burial is that the purity of the land must be maintained. This is why our paragraph closes with Moses' words, "You shall not defile your land that the LORD your God is giving you for an inheritance" (21:23c).

Sandwiched between the first and third part of verse 23 is a statement about those who are hanged: ". . . for a hanged man is cursed by God." We are not told exactly why such a person is cursed by God. Probably it means that one who was executed for serious sin and kept for public viewing as a deterrent to sin was surely one who was cursed by God. The church began to use this statement when looking at the significance of the death of Christ. Paul said, "Christ redeemed us from the curse of the law by becoming a curse for us—for it is written, 'Cursed is everyone who is hanged on a tree'" (Galatians 3:13). Peter may have been alluding to this when he said, "He himself bore our sins in his body on the tree, that we might die to sin and live to righteousness" (1 Peter 2:24). As Peter Craigie put it, "His separation from the family of God made possible our admission to the family of God, because the curse of the broken law—which would have permanently barred admission—had been removed." Today there is a lot of haziness about the idea of Christ being our substitute, about his bearing our sins in his body as Peter said, about God making him to be sin for our sake as Paul said (2 Corinthians 5:21). Looking at the way the New Testament writers used Old Testament texts in explaining the death of Christ would take away any ambiguity about what was achieved on the cross.

In a most amazing twist we find in this difficult passage a doorway to understanding the nature of God. Deuteronomy 21:18–21 portrays God's asking a father to bring his rebellious son for execution in order that the nation may be kept pure. People would ask, "What kind of God would permit a father to hand over his own son for execution?" We answer, "The God who himself handed over his own son to be a curse for us all."

46

Rules for an Orderly and Healthy Society

DEUTERONOMY 22:1–12

RECENTLY THERE HAS BEEN a fresh realization of the need for civility if we are to have healthy, orderly societies. If people are to live in harmony, they must be sensitive to the needs and scruples of others. Civility is defined as "the act of showing regard for others."[1] This is generally extended to cover courtesy and politeness also.[2]

As a young man, George Washington wrote 110 "Rules of Civility and Decent Behavior in Company and Conversation," and that work is still available, with Amazon.com advertising at least ten different editions. Johns Hopkins University started a civility project in 1997, and its co-founder, Professor P. M. Forni, has written a book entitled *Choosing Civility: The Twenty-Five Rules of Considerate Conduct.*[3] The publisher's description of this book begins with the words, "Most people would agree that thoughtful behavior and common decency are in short supply, or simply forgotten in hurried lives of emails, cell-phones, and multi-tasking." Technological advances have rushed our lives to such an extent that we are no longer used to doing inconvenient things and adjusting our behavior out of concern for our neighbors.

Our passage gives several rules intended to help keep a society harmonious and healthy.

Helping Restore Lost Property (22:1–4)

The rules of verses 1–4 show concern not only for human beings but also for animals. If an owner carelessly loses track of an animal belonging to him, someone in the community who finds the animal must care for the animal and restore it to the rightful owner. The first rule is straightforward: "You shall not see your brother's ox or his sheep going astray and ignore them. You shall take them back to your brother" (22:1). Next, Moses brings up situations where the owner is not immediately accessible: "And if he does not live near you and you do not know who he is, you shall bring it home to your house, and it shall stay with you until your brother seeks it. Then you shall restore it to him" (22:2). Moses then extends this rule to apply to a lost "donkey," "garment" and "any lost thing of your brother's" (22:3).

Then Moses says we must help when a "donkey" or an "ox" belonging to a brother is "fallen down by the way." If the donkey was carrying a heavy load, it would have been difficult for the owner to lift it up alone. So if someone sees this, he must "help him to lift them up again" (22:4). This means helping another with an emergency. As Warren Wiersbe says, "Emergencies don't make people; they show what people are made of." Wiersbe says that when a terrible storm destroyed thousands of trees in his town, "some people took advantage of the situation and used their chain saws to collect exorbitant fees from helpless people. Love of money won over love for their neighbors. But others, including many teenagers, went from place to place donating their services to help those who couldn't help themselves."

A Christian missionary and companions in Africa were traveling on a rough road when their vehicle got stuck. Unable to get the vehicle out of the mud, they hailed a vehicle that was passing by to get help. Those in the vehicle ignored the request and went merrily along. They finally got their vehicle out of the mud and proceeded with the journey. Sometime later they encountered the vehicle that had ignored their request for help stuck on the road. The driver said, "Ah, here's our chance to get even with these rascals." But the missionary told the driver to stop their vehicle and proceeded to help those people. When they were driving away after helping them, the driver of the vehicle told the missionary, "Now I see the difference between my religion and yours. We try to repay evil for evil. You return good for evil."[4]

Three times in these verses Moses uses a word translated by most modern English translations as "ignore" (22:1, 3, 4). Literally this should read, "Do not hide yourself from . . . " The natural tendency of most people is to leave the scene when they encounter a need they could help meet. The priest and the Levite did something similar in the parable of the good Samaritan when they "passed by on the other side" (Luke 10:31, 32). God's people must not do that. There is a common saying today: "Each man for himself and God for everybody," but that is not acceptable to Christians.

What this passage commands (not just recommends) is very inconvenient. Moses is asking the people to be concerned about the needs of people who do not have any ongoing relationship with them. This is the theme of Jesus' parable of the good Samaritan. Christians must be known for being considerate people who help others. This is the impression that our neighbors should have about us. The command to love our neighbor as ourselves appears nine times in the Bible,[5] but the Bible does not specify and say that we are to love only the neighbors we like. This covers *all* neighbors. Exodus 23:4, 5 has a command similar to that in Deuteronomy 22 relating to property belonging to our enemies. We cannot say things like, "I know how he treated me. So I am not going to help him." Sadly, however, we often hear even Christians saying things like this. Our society is weak when it comes to the ability to be patient with inconvenience caused by others. God's people should be different.

We may think we hide ourselves in peace when we ignore the needs of others. This kind of hiding is like the hiding that Adam and Eve did when they moved away from God's way. God has made human beings to be sacrificially loving just like him. When we do not act that way, presumably so we can be at peace without being troubled by others, what actually happens is that our peace is taken away. In fact, we are usually annoyed with the person in need who took away our peace by exposing us to his or her need. So our impatience increases our stress and unhappiness. This unhappiness becomes even more marked if we lose our temper and lash out at those neighbors, for then our guilt is compounded. Ultimately, a life of selfish disregard for our neighbors' needs only serves to make us unhappy.

Such selfishness also affects our testimony. John says, "But if anyone has the world's goods and sees his brother in need, yet closes his heart against him, how does God's love abide in him?" (1 John 3:17). John is saying that it is inconceivable that a Christian should act in such a selfish way. Christians have earned the criticism of being judgmental and arrogant because we stand against things that others accept for supposedly "humanitarian" reasons— abortion, euthanasia, homosexual practice, the idea that all religions are ways to salvation, and so on. One way to overcome this criticism is to live lives of radical concern even for those who oppose us. Then though they may resent our beliefs, they will be impressed by our behavior and possibly even become open to the gospel.

I am from the Sinhala race, and we had a three-decade war in Sri Lanka between the predominantly Sinhala army and rebels from the Tamil minority. When something unpleasant happens, the Tamils in our city are vulnerable to attack by angry Sinhala mobs. My wife and I try to do all we can to protect such people. So when we know that something like that could happen, we visit our Tamil friends, pray with them, and assure them that they can stay in our home if there is trouble. A young man who was converted from Hinduism through our ministry stayed with us for six months along with his mother after their home was burned in a riot. He was the only Christian in the family. Before they left our home both his mother and sister (who was living somewhere else) were baptized in our church. Another brother followed a little later. This is just one example of how caring for others can be an opportunity for gospel witness.

Our passage does not mention any punishment for failing to help our brothers when they lose something. It is not a crime to ignore the needs of our brothers, but it is unholy and wrong from God's perspective. We must go beyond what the Law requires and go the second mile in helping our neighbors (see Matthew 5:40–42).

Maintaining Gender Distinctions (22:5)

Verse 5 prohibits what we today call cross-dressing: "A woman shall not wear a man's garment, nor shall a man put on a woman's cloak, for whoever does these things is an abomination to the LORD your God." The word translated "garment" here literally means "article, utensil, or implement." Therefore, the word could cover not only clothes but also "anything worn that is a symbol of maleness" (Hall). In those days people may have done this for emotional or sexual (possibly homosexual) gratification, and it is known as transvestism. This practice may even have been part of a pagan temple ritual.

This chapter prohibits breaking God's order in the areas of agriculture (22:9, 10), clothing (22:11), and sexual behavior (22:13–30). Therefore, it is possible that the point addressed here is breaking God's order for gender distinction. Of course, we know that in Christ male and female are equal (Galatians 3:28). But equality in status does not eliminate differences in physical matters and roles. When it comes to clothes, norms as to what is feminine and what is masculine vary according to culture. Scottish people wear kilts, which is a pleated skirt. When I was a student in the USA and wore a sarong, which men in Sri Lanka wear when relaxing, my friends would say, "Ajith is wearing his skirt!" Sometimes people accuse women of immodesty when they wear slacks as they are predominantly worn by men. But in many cultures wearing slacks is the most modest way for women to dress. So we must beware of making rules about clothing without thinking of the cultural backgrounds.

This verse says, ". . . whoever does these things is an abomination to the LORD your God." "Abomination" is a strong word! This would drive us to be careful about maintaining gender distinctions today. Some have mistaken sameness for equality and insisted that men should have the freedom to do all that women do and vice versa. The strong words of our verse should be a warning to us about the dangers of such thinking. Leviticus uses the word "abomination" in connection with homosexual behavior (18:22; 20:13). Having lost their purity, people have found gratification in the sexual realm from many things that do not please God (see Romans 1:26, 27). As many consider these things normal today, it is easy for Christians also to be dragged into attitudes that regard deviant sexual behavior as normal. With such attitudes, we, too, can fall into some of these abominable sins, especially because of the power of sexual temptation.

May we always hate what God hates! May we never forget that we live in a sexually charged era, making us all vulnerable to sinful sexual attitudes and practices. It is considered normal to find sexual satisfaction from the body of someone who is not our spouse, not only through pornographic sites but even through supposedly safe family entertainment. This violates God's standards. May we daily ask God to keep us pure and avail ourselves of the strength he gives to battle for sexual purity in our lives. Paul's autobiographical statement in 1 Corinthians 9:27 surely applies to the sexual realm, too: "I punish my body and enslave it, so that after proclaiming to others I myself should not be disqualified" (NRSV). Usually failure in this area first hits us almost imperceptibly with small compromises along the way. This gives "the devil a foothold" (Ephesians 4:27, NIV), and he will begin to work on us until we lose control of ourselves and are led to sin like oxen to the slaughter (Proverbs 7:22). The key is to be watchful so that our minds and thinking always reflect God's abhorrence for things that are an abomination to him. Here Moses is particularly talking about gender attitudes and sexual practices that violate God's order.

Protecting Food-Producing Species (22:6, 7)

The next rule is about what to do when one encounters a bird's nest with a bird sitting on her young or on eggs. "If you come across a bird's nest in any tree or on the ground, with young ones or eggs and the mother sitting on the young or on the eggs, you shall not take the mother with the young. You shall let the mother go, but the young you may take for yourself" (22:6, 7a). This is similar to the law regarding the cutting of fruit trees in 20:19, 20. If the mother is also taken for food, then the population of birds would be depleted, and food would become scarce. This rule paves the way for the many hunting rules in operation today that regulate how many animals of a given species may be killed in a given season.

Many people who know that unregulated harnessing of natural resources and polluting of the atmosphere reap adverse effects for future generations still do not think twice before doing something irresponsible because of short-term convenience for themselves. We must present such issues as being an essential part of the life of obedience to God. Sadly, many don't associate Christianity with these matters.

Animals are part of God's creation, and we have been given the responsibility to care for all creation (Genesis 1:28–30; 9:2, 3). Principled living goes beyond our attitude toward the nonhuman aspects of creation. We must remember that Jesus said that God feeds the birds and clothes the grass (Matthew 6:26–30). He is concerned for these parts of creation, too. So it is not surprising to find in our passage that the proper carrying out of these rules is a condition for God's blessings. Moses says that the result of keeping them is "that it may go well with you, and that you may live long" (Deuteronomy 22:7b).

Constructing Safe Buildings (22:8)

This chapter has been a revelation to me of the way Deuteronomy provided guidelines for legislation in society for the more than three millennia since these laws were first given. Verse 8 gives another rule that is reflected today, this time in building regulations: "When you build a new house, you shall make a parapet for your roof, that you may not bring the guilt of blood upon your house, if anyone should fall from it." The roofs of Middle Eastern houses were flat, and people used them for different activities. They even slept at night on their roofs during the hot season. David sadly fell into temptation when he was on the rooftop (2 Samuel 11:2–4), and Peter received a historic message from God on a rooftop in Joppa that opened the door to Gentiles coming into the church (Acts 10:9–20). Owners would know the boundaries of the roof of their home, but visitors would not. This law helps protect visitors.

Christians need to be concerned for the safety of others. So often people neglect the safety of others to make a bigger profit or for their personal convenience or simply because they don't want to be bothered. We let our factories and vehicles emit harmful toxic fumes or waste. We drive or ride recklessly or have vehicles without proper brakes. All these violate the spirit of this law. Christians must not be responsible for situations that jeopardize the safety of others.

Unhealthy Mixing (22:9–11)

Verses 9–11 have three prohibitions that are difficult for us to understand today. Scholars are uncertain about the reasons for these prohibitions. Some think that all three or some of these prohibitions have to do with pagan practices of the day (which we do not know) that must be avoided. Others think this is given to maintain God's order for creation without confusing it through mixing. The first prohibition is the sowing of two kinds of seed in a vineyard: "You shall not sow your vineyard with two kinds of seed, lest the whole yield be forfeited, the crop that you have sown and the yield of the vineyard" (22:9). The idea of forfeiting the two crops suggests that this prohibition relates to some sort of ceremonial impurity through mixing the crops.

The second prohibition, "You shall not plow with an ox and a donkey together" (22:10), also seems to suggest the ceremonial impurity theme because the ox was a clean animal and the donkey an unclean animal. Could this be a parable to them against syncretism? Just as clean and unclean food was to distinguish the Israelites from others and mark their unique identity (14:3–21), could the prohibition against mixing clean and unclean animals be a reminder of the principle of ceremonial separateness? It could be, but we are not sure. Wiersbe remarks, "From a practical point of view, the animals have different temperaments, and their being yoked together could only create problems." The third prohibition, "You shall not wear cloth of wool and linen mixed together" (22:11), could also be viewed as a symbolic warning against mixing.

As I am uncertain of the meaning behind these rules, I am reluctant to make any direct applications. If this passage does mean that these are reminders to help the people avoid syncretism and to affirm their unique identity, then our comments on 14:3–21 apply here, too.

Tassels (22:12)

The last rule in this section is about tassels: "You must put four tassels on the hem of the cloak with which you cover yourself—on the front, back, and sides" (22:12, NLT). The tassels mentioned here are probably the same as those mentioned in Numbers 15:37–41, though a different Hebrew word is used there. There we have a record of God telling Moses, "The tassels will remind you of the commands of the LORD, and that you are to obey his commands instead of following your own desires and going your own ways, as you are prone to do. The tassels will help you remember that you must obey all my commands and be holy to your God" (Numbers 15:39, 40, NLT). They are aids to obedience—to remind the people of God's commands and that they should obey these commands.

Deuteronomy 6:8, 9 presents a different set of visual aids to obedience: tying the commands to their hands, wearing them on their foreheads, and writing them on their doorposts and gates. What we said in our discussion of these two verses applies here, too. As we are so prone to forget God's commands, the more aids we can find to remember them and motivate obedience the better. Our greatest battle in life is the battle for obedience. Disobedience is the only thing of which we can be legitimately afraid. God is greater than everything we face, and he can lead us victoriously through each challenge. The one time he will not give us his triumph is when we forfeit it through disobedience. Therefore, we should give serious attention to how we can be obedient, and we should find creative ways — today's equivalents of tassels — to help motivate us along the path of obedience.

Actually for those whose goal in life is to be obedient to God, adjusting their lifestyle and practices is not a big problem. But today when rules like what we looked at are presented, some angrily cry out that their freedoms are being violated. In fact, even in some churches, if the leadership tried to call for abiding by the rules in this chapter, they might end up having to go to court to defend their right to make such a call! This comes from a very weak understanding of freedom. Freedom that does not know how to sacrifice for the sake of society, of principles, and of other people is not freedom — it is bondage to an unfulfilling lifestyle that is wrongly associated with the noble term *freedom*.

47

Upholding the High Value of Sex

DEUTERONOMY 22:13–30

WHETHER ONE COMES FROM the East or the West, whether one is rich or poor, most would agree that we are living in a sex-saturated era. The result of this preoccupation with sex has been an undervaluing of it. Many think that those who uphold traditional morality downplay the value of sex. On the contrary, Biblical Christians have such a high view of sex that we see it as operating only within parameters that uphold its great value as one of God's choicest gifts to humanity. Christians are committed to holy sex. We believe that only by confining its use to the boundaries drawn up by God can people experience completely the fulfillment God intended us to have through it.

These days we often hear the Puritans mentioned in a disparaging way as people who did not really enjoy life, especially sex. But as Leland Ryken has shown in his book *Worldly Saints: The Puritans as They Really Were*, this was very far from the truth. This is what Ryken says about the idea that the Puritans were against sex: "Ridiculous. An influential Puritan said that sexual intercourse was 'one of the most proper and essential acts of marriage' and something which a couple should engage in 'with good will and delight, willingly, readily, and cheerfully.'"[1] The Old Testament is very eager to maintain this perspective on sex. Proverbs[2] and the Song of Solomon[3] have unbridled expressions of the sheer delight of the physical pleasure one finds from one's spouse's body.

According to the Bible, the sexual relationship is designed for marriage, and people miss God's plan for fulfillment through sex when they experience it outside of marriage. Yet the sexual urge is very strong and can easily express itself in wrong ways if not kept under control. So the Old Testament warns us in strong language about the dangers of sinful sexual practices and prescribes severe punishment that could act as a deterrent to sexual sin. Some of this may seem strange to us today. Because of this, we should carefully study these passages, for they show us how far our society has moved away from God's ways. Deuteronomy 22:13–30 is one such passage.

It would be good for us to study this passage from the background of knowing that the sins condemned here are poor substitutes to the beautiful plan God has for human sexual fulfillment. It is because God wants people to enjoy this in the proper way and because improper ways are so harmful that God speaks so strongly against them.

The Seriousness of False Accusations (22:13–19a)

The first group of rules here is intended to protect a bride from false accusations brought against her by her groom. Marriages in those days were usually "arranged," and the bride and groom sometimes hardly knew each other until their wedding day. What if the husband does not like his bride after the wedding? That is the situation envisaged here: "If any man takes a wife and goes in to her and then hates her . . . " (22:13). Implied here is that the first sexual experience is not a good one. We know that the first sexual experience is usually not a good gauge of what kind of sexual life a couple will have in the future. One has a whole lifetime to learn and improve in this area. And research has shown that generally couples experience their most fulfilling sexual experiences many years after their wedding. Later we will see that "wedding night blues" is not an adequate reason for breaking up the marriage (22:19).

Because of hating his bride he "accuses her of misconduct and brings a bad name upon her, saying, 'I took this woman, and when I came near her, I did not find in her evidence of virginity'" (22:14). His claim is that she has had sexual relations before marriage with someone else. He accuses her, and if it is true, he can divorce her and get back the dowry he gave to her family. He would not get that in a normal divorce! Giving a girl a bad name, however, is a serious thing. The charge must be substantiated, and the bride's family must be given the opportunity to defend her honor. So the Law says, ". . . then the father of the young woman and her mother shall take and bring out the evidence of her virginity to the elders of the city in the gate" (22:15). The city gate in those days was where legal matters were dealt with. What is this "evidence of her virginity"? It could be a stain of blood on the sheet through the rupturing of the hymen on the wedding night. This is troubling, as the hymens of women who are virgins sometimes get ruptured before their first sexual experience (e.g., when playing as a child). In that case, the family would have to find another way to prove that she is a virgin. The blood would have been a foolproof test. This phrase translated "evidence of her virginity" could also be a translated "evidence of adolescence." Such evidence of adolescence would be the menstrual blood that is produced with the onset of adolescence. In this case the parents would produce evidence of the girl's not being pregnant through a cloth stained with recent menstrual blood.[4]

The girl's father is to tell the elders, "I gave my daughter to this man to marry, and he hates her; and behold, he has accused her of misconduct, saying, 'I did not find in your daughter evidence of virginity'" (22:16, 17a). Then he will "spread the cloak before the elders of the city," saying, "And yet this is the evidence of my daughter's virginity" (22:17b). Once the accusation has been proven to be wrong, "the elders of that city shall take the man and whip him, and they shall fine him a hundred shekels of silver and give them to the father of the young woman, because he has brought a bad name upon a virgin of Israel" (22:18, 19a). This is a huge fine—twice the bride-price required in 22:29.

The point here is that a man cannot get away with making false accusations against a woman. Sadly, however, usually when an accusation of a sexual nature is made against another—especially a Christian—it spreads like wildfire, and it is very difficult to contain it, even if it is totally untrue. Sometimes when a woman accuses a man of improper behavior toward her, he tries to negate the accusations by insinuating she is an immoral person, so that she is the offender, not him. I heard about a successful pastor who had to leave the ministry because his secretary accused him of impropriety, the church ruled that the accusations were true, and he had to resign. Several years later she admitted that she was the one who had tried to be intimate with the pastor and not vice versa. The accusations were her angry response to his rejection of her advances.

The fact that false witness was included in the Ten Commandments shows how seriously God views this sin (Exodus 20:16). We should not tolerate false accusations, and we must adopt careful procedures to determine whether an accusation is true or false. The severity of the punishment prescribed here is intended to be a deterrent to spreading slanderous stories about people and also a just sentence for the wrong done. Today we hardly subject to discipline people in the church who slander others. Perhaps by adopting such disciplinary processes we can minimize the circulation of unsubstantiated slanderous stories in the church. I think the command about false witness is one of the least kept commands among the Ten Commandments in the church today.

The Seriousness of Covenant Commitments (22:19b)

The Law goes on to say, "And she shall be his wife. He may not divorce her all his days" (22:19b). Many today would react to this statement with shock and incredulity. Why should a man be forced to live until death with a woman he "hates" (22:13)? Should not the couple divorce because they are so incompatible? Incompatibility seems to be an almost universally accepted ground for divorce today. Billy Graham's wife, Ruth, made popular the idea that incompatibility can be a plus point in a marriage. Billy Graham once described the secret of their more than sixty-year marriage by saying, "Ruth and I are happily incompatible."[5] Chuck and Barb Snyder, who describe themselves as "the world's most opposite couple," have written a helpful book, *Incompatibility: Still Grounds for a Great Marriage*,[6] which, they say, explains "how they have survived almost 50 years of marriage—and enjoyed the journey."[7]

When a couple marries, they make a solemn covenant before God and human witnesses to be faithful to each other until they die. That is a serious undertaking. If people keep breaking their covenant commitments, we are going to end up with a very insecure society in which no one trusts anyone and authentic community life becomes extinct. Sadly, this seems to have happened already, and the world is filled with insecure, unhappy, and restless people—missing the enriching life in community that God intended for them. The idea of lasting commitment has gone out of fashion. When people find their church does not meet their particular needs (incompatibility), they move to another church, forgetting that the key to their church membership is not their needs but the fact that they have become part of that body. Imagine a body having to amputate its members all the time. Today's church-hopping culture has made the body metaphor for the church very difficult to sustain!

The principle of commitment to people despite their weaknesses and failures finds its fullest expression in marriage. Christians do not practice this commitment only by stoically clinging to an unhappy and gloomy marriage out of an obligation to be faithful to vows made at the wedding. The Christian view of patience is much more positive, and it is based on the belief that God turns everything to good (Romans 8:28). We are patient with people because that is the best possible thing to do. If the Old Testament is any indication of what a good family is, then joy is an important feature of the marriage relationship. When Christians exercise patience with their spouses, they are fired by an ambition to see their family life joyful just as God intended it to be. They know that God can help them achieve this joy.

With such ambition, Christians exercise patience as part of a concerted effort to work at improving their marriage relationship. Over the years I have worked with a few couples who looked like they were very incompatible with each other. Some had come from dysfunctional backgrounds that had left serious psychological scars in their personalities. At times it looked like there was no hope of salvaging these marriages. However, as they persevered in obedience to God and with an ambition to make their marriages work, I have seen them emerge with beautiful testimonies to how the sufficient grace of God helped them forge stable marriage relationships.

I am not saying that there is no place for divorce in the Christian church. We know that sometimes devout, holy Christians have to resort to divorce because of an impossible relationship in which one partner refuses to work toward a resolution. What I am saying is that far too many battles to save marriages are abandoned too early. God can make incompatible people happy. However, for all this to make sense, we must first bring back to the thinking of Christians the utmost importance of commitment as a key Christian value. Jesus said, "What therefore God has joined together, let not man separate" (Matthew 19:6).

The Seriousness of Sexual Relations outside Marriage (22:20–30)

The rest of the chapter describes procedures for dealing with six different kinds of sexual relationships outside marriage.

Six Situations

We have already been looking at the situation of a groom accusing his bride of not being a virgin. Moses says, "But if the thing is true, that evidence of virginity was not found in the young woman . . . " (22:20), a severe punishment is decreed: "then they shall bring out the young woman to the door of her father's house, and the men of her city shall stone her to death with stones, because she has done an outrageous thing in Israel by whoring in her father's house. So you shall purge the evil from your midst" (22:21). Note how sexual promiscuity before marriage is called "an outrageous thing in Israel." Sadly, this kind of behavior no longer causes outrage today. This has prompted the writing of the book titled *The Death of Outrage: Bill Clinton and the Assault on American Ideals*.[8]

The second situation is what we would call adultery: "If a man is found lying with the wife of another man . . . " (22:22a). This was discussed at length in our study of the seventh of the Ten Commandments (5:18). Here the punishment for the sin is also given: ". . . both of them shall die, the man who lay with the woman, and the woman. So you shall purge the evil from Israel" (20:22).

Three times in this passage the punishment for three different kinds of extramarital sex is described with the words, "You shall purge the evil from your midst [or from Israel]" (22:21, 22, 24). The same thing is said of false prophets, idolatry, and murder.[9] Sex outside marriage makes the people of God unclean. It must be dealt with forthrightly and swiftly. Paul counseled regarding the sexual offender in the Corinthian church, "Deliver this man to Satan [that is, excommunicate him] for the destruction of the flesh, so that his spirit may be saved in the day of the Lord" (1 Corinthians 5:5). Some say that we should keep such people in the church because we may lose them if we discipline them. Paul is implying just the opposite. Unless we deal with his sin severely he will not have an occasion to flee from it in fear. The end of the discipline is that he will be "saved in the day of the Lord."

The third situation is when a man has sexual relations with a betrothed virgin: "If there is a betrothed virgin, and a man meets her in the city and lies with her . . . " (22:23). Again, as with adultery, both are to be killed: "then you shall bring them both out to the gate of that city, and you shall stone them to death with stones, the young woman because she did not cry for help though she was in the city, and the man because he violated his neighbor's wife. So you shall purge the evil from your midst" (22:24). Note that the virginity requirements are not only for women but for men also. Though technically the offending man may be married, the implication is that the same standards of morality are required of men and women and the same punishments are given—something that is missing in the strict rules concerning sexual sin in many societies, where the law often gives the man an unfair advantage. If the woman had cried out for help, she would have been released. Unlike in modern affluent societies, in the cities of those days and in much of the less affluent world today, houses are close to each other, so if a woman cries for help it would be known. What Moses says here may suggest that a woman would be punished if she cried but her cry was not heard. This brief summary statement does not include things that would be done in situations like that to ensure that justice is served.

The fourth situation is when a betrothed woman is raped. "But if in the open country a man meets a young woman who is betrothed, and the man seizes her and lies with her . . . " (22:25a). In verse 23 the man "meets" the woman, here he "seizes her." The NIV rendering, "rapes," correctly interprets the Hebrew. In this case, "only the man who lay with her shall die" (22:25b). She had no chance of getting help from another: "But you shall do nothing to the young woman; she has committed no offense punishable by death. For this case is like that of a man attacking and murdering his neighbor, because he met her in the open country, and though the betrothed young woman cried for help there was no one to rescue her" (22:26, 27).

We contrast this treatment of the raped woman with a recent happening in a Middle-Eastern country, where a teenage girl was raped. Her brother tied her to a chair and killed her by slashing her throat. He said he did it to protect the honor of his family.[10] Such honor killings are considered acceptable in some shame-based cultures. Shame and honor were important criteria for determining right and wrong in ancient Israeli culture, also. But the criteria for shame and honor were God's holiness and love and not the kind of shame for which the shamed person was not responsible. It is important for us to learn God's criteria for shame and honor—they have to do with God's unwavering principles rather than with appearance. While society may reject an innocent woman who is raped, God's people must do all they can to ensure her welfare and healing.

The fifth situation is also a case of rape, as the word "seizes" (also see 22:25) used here suggests: "If a man meets a virgin who is not betrothed, and seizes her and lies with her, and they are found . . . " (22:28). The man has to take responsibility for his actions: ". . . then the man who lay with her shall give to the father of the young woman fifty shekels of silver, and she shall be his wife, because he has violated her. He may not divorce her all his days" (22:29). Here a woman's life has the potential of ruin. No one may marry her because she has been "violated." If she has children from this relationship, they, too, are severely handicapped. So he has to take responsibility for his actions and marry her. The "fifty shekels of silver" is probably the bride-price spoken of in Exodus 22:16.

Sadly, today, we have too many situations of men having their "fun" with women by exploiting them sexually without any intention of a permanent commitment. They move away when they get tired of the woman. And the woman is deeply hurt as she was hoping for a permanent relationship. This would have been the case then, too. Such actions are not tolerated in the Bible. Along with the sex act go many responsibilities because, as we saw in our discussion of the seventh command (Deuteronomy 5:18), two bodies have been permanently united. The Bible intends that union to be for life. To have sex just for fun without taking on the accompanying responsibilities is a despicable act of wickedly exploiting a woman and cheapening one of life's most valued treasures. This must not be tolerated.

Today we see a lot of people cohabiting without getting married. What we said about the permanency of sexual relationships suggests that we should counsel them to marry, as now they have already entered into a key aspect of marriage. But because sex outside marriage is sin, our counsel to such couples is to repent of their sin, live apart immediately, and prepare for marriage without having further sexual contact until their wedding day. I understand that some who have had sexual relations should not get married for practical reasons. What this passage says is that we must consider the sex act as something extremely serious and take responsibility for it.

The final situation probably refers not only to having sexual relations but also to marrying one's father's wife: "A man shall not take his father's wife, so that he does not uncover his father's nakedness" (22:30). The expression "uncover his father's nakedness" (literally, "uncover his father's skirt") probably means to bring severe dishonor to the father. The woman is probably his stepmother, the father having married a person possibly much younger than he. The other possibility is that she is a wife in a polygamous situation. Leviticus 18 gives other types of prohibited incestuous behavior. The same variety of incest was found in the Corinthian church, and Paul says it is not even tolerated by pagans (1 Corinthians 5:1). The seriousness of incest is that it is a direct attack on one of the most, if not *the* most, important institutions in society—the home. When the family is attacked, it is a huge and serious assault on the whole of society.

In the relatively small homes in which most people lived in those days, people could be more vulnerable to incest than in many affluent homes today. However, as the media have gone more and more into giving entertainment through aberrations of normal sexual behavior, incest also has come into films (it appeared in literature for many centuries).[11] Actually, there seems to be a concerted effort to take away the designation of heterosexual relationships between married couples as the normal sexual relationship. Once when I was visiting England, the press gave a lot of prominence to the case of a father who was having a full-blown affair with his son's wife while the son was at work. I realized that this prominence was given not because they thought it was wrong, but because of the novelty of the relationship. Soon, however, this novelty will become normal, and people will start looking for a new frontier of decadence to satisfy their lustful curiosity. The prohibition in Deuteronomy 22:30, therefore, has much relevance today also.

Virginity

Before proceeding any further in this discussion, I need to say that when we speak about virginity we must apply it to both males and females, which is how this chapter addresses it. To apply it only to women would make us guilty of demeaning women.

All this talk about virginity seems strange in an age when, in many circles, being a virgin is considered a thing of which an adult should be ashamed! The stunning statistic released by the U.S. government that unmarried mothers gave birth to about 40 percent of the children born in the U.S. in 2007 gives evidence of how this generation has rejected the Biblical teaching about sex and marriage. In 1940 that figure was 3.8 percent.[12] Even more stunning is the statistic that 31 percent of the congregations in the U.S. would accept a member of a cohabiting unmarried couple as a lay leader.[13] There is a lot of legitimate concern among Christians today about the growing acceptance of homosexual lifestyles. But I believe heterosexual sin is a far more prevalent problem in the church, and there is a corresponding lack of emphasis on this problem. When advocates of homosexual lifestyles see opponents of such lifestyles paying so much attention to this issue without giving correspondingly serious attention to highly prevalent heterosexual sins, they could justify their branding us homophobic—haters of homosexuals.[14]

It would be true to say that in some areas we who are under the new covenant need a somewhat different approach to sexual sin than what is found in the Old Testament. We know that the days of severe punishment for extramarital sex are over, and under the new covenant sinners can receive forgiveness for their sins and start a new life, knowing that God has not only forgiven but has also forgotten their sins (Jeremiah 31:34). A woman who had lived a very promiscuous life exclaimed after her conversion, "In God's sight, I am a virgin."[15] That is how her fiancé should regard her before marrying her. Some are calling this "second-time virginity."[16] It is significant that of the five women mentioned in Jesus' genealogy, except for Ruth and Mary, three were adulterers (Matthew 1:1–16). Tamar disguised herself as a prostitute and got Judah to impregnate her because he did not keep his promise to give her his third son. Rahab was a prostitute. Bathsheba's name is not given, but she is mentioned as "the wife of Uriah" (v. 6), whom David stole from Uriah in a most shameful way.

Yet the promise of forgiveness for extramarital sex does not take away from its seriousness. Jesus told the woman "caught in the act of adultery" (John 8:4), "Neither do I condemn you." But immediately after that he also told her, ". . . go, and from now on sin no more" (John 8:11). Paul said, "neither the sexually immoral . . . nor adulterers . . . will inherit the kingdom of God" (1 Corinthians 6:9, 10). Then he says that some of his readers were also like this, but now they have been "washed . . . , sanctified . . . , justified" (1 Corinthians 6:11). Hebrews 13:4 upholds the honor of marriage in relation to extramarital sex when it says, "Let marriage be held in honor among all, and let the marriage bed be undefiled, for God will judge the sexually immoral and adulterous." Adulterers and fornicators must give up their sin when they come to God and plan never to return to it; otherwise, a severe judgment awaits them.

In his book *True Sexual Morality: Recovering Biblical Standards for a Culture in Crisis,* Daniel Heimbach shares great wisdom on why adultery is so serious in the Bible. I will close this chapter with some of his comments.

> Without marriage, sex is simply wrong, and God takes it so seriously he makes adultery the ultimate paradigm for breaking faith with himself. . . . God's prohibition of sex outside marriage is stated so clearly and repeated so often, God seems to have taken extra steps to make sure we do not miss its importance.[17]
>
> The positive principles at stake seem to be that sex outside of marriage erodes and ultimately destroys the precious value of exclusivity and selflessness in the sexual relationship. . . . Adulterous sex can never be exclusive and selfless. By its very nature, adulterous sex rejects the value of keeping sex exclusive and is driven by self-centered interests that preempt our responsibility to always do what is best for others—in this case those depending on us in the areas of marriage and family life. But the value of exclusive, selfless sex is so good that God never allows less. He prohibits sex outside of marriage to keep us from losing what is best.[18]

48

Rules for a Holy Society

DEUTERONOMY 23:1–14

AT DIFFERENT TIMES IN HISTORY God's people had some practices that were crucial to defining their identity. In a later era this was no longer the case, and people wondered why those in earlier times made such a fuss about those things. Today evangelical Episcopalians wonder why evangelical Anglicans a century or two before them fought so vehemently over things like the use of vestments by priests in worship. To us this seems to be a minor issue. But at that time in the history of the church they represented serious issues that defined faithfulness to Biblical Christianity for many. This is the case with many of the ceremonial laws in the Old Testament. We wonder why they were considered so important, especially after Christ annulled some of them.

The fact is, during a certain period of the history of God's people these laws represented key aspects of the identity of the people of God. Once the lesson they were supposed to teach had entered into the minds of the people, these laws were annulled because they were not moral laws that involved doing something ethically wrong but ceremonial laws that symbolized a spiritual reality to the people. The laws described in our passage come under this category of ceremonial laws. Yet when studying these we must not miss the many helpful principles that can be learned from them that are useful to us today. When I started studying this passage I thought I could complete the whole chapter in one study. But there were so many helpful truths here that I decided to divide it into two studies, in order to give adequate space to helpful principles.

We call the process of God's revealing his will and ways in stages progressive revelation.

523

People Excluded from and Included in the Assembly (23:1–8)

The Assembly of the Lord

The first section is about people who can and cannot "enter the assembly of the LORD" (an expression that appears five times in these verses: 23:1, 2a, 2b, 3, 8)[1]. "The assembly of the LORD" (or "assembly of Israel") "is a technical term for all those adult males who are enfranchised to make decisions, participate in cultic activities and serve in the military of Israel (Micah 2:5)."[2] The exclusion of some from this assembly had to do with the fact that Israel was a covenant people, called to be "to [God] a kingdom of priests and a holy nation" (Exodus 19:6). Maintaining ritual purity was an important aspect of this unique identity. So when they met at certain crucial times, people viewed as ritually unclean were excluded from the gatherings.

We will see below that some of the exclusions in this passage were revoked later on in Israel's history. Now, however, at this early stage of their national history, when their identity as the holy priesthood was being forged, "external, physical, and material means had spiritual significance and were used to teach lessons on the nature of their relationship to the Lord and the nature of the holiness that was required of them" (Kalland). In different times during the progress of God's revelation of his will and ways to the human race, God used spectacular means to reveal his truth. In certain periods miracles were very marked. So was prophecy, which ceased for 400 years until John the Baptist burst onto the scene to signal the birth of the greatest revelatory period that came with Jesus. At the start of the life of the church Ananias and Sapphira died after lying so that God could show his abhorrence of lying. He still hates lying, but believers who lie are not usually punished in that way today, this side of the final judgment.

In the same way for several centuries there were restrictions that drove home vividly to the people of this "new" nation that God would not tolerate certain attitudes and practices. Those associated with these, therefore, were excluded even though some of them may not have been responsible for the state in which they were.

Eunuchs (23:1)

The first kind of person excluded was "one whose testicles are crushed or whose male organ is cut off" (23:1). These eunuchs became so because of a ritual of dedication to a god or because they had a special official position in the king's service or because of deliberate mutilation. These practices were abhorrent to God. This terrible practice had to be stopped by severe action, and this would act as a deterrent to others trying to do it. It would also save future sons of Israel from being subjected to this painful and inhumane treatment, thus making this a compassionate law in the long run.

Children Born of a Forbidden Union (23:2)

The second kind of person excluded was "one born of a forbidden union" (23:2a). Here the exclusion extended beyond the person: "Even to the tenth generation, none of his descendants may enter the assembly of the LORD" (23:2b). This includes those born out of wedlock, those born through incest, and those born to marriages that broke God's Law. Leviticus 18:6–20 and 20:10–21 gives a long list of incestuous, adulterous, and ceremonially unacceptable sexual unions. I found seven places in the Old Testament where there is a prohibition against marrying people of other nations because the foreign spouse will turn the heart of the Israelite spouse from the Lord.[3] Today that would translate to the act of marrying an unbeliever—one who does not belong to the new-covenant community, the body of Christ. We usually use only 2 Corinthians 6:14 when arguing for the inadvisability of marrying unbelievers: "Do not be unequally yoked with unbelievers. For what partnership has righteousness with lawlessness? Or what fellowship has light with darkness?" This verse can legitimately be interpreted as implying a ban on Christians marrying unbelievers. The Old Testament passages, however, are much more explicit.

Is it not unfair to punish children in this way for their parents' acts of disobedience? Again, we interpret these laws as being so harsh because of their deterrent value. The value is of this is seen today when (as we showed in the previous study) as many as 40 percent of the children born in the United States are born outside of marriage.[4] Sex is a powerful force that can easily run out of control. Therefore, humans need strong deterrents to keep them self-controlled when they are under the force of temptation. This is why many Christians (including myself) use accountability software to report on their Internet use to accountability partners, because it is so easy to go to sexually explicit sites. The fact that the accountability partner will find out acts as a deterrent to this sin.

In the New Testament if the spouses of converts to Christianity did not convert with them, there was no ban on the convert coming into the full fellowship of the church. In fact, Peter gives guidelines on how unbelieving husbands "may be won without a word" through the submissive and loving conduct of their wives (1 Peter 3:1–6, esp. v. 1). However, that does not give an excuse for those who are believers before marriage to marry unbelievers. Indeed, those who did this may enter into full church fellowship after repenting and may be effective ministers if they are willing to tell others that they made a mistake in their choice of a marriage partner. However, the Old Testament principle that religious intermarriage is prohibited clearly applies. The New Testament hails the destruction of race, caste, and class barriers as a major result of the work of Christ (e.g., 2 Corinthians 5:14–17; Galatians 3:28; Ephesians 2:11–22). But it never extends that to the breaking of the religious divide between believers and unbelievers.

Ammonites and Moabites (23:3–6)

Next in the list of people excluded from the assembly are Ammonites and Moabites. Here, too, the exclusion is "even to the tenth generation," and here the words "none of them may enter the assembly of the LORD forever" (23:3) are added. The reason for this is then given: "because they did not meet you with bread and with water on the way, when you came out of Egypt, and because they hired against you Balaam the son of Beor from Pethor of Mesopotamia, to curse you" (23:4). The Ammonites and Moabites lived in areas that were not going to be given to Israel, so God asked the people to go through this land without any conflict, but only to be able to purchase food and water from them. But those peoples refused to sell these provisions and did not extend hospitality to the Israelites, though the Bible mentions only the refusal of the Moabites (see Deuteronomy 2). Numbers 22—24 describe the incident where the king hired Balaam to prophecy against Israel, but God prevented him from doing so and instead made him to bless the Israelites. Deuteronomy 23:5 summarizes this, saying, "But the LORD your God would not listen to Balaam; instead the LORD your God turned the curse into a blessing for you, because the LORD your God loved you." Moses even goes on to say, "You shall not seek their peace or their prosperity all your days forever" (23:6).

Why was the sin of the Moabites and the Ammonites so serious that it provoked such a hard attitude against them? In his parable of the separation of the sheep and the goats, Jesus also said that not helping God's people in their time of need is a serious sin. In this parable people were excluded from the kingdom because they did not help God's needy people (Matthew 25:31–46). This shows us how important it is to help our neighbors in need. Jesus illustrated how this is done with the parable of the good Samaritan (Luke 10:25–37). Clearly this is an important Christian value. Its importance is evidenced by the fact that the command to love our neighbors as ourselves appears nine times in the Bible.[5] Its inclusion here suggests that it is something that we could neglect doing.

Sadly, sometimes those who have a more liberal approach to Biblical truth are often known to be more helpful to people in need than evangelicals are. Albert Schweitzer, the great organist, medical doctor, theologian, and missionary, was my hero in my youth because of his sacrificial service in Africa among needy people and because of his great skill in playing the organ. How sad I was when I found out in seminary that some of his views about Jesus were not orthodox. Schweitzer exemplified this Christian virtue of helpfulness. On his only visit to Chicago, a prominent group of leaders came to the train station to welcome him. However, they noticed that he looked beyond them and hurried over to an elderly woman who was staggering under her load of heavy suitcases and extra bundles. He grabbed her luggage and led her to her train carriage. After placing her bags on the overhead rack and wishing her a good journey he hurried back to the stunned reception committee and apologized for keeping them waiting![6]

Going to a soothsayer like Balaam, of course, is a very serious act, the seriousness of which we discussed in our comments on 12:32—13:18 (chapters 34, 35 of this book). There we showed how easy it is to fall into the trap of seeking such help when we are in a hurry to get something personal. Perhaps the most serious use of this is to harm God's people. This is sometimes done against Christians by Christians and by non-Christians. They may go to a medicine man or one who makes charms in their eagerness to harm the person targeted. We would simply say here that those who go to such people are playing with fire and are accumulating the full severity of God's wrath in judging sin.

Inclusion Later on in History

Isaiah 56:3–8 talks about how righteous foreigners and eunuchs will be welcome in the temple. In fact they are given "a name better than sons and daughters" because of their righteousness (Isaiah 56:5). Ruth, the Moabitess, became the ancestor of Israel's greatest king, David, and even of the long-awaited Messiah (Matthew 1:5). The coveted position of being the first Gentile convert—the first fruit of the greatest harvest in history—was graciously given by God to an Ethiopian eunuch (Acts 8:29–39).

This trend of progressively doing away with the ceremonial distinctives of the people of God reached its fullest expression in the new covenant. The call to take the gospel to all the nations or all the world appears in four of the statements of the Great Commission (Matthew 28:19; Mark 16:15; Luke 24:47; Acts 1:8). The disciples had to receive special divine guidance to accept Gentiles into the fellowship of the church, and conflicts arose in the outworking of this. But with the Council of Jerusalem (Acts 15:1–35) and the refusal of Paul to bow down to the Judaizers, the church universally accepted that the three markers that characterized those who belonged to the people of God in the Old Testament—circumcision, Sabbath-keeping, and kosher food laws—were not essential for Gentile converts.

Incorporation to the church—the body of Christ—also became something that took place primarily through an inner change brought about by the Holy Spirit, resulting in one's being born again (John 3:1–15). In this new community the past is no longer significant as people are new creations, with the passing away of the old and the coming of the new (2 Corinthians 5:15–17). Now God's kingdom incorporates eunuchs (Acts 8:29–39) and repentant people who once committed sins that should disqualify them from entrance into the kingdom (1 Corinthians 6:9–11). This great multitude that no one could number consists of the redeemed from every nation, tribe, people, and language (Revelation 7:9). As a prelude to this trend, when Jesus was on earth he hung around with tax collectors and sinners, to the horror of the religious establishment of the day. But these formerly sinful people, including Zacchaeus, Matthew, the woman caught in adultery, and the thief on the cross, gave up their sin and became righteous followers of Jesus.

As in Old Testament times we today must reject lifestyles that are abhorrent to God. But we will pursue those committing these sins until they also bow their knee to Jesus.

Excluding Members Today

Even though the ritual factors influencing exclusion from the assembly do not have direct reference to the Christian church today, we are today's "assembly of the LORD." The Septuagint (the Greek translation of the Old Testament) uses *ekklesia* for "assembly" in Deuteronomy 23, which is the word the New Testament generally uses for "church." The church expresses its holiness more through moral purity than through ritual purity. Just as they were a chosen people who needed to be different from their neighbors, we need to be different from our neighbors. That is our identity as Christians—Christ-people, the bearers of his name. We must be holy just as Jesus was holy. The call appearing at least six times in the Old Testament to be holy as God is holy[7] is given to the church in the New Testament. Peter says, ". . . as he who called you is holy, you also be holy in all your conduct, since it is written, 'You shall be holy, for I am holy'" (1 Peter 1:15, 16). Later, again in words reminiscent of the Old Testament, he says that we are "a holy priesthood" (1 Peter 2:5) and "a holy nation" (1 Peter 2:9).

When the New Testament uses "holiness" in connection with the church, it is referring primarily to moral purity. So when there is exclusion from the church today it should be when people violate their identity by unholy living. Paul said that the one committing incest in Corinth and Alexander and Hymenaeus (probably in Ephesus), who blasphemed through rejecting the faith, must be delivered to Satan (1 Corinthians 5:5; 1 Timothy 1:20), that is, excluded from the fellowship. This does not mean there will be no contact with them. It means they cannot come under the protection of the assembly with all its privileges and responsibilities. In both these cases the context shows that one reason for exclusion is that the pain of it would cause them to repent and return to holiness.

It is not easy to combine this dual commitment to the restoration of the sinner and maintaining the purity of the church. On the one hand, we could reject the sinner, consider him an enemy, have nothing to do with him, and not labor for his restoration after his exclusion from the fellowship. On the other hand, we could take no action on the grounds that by our acceptance of him as a person we would open the door for his return to holiness. I remember a church leader talking to me about unmarried couples who live together who come to his church. He came from a liturgically oriented church that gave Communion every Sunday. He said that they decided to give Communion to these couples because if they didn't, those couples might stop coming to church and there would be no influence toward God's ways in their lives. This is not in line with the Biblical view.

In the Youth for Christ ministry in Sri Lanka, we discipline our staff and volunteers regularly. I have never encountered a discipline situation that went perfectly smoothly. Disciplining is a messy business! Everybody in the group will not fully understand the decisions made and the procedures adopted. Leaders cannot divulge all the facts because that could be harmful to the sinner and his or her family. Yet if a procedure has been set in place, the confusion and discontent is greatly reduced, and the offender will have a better chance of getting a fair hearing. We have found that most of the people we disciplined remained in our work and were restored to ministry

The Edomites and the Egyptians (23:7, 8)

The people are then told, "You shall not abhor an Edomite, for he is your brother" (23:7). The Edomites were descendants of Esau and thus were Semites with a language that was closely related to Hebrew. Though they were often enemies of Israel in history, the Israelites needed to have a special attitude toward them. An Egyptian also was not to be abhorred "because," says Moses, "you were a sojourner in his land." Though the latter part of that time was very unpleasant, they are not to forget the kindness shown to them earlier on. In view of this relationship with these two nations, "children born to [Edomites or Egyptians] in the third generation may enter the assembly of the LORD" (23:8). Three generations would be sufficient for these people to be fully assimilated into Israel.

Remembering History

The teaching of verses 3–8 presents several challenges we face in an era when memory is often a source of both vengeful and benevolent attitudes toward others. One thing to remember is that early in the history of the people who were to give to the world the knowledge of the ways of God some truths were vividly portrayed so that the principles behind them might be remembered.

We learn that people do not forget what was done to them in history. Therefore, one generation cannot say that they are not responsible for the wrong behavior of their ancestors and ignore the anger of people who were hurt. There must be an honest admission of wrong from the next generation, if necessary. This seems strange to those from individualistic cultures. That is because they do not realize the real sense in which people are connected with their ancestors in cultures where community solidarity is a key value. We discussed this in our comments on 9:16, 17. We said that in the latter part of the last century, when Japanese Christians met with other Asian Christians at conferences, it was quite common to see them enact some formal rituals of apologizing to the people and seeking their forgiveness for the atrocities the Japanese committed in their nations about fifty years earlier. This is an important step in the healing of wounds inflicted by ancestors upon another group.

The special place given to Egyptians in this passage shows that one must also remember with gratitude help given in the past. And this was even though the Israelites were ill-treated during the last years of their sojourn in Egypt. Either because of a few incidents that detract from gratitude or because people are fixated on what is happening now and tend to disregard history, sometimes people today neglect gratitude to those who have helped them in the past. People who disregard help given to their ancestors are dishonorable people.

Higher education in Sri Lanka is inseparably linked with the name of Sir Ivor Jennings (1903–1965) who founded the first university here. When university students vehemently protested when a building in the university was named after Jennings, I was deeply ashamed. True, he was British, and I, like most Sri Lankans, am not happy that the British ruled our nation. But that does not mean we must forget the good that many British people did for us. In the same way, I think it is wrong to despise the missionaries who, though coming from ruling nations, served us at great cost and brought us the message that gave us salvation. True, they made many mistakes, but they sacrificed their lives for our salvation.

It is important for nations and people to have memories of key historical events, but what if those nations and people cause bitterness that will hinder peaceful coexistence among communities and nations? I believe this is one of the sections in Deuteronomy that need to be applied with reserve as our situation is very different from the unique situation of the first Israelites who settled in Canaan. With the coming of Christ, a new age of grace has dawned with the mandate to the church to take the gospel to the whole world. We need to develop strategies of leaving behind past hurts in forgiveness. This way nations and peoples can live as a global family in which each helps the other and secures a peaceful and prosperous world. This issue has been explored in depth by Miroslav Volf who grew up in the former Yugoslavia and saw much ethnic hatred and violence. In his book *The End of Memory: Remembering Rightly in a Violent World*[8] he shows how we can remember wrongly and provides suggestions of ways to remember rightly in order that wounds of atrocities may be healed.

Purity of the Camp at Wartime (23:9–14)

The next group of rules has to do with the purity of the camp at wartime. Verse 9 says, "When you are encamped against your enemies, then you shall keep yourself from every evil thing." The word "evil" does not necessarily mean moral evil, but evil more in a ceremonial sense as the war is God's war, and the presence of God in the camp requires that the camp be a ceremonially holy place. This is stated in verse 14: "Because the LORD your God walks in the midst of your camp, to deliver you and to give up your enemies before you, therefore your camp must be holy, so that he may not see anything indecent among you and turn away from you." The indecent things, which would not be in keeping with a place where God's presence dwelt, are mentioned in verses 10–13.

The first kind of impurity is when "any man among you becomes unclean because of a nocturnal emission" (23:10a). The words translated "nocturnal emission" are literally "what happens at night" in the Hebrew. It could refer to what we usually call a nocturnal emission of semen, or it could refer to urinating inside the camp at night without going outside the camp. Whatever its exact meaning may be, it brought about ceremonial uncleanness. The remedy is then given: ". . . then he shall go outside the camp. He shall not come inside the camp, but when evening comes, he shall bathe himself in water, and as the sun sets, he may come inside the camp" (23:10b, 11). The refusal of

Uriah the Hittite to go home to his wife Bathsheba for the night when David summoned him to Jerusalem from the battlefield could be because he did not want to become ceremonially unclean during wartime and disqualify himself from going back to the battle. David responded to such amazing loyalty with shameful treachery (2 Samuel 11).

The next rule has to do with making provision for the proper disposal of excrement. They must "have a place outside the camp" and are to "go out to it" (23:12). Instructions are given about sanitary procedures: "And you shall have a trowel with your tools, and when you sit down outside, you shall dig a hole with it and turn back and cover up your excrement" (23:13). Not only is this of ceremonial significance, it is also useful for health reasons. Insects can cause infection with excrement left in the open. Yet today excrement is often seen open to the elements in overcrowded housing estates of the poor. This can be very harmful health-wise. Governments and social service agencies need to act quickly to build adequate lavatories in such places. In fact, this could be an assignment Christians can do on behalf of their needy neighbors.

While there is no direct application of the ceremonial purity principle to us today, some principles are implied by the teaching here. Places indwelt by God should not have things that are unbecoming of God. Sometime after a young man had left home for college, his mother visited him and found several pictures of scantily clad women on his wall. She did not say anything about this to him, but after she went back home she mailed him a framed picture of Jesus. He happily hung it just above his desk. That night when he went to bed he noticed the incongruity of having a pinup girl's photo next to that of Jesus. He took down the pinup's photo and in time continued to take down all the inappropriate photos. Jesus cannot coexist with filth—which is what sexually suggestive photos of women are, for a woman's sexual beauty is for her husband to enjoy, not outsiders!

We should seek to have nothing in our possession that will make God turn away. How sad that sometimes we will hide things in our computers, drawers, and under our beds so others will not see them even while we claim that the all-seeing God lives with us. Talismans and charms, statues, items belonging to our workplace, income tax returns that are not quite accurate, unwashed bodies and unclean homes . . . these are all incompatible with the holiness of God who lives in us and with us. May this cause us to have only possessions that honor God.

This passage that at first sounds somewhat strange to us has some abiding values to teach us. Foremost among these is that we must not permit anything to enter our lives that is unbecoming of followers of the holy God we worship.

49

Rules for a Considerate Society

DEUTERONOMY 23:15–25; 24:19–22

IN OUR STUDY OF 22:1–12, we described the need for a return to being considerate toward others in society. Deuteronomy gives plenty of data to spur us on in the pursuit of civility. Many people think that Old Testament religion was characterized by a harsh and unbending legalism. We will show in this study that this characterization is far from the truth. The rules of Deuteronomy were intended to give joy and stability to Israel, among other things—to make it a pleasant place in which to live. We will see this repeatedly as we look at these chapters detailing the Law.

Protecting Slaves from Harsh Masters (23:15, 16)

Chris Wright describes the first law in this section as "astonishing." Verses 15 and 16 say, "You shall not give up to his master a slave who has escaped from his master to you. He shall dwell with you, in your midst, in the place that he shall choose within one of your towns, wherever it suits him. You shall not wrong him." The implication here is that the master of the slave has been harsh, and this has motivated the slave to escape. If he comes to an Israelite home seeking "refuge" (NIV), they must give him refuge. The person must take the risk of angering the former master by refusing to send the slave back to him. Instead, he must give the slave freedom to choose to serve "in the place that he shall choose . . . wherever it suits him." The surrounding nations may consider slaves as having no rights, but God's people are to treat them as humans, created in the image of God. An important feature of humanness is the freedom to make choices regarding one's destiny.

This law shows us that slavery in the ancient world, especially in Israel, was often more humane than slavery in the modern world. Slaves could buy back their freedom, and they were sometimes more educated than their masters. The feature that marked them out was total dedication to their masters.[1] This may be one reason why the church in Biblical times did not immediately work for the abolition of slavery. However, the Biblical teaching of the value of every human being had within it the seeds for the abolition of slavery, especially the dehumanizing slavery that appeared in the modern era. The two great heroes of the movement that led to the abolition of slavery in Britain and its colonies and in the United States were William Wilberforce and Abraham Lincoln, respectively. Both of them worked out of strong Christian convictions.

When people who call themselves Christians do not treat with respect and kindness those whom the world considers weak and insignificant and those who are supposedly their "subordinates," we can say that they are not genuine Christians. Even today we see powerless people exploited by powerful people. Unreasonable demands are made on workers that are not good for their emotional and physical well-being. It is not easy for relatively wealthy Christians to rise up against this, especially if they are friends with the perpetrators of this injustice. Sometimes these unjust people are even respected members of and generous donors to our churches. Biblical Christians must speak up for those who have no voice and pay the cost of standing up for their rights. Preachers must preach that exploiting the poor is wrong.

We sometimes find successful businesspeople, who after hearing the message of the gospel, give their lives to Christ, but they are not told that Christians must not exploit the poor. The late James Boice has been credited with the statement, "What you win them by, you win them to." If people are won to Christ by a gospel that ignores the sin of exploitation (and other social sins), they will see Christianity as a religion that does not address such social issues and will not feel guilty of perpetuating the exploitation prevalent in society. This has happened often. In fact, sometimes preachers deliberately avoid bringing up such topics because they know if they do, so some people will be turned off. This is sheer irresponsibility and a violation of gospel truth.

Sometimes a society does not make a big fuss about some form of injustice for a time. And Christians sometimes perpetuate this injustice. But later this injustice gets highlighted and becomes unpopular. Then great dishonor comes to Christ because Christians are guilty of the sins highlighted. This happened with segregation in the United States and apartheid in South Africa. The people who had been unjustly treated could become hostile to the gospel. Islam is making great strides among people who have such a history of being unjustly treated by Christians. I fear that some Christians in business in Asia are also guilty of ignoring justice issues.

Staying Clear of Prostitution (23:17, 18)

The next law tackles prostitution. First, it talks of cult prostitutes: "None of the daughters of Israel shall be a cult prostitute, and none of the sons of Israel shall be a cult prostitute" (23:17). Such prostitutes were involved in the fertility rituals of Israel's neighboring nations. "Whole guilds of male and female temple personnel participated in grossly sexual rituals designed to induce the various gods and goddesses to release their procreative powers on the earth."[2] The Scriptures ban this practice on religious and moral grounds. Next, using a different word for "prostitute," the Law tackles prostitution in general: "You shall not bring the fee of a prostitute or the wages of a dog into the house of the LORD your God in payment for any vow, for both of these are an abomination to the LORD your God" (23:18). "Dog" here seems to mean "male prostitute." Gifts associated with vows were an expression of gratitude to God for his provision. God does not provide to people through prostitution or other illegitimate means. Therefore, wages from prostitution are not to be brought to fulfill vows.

When Zacchaeus was converted, he paid back the money he stole, and justice was restored by that (Luke 19:8, 9). A similar attitude is found here toward gain from prostitution. Prostitution is "an abomination to the LORD," and therefore no one is to bring to the Lord's house money earned from it. Recently in Sri Lanka a person won a large sum in a lottery and brought a big gift out of it to the church. The minister denounced her for indulging in gambling, and I believe the gift was lost to the church. The Lord does not need money earned in the wrong way. People who come to God in conversion, after having become rich through dishonesty or sexual immorality or some other thing abhorrent to God, must seriously ask what they should do with their wealth! Sometimes the church is reluctant to speak against injustice and unrighteousness as it depends financially on people who earn income through unjust means. We must remember that God does not need money, as he owns everything on earth. Therefore, we do not need to compromise our principles in order to fund the work of God.

While prostitution is "an abomination to the LORD," perhaps we should say something about the value of a prostitute in God's sight. The genealogy of Jesus reveals God's grace to prostitutes, for in it Rahab, a prostitute, appears as an ancestor of Jesus (Matthew 1:5). Very often today vulnerable young men and women are pushed into prostitution forcibly by unscrupulous people who promise jobs for them in the city or in another country. Prostitutes are often subject to terrible physical abuse and frustration. Like any other sinners, they need Jesus. Therefore, though we do not condone their profession, the church must share the gospel with them and look for ways to win a hearing for the gospel. We should try to rescue them from prostitution and find alternative ways for them to earn an income. We should pray that God would call some of his people to the specific task of ministering to prostitutes.

No Interest from Brothers (23:19, 20)

The next command sounds strange because today people can borrow on interest in a way that is beneficial to both the lender and the borrower: "You shall not charge interest on loans to your brother, interest on money, interest on food, interest on anything that is lent for interest. You may charge a foreigner interest, but you may not charge your brother interest . . . " (23:19, 20a). By giving permission to take interest from foreigners, the Bible shows that interest is not wrong per se. Lending as a business is permissible. Therefore, banking today is not un-Biblical. What is wrong is exploiting a needy person. As inflation in those days was negligible, it would not be a big sacrifice for a person of means to help a needy brother without asking for interest. But an unkind person could exploit a poor person in desperate need of funds by giving him money at exorbitant interest. The borrower would take the money because of his emergency and end up being enslaved to the lender, sometimes for life.

This happens today also. The poor are usually unable to satisfy the criteria that banks and other lending institutions ask for in order to lend money. Even if they did meet these criteria, they are so intimidated by the paperwork required to apply for a loan that they do not even attempt to fill out the forms. Instead, they resort to unscrupulous moneylenders who charge huge interest and often take something valuable, such as jewelry, as security. I know many people who have had to forfeit what they gave as security because they could not pay back the loans they took! This is why one of the most important things that people who are more educated can do is to help the poor get what they can by making them aware of those opportunities and helping them apply for financial assistance.

The other thing we can do for people in need of money is to give to those who ask, as Jesus commanded (Luke 6:30). Jesus went on to present an attitude of radical generosity to the poor:

> And if you lend to those from whom you expect to receive, what credit is that to you? Even sinners lend to sinners, to get back the same amount. But . . . lend, expecting nothing in return, and your reward will be great, and you will be sons of the Most High, for he is kind to the ungrateful and the evil. Be merciful, even as your Father is merciful. (Luke 6:34–36)

As God was merciful with us, we should be merciful with the poor and should be willing to give to those who cannot repay. This does not mean that we must encourage irresponsibility by giving to those who ask us with no plan to pay us back. We must help people learn to live within their means. But sometimes we need to suspend those principles when people in desperate need come asking for our help.

As Jesus did in Luke 6:35, Moses promises a reward to those who lend to the poor without interest: ". . . that the LORD your God may bless you in all that you undertake in the land that you are entering to take possession of it" (Deuteronomy 23:20b). This is the clear teaching of the Bible. Proverbs 19:17 promises, "Whoever is generous to the poor lends to the LORD, and he will repay him for his deed." We can share many stories of how God provides to those who help the needy.

When Hudson Taylor, missionary to China, was a young man, he worked for a Christian medical doctor, Dr. Robert Hardey, as part of his medical training. Dr. Hardey agreed to give him his allowance and rent once in four months, but he would often forget about this and delay giving it. Taylor decided that he would not ask Dr. Hardey for the money but would wait on the Lord until he gave it. Once he was running low on money, and he planned to live frugally until the funds came. That day Dr. Hardey told him not to let him forget to pay him on time. But Dr. Hardey did forget and had still not paid him a week after the scheduled payday. Taylor had only a half-crown coin with him. It was Saturday night, and he needed to pay his rent the next morning, and that came to more than half a crown. Taylor pleaded with God to remind Dr. Harley, but he did not do so himself.

When going to church the next morning, he had to pass through a rough neighborhood. A poor man, recognizing Taylor and knowing that he was a godly man, grabbed him by the arm and pulled him into an alley. He told him that his wife was dying and asked him to come and pray for her. She had bled profusely, probably following childbirth, and Taylor realized that she was at death's door. There were also five other children in this desperately poor home. After Taylor prayed, the man asked him for some financial help, and Taylor knew that he should give some money to this family. But he had only one coin. He wished he had three coins adding up to half a crown. He remembered the statement of Jesus to give to him who asks (Luke 6:30). The battle of faith was won, and he gave the man his solitary coin. He joyfully left that home singing hymns as he walked.

The next morning he heard the mail carrier knock at the front door, but as he did not usually get letters on Mondays, he assumed the letter was not for him. But his landlady came and gave him a letter that had come in the mail. As he opened it, a nice pair of gloves fell out. He was looking to see who had sent this letter when a half-sovereign coin also fell on the floor from the envelope. That was worth four times the half-crown that he had given away. He never knew who had sent it! Later he was surprised to learn that the woman for whom he'd prayed had not died as expected but had been healed.[3] Jesus said, ". . . give, and it will be given to you. Good measure, pressed down, shaken together, running over, will be put into your lap. For with the measure you use it will be measured back to you" (Luke 6:38).

It is interesting that research is showing that the poor are more generous givers than the rich. In the United States, for example, government statistics show that the poorest 20 percent of the population contributed about 4.3 percent of their income to charitable organizations, while the richest 20 percent gave less than 2.1 percent.[4] No wonder Paul especially tells the rich "to do good, to be rich in good works, to be generous and ready to share, thus storing up treasure for themselves as a good foundation for the future, so that they may take hold of that which is truly life" (1 Timothy 6:18, 19).

The Seriousness of Vows (23:21–23)

The next law is about voluntary vows and is more of an exhortation than a law: "If you make a vow to the LORD your God, you shall not delay fulfilling it, for the LORD your God will surely require it of you, and you will be guilty of sin" (23:21). Ecclesiastes 5:4–7 gives the teaching of this law in detail:

> When you vow a vow to God, do not delay paying it, for he has no pleasure in fools. Pay what you vow. It is better that you should not vow than that you should vow and not pay. Let not your mouth lead you into sin, and do not say before the messenger that it was a mistake. Why should God be angry at your voice and destroy the work of your hands For when dreams increase and words grow many, there is vanity; but God is the one you must fear.

People take vows when asking God to do something for them or as an expression of devotion. So parents might ask God to heal a sick child or give them a child and promise to offer sacrifices when that is fulfilled. An example of an expression of devotion could be taking a Nazirite vow (Numbers 6:2, 5, 21). Sometimes a pledge for service is made if a request is granted. Hannah vowed that if God gave her a child, she would give him to God for life (1 Samuel 1:11). And she did that when Samuel was a little boy.

Vows are not very popular now, especially among evangelical Christians. But considering how weak we are in our faith and our resolve to obey, they could be useful for us, too. Paul cut his hair to fulfill a vow he had made (Acts

18:18), and he helped four people fulfill their vow by paying their expenses and joining them in the temple (Acts 21:23–26). A person addicted to lying could vow that every time he tells a lie, he will miss a meal. That would help him overcome his weakness.

Our passage says that vows are deadly serious. They are voluntary acts, and there is no compulsion to do it. So Moses says, "But if you refrain from vowing, you will not be guilty of sin" (23:22). If a vow is made, the person must "not delay in fulfilling it" (v. 21). To delay would be to insult God by saying that our relationship with him is not a priority. The fact that we make vows to God makes it all the more serious: "You shall be careful to do what has passed your lips, for you have voluntarily vowed to the LORD your God what you have promised with your mouth" (23:23). If one cannot fulfill a vow, it would be better not to have made it at all. Sadly, we are sometimes afraid to break a promise made to a powerful person and unafraid to break the promises we make to God. This passage challenges us to take our relationship with God more seriously.

Why is the breaking of vows so serious? The covenant culture of the Bible makes words absolutely important. God made promises, which he will surely fulfill. Paul said, "For all the promises of God find their Yes in him. That is why it is through him that we utter our Amen to God for his glory" (2 Corinthians 1:20). God's gift of Jesus consummated this, so that in Jesus we have the most tangible evidence that God will fulfill his promises, even to the extent of giving us his Son. Paul said, "He who did not spare his own Son but gave him up for us all, how will he not also with him graciously give us all things?" (Romans 8:32). The giving of Christ is absolute proof that God will look after us. James says that with God "there is no variation or shadow due to change" (James 1:17). Paul says in a verse quoted earlier (2 Corinthians 1:20) that when we use the popular word *amen* we proclaim God's absolute reliability and bring glory to him. *Amen* is a Hebrew "word meaning 'true,' 'trustworthy'; suggesting solidity, firmness, and [is] used as a strengthening and confirming statement."[5]

When we make a vow and do not fulfill it, we make a mockery of truth and insult God. We contribute to the creation of a culture in which faithfulness is not an important value. In fact, in a culture in which people do not take their vows seriously, faithfulness will become an alien concept, and people will find it difficult even to trust God to look after them. That is a major catastrophe. How often we encounter people who find it difficult to believe that God works for their good. They cannot believe that God will keep his promises. So the Bible asks us to be reliable in fulfilling our promises. James exhorts, ". . . let your 'yes' be yes and your 'no' be no, so that you may not fall under condemnation" (James 5:12). David says God accepts the one "who swears to his own hurt and does not change" (Psalm 15:4). Even if it hurts him, he will keep his promises.

This kind of commitment to absolute truthfulness is going to become more and more difficult in the Western world because it is rejecting the idea that there is a supreme God to whom we are accountable. This was the base upon which the Western emphasis on trustworthiness and honesty was built. Now the criteria for determining right and wrong are becoming anthropocentric (human-centered) rather than theocentric (God-centered). The issue often is not whether an action violates God's Law but whether it hurts someone else or society. Our Sri Lankan culture has not been built on the belief in a supreme and holy God, and lying is rampant, and promises are sometimes made without any intention of fulfilling them. For example, people might say, "I'll come and see you soon" with no intention to do so! The restoration of the value of words is an urgent need all over the world, and a way to help in that is to keep our promises.

The Generosity of Farmers (23:24, 25; 24:19–22)

The next law refers to generosity by farmers: "If you go into your neighbor's vineyard, you may eat your fill of grapes, as many as you wish. . . . If you go into your neighbor's standing grain, you may pluck the ears with your hand" (23:24a, 25a). Many scholars think this law is primarily for the benefit of travelers, and we know that Jesus' disciples made use of it one Sabbath when they were hungry (Luke 6:1). Using the word "neighbor" gives this law a wider application, though it may primarily apply to travelers. The similar law in Deuteronomy 24:19–22, which we will also consider, extends the benefit of the farmer's generosity to "the sojourner, the fatherless, and the widow," that is, the needy.

Some could exploit the generosity of the farmer and take more than they should. So both these verses have a clause limiting how much one could take: ". . . but you shall not put any in your bag . . . you shall not put a sickle to your neighbor's standing grain" (23:24b, 25b). As David F. Payne says, this is "a commonsense law . . . to discourage meanness and greediness on the part of farmers, and theft on the part of passers-by." Today house owners get stingy, and passers-by get exploitative. So we have high walls protecting residences and properties that show that generous neighborliness is outdated. We must find ways of generosity that make it easy for the truly needy to find help and make it difficult for exploiters to take the generous for a ride. Because of this we need to have specific rules like those in these two verses aimed at preventing abuses.

I am going to look at this law along with a similar law in 24:19–22 that applies to a time a little later in the agricultural cycle than this one—after the grain, olive, and vineyard harvests. What is missed in the original harvesting is to be left for the needy to take.

> When you reap your harvest in your field and forget a sheaf in the field, you shall not go back to get it. It shall be for the sojourner, the fatherless, and the widow, that the LORD your God may bless you in all the work of your hands. When you beat your olive trees, you shall not go over them again. It shall be for the sojourner, the fatherless, and the widow. When you gather the grapes of your vineyard, you shall not strip it afterward. It shall be for the sojourner, the fatherless, and the widow. You shall remember that you were a slave in the land of Egypt; therefore I command you to do this. (24:19–22)

As we have already said, here the law specifically mentions the needy—"the sojourner, the fatherless, and the widow"—as beneficiaries.

What is described here is a pleasant neighborhood where people think it is a normal part of life to help others and do not think it is a big deal when they have done so. This comes out of the Biblical attitude toward possessions, which says that everything we own ultimately comes from God and has been given to us to use as he wishes. In the early church, "no one said that any of the things that belonged to him was his own" (Acts 4:32). We do not cling to any possession with the idea that it is exclusively ours. Some Christians do not have this mind-set today, but they will never be happy, for it is only as we allow love to flow out of our lives that we find the satisfaction of living life to the full. Yet to do this we must first surrender our lives to God. Once this has been done, there is a deep sense within us that true satisfaction can only be found in God's way, and that therefore we will give anything to anybody whom God asks us to help. When people benefit from another's generosity, they are happy. The giver is happy, the receiver is happy, and the result is a happy society.

Our passage teaches that the basic Biblical attitude to neighbors is not "How can I protect myself from them?" but "How can I be a blessing to them?" W. E. Sangster was a famous British Methodist preacher who tried to approach every encounter he had with someone by asking the question, "How can I help this person?" When Sangster died, his wife received about 1,400 letters of condolence, and in about 1,000 of them the writers mentioned some specific help they had received from Dr. Sangster.[6] That is how we should look at our neighbors. We should always ask, "How can I help them?" The evangelistic value of such an attitude cannot be underestimated, especially in this era when those committed to evangelism are viewed as being arrogant.

The Pharisees were legalistic when they came to the application of the teaching of our passage. When the hungry disciples of Jesus "plucked and ate some heads of grain, rubbing them in their hands," the Pharisees complained that the disciples did this on the Sabbath day (Luke 6:1, 2). Isn't it strange that people can become legalistic when applying provisions made for expressions of kindness! The society envisaged for Old Testament Israel, contrary to what many think today, was a pleasant place. No wonder its hallmark was joy. There are twenty-three different Hebrew words for joy in the Old Testament, which according to some is the greatest number of words for joy in any language.

This study showed that God intended us to have societies where people are considerate toward others and faithful in fulfilling what they pledge. That would result in happy neighborhoods because people are considerate and stable neighborhoods because people are faithful.

50

Generous Justice

DEUTERONOMY 24:1–22

THE USUAL PICTURE WE HAVE of justice is of an unbending system that deals with all people alike regardless of their circumstances. That is not the picture of justice that we get in the Bible. In our study of Deuteronomy 15:1–18, we said that the Bible goes beyond strict justice. We said that the depiction of the law as a blindfolded woman (without prejudice) holding up a pair of scales (strictly enforcing justice in the same way to all) does not fit in well with the Biblical teaching about justice. When making demands on people, Biblical justice takes seriously the situations in which they are found. The Bible does not envisage the situation common today of the weak and poor having the law brutally thrown at them, leaving them with no hope of relief from their desperate personal circumstances. Timothy Keller has written a book on this called *Generous Justice: How God's Grace Makes Us Just.*[1]

Biblical justice reflects God's holy and loving nature. As we shall see in this study, God's righteousness is expressed not only in opposing wrong but also in merciful love to the needy, taking into account their extreme circumstances. In our passage the word "righteousness" is used for returning a cloak taken as a pledge for a loan so that the borrower will not be cold (24:13). Referring to a similar scenario, it talks about "the justice due to the sojourner or to the fatherless" (24:17). Deuteronomy 24 shows the loving side of God's righteousness in concessions made to the newly married (24:5), the needy who take loans (24:6, 10–18), and the sojourners, the widows, and the fatherless who live near agricultural lands (24:19–22). As Chris Wright puts it, "The majority of laws in this chapter have to do with restraining exploitation and greed for the sake of protecting the needy." They are comprehensive in scope, covering family life, business, and agriculture.

Prohibition against Marrying a Former Wife (24:1–4)

First, we have a law about ex-husbands remarrying their ex-wives. This law deals with very specific circumstances and is not primarily about the rights and wrongs of divorce and remarriage. This is indicated by the presence of the word "if" three times (24:1, 2, 3) and "then" twice (24:1, 4) in key places. These are called casuistic laws, which is the name given for laws that apply general laws to specific circumstances. The first situation is where a crisis has arisen in a marriage because of a problem with the wife: "When a man takes a wife and marries her, if then she finds no favor in his eyes because he has found some indecency in her . . . " (24:1a). We cannot be sure what the indecency was, for the text does not state that. It was not adultery because that would bring the death sentence. Most commentators think that some immodesty or indecent behavior is involved.

When the husband encounters this problem, "he writes her a certificate of divorce and puts it in her hand and sends her out of his house, and she departs out of his house" (24:1b). Note that the husband is not told to divorce her. Hosea did not divorce his wife when she did much worse things. This passage describes what should happen if the husband decides to divorce her. The next scenario is that this divorced woman marries another man (24:2) who could come to the state where he "hates her and writes her a certificate of divorce and puts it in her hand and sends her out of his house" (24:3a). Another possible situation is that "the latter man dies" (24:3b). This law prohibits her first husband from marrying her again: ". . . then her former husband, who sent her away, may not take her again to be his wife, after she has been defiled, for that is an abomination before the LORD" (24:4).

This law says "she has been defiled." This does not mean she is immoral. It means that as far as the first husband is concerned she is out of bounds or ritually unclean.[2] In fact the strong words, "that is an abomination before the LORD" are usually used in ceremonial or cultic settings.[3] The paragraph concludes with the statement, "And you shall not bring sin upon the land that the LORD your God is giving you for an inheritance" (24:4b). That is, the course of action prohibited has a very bad influence upon the land.

At first it may seem that the wife is being given shoddy treatment here. Actually this law is intended to protect her. In those days marriages and divorces were not performed by government authorities or authorities accredited by the government, which is what officiating ministers at weddings are today. They were domestic matters, and all that the husband needed to do was to tell her wife that he was divorcing her. The Bible brought in laws to protect the wife, which is what the "certificate of divorce" (24:1) does. Without something in writing that she was divorced, she would be accused of adultery if she marries again. This law "provides guideposts" for divorce.[4] There had to be adequate grounds for divorce, and a legal document was required. This law makes divorce a serious matter. In those days a woman could be easily transferred from man to man. She could be discarded by her husband without adequate reasons.

What this law says is that a man cannot just change his mind after divorcing his wife and simply take her back. It forces the man to think more seriously, before divorcing, of the implications of divorcing his wife. Jesus raised the standard even higher by saying that divorce was a concession granted by Moses "because of [their] hardness of heart" (Matthew 19:8). This is very relevant today because I believe some people divorce for inadequate reasons. Recently I have been told of several people who could have saved a marriage but rushed into divorce too quickly. This problem is found among evangelical Christians, too. A recent survey showed that about 26 percent of married evangelical Christians in the United States have divorced. Though this is lower than the national average of 33 percent, it is still high.[5] While the Bible permits divorce, it recommends a greater hesitancy to doing this than is seen in the world.

This law is evidence that the Bible has a higher standard of marriage than the cultures of the neighboring people. History shows that in many cultures there were practices that demeaned marriage, before they were influenced by the Christian culture. The presence of Christians helped raise the value of marriage. This was certainly true in Sri Lanka. Even though large numbers of people did not become Christians under colonial rule, the colonial rulers from nations influenced by Christianity brought in rules that raised the standard of marriage, such as introducing monogamy as the only acceptable form of marriage.

Enjoy Your Wife (24:5)

The next command in this section on generous justice is about newly married men: "When a man is newly married, he shall not go out with the army or be liable for any other public duty. He shall be free at home one year to be happy with his wife whom he has taken" (24:5). In those days many in the national army were not full-time soldiers. When there was a war, they left their usual professions to participate in the battle. Newly married men are exempted from battles and from special civic duties. Presumably during this year the man will still do what he usually does to earn a living. One reason for this exemption ought to be that he can have a child to ensure the continuity of his family, as there is the possibility of his dying in the battle. The reason given here, however, is, "to be happy with his wife." This should more accurately read, "bring happiness to the wife he has married" (TNIV).

Someone has quipped that marriage is a three-ring circus. First, you have the engagement ring, then you have the wedding ring, and finally you have the suffering! That is *not* the Biblical idea of marriage. The Biblical picture of marriage is that of a joyous relationship. Note that the husband has the responsibility to make his wife happy. Research has shown a common scenario in marriages. During the first few years of marriage the husband is so busy with the task of laying a good foundation in his career that he does not give sufficient attention to showing affection to his wife. The wife, after looking for affection from her husband and not getting a satisfactory response, soon begins to pour her love and her energies into her children. When the husband reaches middle age, he has a general picture of the course his career will take. He realizes that he has neglected the most important things in his life, such as showing affection to his wife. When he turns to his wife with affection, he finds that she has now gained new interests and does not respond as he wishes. Having been hurt by her unrealized expectations and having raised children to relative independence, she is ready now to pursue a career and things she considers to be fulfilling.[6]

It is not accidental that the primary advice to husbands regarding marriage in the New Testament is that they love their wives (Ephesians 5:25; Colossians 3:19; see 1 Peter 3:7). I have heard of many wives who said that their first year of marriage was a terrible ordeal. There were so many new responsibilities, so many areas of incompetence were revealed, trying to understand the husband's behavior was often a huge challenge, and many times his behavior hurt her. This is inevitable in any marriage. The process of two becoming one does not occur automatically! It has to be worked at. How much easier this is if the husband makes it his aim in life to love his wife and make her happy. And that squares with what the Scriptures teach. First Corinthians 14:1 asks us to "pursue love," and one with whom we should do that most conscientiously is our spouse.

Again the Biblical ethic proves to have a higher standard than the surrounding culture. Even today in some circles people think the wife's job is to serve and make her husband happy. Here the reverse is commanded.

Four Laws about Loans and Pledges (24:6, 10–13, 17, 18)

In this chapter we find several laws to protect the needy. Four of these laws are about protecting the needy when they give a pledge as security for a loan.

The Bible commends lending to the poor (Psalm 15:5), but greed can cause the lender to "squeeze and exploit"[7] debtors. This is why moneylenders have been caricatured as unkind and have been disliked in literature and drama throughout history. Our passage talks about limits to what lenders can do with pledges taken with the loans. Though the Israelites could not take interest on their loans, they could take pledges as security to ensure repayment.

The Laws

First, Moses says, "No one shall take a mill or an upper millstone in pledge, for that would be taking a life in pledge" (24:6). The poor could not purchase processed grain from others. So they had to grind grain at home using a mill that had a heavy lower millstone and a lighter upper one. If the upper stone was taken, the mill could not be used. Without the mill, they would not be able to make bread, which was an essential part of their daily food. Of course, if the lender takes the mill or millstone as a pledge, the borrower would return the money soon. A conscientious Christian lender must think of the welfare of the borrower and try to ensure that his life is not ruined because of the loan he takes. That is the Biblical way, even though it sounds strange to our ears today.

This is, however, a complex issue because some borrowers could exploit the lender, sometimes quoting Scripture to force the person to give. My wife and I have found that some Christians habitually borrow money from other Christians and never pay back the money. This is very damaging to the person. In fact, I think I am correct in my observation that such people have little chance of succeeding economically because they are irresponsible. Sadly, they give a bad example to their children, who also often grow up to be irresponsible people who stand little chance of progressing in life economically.

Not only must the lender think of the borrower's welfare, he must make sure that he can "borrow with honor."[8] In the second law Moses says, "When you make your neighbor a loan of any sort, you shall not go into his house to collect his pledge. You shall stand outside, and the man to whom you make the loan shall bring the pledge out to you" (24:10, 11). This at first seems strange in our cultures where the Western understanding of privacy is not a premium value and people go in and out of houses freely. We saw this happening in the ministry of Jesus (see Matthew 26:7). As the lender has power over the desperate borrower, he could go into the house and demand something from the house, demeaning the borrower in the process. He is in a very vulnerable situation and is at the lender's mercy. But he is a person made in the image of God. The lender has the responsibility of protecting the borrower's honor. This, too, is an approach to lending that we do not see very often today. Actually this law implies that when we help the poor in any way, we should not do so in a way that makes them feel small. This happens often, and because of that social workers are often intensely disliked by the people they help.

I believe this principle also applies to other situations when we deal with needy people. For example, we should speak respectfully to a man in front of his children, and if we have to rebuke him, do it when he is not with his children.

The third law says, "And if he is a poor man, you shall not sleep in his pledge. You shall restore to him the pledge as the sun sets, that he may sleep in his cloak and bless you" (24:12, 13a). The item in question was like a blanket and was used as a cloak during the day and as a covering at night. If the lender gets a cloak as a pledge, he must not keep it overnight. The borrower must have it to keep himself warm. The giving of the cloak shows how genuine the borrower is. He has given something that is very precious to him. Such sincerity should be rewarded by returning the cloak to him. Again the welfare of the borrower is uppermost. The powerful person is to be sensitive to the needs of the weak person and make allowance for those needs. But does this not violate principles of responsible lending? Moses seems to think that this so-called violation actually becomes righteousness to the lender, as the second part of verse 13 says: "And it [restoring the pledge] shall be righteousness for you before the LORD your God." Here is an instance of what we have called generous justice. Our righteousness must be like God's righteousness, in which mercy and grace are important aspects. A holy person is one who has a special concern for the needy. Sadly, this is often left out when we define personal holiness.

Before the fourth law about pledges we see a general statement: "You shall not pervert the justice due to the sojourner or to the fatherless" (24:17a), which is in keeping with the theme we are looking at here. Then Moses gives the fourth law, saying, ". . . or take a widow's garment in pledge" (24:17b). This is very similar to the third law.

Grace Is Given Freely after Grace Is Received Freely (24:18)

What follows the fourth law is particularly significant: ". . . but you shall remember that you were a slave in Egypt and the LORD your God redeemed you from there; therefore I command you to do this" (24:18). A similar statement is made after the last law in this chapter (24:22). Remembering God's gracious redemption from Egypt is a foundational principle governing the lending process. In fact, it is a foundational principle governing all behavior. I found this idea repeated twenty-eight times in Deuteronomy.[9] As we face pressures and disappointments in life it is easy to forget the fact that we are a redeemed people. Our redemption is an even more spectacular one than that of the Jews because God's Son himself died in order to redeem us. We must always remember that we have huge riches that we don't deserve. This makes us joyously grateful to God for his kindness, and this gratitude nurtures an attitude of graciousness within us. We help people not out of a sense of duty but out of the overflow of joy in our lives. Naturally we would not want to put burdens upon those we help.

The covenant community is a grace-filled community. However, when we lose sight of grace, life is no longer sweetened by joy and gratitude. Then we become angry over people exploiting us and about not being given the recognition we believe we should receive. We may work hard and help others, but we are angry people. The anger will soon spill out, and we end up hurting others.

There is another significant thing about remembering our past bondage and present redemption. Sometimes people who have been liberated from oppression and poverty try to deny or hide their past. They fear that the past will adversely affect their identity. Some become oppressors themselves. Some refuse to go back to their old neighborhoods or to think about the needs of those who are needy just as they once were. Moses says that redemption from a needy past makes us more considerate and caring of the needy. People who try to deny their past end up being bound to that past on the inside even though they were liberated from it on the outside.

We need to discuss one more aspect of helping the poor and making concessions for them. When we help the poor, we are in danger of fostering a welfare mentality that cripples many societies. The poor, having lost their sense of responsibility, think that affluent individuals or the government or the church must look after them. They do not work hard to come out of poverty and to repay their loans. The Bible is alert to this problem. This is why Paul says that only those who qualify should be included in the list of widows to be helped by the church (1 Timothy 5:3–16). He says that if you give charity to widows who can work, "they learn to be idlers, going about from house to house" (1 Timothy 5:13). We must be wise in the way we give. We must not create an unhealthy attitude of dependence that discourages hard work among the poor.

Yet the abuse of charity by some should not cause us to be insensitive to those who are truly needy. In fact, sometimes we may need to help children of irresponsible parents because we do not want the sins of parents to result in their children being malnourished.

The lending laws of this chapter raise some difficult questions. In answering them we must put the needs of people uppermost in our thinking. We are graced people who want to be gracious to others. Moreover, when we help people we must never cause those receiving help to feel small, and we must do all we can to protect their honor in their time of need.

Two More Laws to Protect the Needy (24:14, 15, 19–22)

Paying a Daily Wage to the Needy (24:14, 15)

The next law is about giving wages daily to the poor: "You shall give him his wages on the same day, before the sun sets (for he is poor and counts on it)" (24:15a). When I first read this, I thought of the many poor people whose misery would have been reduced if some concessions were made for them. I am thinking about wives of drug addicts or alcoholics and of others who struggle to survive because of economic circumstances. Often the poor have to wait until the end of the week or month to get paid. Therefore, they have to borrow money from unscrupulous moneylenders who lend them money with very high interest. This begins a process of bondage from which they will never escape. Another problem is that often the poor spend in a week what they were paid for the month because they have not learned to use money responsibly. This law shows us that God has thought about the circumstances of the poor and has given laws appropriate to them.

I think of the poor in need who come and ask for something that they could legitimately receive but that if given at this time would require a little extra work by the people administering the process. Some poor are not educated enough to fill out a form properly. How good it would be if the administering officer goes that extra mile and fills it out for him. After all, these officers often make all sorts of exceptions to help the rich and influential! The spirit of the present law would imply that authorities should do extra work to help the poor.

The Biblical verdict on those who do not make concessions for the poor in the way mentioned above is very sobering. Just before stating the law about paying the poor daily, Moses says, "You shall not oppress a hired worker who is poor and needy, whether he is one of your brothers or one of the sojourners who are in your land within your towns" (24:14). This means that the failure to make concessions for the poor is a form of oppression! Then Moses says, ". . . lest he cry against you to the LORD, and you be guilty of sin" (24:15b). If by our negligence we have given a poor person occasion to cry out to God for help, we become guilty of sin and are liable to God's punishment.

Most people do not care to go out of their way to help the needy because they think there is nothing to gain from doing so. The rich, however, are influential, and people would be afraid not to help the rich. What Moses is saying is that there is everything to lose by not helping the poor. We provoke the Lord God Almighty to anger and expose ourselves to his awesome punishment. The power of the most powerful person in the world is insignificant in comparison with God's power. Proverbs 22:22, 23 says, "Do not exploit the poor because they are poor and do not crush the needy in court, for the LORD will take up their case and will exact life for life" (TNIV). When we exploit the poor, we are going to take on God—and there is no doubt over who will win! Shrewd people will make special concessions to the powerful for fear of displeasing them. God's people make concessions to the poor for fear of displeasing God. Though those who help the poor may look like fools, they are making a very smart choice.

The Farmers' Generosity (24:19–22)

The next law to protect the needy is given to farmers. Deuteronomy 24:19–22 says that after the harvesting of grains, olives, and vineyards, the farmers must leave what is missed in the original harvesting for the needy to take. We looked at this law along with our discussion on 23:24, 25. Note that here, too, there is an exhortation to remember their deliverance from Egypt: "You shall remember that you were a slave in the land of Egypt; therefore I command you to do this" (24:22).

Three More Laws (24:7–9, 16)

Three more laws from chapter 24 remain to be discussed.

Kidnapping (24:7)

Verse 7 presents a law that seems so distant to our world that we might ignore it. It is about kidnapping people to sell as slaves: "If a man is found stealing one of his brothers of the people of Israel, and if he treats him as a slave or sells him, then that thief shall die" (24:7a). This is the only form of stealing that merits a death penalty in the Mosaic Law. Though slaves were bought and sold in the world that the Israelites lived in, stealing people to sell as slaves was never permitted even among Israel's neighbors.[10] Kidnapping still takes place today, now for a ransom.

Another practice similar to what is condemned here goes on unabated today. People, especially women and girls, from desperately poor backgrounds are taken away with the promise of employment and are forced into prostitution, sex slavery, and forced labor. People are taken from rural areas to urban areas and from poorer nations to nations that are more affluent. There is a wide variation in the figures about the numbers of people being trafficked. This is partly because it is difficult to track this, as it is done by illegal, underground organizations. A conservative figure often cited is from a 2005 United States State Department Report that 600,000 to 800,000 people are trafficked across international borders for all kinds of forced labor including sexual exploitation.[11] The figure of people trafficked within a nation could also be staggering.

Moses says about the punishment for kidnapping for slavery, "So you shall purge the evil from your midst" (24:7b). Like some other serious sins about which this statement is made (17:7, 12; 19:19; 21:21; 22:21; 24:7), kidnapping is a sin that defiles a nation. Something must be done about it. This is how the Bible would describe the selling of helpless people into sexual slavery. May some of God's people respond to this need and do all they can to rescue such people. There are encouraging stories of Christian ministries among sex slaves that help rescue them and find alternate lives for them.[12] The work is slow and hard, but surely it would be in keeping with the spirit of Deuteronomy, which gives great emphasis to protecting people from exploitation.

Leprous Diseases (24:8, 9)

The next command sounds more like an exhortation than a law, and it seems to be out of place in a section with laws describing ethical behavior. It is about leprous diseases—which in the Bible usually includes several skin diseases in addition to what is called leprosy today. There were detailed regulations about these diseases in Leviticus 13, 14. Here Moses summarizes saying, "Take care, in a case of leprous disease, to be very careful to do according to all that the Levitical priests shall direct you. As I commanded them, so you shall be careful to do" (Deuteronomy 24:8). Probably this call to be careful is because the lack of care could result in an epidemic. There were no doctors in those days, and the people had limited medical knowledge. So they are commanded to take the patient to the Levitical priest who should have better knowledge. He will give instructions about what to do. We can see that the issues involved here are ethical ones. Therefore, this exhortation is not out of place in this chapter.

The application for us today is that we must be careful when people get infectious diseases. Sometimes in our ministry we might have a young person with a highly contagious fever come to a camp. The campers spend a lot of time close to each other. The infection could spread like wildfire. A child who goes to school with a contagious eye infection could also have such an effect. Parents and citizens should be alert to prevent people from unnecessarily spreading infection. Medical personnel, especially those in community medicine, could render a great service by preventing the spread of diseases.

Verse 9 also seems to have an ethical edge: "Remember what the LORD your God did to Miriam on the way as you came out of Egypt." We cannot be sure what lesson Moses intends us to get from remembering Miriam's leprosy. Could it be that Moses is saying that if such a high person in society as Miriam could get this, then normal people, too, could get it and we should be alert to the possibility of infection? Another possible application is that just as Miriam broke out with a leprous disease, we also could get sick if we go on making false accusations against people (Numbers 12). We make a similar application from 1 Corinthians 11:28–30 where Paul calls on people to examine themselves before participating in the Lord's Supper and then says, "For anyone who eats and drinks without discerning the body eats and drinks judgment on himself. That is why many of you are weak and ill, and some have died."

Individual Responsibility (24:16)

Deuteronomy 24:16 says, "Fathers shall not be put to death because of their children, nor shall children be put to death because of their fathers. Each one shall be put to death for his own sin." Often in our study of Deuteronomy we have highlighted the strong bonds of corporate solidarity that existed in the Israelite community. Israel is presented "as almost a corporate personality."[13] We discussed this in our study of 9:16, 17. So sometimes when one person sins, it is as if the whole community has sinned. When Achan sinned, the whole of Israel was punished (Joshua 22:20). But that is not the way God acts every time somebody sins. Usually an individual is punished for his or her sins, and others are not held responsible.

We saw in our study of Deuteronomy 5:3–5 that ultimately individuals and not others are responsible for their own behavior. The law we are looking at says that fathers should not be put to death because of their children and children should not be put to death because of their fathers. There is individual responsibility in the Biblical community while it practices corporate solidarity. Those who say that Deuteronomy was written much later than the traditional date say this is evidence of the late date—that the concept of individual responsibility emerged much later in Israel's history. Indeed, there is a strong statement about individual responsibility in the description of the new covenant by the prophets (Jeremiah 31:34; see Ezekiel 18). But this is a principle that was already evident in the early years of Israel's history (see Exodus 21–23).[14]

Applying this verse today, we could say that we should not hold family members responsible for the sins of one member of the family. Often unruly and lawless children emerge from seriously deficient families. Sometimes such a son may come out of a family with good and godly parents. The suffering those parents endure because of their child's behavior is huge. We do not need to add to that by blaming them for their children's behavior. One of Jesus' twelve disciples was Judas. He betrayed Jesus, and Jesus said that it would have been better if he had not been born (Matthew 26:24). Jesus was the greatest discipler ever, and he had a Judas. In the same way, good parents may sometimes have rebellious children. Just like many of the laws in this chapter, this law is also concerned with protecting the vulnerable—in this case the family members of a wrongdoer.

I have worked on this book for many years, and throughout this period people have tried to communicate to me the idea that they think there is very little value for today in the book of Deuteronomy. The more I study this book, the more I realize how wrong they are. Many have asked me why I took on this project. Again the idea is that I could have chosen a more exciting and helpful book. Always my response to that question is that I took it on because Deuteronomy influenced me greatly in my formative years in ministry. Deuteronomy influenced many of the lifestyle choices my wife and I made, especially in our attitude toward people who are needy and vulnerable to exploitation. Many of the individual laws do not need to be fully observed by those who are non-Jews living under the new covenant, but these laws tell us about the mind of God. They tell us the things that God hates and the things that God loves. Chapter 24 is a good example of how Deuteronomy gives practical hints into how God wants us to think and act.

51

Concern for Humans and Animals and Honesty

DEUTERONOMY 25:1–19

IN THIS DETAILED LAW SECTION OF Deuteronomy I am amazed at the recurring serious desire to ensure that the Israelite nation does not neglect any needy or disadvantaged person. There is so much to learn from this emphasis on making concrete plans to help people who are vulnerable to exploitation and neglect. Deuteronomy 25 refers to concerns about wrongdoers who are being punished, oxen used for work, women whose husbands die without leaving an heir, men involved in a conflict, and consumers. No wonder some have described Deuteronomy as the constitution of the Israelite nation.

Regulating Punishment (25:1–3)

The chapter begins by presenting something that often happens today: "If there is a dispute between men and they come into court and the judges decide between them, acquitting the innocent and condemning the guilty . . . " (25:1). The punishment prescribed here is what we call corporal punishment: ". . . then if the guilty man deserves to be beaten, the judge shall cause him to lie down and be beaten in his presence with a number of stripes in proportion to his offense" (25:2). Corporal punishment was a very common form of punishment everywhere in those days. What is special about this law is what comes next: "Forty stripes may be given him, but not more, lest, if one should go on to beat him with more stripes than these, your brother be degraded in your sight" (25:3). In the laws of the Babylonian King Hammurabi (1792–1750 BC) and the Middle Assyrian Code (1000–612 BC) the number of lashes range from twenty to sixty.[1] Here the maximum permitted is forty lashes. Later the limit was reduced to thirty-nine "to err on the safe side."[2] Paul says, "Five times I received at the hands of the Jews the forty lashes less one" (2 Corinthians 11:24).

While all this may sound very cruel to us today, the purpose of the law we are studying is to restrict the punishment to a bearable intensity so as to prevent, as Moses says, the person being "degraded in [their] sight" (Deuteronomy 25:3). The Hebrew word translated "degraded" carries the idea of putting a person "in an unwarranted social position."[3] One cannot do that to a "brother" even though he may have caused him some harm. Punishment must not violate the dignity of a human being made in the image of God. One aim of punishment is correcting the person's sinful weaknesses. That will not happen if the punishment makes one feel subhuman. Sometimes parents and teachers make statements like, "You have no hope of doing well in life" or, "You are useless" or, "You come from the gutter." Such statements degrade those children.

One way to motivate people to seek what is good is to show them that as children of God they are too exalted to be satisfied with sin, that God made them for something much greater. In 1 Timothy 1:18, using a tender word meaning "beloved child" and a strong word meaning "command or charge," Paul told his spiritual son Timothy, "This charge I entrust to you, Timothy, my child, in accordance with the prophecies previously made about you, that by them you may wage the good warfare." This is a good model for parents to adopt when disciplining their children. Paul gives a firm charge to his beloved child, but he does so "in accordance with the prophecies previously made about" Timothy. These prophecies would have fueled Paul's ambition to see Timothy being greatly used by God. When Paul spoke sternly to Timothy, he also reminded him of his great potential, so that he would realize that the sternness was aimed at helping him achieve his fullest potential.

The recent moves to outlaw corporal punishment in many countries were motivated by the degrading way it is often meted out. People in a rage can lose control and cause harm to the punished person that outweighed the good the punishment was intended to achieve. Parents sometimes destroy a child's sense of self-esteem by angrily screaming at him or her, by lashing out unmercifully and causing grievous physical and mental harm. The pressure of our fast-moving society triggers stress in people. Unlike earlier times, many parents do not have the support of members of their extended family who live nearby and can help in nurturing and caring for little children. Parents are generally more stressed today than in earlier generations. They sometimes react in an extreme way when provoked by the behavior of their children.

Though corporal punishment has been outlawed in many places, it is still important for Christians to use utmost care when disciplining people and resolving conflicts. Deuteronomy 25:1–3 gives principles that govern and moderate their reactions to conflicts. For example, the principle recommended here, of bringing the problem to a group similar to the elders, is helpful in serious cases. Parents would do well to consult each other and come up with a mutually agreed upon strategy for disciplining a child about a given issue. To ensure that we do not degrade a person, it is good to control ourselves when we are angry and wait until the anger subsides because in our anger we may say and do things that cause more harm than good. For example, we can say insulting things to children that will cause deep wounds and make it difficult for them to believe they are significant and loved.

A magician named Elymas opposed Barnabas and Paul when they were sharing the gospel with a Roman official named Sergius Paulus. He tried "to turn [him] away from the faith" (Acts 13:8). Paul rebuked Elymas, who then went blind. Before reporting the rebuke, Luke says, "Paul, filled with the Holy Spirit, looked intently at him" (Acts 13:9). This was a case of a special filling of the Spirit for dealing with a hostile situation. Rebuking and punishing are intensely spiritual activities. We need God's help and infilling when we do such things.

Being Considerate of Working Animals (25:4)

The next law was used by Paul as an illustration when talking about the payment of ministers of the gospel (1 Corinthians 9:9; 1 Timothy 5:18), but that should not make us ignore the original intention of this law. It says, "You shall not muzzle an ox when it is treading out the grain." This law is given out of concern for the welfare of animals. "Oxen were used to plow fields and to pull threshing sleds to crush the stocks of grain once they were harvested. At the threshing floor, the grain would be laid in such a way that a heavy sled could be driven over it. The hooves of the oxen would also aid in the processing of the grain."[4] The oxen were permitted to eat some of the grain as their "wage."

We have already mentioned that the concern for animals is a unique feature of the Israelites among the ancient Near Eastern nations (see the discussion on 5:14; 22:1–4). We cited Proverbs 12:10: "Whoever is righteous has regard for the life of his beast." We pointed out that the Royal Society for the Prevention of Cruelty to Animals (RSPCA) was founded in England in 1824 by Arthur Broome, an Anglican clergyman, with the aid of the evangelical social reformer William Wilberforce and his friends.[5] Christians adopt a humane approach to animals and humans because they believe that these have been created by God and that God has given humans the responsibility of caring for all of creation (Genesis 1:28; 9:2, 3).

The Bible does give permission for the killing of animals for sacrifices and food, but we must balance this with the call to be considerate to animals. Any form of killing animals that causes great pain to them would be unacceptable to Christians. This is why it is not surprising that in several countries Christians, though a minority, have been in the forefront of advocating humane ways to slaughter animals.

Levirate Marriage (25:5–10)

Verses 5–10 give instructions for what we call levirate marriages. The word *levirate* comes from a Latin word that means a husband's brother and refers to a marriage where a widow marries her late husband's brother. Levirate marriage was a common practice in the ancient Near East. Our passage deals with a very restricted and specific situation. Verse 5 says, "If brothers dwell together, and one of them dies and has no son, the wife of the dead man shall not be married outside the family to a stranger. Her husband's brother shall go in to her and take her as his wife and perform the duty of a husband's brother to her." The brothers must "dwell together" before one dies. This suggests that the father has died before the property had been divided, and the children were thus living in an undivided property. This law also is for a situation where the person who dies "has no son." This means that someone was needed to carry on her husband's name. Verse 6 says, "And the first son whom she bears shall succeed to the name of his dead brother, that his name may not be blotted out of Israel." By marrying the widow the brother is "providing a family heir or . . . [is] passing on property in an orderly fashion."[6] With time levirate marriage became less common, especially as daughters began inheriting property.[7]

There is no insistence here that the brother must marry his widowed sister-in-law. The possibility of the brother refusing to do this is mentioned next: "And if the man does not wish to take his brother's wife . . . " (25:7a). While taking his brother's wife is desirable, it is not compulsory. An unnamed relative refused to marry Ruth when she came to Israel as a widow because it would threaten his inheritance (Ruth 4:1–6). So the next in line, Boaz, took her as his wife.

If the brother-in-law refuses to marry the widow, this would be a setback to her. So she is given an opportunity to appeal to the elders of the community about his decision: ". . . then his brother's wife shall go up to the gate to the elders and say, 'My husband's brother refuses to perpetuate his brother's name in Israel; he will not perform the duty of a husband's brother to me'" (25:7b). He may refuse even after the elders appeal to him: "Then the elders of his city shall call him and speak to him, and if he persists, saying, 'I do not wish to take her' . . . " (25:8). They cannot force the brother-in-law if he refuses. But the disappointed widow can express her disappointment and dishonor him for refusing to take up his moral responsibility: ". . . then his brother's wife shall go up to him in the presence of the elders and pull his sandal off his foot and spit in his face. And she shall answer and say, 'So shall it be done to the man who does not build up his brother's house.' And the name of his house shall be called in Israel, 'The house of him who had his sandal pulled off'" (25:9, 10). The act of pulling the sandal off his feet could be a sign of his renouncing his property rights or it could be a way of humiliating him. Certainly spitting in his face humiliates him.

You cannot force a person to marry someone he does not want to marry. A few times over the past years I have had the difficult task of trying to convince a young woman that the person she was planning to marry was not going to marry her. It was very painful, especially because in our culture a woman who does not marry after being engaged to a man is at a big disadvantage. I always tell our men that it is wrong to give a woman false hopes and then to suddenly drop her. But I know that I cannot force a person to marry someone whom he does not want to marry. I also believe that it is wrong to delay communicating that to the woman, for that would increase her misery. Because I have insisted that this should be communicated quickly, I have sometimes been accused of being the one responsible for breaking the engagement! But I have always felt that this is something we must do on behalf of the woman, though she might end up blaming us for the breakup!

A similar situation exists here. Though there is a moral responsibility to marry her, the law cannot force a man to marry his widowed sister-in-law. The law, however, must do all it can to protect the vulnerable. So it permits her to express her outrage in a concrete way. This could be a step in healing the pain of this unfortunate widow. She has lost her husband and has now been rejected by his brother. She is given an opportunity to express her rage.

I have found exit interviews with staff that leave us angrily very painful to endure. The exiting staff workers are vulnerable at that time because they are going into an uncertain future. Therefore, I believe it is necessary to patiently listen to them expressing their anger—often against me! My hope is that having released their anger, they are now ready to start a new chapter in their lives. I have found that these staff, who scolded me quite severely at the time they left, are all friendly with me now. And I have tried to do my part to help secure a good future for them. If they do not get an opportunity to say what they want to say, they could go through life with an unhealed wound that adversely influences their attitudes and actions.

This law is sensitive to the needs of the widow and does all it can to see that she is cared for. We, too, have a similar responsibility to widows—especially those without children who can take care of them. This is such an important value that, in a discussion on caring for widows, Paul says, "But if anyone does not provide for his relatives, and especially for members of his household, he has denied the faith and is worse than an unbeliever" (1 Timothy 5:8).

Hurting the Genitals of a Man (25:11, 12)

The next law seems strange and out of place in this section of Deuteronomy. Because of its many difficulties, Jewish scholars have debated the meaning and intent of this law extensively.[8] It speaks of a situation where a wife comes to help her husband in a conflict: "When men fight with one another and the wife of the one draws near to rescue her husband from the hand of him who is beating him and puts out her hand and seizes him by the private parts . . . " (25:11). At first this looks like a noble act of rescuing a husband who is in serious trouble. However, the punishment is surprisingly severe: ". . . then you shall cut off her hand. Your eye shall have no pity" (25:12). Apart from the *lex talionis* or "an eye for an eye" law, this is the only law that calls for any form of physical mutilation, a punishment that was common in neighboring countries. This was probably a rare occurrence,[9] so the severity of the punishment would primarily serve as a deterrent.

Why does hurting a man's testicles earn such a severe punishment? It could be because this was an act of gross indecency. More probably it may be because the man's genitals could be injured so that he would not be able to father children. The issue of fathering children was the topic of the levirate marriage law just before this. In movies today we see instances of people hurting a man's genitals by kicking them or hitting them in some other way. In the spirit of this law, we can say that such practices are abhorrent to God.

Honesty (25:13–16)

Over the centuries people in every society have tried to cheat others for economic gain. Verses 13–16 tackle the problem of dishonesty. Moses says, "You shall not have in your bag two kinds of weights, a large and a small. You shall not have in your house two kinds of measures, a large and a small. A full and fair weight you shall have, a full and fair measure you shall have . . . " (25:13–15a). Unscrupulous traders had two kinds of "weights" (literally, "stones") and "measures" (literally, "ephahs") — large ones for buying and small ones for selling. The Hebrew word (*tsedeq*) translated "fair" in the ESV ("honest," TNIV) for the weights and measures one should have is a common word usually translated "righteousness" or "justice." Honesty in all our business dealings is an essential feature of our walk with God and is a requirement for a right relationship with him. We sometimes meet people in the business world who testify to God's goodness in life while continuing unethical business practices. This is a contradiction and, as we shall see, a huge insult to God.

In spite of the strong prohibition of dishonest trade here and in Leviticus 19:35–37, this continued to be a problem in Israel. It is mentioned in Proverbs (11:1; 16:11) and by the prophets (Amos 8:5; Micah 6:11). The tendency to be dishonest, especially when everyone else around us is, is so strong that it can silence the voice of conscience. In many cultures with a so-called shame and honor orientation, people view being shamed as being the biggest evil that can happen to a person. So when one gives into the natural tendency to dishonesty there is no inclination to own up to it when confronted because the shame of being called a liar or a thief is viewed as a greater evil than being a liar or a thief. Parents, therefore, will defend their children to school authorities when they are accused, without determining whether or not the accusation is true. They feel they must not permit their children to be shamed. By doing this they help entrench dishonesty in their children's personalities.

Abraham Lincoln, whom many regard as the greatest American President, was known as "Honest Abe" because of his commitment to honesty. He had a motto: "I am not bound to win, but I am bound to be true. I am not bound to succeed, but I am bound to live up to the light I have."[10] When success becomes more important than our principles, we succumb to the temptation of dishonesty. As a young man Lincoln served as a store clerk, and at the end of the day a woman came in and bought half a pound of sugar. It was the last sale for the day. The next morning when he came to the shop he found that there was a four-ounce weight on the scales, which meant that he had given the woman only four ounces of sugar the day before. He promptly weighed out the balance that he had not given, closed the shop, and took the sugar to the woman's home.

There are ways in which those who are not traders also can violate the spirit of this law.

- Selling a vehicle that has been involved in a big accident without telling the buyer about the accident.
- Not telling a potential buyer of a motorcycle about a defect in the engine.

- Not doing a full day's work but accepting a full day's salary.
- Missing work in order to do something and saying you are sick because that would be the only way you can get time off.

Everyone else may do these things, but Christians cannot.

Moses goes on to describe the consequences of honesty: ". . . that your days may be long in the land that the LORD your God is giving you. For all who do such things, all who act dishonestly, are an abomination to the LORD your God" (25:15b, 16). Under the new covenant, we would interpret the lengthening of days in the land as the blessing of God upon our lives. This is the stark reality: God will not bless those who are dishonest. But there is something even more serious: dishonest people "are an abomination to the LORD." That is, they bear his name, but their actions "are insulting to his character."[11] What a serious thing that is: they insult God! The implication is that they are headed for God's judgment.[12] Having grappled with the question of dishonesty in our land, even among Christians, for a long time, I have concluded that one of the greatest deterrents to dishonesty is the prospect of judgment by the holy, awesome, and almighty God.

This will soon become a serious problem in the West where for generations the culture (unlike Sri Lankan culture) was influenced by the prospect that people are accountable to a holy God before whose judgment they must someday stand. The core to social life in the West was built on this. Supermarkets and general human transactions operated based on trust. Millions of dollars being spent on surveillance and other instruments to prevent dishonesty shows that such trust is eroding. So does the fact that contracts are getting more and more complex to ensure that there will not be a breaking of trust. The idea of a "gentlemen's agreement" is fast becoming outdated.

I believe a major reason for the loss of trust is that Westerners do not believe anymore that they are under a supreme and holy God to whom they are accountable and who will judge their actions one day. Some have an idea of God as being a benevolent father whose nature they define purely by a warped understanding of love. Some have discarded monotheism, the belief in one God, for pantheism where everything, including ourselves, is God and the divine is more a life force than a person to whom humans are accountable. Some are practical atheists—if there is a God, his existence does not concern us (like the deists of two centuries ago)—or dogmatic atheists who publicly state that there is no God. This does not bode well for Western society.

Annihilate the Amalekites (25:17–19)

We are coming to the end of a long list of stipulations that formed a key part of the covenant relationship between Israel and God (12:1—26:19). The last command in this chapter is to completely annihilate the Amalekites after the Israelites have taken possession of the land. Verse 19 says, "Therefore when the LORD your God has given you rest from all your enemies around you, in the land that the LORD your God is giving you for an inheritance to possess, you shall blot out the memory of Amalek from under heaven; you shall not forget." The Amalekites were a nomadic group of people who roamed around in the area called the Negev, south of Palestine where Israel would live. They were to be exterminated in the same way as the other nations that were "devoted to destruction" as we saw in our discussions of chapters 7 and 20. This did not take place, and therefore the Amalekites were a problem to Israel for many centuries to come (Judges 6:3; 1 Samuel 30:1; 2 Samuel 8:12; 1 Chronicles 4:43). They figure again in 1 Samuel 15:2 and 3 where the term "devote to destruction" is specifically used for them.

The reason given for their extermination is the terrible way in which they attacked Israel when they were passing their area. This battle is described in Exodus 17:8–16, which tells how Joshua defeated them while Moses prayed with his arms outstretched with the aid of Aaron and Hur. The Deuteronomy passage gives some details of their wickedness: "Remember what Amalek did to you on the way as you came out of Egypt, how he attacked you on the way when you were faint and weary, and cut off your tail, those who were lagging behind you, and he did not fear God" (25:17, 18). We discussed the reasons why these nations "devoted to destruction" needed to be exterminated in our discussions of Deuteronomy 7 and 20. Just like the people during Noah's time (Genesis 6:5–7) and in Sodom and Gomorrah (Genesis 18:20, 21; 19:24, 25), "their incorrigible wickedness was such that annihilation was necessary."[13]

This brings us almost to the end of the section outlining detailed laws (chapters 12—26) that give us an idea of what kind of behavior was expected in the new nation of Israel. One more set of instructions remains to be given about firstfruits and tithes. We've seen laws about

- acceptable and unacceptable worship
- festivals
- diet
- giving to God and the needy
- protecting the vulnerable
- leadership and legal procedures
- warfare and trade
- marriage, sex, and divorce

- animals and plants
- combating wrong influences from neighboring nations
- health and hygiene

What a comprehensive list this is! It shows that God is interested in all of life. We are to follow him in everything we do and to reflect both his love and his holiness. The result will be a happy society where people live in harmony and the needy are cared for.

52

The Heart of a Biblical Giver

DEUTERONOMY 26:1–19

WITH CHAPTER 26, we end the largest section of Deuteronomy (12:1– 26:19), which gave detailed covenant stipulations or laws that would govern the life of the people of Israel. At the heart of the factors influencing the life of this society is its relationship with God. That is best expressed in worship. So Moses actually finishes the typical lawbook type of laws in chapter 25 and ends this sub-section the way he started it (chapter 12)—by discussing something to do with the worship of the people (chapter 26). In the laws that are found in the chapters between chapters 12 and 26 are many references to worship, especially during the festivals, which were primarily worship festivals.

The particular form of worship described here is the offering of firstfruits and tithes. Giving thank offerings to God is a fitting way to end the laws to govern living in the land that God miraculously gave to the people.

Firstfruits to Honor God (26:1–11)

The first ceremony described is the offering of firstfruits. This actually could have come in the section on the Feast of Weeks (or Pentecost), which was when the firstfruits were offered (16:9–12). But the description of the law about firstfruits is postponed until now. Gordon McConville says, "The reason for keeping it until now is that the offering of the firstfruits had special significance the first time that it was done in the new land. The present law is thinking primarily of that very first offering of the fruits of harvest" after the people settled in the land.[1]

The Procedure

The offering is to be made "[w]hen you come into the land that the LORD your God is giving you for an inheritance and have taken possession of it and live in it" (26:1). It is to take place after the first harvest in the new land. Verse 2 says, "You shall take some of the first of all the fruit of the ground, which you harvest from your land that the LORD your God is giving you, and you shall put it in a basket, and you shall go to the place that the LORD your God will choose, to make his name to dwell there." The offering must represent "all the fruit of the ground." It "was obviously only a sample of the various agricultural products that had been grown on the land."[2] God is identified as "the LORD your God" nine times in this paragraph (26:1, 2 [twice], 3, 4, 5, 10 [twice], 11) to highlight the fact that it is God who gave the fruit and not the pagan gods, to whom their neighbors looked for fruit.

They are to go to the place chosen by God "to make his name to dwell there" (26:2). We looked at the significance of this place in our discussion on 12:5. We said that three factors are communicated by this. First, this is a place chosen by God and not by humans. Second, by putting his name there, God wanted this place to signify his exclusiveness. The worship of no other god is permitted. Third, this place signifies the presence of God among the people. They are to "go to the priest who is in office at that time" (26:3a), and, says Moses, he will "take the basket from your hand and set it down before the altar of the LORD your God" (26:4).

The giver has to make a declaration before the giving of the basket: "I declare today to the LORD your God that I have come into the land that the LORD swore to our fathers to give us" (26:3b). As Chris Wright says, this statement "is not a *claim*—'I own this land because I conquered it' but an *acknowledgment*—'I have come because God gave it.'"[3] The giver has to express another longer narrative, which is like a confession of faith, after giving the basket. It recounts the history of Israel from the time of the fathers of the race. It begins with the statement, "A wandering Aramean was my father" (26:5a). What became Aram is where the roots of Israel lie, with Abraham's brother remaining there and Isaac and Jacob finding their wives from there. The "wandering Aramean" was probably Jacob who traveled there and back and then came to Egypt, as the text goes on to say: "And he went down into Egypt and sojourned there, few in number, and there he became a nation, great, mighty, and populous" (26:5b).

Then there is a description of the enslavement and liberation of the people:

And the Egyptians treated us harshly and humiliated us and laid on us hard labor. Then we cried to the LORD, the God of our fathers, and the LORD heard our voice and saw our affliction, our toil, and our oppression. And the LORD brought us out of Egypt with a mighty hand and an outstretched arm, with great deeds of terror, with signs and wonders. And he brought us into this place and gave us this land, a land flowing with milk and honey. (26:6–9)

Again the focus is on God's grace. The giver is saying in essence, "I am here because God has saved and looked after me." In our study of the pilgrimage festivals in Deuteronomy 16, we looked at the value of recounting history during times of public worship. Our history binds us together and feeds our faith by reminding us that we are putting our trust in a mighty God who has done much to help us.

Only after this long declaration does the giver mention his reason for coming—to offer firstfruits. He says in verse 10a, "And behold, now I bring the first of the fruit of the ground, which you, O LORD, have given me." Again the focus is on God. He does not say, "I bring the fruit of my labor." He acknowledges that it was given by God. Next, Moses instructs, "And you shall set it down before the LORD your God and worship before the LORD your God" (26:10b). It is implied, of course, that he sets it down through the priest. How different this is to a lot of our reflections when people give to the Lord. We focus on human factors. Here it is primarily on God's provision.

The natural consequence of focusing on God's provision rather than on human merit is joy. So Moses says that the whole household, including the Levite and the sojourner, "shall rejoice in all the good that the LORD your God has given to you and to your house" (26:11). In the Bible, times of giving are not grim occasions focusing on obedience to God's command to give; they are times of joyous celebration of God's provision. In our discussion on 16:11, 14, when we looked at the reference to the sojourners' presence in the festival meals, we looked at the significance of sojourners rejoicing with them. God's people do not accept the class distinctions of the rest of society, and at times of celebration—the times people like to be with their own kind—they include outsiders.

The Significance of Offering Firstfruits

David Payne says, "Even today a keen gardener takes a special pleasure in the first crop of the season, but perhaps in this scientific age, we have rather lost the wonder of it." On the other hand, "Ancient man . . . still felt awe at the workings of nature and was quick to show his gratitude to the divine powers he believed were responsible." One of the greatest setbacks of modern technological advancement has been the loss of wonder among people. We seem to be able to explain everything through science. We do not realize that God is the creator and sustainer of the whole universe. Hebrews 1:3 says Jesus "upholds the universe by the word of his power." Paul says, "In [Christ] all things hold together" (Colossians 1:17). If God took his sustaining hand out of the universe, everything would disintegrate into smithereens. We think we know the operations of the world so well that we almost feel we can control nature. Therefore, blinded by our own sense of self-importance, we lose sight of the wonder of God's provision. I know of a situation where an unbelieving husband got angry when his wife gave God the credit for some success of his. He felt he had achieved that through his own effort and ability.

The Biblical attitude toward creation is well expressed in something that G. K. Chesterton said, which Darrell Johnson cites in his new book *The Glory of Preaching*: "As G. K. Chesterton suggested, each new day is not just the product of an inexorable mechanical process; rather, each new day is the result of God saying, to the sun, 'Do it again!' To the moon, 'Do it again!' To my heart, 'Beat again!' To your lungs, 'Breathe again!'" Johnson then comments, "Which is why 'thank you' is the most appropriate response for human beings to speak at the beginning, middle, and end of the day."[4]

The poor often take to wonder better than affluent, self-sufficient people. I have worked with the poor all my life and have sometimes despaired at our attempts to get them to give up some of their pre-Christian habits, such as lying. However, I have always been challenged by their trust in God. Not possessing many things to give them false confidence, they are free to appreciate the greatness of God and to depend on him. Along with wonder comes response—the response of adoration and thanksgiving over his involvement in our life. The giving of the firstfruits is an expression of this thanksgiving.

Of course, these rituals of offering could become meaningless rituals. They could even become substitutes for obedience. We know of unscrupulous traders who make frequent vows in shrines and give large donations to religious causes in the hope of receiving business success as the reward for their gifts. This is like bribery. Without living in obedience, which is the condition for success, these people try to take short-cuts by giving gifts as substitutes for obeying the rules. Of course, God does not bless such people, so the bribing yields no results from God—though Satan may answer some of their prayers to entrench them in their sin. It is easy for rituals involving thank-offerings to take on a superstitious shape and become actions people do to earn favors from God. In the Bible they are expressions of thanksgiving in response to God's favor.

Unscrupulous religious leaders can exploit the superstitions of people to raise funds, by offering people blessings in return for their thank-offerings. Sadly, this happens in both non-Christian and Christian circles. Martin Luther rebelled against the sale of indulgences that the Roman Catholic Church of his time offered the people with the promise of a reduced stay in purgatory. Evangelists advertise the opportunity of "investing" in their ministries through donations, which are sometimes called "blessing shares." God is said to unleash blessings on the givers through those donations. Non-Christian clergy motivate people to give to their ministries by promising them the prospect of continued success in business or some other aspect of life in return for gifts given at their shrines.

Wonder, then, makes us want to acknowledge God as the giver of all good gifts. And this is the purpose of giving firstfruits to God. Proverbs 3:9 says, "Honor the LORD with your wealth and with the firstfruits of all your produce." When the Israelites gave their firstfruits to God they affirmed that

- God is the Lord of their life who has provided all they have;
- everything belongs to God, and what they are giving is a token and an affirmation of that;
- they are grateful to God for his grace and provision;
- giving to God is the priority in connection with their attitude toward and use of possessions.

Because most of us do not live in agricultural societies, the practice of giving firstfruits does not directly apply to us. However, the firstfruits idea can have many practical applications in the lives of non-farmers, too. Once during a time of crisis in our ministry, we decided as leaders that to solve a certain problem I would find a substantial sum of money and pay it personally without asking YFC for it. This was not because of any dishonesty but because of a commitment made that did not meet the approval of the whole leadership team. I did not know where I would get this money. While I was at the meeting that made this decision, a person to whom I had ministered during his youth called me saying he would like to meet with me. We decided to meet in about an hour. He brought the second salary he received from his new job and gave it as a gift to me (he had used his first salary for an emergency, though giving me his first salary was his original idea). When he left, I opened the envelope and found almost the exact amount I had agreed to pay a short while before. My friend decided to give his firstfruits to an equivalent of a Levite in his life.

The firstfruits idea should spill over into our response to receiving something. When we get our salary or a gift or the proceeds from a sale of land or any other kind of wealth, the first thing we do should be to ask how much of that we will give away—for God's work and for the needy. This becomes an ambition in life—using God's provision to give to God's work and the needy. I got to know the founding president of Youth for Christ, the late Dr. Torrey

Johnson, when he was in his seventies. I had the joy of meeting him several times after that. He would often tell me about dreaming of receiving a million dollars so he could give it all to missions. I never left a meeting with Dr. Johnson without being fired up for the work of the gospel.

When we acknowledge that God has given us all our possessions, and when we desire to always give God the glory through our actions, especially through our giving, then giving becomes a joy. The result of giving is, "And you shall rejoice in all the good that the LORD your God has given to you and to your house, you, and the Levite, and the sojourner who is among you" (26:11). You join with others and are happy! Giving is not a burden — a rule to reluctantly obey; it is a joy. Clearly that is how Dr. Johnson saw his giving — as an ambition that brought him great joy. Joy is made complete when it is shared. So the joy of giving firstfruits is shared with family and friends.

Some people cling to what they get so tenaciously that they fear to give in this way. Thus, they miss the joy of giving. Did not Jesus say, "It is more blessed to give than to receive" (Acts 20:35)? Those who cling to their wealth become unhappy people. They become preoccupied with a fear of losing it, a fear of being exploited by others, and the need to protect and invest their money. Recent events have shown how earthly wealth is an unsatisfactory source of security. As Jesus said, earthly treasure rusts, is eaten by moths, and is sometimes stolen by thieves (Matthew 6:19–21). May we experience the freedom that comes from not clinging to our wealth but from joyfully giving it away. This freedom comes from acknowledging that all our wealth is provided by God and belongs to him.

King David's prayer when he made an offering for the temple that Solomon was going to build illustrates the attitudes that lie behind the giving of the firstfruits:

> Blessed are you, O LORD, the God of Israel our father, forever and ever. Yours, O LORD, is the greatness and the power and the glory and the victory and the majesty, for all that is in the heavens and in the earth is yours. Yours is the kingdom, O LORD, and you are exalted as head above all. Both riches and honor come from you, and you rule over all. In your hand are power and might, and in your hand it is to make great and to give strength to all. And now we thank you, our God, and praise your glorious name. But who am I, and what is my people, that we should be able thus to offer willingly? *For all things come from you, and of your own have we given you.* For we are strangers before you and sojourners, as all our fathers were. (1 Chronicles 29:10–15a, italics mine)

A great king is making a huge contribution for the temple, but the tone of his prayer is self-effacing and God-honoring. He acknowledges God's great-

ness and his own utter unworthiness, and he says that what he is giving came
from God and still belongs to God.

The Three-Year Tithe: Giving out of a Life of Obedience (26:12–15)

In our discussion of 14:28, 29 we looked at the tithe that is given at the end
of three years. We said that we cannot be sure whether this tithe is in addition to the annual tithe or whether it is a substitute for it in the third year.
Deuteronomy 26:12 says, "When you have finished paying all the tithe of
your produce in the third year, which is the year of tithing, giving it to the
Levite, the sojourner, the fatherless, and the widow, so that they may eat
within your towns and be filled. . . . " The tithe is given for the needs of
vocational religious workers (the Levite) and the needy (the sojourner, the
fatherless, and the widow). In our discussion of 15:1–18 we looked at the
importance of helping the needy.

Once the tithe has been given, the giver has to make a declaration that
the giving was made in the right way. Far from the giver acting like a big
shot because he is giving funds, he has to humbly assert that he has not done
anything wrong in the way he gave it. Because God is so great and awesome,
we must be careful about the way we give to God. First, he says, "I have
removed the sacred portion out of my house, and moreover, I have given it
to the Levite, the sojourner, the fatherless, and the widow, according to all
your commandment that you have commanded me" (26:13a). The giver must
describe his giving as removing "the sacred portion out of [his] house." By
describing it as a "sacred portion," he is saying that it "specially belongs to
God."[5] The idea is of something that sticks out as not belonging to the home,
something that does not harmonize with the surroundings. If someone were to
see it in our home, he or she could ask, "This belongs to God, what is it doing
here?" When Malachi said that the failure to tithe was robbing God (Malachi
3:8–10), he was expressing the sentiments described in Deuteronomy 26:13.
I sometimes delay giving my monthly gift to our church because I often travel
on weekends. I realize that I need to feel uneasy when that money is in my
house. After studying this text, I decided that I must take more seriously the
sense of unease I should feel if I have not sent my contribution to church at
the beginning of the month. We solved this problem by having my wife take
the responsibility of giving our monthly offering to the church.

The giver continues his declaration, saying, "I have not transgressed any
of your commandments, nor have I forgotten them" (26:13b). Living in obedience to God and our giving are intertwined. We cannot have one without

the other. The giver goes on to say that he was ceremonially clean when he came into the sanctuary with the gift:

> I have not eaten of the tithe while I was mourning, or removed any of it while I was unclean, or offered any of it to the dead. I have obeyed the voice of the LORD my God. I have done according to all that you have commanded me. (26:14)

Ceremonial cleanness was a special feature of Jewish worship. While it does not directly apply to us, it underscores the fact that our lives should be pleasing to God when we come with our gifts.

As we saw above, many people who live unrighteous lives give to religious causes, sometimes to assuage the voice of conscience and sometimes to get some good luck. This practice is very common today, but it does not please God. Christianity is a holistic religion. The God who receives our gifts desires our total commitment in all that we do. Otherwise our giving is meaningless. Jesus said, ". . . if you are offering your gift at the altar and there remember that your brother has something against you, leave your gift there before the altar and go. First be reconciled to your brother, and then come and offer your gift" (Matthew 5:23, 24). Jesus does not say that *we* have something against our brother, but that *our brother* has something against us. We may think we are fully innocent, but it is an insult to God to give a gift while we have a relationship problem that has not been cleared up.

Finally, the giver says, "Look down from your holy habitation, from heaven, and bless your people Israel and the ground that you have given us, as you swore to our fathers, a land flowing with milk and honey" (26:15). The faithful giver is emboldened to ask for God's blessing. We do not earn God's blessing through our gifts and obedience, but they take away the hindrances to God's blessing us. Isaiah said, "Behold, the LORD's hand is not shortened, that it cannot save, or his ear dull, that it cannot hear; but your iniquities have made a separation between you and your God, and your sins have hidden his face from you so that he does not hear" (Isaiah 59:1, 2).

Youth for Christ helped give birth to another movement, and we pledged to support that movement with a substantial financial grant each month for a few years. Soon after we took this decision, our ministry was in such a severe financial crisis that we wondered how we were even going to pay our own salaries. Some people felt that we should look after our needs first and then pay the other group. Others felt that we should fulfill our obligation to the other group first and then see about ourselves. I felt strongly that the latter is what we should do. We were going to decide on this at a crucial meeting of our leadership.

I became ill with chicken pox the day before that meeting started. The leaders had to make the decision without my input. They decided they would give the grant first and then think about our needs. The day after that decision was made, a huge contribution came our way that cleared about 50 percent of our deficit, and with it came the promise of more regular support. There had been a problem with the address on the envelope that contained this check. It had been delivered to two past addresses of our office and returned to the postman. After roaming from place to place in our city for two weeks, the letter made its way to our office just after our leaders had decided to give to the other movement first. God honored that decision with a great provision to us.

More important than asking for blessing is asking God to help us to obey. Some who do not receive what they ask for blame God when they should be looking inside and asking whether there is something in them that is hindering God's blessings. Sadly, many refuse to do that because they do not want to give up their sinful attitudes.

Conclusion to the Declaration of the Law (26:16–19)

Moses now concludes the longest section in Deuteronomy (12:1 – 26:19), which presented the specific covenant stipulations that govern the life of the people. He does so with five affirmations, all of which have obedience as their key (26:16–19).

- First, we have a call to "do" the "statutes and rules," and that is followed by the familiar call to be careful to do them with our whole being: "This day the LORD your God commands you to do these statutes and rules. You shall therefore be careful to do them with all your heart and with all your soul" (26:16).
- Next, there is a reminder of their declaration to be faithful: "You have declared today that the LORD is your God, and that you will walk in his ways, and keep his statutes and his commandments and his rules, and will obey his voice" (26:17).
- Then comes Moses' declaration that those who are completely obedient are God's "treasured possession": "And the LORD has declared today that you are a people for his treasured possession, as he has promised you, and that you are to keep all his commandments" (26:18).
- Fourth, there is the reminder of the promise of honor and fame as a consequence of their faithfulness declared by God: ". . . and that he will set you in praise and in fame and in honor high above all nations that he has made . . . " (26:19a).
- Finally, there is an affirmation that these people will be God's people: ". . . and that you shall be a people holy to the LORD your God, as he promised" (26:19b). This is both a responsibility and a privilege.

The theme of future reward for faithful obedience is a key aspect of the Biblical worldview. It is fitting that it should close out this section. Often people move away from God when they do not see the rewards of obedience. The key to rewards in the Bible is the future. This theme is treated much more comprehensively in the New Testament. Paul said about his battle for obedience, "Not that I have already obtained this or am already perfect, but I press on to make it my own, because Christ Jesus has made me his own. Brothers, I do not consider that I have made it my own. But one thing I do: forgetting what lies behind and straining forward to what lies ahead, I press on toward the goal for the prize of the upward call of God in Christ Jesus" (Philippians 3:12–14). Our call today is to battle for obedience—a major challenge considering our inclination to sin. But one day we will see that it was worth it all. Amy Carmichael was a missionary to South India from Ireland who spent her life giving a future to children who had been discarded by their families. Scottish missionary Robert Moffatt (1795–1883), who served in Africa for over fifty years, once said, "We have a whole eternity to celebrate our victories, but one short hour before sunset in which to win them."

53

Acts That Help
Refresh Commitment

DEUTERONOMY 27:1–10

MOSES' AIM IN THESE farewell messages was to help the people to be faithful to their covenant with God after they settled in the promised land. We have said that because of this Deuteronomy is structured like a typical covenant-making ritual from that period. After a brief introduction that parallels the preamble sections of ancient covenant treaties (1:1–5), there is a historical summary of the way God had led the people up to that point (1:6—4:43), again typical in covenant-making rituals. Then we had the huge section detailing the conditions related to the covenant (4:44—26:19). This was divided into a general description of what obedience looked like (5:1—11:32) and a listing of the detailed laws that governed the life of the people (12:1—26:19). Deuteronomy 27:1–10 represents another important feature of covenant rituals: making provision for the laws to be written down. The next two studies will look at yet another feature: pronouncing blessings for faithfulness to the covenant and curses for unfaithfulness (27:11—28:68).

Stones and an Altar to Aid in Obedience (27:1–8)

The first paragraph (27:1–8) talks about setting up some stones and an altar on Mount Ebal. The purpose of these two structures was to aid obedience. Verse 1 says, "Now Moses and the elders of Israel commanded the people, saying, 'Keep the whole commandment that I command you today.'" How often exhortations to obey the commands appear in Deuteronomy! Obedience is a key theme of this book. As Moses gets ready to leave, his greatest desire

575

seems to be to motivate the people to obey God's will, so they will not forfeit God's promised blessings.

Here, of course, Moses will go on to give instructions on the covenant-renewing ritual they will have after they enter the section of the promised land west of the Jordan. But he says, "Keep the whole commandment," suggesting that the meaning of details must be understood against the backdrop of the whole.[1] Whether we are singing a song or leading a time of worship or rededicating ourselves to God at an anniversary celebration or revival meeting, the background of that action is a life of total obedience to all of what God says. This is why it is demeaning to our covenant relationship with God when public acts of dedication use those who are not committed to God to do some of the key functions, such as performing musically.

As is often the case in Deuteronomy, the commands to obedience are given in the context of the promise of God's blessing for obedience. Here Moses points to the blessing by describing the promised land as ". . . the land that the LORD your God is giving you, a land flowing with milk and honey, as the LORD, the God of your fathers, has promised you" (27:3b). There is a message here for us. When we think of obedience and when we urge others to obedience, we should not simply do it as a motivation to duties we have to perform for God. We must emphasize the fact that this is the wisest and best thing for us to do. Obedience opens the door to God's blessings, and disobedience results in our forfeiting those blessings. This truth is given with vivid emphasis in 27:11—28:68 through the ritual of public recitation of blessings and curses.

In addition to presenting the blessings and curses to motivate obedience, Moses emphasizes the fact that these people are God's own people. The expression "LORD your God" appears eight times in verses 1–10, and in verse 3 Moses says, ". . . as the LORD, the God of your fathers, has promised you." Clearly, Moses is encouraging obedience by reminding them that the mighty God has chosen to call them his own possession. Surely the God who can do all things will care for his own. The connection between ownership and obedience is spelled out in verses 9, 10:

> Then Moses and the Levitical priests said to all Israel, "Keep silence and hear, O Israel: this day you have become the people of the LORD your God. You shall therefore obey the voice of the LORD your God, keeping his commandments and his statutes, which I command you today."

The command to set up stones appears twice. Verse 2 says, "And on the day you cross over the Jordan to the land that the LORD your God is giving you, you shall set up large stones and plaster them with plaster." Verse 4 says, "And when you have crossed over the Jordan, you shall set up these stones, concerning which I command you today, on Mount Ebal, and you shall plaster them with plaster." Mount Ebal lies some distance north-northwest of Jericho. So Jericho must be first defeated before the altar is built, as the record of this event in Joshua 8:30–35 shows. When Moses says that this must be done "on the day you cross over the Jordan to the land" (Deuteronomy 27:2a), he refers "not necessarily [to] the precise day" that they cross over, "on the day" "simply meaning 'when'" here.[2]

Twice Moses says that they must "write on [the stones] all the words of this law" (27:3a, 8). Twice they are told to "plaster [the stones] with plaster" (27:2, 4). "Engraving in stone could be very time-consuming, so one variation for longer inscriptions was to coat the stone surface with plaster and then write in the soft plaster."[3] This is yet another example of using visual aids to place before the people the teaching of the Law, as we saw in our discussion of 6:6–9.

The second instruction about writing the words on the stones adds that they must be written "very plainly" (27:8) or "very clearly" (TNIV, NRSV). The Hebrew word used here means "to make plain" or "to make clear." The Word of God does not consist of hidden sayings offered only to a spiritual or intellectual elite. It is available to all to access fully. This is so for the whole Bible. Actually people think that Deuteronomy is not very accessible, but that is because they have not spent time in it and listened to its message. We contrast this with the teachings of the Buddha whose highest teachings were understandable only to the intellectual elite. So were the teachings of the great philosopher Plato. The Qur'an is generally read in Arabic, and reading translations, though permitted, is not the preferred way for a devout Muslim to study it.

In our discussion of 6:7, I mentioned that my mother has been the most influential Bible teacher in my life even though she converted to Christianity from Buddhism in her teens. She had little background in Christian truth and, as far as I know, never took a course on how to study the Bible. But she is a woman who is mighty in the Scriptures. The deepest truths of the faith are available to the simplest person. This is why some of the great saints in the history of the church and today are people with minimal education who studied the Word and obeyed it. We, too, must seek to make the Word plain for all to read and learn and grow in godliness.

In addition to the stones, the people are to build an altar: "And there you shall build an altar to the LORD your God, an altar of stones. You shall wield no iron tool on them; you shall build an altar to the LORD your God of uncut stones" (27:5, 6a). The Pentateuch records Noah, Abraham, Isaac, Jacob, and Moses building altars usually after some special event or victory.[4] E. M. Blaiklock says, "The patriarchs seem to have set up altars as symbols of some notable encounter with God and memorials of spiritual experience."[5] Not only does this help motivate people to obedience, it is also a key to helping people acknowledge that the victory was a gift from God. It is very important for God's people to mark their successes with a major expression of thanks to God and the pivotal points in their life with acknowledging God's lordship in all they do. In those days the people built an altar to do that.

Two kinds of sacrifices were to be offered at the altar at Mount Ebal. It is most appropriate that there should be sacrifices after the Law is stated. Paul said, "For by works of the law no human being will be justified in his sight, since through the law comes knowledge of sin" (Romans 3:20). The reading of the Law would bring guilt over sin. The sacrifices would bring forgiveness for those sins. First, the people offer burnt offerings (Deuteronomy 27:6b), and, as Warren Wiersbe has pointed out, those offerings would signify total dedication to God by the people. The second offering is the peace offering. Verse 7 says, ". . . and you shall sacrifice peace offerings and shall eat there, and you shall rejoice before the LORD your God." The offering and the joyous fellowship meal signify "joyful celebration of God's blessing."[6] Joyful celebration is a key sub-theme of Deuteronomy (12:7, 12, 18; 16:11, 14, 15).

The altar, then, was set up to acknowledge God's provision and lordship over their lives and to thank God and celebrate in community. Today we can get together at crucial times in the life of a community or family to do the same. The dedication of a building, the celebration of a special providence by God, a special birthday, a wedding, or even a funeral can all be transformed into opportunities to glorify God in this way. May we be on the lookout for opportunities to rejoice and dedicate ourselves afresh along with the whole community to which we belong. And, as here, it would be a good idea to cap the celebration with a hearty meal!

Here are some key principles about motivation to obedience from verses 1–8:

- Charges to obedience need to be given often.
- Specific instructions for events are given from the backdrop of a commitment to total obedience.
- These charges are not given simply as charges to do one's duty. They must be accompanied by descriptions of the blessings of obedience and how disobedience forfeits blessings.
- The people must be reminded of their security as God's own possessions.
- Use creativity to keep the truths of the Word before the eyes of the people.

- The Word of God must be presented in a way that is accessible to all.
- Convert special occasions in the life of a community into opportunities to acknowledge God's lordship over our lives, to recommit ourselves to God, and to rejoice together over his provision.

Becoming God's People Again (27:9, 10)

Two Covenant Renewals

Moses is speaking from the plains of Moab before he dies. The people will enter the promised land after he dies. They will renew the covenant after they enter the promised land, and Moses has just given instructions about how they are to perform that renewal of the covenant. He will continue with those instructions in the rest of chapter 27 and in chapter 28. However in 27:9, 10 he gives instructions about another renewal, which happens in chapter 29. Moses himself will lead them in this renewal before he dies.

Silence before the Word of God

First, Moses and the Levitical priests tell the people, "Keep silence and hear, O Israel" (27:9a). When it comes to the Law of God, there is no place for arguing or adding or taking away. When God's Law is given, the people must humbly listen. The Bible refers to the faithful as those who "tremble at his word" (Isaiah 66:5) and "tremble at the commandment" (Ezra 10:3). Habakkuk 2:20 says, ". . . the Lord is in his holy temple; let all the earth keep silence before him." Hebrews 12:28b, 29 counsel, ". . . let us offer to God acceptable worship, with reverence and awe, for our God is a consuming fire." Oh, that we may all develop an attitude of humble, urgent expectancy so that nothing would hinder us from hearing from God.

Sometimes we see Christians approach the Bible like critics whose wisdom is above that of this primitive book, the Bible. They are quick to criticize things stated in the Bible. They say they know that some events recorded in the Bible could not have happened but rather reflect a magical view of things typical of primitive peoples. They reject teachings in the Bible, especially in the severe passages of the Old Testament, stating that enlightened modern humans do not hold such primitive views. They say that now we know that the God of the Old Testament is different from the Father of Jesus in whom we have come to believe.

Several years ago I spoke at a theological seminary on the uniqueness of Christ. The students and some faculty responded with disdain to what I had said. What worried me most was the scant respect they showed to the Bible. They seemed to imply that modern scholarship has mandated that many things stated in the Bible should be discarded. The arrogance of the students was frightening. I tried to take each question on its merits and answer them one by one. But at the end of it I felt I had made little progress in communicating what I wanted to tell them. A young person I took with me for this event could not believe that these people are one day going to be ministers in churches!

I could not in good conscience describe to the students an alternative approach to Scripture that day. If I had a chance, I would say that true humility would bow in submission to the Word of God. We will labor to find explanations for the things we cannot explain. If we do not find a satisfactory explanation, we will postpone judgment on the text and keep the issue unresolved until we find an explanation on earth or perhaps in Heaven. But we will not arrogantly discard what is in the Word because it does not square with the way our small minds think! We must always have the attitude Moses recommended here: "Keep silence and hear, O Israel."

When Jesus dealt with a controversial statement in Psalm 82:6 ("I said, you are gods"), his basic attitude was expressed in his statement, ". . . and Scripture cannot be broken" (John 10:35). We are not closing our minds when we do that. We open our minds to grapple with difficult statements, seeking to find a solution to the problems we encounter. But we do so with an attitude of humility that causes us to say that we will leave the question open, without rushing to the conclusion that the statement in the Bible is wrong.

Affirming Again That We Belong to God

What then is the vital message that comes from God for which the people are asked to be silent? Moses and the priests say, ". . . this day you have become the people of the LORD your God" (27:9). Doesn't Deuteronomy assert often that they are already God's people (4:20; 7:6, 7; 9:26–29; 10:15; 14:2; 21:8)? Did they not enter into a covenant relationship with God at Sinai (Exodus 24)? At this time of covenant renewal, they will affirm afresh that they are God's people. People can lose this sense and live as if they do not belong to God. They could forget the covenant promises and live as poor people not having joyous confidence and satisfaction over their wealth in God that is their right. This is why renewal of the covenant was important. It was a time when they were reaffirmed as God's people.

This happens to us often. When we face a big problem, we forget all that God has done to and for us, and we lose our joy. We feel let down by God, and an attitude of complaining takes over. This can happen because of our own carelessness, too. For example, if we get so busy that we neglect the basic Christian disciplines of Bible reading, personal prayer, corporate worship, fellowship, witness, and service, then, too, we will end up acting as people without the security of belonging to God. When we are like this, God speaks to us through some means, and we realize how wrong our attitude was. We rush back to God, we confess our sin of unbelief, and we reaffirm the fact that we are God's and that he will look after us. Our joy returns as we return to an attitude of being children of God.

Belonging Means Obeying

But more serious than living in poverty through forgetting our identity is violating our identity by living in disobedience. Therefore, as soon as the identity of the Israelites as God's people is reaffirmed, they are commanded to obey God's voice: "You shall therefore obey the voice of the LORD your God, keeping his commandments and his statutes, which I command you today" (27:10). At the start of chapter 27, the people are told, 'Keep the whole commandment that I command you today'" (v. 1). After that command, which was for the present day, verses 2–8 give them instructions of what they should do at a future date after they enter the land. After those instructions, the section ends as it began—with a command to obey.

John says, ". . . whoever says he abides in him [Christ] ought to walk in the same way in which he walked" (1 John 2:6). John's point is that it is through such obedience to Christ that "we may know that we are in him" (1 John 2:5). When we disobey, we do not feel like God's children. Then we find it difficult to believe that God will look after us. In unbelief we resort to wrong means for getting the things we want. This is why we need to keep renewing our commitment and refreshing our identity through concrete affirmations that we belong to God.

Note that it was for a message about their identity that the people were all asked to be in silent anticipation. This shows how important it is to get this truth about our identity into our minds. Sadly, many Christians seldom act like they belong to God. They see the power of temptation or of the misfortunes that they have encountered as being so great that they never possess this great treasure of royal identity. Temptation causes them to act like Satan's children. Misfortunes cause them to act as beggars who have been given a raw deal in life. For all of us, we pray that Obadiah 17 would be true: ". . . and the house of Jacob shall possess their own possessions."

The way to continue with the rich confidence of belonging to God is to obey him. When we obey him, we can, as John said, "know that we are in him" (1 John 2:5). In our discussion on Deuteronomy 2:4–6 I mentioned a drug rehab worker who did not hit back after he was assaulted, even though he was a former gang leader and earlier hitting back would have been the natural response. I described how after this event he told me, "Now I know I am a real Christian." When he behaved as Jesus behaved, he knew that he did, indeed, belong to God.

We keep renewing our covenant to remind ourselves of our identity and the need to obey. Obedience, on the other hand, confirms our identity in our hearts. It is vital for our health and joy that we always revel in the fact that we belong to God. It would be helpful to refresh our identity often by renewing our covenant with God and, after doing that, to follow through on the renewal with lives of obedience. If we disobey, we lose our sense of identity, and that could entrench us in more disobedience and unhappiness.

54

Can We Curse People Today?

DEUTERONOMY 27:11–26

WE NOW COME TO A relatively large section of Deuteronomy that also fits in with the form of covenant-making rituals of the ancient Near East. Deuteronomy 27:1–8 gave us an example of making provision for the laws to be written down, which is also part of the covenant-making format. This next large section is about blessings for obedience and curses for disobedience. The people needed to proclaim blessings and curses as part of the covenant-making rituals.

Two Mountains with Two Messages (27:11–14)

Moses is preparing the people to enter the promised land. We know they entered by crossing the Jordan River somewhere near Jericho. The conquest of Jericho is the first major victory to occur after crossing the Jordan River (recorded in the book of Joshua). Moses says that after they have crossed the Jordan, they are to set up an altar on Mount Ebal and to inscribe the Law on the stones of which this altar is made (27:8). We said in the last study that this event actually would have taken place after the defeat of Jericho.

In verse 11 Moses begins a new section of pronouncing blessings and curses. He first says that after crossing the Jordan, the tribes of Israel must be divided into two. The first group is to stand on Mount Gerizim, which is a little south of Mount Ebal. Verse 12 says, "When you have crossed over the Jordan, these shall stand on Mount Gerizim to bless the people: Simeon, Levi, Judah, Issachar, Joseph, and Benjamin." Their task is "to bless the people," but the next group of tribes was to stand on Mount Ebal to pronounce a curse. "And these shall stand on Mount Ebal for the curse: Reuben, Gad, Asher, Zebulun,

Dan, and Naphtali" (27:13). Gerizim, which represented the blessings, was a "luxurious" mountain, while Ebal was "barren."[1] Next Moses says, "And the Levites shall declare to all the men of Israel in a loud voice" (27:14) the curses (27:15–26).

The details of this ceremony are not at all clear. Perhaps the people of the tribes did not actually declare the blessings and curses because the Levites made that declaration (27:14). Perhaps these two tribes were asked to line up in this way to be a vivid symbol of blessings and curses.

A lot of trouble was taken to present this message of blessings and curses in such a vivid way. The reason is to leave the people with no doubt that sin will be punished and righteousness will be blessed. Is it not a mystery then that we hardly even mention this dual motivation to righteous living? Christians talk about blessings for righteousness but most almost never talk about curses for disobedience. Surely this is an area in which we need to change our attitudes and conversation markedly.

The Sins That Trigger Curses (27:15–26)

And All the People Said, "Amen"

Some Christians today have a practice of affirming some truth when gathered together by saying, "Amen." Usually the leader or someone else affirms a truth, and the leader says, "And all the people said . . . " and the people respond by saying, "Amen." Usually the truth affirmed is something positive, something encouraging, such as a testimony or a promise from the Word. In Deuteronomy 27, however, this "Amen" formula appears in connection with curses for disobedience.

This practice of responding to an affirmation with "Amen" appears often in the Bible. It is a way to stress the seriousness of the affirmation being made. I found expressions like the formula we have just described, with people responding to a statement by saying, "Amen" in eight places in the Old Testament. One of those times is a somewhat cynical remark from Jeremiah to a prediction of blessing made by a false prophet while Jeremiah was predicting punishment and not blessing (Jeremiah 28:6). If we disregard that reference, the figure goes down to seven. Of these seven occurrences, three are in responses to statements of praise to God (1 Chronicles 16:36; Nehemiah 8:6; Psalm 106:48). Only once does it come after referring to how God will bless his people (Jeremiah 11:5). This is how we normally use it. The remaining three times are in response to a proclamation of curses for disobedience (Numbers 5:22; Deuteronomy 27:26; Nehemiah 5:13). In our passage the statement appears twelve times, and if we take each of these as a separate instance, then the formula occurs eighteen times in the Old Testament with fourteen of them in connection with curses!

Today we almost never use this Amen formula in this way. This is another indication of how far our thinking has moved from the spirit of the Word of God. Some may say that such discourse has been superseded by the revelation in the New Testament. But the New Testament also has statements like this. For example, Paul said, "Note then the kindness and the severity of God: severity toward those who have fallen, but God's kindness to you, provided you continue in his kindness. Otherwise you too will be cut off" (Romans 11:22).

The Meaning and Purpose of Biblical Curses

Many today interpret the term *curse* from the background of what it has come to mean in the behavior of people today. They interpret concepts like God's wrath and punishment in this way also. Generally such words remind us of angry outbursts by bitter people bent on revenge for a wrong done against them or furious with annoyance over an inconvenience faced. We think of people who go to medicine men, a spirit medium, or the shrine of a god to cast a spell and curse an enemy. But that is not the way the pronouncing of Biblical curses is understood.

When thinking about Biblical curses we note, first, that it is God who curses people for wrong, not us. Those who legitimately pronounce curses in the Bible do so under the inspiration of God or in keeping with the revelation of God and as God's representative. Today we can warn people that if they persist in disobedience to God, they will be under God's curse. We do not say, "Curse you"; we say, "You will be cursed," which is what our Deuteronomy passage is also saying. We can do so with confidence, knowing that what we are saying is in keeping with the Word of God. This would keep us in line with Jesus' command to us not to judge (Matthew 7:1) and to "bless those who persecute [us]; bless and do not curse them" (Romans 12:14).

Second, when the righteous pronounced curses, these were not vindictive acts of revenge. Instead, they were a way of upholding the glory of God and the integrity of the covenant. If God did not punish violations of the covenant, justice would be mocked. Justice is a key feature of a good world. Paul said, "Do not be deceived: God is not mocked, for whatever one sows, that will he also reap" (Galatians 6:7). Goodness and evil must receive their just rewards if there is to be justice in the world. Even when God forgave us, justice was satisfied by the offering up of his Son as a punishment for our sin. Paul said, "God put forward [Jesus] as a propitiation [that is, one who took upon himself God's wrath over sin] by his blood, to be received by faith. This was to show God's righteousness . . . so that he might be just and the justifier of the one who has faith in Jesus" (Romans 3:25, 26; see also 1 John 1:9). When God forgave us, his wrath was spent and his justice was satisfied. Paul said, "Christ redeemed us from the curse of the law by becoming a curse for us" (Galatians 3:13).

For the same reason we could say that curses uphold the glory of God. If God did not punish things that damaged the goodness of this world, he would not be good or glorious. The imprecatory psalms, in which the psalmists utter curses upon the unrighteous, were prayers of people who were desperate to uphold the glory of God in a world where scant attention was paid to it and where people acted as if sin was more profitable and worthwhile than righteousness.

Third, curses reflect the value of the human being. When a human does wrong, that is significant because humans are significant. If people simply ignore the wrongs committed by a child without taking them too seriously, that child could end up as a delinquent—doing spectacular acts of wrong to win the attention of people, as has been so capably pointed out by child psychiatrist James Dobson.[2]

Fourth, pronouncing curses has a deterrent value because they warn people that sin will be punished. As such they are acts of love, for they could result in sinners' salvation. Ezekiel 3:16–21 speaks in vivid language of the responsibility that Ezekiel had to warn the wicked. If he failed to do that, he would be held responsible for a serious sin of omission.

Fifth, pronouncing curses is a encouragement to the righteous to persevere along the path of obedience at a time when the wicked seem to prosper and the righteous don't. The prophets and the psalmists grappled with this problem. Psalm 73 faces this issue squarely. After describing the paradox of the righteous suffering while evil people prosper, the psalmist said, "All in vain have I kept my heart clean and washed my hands in innocence" (v. 13). The psalm continues with the psalmist looking at things from God's perspective after going "into the sanctuary of God" where he "discerned their end" (v. 17). He goes on to talk about the judgment that the wicked will face one day (vv. 18–20). Though they are now not suffering in the way the covenant curses predict, one day they will have to face God's judgment. In other words, the covenant will be upheld when covenant-breakers are finally punished.

The approach of Psalm 73 to blessings and curses is a good way for us also to look at this issue. This teaching is even more marked in the New Testament, which teaches, ". . . it is appointed for man to die once, and after that comes judgment . . . " (Hebrews 9:27). The curses teach us that in today's world, where evil seems to flourish and honesty does not seem to pay, it is still worth being righteous. Paul said, "For we must all appear before the judgment seat of Christ, so that each one may receive what is due for what he has done in the body, whether good or evil" (2 Corinthians 5:10). In the verse that follows, Paul says that fear over this prospect of standing before the judgment seat motivates him to obedient action: "Therefore, knowing the fear of the Lord, we persuade others" (v. 11).

Pronouncing Curses as an Expression of Solidarity

We have already said that it is surprising that the sequence of "and all the people said" and "Amen" appears in a listing of curses. This practice of public proclamation of lists of sins and curses can teach us something today. The Israelites had a strong sense of community solidarity, as opposed to the radical individualism we see in modern Western society. This is an area of which Christians all over the world need to be aware. Western Christians face a huge challenge to Christian thinking from the un-Biblical, radical individualism that prevails in society. People in the East are also moving in this direction, as Western values are having a sweeping effect all over the world, especially in urban areas. In Biblical Israel shame and honor were very important values determining what is right and wrong, desirable and undesirable. We could classify much of the non-Western world today as having shame-honor oriented cultures. The Western world needs to relearn the importance of communities influencing and playing a key part in determining the values that govern one's personal behavior, as that is a Biblical value.

The ritual of pronouncing curses is an exercise in affirming the solidarity of the community in its opposition to wrong. The things for which a curse is pronounced are shameful and thus unacceptable for people belonging to this community. To indulge in those is to shame themselves and the community and do great harm both to individuals and to the community. Paul often uses shame categories in his strategy to motivate Christians to godly living. Here are some of his statements:

- "But sexual immorality and all impurity or covetousness *must not even be named among you, as is proper among saints*" (Ephesians 5:3).
- "Let there be no filthiness nor foolish talk nor crude joking, *which are out of place*" (Ephesians 5:4).
- "Wake up from your drunken stupor, as is right, and do not go on sinning. For some have no knowledge of God. *I say this to your shame*" (1 Corinthians 15:34).
- "If anyone does not obey what we say in this letter, take note of that person, and have nothing to do with him, *that he may be ashamed*. Do

not regard him as an enemy, but warn him as a brother" (2 Thessalonians 3:14, 15).

- "But if anyone does not provide for his relatives, and especially for members of his household, he has denied the faith and *is worse than an unbeliever*" (1 Timothy 5:8).

So when the pronouncements are made about sins cursed, it was an expression of community solidarity in their opposition to the sins mentioned. When the community was making pronouncements of curses, they were proclaiming aloud among themselves that these sins were simply not acceptable in the community. As Christians face more and more isolation from the rest of society because of their views, perhaps they too need to have expressions of solidarity about the things that are commonplace in society but not acceptable in Christianity. This is especially needed as the push for new ethical norms is coming in very attractive packages in the media. We will look at some of those issues below.

Kinds of Sins That Are Cursed

A wide variety of sins is mentioned in the list in Deuteronomy 27:15–26. Many more could be mentioned. It looks like what we have here is a representative sample. So we will look at the categories of sins mentioned and look for contemporary equivalents of them.

The first and the tenth sins are specifically described as having been done "in secret" (27:15, 24). Most of the other sins can also be done without society or the church knowing anything about it. The conditions are such that they would not get caught if they committed the sins, so they think they can get away with it. "The theme of secrecy . . . shows that even if a person's crime may be undetected, that person remains under God's curse."[3] We should battle injustice, exploitation, and other forms of sin. We should do all we can to prevent it, but we do not need to be bitter about sinners not being caught. That will sour our lives and reduce our effectiveness. Those people do not deserve the honor of having done that to us. The doctrine of judgment not only acts as an incentive to holiness, but as John Piper has shown in his book *Future Grace*, it helps us overcome bitterness over wrongs done in this world.[4] As for us, we too must beware of secret sins. It is amazing that sometimes we are more afraid of sinning in front of people than in front of God. May God press home to our warped minds that the most serious thing about sinning is that it is done before God!

Can we curse people today? No, we cannot! But we can warn them of the way God responds to their sins.

Figure 54.1: Sins and Curses in Deuteronomy 27 and Today

Reference	Category	The Sins	Contemporary Equivalents
27:15	Religious	Making idols and setting them up in secret	Looking to sources in other religions for help, e.g., astrologers, idols, psychic healers and counselors, TM, medicine men, séances, etc.
27:16	Family	Dishonors father or mother	Treating parents with disrespect; rebelling against parents when under their care; making important plans for our lives without consulting parents; not caring for parents when they are old; doing things that harm parents
27:17	Neighborhood	Moves neighbor's landmark	Doing something for ourselves that will hurt our neighbor, e.g., moving boundary of property (sadly, this still happens among Christians), throwing trash into neighbor's property
27:18	Handicapped	Misleads a blind man on the road (the blind person would not be able to identify the culprit and bring a charge against him)	Exploiting the handicapped and vulnerable knowing they do not have the ability to hit back, e.g., exploiting children, employees, or others who are too weak to resist— sexually, economically (underpaying), through oppressive workload, etc.; extorting from a person using a vulnerable thing in that person (something he or she wants to hide); taking advantage of the trust of a widow, an orphan, or an elderly person and exploiting for personal gain under the pretext of helping that person
27:19	Social justice	Perverting justice to sojourner, fatherless, and widow	Not giving what vulnerable persons should get, e.g., government officials not speedily expediting their requests when they come to get something done; employers underpaying and overworking powerless employees; authorities taking bribes from a rich person and taking his side in a conflict with a poor or vulnerable person
27:20–23	Personal sexual morality	Sex with stepmother, an animal, a family member, mother-in-law	All kinds of homosexual relations, heterosexual relations outside marriage, and all other perversions of God's ideal for sex, including pornography and sexual abuse of weak and vulnerable people such as children
27:24, 25	Crime in society	Striking down a neighbor in secret; taking a bribe to shed innocent blood	All forms of murder, especially murder done secretly, contract killings, underworld activity
27:26	Personal commitment	Not conforming to the words of the Law by not doing them	Not being personally committed to Christian ethical principles and disobeying what the Bible teaches

55

Kinds of Blessings and Curses

DEUTERONOMY 28:1–68

THE THEMES COVERED IN chapter 28 have already been addressed several times in the book of Deuteronomy. Here they are condensed into a list of blessings and curses. Therefore, I will not do a detailed verse-by-verse exposition of this passage. Instead, I will attempt to glean theological principles from this passage and to discuss what truths this section teaches about the life of faith.

Kinds of Blessings (28:1–14)

Complete Obedience

Deuteronomy 28:1–14 contains a list of the blessings the nation Israel will receive if they obey God fully. At the start and end of this section are statements that the blessings are only for those who completely obey. In two places in the body of the passage are two more statements reminding us that the condition for the blessings listed is obedience (28:2b, 9b). The emphasis on *complete* obedience in the beginning and end is significant. I have italicized the words that point to the need for complete obedience. Verse 1 says, "And if you *faithfully obey* the voice of the LORD your God, *being careful to do all his commandments* that I command you today, the LORD your God will set you high above all the nations of the earth." Verses 13b, 14 say, ". . . if you obey the commandments of the LORD your God, which I command you today, *being careful to do them*, and if you *do not turn aside from any of the words* that I command you today, *to the right hand or to the left*, to go after other gods to serve them . . . "

The sad truth is that all of us have areas in our lives in which we are not fully obedient. A denominational leader responsible for supervising pastors once told a pastor friend of mine that after years of dealing with issues pertaining to Christian ministers, he has concluded that everyone has a dark side that is hidden from the public image that he or she projects to the world. I think he is right. The key issue is how we deal with our dark side. Are we battling it vigorously and with the help of brothers or sisters whom we can trust and to whom we are spiritually accountable, or are we grappling with it alone? When we do so alone, there is the possibility of cultivating a secret life, which is extremely dangerous. Many of the prominent leaders whose fall into serious sin brought great dishonor to God were having a secret life of sin long unknown to their Christian acquaintances before the sin became public.

When we see an area of disobedience in our life, may we hasten to deal with it. And may we continue to deal with it, because Satan has a way of tempting us in areas where we are vulnerable. The command of God is for his people to be totally obedient.

The List of Blessings

Here we will give only a summary list of the blessings mentioned in verses 1–14.

- The nation will be "set . . . high above all the nations of the earth" (28:1).
- "All these blessings [will] come on [them] and overtake [them]" (28:2).
- The blessings will be everywhere: "in the city" and "in the field" (28:3).
- Their wombs, their plants, and their livestock will be fruitful (28:4). This is repeated in 28:11.
- Their work at home—with basket and kneading bowl (for making bread)—will be blessed (28:5).
- They will be blessed when they "come in" and when they "go out" (28:6).
- Their enemies will be defeated and scatter as they flee (28:7).
- God commands blessing on them in their barns and in all they undertake (28:8a).
- God will bless them in the land he is giving them (28:8b).
- God will establish them "as a people holy to himself" (28:9a).
- The other nations will see that they are called by God's name and will be afraid of them (28:10).
- They will abound with prosperity with the fruit of their womb, their ground, and their livestock (28:11, also mentioned in v. 4).
- God will bless them with abundant rain (28:12a).
- Economic prosperity: they will "lend to many nations, but . . . not borrow" (28:12b).
- God "will make [them] the head and not the tail," and they will "only go up and not down" (28:13).

This is a comprehensive list encompassing all of life—fruitfulness, productivity, economics, war, and reputation.

Is Prosperity Assured Today?

Proponents of prosperity theology use passages like this one to claim that we may today expect the kind of prosperity described here. Indeed, prosperity is a key theme in this passage. Verse 11 says, "And the LORD will make you abound in prosperity." Yet we must remember two things. First, these promises are to a righteous nation under the old covenant. Second, while the principle of prosperity for the obedient is applied in some passages to individuals under the new covenant, other passages show that the path to prosperity may sometimes be through deprivation and suffering. In fact, we see this in many instances with individuals under the old covenant too, as Psalm 73 and the book of Job show. Here righteous people struggle with their apparent lack of prosperity and even wonder whether God has forsaken them.

In Christ's basic call to discipleship recorded in the Synoptic Gospels, he promised his followers life and victory and vindication ultimately when he comes with his holy angels (Mark 8:35–38). Eternal prosperity is assured for faithful followers of God. But the path to prosperity may be one of suffering and self-denial. So before those promises Jesus said, "If anyone would come after me, let him deny himself and take up his cross and follow me" (Mark 8:34). Then he said, "For whoever would save his life will lose it, but whoever loses his life for my sake and the gospel's will save it" (8:35). It is always worthwhile and incomparably rewarding to live the life of obedience.

During the time of obedience, we may not have some of the material blessings that people use to measure prosperity. But we will have the abundantly full life that Christ came to give us (John 10:10) with the fullness of Christ's joy (John 15:11) and "the peace of God, which surpasses all understanding" (Philippians 4:7). We may or may not have material prosperity here, but we have this abundant life because of the presence of God with us here and will surely have an eternal reward that surpasses all earthly prosperity. Speaking of life under the new covenant, Paul said, ". . . godliness is of value in every way, as it holds promise for the present life and also for the life to come" (1 Timothy 4:8). The righteous are the ones who really have the best of both worlds.

Kinds of Curses (28:15–68)

Three Introductory Statements (28:15–20)

Whereas 27:15–26 gave a list of the sins that merit curses, the list in chapter 28 describes how these curses will be expressed on earth. Before the list, however, we have three introductory statements. First, it says that the curses will come if the nation refuses to obey God: "But if you will not obey the voice of the LORD your God or be careful to do all his commandments and his statutes that I command you today, then all these curses shall come upon you and overtake you" (28:15). Then there is a general statement that the nation will suffer comprehensively in every area of life for this failure to obey:

> Cursed shall you be in the city, and cursed shall you be in the field. Cursed shall be your basket and your kneading bowl. Cursed shall be the fruit of your womb and the fruit of your ground, the increase of your herds and the young of your flock. Cursed shall you be when you come in, and cursed shall you be when you go out. (28:16–19)

There is a parallel section about how comprehensive the blessings will be in the blessings passage (28:3–6).

The third general statement in verse 20 gives four stages of the way the final curse is enacted. First, "The LORD will send on you curses." Second comes "confusion," which is what God did to enemies when he handed them over to Israel (7:23). They do not know what to do and where to turn as they face God's wrath. Third, they face "frustration in all that [they] undertake to do." When God's wrath is upon them, nothing they do will succeed. The word translated "frustration" could mean "rebuke" (NIV and others), in which case what is meant is that everything they do is rejected by God and receives a rebuke from him. Finally, this will go on "until you are destroyed and perish quickly on account of the evil of your deeds, because you have forsaken me." This is a comprehensive failure of all they do, until they are destroyed.

A List of Curses (28:21–44)

Next, we get a listing of the curses, and we will only give a summary here.

- Drought, pestilence, and disaster to the land and the food supply (28:21–24).
- Defeat in war (28:25).
- Personal disasters: unburied corpses open to animals, illness, weakness, death, mental illness, blindness, being oppressed and robbed with no one to help, interrupted marriage arrangements, interrupted housing plans and harvests, loss of livestock to others, children dragged away from parents (28:26–32), people being driven to insanity, and grievous boils (27:34, 35).
- Oppression by a foreign nation (27:33).
- Exile, being taken to another nation, serving other gods (28:36, 37).
- Becoming a talking point among people of other nations (28:37).
- Frustrated efforts at farming (28:38–40, 42).
- Frustrated efforts at parenting because children are taken into exile (28:41).

- Sojourners rising while the Israelites go down (28:43, 44; see the parallel blessing in 28:13).

An Explanatory Interlude (28:45–47)

After this long list of curses (28:21–44), there is an interlude with a general statement giving the cause for the curses. Verse 45 says, "All these curses shall come upon you and pursue you and overtake you till you are destroyed, because you did not obey the voice of the LORD your God, to keep his commandments and his statutes that he commanded you." There will be no escape. Today the disobedient may confidently go about doing wrong, leaving the righteous confused and discouraged. But one day their sins will catch up with them. Verse 46 says that these signs will "be a sign and a wonder against you and your offspring forever." Just as the miracles God performed at the exodus from Egypt and during the journey so far were a sign and a wonder to the people, the curses to the disobedient will serve as a sign and a wonder to the present generation and to future generations. They will realize that the miraculous power of God has been at work in punishing the disobedient.

Verse 47 is a spiritual gem, giving the reason for their moving away from God. Moses says that the curses are "because you did not serve the LORD your God with joyfulness and gladness of heart, because of the abundance of all things." When they became rich, they forgot God, and as a result they lost their "joyfulness and gladness of heart." Preoccupation with their abundant possessions and the loss of joy and gladness from their life left them with no time or inclination to serve God.

The progression implied here is all too common among Christians. I have seen this with so many Christians who had very little when they first came to Christ. After becoming Christians they began to live responsibly and gradually acquired possessions. Those possessions became an idol, which took away their joy. They constantly got upset when there was any problem relating to their possessions. Having acquired the taste of what it means to have some earthly possessions, such as their own house, they began to desire improvements to what they had. It is amazing how people's catalog of what is considered essential for a healthy life gets so much bigger when they become more affluent. Their giving decreases. They get entangled in a huge burden of debt by trying to fulfill their new ambitions. Their bondage to possessions takes away their joy. That means they lost their spiritual freedom and the strength to serve God joyfully. Or as Moses put it, they can no longer "serve the LORD [their] God with joyfulness and gladness of heart, because of the abundance of all things."

In the parable of the sower, Jesus said that the seed that fell among thorns represented the experience of "those who hear the word, but the cares of the world and the deceitfulness of riches and the desires for other things enter in and choke the word, and it proves unfruitful" (Mark 4:18, 19). Do we ever think of possessions as means to curses coming to our lives? What folly this is—no joy in the present and a curse awaiting them in the future!

Another List of Curses (28:48–68)

After that brief interlude, Moses again lists some curses.

- Oppression and deprivation under a brutal enemy nation will ultimately result in total destruction, leaving nothing of the resources of the land until they have perished (27:48–51).
- The towns will be besieged by this nation (27:52), and in desperation the people will start eating the flesh of their own children (27:53). Even the most gentle and refined people will resort to brutal cannibalism (27:54–57).

Verse 58 is another general statement that presents the cause for the curses: "If you are not careful to do all the words of this law that are written in this book, that you may fear this glorious and awesome name, the LORD your God . . . " Further curses follow that statement:

- Severe afflictions and sickness—the diseases of Egypt that they dreaded (28:59, 60)—will come on them until they are destroyed (28:61).
- Though they were numerous as the stars, only a small remnant will remain (28:62).
- Verse 63a is remarkably vivid and forceful: "And as the LORD took delight in doing you good and multiplying you, so the LORD will take delight in bringing ruin upon you and destroying you." We will look at this verse further later.
- They will be plucked off the land they are just going to enter (28:63b) and scattered to the ends of the earth (28:64a). They will worship the strange gods of these nations (28:64b). In those nations they will have no respite to their suffering and fear (28:65, 66) despite their eager desire for relief (28:67).
- They will have a return journey to Egypt, despite the promise that this would never happen (28:68a). There they will try to sell themselves as slaves, but no one will want to purchase them (28:68b).

I trust that the rapid listing of these curses has given a sense of their horror. I believe this is the effect that Moses' extended listing would have had on his original audience. After all this they disobeyed the words of the Law! As Jeremiah said, "The heart is deceitful above all things, and desperately sick;

who can understand it?" (Jeremiah 17:9). It makes us lose our better judgment and do such stupid things!

The Curses and Israel's Subsequent History

David Payne wrote that if verses 1–14 are a picture of what might have been, the rest of the chapter is largely a picture of what actually *did* happen to Israel. The four books that follow Deuteronomy—Joshua, Judges, Samuel, and Kings—tell a story of political ups and downs, to be sure, but include many unhappy experiences for Israel and end with total disaster. Therefore, these curses are not unfounded threats given just to frighten people—like those of a mother who tells her daughter that the bogeyman will take away her away if she does not drink her milk. They really did take place in Israel's history. As Payne points out, "The real power of Deuteronomy . . . can perhaps be best seen in the fact that after the Exile, the Jewish people became more and more dedicated to keeping the Law enshrined in it." We know, for example, that, though the people may have had many non-religious idols, they never lapsed into making idols for worship after the exile.

Are These Curses for Today?

What we said about how the promises of prosperity apply today can also be said of the predictions of curses. First, these curses were for the nation of Israel under the old covenant. Second, some individuals under the old and new covenants may or may not be punished here on earth for their wrongdoing, but they will surely be punished in the next life. Paul's threat is true for old covenant and new covenant nations and individuals: "Do not be deceived: God is not mocked, for whatever one sows, that will he also reap" (Galatians 6:7). But the time of reaping curses may be postponed for the final judgment. As Paul said, "For we must all appear before the judgment seat of Christ, so that each one may receive what is due for what he has done in the body, whether good or evil" (2 Corinthians 5:10).

The Curses Are from God Himself

It is interesting that the curses here are described as coming from God himself. Here is a sampling of evidence for that:

- The LORD will send on you curses, confusion, and frustration in all that you undertake to do (28:20);
- The LORD will make the pestilence stick to you (28:21);
- The LORD will strike you with wasting disease and with fever, inflammation (28:22);
- The LORD will make the rain of your land powder (28:24); and

• The LORD will cause you to be defeated before your enemies (28:25).

Statements like this appear nineteen times between verses 20 and 68. The most vivid statement is in verse 63a: "And as the LORD took delight in doing you good and multiplying you, so the LORD will take delight in bringing ruin upon you and destroying you." This is not to say that God loves to destroy in the same way that he loves to bless. Elsewhere we see how painful it is to God to punish his people. Hosea 11:8 says, "How can I give you up, O Ephraim? How can I hand you over, O Israel? How can I make you like Admah? How can I treat you like Zeboiim? My heart recoils within me; my compassion grows warm and tender." Ezekiel 18:32 states, "For I have no pleasure in the death of anyone, declares the Lord GOD; so turn, and live." Peter says, "The Lord is not slow to fulfill his promise as some count slowness, but is patient toward you, not wishing that any should perish, but that all should reach repentance" (2 Peter 3:9).

If God dislikes punishing sinners, how should we understand the statement about God delighting to destroy the rebellious people? It must mean that God likes to do what is right and good. It is good to punish evildoers, so God likes to do it, even though it hurts his heart to do so. As James Orr put it, "God must approve of, yea, rest with satisfaction in, every exercise of his perfections, even in the infliction of judgment."[1] Orr points out that this "verse, in any view of it, is a very terrible one in its bearings on the prospects of the wicked." This is a message we must not hold back from giving to people. If God hates disobedience, we have the responsibility to share that with people, for the consequences of disobedience are tragic.

There has been a tendency among scholars to separate the wrath of God from his love. Marcion, who was condemned as a heretic in the second century, separated the God of the Old Testament from the heavenly Father of Jesus described in the New Testament. He said the God of the Old Testament "is legal-minded, violent, vindictive. The religion of this God is oriented around laws and demands." On the other hand, "the God of Jesus Christ . . . is the opposite. He is the forgiving and saving God. . . . And in Jesus he is revealed as pure love and mercy."[2] In the mid-twentieth century scholars such as A. T. Hanson and C. H. Dodd sought to take away the idea that the wrath described in the Bible is part of the nature of God. Hanson says that wrath "does not describe an attitude of God but a condition of men."[3] In the words of Dodd, "Wrath is the effect of human sin: mercy is not the effect of human goodness, but it is inherent in the character of God." They made wrath into an impersonal process of cause and effect that operates somewhat like the force of karma in Buddhism and Hinduism. Dodd claimed that wrath is retained in the New Testament "not to describe the attitude of God to man, but to describe the inevitable process of retribution."[4]

This attitude is common today also. When some Christians think of God's wrath they say something like, "Ah, but that's the God of the Old Testament, not of the New." However, as in the Old Testament, wrath is clearly connected with the nature of God in the New Testament also. Just look at a few verses from the epistle to the Romans:

- For the *wrath of God* is revealed from heaven against all ungodliness and unrighteousness of men (1:18).
- But if our unrighteousness serves to show the righteousness of God, what shall we say? That *God* is unrighteous *to inflict wrath* on us? (I speak in a human way.) By no means! For then how could God judge the world? (3:5, 6).
- What if God, desiring to show *his wrath* and to make known his power, has endured with much patience vessels of wrath prepared for destruction . . . (9:22).

I remember a sensitive ten-year-old boy in a Sunday school class I taught several years ago asking me, "If Jesus was a good man, how could he have acted the way he did at the temple?" He was referring to the cleansing of the temple. He simply could not reconcile that outburst of wrath with his idea of the goodness of God. But Jesus often acted with wrath over the way people, especially the Pharisees, rejected the truth. Matthew 23 is a vivid example of this. We see seven woes there. Jesus calls the scribes and Pharisees "hypocrites" six times, "blind" five times. Jesus says, "Woe to you, scribes and Pharisees, hypocrites! For you are like whitewashed tombs, which outwardly appear beautiful, but within are full of dead people's bones and all uncleanness" (v. 27). Again, "You serpents, you brood of vipers, how are you to escape being sentenced to hell?" (23:33).

Sadly, when we think of wrath we think of human outbursts of uncontrolled, selfish passion, which do more harm than good. Leon Morris was an Australian scholar who has written a lot on this topic. He says, "Nobody wants to attribute to God the weakness we know so well from human anger."[5] What we see in the Bible is God's attitude toward evil. If God condoned evil, he would not be just or good. It is good to punish evil so that goodness will remain good. So when he punishes evil, he does what is good. His wrath is a part of his good nature.

God's wrath could even be regarded as the flip side of his love. If God did not get angry at our sin, he would be insulting us by saying that we are so insignificant that our deeds do not matter. God's wrath elevates humans to a high level of significance, for it tells us that our actions do matter to God. Leon Morris says, "We sometimes find among men a love which is untempered by a sterner side, and this we call not love but sentimentality." Morris goes on to say, "It is not such that the Bible thinks of when it speaks of the love of God, but rather love which is so jealous of the loved one that it blazes out in fiery wrath against everything that is evil."[6] We need to be faithful in making people aware of this side of God's nature.[7]

Why Is More Space Given for the Curses?

It is significant that more space is given for the listing and description of the curses than for the blessings. This follows a pattern found in the Bible. A. W. Pink has been credited with the observation that the Bible has more references to the wrath of God than to the love of God. In the recorded statements of Jesus, there are more references to Hell than there are to Heaven. I believe the reason for this is that people naturally tend to ignore unpleasant things and focus on more pleasant things. We are taught to "think positive."

An American entertainer who had lived a godless life was interviewed by a TV reporter during the advanced stages of a terminal illness. The interviewer asked whether, now that he knew he was going to die, he was afraid of anything. He replied, "That there is a hell." But he quickly added, "I think it will work out well in the end." The human heart has a way of turning our legitimate fears into things we can ignore. Paul said of rebellious humanity, "Though they know God's decree that those who practice such things deserve to die, they not only do them but give approval to those who practice them" (Romans 1:32). Within everyone is the sense that sin should be punished. But many suppress that sense and continue in sin. Our calling is to resurface that awareness so that people will realize that a life of sin does merit a curse.

John the Baptist spoke about people being "warned [to] flee from the wrath to come" (Luke 3:7). May we be faithful in telling people, and in reminding ourselves, of the promise of blessings for the obedient and the prospect of curses for the disobedient.

56

Keys to Renewal

DEUTERONOMY 29:1–29

D. L. MOODY (1837–1899) was the most prominent evangelist of his era and was a colorful figure known for his apt and pithy statements. He placed great stress on the need for the fullness of the Spirit for ministry. He is reported to have said that he needed to keep being filled with the Spirit because leakage tended to take place in his spiritual life. Paul tells the Ephesians," . . . be filled with the Spirit" (Ephesians 5:18), implying that the filling is something we continually need to seek. Renewal, therefore, is a key Christian issue.

The Old Testament had a good way for the people to renew their commitment to God and the covenant they made with him. They had frequent covenant-renewal rituals that followed the same format as the original covenant-making ritual. Deuteronomy 29:1 talks about "the covenant that the LORD commanded Moses to make with the people of Israel in the land of Moab, besides the covenant that he had made with them at Horeb." Horeb or Sinai was where the major covenant was made. Now, before Moses dies, God commands him to "make" another covenant in Moab, which is where Moses was even at the start of this book (1:5). This covenant was not different in nature from the covenant made at Sinai; it was a renewal of that covenant. Joshua will lead the people in another renewal of this covenant after they have entered the promised land (Joshua 8:30–35). Moses' words in preparation for this covenant renewal in Moab appear in Deuteronomy 29, 30. These words are actually a summary of the whole message of Deuteronomy, because they present the features that should be included in the act of renewing the covenant.

Several times in this book we have referred to how the Hebrew word *shamar*, meaning something like "being careful to attend to," is used in

Deuteronomy in connection with obedience. Despite all the commands to be careful to obey, like the Israelites, we also tend to get careless about features in our walk with God. We end up disobeying. This may happen with our devotional life—the daily time we spend with the Bible and in prayer. We may get careless with our Internet use or TV watching and break some of the rules we made about that. The carelessness may slip into our behavior at home or school or work. Each Christian has areas about which he or she needs to be vigilant.

Renewing our covenant with God is an excellent aid to coming back to the path of obedience, of reaffirming that we are going to be serious about being careful to follow God's will in all we do. However, a simple prayer or rededication may not have the desired effect, because wrong habits may be ingrained into our behavior patterns. So the Bible describes a more elaborate ritual of commitment to burn into our hearts the full implications of the recommitment we are making. When this is done as a community, there is the added incentive of community solidarity to help us stick to the commitments we made. In the comments on 4:23 I referred to my favorite church service of the year, the Methodist Covenant service, usually held on the first Sunday of the year. It details many aspects of our commitment and ends with a very meaningful prayer of rededication. This renewal of our covenant could also take place through a day spent in fasting and prayer, alone or with a group, which buttresses the urgency and seriousness of what we are doing. It is good for us to develop regular renewal rituals for our lives.

Deuteronomy 29 describes the words Moses said just before his parting act of covenant renewal. We find some important keys to renewal here.

Recounting History and Possible Responses (29:2–9)

The first four chapters of Deuteronomy had a somewhat detailed recounting of the recent history of the people by Moses. In 29:2–9 we have an abbreviated version of this. Elsewhere we have described the value of recounting our history of God's dealings with us (see the discussions on 4:9b–14; 6:20–25; 10:20–22). Here we will simply follow the text and comment on important themes. Moses divides this section and gives three stages of God's recent actions in delivering the nation. Each division is followed by a possible response to the history.

First, Moses talks of "the great trials" that Egypt faced before they released the Israelites. They are referred to as "the signs, and those great wonders." Verses 2, 3 say, "And Moses summoned all Israel and said to them: 'You have seen all that the LORD did before your eyes in the land of Egypt, to

Pharaoh and to all his servants and to all his land, the great trials that your eyes saw, the signs, and those great wonders.'" The response mentioned here is one that should not have taken place: "But to this day the LORD has not given you a heart to understand or eyes to see or ears to hear" (v. 4). There is a sad and ironic play on words here. Verse 2 says, "*You have seen* all that the LORD did *before your eyes . . .* " Verse 2 talks of "the great trials that *your eyes saw.*" But their response is not seeing. Moses says, ". . . the LORD has not given you a heart to understand, or eyes to see or ears to hear" (v. 4). This should be interpreted as God's verdict on their rejection of his ways. Romans 1:24, 26, 28 talk of God giving up people who had refused to acknowledge him to do the terrible sins they wanted to do. Similarly, as the Israelites rejected his ways, God confirmed that choice by not giving them hearts, eyes, or ears to receive his message.

Even today people see God act in amazing ways and yet refuse to acknowledge God and yield to him. This is what was so hard for Moses to bear. He complained to God and asked for release from the responsibility of leading such a stiff-necked people, even asking God to kill him rather than have him as the leader of Israel (Numbers 11:10–15; see also Numbers 20:10). We will always mourn the unbelief of our people. But we must not get overly discouraged when people reject God's ways after they have seen God acting among them in such clear ways. How could people be so stubborn and unresponsive to such spectacular acts of deliverance? The next response mentioned helps us answer this question.

The second stage of their recent history was God's provision in the wilderness. The focus is on God's providing clothes and shoes that did not wear out for forty years and manna from Heaven instead of earthly food and wine. Deuteronomy 29:5, 6a says "I have led you forty years in the wilderness. Your clothes have not worn out on you, and your sandals have not worn off your feet. You have not eaten bread, and you have not drunk wine or strong drink." The response described here is a desired response: ". . . that you may know that I am the LORD your God" (29:6b). They had enough evidence to show that that God was with them and for them. They should have rejoiced over being God's people. Yet they behaved as if God had rejected them. They continued with their grumblings. Why? They were not in an ideal situation yet. They were in the wilderness; they did not have homes of their own and many of the things that people would have associated with prosperity. They focused on the things they did not have and adopted an attitude of murmuring.

While we are on earth, even those who belong to God will never have what is viewed as an ideal life by human standards. This is why Peter, just after saying, ". . . but now you are God's people" (1 Peter 2:10), goes on to say, "I urge you as sojourners and exiles . . . " (1 Peter 2:11). Paul says that because "the creation was subjected to futility" or "frustration" (TNIV), not only the whole creation but believers also "groan inwardly as we wait eagerly for" the coming redemption (Romans 8:20–23).

We can decide what we will do with the frustrating things that we encounter in life. Some reckon that because God has done so much for them already—especially in giving them eternal salvation—they can trust his promise to turn everything to good. They will choose to relish their joy in the Lord and act with hope, knowing that the frustration will yield something good. Their personal and corporate history to date enables them to say that they "know that [God is] the LORD [their] God." The trial deepens their faith, refines their character, and increases their joy.

Others will use the frustrating thing as a reason for complaining. They choose not to take into account all of God's goodness up to that point, and they say that God has not looked after them. People with such an attitude will always have something about which to complain. Frustration can challenge us to deeper exploration into God and his ways or it can feed despair and unbelief. We have a choice to make!

The third stage of Israel's history that Moses mentions is the conquest of the lands east of the Jordan River and the nations that lived in them, which two and a half tribes would occupy. Verses 7, 8 say, "And when you came to this place, Sihon the king of Heshbon and Og the king of Bashan came out against us to battle, but we defeated them. We took their land and gave it for an inheritance to the Reubenites, the Gadites, and the half-tribe of the Manassites." The response mentioned here is the main theme of this book and is presented as a command: "Therefore keep the words of this covenant and do them, that you may prosper in all that you do" (29:9). God's providence in our history assures us that we belong to God (29:6) and encourages us to live in faithful obedience to the one who has redeemed us and to whom we belong. There is another reason for being obedient. Just as God has helped us in the past, he will bless us in the future also, if we are obedient, and we will "prosper in all that [we] do" (29:9).

The Need for Renewal: A Great Equalizer (29:10–15)

The first key to renewal we looked at was the evidence of history, which encourages commitment to God and his ways. The second key is recognizing that we all need renewal. This is the theme of verses 10–15. Verses 12, 13 describe what will happen at the renewal ritual: ". . . so that you may enter into the sworn covenant of the LORD your God, which the LORD your God is making with you today, that he may establish you today as his people, and that he may be your God, as he promised you, and as he swore to your fathers, to Abraham, to Isaac, and to Jacob." They enter into a sworn covenant. Verses 10, 11 list who will participate in this ceremony: "You are standing today all of you before the LORD your God: the heads of your tribes, your elders, and your officers, all the men of Israel, your little ones, your wives, and the sojourner who is in your camp, from the one who chops your wood to the one who draws your water." Those who chop wood and draw water are the lowliest people in that society, and they were probably the sojourners mentioned here. These were non-Israelites or, as the TNIV translates it, "foreigners." Verses 14, 15 say that this covenant will also apply to those in the community who are not there—that is, those who are not yet born: "It is not with you alone that I am making this sworn covenant, but with whoever is standing here with us today before the LORD our God, and with whoever is not here with us today."

The covenant is a great equalizer. Chris Wright says that this act of "standing . . . before the LORD" (29:15) is "a radically leveling posture." Here the equality is not only in the fact that they stand before God but also that they all are in need of renewing their covenant. We have hierarchies based on responsibility and other factors, and those are needed for the smooth running of church, family, and society. So we have leaders and those who follow the leaders. We have directors and managers and those who are responsible to report to them. The Bible asks us to honor parents (5:16) and to "stand up before the gray head and honor the face of an old man" (Leviticus 19:32). We will gladly submit to these conventions, especially if the people we respect are honorable and good. Before God, however, we are all needy people, equally in need of renewal.

When great leaders of God's people like Isaiah, Daniel, and John had a glimpse of the nature of God, they were overwhelmed by a sense of inadequacy and awestruck by his holiness and greatness (Isaiah 6:1–5; Daniel 10:1–9; Revelation 1:9–17). We will not reach absolute perfection this side of Heaven. So even the godliest Christian will always be humbly desperate for God. The four opening statements of Jesus' kingdom manifesto (Matthew 5:3–6), in the Sermon on the Mount, describe true greatness in God's kingdom:

- Blessed are the poor in spirit, for theirs is the kingdom of heaven;
- Blessed are those who mourn, for they shall be comforted;
- Blessed are the meek, for they shall inherit the earth; and
- Blessed are those who hunger and thirst for righteousness, for they shall be satisfied.

The common denominator in this list is a sense of need. Actually God is so great and holy that the closer we get to him, the more we see our own unholiness. As we join in rituals of renewal, we all confess our need for more of God. The moment we stop having this sense of being needy, we stop growing. The former chaplain to the United States Senate, Richard C. Halverson, once said that the growing edge of the Christian life is need. When we come to renew our covenant with God, we all come as people needing desperately to live faithful lives.

As you look at some of the heroes of the Bible, you see that they were all weak people, many of whom easily went astray.

- Abraham gave in to fear and on two occasions was willing to give his wife to a king's harem by calling her his sister.
- Moses struggled with impatience with his people and sometimes made rash decisions.
- Aaron and Miriam became jealous of their brother Moses and tried to rebel against him.
- David gave in to lust and ended up committing adultery and murder.
- Elijah got so depressed that he wanted to die.
- Jeremiah got so depressed that he wished he'd never been born.
- Peter made promises of fearless devotion to Christ but soon after that denied Christ.

Truly great people always sense their need for more wisdom, more holiness, more of God. The first major international conference at which I spoke was the Amsterdam '83 International Conference for Itinerant Evangelists organized by the Billy Graham Evangelistic Association. I was thirty-four years old, and I spoke about encouraging younger evangelists. I described how Paul took younger evangelists with him in his travels and then told how I, too, had traveled with older evangelists and learned so much from them. I challenged the evangelists there to take younger people with them when they go on their ministry assignments. After I finished speaking, Billy Graham, who had been watching the talk from a television in another room, came up to the stage and spoke to me. Sadly, no one was there to photograph this great event in my life! But what he told me shocked me. He said that he would like to travel with me in order to learn how to preach to Asian audiences!

Clearly Dr. Graham was trying to encourage me. Behind this statement, however, I could see a humility that was desirous of more knowledge even from an unknown young preacher like me. I am not surprised when people say that one of the main reasons God entrusted Dr. Graham with the huge responsibility of being the world's most prominent Christian preacher was his humility. Before God we are all needy people, always needing renewal.

Rebels in the Community (29:16–19a)

The next paragraph warns about the possibility of being led astray by others in the community. First, Moses reminds the people that they know the horror of idolatry, which they'd seen in Egypt and in the nations they had encountered on their journey from Egypt. Verse 16 says, "You know how we lived in the land of Egypt, and how we came through the midst of the nations through which you passed." What they saw was detestable. Verse 17 says, "And you have seen their detestable things, their idols of wood and stone, of silver and gold, which were among them."

Then Moses warns the people of the influence of rebels within the community: "Beware lest there be among you a man or woman or clan or tribe whose heart is turning away today from the LORD our God to go and serve the gods of those nations" (29:18a). The rebellion could come from an individual or a group from within a tribe or from a whole tribe. This has been happening among God's people over the more than three millennia since this statement was made. Sometimes an individual who has the power to persuade others is the key source of rebellion. Sometimes it is a smaller or larger group that already had some special solidarity or that has come together because of the issue over which they are rebelling. Their power is immense, so Moses says, "Beware lest there be among you a root bearing poisonous and bitter fruit" (29:18b). As Gary Hall puts it, "A root that would remain after a tree was cut down could sprout again (Isaiah 11:1, 10) and would be difficult to eradicate. We would say that one rotten apple spoils the whole container." The phrase "poisonous and bitter fruit" gives an indication of the extent of the damage done. Those who sow discord and discontentment can cause havoc among God's people because often people respond affirmatively to any wave of influence that may harmonize with the discontentment that is in their hearts. As soon as leaders see what is happening, they must meet and talk to the rebellious individual or group.

Deuteronomy 29:19 describes the nature of their rebellion. Before looking at this, I must clarify that we are not talking about people who are questioning the status quo and want change that could be good for the organization or church. Organizations and churches need to adapt to demands made by the particular environment and the stage of their history in which they are. Principles and practices that were helpful in the early years of a movement may no longer be helpful. Major or minor changes may need to be introduced to meet new challenges. Often this need for change is advocated by younger people, sometimes referred to as rebels within the movement because of some of their radical ideas. We need these kind of radicals if we are to be organizationally at the cutting edge.

The rebellion Moses is talking about has to do with basic Biblical rules of conduct. He describes the rebel as "one who, when he hears the words of this sworn covenant, blesses himself in his heart, saying, "I shall be safe, though I walk in the stubbornness of my heart'" (29:19a). This person is claiming that it is not necessary to obey the laws of the covenant and that no harm will come because of this. Such people can have a huge impact because of the attractiveness of sin and a relaxed attitude toward rules. Why carry out this huge battle against temptation when we there is no harm done by giving in to it? The statement "blesses himself in his heart" is an expression of pride. The sinner misleads others by his sheer confidence that he can sin boldly and enjoy sin. It is like saying, "Why are you so uptight as to stick to these outmoded rules that even our parents found impossible to keep? Wake up! You're living in the twenty-first century." It suggests an enthusiasm to propagate the new lifestyle. This is exactly what we are seeing today. The zeal of advocates of the new morality is having a huge impact among Christians, especially as it has the backing of the media.

We will take the new sexual ethic that is being propagated today as an example of this phenomenon. The Bible unambiguously condemns all sex outside of marriage as sin. Yet society almost trains young people to have premarital sex through today's sex education programs. Those who are virgins are made to feel ashamed of their "sexual inexperience." The power of sex is immense, and unmarried Christian couples have to use severe restraint to maintain their commitment to sex being only within marriage. They need to have strict rules about their behavior with each other. They need to be careful not to find themselves in places and situations where they would be vulnerable to sinful sexual activity. They have accountability partners who monitor their activity as they wade through these difficult waters.

But the new morality is saying, "It's OK. Just enjoy yourself! All this fuss about chastity is an unnecessary vestige of a bygone era." The church is also wavering on this issue. It talks about the evils of adultery—of married people having extramarital sex. But it does not talk much about premarital sex, possibly because many of the people in the pews are indulging in it and would stop coming to church if there is too much talk against it. With the loss of the old taboos in society and the silence of the church, there isn't much to restrain Christians who are struggling with the huge pressure of sexual feelings.

How important it is for the church to counteract the push that is coming from the world to legitimize what the Bible clearly calls sin. This is the same danger that Moses is talking about in our passage. We must push back wisely. We must do it intelligently. We must find answers to the claims made by proponents of the new morality. We must do all this in a way that will make sinners feel welcome in the church while being challenged to repent of their sin. But if people within the church try to advocate or be lenient about the new morality, we must respond with firm opposition. In the verses that follow, Moses is unafraid to say that the person advocating sin is on a very dangerous course.

The Consequences of Abandoning the Covenant (29:19b–28)

The second part of verse 19 is difficult to interpret: "This will lead to the sweeping away of moist and dry alike." Whatever the exact meaning, we can safely say that it is talking about the disaster that awaits every individual or community that rejects God's covenant. Moses goes on to describe the fate of the one who rebels against God's covenant.

> The LORD will not be willing to forgive him, but rather the anger of the LORD and his jealousy will smoke against that man, and the curses written in this book will settle upon him, and the LORD will blot out his name from under heaven. And the LORD will single him out from all the tribes of Israel for calamity, in accordance with all the curses of the covenant written in this Book of the Law. (29:20, 21)

As in the previous chapter we see that God is personally angry about this abandoning of the covenant. These verses speak of "the anger of the LORD and his jealousy." He loved Israel and committed himself to caring for and prospering her. But the love is not reciprocated. It is given instead to worthless and "detestable" idols (v. 17). Naturally, his anger and jealousy, or as Eugene Merrill paraphrases it, "his zealous wrath," burns. Love burns with anger when the object of love chooses a path of destruction. Moses says, "The LORD will not be willing to forgive him," probably because in his arrogant attitude of rebellion he is not willing to repent.[1]

Verses 22–24 say that the next generation of Israelites and foreigners who come from afar are going to marvel and ask why this happened.

> And the next generation, your children who rise up after you, and the foreigner who comes from a far land, will say, when they see the afflictions of that land and the sicknesses with which the LORD has made it sick—the whole land burned out with brimstone and salt, nothing sown and nothing growing, where no plant can sprout, an overthrow like that of Sodom and Gomorrah, Admah, and Zeboiim, which the LORD overthrew in his anger

and wrath—all the nations will say, "Why has the LORD done thus to this land? What caused the heat of this great anger?"

The answer to the question about the reason for this fate is that they abandoned the covenant by worshipping other gods.

> Then people will say, "It is because they abandoned the covenant of the LORD, the God of their fathers, which he made with them when he brought them out of the land of Egypt, and went and served other gods and worshiped them, gods whom they had not known and whom he had not allotted to them." (29:25, 26)

As a result the Lord's anger was kindled against the people, and the curses described in the covenant were enacted, especially the curse of the driving of the people of Israel into another land: "Therefore the anger of the LORD was kindled against this land, bringing upon it all the curses written in this book, and the LORD uprooted them from their land in anger and fury and great wrath, and cast them into another land, as they are this day" (29:27, 28). About the exile, it is said, "as they are this day." Some use this as evidence that Deuteronomy was written during the time of the exile. In answer we say that here Moses is describing, before the event, what people will say when they see Israel exiled. It is not difficult to believe that Moses himself would say such a thing in his prophetic description.

What a contrast there is between the arrogance of the rebel before God deals with him and his sheer debasement after exposure to God's wrath. Today's inclusive world loves to include as legitimate what we consider to be sin. When people insist on righteousness in morality, some protest, saying that this is incompatible with the value of inclusiveness. In such an environment those who peddle the attractiveness of disobedience to God's Law may seem very powerful. We must not be rattled by the falsely confident moral high ground that advocates of moral relativism are projecting today. Their power and confidence are fleeting, and they are headed for a terrible downfall. The smiles and the attractive mirage of wholesomeness that they project in the media hide the sordid confusion their lifestyles create. We must not be fooled. Instead, we must faithfully warn people about the peril of rejecting God's ways for this alternate morality.

God's Secrets and Revelation (29:29)

The last verse of this chapter is different from the rest in that it gives a stand-alone theological principle. It is related to the rest of the chapter because this principle lies behind the life of obedience to God. "The secret things belong to the LORD our God, but the things that are revealed belong to us and to our children forever, that we may do all the words of this law" (29:29). Our knowledge is not complete, but it is sufficient for obedience. That knowledge comes from revelation, and it is for us "forever." The Word of God will never change; it will always be relevant. The eternity of the Word is a theme that appears several times in the Bible. Isaiah said, "The grass withers, the flower fades, but the word of our God will stand forever" (Isaiah 40:8)—a statement that Peter quoted (1 Peter 1:24, 25). Jesus said, "Heaven and earth will pass away, but my words will not pass away" (Mark 13:31). According to Deuteronomy 29:29, the purpose of God's revelation is "that we may do all the words of this law." God has given us enough knowledge to help us live an obedient life.

Yet by saying, "The secret things belong to the LORD our God," Moses is saying there are some things we do not know, things that God has chosen not to reveal to us, as they are not necessary for the main purpose of God's revelation—to lead us to know and obey God. Among those things are the details of what God is going to do in the future. Much has been said about the end times in the Bible, but the purpose of that revelation is to help us to be obedient to God. Mark 13, known as "the Little Apocalypse" or "the Olivet Discourse," is one of the key passages about the end times in the Bible. Jesus starts this discourse with an imperative: "See that no one leads you astray" (13:5) and ends it with an imperative: "Stay awake" (13:37). The body of the discourse is loaded with imperatives. Jesus is describing what is going to happen in the future with the aim of urging the people to be obedient. Matthew's version of this discourse gives us a grand theme that should fire our lives with ambition to do what we can do to hasten the end: "And this gospel of the kingdom will be proclaimed throughout the whole world as a testimony to all nations, and then the end will come" (Matthew 24:14).

Yet throughout history people have had a thirst for details of future events. People go to astrologers, psychic readers, and soothsayers to learn what will come. The prophecies like those of Nostradamus never fail to win a wide and enthusiastic audience. Even Christians are sometimes not content with what is given in the Bible. Many extrapolate the teachings of the Bible to draw conclusions that are not warranted from a Biblical perspective. For example, over the years people have been predicting the date of the coming of the end or the return of Christ. In the Olivet Discourse Jesus explicitly said, "But concerning that day or that hour, no one knows, not even the angels in heaven, nor the Son, but only the Father" (Mark 13:32). When the disciples asked about this, Jesus gave them a mild rebuke saying, "It is not for you to know times or seasons that the Father has fixed by his own authority"

(Acts 1:7). Immediately following that, he gives the Great Commission (Acts 1:8), which tells them what they *should* be concerned about.

Why then do Bible-believing teachers persist in going beyond what the Scriptures permit to make specific predictions about the future? Should they not have learned a lesson from the many people who have done this throughout the centuries and ended in disrepute because their predictions did not come to pass? I cannot say with certainty why this is so. But God's Word is being violated, and sincere people are being misled. Therefore, we must roundly condemn this. Perhaps there is a marketing reason for the popularity of these predictions about the end times. Throughout the centuries people have wanted to know about the future. One of the keys to marketing is giving what people need and arousing in people a sense of need for a specific product. Those who talk about the future beyond what Scripture teaches can be sure of a ready audience.

How much safer it is for us to say that we do not know the answer to questions relating to specifics of the end times than to run the risk of rebelling against God by going beyond where the Bible permits us to go.

The long-term damage of such unfulfilled predictions can be very serious. The value of words has been greatly reduced in this postmodern generation. Sadly, our generation does not trust language. The idea of fashioning our lives according to objective truths in the Bible sounds insane to many ears. But God has spoken to us through language. Christianity rests on certain objective facts upon which we pin our hope. One of our greatest apologetic challenges in this era is to convince people that there is such a thing as truth and that it is worth banking our lives on the truths of God's Word. What if those who claim to speak on the authority of God's Word are shown to have been mistaken on a lot of things? People will see in this another reason for not believing the Bible. The end-time scenarios being propagated these days could do much to increase the distrust of truth in our generation.

Despite our terrible performance as guardians of orthodoxy, the truth of God will abide forever. But our presumptuous pursuit along illegitimate paths in search of the secrets of God will cause many to stumble and miss the truth.

Let's recap the keys about renewal that this passage teaches.

- It is wise to be open to frequent acts of renewing our covenant with God because we can grow cold in our commitment to God.
- History should drive us to obedience, but some people may continue to disobey God by choosing not to accept the implications of God's actions in history. They could focus on the inevitable frustrations of life and use them as an excuse to opt out of covenant living.

- The thirst for renewal is a great equalizer. Whatever our status on earth, we are needy people in God's sight. We must never lose the holy dissatisfaction that drives us to want more of God.
- We must beware of the insidious and powerful influence of rebels who confidently proclaim that we can, without harming ourselves, reject the Biblical way of life.
- The revealed Word of God is what spurs us on to obedience. We must be careful to avoid delving too much into areas about which God has chosen not to inform us. A renewal of prophetic frenzy is not the same as the renewal of the church.

57

The Path of Repentance

DEUTERONOMY 30:1–20

R. A. TORREY (1856–1928) was a scholar, Bible teacher, and evangelist who exercised a wide teaching and preaching ministry all over the world. He was the first head (after founder D. L. Moody) of what became Moody Bible Institute and later president of what became Biola University. When he conducted evangelistic campaigns in a city, the city would often be saturated with posters and banners with the words, "Get Right with God." The people were confronted with the stark reality of the urgency of making peace with God. Such urgency is seen in Deuteronomy 30, which presents two major themes: the promise of restoration and the wrongness of rebellion. The chapter starts with a description of what will happen to the people after they return to God. But it ends with an urgent description of the stark choice the people have between obedience, which brings blessing, and disobedience, which brings punishment.

The Anatomy of Repentance (30:1–10)

Verses 1–10 are a beautiful description of what happens when a lapsed group or individual returns to God. This may not be the exact order in which the steps take place. I think the order may differ with different people. In fact, in this passage we find the same steps mentioned several times in different places.

The People Remember the Word (30:1)

The repentance takes place after the Israelites have rebelled against the covenant. Moses describes the situation saying, "And when all these things

come upon you, the blessing and the curse, which I have set before you . . . "
(30:1a). The implication is that they are now miserable and under the curse.
In that situation they are going to remember what the Word has said about
blessings and curses. Moses says, ". . . you call them [that is, the blessing
and the curse] to mind among all the nations where the Lord your God has
driven you . . . " (30:1b). That triggers the process of repentance. When people
recognize the folly of their ways, they are in a receptive mood to hear what
the Word of God says.

The Bible teaches that the Word of God can keep a person from sinning.
Psalm 119:11 says, "I have stored up your word in my heart, that I might
not sin against you." The Word stored up in the heart can also help a person
who has sinned to repent! The biographies of some famous Christians who
came to Christ only after a time of sinful rebellion against God show that
the truths that they had been taught, often in their childhood, had a part to
play in their return to God. Today some Christians say that people are not
interested in Bible exposition and that the push for relevance would dictate
that preachers look for other ways of preaching. Indeed, we have to adapt to
our audience, and our styles may change. But our content must always come
from the Bible.

Preaching can be so supposedly "relevant" that people are so comfortable
with it that they do not feel convicted to turn from their sin to God. Stephen's
message (Acts 7) was both very Scriptural and very relevant. The relevance,
however, was a prophetic relevance. It demonstrated that God acts powerfully
outside Jerusalem and its temple. This opened the church to the idea that it
should go beyond the geographical confines of Israel, as the narrative in Acts
following Stephen's death shows (Acts 8—28). Stephen also became the
model of the great apologists of the first three centuries of the church. This
message enraged his opponents so much that they killed him. The church
is always called to be prophetic. We are countercultural, but what makes us
relevant is that our message cuts through to the hearers. Some accept it, while
others reject it.

The Bible teaching ministry is costly in an age when preachers are too
busy to do careful study of the Word and hearers may not be as interested in
what the Bible says as before. It requires extra time to be devoted not only
to study the text but also to make sure that the Biblical content is presented
relevantly, practically, and attractively. I have been spurred on in this enterprise through the thought that the silence of the Bible in the church is a sure
sign of the need for revival in the church. We must teach the Bible, and we
must believe that it will one day trigger revival. Once revival comes, the
people will thirst for the Scriptures. Our task is to help foster a thirst for the

Word. The great historian of revival, J. Edwin Orr, has said that a theological awakening must precede a revival of religion. Dr. John Mackay writes, "First the enlightened mind, then the burning heart. First a revival of theological insights, and then the revival we need."[1] This is what happened under King Josiah when a newly discovered book of the Law was read and a mighty revival was sparked off (2 Kings 22, 23). The same thing happened when Ezra read the Law and others helped the people to understand it. First there was great weeping among the people, and then there was great rejoicing as they experienced God's grace (Nehemiah 8). The principle we glean, then, is that if we wish to prepare for revival and repentance, we should be faithful in teaching the Word to our people. We teach the Bible to help trigger a revival, and after people are revived they will come because they want to hear the Word taught.

Being genuinely prophetic has never been popular and lucrative. Marketing has influenced our understanding of significance so much that those who do things that are not very popular would not be considered significant in many circles. A book on a hot subject would be more popular than a Bible study book. A Bible teacher may be tempted to write popular books rather than books on Biblical topics. Indeed, we must labor to write Biblical books attractively so people will want to read them. But they will rarely be best sellers. That should not bother us. Our task is to be faithful and to contribute to God's plan to renew his church.

The People Return to God (30:2a, 6, 10b)

After the people remember what the Word said, Moses tells them they will "return to the Lord your God, you and your children" (30:2a). Verse 10b says, ". . . when you turn to the Lord your God with all your heart and with all your soul," he is talking about repentance. We have looked at this in some detail in our study of 4:29–31.

Moses tells the people that when they move away from God, they will face the full severity of the curse "among all the nations where the Lord your God has driven you" (30:1). While suffering utter humiliation in exile, the people lose their pride. They turn to God out of a sense of hopelessness. Some may scoff at such repentance saying that it is dishonorable, merely the result of people in utter desperation turning to God, realizing they have nowhere else to go. Those who speak like this do not fully understand the mercy and grace of God. Turning to God is never a thing about which a person can boast. We all come as sinners in need of God. We are forgiven not because we are worthy of it but because of the sheer mercy of God.

The People Obey Wholeheartedly (30:2b, 8, 10)

The people do not only return to God, they also become obedient to God. Our paragraph mentions this three times:

- Verse 2 says they will ". . . obey his voice in all that I command you to-day, with all your heart and with all your soul" (30:2b).
- Verse 8 says, "And you shall again obey the voice of the Lord and keep all his commandments that I command you today."
- Verse 10 says, ". . . when you obey the voice of the Lord your God, to keep his commandments and his statutes that are written in this Book of the Law, when you turn to the Lord your God with all your heart and with all your soul."

Obedience is the sign of true repentance. John the Baptist called for the people to "bear fruits in keeping with repentance" (Luke 3:8). The surest fruit of repentance is a heart desiring to obey God. Note how Moses says that they must obey with "all your heart and with all your soul" (30:2). To obey in this way is to desire to obey. We obey not only because it is our duty and because the Word says to do it, we obey because we want to obey. We will see below that God gives us this desire as our hearts are filled with a love for him. Indeed, there are times when earthly desires overcome us and we desire things that are not of God. But deep down we want to please God. So we ask God to give us godly desires. I have pasted a little prayer by Robert Tuttle where I pray at home: "Lord God, I want to want what you want for me!"[2] As we will see, God gives us the ability to desire the right things by circumcising our hearts (30:6). We are always what we are because of the mercy of God. Jesus himself said that what we need is faith like a grain of mustard seed (Matthew 17:20), indicating that it is all of God. What God wants is our openness to him like a seed is open to the nutrients which will help it germinate and grow. And he wants our willingness to obey his voice in all that the Word commands us (Deuteronomy 30:8).

Having worked with people with addictions, I know that some really want to overcome their addiction but keep going back. I have also seen some giving up the habit for good after sometimes as many as ten lapses. Other Christians were involved in helping these people come into this victory. They availed themselves of the different means that God uses to help people overcome sin and to mediate his grace—such as prayer, Bible reading, corporate worship, the Lord's Supper, spiritual accountability, group Bible study, and fellowship. Whatever the means used, the initial return needs to be with one's whole heart. That is, the person comes back saying he or she will never go back to drugs or idolatry or extramarital sex or dishonesty or lying or whatever it is that keeps him or her away from God. God can take that resolve and infuse it with his sufficient grace, using different means of grace. Without a willingness to give up sin totally, there is little hope of a genuine return to God.

When lapsed Christians return to God after messing up their lives, we must welcome them with open arms and fight the cynicism that tells us it won't last. We do so with our belief in the power of God's grace to change the person completely. But we must also help these people follow the path of obedience and make the tough choices that will help them leave their past and obey God totally.

God Makes the Change Possible (30:6a)

Can sinful people come back to God and change their behavior? They cannot on their own, but they can with God's help. That is what verse 6 says: "And the LORD your God will circumcise your heart and the heart of your offspring, so that you will love the LORD your God with all your heart and with all your soul, that you may live." Circumcision was the outward sign of their belonging to the people of God. They could be circumcised physically without an inward acceptance of God as their Lord. God makes them real followers by circumcising their hearts. This was fully achieved under the new covenant, which Jeremiah describes: "I will put my law within them, and I will write it on their hearts. And I will be their God, and they shall be my people" (Jeremiah 31:33).

God changes us from the inside by circumcising our hearts and filling us with a love for him. This in turn expresses itself in obedience. The friends of a Muslim university student who became a Christian were very surprised by his conversion. They told him, "Ahmed, we hear you have changed your religion." He responded, "Oh no! You have it all wrong. I have not changed my religion. My religion has changed me."[3]

They Love God Totally (30:6b)

The result of God's circumcising their hearts is that they love God: ". . . so that you will love the LORD your God with all your heart and with all your soul" (30:6b). Loving God is the key to the life of a believer. This passage teaches that the surest sign of loving God is obedience to his commands. As Jesus said, "If you love me, you will keep my commandments" (John 14:15). Or as John said, "For this is the love of God, that we keep his commandments" (1 John 5:3). You cannot have one without the other. You cannot love without obedience; and if you obey without love, it is not true Christian obedience, for it lacks what our next point talks about.

They Will Live (30:6c)

Moses says that the fruit of having hearts circumcised and of loving God is that we live: "the LORD God will circumcise your heart . . . so that you will love the LORD your God . . . that you may live" (30:6). In both the Old and the New Testaments, at the heart of the life God gives us is a love relationship with him. Jesus explained, "And this is eternal life, that they know you the only true God, and Jesus Christ whom you have sent" (John 17:3). The heart of Biblical religion is turning to God and experiencing the work he does in us. Such a relationship with God gives us a desire to obey him, and so the relationship results in obedience.

God Restores their Fortunes (30:3–5, 7, 9)

We saw that God circumcises the hearts of the people in order to enable them to turn to God and to love and obey him (30:6). Once that step is completed, Moses says that God will restore their fortunes.

> . . . then the LORD your God will restore your fortunes and have mercy on you, and he will gather you again from all the peoples where the LORD your God has scattered you. If your outcasts are in the uttermost parts of heaven, from there the LORD your God will gather you, and from there he will take you. And the LORD your God will bring you into the land that your fathers possessed, that you may possess it. And he will make you more prosperous and numerous than your fathers. (vv. 3–5)

First, God will gather the people from the ends of the earth to which they have been scattered. Wherever they are—even if they are "in the uttermost parts of the heavens"—they will be brought back to the land of their fathers. They will be prosperous and multiply in this land.

Verse 7 says that their enemies will experience the curses with which they were cursed: "And the LORD your God will put all these curses on your foes and enemies who persecuted you." Verse 9 expands on the promise of prosperity: "The LORD your God will make you abundantly prosperous in all the work of your hand, in the fruit of your womb and in the fruit of your cattle and in the fruit of your ground. For the LORD will again take delight in prospering you, as he took delight in your fathers." We have already discussed the issue of the promises of prosperity in our comments on 28:1–14.

God's Loving Attitude toward Them (30:3, 9)

Tucked inside these promises of what God will do to the people are two thoughts that tell us of God's attitude toward the people. The first is in verse 3, which says that God will "have mercy" or "pity" (NJB) on them. The Hebrew word translated "have mercy" belongs to a group of words that is frequently used of God. It carries the idea of "God's deep and tender love."[4] Salvation and forgiveness originate in the deep love that God has for us. Later revelation shows that God demonstrated this love in the giving of his own Son to die for us "while we were still sinners" (Romans 5:8).

The second thought is another expression of God's deep and tender love to us. Verse 9b says, "For the LORD will again take delight in prospering you, as he took delight in your fathers." This wonderful theme lies at the heart of the Old Testament emphasis on joy. We often talk about our delighting in God and his Law. But we do not talk as much of an even greater truth—God delighting in us! I found seven places in the Old Testament where it says that God delights or takes pleasure in us.[5] I found three instances, including the verse we are looking at, that say God takes delight in loving and blessing us (Deuteronomy 28:63; 30:9b; Micah 7:18). I also found one statement that God delights in our welfare (Psalm 35:27). This means there are eleven references proclaiming that God's children bring delight to him. That is the way good fathers are. Observing and thinking about their children brings them great joy.

Zephaniah 3:17 vividly expresses the idea of God delighting in us: "The LORD your God is in your midst, a mighty one who will save; he will rejoice over you with gladness; he will quiet you by his love; he will exult over you with loud singing." The *New American Standard Bible* translates that last phrase, "He will rejoice over you with shouts of joy." We can picture a father at a school play in which his little daughter is acting. She does a great job, and the proud and happy father feels like shouting, "That's my girl!" That is how God thinks of us when we return to him after a time in the far country. This was the attitude of the father of the prodigal son in Jesus' famous parable.

I believe one of the greatest challenges in Christian discipleship is learning to believe that God delights in us in this way. We have faced so much disappointment, rejection, and pain from people who we thought were committed to us that we cannot think that anyone, even God, loves us enough to be thrilled about us. Until we come to accept this truth about God, we will never know the joy about which the Bible talks so much. When the most significant person in your life is thrilled about you, you will really be happy. When you realize that this person is the Lord of the universe, you will be thrilled. Let us make understanding the extent of this amazing love of God one of our main pursuits in life.

The Accessible Word (30:11–14)

Moses has just described the process of the people returning to God and obeying the Word through God's circumcising their hearts. Now he goes on to say something about the Word that they will obey. He says, "For this commandment that I command you today is not too hard for you, neither is it far off" (30:11). It could be that people objected that the Word was too difficult to understand and too difficult to practice. Moses is answering both those questions when he says that it is "not too hard." We already saw in 27:8 that the Word had to be written "very plainly" so that all could read it. It needed to be accessible to everyone. In our discussion of 27:1–8 we said that the simplicity of the Word contrasts with the complexity of the scriptures of other religions.

A pastor once told me that it is difficult to talk about corruption from the pulpit because it is impossible for people living in society to survive if they are totally honest. Many preachers do not talk about the Biblical attitude toward possessions or the poor or social justice or sexual morality because they think these teachings are impractical today. Moses, however, says that God's commandment "is not too hard for you." If we open up our heart to God and let him circumcise it, then he will help us obey. This teaching is taught more clearly in Romans 8 as a part of the work of the Holy Spirit. There is hope for the sincere Christian who is caught up in a sin or is addicted to a habit and is finding it difficult to give it up. The Bible says we can do what God commands us to do! The Holy Spirit is there to help us. We can hope that we will be freed! We may fall in spite of our resolutions, but there is no excuse for falling. The grace of God is there to forgive and to help us start again, believing that we can win this battle.

Verse 12 says, "It [the commandment] is not in heaven, that you should say, 'Who will ascend to heaven for us and bring it to us, that we may hear it and do it?'" All through history there has been a tendency to look to special media of revelation. Indeed, God worked through special messages to prophets to tell us his will. But they were not mystics who gave us esoteric messages. Especially now that we have a complete Bible, we can say that we can find all that we need for obedience from the Word.

Preachers will help people understand by expounding the Word. Some people who walk very close to God see things that others do not see through spiritual eyes that have been enlightened by hours spent in the presence of God. The Bible, however, does not encourage the nurturing of a class of mystics who receive special messages from God. This was seen in a big way in the period when the heresy Gnosticism was popular in the church. We see it today sometimes when people claim to have special spiritual interpretations of the Word that come through heavenly revelations. The Word is plain for all to read and learn.

Verse 13 says, "Neither is it beyond the sea, that you should say, 'Who will go over the sea for us and bring it to us, that we may hear it and do it?'" Indeed people can cross the seas to learn from good teachers. I did that when I went to the United States for my theological studies. But here I think the idea is of people saying that there is a special revelation in some special place and we must go there to experience that, and those who do not go are somehow considered deprived. This practice of people making spiritual pilgrimages to holy sites takes place when something spectacular is happening in a given place. People from all over the world flock to that place to be part of the phenomenon. Again I must say that it is not wrong to learn from a place where God is working. The problem is when the focus moves from obedience to exotic experiences and revelations. Then we have moved away from the central focus of the Bible, which is to help people to obey God.

One of the best preachers I have heard was an Indian evangelist called Samuel Ganesh who preached in the Tamil language. He stayed in our home during a visit to Sri Lanka. He is not skilled in English, and he told me that he deeply regretted that, because he could not learn from all the scholarship that comes from the West. I thought, however, that his brilliance as a preacher was because he was steeped in the Bible and the world of the Bible and because he was able to present the Biblical message in a culturally skilled way to the Tamil people. I feared that if he had too much Western education he might lose some of the brilliant artistry and relevance of his preaching. We can go elsewhere to learn. But we must not forget that the Bible is fully accessible to all people in every country where it has been translated.

Verse 14 says, "But the word is very near you. It is in your mouth and in your heart, so that you can do it." The Bible is eminently accessible to all people. Paul quotes this passage in Romans 10:6–8 to show that the Israelites already had the message of faith through the Scriptures. When we go to the Word with circumcised hearts, we can receive from God what he wishes to give us, and that can change our lives. Of course, we must live close to the Word as Deuteronomy has often told us (see especially 6:6–9).

Moses mentions three things that we can do with the Word that is near us. First, the Word must be "in your mouth." We must talk about the Word. There are few pleasures in life as rich as what might be called holy conversation—Christians chatting about the things of God as found in the Word. As we do that we learn from each other, and our active involvement through conversation helps the Word get embedded in our hearts. There is a lot of superficial talk when Christians get together these days. That is not bad in itself, especially if we can have a good laugh. Does not the Bible say that "a cheerful heart is good medicine" (Proverbs 17:22, NLT)? But there is also deep, deep satisfaction from talking about eternal truth with fellow pilgrims. This is a practice that can bring great richness and depth to our lives.

Second, Moses says the Word "is . . . in your heart." This should refer to understanding the Word and storing it for use when needed, and possibly also to meditating on the Word. Third, this close contact with the Word results in our obeying the Word. So Moses says, ". . . so that you may do it." All study, conversation, and meditation on the Word must result in obedience to the Word.

If the Old Testament is so confident about the accessibility and practicability of the Word, how much more confident we can be, now that we have the whole Bible. Jesus said, "When the Spirit of truth comes, he will guide you into all the truth" (John 16:13). Now we have God's complete revelation. Let us spend time with this book and focus on how to obey what it teaches. It will speak to us and help transform our lives. An African woman was asked if she enjoyed reading her new Bible. She replied, "Sir, I am not reading this Book. This Book is reading me!"[6] That is how relevant and accessible the Bible is.

A Stark Choice[7] (30:15–20)

Verses 15–20 bring to an end the relatively short speech of Moses that covers chapters 29, 30. Most of the content of this sermon has already been given in Deuteronomy. In fact, chapter 30 is a summary of the essential message of Deuteronomy. But we have a new slant or fresh emphasis in the main points made in this chapter. The first section was on how the people will return to God and their land (30:1–10), giving us an outline of repentance. The section on the Word (30:11–14) focused on the accessibility of the Word. This last section (30:15–20) presents the two alternate possibilities of obedience and disobedience, which appear so often in this book. This time they are presented as a stark choice placed before the people.

Life and Death, Good and Evil (30:15)

Verse 15 says, "See, I have set before you today life and good, death and evil." Is the acceptance or rejection of God's way such a serious matter? It is! And we who live in the post-New Testament era know this even more clearly. The gospel is a matter of life and death. John puts this in unmistakable terms when he says, "And this is the testimony, that God gave us eternal life, and this life is in his Son. Whoever has the Son has life; whoever does not have the Son of God does not have life" (1 John 5:11, 12). It is a choice between life and death, between salvation and damnation.

How about the words "good" and "evil"? Surely, there are non-Christians who live good lives from which we can learn much. Can we call them "evil"? I have learned many good things about neighborliness from my Muslim neighbors. Indeed, some non-Christians may exceed us in showing good character—I say this to our shame. But the most serious wrong that one could do is to spurn God's offer of salvation and use other methods to save ourselves and govern our lives. He is the Creator and Lord of the universe; to rebel against his chosen way to run this world is treason—a serious crime, indeed. Yes, we can call it evil! That does not mean that we do not appreciate the good there is in others. We can affirm all the good there is in them, learn from them, and express our gratitude to them. Having been made in the image of God, they are able to develop some innate characteristics in admirable ways. But these don't give them salvation. We must also do all we can to bring them to accept the way of their Creator.

The Path of Obedience (30:16, 20)

Verses 16, 20 describe four features of the life that results from choosing "life and good" (30:15). First, Moses says they must "obey the commandments of the LORD your God that I command you today" (30:16a). Verse 20 describes it as "obeying his voice." That second expression suggests that they are constantly listening to the voice of God. This is borne out in the many passages in Deuteronomy that tell the people they must live close to the Scriptures (6:6–9).

Second, the way to obey the commands is "by loving the LORD your God, by walking in his ways, and by keeping his commandments and his statutes and his rules" (30:16b). This is a comprehensive way to describe Biblical obedience. Both verses 16 and 20 mention loving God, which is a key motivation for obedience. Because we love God, obedience is not just some duty that we perform to satisfy the authorities. We want to please the one we love. Then it involves "walking in his ways." We have chosen God's way as our way, the way we love to live. As Paul put it, we "walk by the Spirit" (Galatians 5:16). This reminds us that we are in relationship with God through the Spirit. To walk in God's ways is to walk with God, as Enoch did (Genesis 5:22, 24). Again, the life of obedience is not simply a bunch of rules—it is a lifestyle of walking with God in his way. Only after these two things—loving and walking—does Moses mention "by keeping his commandments and his statutes and his rules." That is just one aspect of something that is much deeper—a love relationship with God that includes listening to him, walking with him, and obeying him.

Yet the distractions are many, and we could backslide away from God. So, third, Moses says that the life of obedience is lived by "holding fast to him" (30:20b). Note that we are holding fast to the one we love. I think of the picture of a child clinging to her father while the wind is blowing hard, afraid to be separated from him. The mood is one of desperation. We love God, we want to obey him, but we know that the temptation to move away from God is severe. So we cling to God in desperation.

Fourth, both verses 16 and 20 give the rewards of obedience. ". . . then you shall live and multiply, and the LORD your God will bless you in the land that you are entering to take possession of it" (30:16c); ". . . that you may dwell in the land that the LORD swore to your fathers, to Abraham, to Isaac, and to Jacob, to give them" (30:20c). This is the standard promise of Deuteronomy.

The Path of Backsliding (30:17, 18)

Verse 17 says, "But if your heart turns away, and you will not hear, but are drawn away to worship other gods and serve them." This accurately expresses the way a person moves away from God. First, the "heart turns away." Other things become more important. It could be work, pleasure, or just self. God is no longer first in his life. One of the saddest things we who are in youth work observe is how some people who were very enthusiastic for God and his work in their youth slowly lose that commitment. They get engrossed in the task of proving themselves in a hostile work environment and of bringing economic stability to the family they have just started. These become more and more important and the things of God get neglected. Gradually there is less time for fellowship, for prayer, for studying the Bible alone and in a group setting. Some stay on the sidelines, missing the potential they had to make an eternal difference. Others move away from God altogether.

Second, Moses says, ". . . you will not hear" (30:17b; NLT: "you refuse to listen"). One of the primary ways to maintain faithfulness to God in Deuteronomy is through hearing the Word. We must hear daily from God through the Word. The world bombards us with a different message in pervasive and subtle ways. If we do not keep hearing from God daily, it is easy to begin to think in ways that do not please God, especially as God's thoughts are so different from ours (Isaiah 55:8, 9).

The next step is outright idolatry, as the persons who are not in tune with God "are drawn away to worship other gods and serve them" (Deuteronomy 30:17c). Then we hear of the consequence of disobedience: "I declare to you today, that you shall surely perish. You shall not live long in the land that you are going over the Jordan to enter and possess" (30:18).

The Herald's Task (30:19)

Verse 19a is a solemn declaration by Moses that he has fulfilled his task to warn and exhort the people about the choice before them: "I call heaven and earth to witness against you today, that I have set before you life and death, blessing and curse." We will mourn if they reject the message and rejoice if they accept it. But the choice is up to them. We must do our work faithfully and let them know that a serious choice confronts them. Ezekiel said, "And whether they hear or refuse to hear (for they are a rebellious house) they will know that a prophet has been among them" (Ezekiel 2:5).

However, the herald's task is not simply to present the two ways and leave it at that. There is a trend to do that today. Some are embarrassed by attempts to persuade people to accept the gospel. Moses would have none of that passionless stating of facts. Moses goes on to call the people to make a decision in response to his message: "Therefore choose life, that you and your offspring may live" (30:19b). That was the way the gospel was proclaimed in Acts, too, where the word "persuade" appears seven times to describe Paul's evangelism.[8] The word "persuade" implies that the person leaves his or her past life and beliefs in order to embrace the way of Christ.

The sense of the urgency of the message we have pervades this passage. This is serious business. And so it is today. Paul said, "For necessity is laid upon me. Woe to me if I do not preach the gospel!" (1 Corinthians 9:16).

58

How to Handle
Leadership Succession

DEUTERONOMY 31:1-29

ALMOST EVERYTHING IN CHAPTER 31 has already been said earlier in Deuteronomy. What makes these words special is the context in which they appear. Here Moses hands over the leadership of the people of Israel to Joshua, after leading them for forty years. This passage is of special significance to me as I get ready to hand over the leadership of Youth for Christ in Sri Lanka after thirty-five years. The emphases in this handing over and commissioning are different from what we often see at such times. So there is a lot that all of us can learn from this.

Moses Goes but God and the Mission Stay (31:1–6)

The chapter begins with similar words to those at the start of the book: "So Moses continued to speak these words to all Israel" (31:1). Actually chapters 1—3 and 31—34 form what has been called the "outer frame" of Deuteronomy. Chapters 1—3 constitute an introduction and 31—34 a conclusion. Moses first says, "I am 120 years old today. I am no longer able to go out and come in" (31:2a). The expression "go out and come in" "is often used in the OT to denote a man's ability to come and go in the affairs of life."[1] Moses cannot lead anymore. Besides, as he often sadly reminds the people (3:26, 27; 4:21, 22; 32:48–52), God has told him, "You shall not go over this Jordan" (31:2b).

While Moses may be leaving, God will not be leaving, and the mission of the group will not change. So Moses says, "The LORD your God himself will go over before you. He will destroy these nations before you" (31:3a). This passage is saturated with God and what he did and will do and with the task ahead, which is to enter the promised land.

- God is the one who has decreed that Moses will not go over the Jordan (31:2).
- God has given instructions (31:3, 5).
- He will destroy the nations (31:3, 4) as he did before (31:4).
- He will give the nations over to the people for them to destroy (31:5).
- He will go over with the people (31:6, 8). He will not leave or forsake them (31:6, 8). He himself goes before the people (31:3, 8).
- He has sworn to give the people the land (31:7).

Indeed, we are talking about leadership change. That, however, is never the main thing. Always in an organization, group, or church, God is the main factor with which we must reckon. Then there is the mission of the group, and here the mission is to possess the land. How sad that often when a leader leaves a group or a church many others also leave. The main features of the group do not change—God and the mission of the group. The style may change; the intimacy individuals have with the leader may change. But the most important things have not changed. So there is no need to leave.

Biblical religion is a covenant faith. In everything we are bound to a covenant—primarily with God. Covenant relationships are a key feature of the culture of a Biblically patterned organization. Christians commit themselves to groups and to each other—not because of the leader but because of God and the mission. Likes and dislikes are not major factors influencing commitment. Sadly, today people join groups and churches with the attitude of consumers. If they like a group, its program, and its leaders, they stay with the group. The moment they think they are more "comfortable" in another group, they leave and join that group. When did comfort become a factor determining the obedience of Christians? Only when they moved away from a Biblical approach to life!

Joshua Must Not Fear (31:7, 8)

Moses' charge to Joshua given "in the sight of all Israel" includes the call, "Be strong and courageous. . . . Do not fear or be dismayed" (31:7, 8). Moses has just told this to the people in general (31:6). Now immediately after that he repeats it to Joshua. The theme of not fearing appears right at the start of the book also, in connection with what lies ahead for the people in conquering the promised land. Moses tells the people, "See, the LORD your God has set the land before you. Go up, take possession, as the LORD, the God of your fathers, has told you. Do not fear or be dismayed" (1:21). This message is repeated several times in the book (3:2, 22; 20:3). If the people are not to be afraid, the leaders must lead in not being afraid. So three times in the book of Joshua, Joshua is told not to fear (Joshua 1:9; 8:1; 10:8).

Joshua is told, "You shall go with this people into the land that the LORD has sworn to their fathers to give them, and you shall put them in possession of it" (31:7b). The leader must lead in fighting the battle. In verse 3 Moses tells the people, ". . . and Joshua will go over at your head, as the LORD has spoken." This is in keeping with the practice in ancient times of the king literally leading the army from the front. A key element of leadership is the ability to inspire others to do great things. The people might get afraid, but when they see the leader take a bold stand, they will follow. If you look at a list of some of the greatest leaders, you will find that they have different types of personalities. Their personalities influence their leadership styles, and the styles are often very different. But all good leaders will have in common the ability to inspire people to greatness. And one of the best ways to do that is by leading from the front.

Leaders can use their authority to avoid getting involved in the battle. It is easy for leaders to become lazy and not do the things they should do, especially because most leaders are not minutely supervised. This is very dangerous. It takes away the motivation of the others. I often call pastors to care for their families without neglecting them because of the ministry. Sometimes laypeople in the audience say that their pastor is at home when he should be working, that his supposed commitment to the family has resulted in his not being committed to his job. This is another kind of laziness—we are called to the tiring task of both caring for our families and for our vocational responsibilities. Such laziness can also open the door to other sins. Not doing what they should be doing, they may end up doing what they should not be doing. This is what happened to David. "In the spring of the year, the time when kings go out to battle" (2 Samuel 11:1), he stayed home and fell into sin with Bathsheba.

What if leaders are afraid of the huge task before them? They must battle that out with God before going to the people. And they do that by reckoning that God is with them in this enterprise. Actually as verse 8a puts it, "It is the LORD who goes *before*" them. Leaders lead from the front. That is how it looks to the people. But actually the one in front is God, and the leaders also are following him. So Moses assures Joshua, "He will be with you; he will not leave you or forsake you" (31:8b). This statement has already appeared in verse 6. It will also appear in the other record of Joshua's commissioning (Joshua 1:5) and will appear again when David gives a charge to the young Solomon (1 Chronicles 28:20).

When we think of courageous leadership, we often think of leaders with a strong personality—what people today call a Type A personality. Gentle and mild leaders could also be courageous. But first they have to be convinced that a given endeavor is from God. That may take some time because of their natural timidity. But once they know that God is in it, not only will they persevere, they will also have the patience to take the time to convince the others that this project is from God. Then the whole group will strive with one heart and mind to achieve the goal. The way different personalities achieve a given goal may differ, but if they believe in God they will finally reach the goal. So leaders must agonize with God until they have the conviction that God is with them. Then their faith in God will open the door to their being endued with God's courage.

You may be a timid person. But God is great. Spend time with him before you launch into any project. The time spent with God will give you security and peace and will help you sense his presence with you in the midst of the battle. Trusting in him and knowing that he will see you through can help you persevere until the battle is won.

Moses' Legacy Was the Word (31:9–13)

Entrust the Word to Leaders (31:9)

People sometimes want to leave behind a legacy when they retire, and they do various things to ensure that their legacy is remembered by succeeding generations. What a waste of precious time, energy, and resources! The legacy we must leave behind is a people who live to honor God. Building monuments to our memory and having plaques with our name on them will not do that! Teaching the people to be obedient to God *will* do that. So as Moses prepares to leave, he writes down the Law and gives it to the leaders: "Then Moses wrote this law and gave it to the priests, the sons of Levi, who carried the ark of the covenant of the LORD, and to all the elders of Israel" (31:9).

Note how he entrusts the Law to the leaders: "to the priests . . . who carried the ark . . . and to all the elders of Israel." The leaders are the ones who will ensure that the ethos of a movement will continue to be guarded. So always, and especially during the last days before they leave, leaders must spend time with the other leaders, hammering home the great features that characterize the movement. This is what Jesus did with what we call the Great Commission. Between the Last Supper and the ascension there are six different statements of this commission.[2] There is a seventh in Acts described by Peter without mentioning when Jesus said it (Acts 10:42). There is no need to be wasting time and energy on the pomp and pageantry of farewells and tributes. What is important is the mission of the movement. Our passion should be to ensure that is kept uppermost in the thinking of the people after the leader leaves. So public relations events are not what are most important. The focus should be on spending time with the leaders, drumming into their hearts and minds the values that characterize the group.

The task of the second-level leaders is to share these truths with the rest of the people. This is the great principle of multiplication that Paul described in 2 Timothy 2:2: ". . . what you have heard from me in the presence of many witnesses entrust to faithful men who will be able to teach others also." According to this verse, truth is transmitted down four generations. (1) Paul taught (2) Timothy, and Timothy must entrust what he had learned to (3) faithful men; they in turn will teach (4) others. Always, from start to finish, a good leader's focus is on the other leaders. This was clearly the focus of the ministry of both Jesus and Paul. Public ministry was important to them, and they did it faithfully; but they spent most of their time discipling their leaders.

Moses learned the principle of delegation, of working through equipping leaders, rather late in his life, as we saw in our study of Deuteronomy 1:9–15. It was a lesson he learned from his father-in-law Jethro (Exodus 18). It is a lesson that is better learned late than never!

Ensure That Leaders Pass It on to the People (31:10–13)

Next, Moses takes steps to ensure that the leaders teach the people the Law. According to Deuteronomy, the basic teaching of the Law takes place in the home, as we saw in our discussion of 6:6–9. But occasional public events must be held where the focus is on explaining the Word. So "Moses commanded [the priests and elders], 'At the end of every seven years, at the set time in the year of release, at the Feast of Booths, when all Israel comes to appear before the LORD your God at the place that he will choose, you shall read this law before all Israel in their hearing'" (31:10, 11). This is a major gathering of the whole nation, held during the sabbatical year about which we read in Deuteronomy 15. Today we would call it a convocation or convention.

Most movements—religious and non-religious—usually have some sort of convocation or convention for their whole membership once in one or more years. We can choose to do various things at these gatherings. But the Biblical model is to saturate these gatherings with aids to help communicate the truths of the faith to the whole body and then communicate it from generation to generation. That this is the aim of this sabbatical gathering is shown in verses 12, 13. Moses says, "Assemble the people, men, women, and little ones, and the sojourner within your towns, that they may hear and learn to fear the LORD your God, and be careful to do all the words of this law, and that their children, who have not known it, may hear and learn to fear the LORD your God, as long as you live in the land that you are going over the Jordan to possess."

I believe focusing on distinctives is the key feature to put at the top of the priorities of all regular convocations of any Christian group. The leaders must pray and think and discuss among each other what emphases should be highlighted at such a meeting. Careful preparation should be done to ensure that those emphases take center stage and are communicated in a way that is appropriate and effective at a large gathering. The leaders of the movement who speak at these gatherings should earnestly seek God for a message to give to the people—a message that will become a key word from God to the people. Preparations should be made with a sense of expectancy and prayerful yearning for God to do a mighty work among the people. History has shown how God has used such gatherings to start great movements among his people. A good example is the gathering of the people of Israel that lasted the whole morning when the Law was read by Ezra and explained to the people by some leaders (Nehemiah 8). There was great weeping among the people when they heard the Law (v. 9).

A revival that took place in Korea in the early twentieth century is a vivid example of how this sequence takes place of God speaking to leaders from his Word and that message going to the people at a holy convocation. There were three waves of revival in Korea in 1903–1904, 1905–1906, and 1906–1907. They followed the sequence of leaders being revived by reading the Word followed by the people being revived, especially at a national convocation. The third and largest wave began with the missionaries meeting for a week of prayer and Bible study in August 1906. They used 1 John as their text for study and meditation and experienced refreshment and a fresh resolve to take the message to the people nationwide. The revived leaders went to their people and proclaimed what they had learned to them, and revival followed with repentance and confession. At the beginning of the year was the annual New Year Bible study convocation to which about 1,500 Christians came from all parts of the country. There God powerfully broke through with revival. The revived leaders went to their towns, and revival occurred there, too. The ultimate result of the revival was a spurt of growth in the young Korean church.[3]

Moses' Great Legacy

So the great legacy Moses left behind was the Law. He told the people how to live in obedience to God. While the immediate generations that followed did not follow through with obedience, Moses' legacy has become the foundational first building block of what we today call the Word of God—a great legacy indeed!

May all leaders today have as their primary goal the task of keeping the movement they lead on track with God's plan and purpose. May they strive to have that as the legacy they leave behind. Many Christians today do not know the name D. E. Hoste. Hoste succeeded Hudson Taylor as the general director of China Inland Mission (now known as OMF) and led the movement from 1900 to 1935. A recent booklet, *Live to Be Forgotten: D E Hoste* by Patrick Fung,[4] the present general director of this movement, shows that Hoste did not seem to want to be remembered. Colleagues remembered D. E. Hoste as one who "lived to be forgotten in order that Christ may be remembered."[5] Was this a correct path to take? While many movements have moved away from the values under which they were founded, the movement that Hudson Taylor founded and that D. E. Hoste led for thirty-five years after Taylor continues to do an amazing ministry in Asia. A feature of their service is that it is done without much publicity.

This lack of emphasis on Moses' achievement is all the more significant when we remember that Deuteronomy stresses the importance of remembering the past. The people needed to remember how they were punished for their sins and how God led them and gave them victory. The man who is so committed to history is not concerned about people remembering the one who was, humanly speaking, probably Israel's greatest history-maker. In his eyes God alone deserved the designation history-maker. As another history-maker said, "When I am gone, speak not of William Carey, but of William Carey's Savior."

God Commissions Joshua (31:14, 15, 23)

Joshua's commissioning takes place in three stages. First, Moses summons and exhorts him to be courageous and assures him of success in taking the people to the land because God is with him (31:7, 8). Second, God asks Moses to summon Joshua to the presence of God: "And the LORD said to Moses, 'Behold, the days approach when you must die. Call Joshua and present yourselves in the tent of meeting, that I may commission him'" (31:14a). In response to this, "Moses and Joshua went and presented themselves in the tent of meeting," which was the place that symbolized the presence of God (31:14b). The result was that God showed up in the miraculously glorious way he was accustomed to using to assure the people of his presence: "And the LORD appeared in the tent in a pillar of cloud. And the pillar of cloud stood over the entrance of the tent" (31:15). The third stage is when God himself commissions Joshua and says something close to what Moses had already said: "And the LORD commissioned Joshua the son of Nun and said, 'Be strong and courageous, for you shall bring the people of Israel into the land that I swore to give them. I will be with you'" (31:23).

The feature of the second and third stages is that the commissioning is presented entirely as an act of God. In both instances there is specific mention of the fact that God is the one who commissions Joshua. It seems that by calling Moses and Joshua to the tent of meeting, God wants to emphasize the fact that this is his appointment rather than a human appointment. The basic assumption when it comes to appointing people to God's service is that the call is entirely God's work. The clear sense of God's calling as opposed to humans aspiring to positions in God's service is also seen in the call of Moses (Exodus 3, 4), Gideon (Judges 6:11–16), Samuel (1 Samuel 3:4–21), David (1 Samuel 16:1–13), Solomon (1 Chronicles 28:6–10), Jehu (2 Kings 9:6, 7), Amos (Amos 7:14, 15), Jeremiah (Jeremiah 1:4–19), Ezekiel (Ezekiel 2:1–10), the twelve apostles, Matthias (Acts 1:23–26), and Paul (Acts 9:1–16).

This impressive list should cause us to see how we, too, must ensure that those we put into leadership positions have been called and commissioned by God. One way the church has tried to do this is by asking other Christians to look for evidence of a call in the person they suggest. Once all those who are qualified for the job are identified, the names are voted on. Nowhere does the Bible say that selection through a vote is wrong per se. But we must ensure that Biblical qualifications for leadership are evident in all the persons presented.

Clearly Joshua had often given evidence of being faithful to God even when others were not, as in the case of the twelve spies (Numbers 14). He was described as "a man in whom is the Spirit" (Numbers 27:18) and as being "full of the spirit of wisdom" (Deuteronomy 34:9). He had an excellent track record as the head of the army and as Moses' faithful assistant. Whatever the method used to select leaders, priority must always be given to ensuring that the person has the spiritual qualifications and required abilities for the job. Paul gave some important lists about this in his Pastoral Epistles (1 Timothy 3:1–7, 8–13; Titus 1:5–9).

Moses Predicts Apostasy (31:16–29)

Some believe that Moses was the greatest national leader in human history. That could well be true. Given his brilliant record of accomplishment in leading such a rebellious people, one would have expected some praise of his leadership when he handed over leadership to his successor. The epistles of Paul and the Song of Solomon leave us with no doubt that praising faithful and good people is a legitimate aspect of Biblical religion. Leaders generally permit some time for praise at their farewell. Paul even says that we should "give recognition" to good leaders (1 Corinthians 16:18). But there was more urgent business to be done on this occasion. What we find is a serious warning that soon the people of Israel will be unfaithful to God.

Whoredom and Punishment (31:16–18)

God introduces to Moses the theme of prostitution, which the prophets will later use often to describe Israel's unfaithfulness (Jeremiah 3:1; Ezekiel 6:9; 20:30; Hosea 2:5–7; 4:15). In Deuteronomy 31:16 God says, "Behold, you are about to lie down with your fathers. Then this people will rise and whore after the foreign gods among them in the land that they are entering, and they will forsake me and break my covenant that I have made with them." Prostitution is an apt way to describe breaking the binding covenant with God of which the covenant of marriage is one of the best illustrations.

God says he will respond to this apostasy by punishing the people: "Then my anger will be kindled against them in that day, and I will forsake them and hide my face from them, and they will be devoured. And many evils and troubles will come upon them, so that they will say in that day, 'Have not these evils come upon us because our God is not among us?' And I will surely hide my face in that day because of all the evil that they have done, because they have turned to other gods" (31:17, 18). What we see here is the opposite of the promise of God's presence and help for conquest that is given several times in this very chapter both before and after these verses (31:3–6, 8, 23). The God who said, "I will not leave you or forsake you," now says, "I will forsake them and hide my face from them. . . . I will surely hide my face in that day."

Often the Bible states a promise and also adds that it won't be fulfilled if the people disobey. The Bible is faithful in giving the other side of the good news. Are we? Often we avoid talking about this, or if we do, we do it so inappropriately (e.g., harshly) that people reject what we say. Some say this is from the Old Testament and therefore does not apply to us today, even though the New Testament also presents these teachings. Thus we develop an understanding of God that does not include his wrath. When we fail to teach the kind of material found in these verses, we will develop a generation that is malnourished and is not equipped for the challenges to their faith that they will surely face.

The punishment convinces them that God has left them. Verse 17b says, "And many evils and troubles will come upon them, so that they will say in that day, 'Have not these evils come upon us because our God is not among us?'" Only now do they realize that God has left them. He had left them much earlier because of their disobedience. But until the punishment comes they assume that God is with them as he was before. So they call him "our God," not realizing that he was no longer their God. This is what happened to Samson. After his hair had been cut in his sleep and the Philistines had come to him, "he awoke from his sleep and said, 'I will go out as at other times and shake myself free.'" The narrator next says something sobering: "But he did not know that the LORD had left him" (Judges 16:20).

This is a frightening thought. Sometimes when caught up in a sin we blind ourselves to the seriousness of the sin and assume that God is with us. We may see some measure of success in what we do, and that further blinds us. Those who have ability and training can do God's work for some time without others realizing that they are living in rebellion against God. But one day their life will catch up with their ministry. Then when they crash and face the full force of the consequences of their sin, they realize that God had left them quite some time before. In the financial world we had an interesting parallel to this in the experience of Bernie Madoff, who defrauded investors of millions of dollars. He recently said that he wished he had been exposed several years before, so that he would not have multiplied his crimes over so many years.

There is a warning for us here. If there is an element of unfaithfulness in our lives, we must move away from it completely without negotiating to see how far we can go into the dangerous field without giving up our faith. Otherwise we may soon realize that God has left us completely.

A Song as a Witness against the People (31:19–22)

God's next assignment to Moses shows the message being given in a way that will penetrate resistant and disobedient people. Moses is to write a song and teach it to the people to ensure that the message resides in the people. God tells him, "Now therefore write this song and teach it to the people of Israel. Put it in their mouths . . . " (31:19a, b). This suggests that it will become part of the folklore of the people. Verse 21c says, ". . . for it will live unforgotten in the mouths of their offspring." The song is to become a vital asset after the people disobey God. God says the people will become unfaithful after they experience prosperity: "For when I have brought them into the land flowing with milk and honey, which I swore to give to their fathers, and they have eaten and are full and grown fat, they will turn to other gods and serve them, and despise me and break my covenant" (31:20; see the discussion on 6:10–25).

After the people turn away from God, they are going to face the consequences of disobedience: "And when many evils and troubles have come upon them . . . " (31:21a). However, though the people have turned away from God, they will still be singing the song Moses taught them because it has become part of the folklore of the people. Verse 21 goes on, ". . . this song shall confront them as a witness (for it will live unforgotten in the mouths of their offspring)." At that time, though they have forgotten God, the song will speak to them and serve as a witness against them. This function of the song is presented twice in this paragraph. Verse 19c says, ". . . that this song may be a witness for me against the people of Israel." Verse 21b says, ". . . this song shall confront them as a witness." They will discover that the song warned about the dangers of apostasy. They have been singing it as a cultural practice without letting its words sink into them. Now in their distress it does sink in.

Here we see the value of getting Christian thoughts into the cultural mainstream. David Payne says that this song of Moses was intended to be like a pop song. I think of the soccer games in Britain where spectators sing old hymns without meaning a word of what they sing. They became part of the soccer culture at a time when the people accepted the truths they conveyed. Then it became part of the folklore. Sometimes we get upset at the way carols are relayed over the media at Christmastime by ungodly people, sometimes in ungodly attire! We can hope that because the words go into the mind of the people, the songs will one day do their work of challenging the people with their message. I have heard stories of people who were living in despair as a result of disobedience whose coming back to God was triggered by hearing a Christian song they knew as a child or when they were earlier walking close to God.

Albert Orsborn (1886–1967) was the most famous hymn-writer of the Salvation Army and was for a time its general. When he was a young officer in London, revival spread in the area where he had been leading. Following this revival an officer came and told him that he heard that the leaders were planning to divide his district. He urged Orsborn not to let it happen. He said that God was blessing his district so much and to divide the district would hinder the work of God. He told him, "I think you ought to fight it." Orsborn replied, "Oh, no. I want to do the will of God and respect my superiors. I will not do that."

Nevertheless, Orsborn began to argue with the leadership about the division of his district. Later he said that the real reason for his arguing was because he had less prestige and power. "Unwittingly I had begun to fight not for the kingdom but for my position in the kingdom, and the Holy Spirit was grieved." He added, "When the Spirit grieves, the Spirit leaves." He said he went through the motions of ministry, but there was a distance between him and God. Deadness had entered his life, and he felt empty inside.

Then Orsborn was in a serious car accident, and he took a long time to recover. God began to work on him. One day he heard some singing in the room next to his in the hospital. He says, "I heard them sing of the glories of God. My heart began to yearn once again for that kind of intimacy with God. I wept my heart out in repentance. God forgave me. And the Spirit came and filled my heart afresh." Thank God, Orsborn ended his life well.[6]

Isaiah 55:8 says, "For my thoughts are not your thoughts, neither are your ways my ways, declares the LORD." The people will reject God's message. However, Isaiah goes on to say about God's Word, ". . . so shall my word be that goes out from my mouth; it shall not return to me empty, but it shall accomplish that which I purpose, and shall succeed in the thing for which I sent it" (Isaiah 55:11). How does it succeed if the people reject it? Second Corinthians 2:15, 16 helps us here. Paul says, "For we are the aroma of Christ to God among those who are being saved and among those who are perishing, to one a fragrance from death to death, to the other a fragrance from life to life." The Word serves to bring salvation to some people and judgment to others. Moses' song will do something like that. It will serve as a witness against the people, showing them that they should have responded positively to the message of God.

There is encouragement here for our call to proclaim the difficult and unpleasant subjects in the Bible. Many who reject the message will realize one day that they should have listened. It will also help them understand the judgment they are facing. Hopefully this will help them return to God. They rejected the message and suffered. But in their suffering they realized the truth of the Word and turned to God.

Verse 21 ends with the sad statement, "For I know what they are inclined to do even today, before I have brought them into the land that I swore to give." Moses knew that their present attitudes were a foreboding of future unfaithfulness.

Moses, of course, as always, promptly does what God asks him to do: "So Moses wrote this song the same day and taught it to the people of Israel" (31:22).

Provision for a Repository (31:24–26)

In typical ancient Near-Eastern, covenant-making style, provision is made for a repository for the Law. First, Moses writes it down: "When Moses had finished writing the words of this law in a book to the very end" (31:24).

We are not told what "this law" is that is written in a book. Perhaps it was a section of the Law. Next "Moses commanded the Levites who carried the ark of the covenant of the LORD, 'Take this Book of the Law and put it by the side of the ark of the covenant of the LORD your God, that it may be there for a witness against you'" (31:25, 26). The Ten Commandments had been placed within the ark (Exodus 25:16). This book is to be placed by the side of the ark.

The idea is that by keeping it in this very important and prominent place the people will be reminded of the importance of obedience to the Law. This is another of the many places in the Pentateuch where the placing of objects in prominent places was intended to remind people of the Law and serve as a motivation to obedience. The most famous statement about such a practice is Deuteronomy 6:8, 9: "You shall bind them [God's commands] as a sign on your hand, and they shall be as frontlets between your eyes. You shall write them on the doorposts of your house and on your gates." Sadly, the repository does not serve as a motivation to obedience as it should. Instead, Moses says it is "there for a witness against you."

This whole chapter shows that Moses was to concentrate on the challenge of continuing obedience to God by the people after he is gone. The particular way he is to do this is to leave behind a written record of God's message to the people. He had to ensure that the form in which it is presented (a song), where it is stored (by the side of the ark), and the method used to communicate it to the people (by teaching it to the leaders) would give the message a long-term impact on succeeding generations. Moses' legacy was the Word of God. Departing leaders should concentrate on ensuring that the ethos of the movement that ignited their life is carried on through succeeding generations. One of the best ways to do this is to leave behind a leadership that is also passionate about this ethos and to leave some concrete verbal expressions of this ethos.

Books and songs proclaiming and explaining the ethos of groups have been used effectively in the past to ensure continued faithfulness. John Wesley knew the need to keep succeeding generations aware of the ethos. So he entered into an ambitious publishing enterprise and published his sermons, journals, and other works and hundreds of Charles Wesley's hymns. Over 200 years later, these writings and hymns continue to have a huge impact on me and on many others. They were among the most effective means God used to help me withstand the liberal theology that swept through my denomination in my younger days. Thankfully, there has been a reversal in the denomination, so that those holding to an evangelical viewpoint are no longer a minority.

Another Witness against Israel (31:27–29)

Next, using slightly different language, Moses repeats the idea that their present attitudes were a foreboding of future unfaithfulness: "For I know how rebellious and stubborn you are. Behold, even today while I am yet alive with you, you have been rebellious against the LORD. How much more after my death!" (31:27). Then Moses calls for an assembly: "Assemble to me all the elders of your tribes and your officers, that I may speak these words in their ears and call heaven and earth to witness against them" (31:28). It is like a court case where God is the plaintiff and Israel is the defendant.[7] Heaven and earth are called to witness against the people.

This is the fourth time witness against Israel is mentioned in this chapter. Twice it is the song of Moses that witnesses against them (31:19, 21), and once it is the book of the Law, which may be the same as the song (31:26). The fourth time is when Heaven and earth are called to witness (31:28). This is an instance of the concern for the reasonableness of justice that characterizes much of the Biblical teaching about judgment. This concern is well represented in the words of Abraham as he intercedes for Sodom: "Shall not the Judge of all the earth do what is just?" (Genesis 18:25). Wilbur M. Smith, a well-known Bible teacher of an earlier generation, has said, "Judgment is hardly ever spoken of in the Word of God unless at the same time it is characterized as *righteous* judgment."[8]

Deuteronomy 31:29a has the sixth prediction of apostasy in this passage: "For I know that after my death you will surely act corruptly and turn aside from the way that I have commanded you" (the others are 31:16, 18, 20, 21b, 27). This is followed by the fourth prediction in the passage of the dire consequences of their apostasy in verse 29b: "And in the days to come evil will befall you, because you will do what is evil in the sight of the LORD, provoking him to anger through the work of your hands" (also see 31:17, 18, 21). Judgment was much more culturally acceptable in the time of Moses than it is today, but Moses needed to use these several repetitions to persuade people about its certainty. How much more important is it for us to work hard at finding the best way to communicate this message to our people!

Why Such an Emphasis on Future Apostasy?

Is it appropriate to have such a strong emphasis on future apostasy in an event of a revered, veteran leader handing over leadership to another? David Payne points out, "Part of the reasoning is to convince the Jews of a later period that their nation's history of disobedience (and disaster because of it) had been no surprise to God." Payne says, "Paul was equally convinced that the widespread rejection of Christianity, in this era, fitted into God's design of history (Romans 9—11)."

The knowledge that God anticipated this apostasy would be an encouragement for the minority who choose to be faithful to God and persevere along the path of obedience when the majority is unfaithful. This noble minority would often be tempted to give up, claiming that the situation is hopeless. The knowledge that God anticipated this apostasy and ordained that the guilty will be severely punished would show them that obedience is the wisest and safest approach to adopt, that the now powerful apostate majority are following a foolish and destructive path.

Let me apply this to two issues facing Christians today. Christians living in nations where spiritual unfaithfulness is rife should remind themselves that the Bible teaches that corrupt people will be severely punished. That should give them courage to persevere along the path of honesty. Christian leaders who talk against extramarital sex and insist on disciplining Christians guilty of it would be considered to be totally out of touch with reality. But they know that their refusal to warn and discipline such people would reduce those individuals' chances of repenting and avoiding a much more severe punishment from God.

Conclusion

This passage gives us the great passion that drives leaders of the people of God. They want to see the people they lead following God's ways. That will be their primary goal at the start and at the end of their ministry. Even their farewell would be dominated by that desire. The place to get to know about how to follow God obediently is the Word of God. Therefore, during their period of leadership and during their farewell, the Word will have a prominent place.

A movement where everything done springs from the Word has a much greater chance of being faithful to its original call over a long period than one that is primarily program-oriented. In a program-oriented movement, the vision often vanishes with the retirement of the driver of the movement. People drop off or lose interest when the leader leaves. The aim of a good Christian leader should be to get people into the habit of receiving instruction and deriving strategy from the Word. That will dominate his or her program during his or her tenure as leader and at the end of it.

59

Moses' Song I:
Scandalous Disobedience

DEUTERONOMY 31:30—32:18

IN OUR DISCUSSION OF chapter 31:19–22 we introduced Moses' farewell song as a "pop song" that would become a part of the culture of the people and act as a witness against them when they move away from God. They would sing the words without meaning them. The words present a strong statement of the folly of disobedience, but disobedient people would be singing it because it had become part of the culture. When they suffer the consequences of their rebellion against God, the words of the song will strike home. Our current passage begins with the announcement, "Then Moses spoke the words of this song until they were finished, in the ears of all the assembly of Israel" (31:30).

There is general agreement among scholars that the form of this song is that of a lawsuit address (known as *rib*, the Hebrew word for "lawsuit"). Such lawsuits were common in international law in the ancient Near East when a controlling power or king (suzerain) had a controversy with a vassal state.

Moses' Wish for the Song (32:1, 2)

Moses expresses his wish for the song using two images: a courtroom and a shower of rain. He first says, "Give ear, O heavens, and I will speak, and let the earth hear the words of my mouth" (32:1). This is the figure of a courtroom where Heaven and earth are called to be witnesses to the words that Moses will present, and it fits in with the lawsuit address (*rib*) format. Unlike other places in Deuteronomy (4:26; 30:19; 31:28) where Heaven and earth are called to testify against Israel, here the function seems to be to listen. "As objective onlookers they would see that God had a case against his people."[1] I have known of situations where non-Christians advise Christians to obey God because they know this is the best thing for the Christian to do! This is such a case. Even someone who does not follow God would, through this song, realize how foolish and dangerous it is for God's people to disobey him.

Next, Moses expresses his wish for the song using the image of a shower of rain. Verse 2 says, "May my teaching drop as the rain, my speech distill as the dew, like gentle rain upon the tender grass, and like showers upon the herb." The song is described as "teaching," reminding us that songs are means of teaching the truths of God. Today we sometimes think of songwriters as entertainers, but a Christian songwriter is also a teacher. A deep desire to help God's people be faithful to God is one of the visions driving a Christian songwriter. The effect of the song is likened here to the health brought to vegetation by a shower of rain. This is a particularly apt figure in the Middle East where in most places there is very little rain.

Verses 1, 2 present two aims of the song. First, Moses wants to show that the folly of disobedience is evident for all to see. Second, he wants the message of the song to go deep into the soil of the culture so as to provide health to the people. In the same way, we first argue for the validity of our message and then present it in such a way that it will penetrate into the innermost life of the hearers and bring them God's health. We pay attention to the content of our message and to the form in which it is communicated.

God's Utter Reliability (32:3, 4)

Knowing Who God Is (32:3)

Beginning with "For," suggesting a connection with what precedes, verse 3 states why the song will be a health-giving resource to the people: "For I will proclaim the name of the LORD; ascribe greatness to our God!" The most important feature of the song is that it expounds on God. To "proclaim the name" of God is to describe the nature of God, as God's name stood for who God is. When the nature of God is described, the result is to "ascribe [literally, "give, ascribe"] greatness" to him. When people realize who God is (through the proclamation of his name), they should stop to acknowledge his greatness. All our teaching should ultimately be aimed at giving people a sense of who God is.

In his classic book on the attributes of God, *The Knowledge of the Holy*, A. W. Tozer said, "What comes into our minds when we think about God is the most important thing about us." Tozer went on to say, "Man's spiritual history will positively demonstrate that no religion has ever been greater than its idea of God."[2] Today we have many, many books, videos, and talks giving human-centered practical teaching about life. They seem to be eminently practical and relevant to our needs. But our greatest need is to know who God is. The most effective practical teaching in the world is teaching that gives people a sense of who God is. That will influence their life in the most important and helpful way possible.

God Is Utterly Reliable (32:4)

The beloved words of verse 4 have made their way into a popular worship song: "The Rock, his work is perfect, for all his ways are justice. A God of faithfulness and without iniquity, just and upright is he." God is described as the "Rock" five times in this song (32:4, 15, 18, 30, 31). It points to God's "utter reliability and unshakeable trustworthiness,"[3] implying that those who go to him are safe and will be delivered from all attacks.

How important it is to drive home the message of God's absolute trustworthiness to Christians. When prayers are not answered in the way they hoped, some Christians resort to other sources of security. They go to an astrologer or a shrine or the underworld for a quick answer to their problem. And sometimes they get the desired result. But they are left to swim unaided in a hostile and uncertain sea. They lose the peace of God and keep going from place to place looking for help in times of crisis. When following Christian principles seems to be disadvantageous, some will abandon these principles and try other means to achieve their ends. They will lie to make a sale or take revenge on someone who has hurt them or slander or hurt another vying for the same promotion at work. What helps us stay clear of such paths of disobedience when they seem to be the natural way to go? It is the knowledge that the good God will not forsake us and will bring us ultimate victory.

The nature of God as Rock is explained in the rest of verse 4: ". . . his work is perfect, for all his ways are justice. A God of faithfulness and without iniquity, just and upright is he." Each of the qualities described here buttresses the idea that God is utterly reliable. First, "his work is perfect." The lexicon defines the Hebrew word used here as "blameless, without defect, perfect."[4] Our knowledge and abilities are limited, but God's are not. We may think that things are not going as we wish and might be tempted to compromise on our commitment to God's ways. But that is folly. God's ways are perfect. That is, they are the best in every way for us and for others. Then Moses says, ". . . all his ways are justice." That means that his will for us will protect our rights. For a time we may think that injustice rules and the righteous are at a severe disadvantage. But that is because of temporary factors. Ultimately we will see that despite all the injustice in the world, God will honor those who follow him by ensuring that they receive justice. Because we are made in the image of God, we also care for justice and get enraged when justice is not served, especially to us. When treated unjustly, we may be tempted to be bitter or to hit back in an unchristian way. At such a time we cling to the fact that God is just and is for us, and we wait for him to act for our vindication. This is why, as John Piper has pointed out, the doctrine of judgment helps take away bitterness in our lives.[5]

But how do we know that the just God will act on our behalf? He is "a God of faithfulness." He is totally reliable and will keep his promises. The people we have worked with in life may not have been faithful, but God is, and God is the most important factor in our lives. In the darkest night, when following God does not seem to be worthwhile, we cling to God's faithfulness and wait for his deliverance to come. Next we are told that God is "without iniquity, just and upright is he." This virtually repeats what has already been said, which is a common feature in Hebrew poetry. There is no doubt about it—God will act in the right way. The one thing we must ensure is that we are obedient to God.

One of the biggest challenges I have faced in my ministry is convincing some people that because God is who verse 4 describes him to be, they can trust God to look after them. Some refuse to believe this and remain trapped in self-pity and in blaming others for their unhappiness. They are almost afraid to come out of their prison and admit that God is going to turn everything they encounter into something good. That would take away the reason for their angry behavior and for their habit of blaming others. Others give up Christian morality because of their inability to believe what verse 4 says about God. They give in to revenge or to trusting in astrologers or to corrupt practices or to unkind and selfish behavior. They say they need to do these things in order to realistically survive in this world. Bitterness and disobedience are ultimately expressions of a refusal to believe that God will be just and perfect in his dealings with us.

How I yearn to find the best way to make people understand the truth of Psalm 34:8: "Oh, taste and see that the LORD is good! Blessed is the man who takes refuge in him!" After making that statement, David goes on to cite the blessing of taking refuge in God: "Oh, fear the LORD, you his saints, for those who fear him have no lack! The young lions suffer want and hunger; but those who seek the LORD lack no good thing" (34:9, 10). Apart from hammering home Scriptural teaching on God's faithfulness, one thing we can do for such people is to be faithful to them. Having experienced human faithfulness they may come to believe that faithfulness is a possibility in this world and become open to accepting divine faithfulness.

A Scandalous Response to God's Reliability (32:5–14)

The People Are Corrupt (32:5)

After describing God's absolute reliability, Moses says that the so-called people of God were the exact opposite of the God they professed to follow: "They have dealt corruptly with him; they are no longer his children because they are blemished; they are a crooked and twisted generation" (32:5). They are a people who have no regard for principles and will break any rule to get what they want. Such people are the most powerful people in many societies. They may be the ruling officials or they may belong to the underworld. But they are powerful, and they usually get their way.

The righteous must not be resentful of the power of these unprincipled people because, as Moses says, "they are no longer [God's] children." They have many earthly privileges, but they do not have the greatest of all privileges: the privilege of being a child of the Ruler of the universe. This privilege only the righteous enjoy. Verses 15–18 describe how their going astray took place after they experienced prosperity. But before that, Moses presents the scandalous fact that they rebelled after God cared for them in an amazing way.

The Folly of Rebelling against God (32:6–14)

The description of God in verse 4 appealed to God's absolute reliability, and verse 5 said the people responded to this reliability with corruption. Now we come to a description of God as Father. It begins with a statement of the utter folly of the people in rejecting their Father: "Do you thus repay the LORD, you foolish and senseless people? Is not he your father, who created you, who made you and established you?" Rejecting the one who has unfailingly cared for them in order to follow a path about which they know very little is sheer folly. As their "father," he shows genuine love for them; and as the one who "created" them, who "made" them, and who "established" them, he knows them better than they know themselves, and he knows what is best for them. No wonder they are called "foolish and senseless."

Is it appropriate to use this kind of language today? The prophets spoke in similar terms to the so-called people of God. I believe we, too, can do so when addressing those who call themselves Christians. With those who have no connection with God's people and his revelation, we would need to argue for the truth in a different way, just as Paul did in Athens when speaking about idolatry. There he used philosophical arguments (Acts 17:16–34). When speaking to the Jews about their idolatry, however, the prophets thundered angrily against them. The Old Testament says several times that fearing God is the beginning of wisdom. Proverbs 9:10 says, "The fear of the LORD is the beginning of wisdom, and the knowledge of the Holy One is insight" (see Job 28:28; Psalm 111:10; Proverbs 1:7; 9:10; 15:33). The Bible also says, "The fool says in his heart, 'There is no God'" (Psalm 14:1; 53:1). This is not dogmatic atheism—the belief that God does not exist; it is practical atheism—acting as if God does not exist. We must show people the folly of disobedience and the wisdom of obedience. Jesus said that the rich farmer who had amassed a large fortune and retired was a fool because he was "not rich toward God" (Luke 12:20, 21).

It is interesting that the focus here is not on the ingratitude of the people after God had done so much for them. Rather, it is on the folly of moving away from one who cares so much for them and has proved that in their history. As John Piper points out in his book *Future Grace*, the so called "debtor's ethic" is not a dominant theme in the Bible.[6] In the debtor's ethic people are motivated to obedience by pointing to the obligation of responding in gratitude to the God who helped them. Rather, the appeal in the Bible is to the wisdom of responding to the God who has proved his love for us. As Romans 8:32 puts it, "He who did not spare his own Son but gave him up for us all, how will he not also with him graciously give us all things?" He can be trusted to supply us with everything we need. We must show people how very foolish it is to reject the God who has faithfully acted on their behalf.

Only a fool would reject God after knowing about him. A person who went on a long journey on a desert road, knowing that the road does not have a gas station, would be a fool if he did not fill up his gas tank before launching on the journey. In the same way those who launch on the journey of life after rejecting the one who can take them to the desired destination are foolish. In verses 28, 29 Moses again points to the folly of rejecting God's way. This is significant because being regarded as fools is one of the most humiliating things righteous people living in an unrighteous world experience. This may trigger within them a strong temptation to move away from God's path. As we showed above, the Bible counters this by showing the folly of rejecting God and the wisdom of following him.

The Bible gives assurance to those who obey God and look like fools for doing so by affirming that they are not fools and that those who have gained earthly success by unrighteous means are stupid rather than successful. Several Christian leaders, including John Wimber and Brother Andrew, have adopted for themselves the slogan, "I am a fool for Christ; whose fool are you?"

In the verses that follow, Moses appeals to the history of God's concern for the people. He tells them, "Remember the days of old; consider the years of many generations; ask your father, and he will show you, your elders, and they will tell you" (32:7). If they are ignorant of their history—which was most unlikely—they should ask their "fathers" and the "elders" in their community. The next two verses describe what the elders would say. They would say that the God who superintended the process of the birth of nations gave to Israel the very special calling of being God's portion and heritage: "When the Most High gave to the nations their inheritance, when he divided mankind, he fixed the borders of the peoples according to the number of the sons of God. But the LORD's portion is his people, Jacob his allotted heritage" (32:8, 9). Being God's "portion" and "heritage" meant that out of all the peoples of the world, they had a position of privilege before God and intimacy with God.

Next Moses, using the picture of caring for the most important and precious part of the eye—the pupil or "the apple of [the] eye"—and of the care of "an eagle" for "its young," he describes the care, protection, and guidance of the Israelites: "He found him in a desert land, and in the howling waste of the wilderness; he encircled him, he cared for him, he kept him as the apple of his eye. Like an eagle that stirs up its nest, that flutters over its young, spreading out its wings, catching them, bearing them on its pinions . . . " (32:10, 11).

Verse 12 says that the foreign gods by whom the people are tempted were nowhere during this time of God's guidance: ". . . the LORD alone guided him, no foreign god was with him." Again we see the folly of disobedience: they have traded the God who has proved himself in history for an unknown god about whom they know nothing. Yet that is the way those who have lost the security of living under God act. They will go from place to place seeking refuge while continuing their disobedient lifestyle. It is no surprise then that dishonest and violent people are some of the most generous donors to shrines, temples, and even churches. They want to buy some protection from a god who will not challenge their lifestyle.

In vivid language verses 13, 14 describe God's provision to the people: "He made him ride on the high places of the land, and he ate the produce of the field, and he suckled him with honey out of the rock, and oil out of the flinty rock. Curds from the herd, and milk from the flock, with fat of lambs, rams of Bashan and goats, with the very finest of the wheat—and you drank foaming wine made from the blood of the grape." All this is to show the scandal of how a people so endowed by God could move away from him. The next paragraph tells us what triggered their apostasy.

Disloyalty Triggered by Prosperity (32:15–18)

Moses goes on to describe how the blessing of God's provision as a result of going to the land flowing with milk and honey was turned into a curse that ensnared them. In our study of 6:10–25 we saw how prosperity can cause a people to move away from God. Deuteronomy 32:15–18 says that this is what happened to the people of Israel. Each of these four verses has a key message.

The Perils of Prosperity (32:15)

Moses begins this section by calling Israel "Jeshurun," which means "the upright one." This seems to have been like a pet name for Israel. Sadly, the people were going to become anything but upright. And Moses' song proceeds to explain how that happened: they became prosperous. "But Jeshurun grew fat, and kicked; you grew fat, stout, and sleek" (32:15a). I do not know the reason for the ESV adopting the word "sleek" here, but the Hebrew word could mean "stubborn" or "headstrong."[7] Fat animals are usually lethargic, but this animal "kicked." This is a sign of their rebellion.

The last part of verse 15 is a sad commentary on the paradox of rebellion against God: "he . . . scoffed at the Rock of his salvation." God is the rock of Israel's salvation, but Israel forgot that. They were now strong and prosperous. They scoffed at the idea of having to depend on God for their existence. They thought they were strong without God. "Scoffed at" is a better translation than the NIV's "rejected," for the Hebrew word has the idea of treating with contempt. In our discussion of 6:13–15 I mentioned how, after I had spoken on the parable of the two sons, a "self-made" businessman scoffed at the idea of his needing God like the prodigal son did. People can become so impressed by their success that they forget the God who gave them success. I have seen people from economically poor backgrounds who, after becoming Christians, prospered and overcame their poverty. Some of these people get proud and start comparing themselves with others who remain poor. "If we could come out of this mess, why can't they?" they say. Their pride gradually leads them to act as if they, not God, were responsible for their success in life.

The Reality of God's Jealousy (32:16)

Verse 16 presents another step in the degradation of the people: "They stirred him to jealousy with strange gods; with abominations they provoked him to anger." David Payne presents three steps of their degradation: "It was a case of prosperity leading to contempt, and contempt to disloyalty—the disloyalty of false worship." They reject the God who was like a Father to them and worship "strange gods." In God's love for the people he responds to this disloyalty with holy jealousy at their rebellion, just as a loving and faithful husband would respond to his wife's unfaithfulness. This is a theme that has already occurred several times in Deuteronomy (4:24; 5:9; 6:15; 29:20) and will occur once more in this chapter (32:21). We are made for loyal commitment to the God who created us, saved us, and made us his own. When someone forfeits that through sin, the loving God is stirred to holy jealousy.

We have already dealt with God's jealousy in our discussions of 4:24 and 5:9 and will do so in the next study. Here let me say that if we have helped someone in the way of the Lord and have seen that person's potential to grow to be a fine Christian, if that person falls from grace, it is right for us to be angry. Today we sometimes view such anger as unworthy of a Christian worker by comparing it to the anger of someone who has lost a battle and is humiliated. Indeed it is humbling to see our work crash as a person we invested in moves away from God. But that is not the primary reason for our anger. The primary reason is the tragedy of what has happened. Here are people who should be living for God, who have experienced God's blessings in their lives. But now they are rebelling against God and destroying their lives. They are bringing great dishonor to the most important value on earth—the honor of God. This is not what they are made for. A child of God is now headed for punishment.

This is why Paul thunders angrily over the abandoning of the faith by the Galatians. In the same book where he expresses outrage over their being led astray he also express a deep yearning love that desires them to grow in Christlikeness. So he tells the Galatians, ". . . my little children, for whom I am again in the anguish of childbirth until Christ is formed in you! I wish I could be present with you now and change my tone, for I am perplexed about you" (Galatians 4:19, 20). Let us not be afraid to express, as our own, God's jealousy over our spiritual children being led astray from God. In a world devoid of deep commitment, where people have tried to numb the pain caused by others, may we love people to the point of being hurt with deep jealousy when they fall prey to the devices of Satan!

The practices that go with the worship of strange gods are called "abominations [that] provoked [God] to anger" (32:16b). We must never lose our sense of disgust over worship that does not honor God. Earlier in Deuteronomy Moses said:

> The carved images of their gods you shall burn with fire. You shall not covet the silver or the gold that is on them or take it for yourselves, lest you be ensnared by it, for it is an abomination to the LORD your God. And you shall not bring an abominable thing into your house and become devoted to destruction like it. You shall utterly detest and abhor it, for it is devoted to destruction. (7:25, 26)

We might not directly express our disgust over these practices to people outside God's covenant community. Instead we might argue for their futility as Paul did in Athens. But in Athens, though he did not express his anger, Paul's "spirit was provoked within him as he saw that the city was full of idols" (Acts 17:16). Idolatry is always abhorrent to God and his people.

The Attraction of New Gods (32:17)

Verse 17 describes the gods the people chose in place of Yahweh: "They sacrificed to demons that were no gods, to gods they had never known, to new gods that had come recently, whom your fathers had never dreaded." Though the Hebrew word translated "demons" appears only in one other place in the Old Testament (Psalm 106:37), this word was commonly used in those days for "a protective guardian mostly concerned with the individual's health and welfare."[8] They are "demons that were no gods" (Deuteronomy 32:17a). They have supernatural powers, and people could be lured by these powers and by the prospect of receiving something they want. We live in an age when people look at alternate supernatural powers as legitimate substitutes for the God of the Bible. It is not politically correct to call them demons. We would be wise to know what words to use with different audiences lest we lose an opportunity to impact an audience through the inappropriate use of a term such as *demon*. But we must never forget the source of all competing supernatural powers—Satan. They are demonic. They may appear to help people to act more righteously and even take on a veneer of holiness, but if they keep people from the one true God they are demonically inspired. Paul said, ". . . even Satan disguises himself as an angel of light" (2 Corinthians 11:14).

Moses says that though they are "demons" they are "no gods." There is only one true God, and he is incomparable. They have power, but their power is limited. They do not have the comprehensive omnipotence or the holy love that characterizes the God of the Bible. Instead, they need to be appeased with sacrifices so they will grant favors to people. They are incapable of caring for people like our God who is our loving Father. Sadly, because the loving Father is also a holy God, some opt for the demons rather than a life of obedience to God's laws.

Next, these gods are described as "gods they had never known." After knowing so much about God and his goodness and what he has done for them in history, how could they go after gods about whom they know nothing? Nathan asked David a question somewhat like this when the king's adultery was exposed:

> Thus says the LORD, the God of Israel, "I anointed you king over Israel, and I delivered you out of the hand of Saul. And I gave you your master's house and your master's wives into your arms and gave you the house of Israel and of Judah. And if this were too little, I would add to you as much more. Why have you despised the word of the LORD, to do what is evil in his sight?" (2 Samuel 12:7b–9a)

This is the power of temptation. We all have areas of vulnerability to temptation in our lives. Examples are the lure of dishonest gain, lust, making more money, revenge, and success attained by neglecting other important things in life such as family, church, and God. These temptations could send us on a path that finally results in our betraying the God who has done so much for us. And the result could be, as Moses says, that we go after "new gods that had come recently, whom your fathers had never dreaded" (32:17c, d). Arrogance does not take away fear. People may rebel against the God of the universe and arrogantly act as if they are in control of things. But deep down there is an insecurity. They have lost the peace—the *shalom*—of knowing that life with God is good. In their insecurity they will turn to other gods and sacrifice to them.

Underworld figures and unscrupulous businessmen are sometimes among the most lavish contributors and "faithful" adherents of shrines, temples, and churches. They live their life of sin, but they give generously to the gods something like an insurance premium. The problem is that the God of the Bible does not operate that way. In his holy love and commitment to us he wants our all. Those who are not willing to give their all to God will resort to a new god who could be appeased by a sacrifice and will not meddle with their personal lives.

The Unfaithfulness of Forgetting God (32:18)

Verse 18 describes the rebellion of the people as a contrast to God's faithfulness to them: "You were unmindful of the Rock that bore you, and you forgot the God who gave you birth." Three pictures are used here of God's concern for them. He was their "Rock," which points to reliability and trustworthiness. He would never disappoint them. He "bore" or "fathered" (NIV, ESV margin) them, which is the picture of a father. Thirdly, he "gave . . . birth" to them—the picture of a mother. The word used here has the idea of the pains of childbirth. On God's side there has been costly, comprehensive commitment to his people. Today we see that commitment in his giving his Son to die for us. Two verbs—"were unmindful" and "forgot"—describe the people's rebellion. Both Hebrew words basically mean "to forget." In the time of temptation they forgot all that God had done for them.

Moses calls the people over and over again in Deuteronomy to remember their past deliverances and their chastisements for disobedience. But when under temptation they forget. Humans tend to forget so easily. When a person who had been a terribly repressive and unjust ruler seeks election after a few years of being out of office, he is voted in. The people forget all his misdeeds and are lured by all the election promises he makes. When people move away from God, usually not only do they forget God, they blame God to justify their rebellion. How can we prevent this? We will do what Moses did. We will attack forgetfulness by calling people to remember God's faithfulness. Paul did the same in the epistle to the Ephesians. He called his readers to remember who they were before conversion:

> Therefore *remember* that at one time you Gentiles in the flesh, called "the uncircumcision" by what is called the circumcision, which is made in the flesh by hands—*remember* that you were at that time separated from Christ, alienated from the commonwealth of Israel and strangers to the covenants of promise, having no hope and without God in the world. (Ephesians 2:11, 12)

Then he reminds them of what God has done in their lives: "But now in Christ Jesus you who once were far off have been brought near by the blood of Christ" (Ephesians 2:13).

Yet there is no guarantee that the people will remember and be faithful. Despite all of Moses' exhortations, the Israelites rebelled. We must not be overly discouraged if we meet the same response to our ministries. Like spiritual parents we will pour our lives into people; but some may rebel against God and us and even accuse God and us of failing them. Just as God did not give up on the Israelites, we must not give up on our spiritual children. And, most importantly, we do not give up on the practice of spiritual parenthood. In our ministry with drug-dependents we have found that many people grow to mature stability in their lives after several lapses into disobedience. They blame us during those disobedient times. But those who persevere in this ministry find that some will make it in the end.

As for our personal lives, may we never forget what God has done for us. That is gross ingratitude and lowly behavior. To forget the one who has saved us at the cost of his own Son and go after other gods and paths is unthinkable for a faithful person. In Christianity, honorable, exalted behavior is faithfulness, even when it costs. In our discussion of 1:28 we referred to Polycarp, who was told that his life would be spared if he disowned Christ. His response was, "Eighty and six years have I served Him, and He never did me any injury: how then can I blaspheme my King and my Savior?" For Polycarp faithfulness to Christ meant martyrdom, but he accepted it as an honor considering all that Christ had done for him. He even ended his life with a doxology, praising God for giving him the honor of martyrdom.

This song of Moses is amazing! It condemns unfaithfulness. People will sing the song while they are unfaithful, but the words will not sink in. Only when they suffer from the consequences of unfaithfulness will that happen. Such is the deceitfulness of the heart that has moved away from God.

60

Moses' Song II: Judgment and Restoration

DEUTERONOMY 32:19–47

AFTER DESCRIBING HOW the people disobeyed God, Moses' song proceeds to a description of God's response to their disobedience. A key theme that occurs here is God's jealousy over his people—resulting in his being provoked to anger and judging the people—and his jealousy for his name—resulting in his restoring the people.

God Is Jealous over Unfaithfulness (32:19–25)

The song uses strong words, indicating deep feelings, to describe God's response to the disobedience of the people. Verse 19 introduces the topic with two strong words, "spurned" and "provocation": "The LORD saw it and spurned them, because of the provocation of his sons and his daughters." This idea is repeated in verse 21: "They have made me jealous . . . they have provoked me to anger." Verse 22 speaks of God's anger burning: "For a fire is kindled by my anger, and it burns to the depths of Sheol." Do we ever think of the sins of those who call themselves Christians as being a means of provoking God, of God burning with anger over them? As this theme is repeated so many times in Deuteronomy and as it is an alien idea to even many Christians today, it merits another discussion by us in this book (see the discussions on 9:7, 8; 28:48–68; 32:16).

The covenant love of God demands exclusive loyalty and faithfulness on our part. God promises that he will never leave us or forsake us (Deuteronomy 31:6, 8; Joshua 1:5). But when we become unfaithful, God's anger is kindled, and he says, "I will hide my face from them; I will see what their end will be" (Deuteronomy 32:20a). Why? "For they are a perverse generation, children in whom is no faithfulness" (32:20b). Real love can never be satisfied with rejection. People must learn to live with rejection when their desires are sometimes rejected by people—for example, when a person does not reciprocate the love of someone who wants to marry him or her. But once a covenant is made—with God or humans—when that is broken, there is anger because of the high place the breaker of the covenant has in our hearts. If a mother is not moved to the depth of her being when her son destroys his life with sinful living, there is something lacking in her love.

If what the Bible says about God's commitment to our welfare and to truthfulness and to justice is true, then he must get angry when his people become faithless and choose one who is "no god" or "idols" (32:21). Warren Wiersbe says, "God's 'jealousy' is that of a loving faithful husband whose wife has betrayed him. (This is the story in the Book of Hosea, and see Jeremiah 2:25)." Yet today many people are surprised when they read about God's wrath. It shows how culturally distant the religion of the Bible is even to Christians. A generation of Christians has arisen that does not know a vital part of Biblical religion: the doctrine that God hates sin and judges it. Because we have seen so much selfish anger that is both damaging and sinful, we tend to forget that wrath is an essential aspect of the love and holiness of God. As J. Orr says, "A God who is incapable of moral indignation would be equally incapable of moral love, and could not, with truth, be spoken of as dispensing mercy. Wrath and love are opposite poles of one affection." Orr goes on to say that neglecting the idea that sin provokes God makes it difficult for us to understand forgiveness: "Where there is no offence, there needs no forgiveness."[1]

Verses 21 says that just as God was made jealous and angry by these people, they will be made jealous and angry by an insignificant and foolish nation: "They have made me jealous with what is no god; they have provoked me to anger with their idols. So I will make them jealous with those who are no people; I will provoke them to anger with a foolish nation." No specific nation is mentioned. We know that several nations did this to Israel. Verse 22 talks of fire that will consume the land: "For a fire is kindled by my anger, and it burns to the depths of Sheol, devours the earth and its increase, and sets on fire the foundations of the mountains." Shifting from the fire image, verses 23, 24 move to several images for what will bring disaster to the land: "And I will heap disasters upon them; I will spend my arrows on them; they shall be wasted with hunger, and devoured by plague and poisonous pestilence; I will send the teeth of beasts against them, with the venom of things that crawl in the dust." One cannot help noting the vividness and the variety in the language used. Arrows, hunger, plague, pestilence, wild beasts, and venomous (probably) "vipers" (NIV) are used. There is a hint for us here, too. Even as we use our creativity to communicate numerous Christian truths, we need to use our creativity to strike home the truth of judgment. C. S. Lewis did this so well. More recently Bill Muir and John Schmidt have produced a short film, *The Crossing*, that did this effectively.

Moses' song shows that no one can hope to escape punishment: "Outdoors the sword shall bereave, and indoors terror, for young man and woman alike, the nursing child with the man of gray hairs" (32:25). It is very hard to live a righteous life in a society where violence, corruption, exploitation, and sexual indulgence thrive. Powerful people in society seem to get away with so much wickedness, and those who challenge their wickedness are crushed and defeated. These powerful people in society seem to be invincible. The righteous could end up very bitter over this. But there is no need for bitterness. These people will be punished severely. There will be no escape for anyone on the day of judgment. We need to keep reminding ourselves of this in order to have the courage to go against the stream and pay the price of righteousness.

God Is Committed to His Honor (32:26, 27)

Speaking very much like a human being, in anthropomorphic language, God says that he felt like totally destroying the people: "I would have said, 'I will cut them to pieces; I will wipe them from human memory'" (32:26). Yet, he holds back because of the implications of such an action—their enemies would think that they, not God, were sovereign over the destiny of Israel: "had I not feared provocation by the enemy, lest their adversaries should misunderstand, lest they should say, 'Our hand is triumphant, it was not the LORD who did all this'" (32:27). Moses himself had previously argued in a similar tone when appealing for moderation in his judgment upon sinful Israel, because the Egyptians would arrive at conclusions that were damaging to God's reputation (9:25–29).

There is going to be a switch from punishment of Israel to salvation for Israel in the song, and the driving force for that is the reputation of God.[2] This passage does not imply that God was taken by surprise by what happened. The words here are, as we said, anthropomorphic. What he is saying is that the damage done by the complete destruction of the people would be too great and too damaging. It would bring dishonor to God that would be damaging all around. The welfare of the world depends on people knowing who God is and what he is like. For people to be deprived of that vision would be a serious problem. Even more serious is the problem created by a very wrong picture of God being communicated by God's own actions. As J. Orr says, "There is more honor to God in saving men than in destroying them." Often, then, God pardons and restores his people, not because we deserve it but because God's name would be irreparably dishonored by our downfall. The church has survived in spite of itself, and only because of the mercy of God.

God Will Give up on Disobedient Israel (32:28–31)

Moses has just said that God will show some restraint and not let the enemies of the people of Israel destroy them totally (32:26, 27). There is some question as to whether verses 28, 29 are talking about Israel or Israel's enemy. The principles about God's dealings with humans given here could be applied to both. So the teaching we glean from these verses would be similar even if we have wrongly identified the subject of these verses. I am taking verses 28, 29 to refer to the Israelites. Moses says, "For they are a nation void of counsel, and there is no understanding in them" (32:28). He says wise people would recognize that there is punishment for disobeying God: "If they were wise, they would understand this; they would discern their latter end!" (32:29).

There is no doubt about whom the next verses speak. Verse 30 says that the defeat of Israel was possible because God had given up on his people. "How could one have chased a thousand, and two have put ten thousand to flight, unless their Rock had sold them, and the Lord had given them up?" The God who is Israel's unshakable, ever reliable Rock (32:4) has chosen to sell them, to give them up. Romans talks about how God gave up on humanity in general after humans chose to dishonor God (1:24, 26, 28). When he gave up on humanity, he did so with the hope of choosing Israel so that Israel would become the means through which God's message would go to the world. But when Israel also rejected God's ways, she, too, was rejected by God. Moses says that though the enemies of Israel seemed to be very powerful, the Rock they depended on cannot be compared to God the Rock: "For their rock is not as our Rock; our enemies are by themselves" (Deuteronomy 32:31). They may sound very confident and look like they are backed by powerful forces, but actually they are "by themselves." And they defeated Israel!

What a tragically contradictory situation we have here. God is the Rock of his people. But his people are defeated by lesser rocks because they rejected God's ways. This can still happen in real life. An Asian pastor smuggled some restricted goods in at a time when imports were severely restricted in his country. When his offense was discovered, he told the customs officials, who themselves were quite corrupt, that he was the Billy Graham of Sri Lanka. He felt that they should give him some special consideration because of this. But they did not do so. And God did nothing to protect him from this humiliating situation. He let the dishonest customs officers fine and expose his own servant. It was even reported in the newspapers. What a dishonor to God! Despite the dishonor, he will not act to protect his disobedient servants. He lets them be brought to shame. I can cite many examples of this—of unrighteous people justly punishing God's people. Oh, may we be careful about the way we live, for God's name is being dishonored through the punishment meted out to his servants. And dishonor coming to God's name is one of the most terrible things that can happen on earth.

God Will Take Vengeance against Israel's Destroyers (32:32–35)

Moses proceeds to describe why the things that these enemy nations who defeated Israel are depending on are not going to help them finally. "For their vine comes from the vine of Sodom and from the fields of Gomorrah; their grapes are grapes of poison; their clusters are bitter; their wine is the poison of serpents and the cruel venom of asps" (32:32, 33). Sodom and Gomorrah, of course, were very wicked and were destroyed by God. Not only do they reap future judgment, they do not even satisfy in the present because "their grapes are . . . poison; their clusters are bitter." Even on earth, powerful people will not be happy. Their victories will turn sour. The fact that they have temporarily defeated the people of God should not cause us to join them. They are not happy in the present and are depending on the wrong things for the future. Let those who envy successful wicked people remember this. Their power is not as powerful as it seems, and their success is not as satisfying as it seems.

God is actually storing up wrath against people who rebel against him. In verses 34, 35 God says, "Is not this laid up in store with me, sealed up in my treasuries? Vengeance is mine, and recompense, for the time when their foot shall slip; for the day of their calamity is at hand, and their doom comes swiftly." Note how God is going to judge because vengeance belongs to him. This may seem to be unworthy of God, for it looks like God is taking revenge against his enemies. This is not revenge in the bad human sense. Justice demands that sin be punished. God will not be holy and good if he does not punish the wicked. This is why after mentioning vengeance the song goes on to say, ". . . and recompense." And verse 41, after talking of vengeance, says "[I] will repay." The vengeance of God is punishment for wrong, a repayment according to the laws of justice.

Today we may revolt against the idea of God's vengeance because of the way humans have taken revenge. We must remember that vengeance is usually used in the Bible to refer to something that God does. If we take the law into our hands and try to take vengeance, we will make a mess of things. So Paul uses the language of verses 41, 42 in his argument for why we should not take revenge: "Beloved, never avenge yourselves, but leave it to the wrath of God, for it is written, 'Vengeance is mine, I will repay, says the Lord'" (Romans 12:19). Sometimes God's vengeance is carried out by humans. Paul says about government authorities, "For there is no authority except from God, and those that exist have been instituted by God" (Romans 13:1). These have been given to carry out God's vengeance ". . . for he [the governing authority] is God's servant for your good. But if you do wrong, be afraid, for he does not bear the sword in vain. For he is the servant of God, an avenger who carries out God's wrath on the wrongdoer" (Romans 13:4; see Numbers 31:2, 3). So we will look at God's vengeance as an expression of his hatred for evil and his commitment to justice.

Soon "their foot shall slip" (32:35). Powerful wicked people usually come to their positions of influence because they are capable, perhaps brilliant. This is why we call some people "evil geniuses." They use their wisdom to cover all their bases so they will not be exposed as being wicked. Even good people bow down to them with respect, recognizing their power and influence. Though God despises them, humans will pay homage to them. But they cannot go on in their wicked ways indefinitely. Eventually their wickedness will catch up with them. A vulnerable situation will emerge, and "their foot shall slip." Often people are forced to join wicked enterprises because of the sheer power of their leaders. Those who refuse to join because of their principles will find themselves exposed to danger. But history shows that the power of such wicked people does not last forever. The names Nero, Hitler, Idi Amin, and Pol Pot are recalled today with revulsion. They have their day for a time, but they will soon be gone. They cannot ultimately cover all their bases. A vulnerable position will emerge, and that will be the beginning of the end for them.

There is a word of comfort and courage to us here. We should not resent the success of wicked people. Actually we should feel sorry for them—something we do not feel inclined to do when they are the ones who are oppressing us. The righteous poet who wrote Psalm 73 experienced this struggle with bitterness over the success of the wicked and the failure of the righteous. He even said, "All in vain have I kept my heart clean and washed my hands in innocence" (v. 13). But he realized that he could not go on harboring such attitudes (v. 15). So he "went into the sanctuary of God" (v. 17a), and his whole attitude changed. There he "discerned their end" (v. 17b). He realized that they are going to crash one day and be destroyed (vv. 18, 19).

Is it right for us to contemplate the destruction of the wicked in this way?

It is! We could easily buckle under the strain of their oppression and corruption and move away from God's path. The doctrine of judgment upon the wicked helps us to remain righteous and not to be bitter about the success of the unrighteous. Just as this song of Moses was going to become part of the folklore of the people, we too must include the fact that the wicked will be judged in our ordinary conversation and singing. The doctrine of judgment is a key feature of the Biblical armor against assimilation into evil world systems.

Preachers who neglect proclaiming this to their people and parents who neglect talking about this to their children are guilty of a serious omission. These are unpleasant topics, and we tend to avoid bringing them up. That is un-Biblical and dangerously wrong. We could mislead people and cause them to develop a false security that could result in their being lured into the evil lifestyle of the world. Christians must always bear in mind that sin will be punished. And sometimes it may be necessary in the face of powerful evil to point to those powerful people and tell the faithful that those people will be punished. It will give wisdom to the faithful about the folly of compromising obedience in order to fall in line with the schemes of wicked people.

God Demonstrates His Sovereignty in Restoring Israel (32:36–43)

Next, Moses says that the God who judged the enemies of Israel will judge Israel, but he will do so in order to vindicate them: "For the LORD will vindicate his people and have compassion on his servants" (32:36a). The word translated "vindicate" also means "judge." Here his judgment is going to result in the restoration of the people. The honor of God's name is wrapped up in the history of the people who bear his name. When they fail, it looks like God has failed. It is therefore desperately important for God's people to be vindicated. But God cannot do this without punishing them for their rebellion. So he first punishes them and then restores them. In this way neither the holiness of God nor his love are compromised.

God shows "compassion on his servants, when he sees that their power is gone and there is none remaining, bond or free" (32:36b). As Chris Wright puts it, "Grace is suffused with pity when God sees the utter destitution of his people." Just as God has pity on his rebellious children, we, too, should be moved with compassion when we see the pitiable state of Christians who rebel against God. They may have said terrible things about us during their time of rebellion. Now when we see them experiencing the consequences of their sin, love comes to the fore, and we yearn for their restoration. This was the attitude of Moses when God struck Miriam with leprosy for rebelling against Moses. The moment he saw it, "Moses cried to the LORD, 'O God, please heal her—please'" (Numbers 12:13). You can sense an urgency in the words of Moses. Love yearns for the restoration of those who have spurned our love and God's love.

Immediately after talking about their coming restoration, Moses' song says, "Then [God] will say, 'Where are their gods, the rock in which they took refuge, who ate the fat of their sacrifices and drank the wine of their drink offering? Let them rise up and help you; let them be your protection!'" (Deuteronomy 32:37, 38). They must be reminded of the folly of their actions. These gods became "the rock in which they took refuge," and they invested considerable resources to feed them: ". . . who ate the fat of their sacrifices and drank the wine of their drink offering." With biting irony God says, "Let them rise up and help you; let them be your protection!" They did not protect the people. These gods failed, as they always do. Chris Wright reminds us, "Such is always the way of idolatry in human society, ancient and modern. False gods never fail to fail. Sadly, we never fail to forget." Because we do forget, we need to be reminded repeatedly of the folly of idolatry in all its forms.

After highlighting the impotence of the other gods, God highlights his own supremacy. First, he says, "See now that I, even I, am he, and there is no god beside me" (32:39a). The surrounding nations believed there were several gods performing different functions. But Israel knows that Yahweh was not just the head of a pantheon. He is the one and only God.

Of course, the Bible recognizes the existence of other powers, and they have some power, as we pointed out in our discussion of the first command-ment (5:7). Their powers are sometimes paraded as being more accessible than Yahweh's power. Sometimes God does not seem to be answering the prayers of Christians, and they cannot do much other than continue in prayer, waiting for God to act. Then they might get restless and go to another god whose services can be more readily accessed by making a payment or offering to that god. Because of that, even believers could be tempted to go to a shrine or to a spiritual advisor, astrologer, or medicine man for a quicker result. The Israelites had done something like this when they went to these other gods.

To keep people from falling into this trap again, God says, "I kill and I make alive; I wound and I heal; and there is none that can deliver out of my hand" (32:39b). In other words, because God is sovereign over history, even the things that happen that do not seem to tally with his nature are done only because he has given them permission to do so. The Jewish view of the sov-ereignty of God was so strong that they attributed the action to God. Besides, God will judge the wicked. Sometimes wicked people will carry out this judg-ment on others on earth. The Babylonians, who in later history gave Israel such a hard time, were punished through Darius. Once again we are reminded that sin is going to be punished and that it is sheer folly to trust in any idol in place of God. When we make an idol of our education or our job or our quest for wealth or pleasure, we are being fools. All these idols are also going to come under God's judgment. How easy to forget that God is sovereign when we are surrounded by other earthly powers that seem to control life on earth right now. The temptation to bow down to those forces is great. We must not be deceived and succumb.

Verse 40 presents words that we do not usually associate with God: we see God taking an oath. God says, "For I lift up my hand to heaven and swear, as I live forever . . . " God's hand is raised as a sign that he is making a sworn testimony. The expression, "As I live forever" is like "As the Lord lives," which people use when taking an oath. God is taking an oath and swearing by himself! Eugene Merrill comments, "The Word of God by itself is sure, but when he swears by his own life and reputation, there can be no doubt about the fulfillment of his intentions." He is talking about the coming judgment upon hostile nations, which he proceeds to describe using vivid language: ". . . if I sharpen my flashing sword and my hand takes hold on judgment, I will take vengeance on my adversaries and will repay those who hate me. I will make my arrows drunk with blood, and my sword shall devour flesh—with the blood of the slain and the captives, from the long-haired heads of the enemy" (32:41, 42). Oh, that those who live in open rebellion against God would realize that God's judgment is sure, that their arrogant disregard for his principles is earning for them a terrible judgment.

Verse 43 presents us with another surprise: "Rejoice with him, O heavens; bow down to him, all gods, for he avenges the blood of his children and takes vengeance on his adversaries. He repays those who hate him and cleanses his people's land." "Heavens" probably refers to nations, which is how Paul renders the quotation of this verse in Romans 15:10 ("Gentiles"). Indeed, we feel sorry when people who are made in the image of God are destroyed. But there are times when people are made to suffer a terrible fate at the hands of terribly wicked people who arrogantly go on flaunting their power. In the Psalms we find the psalmists crying out, "How long, Lord?" eight times[3] as they long for his intervention while his people suffer. Psalm 73:12, 13 present a familiar dilemma faced by righteous people as they conscientiously try to obey God in a fallen world: "Behold, these are the wicked; always at ease, they increase in riches. All in vain have I kept my heart clean and washed my hands in innocence." To people who struggle in this way, God says that it is not in vain, swearing that the wicked will be punished.

God's Word Is a Matter of Life and Death (32:44–47)

Finally, the song is over. Verse 44 says, "Moses came and recited all the words of this song in the hearing of the people, he and Joshua the son of Nun." The song was intended to motivate faithfulness to God and his Law. Therefore, Moses gives an exhortation to vigilance and obedience (32:44–47). When I was a seminary student I had the privilege of traveling often for missions conferences during the weekends with my missions professor, Dr. John T. Seamands. Once after I had finished preaching he told me something that I will never forget. He told me that I gave a good message but I just left it there. "Truth demands a verdict. You must call people to act upon what you said." I determined that day that I will always end my messages by giving people the opportunity to make a decision about how they will respond in life to what I had preached.

Before the exhortation there is a summary of what happened in the reciting of the song: "Moses came and recited all the words of this song in the hearing of the people, he and Joshua the son of Nun" (32:44). Then after an introduction (32:45, 46a), there is an exhortation to the people to be faithful to the Word: "Take to heart all the words by which I am warning you today, that you may command them to your children, that they may be careful to do all the words of this law" (32:46b). He has extended his exhortation to "all the words of this law." The song was intended to lead people to the whole Law. It was intended to help create an attitude of devotion and obedience, which would lead people to the whole Word. That is an important aim of preaching and singing. We could never tell people everything there is to say. But we can point them to the path of faithfulness, so that they will enter into a lifetime of study of and obedience to the Word. They are to "take to heart all the words," which not only involves hearing and reading but also letting it go deep inside and result in obedience.

Then Moses says, ". . . command [the words] to your children, that they may be careful to do all the words of this law." Parents have the responsibility to pass on the truths of God to their children. They cannot just expect the church to do this and blame the church if their children go astray. This is primarily their responsibility. And why is that so important? Moses says, "For it is no empty word for you, but your very life, and by this word you shall live long in the land that you are going over the Jordan to possess" (32:47). One of my saddest experiences as a youth worker has been seeing Christian parents who are more interested in their children's advancement in society than in the kingdom of God. They very grudgingly send them to youth programs and get upset when they see their children spending time reading the Word at home. They want them to study and to be active in school societies that will give them a good standing when they graduate from school. Those children need to know that all the achievements in the world are for a short time, but God's Word is their "very life." If they do not live in obedience to the Word, they will land in Hell, and Hell is forever. Someone has estimated that over 80 percent of committed Christians in churches in the United States made their commitment to Christ before they were eighteen years old. I believe some of them do so despite their parents and not because of them.

The statement that the Word is "your very life" implies that in it is everything necessary for a meaningful life. Though written so long ago, it still shows us the way to salvation and gives us the principles by which we should make all our decisions. It tells us how we are doing in our life—showing us when we go wrong and pointing us to the right way to go. It nourishes us so we can be strong to do the right things. And the result of obeying it is a prosperous life (32:47b). As shared earlier, an African woman was asked if she enjoyed reading her new Bible. She replied, "Sir, I am not reading this Book. This Book is reading me!"[4] John Wesley expresses the power of and dependence on the Word well in the preface to his book of sermons:

> To candid, reasonable men, I am not afraid to lay open what have been the inmost thoughts of my heart. I have thought, I am a creature of a day, passing through life as an arrow through the air. I am a spirit come from God, and returning to God: Just hovering over the great gulf; till, a few moments hence, I am no more seen; I drop into an unchangeable eternity! I want to know one thing—the way to heaven; how to land safe on that happy shore. God himself has condescended to teach the way: For this very end he came from heaven. He hath written it down in a book. O give me that book! At any price, give me the book of God! I have it: Here is knowledge enough for me. Let me be *homo unius libri* [a man of one book].[5]

Moses' song was intended to point people to God and his ways. Like the Bible it would be ignored by disobedient people. But within it is the key to life. Some disobedient people would one day realize the folly of their ways and turn to God through it. So let us not get tired of teaching the Bible. People may reject what we say, but when they see the folly of their ways, our words may be what God uses to get them back on track.

61

The Art of Blessing People

DEUTERONOMY 32:48—33:25

WE NOW COME TO the last thing that Moses, the great leader, did as a leader. He has handed over the leadership to Joshua, and he has taught the people a song that is aimed at helping them be faithful to God and to return to God when they have been unfaithful. His last act as a leader is to bless the people he had led for over forty years. There will be separate blessings for each tribe. Before that, however, Moses is reminded again that he cannot go to the promised land.

A Great Man Is Chastised (32:48–52)

The events recorded here take place on the same day that Moses presented the song to the people: "That very day the LORD spoke to Moses. 'Go up this mountain of the Abarim, Mount Nebo, which is in the land of Moab, opposite Jericho, and view the land of Canaan, which I am giving to the people of Israel for a possession'" (32:48, 49). After forty years of leading the people toward the promised land, Moses will only get a visual glimpse of the land. After that God tells him that he is to die. "And die on the mountain which you go up, and be gathered to your people, as Aaron your brother died in Mount Hor and was gathered to his people" (32:50). Now that his work is over, he can die.

For the fourth time in Deuteronomy we are told that Moses cannot go to the promised land because of his wrongdoing. "For you shall see the land before you, but you shall not go there, into the land that I am giving to the people of Israel" (32:52; see 1:37; 3:23–28; 4:21, 22; see also Numbers 20:12; 27:13, 14). Two reasons are given for this prohibition. First, God says, ". . . because you broke faith with me in the midst of the people of Israel at the waters of Meribah-kadesh, in the wilderness of Zin" (32:51a). The second reason God gives is, ". . . and because you did not treat me as holy in the midst of the people of Israel" (32:51b). This second reason is related to the first in the original description of this event in the book of Numbers. There God tells Moses and Aaron, "Because you did not believe in me, to uphold me as holy in the eyes of the people of Israel, therefore you shall not bring this assembly into the land that I have given them" (20:12). The people were grumbling because of the lack of water. God told Moses and Aaron to speak to the rock. God's word is powerful, and if Moses spoke on behalf of God, water would have gushed out. But they "did not believe" God, so Moses struck the rock.

Believers find it difficult to believe God and trust him to look after them. So they try to get what they want by doing some extra things. When leaders also do the same thing, it is very serious. Leaders must take the lead in showing people that they can indeed be obedient in this world. But in order to be obedient they must believe that God will look after them. The leaders were supposed to demonstrate that in their lives. But Moses' action did not demonstrate that. That is very serious, because the responsibility of leaders is to lead the way in encouraging the people to trust God. When leaders do not trust God, the faith of many people is affected. Our passage from Deuteronomy says, ". . . they broke faith with me in the midst of the people of Israel" (32:51a). "Broke faith" translates "a strong term denoting an act tantamount to apostasy."[1] It "is used, to describe a wife's unfaithfulness to her husband (Numbers 5:12), the treachery of Israel when she forsook the Lord (Leviticus 26:40), and Achan's 'breaking faith' with the Lord (Joshua 22:16, 20)."[2]

As we said above, the second reason given for the prohibition against going into the promised land is directly connected to the first. In their action of breaking faith, they also "did not treat [God] as holy in the midst of the people of Israel" (32:51b). The NLT illuminates this: "You failed to demonstrate my holiness to the people of Israel there." When God's servants disobey God, submission to the supremacy of the sovereign God is compromised. Supremacy and sovereignty are aspects of God's holiness. Moses behaved as if God was not supreme or sovereign. He took matters into his own hands and did things his way. Always in the history of Sri Lanka people in power have broken the law. But they did it inconspicuously. They hid their wrongdoing because they knew that what they did was wrong. However, there have been times in the history of Sri Lanka when national leaders openly broke the laws, acted contrary to the constitution for all to see, and got away with it. I felt this was one of the most serious threats to the welfare of our country. The message is communicated that the constitution is not practical, that acting against it is acceptable. A similar thing happens when Christian leaders disobey God in front of the people. They bring down the standard of God's holiness by communicating the idea that it is acceptable to disobey God. Such actions need to be severely condemned in order to restore the dignity of God before people.

Though Moses did not have the joy of leading the people to the promised land, this was only a chastisement that did not negate the opinion of the Bible that he was a great person and the great eternal rewards he would receive. Actually the frequent mention of this is itself a sign of Moses' greatness. He was so eager for the people to be obedient that he was willing to use his failures and the consequences of them as a motivation to be obedient.

In the era of the New Testament, the Old Testament was divided into two sections—the Law and the Prophets. But seven times in the New Testament we find Jesus and others in the New Testament substituting "Moses" for the Law, resulting in the familiar expression, "Moses and the Prophets."[3] Then Moses, along with Elijah, had the great honor and privilege of being one of those chosen to encourage Jesus on the Mount of Transfiguration as he contemplated his coming death (Matthew 17:3; Mark 9:4; Luke 9:30). Great leaders make mistakes and have to face the consequences of those mistakes. But the merciful God uses their work to leave behind a legacy of blessing on earth. The most severe example of this was David after whose adultery with Bathsheba and murder of Uriah life turned very sour. Nevertheless, he is viewed as Israel's greatest king, and it is from his line that the Messiah came. Even after the event, he is referred to as "a man after [God's] heart" in the New Testament (Acts 13:22).

Blessings from a Man of God (33:1–25)

Moses: the Man of God (33:1)

In the book of Deuteronomy, we have often seen what a great person Moses was and how he exhibited the qualities of godly leadership. We have already said that the marked feature that characterized his retirement and handing over leadership to Joshua was not a desire to have people remember his legacy, even though the idea of remembering the past was very important to the Israelites (see the discussion on 31:9–13). In his handing over leadership and in the song he taught the people, he warned the people about the dangers of disobedience and urged obedience. Now he is ready to die, and again we see that the major concern he has is the welfare of the people: he blesses them. Here we see the two great burdens of great and godly leaders. They want their people to be faithful to God, and they want God to bless them.

An editorial note introduces the blessing: "This is the blessing that Moses, the man of God, gave to the people of Israel before his death" (33:1, NLT).

Moses is called "the man of God" (here and in Joshua 14:6). This term was generally used of prophets and most frequently of Elijah and Elisha.[4] Moses, of course, was the preeminent prophet. Among the people of God, some persons stand out so much that they are described as men and women of God. People see them as being close to God and as representing God well by their words and actions. Would that all Christian leaders were known to be like this! A fuller description of the uniqueness of Moses is given in Deuteronomy 34:10–12.

Praise for God's Activity (33:2–5)

The blessing opens and closes with passages that praise God for his activity among them in recent history (33:2–5; 26–29). Verses 2, 4 refer to events surrounding the giving of the Law on Mount Sinai (usually called Horeb in Deuteronomy). Moses said, "The LORD came from Sinai and dawned from Seir upon us; he shone forth from Mount Paran; he came from the ten thousands of holy ones, with flaming fire at his right hand . . . when Moses commanded us a law, as a possession for the assembly of Jacob." Verse 4 refers to Moses in the third person, even though this is his blessing. It could be that verses 3–5 are a response of the people to the opening statement of verse 2, or it could be that Moses used the third person for some stylistic reason.[5] Verse 3 grounds this activity of God in his love for and close relationship with Israel: "Yes, he loved his people, all his holy ones were in his hand; so they followed in your steps, receiving direction from you."

Verse 5 says, "Thus the LORD became king in Jeshurun [another name for Israel], when the heads of the people were gathered, all the tribes of Israel together." This is probably a reference to the covenant-making or renewal that took place in Sinai or Moab. The covenant affirmed that God was the king of the people and that they would obey and be faithful to him at all times. Sometime after Moses and his successors, the people asked for a king so that they could be like the other nations. Even then the king was a representative of the real King of Israel who is God. Though Israel had a king, at least in theory, Israel remained a theocracy—that is, a nation governed "by officials who are regarded as divinely guided."[6]

Verses 2–5 give three points that are the grounds for the blessing Moses will give. These are, first, God's love for the people (33:3), second, God's actions in history (33:2, 4), and, third, the covenant that the people have made with God (33:5). This is not simply a case of wishful thinking. It is hope based on the record of God's faithful, powerful love for his people, and it is conditioned upon the people keeping the covenant they made with God. Similarly, we, too, can bless people, based on God's love for them and in the hope that they will be faithful to their covenant with God. Moses' blessing is well thought out and appropriate to the object of blessing.

In the same way, we leaders can bless our people as we think of the future prospects for their lives. In the blessing we could include the prayer or hope that the people will remain faithful to God. Generally, in addition to getting to know the background of the people, I pray asking God for guidance about what I should say in the blessing. These are serious times, and we do not want to mouth words that have no real meaning. We want to be agents of God who communicate his thoughts. When I send a birthday greeting to someone close to me, I usually first pray asking the Lord what I should wish for this person for the new year in his or her life. Then after thinking for some time I give what I think is appropriate as my blessing to this person.

Moses gives specific blessings for each tribe except Simeon. Simeon seems to have been absorbed into Judah at an early stage of Israel's history in Canaan (see Joshua 19:1–9). Gary Hall explains, "Judah and Simeon campaigned together early in the settlement period (Judges 1:3, 17). Therefore, the poem seems to reflect the fact that Simeon had little independent status."[7]

Reuben: Muted Blessing (33:6)

The blessing to Reuben is somewhat muted by a qualification: "Let Reuben live, and not die, but let his men be few" (33:6). This is in line with Jacob's words about Reuben in the blessing he gave before his death, in which Jacob said Reuben "shall not have preeminence because [he] went up to [his] father's bed" (Genesis 49:4). This refers to Reuben having sexual intercourse with Bilhah, Jacob's concubine (Genesis 35:22).

Is it fair for later generations to suffer for the sins of the leader of an earlier generation? Could we apply this to a church or Christian organization today? Should later generations suffer for the wrongdoing of an earlier leader? History shows that this is what has happened. God will bless individuals who are faithful to God within the group. But the group itself would suffer for the sins of the earlier leader. Of course, we know of situations where God turns around the fortunes of a group through the leadership of faithful reformers. We saw this happen recently with the Worldwide Church of God, which we regarded as a cult about thirty years ago. A later generation of leaders studied the Word and came to believe in the Trinity. There followed a painful process of jettisoning the wrong doctrines and embracing right doctrines. Not everyone agreed, so splits emerged in the movement. But in the group that stood with the reformers, orthodoxy won the day![8]

Judah: Victory in Battle (33:7)

Judah's blessing is probably connected to what Numbers 2:9 says; that tribe "was to march at the head of the army as the vanguard. In this role Judah would hold a very dangerous place in battle."[9] So Moses prays, "Hear, O LORD, the voice of Judah, and bring him in to his people" (33:7a). If this interpretation is correct, the prayer is that they be brought back safely to their people despite being in this dangerous place during the battle. Then there is a prayer for God's intervention in bringing victory against enemies: "With your hands contend for him, and be a help against his adversaries" (33:7b). There are many interpretive problems with this verse, but the general idea is that Moses is praying for victory in battle.

Applying this to our situation we would pray that those we bless will conquer the various battles they face in life—physical, intellectual, spiritual, moral, interpersonal, vocational, and social. Countless stories could be told about how deeply discouraged people ready to give up were spurred on to persevere until the battle was won after someone prayed over them.

Levi: Effective Priests (33:8–11)

As with Judah, the blessing to the tribe of Levi is connected with its unique role in the nation. Levi was the priestly tribe. These verses give a good description of who a good priest is today, too. Under the new covenant, all Christians, especially those in full-time ministry, are priests (1 Peter 2:9; Revelation 1:6). Moses first says, "Give to Levi your Thummim, and your Urim to your godly one" (Deuteronomy 33:8a). The Thummim and Urim were possibly two flat stones, used for drawing lots, in order to find the will of God after all other checks had been made and two or more possibilities were found in keeping with God's principles (see Numbers 27:21). Such devices were used only after all the homework was done to find which options were in keeping with the revealed will of God. We must first do our Word-related homework even today when we ask God for guidance.

Today this may mean that as God's priests we help people find out what is God's will for their lives. We may do this through supernatural gifts such as the gifts of discernment, knowledge, and prophecy. We will always ask God to lead us. But now, more than in the time of Deuteronomy, we have a completed canon of Scripture that is "profitable for teaching, for reproof, for correction, and for training in righteousness, that the man of God may be competent, equipped for every good work" (2 Timothy 3:16, 17). So now we generally give guidance to people by mastering the Scriptures and by knowing how to apply them to the lives of people. Therefore, we study the Word, and we work with people and develop, through practice, the skill of letting the Scriptures address the issues they face.

Next Moses describes the Levites by saying, ". . . whom you [God] tested at Massah, with whom you quarreled at the waters of Meribah" (33:8b). Exodus 17:1–7 refer to "Massah" and "Meribah" in connection with an event when the Israelites tested God and not where God tested the Levites as described in this verse. This verse may be referring to an event other than that described in Exodus 17, or it may be using Moses as the spokesman for the whole tribe of Levi who were in turn the spokesmen of God. Thus, while the people were testing God, God also was, through Moses, testing the people on this occasion. If this is the interpretation, then it accords with the next verse (Deuteronomy 33:9), which describes what happened after the golden calf incident. "Moses stood in the gate of the camp and said, 'Who is on the LORD's side? Come to me.' And all the sons of Levi gathered around him" (Exodus 32:26). The Levites carried out God's judgment upon the rebellious people, and they did so impartially, not hesitating because of things like family ties. So Moses says of them in the blessing: ". . . who said of his father and mother, 'I regard them not'; he disowned his brothers and ignored his children. For they observed your word and kept your covenant" (33:9).

God's representatives must carry through with God's justice even when people close to them are involved. This is something that is often sadly lacking today. Leaders tend to overlook the sins of their family members and not follow through with the usual thoroughgoing disciplinary procedures. This will act like a cancer in a church as sin has been overlooked, and this one compromise will lead to others. If leaders cannot act impartially when it comes to their family members, they should opt out of the process and let others handle the issue. The Levites are commended because they obeyed God even when it meant punishing family members, an action that would have hurt them deeply. The height of such commitment comes in the case of God who punished his own, perfectly innocent Son on behalf of our sins.

Verse 10 describes the role of the Levites as teachers of the Law and as leaders in the worship of the people: "They shall teach Jacob your rules and Israel your law; they shall put incense before you and whole burnt offerings on your altar." We have already discussed how important the ministry of the Word was then and is now (see the discussions on 5:31; 6:7; 17:18, 19; 31:9–13). The setting apart of a special group of people to lead in worship may have something to say to us today. Indeed, we are all priests now; therefore one does not need to belong to any class of person in order to qualify for leading worship. However, in the Old Testament the Levites were trained and equipped to lead worship. They needed to purify themselves and prepare for this task. This would say something to us about our indiscriminate assigning of people to lead worship. As this is an awesome responsibility, I believe the church should carefully screen those leading worship to ensure that they are gifted in this activity, that they are worshipful individuals in their personal lives, and that their behavior becomes one who represents God before the people and the people before God.

Verse 11 is a prayer for God's blessing to come upon the Levites: "Bless, O Lord, his substance, and accept the work of his hands; crush the loins of his adversaries, of those who hate him, that they rise not again." The ESV translation "substance" (as in NASB, NRSV; "possessions," HCSB) suggests that this is a prayer about the material needs of the Levites. We must pray for and ensure that the needs of God's servants are met. Paul highlights this need (1 Timothy 5:17, 18; see 1 Corinthians 9:6–11). Sadly, some workers exploit this teaching to make dishonest gain through the gifts of others. And other workers are exploited and made to do the Lord's work without adequate remuneration.

However, the Hebrew word translated "substance" could also mean "skills" (NIV). In this case, it would be a parallel expression to the next statement, "and accept the work of his hands." It is important that God's public representatives reflect the glory of God in the way they perform their duties. Today that would include music, preaching, reading, praying, and publishing. We must pray for excellence and effectiveness in the way God's servants carry out their duties. Few things dishonor God as much as unprepared and incompetent preaching, teaching, and worship leading. Paul often asked for prayer for his ministry (2 Corinthians 1:11; Ephesians 6:19; Colossians 4:3, 4; 2 Thessalonians 3:1). In eight of his thirteen letters, he asks his readers to pray for him. We should urge Christians to pray regularly for those who minister to them.

Paul also often asks for prayer for deliverance from enemies and other forms of opposition. After asking the Thessalonians to pray for his ministry of the Word, he writes, "and [pray] that we may be delivered from wicked and evil men" (2 Thessalonians 3:1, 2; see also Philippians 1:19). This is the topic of Moses' next blessing to the Levites: ". . . crush the loins of his adversaries, of those who hate him, that they rise not again" (Deuteronomy 33:11c). Few things hurt Christian workers as much as the experience of being abandoned by those they serve when they are under attack. This happens often because people do not like to get involved in controversy because usually it is too costly to do so. That is wrong! Those who serve God must be protected from enemies. And Moses' blessing expresses this concern using vivid language. It almost looks like Moses is talking about revenge. But what he is talking about here is justice. Wrong should be punished; and those who hurt God's servants should punished.

Benjamin: Protection in Battle (33:12)

The tribe of the youngest brother, Benjamin, has a short blessing that focuses on protection: "The beloved of the LORD dwells in safety. The High God surrounds him all day long, and dwells between his shoulders" (33:12). It is a proclamation of security: God loves Benjamin, "the beloved of the LORD," and "surrounds him all day long." The next statement can be translated as ". . . and dwells between his weapons."[10] This blessing describes the security God gives to a warrior. Jacob's blessing to Benjamin in Genesis 49:27 describes Benjamin as a warrior: "Benjamin is a ravenous wolf, in the morning devouring the prey and at evening dividing the spoil." Deborah's song after her great military triumph specifically mentioned the role of Benjamin (Judges 5:14).

Those who launch out into battle for God are the ones who experience God's security most markedly. We are in a battle for God against the forces of darkness. As we launch into dangerous exploits for God, we will experience his mighty deliverance. Some stay uninvolved on the sidelines of the battle because of security concerns—they do not experience God's security, and so their fear increases. Because of being scared to join in the battle, they remain scared about life. The decisions they make in their quest for peace results in their losing Biblical peace. In the Bible, peace is not the mere absence of conflict; it is the sense of completeness that comes from the realization that God is with us. That realization is enhanced when we experience his deliverance from dangerous situations. So battling for God enhances our experience of peace, for then we experience the truth that "the High God surrounds [us] all day long, and dwells between [our] shoulders."

Joseph: Prosperity and Military Strength (33:13–17)

Like Levi, Joseph gets a long blessing, probably in keeping with the prominent place Joseph had in the early history of Israel.[11] It is marked by lofty, lyrical language. First, Moses proclaims that Joseph will enjoy prosperity through the yield of the land.

> And of Joseph he said, "Blessed by the LORD be his land, with the choicest gifts of heaven above, and of the deep that crouches beneath, with the choicest fruits of the sun and the rich yield of the months, with the finest produce of the ancient mountains and the abundance of the everlasting hills, with the best gifts of the earth and its fullness and the favor of him who dwells in the bush. May these rest on the head of Joseph, on the pate of him who is prince among his brothers. (33:13–16)

Can we pray for such prosperity for people today? The Bible does have many such prayers, and that would suggest that we can. But prosperity theology goes wrong when it puts the emphasis too much on material prosperity and when it does not take sufficiently into account that sometimes God's choicest blessings come to us through suffering. We can pray for material prosperity with the assurance that if he does not answer as we ask, it is because he has something better in store for us.

The blessing starts by affirming that it is God who will give everything to Joseph: "Blessed by the LORD be his land . . . " (33:13a). Later God is described as the one who "dwells in the bush" (33:16). The NIV adds "burning" to bush because Moses is talking about the burning bush. This great God who rules over nature is the God who met Moses by the burning bush and unveiled his plan to liberate Israel from bondage. The use of this expression accords with the Biblical practice of looking back to the events that won our redemption, which is the basis of all that happens to us after that. When we are prosperous, surrounded by the trappings of success, we can forget our salvation from the wretched slavery to sin. So we must constantly go back to the great redeeming events that form the basis of our life; otherwise we could get blinded by our present successes and lose what is most important to us. As the old hymn puts it:

> Lest I forget Gethsemane,
> Lest I forget Thine agony,
> Lest I forget Thy love for me,
> Lead me to Calvary.[12]

Verse 16b describes the preeminence of Joseph over his brothers: "May these rest on the head of Joseph, on the pate of him who is prince among his brothers." The language is taken directly from Jacob's blessing (Genesis 49:26b) and reflects Joseph's dream (Genesis 37:5–11), the events in Egypt,[13] and the prominent place that the tribes coming from Joseph would play in Israel's history as the largest of the northern tribes. Deuteronomy 33:17 calls him "a firstborn bull" and says, "He has majesty" (some think this designation is for Ephraim and not Joseph). This is an example of how "firstborn" is used in the Bible to refer to preeminence rather than the first to be born. Groups like the Jehovah's Witnesses use the references to Jesus as "firstborn" (e.g., Colossians 1:15) to say that he was a created being. But the reference in those texts is to Jesus' preeminence.

Verse 17a refers to Joseph's military strength like that of a wild ox: "A firstborn bull—he has majesty, and his horns are the horns of a wild ox; with them he shall gore the peoples, all of them, to the ends of the earth." Then it talks of the two tribes that came from the two sons of Joseph, Ephraim and Manasseh: ". . . they are the ten thousands of Ephraim, and they are the thousands of Manasseh" (33:17b). Ephraim is the second son, but he is mentioned first and has "ten thousands" while Manasseh has "thousands." This reflects the event recorded in Genesis 48:8–20 when Jacob reversed the order and gave Ephraim the honor of the firstborn. It is interesting to note that Israel's great soldier Joshua belonged to the tribe of Ephraim (Numbers 13:8).

Zebulun and Issachar: Thanksgiving for Prosperity (33:18, 19)

Zebulun and Issachar are blessed together. First, there is a call to rejoice, which implies that they are going to be blessed: "And of Zebulun he said, 'Rejoice, Zebulun, in your going out, and Issachar, in your tents'" (33:18). The combination of "your going out" and "in your tents" is probably equivalent to what is elsewhere expressed as "go out" and "come in" (28:6). If so, this is a call to rejoice over every part of their daily life. Paul echoed this sentiment when he wrote, "Rejoice in the Lord always; again I will say, Rejoice" (Philippians 4:4).

Not only will they rejoice personally, but the blessing goes on to say that they will have services of thanksgiving for their prosperity and will invite Israelites from other tribes ("peoples") to join them in these. Deuteronomy 19 says, "They shall call peoples to their mountain; there they offer right sacrifices; for they draw from the abundance of the seas and the hidden treasures of the sand." Here we see the obligation of those who have been blessed by God to have occasions devoted to thanksgiving and praise to God for his goodness. These thanksgiving services should not focus on boosting persons or organizations, on being public relations events. Rather, they should be times devoted to praising God along with people who can join heartily in genuine thanksgiving and praise.

Gad: Warrior who Helped in His Brothers' Battles (33:20, 21)

The blessing to Gad begins with a blessing either to Gad or to the persons who help Gad prosper: "Blessed be he who enlarges Gad!" (33:20a). Then Gad is presented as a warrior: "Gad crouches like a lion; he tears off arm and scalp" (33:20b). Next, there is a reference to the land allotted to Gad: "He chose the best of the land for himself, for there a commander's portion was reserved" (33:21a). This land was east of Jordan and therefore already occupied. Moses commends them for participating in the conquest for the land west of Jordan for their brothers though they were secure in their own land: ". . . and he came with the heads of the people, with Israel he executed the justice of the LORD, and his judgments for Israel" (33:21b). The conquest is described as an executing of the "justice" and "judgments" of the Lord. It seems that Gad is given a special portion of land known as "a commander's portion" (33:21a) for participating with distinction in this battle.

The people of Gad are commended for risking their own security by joining in the battle of their brothers. Some people, once they have found a secure position, remain there without helping others who have needs like they once had. For example, in Sri Lanka housing is a serious problem for many. House rents in the city are exorbitant, and many cannot afford them. Should not one who has his own house do all he can to see that others in his fellowship also get such houses? Christians never know security in terms of a quiet life separated from the pain of people. Our security in Christ gives us the boldness to risk helping others who are in need. A man is reported to have prayed the following prayer:

> God bless me, my wife Mary; our son John, and his wife Jane.
> Us four and no more forever more. Amen.

That is not the Christian attitude!

Dan: Future Potential (33:22)

The blessing for Dan, like that for Reuben, is very short: "Dan is a lion's cub that leaps from Bashan." Being "a lion's cub" points to future potential. Though they may look timid when cubs, lions grow to be very strong. The next expression, which the ESV translates as "leaps from Bashan," is difficult to understand. It may mean ". . . shies away from the viper" (see Craigie, Kalland, et al.). If that is correct, then it means that now it may be too timid to face a viper, but that will not be so when it is full-grown.

Good leaders pray and act with a focus on the hope they have for the potential of the people they lead. Paul told Timothy, "This charge I entrust to you, Timothy, my child, in accordance with the prophecies previously made about you, that by them you may wage the good warfare" (1 Timothy 1:18). Prophecies made about Timothy became the base of Paul's ambitions for Timothy, and he charged him with a view to helping him achieve those heights. May we learn to look at people with the eyes of hope, just like Jesus looked at Peter, the one who seemed so unstable, and saw one who would be like a rock. He told him, "'You are Simon the son of John. You shall be called Cephas' (which means Peter [rock])" (John 1:42). Good leaders pray for a vision of the potential that lies behind those they lead. That potential becomes a personal ambition that drives them in the way they lead those people.

Naphtali: Blessed to Possess (33:23)

Naphtali is given a blessing described in terms of possessing land. "O Naphtali, sated with favor, and full of the blessing of the LORD, possess the lake and the south." "Lake" could also be translated "west." The exact meanings are not clear. What is clear is that Naphtali will possess land. This is the aim of all the tribes other than the tribes east of the Jordan that had already possessed their lands.

Asher: Fertility and Security (33:24, 25)

Asher's blessing has four parts. The first and the last are new, and the middle two have already figured in other blessings. First, Moses says, "Most blessed of sons be Asher; let him be the favorite of his brothers" (33:24a). I suppose being a favorite among brothers would not cause the problems that Jacob, the father of these tribes, caused by favoring some of his children. This is affection willingly given by brothers, whereas the former favorite affection by the father caused the brothers to be angry with Joseph. Second, there is a wish for fertility of the land that belonged to Asher: ". . . and let him dip his foot in oil" (33:24b). The oil is from the olive trees that were found in upper Galilee where Asher would settle. "The picture of bathing feet in oil is one of extravagance, betokening great prosperity."[14] The third blessing is for security from enemies through strong fortifications: "Your bars [metal door-bolts[15]] shall be iron and bronze" (33:25a).

The fourth blessing is, ". . . and as your days, so shall your strength be" (33:25b). Can we say this today to all faithful people? How about faithful servants of God who spend their last few years in bed paralyzed by a stroke or who are mentally blank because of Alzheimer's disease? These are exceptions to the normal rule, permitted by God in order to achieve a higher end that we may not see at once. Such a perspective on physical debilitation enables those who are sick and those caring for the sick to remain joyful because they know that God is fulfilling some presently unseen purpose through their suffering. Wiersbe's comment on this verse helps us include those exceptions. He says, ". . . the Lord would give them daily strength to accomplish their work." We are reminded of the words of Jesus regarding Peter's last days: "Truly, truly, I say to you, when you were young, you used to dress yourself and walk wherever you wanted, but when you are old, you will stretch out your hands, and another will dress you and carry you where you do not want to go" (John 21:18). That seems to be a sad end for a heroic servant of God. But John's comment on this was, "This he said to show by what kind of death he was to glorify God" (John 21:19).

This brings to an end Moses' career as the leader of the people. Deuteronomy 33:26–29 is a part of the blessing, but it is not directly related to the individual blessings on the tribes. It is a song praising God, to whom Moses is entrusting the people. Therefore, I will discuss it in the next exposition describing the death of Moses. How beautifully Moses ends his career as a leader. First, he hands over to his leadership to Joshua and, without wasting time on tributes to his leadership, gets the leaders together and exhorts them about how to teach the Word to the people (Deuteronomy 31). Second, he teaches them a song that would become like a pop song and help the people to be obedient to God and return to God when they are suffering the consequences of disobedience (Deuteronomy 32). Third, he gives a blessing to each of the tribes of Israel (Deuteronomy 33).

Here we see the three primary passions of a great leader: first, to equip the next level of leaders; second, to hammer home the importance of obedience to God; and third, to yearn for God to bless the people, to have ambitions of seeing them become great people. The job descriptions of the people can be included in these three passions. That, however, is not what is primary. Great leaders yearn for the people they lead to become great, and they do all they can to enable this. They define greatness as obedience to God and receiving God's blessings. In the process, because the people are motivated to serve God, a lot of work is also accomplished!

Once he has finished all his work, Moses indulges himself in an ecstatic song of praise to the God who made it all possible (33:26–29)! We will look further into that in our next study.

62

Moses' Last Outburst of Praise

DEUTERONOMY 33:26–29

THE LAST WORDS a person says before dying are very significant, especially if the person was mentally alert during those last moments on earth. I have a book by Herbert Lockyer entitled *Last Words of Saints and Sinners*, which demonstrates the difference that hoping in Christ makes on the way one dies.[1] We see such hope in the last recorded words of Moses. He has finished pronouncing his blessings on the people. Now he can indulge in an extravagant expression of praise to God and of his confidence that God will look after the nation of Israel. The fact that he is not permitted to enter the land is not going to cloud his meditation on the goodness of God. There is a lesson here for those who die without fulfilling all the earthly dreams they had. Those dreams pale into insignificance in the light of God's goodness. We can all end our lives praising God!

The Majestic Helper of an Upright Nation (33:26)

Moses' song of praise is addressed to Israel, which is called "Jeshurun," meaning "upright one." Earlier this same name was used in a sarcastic manner of a rebellious nation (32:15). Now it is used positively. But perhaps there is a hint of exhortation to Israel, telling them that the uniqueness of God described here is available only to an upright nation. The Bible moves much more comfortably than we do from the importance of holiness among the people to praise for God. Times of praise today are sometimes so silent about holiness that some have suggested that praise is like an opiate that gives people an emotional high without challenging them to live transformed lives. The Bible talks about praise to a holy God who requires holiness of those who worship him. David said, "Who shall ascend the hill of the LORD? And who shall stand in his holy place? He who has clean hands and a pure heart, who does not lift up his soul to what is false and does not swear deceitfully" (Psalm 24:3, 4).

The upright nation is told that God is unique. "There is none like God, O Jeshurun." This uniqueness is because God "rides through the heavens to your help, through the skies in his majesty" (Deuteronomy 33:26). "The figure of deity riding on a chariot through the heavens is an ancient Near Eastern motif known to the Canaanites, but occurring also in the Old Testament (Psalms 18:10; 68:33; Isaiah 19:1; Ezekiel 1)."[2] The Canaanites would have sung that Baal rode in triumph through the heavens. But they were wrong. The God of the Israelites is unique—Baal or any other God cannot be compared with him. Victory belongs to God. I write this a few hours after hearing of a major triumph of some corrupt and lawless forces in our land. My reaction was to despair and be angry. But the forces of evil that seem to be so strong cannot be compared to the God who is with us if we are upright. At the moment those who live strictly according to the principles of the Bible may look like fools, and the temptation to compromise our principles is great. But to do so would be to reject the Lord of the universe who is incomparable for a lesser deity that is destined for destruction. What folly that would be!

The Eternal God Who Is Refuge and Sustainer (33:27)

Though God is unique, it sometimes looks like the wicked are so much in control that they can adopt an attitude of arrogant disdain toward the righteous. That picture is deceptive. Isaiah 48:22 says, "'There is no peace,' says the LORD, 'for the wicked.'" On the other hand, Psalm 119:165 affirms, "Great peace have those who love your law." How can they have such peace even while evil forces raise their ugly heads? The next verse in Moses' song of praise answers that: "The eternal God is your dwelling place, and underneath are the everlasting arms" (Deuteronomy 33:27a). The background of this verse is that God drove out Israel's enemies. Verse 27 goes on to say, "And he thrust out the enemy before you and said, 'Destroy.'" The God who protects the righteous is the one who will chase away their enemies. He rides through the storm, and he also becomes a secure refuge.

There is a word here to our mobile generation in which people's moving from place to place results in their losing the security of an unchanging environment in which to grow and a group of acquaintances in whom they can trust. Our dwelling-place is the eternal God! Homes, jobs, schools, friends, and circumstances may change, but we live in God, and he does not change. Homes for the elderly were dreary places some generations ago. At one such facility a visitor went up to an old and feeble man who was seated and bent in two. He told him, "I am sorry to see you living in the workhouse." The old man slowly raised himself and said, "I don't live in the workhouse. I live in God."[3]

Our problem is that though we may mentally accept this idea, we do not believe that in our heart. We lose our peace and behave as if God is not with us. What a contrast God's peace is to the sources of security people go to when they lose their trust in God. About 200 years ago, Adam Clarke wrote about this verse, "He who was of *old*. Not like the gods which were *lately* come up. He who ever was and ever will be; and He who *was, is,* and *will be* unchangeably holy, wise, just, and merciful." Great joy and security come from contemplating the majesty of God's eternity. And how wonderful it is to know that this majesty is directed toward us!

Moses also says, ". . . and underneath are the everlasting arms" (33:27a). Hall points out that "usually, references to God's arm in Deuteronomy are about his powerful ability to rescue Israel from Egypt (4:34; 5:15; 7:19; 26:8 . . .). However, here it refers to God's eternal care and protection." The Hebrew word is usually used metaphorically, as here, to refer to strength, power.[4] Earlier this verse described God as being "eternal." That Hebrew word has more the idea of ancient, referring to the God who has shown himself in history. Now God's arms are described as "everlasting." This word has more the idea of "forever." This verse then is telling us, first, that the God who has proved himself in history is our refuge. When we go to him, we do not simply wait passively in this place of refuge. Second, this verse tells us that underneath us and sustaining us are the strong arms of God that will hold us forever. Sometimes we run to our refuge so battered and bruised that we feel that we do not have the strength even to stand. But as John Wesley explains, having the everlasting arms under us means that we have "the almighty power of God, which protects and comforts all that trust in him, in their greatest straits and distresses."

John Paton (1824–1907) left a comfortable life in Scotland with his young wife in 1858 for the New Hebrides Islands (now called Vanuatu). There his faith was severely tested as he faced a people whose behavior did not seem to be even remotely close to accepted norms in the West. He wondered whether he had made the right decision to give "up [his] much beloved work and dear people in Glasgow, with so many delightful associations to consecrate [his] life to these . . . people." Three months after arriving, his wife and baby died, and he had to dig with his own hands the lonely grave where he buried them. He says, "I was stunned: My reason seemed almost to give way." But, he says, "I was never altogether forsaken. The ever-merciful

Lord sustained me to lay the precious dust of my loved ones in the same quiet grave. But for Jesus, and the fellowship he vouchsafed me there, I must have gone mad and died beside that lonely grave."[5] Strengthened by God, Paton stayed on there several years. He took a few years' break for raising support and people for this mission. Following his return in 1866, he saw most of the islanders turn to Christ.

Israel's Security and Prosperity (33:28)

With the majestic and eternal God as helper, refuge, and sustainer, Moses can anticipate Israel's security and prosperity and present it as if it has already happened. The first part of verse 28 speaks of security: "So Israel lived in safety, Jacob lived alone [untroubled, HCSB]." The second part of verse 28 speaks of prosperity: ". . . in a land of grain and wine, whose heavens drop down dew." Because God is with them, they can be sure of both security and prosperity.

This promise is given to the nation of Israel. Does it apply to faithful Christians today living in desert lands that cannot yield the harvests envisaged in this verse? How about a Christian languishing in a brutal prison for preaching the gospel? In this post-New Testament era, we know that God's path to prosperity may include enduring the cup of suffering. I was at a meeting in Sri Lanka where the well-known international Christian leader Brother Andrew fielded questions after speaking. Someone asked him what he thought about prosperity theology. His answer was that this theology does not fare well in countries where Christians are being persecuted.

Does God not prosper the faithful today? The book of Revelation presents the greatest prosperity that one could imagine in its description of the new heaven and the new earth. The faithful in Old Testament times knew little or nothing about these future glories. A special place is described in Revelation for the glorious rewards reserved for martyrs. Jesus told the suffering Christians of Smyrna, "Be faithful unto death, and I will give you the crown of life" (Revelation 2:10). "In Revelation martyrdom is seen as a victory over Satan, not a defeat."[6] As Revelation 12:11 puts it, "And they have conquered him by the blood of the Lamb and by the word of their testimony, for they loved not their lives even unto death." So our applications of the idea of God prospering us may differ from those in Moses' time. But we have the same basic faith in God that believes he will give us what is best for us. That best may involve martyrdom. The security God gives may include battling Satan's forces and dying. But even the dying is a victory.

The Joy of a Saved People (33:29)

After describing all that God would do to them, Moses gives the natural human response to his actions. Verse 29a says, "Happy are you, O Israel! Who is like you, a people saved by the LORD." The word translated "happy" here (ESV, HCSB, NRSV) is translated as "blessed" in most other English translations (NJB, NIV, NLT, NASB). Happiness is the natural response to being blessed; so the one term came to mean both in the Hebrew. The *Hebrew-English Lexicon* defines it as "blessed!, happy!, a heightened state of happiness and joy, implying very favorable circumstances, often resulting from the kind acts of God." Moses says this blessing of God makes the Israelites a unique people: "Who is like you, a people saved by the LORD." In this world where costly commitment is getting rarer and rarer, people face insecurity as they do not know who will stand up for them when they are in need if there is nothing to gain in helping them. The Israelites have no such fear, for "the eternal God is [their] dwelling place" (33:27), and that makes them unique in the world.

Moses is pointing to the great acts of God in the recent history of the Israelites, which includes the deliverance from Egypt, the miraculous provision in the wilderness, and the upcoming conquest of the land of Canaan. These acts give joy and the confidence of future protection. Today we would call this the joy of salvation. As Psalm 20:5 puts it, "May we shout for joy over your salvation, and in the name of our God set up our banners!" This is the joy of having been shown costly love. The day before I left Sri Lanka for what became a four-and-a-half-year period for my studies in the United States, a friend of mine made a four-hour journey by bus from the theological college where he was studying, said good-bye to me, prayed with me, and took the bus back to his college the same day. When I remember this, almost forty years later, joy wells up in my heart. Costly commitment elicits joy in the beneficiary.

Just as the Israelites remembered pivotal events in history that filled them with joy over salvation, Christians, too, must focus on those pivotal events on which our joy and our hope are founded. Most new converts to Christ were initially attracted because Jesus met a felt need—such as the need for healing, financial help, direction in life, and success in a career. There is no guarantee that such blessings will be specifically given to us by God. Sometimes his blessings come through hardship in the very area where God's intervention resulted in our turning to God. I know of a national cricketer who came to Christ through the healing of an injury but had to give up cricket several years later (after a superb career of representing Sri Lanka) because of an injury that did not heal. Fortunately, his faith was strong enough to help him weather that storm. I know others who ended up disillusioned with God when such prayers did not yield the desired results.

The most important events bringing joy to the Christian are the events that resulted in our salvation: the work of Christ through which we received forgiveness of sins and eternal life, through which we were transformed from Hell-bent sinners to Heaven-bound saints. Admittedly, because these blessings do not have the immediacy of miracles such as healing and the provision of urgent physical needs, the joy that results from salvation may not be as ecstatic as the joy from the meeting of immediate needs. But it is deep and abiding. It can become ecstatic if we begin to meditate on the glory of salvation and the God who saves us. There is a danger that we may let the ecstasy resulting from the meeting of immediate needs overshadow the deep joy of salvation. Sadly, the meeting of immediate needs is more attractive to people than the gift of eternal salvation. This can result in churches making a marketing decision to give more prominence to less important things.

The result of this neglect of eternal salvation will be a people who are insecure and ill-equipped to face the storms of life. They would not have the confidence that Moses expressed in the last two statements of this blessing. First, he described God as "the shield of your help, and the sword of your triumph!" (33:29b). As our defender he is like a "shield" to help us ward off the darts of the enemy who attacks us. At other times he acts in offense as a "sword" that destroys obstacles along the path to "triumph." This is comprehensive protection and assistance. Second, he says, "Your enemies shall come fawning to you, and you shall tread upon their backs" (33:29c). The NLT gives the sense of this more graphically: "Your enemies will cringe before you, and you will stomp on their backs!"

Our enemies are powerful and fearsome. How can we be sure of victory, as Moses was here? Moses was sure because of the great events of Israel's deliverance: exodus, provision, and conquest. We are sure because of the great events of our salvation: the work of Christ and our own experience of the salvation it brings. As Romans 8:32 says, "He who did not spare his own Son but gave him up for us all, how will he not also with him graciously give us all things?" Everything we need will be given to us. If we think that God has not given us something that we need, we trust his wisdom. The wisdom of the almighty God who loves us so dearly can surely be trusted to do what is best for us.

What a Wonderful Way to Die!

Moses had faced so much pain in his life. People had failed him often. His action of defending an Israelite resulted in a hostile word from another

Israelite that led him to flee Egypt and stay away for forty years. During the next forty years, he led a rebellious people who kept grumbling despite many spectacular expressions of God's concern for them. His own brother and sister rebelled against him. For much of his life as a leader the people acted as if they were ungrateful for his amazingly skillful and devoted leadership. Now as he is ready to die he is painfully aware that someone else will lead the people into the promised land because of his rash reaction to the rebellious behavior of the people. Moses has many things about which he could be bitter. But those things are now all forgotten. He is extravagant in his choice of words as he praises God.

St. Francis of Assisi (c. 1181–1226) has a beautiful verse about death in his immortal hymn, "All Creatures of Our God and King:"

> And thou, most kind and gentle death,
> Waiting to hush our latest breath;
> O praise Him! Alleluia!
> Thou leadest home the child of God
> And Christ our Lord the way hath trod.
> O praise Him! O praise Him!
> Alleluia! Alleluia! Alleluia!

Not only can we die well, we can die with a song of praise on our lips! Indeed, some faithful Christians may sometimes be upset at the time of death as they suffer from severe pain or concern for the ones they are leaving behind. We should not condemn them. God understands how extreme situations can trigger a temporary loss of peace even among the godly. We do not need to doubt that now they are resting with their Lord in the joyful security of Heaven. But these exceptions to the rule do not take away from the fact that Christians can joyfully praise God in the face of death. William Barclay says, "The thing which amazed the heathen in the centuries of persecution was that the martyrs did not die grimly, they died singing. One smiled in the flames; they asked him what he found to smile at there. 'I saw the glory of God,' he said, 'and was glad.'"[7]

63

The Death of a Great Leader

DEUTERONOMY 34:1–12

CHAPTERS 29—33 OF DEUTERONOMY have been devoted to the way Moses prepared for his death. Chapter 34 describes his death.

Preparing Comprehensively for Death (29:1—33:29)

The past few expositions have shown the way Moses prepared for his death. Chapters 29, 30 record Moses' exhortation to the people he led to be faithful to the covenant. Chapter 31 tells us how Moses' successor was selected. Chapter 32 is a song that the people are to remember that will help them along the path of obedience to God. Chapter 33 is a blessing to the people that concludes with a final outburst of praise. Now he is ready to die. This reminds us of the way Jesus also prepared his disciples fully for his crucifixion. Do we prepare for our death in this way?

There is a natural hesitancy among people to talk about their impending deaths. Sometimes family members have to go through a lot of inconvenience because a family member who died had not prepared for death. Perhaps the person did not write a last will, and a lot of confusion and legal proceedings go into trying to divide the wealth of that person. Family members are hesitant to talk about a will for fear that the dying person might get upset and accuse the people of being more interested in his or her wealth than in his or her health. Some who have hidden their ill-gotten gains in secret bank accounts die suddenly, and no one knows where the money is hidden. Actually, the family of the dead person is fortunate not to know this because there is no real gain from ill-gotten wealth.

Some Christians avoid facing up to the issues concerning their death because they say they must not think negative thoughts. However, for Christians, dealing with death is not a negative matter. Moses knew so much less about the afterlife than we do today, but he was not afraid of death. That is because he had walked with God for a long time, and he was still in a good relationship with God. As a gospel chorus puts it, "With Christ in the vessel, I'll smile at the storm." A famous evangelist who gave up the faith and went on to speak and write things against the gospel was asked about Jesus Christ shortly before his death. His answer was, "I miss him."

Not only do we have Jesus with us, we also know the glory of Heaven that awaits us, something only hinted at in the Old Testament. Dietrich Bonhoeffer, who was killed by the Nazis for his opposition to their program, wrote from prison, "Death is the supreme festival on the road to freedom."[1] People with such faith do not need to fear death. They can prepare for it, so that those who remain will not be inconvenienced but will be inspired to follow in their path of devotion to God. If you are past middle age, perhaps it is time to write your last will and testament!

The Faithful Are Satisfied with Firstfruits (34:1–4)

God had promised Moses that though he would not enter the land, he would see it before he dies (32:52). Now that time has come. He does not rebel against his fate of only seeing without entering. He follows God's instructions and climbs Mount Nebo. "Then Moses went up from the plains of Moab to Mount Nebo, to the top of Pisgah, which is opposite Jericho" (34:1a). The highest peak of the mountain range was Pisgah. There he is given a glimpse of the promised land. "And the LORD showed him all the land, Gilead as far as Dan, all Naphtali, the land of Ephraim and Manasseh, all the land of Judah as far as the western sea, the Negeb, and the Plain, that is, the Valley of Jericho the city of palm trees, as far as Zoar" (34:1b–3). After bringing him to the mountaintop, "the LORD said to him, 'This is the land of which I swore to Abraham, to Isaac, and to Jacob, "I will give it to your offspring." I have let you see it with your eyes, but you shall not go over there'" (34:4).

It would probably not have been possible for Moses to see the full extent of the land from the point where he was. But as J. A. Thompson explains, it could be that "the portion that was visible symbolized the whole." As Telford Work explains, God "must be showing him a vision perceptible only with the eyes of hope." Work explains that it was necessary for him to go up to the mountain "because hope sees through the visible to the invisible. It is not blind faith or obvious inference but insight grounded in experience." Moses had walked with God for several decades; he knew that God would keep his word to give Israel the full land, though God had told him that he himself would not enter the land. However, the faithful God lets him see enough of the land, a significantly vast extent, to enable him to, in a sense, experience the whole.

This whole episode is an illustration of the Biblical principle of first-fruits. In Romans 8:18–23 Paul explains that in this life we groan as we live in a world that has been subjected to frustration. But that groaning is like the groanings of one with the pains of childbirth, for we know what is coming. Paul says, ". . . but we ourselves, who have the firstfruits of the Spirit, groan inwardly as we wait eagerly for adoption as sons, the redemption of our bodies" (v. 23). We have a foretaste of the glory to come through experiencing the firstfruits—the Holy Spirit. That is a guarantee of the coming harvest. Paul also said, "For while we are still in this tent, we groan, being burdened—not that we would be unclothed, but that we would be further clothed, so that what is mortal may be swallowed up by life. He who has prepared us for this very thing is God, who has given us the Spirit as a guarantee" (2 Corinthians 5:4, 5). For us, who live in the era of the Spirit, what is true for Moses in this one episode is true every day, for we have the Spirit abiding in us.

What if Moses had disobeyed and refused to go up to the mountaintop? Many Christians would do something like that if they have not been granted a personal request. If Moses had done this, he would have missed the glorious vision that the faithful who hope in God receive. For the faithful, life is always meaningful, whether or not our requests have been granted. Amidst deep frustration, they see glory through the eyes of hope, and they have joy and peace. Paul said, "May the God of hope fill you with all joy and peace in believing, so that by the power of the Holy Spirit you may abound in hope" (Romans 15:13). The disbelieving do not know this joy and peace. By refusing to believe, they forfeit the experience of abounding in hope. Life becomes dreary as they focus on what they do not have rather than on what they already have through the Holy Spirit and what they will have in glory.

An old man lay dying in bed when his doctor visited him and examined him. He whispered something to the person who was looking after him before leaving. The ill man asked what he had said. The man told him that the doctor said he had only a few minutes left to live. The old man said, "Then quick, get me on my knees, so I can spend my last moments praying for the salvation of the world." He had a passion for God's program for the world that did not leave him even when he came to the last moments of his life. These are the blessings of walking in obedience to God.

After leading his people for forty years as they journeyed to the promised land, Moses did not have the joy of seeing the people enter the land. However, he had the confidence of knowing that he was serving the God of history who will culminate history in his way and time. When we live with the perspective of being servants of an eternal God, we see all our work as part of a process that will climax in the eternal triumph of the Lord Jesus Christ. We may not achieve many of our personal goals in life. But we do our best and know that Jesus will conquer in the end. We die happily, knowing that we followed the greatest leader and were involved in the greatest cause.

I have a dream that my country will see a real revival someday. I am speaking of a spiritual awakening where the church is purified and the holy fire that results will bring many lost people into the kingdom. I have entertained this dream of revival for about thirty-five years, ever since I audited a course at Fuller Seminary on spiritual awakenings by the great historian of revival, J. Edwin Orr. During that time I got a chance to talk to Dr. Orr. When I told him that I was from Sri Lanka, he told me that Sri Lanka was one of the few nations in the world in whose history there is no record of major spiritual awakening. I decided to pray for such a revival in Sri Lanka, and I hope that this will happen during my lifetime. At different times I saw what looked like mercy drops. But I have not seen the showers for which I have pleaded to God.

Early in this pilgrimage of prayer for revival, I read in a book by Dr. Orr in which he said that before major revivals there is usually faithful Bible teaching over an extended time.[2] I decided that is what I will try to do for my nation: to teach the Bible to our people. I have been praying for thirty-five years, and I have not yet seen the hoped-for revival. But I will keep praying and teaching the Bible to our people. I might not see revival in Sri Lanka in my lifetime; but if I am faithful to the end, I can die with joy, for I will have done my part in the progress of the eternal kingdom. I even may have been a small instrument in a revival that may come after I die.

What an exciting way this is to live! We know that we are serving the eternal God who has a glorious plan for the world. And we know that he is slowly but surely working out that plan and that our feeble efforts at service will contribute to fulfilling it.

A Godly but Very Human Leader Dies (34:5–8)

The Servant of the Lord (34:5)

Verse 5 says, "So Moses the servant of the LORD died there in the land of Moab, according to the word of the LORD." Other Biblical figures have also been called God's servant. Yet Moses is the one who is called this most often. I counted thirty-nine references to Moses as God's servant. Clearly this frequency is significant. God's response, when Miriam and Aaron rebelled against Moses, shows something of the significance of this title. In Numbers 12:6–8a God says, "Hear my words: If there is a prophet among you, I the LORD make myself known to him in a vision; I speak with him in a dream. Not so with my servant Moses. He is faithful in all my house. With him I speak mouth to mouth. . . ." The key here is faithfulness, which enabled God to give Moses the blessing of intimate conversation. Often in this book we have said that Moses was one of the greatest (if not the greatest) national leaders in history. But the Biblical writers saw his servanthood as the key feature of his life. Numbers 12:7 defines servanthood as being "faithful."

Faithful Christians do what God asks them to do. They do not give up halfway because there are problems. Whatever the problems, they somehow complete the task assigned to them. Florence Nightingale (1820–1910) has been credited with founding the modern nursing profession. Toward the end of her career, she was asked her life's secret. "Well, I can only give one explanation. That is, I have kept nothing back from God." She did not claim to be highly gifted. Once she said, "If I could give you information of my life, it would be to show how a woman of very ordinary ability has been led by God in strange and unaccustomed paths. . . . God has done all, and I nothing." The key was not her ability but her availability to God. At the age of thirty she wrote in her diary, "I am thirty years of age, the age at which Christ began His mission. Now no more childish things, no more vain things. Now, Lord, let me think only of Thy will."[3] Commitment to do God's will and persevering in doing it are the keys to being a servant of God.

A Servant with Human Frailty (34:5b)

Once again we are given the reason for Moses' dying before the conquest. Verse 5 says, "Moses . . . died there in the land of Moab, according to the word of the LORD." Deuteronomy will not let us forget that this great, great leader was a man with human frailties. The sin itself seems to be minor and not deserving of such punishment. But when leaders sin, it is more serious than when others sin. James 3:1 says, "Not many of you should become teachers, my brothers, for you know that we who teach will be judged with greater strictness." Then James says, "For we all stumble in many ways" (v. 2). We are all fallible people. We all can fail, and if we are leaders, the chastisement for it may be severe. To our eyes, this might seem unreasonably severe. Yet, when we think of Moses, what comes to our minds are not his failings but his faithfulness to God and his massive legacy.

Sometimes I wonder whether the reason why I may not see revival in Sri Lanka in my lifetime is my many failings as a Christian and as a leader.

Yet I can thank God that his grace is greater than my sin (Romans 5:20). The eternal God, who in Christ has offered an eternal sacrifice (Hebrews 13:20), will ensure that in eternity what is remembered about his servants are not the ravages of sin but the marvels of God's grace to them. Though faltering often along the way, they sought, in their weakness, to follow their Master, and they will have the thrill of hearing their Master say, "Well done, good and faithful servant. You have been faithful over a little; I will set you over much. Enter into the joy of your master" (Matthew 25:23).

But always all the glory will go to God. Paul was clear that our weakness serves to magnify the name of God. He says, "But we have this treasure in jars of clay, to show that the surpassing power belongs to God and not to us" (2 Corinthians 4:7). I have in these past few chapters often referred to the greatness of Moses. Deuteronomy 34:5 is a corrective to the possibility of an overemphasis on Moses' greatness. As Chris Wright points out, "For all his greatness, Moses is no more and no less the servant of the Lord." The key is that Moses served a great God!

His Burial Place Unknown (34:6, 9b)

The record of the burial of Moses is also significant: ". . . and he buried him in the valley in the land of Moab opposite Beth-peor; but no one knows the place of his burial to this day" (34:6). There has been some discussion about who the "he" is who buried Moses. The text does not make it abundantly clear. The writer/editor who inserted this last part to Deuteronomy could be saying that God buried Moses. Joshua is also mentioned in this passage often, and it could be him. The writer could even be using "he" as a collective term to refer to the people of Israel.[4]

Is it not interesting that the burial place of Moses is not known? Chris Wright points out that some later Jewish interpreters saw this as a balance to the emphasis in Deuteronomy on the closeness of Moses to God. He explains, "There is danger that one who had spent so much time face to face with God (v. 10), one who spoke for God almost interchangeably at times, one who had mediated the blessings and the judgements of God, might come to be unduly venerated." However, there is no grave that would tempt the people to have an idolatrous shrine for Moses.

I am writing this from Cairo, Egypt where the story of Moses began. We have a free day, and some of the participants of the meeting I am here for are visiting the pyramids. The ancient Egyptians made sure that there were monuments to their great kings and queens. Moses' great legacy was the Word. He had no interest in any other ongoing legacy. Then and now people speak of dynasties. Leadership is passed on to the children of leaders after they complete their term of office. While this is not necessarily wrong, it is never an important factor determining the choice of leaders. The qualifications for Christian leadership are devotion to God and the ability to lead people to follow God and his ways. If the child of a leader is most qualified, then he or she can be appointed. But Moses left no dynasty. His successor, Joshua, was not related to him. He did not even belong to Moses' tribe (Levi); he came from the tribe of Ephraim (Numbers 13:8). Yet, our passage later says, ". . . the people of Israel obeyed [Joshua] and did as the LORD had commanded Moses" (Deuteronomy 34:9b). When the people obeyed Joshua, they were actually doing as the Lord had commanded Moses. Moses' great legacy was the Word. As we have said before, that is the legacy we must seek to leave behind—not great books that we have written, not books written about us, not buildings that bear our name, but people who seek to faithfully follow God.

I believe almost everything I do in ministry—especially in studying, teaching, and preaching the Word—has been influenced by my mentor during my graduate studies, Dr. Dan Fuller. He has a brilliant mind and an amazing grasp of the Bible. I am greatly embarrassed that he is not too well known today, while I have received a measure of recognition, even though I see myself as a dwarf in the fields of Bible and theology in comparison to him. Seminary authorities sometimes questioned Dr. Fuller about why he was not writing more. This is something that seems to be required of seminary professors nowadays. He would respond that he was writing people books! One of the students he influenced is John Piper, one of the most prolific and influential writers in the church today.

The record of the end of Moses' life shows what we should have as a primary ministry aspiration: to get people into the Word and to teach them to obey the Word. Earthly monuments will be insignificant in light of the glory of eternity. In one of the few glimpses of Heaven we have in the Bible, the twenty-four elders "cast their crowns before the throne, saying, 'Worthy are you, our Lord and God, to receive glory and honor and power' . . . (Revelation 4:10b, 11). Only God is worthy of glory. The thrill of seeing our God face-to-face will be so great that we would gladly lay the rewards for our service—our heavenly crowns—at his feet. Let us not waste our precious time and energy trying to leave legacies on earth that will make people remember us.

In all we do, the only ultimate vision or primary motivation we should have is the glory of God. And if we have lived with that as a goal, we have lived well. The great composer Johann Sebastian Bach often wrote at the end of the musical scores of his compositions the initials, S.D.G., for *Soli Deo*

Gloria, meaning "To God alone, the glory." Yet he knew that he could not do this work of glorifying God in his own strength. So he would often initial his blank manuscript pages with the marking "J.J.," for *Jesu Juva*, meaning "Help me, Jesus."[5] May that be our prayer too as we spend our remaining days on earth with a passion to bring glory to God alone: "Help me, Jesus!"

Mourning for Moses (34:7, 8)

Verse 7 gives the state of Moses' health when he died: "Moses was 120 years old when he died. His eye was undimmed, and his vigor unabated." My initial personal response to this statement is, this man is twice my age and more healthy and vigorous than me! Possibly this is the fruit of a rugged life lived so much in the outdoors. More likely, it was due to divine provision!

Verse 8 says, "And the people of Israel wept for Moses in the plains of Moab thirty days. Then the days of weeping and mourning for Moses were ended." Setting aside national periods of mourning for national leaders was common in Israel. There were thirty days of mourning for Aaron also (Numbers 20:29). The mourning period for Jacob and Saul was seven days (Genesis 50:10; 1 Samuel 31:13). The Old Testament gives an important place to the practice of mourning and lamenting over death and disaster. This is carried over to the New Testament also. After Stephen died, "Devout men buried Stephen and made great lamentation over him" (Acts 8:2). When Peter went to the funeral home of Tabitha, or Dorcas, in Joppa, "all the widows stood beside him weeping and showing tunics and other garments that Dorcas made while she was with them" (Acts 9:39).

There is a danger of losing this aspect of mourning the dead as we emphasize the glory of the Christian hope of resurrection and Heaven. Indeed, we should emphasize the latter, but we should also honor and mourn for the dead whose passing away brings great sorrow to us. That would be an appropriate way to express appreciation and gratitude to the person who has died. Furthermore, the open expression of pain could go a long way toward comforting us when facing the loss of a loved one. As I have mentioned in our discussion of 14:1, we must look for ways to bring back the Biblical understanding of mourning to our funeral activities.

Joshua Carries on Moses' Work (34:9)

Next we have a brief description of Moses' successor: "And Joshua the son of Nun was full of the spirit of wisdom, for Moses had laid his hands on him" (34:9a). A "spirit of wisdom" is needed for leading well. A leader must not only know what the Word of God says but also how to apply it in life and work. That is what wisdom gives.

Here "the spirit of wisdom" in Joshua is related to Moses' laying hands on him. When people are appointed to a task by God, he anoints them with the ability to perform that task. That anointing is passed on through the laying on of hands. Laying on of hands when inducting people to new roles was a common practice both in Old Testament and New Testament times (Numbers 8:10; 27:18–23; Acts 6:6; 13:3). Timothy was told that his gift was "in [him] through the laying on of [Paul's] hands" (2 Timothy 1:6). We do not need to be superstitious about the practice of laying on hands and conclude that if people were not properly inducted by the leaders they cannot fulfill their tasks properly. God can compensate if a sincere Christian misses something needed for his or her work because of the negligence of others. Yet the Bible teaches that when leaders induct people to do a work through the laying on of hands, anointing for that work is passed on to that person. So we should do this when we appoint people to different tasks.

The second part of verse 9 describes the effectiveness of Joshua's leadership: "So the people of Israel obeyed him and did as the Lord had commanded Moses." Joshua did not create new paths for them to obey. He led them to obey the Word of God communicated through Moses. Obeying Joshua was equal to obeying the things that God had commanded his predecessor. So after the description of the covenant renewal ceremony in which Joshua led the people, it is recorded, "There was not a word of all that Moses commanded that Joshua did not read before all the assembly of Israel" (Joshua 8:35a). Joshua 11 describes the military conquests of Joshua. Five times that chapter says that Joshua did as the Lord commanded him. Four of these five occurrences mentions that Joshua actually obeyed what God had told Moses (Joshua 11:12, 15, 20, 23; cf. v. 9).

There is a craze today for novelty in the church. Theologians are not considered significant if they do not come up with something new. Indeed, those who represent the Creator God should use their creativity in leading people into action—the work of leaders, or thinking—the work of theologians. However, creativity is never an end in itself. The end is to help people follow God's ways that are given to us in the completed canon, the Bible. Would that this would be the benchmark used for the evaluation of leaders and theologians. The church would be spared so many unnecessary and damaging programs and ideas that resulted from innovation rather than obedience being the primary aim!

Moses' successor Joshua is, like Moses, considered a truly great leader. Moses was used by God to help reveal the Word to the people. Joshua was used to help the people obey it. He did not try to supersede Moses. He taught the people to follow God's teachings. Moses had mentored Joshua well.

The Uniqueness of Moses (34:10–12)

Verses 10–12 are like an epitaph for Moses. First, the writer comments on Moses' uniqueness: "And there has not arisen a prophet since in Israel like Moses" (34:10a). Two reasons are given for his uniqueness. First, he was one "whom the LORD knew face to face" (34:10b). Others could not stand the sight of God, but Moses could. In fact, when Moses came from meeting God he had to wear a veil, because the people could not bear the sight of God's glory that he reflected (Exodus 34:33–35). Our text does not say that Moses knew God face-to-face, though, of course, that is implied. Rather it says that God "knew Moses face to face." In Numbers 12:8, while defending Moses before Miriam and Aaron, God proclaimed that Moses was unique among God's servants: "With him I speak mouth to mouth. . . ." Clearly, Moses had such an intimate relationship with God that God would openly speak to him. Thus, it is not surprising that such a large chunk of the Bible should come through him. The Pentateuch leads us to God's mind because it was written by a person who was close to God's mind.

The Bible is now complete, and we will not be agents of God's revelation in the way that Moses was. Now that we have the Bible, we need to be spending extended time with it because that is the primary way God speaks to us today. As an old hymn puts it:

Break Thou the bread of life,
Dear Lord, to me,
As Thou didst break the loaves
Beside the sea;
Beyond the sacred page
I seek Thee, Lord;
My spirit pants for Thee,
O living Word![6]

Moses sometimes worked too hard. So his father-in-law led him to delegate some of his duties to others (Exodus 18:13–26). Even after delegating his responsibilities, he was the leader of a large nation. Yet he would go and spend extended times alone with God. Twice he spent forty days alone with God (Exodus 24:18; 34:28). As he represented God before the people, he needed to remain close to God in order to know God's mind. That is necessary for all leaders. That is why the first structural change in the early church was to bring in a group of people to help with administrative tasks so the apostles could concentrate on prayer and the ministry of the Word (Acts 6:1–7). Anyone who wants to be a Christian leader needs to pursue intimacy with God.

Second, we are told that Moses was unique in the way God used him to express God's power through signs and wonders among the Egyptians. Deuteronomy 34:11 says there were ". . . none like him for all the signs and the wonders that the LORD sent him to do in the land of Egypt, to Pharaoh and to all his servants and to all his land." This would refer to the story of the exodus from Egypt and the plagues connected with it and to the events that took place in connection with the crossing of the Red Sea.

Third, Moses was unique because of the many powerful things that happened among the Israelites between the exodus and the death of Moses. Verse 12 says, ". . . and for all the mighty power and all the great deeds of terror that Moses did in the sight of all Israel." Other prophets also did great things and performed miracles. But they did not come close to Moses in the volume and impact of their miracles.

Can we apply these statements about signs and wonders to our understanding of Christian leadership today? Can we ask God to do the same now? In the prayer of the early church soon after speaking or teaching in the name of Jesus was prohibited, the believers told God ". . . while you stretch out your hand to heal, and signs and wonders are performed through the name of your holy servant Jesus" (Acts 4:30). We know that at different times God acts in miraculous ways to reveal something to his people. We can ask, but we must leave it in the hands of the sovereign God to do what he wishes with our request.

While Moses was unique in the Old Testament, he looked forward to the coming of a Prophet like him (Deuteronomy 18:15–18). The Jews had this hope during the time of Jesus, as is evidenced by the question asked of John the Baptist, "Are you the Prophet?" (John 1:21). Philip told Nathaniel, "We have found him of whom Moses in the Law and also the prophets wrote" (John 1:45). The New Testament presents Jesus as superior to Moses in every way. Hebrews 3:3 says, "For Jesus has been counted worthy of more glory than Moses—as much more glory as the builder of a house has more honor than the house itself." He, too, did great miracles. Moses only mediated the Word of God, but Jesus was the Word (John 1:1). Jesus was to go through an exodus greater than that of Moses, one to which the revelation through Moses looked forward. The next time Moses appears in the Bible is also on a mountain—the Mount of Transfiguration. There, at a crucial time in the ministry of Jesus, "Moses and Elijah . . . appeared in glory and spoke of his departure (literally, "exodus")" (Luke 9:30–31). What an honor this was for Moses! He paved the way for the Savior of the world by being the mediator through whom the Law was revealed. Then he was chosen to encourage the Savior when Jesus faced the great exodus that would bring salvation to the world.

All of this was because Moses was a servant of the Lord. God may not call us to become famously great, having a spectacular role in history like Moses did. But we can all have the key to Moses' life that was also the key to his greatness: we can be servants of God, people who are totally devoted to him.

Soli Deo gloria!

Notes

1. Ajith Fernando, *The Supremacy of Christ* (Wheaton, IL: Crossway, 1995; London: Hodder & Stoughton, 1997; Secundarabad, India: OM Books, 2005).

2. Ajith Fernando, *Sharing the Truth in Love: How to Relate to People of Other Faiths* (Grand Rapids, MI: Discovery House, 2001; Manila, Philippines: LifeChange Publishing, 2003; Mumbai, India: GLS, 2006).

3. Gordon D. Fee and Douglas S. Stuart, *How to Read the Bible Book by Book: A Guided Tour* (Grand Rapids, MI: Zondervan, 2002), pp. 56, 57.

4. Christopher J. H. Wright, *Ambassadors to the World: Declaring God's Love* (Leicester, UK: InterVarsity Press, 1998), p. 12.

5. These figures are from J. A. Thompson, *Deuteronomy: An Introduction and Commentary*, Tyndale Old Testament Commentaries (Leicester, UK and Downers Grove, IL: InterVarsity Press, 1974), p.11, Logos Bible Software (Bellingham, WA: Logos, 2002–2009), software.

6. Paul Barker, *Deuteronomy: The God Who Keeps Promises* (Brunswick East, Australia: Acorn Press, 1998), p. 1.

7. Ibid., p. 3.

Chapter One: Deuteronomy: Highly Relevant History

1. See also Matthew 19:7, 8; Mark 10:3–5; 12:19; John 5:46, 47; Acts 3:22; 7:37, 38; Romans 10:19. See Earl Kalland, "Deuteronomy," in *The Expositor's Bible Commentary*, ed. Frank E. Gaebelein (Grand Rapids, MI: Zondervan, 1992), Zondervan Interactive (Grand Rapids, MI: Zondervan, 2007), Pradis 6.0 software.

2. J. G. McConville, "Deuteronomy," in *New Bible Commentary: 21ˢᵗ Century Edition*, ed. G. J. Weham, J. A. Motyer, D. A. Carson, and R. T. France (Leicester, UK and Downers Grove, IL: IVP Academic, 1994), Logos Library System, The Essential IVP Reference Collection (Bellingham, WA: Logos, 1985–2002), software.

3. K. A. Kitchen, *On the Reliability of the Old Testament* (Cambridge, UK and Grand Rapids, MI: Eerdmans, 2003), p. 285.

4. Ibid., p. 287.

5. Ibid., p. 288.

6. For a refreshing study of the Pentateuch using an avowedly canonical approach by one who thinks that the historical accuracy of the statements made is important, see John H. Sailhamer, *The Pentateuch as Narrative: A Biblical Theological Commentary* (Grand Rapids, MI: Zondervan, 1992).

7. See S. Wesley Ariarajah, *The Bible and People of Other Faiths* (Geneva: World Council of Churches, 1985).

8. For studies on the Old Testament, see Kitchen, *On the Reliability of the Old Testament*; and Walter C. Kaiser Jr., *The Old Testament Documents: Are They Reliable and Relevant?* (Leicester, UK and Downers Grove, IL: InterVarsity Press, 2001). For studies on the New Testament see Craig L. Blomberg, *The Historical*

Reliability of the Gospels (Leicester, UK and Downers Grove, IL: InterVarsity Press, 1987); F. F. Bruce, *The New Testament Documents: Are They Reliable?* (Leicester, UK and Downers Grove, IL: InterVarsity Press, 1960); and Paul Barnett, *Is the New Testament History?* (London: Hodder & Stoughton, 1986).

9. Eugene Merrill, *Deuteronomy,* The New American Commentary, vol. 4 (Nashville, TN: B&H, 1994), WORDsearch 7.0 (Austin, TX: WORDsearch, 2005), software.

Chapter Two: Keys to Launching out into Fresh Exploits

1. Numbers 21:34; Joshua 2:10; 9:10; 12:2–5; 13:10–12, 21; Judges 11:19–22; 1 Kings 4:19; Nehemiah 9:22; Psalm 135:10–12; 136:17–22.

2. Exodus 3:6, 15, 16; 4:5; 6:3, 8; 33:1; Leviticus 26:42; Numbers 32:11; Deuteronomy 1:8; 6:10; 9:5, 27; 29:13; 30:20; 34:4; 2 Kings 13:23; Matthew 22:32; Mark 12:26; Luke 20:37; Acts 3:13; 7:32.

3. The original Hebrew Bible did not have vowels and scholars have suggested different combinations of vowels for the word that appears in the original as *yhwh*.

4. Deuteronomy 1:7, 24, 40; 2:1, 3, 8; 3:1.

5. Earl Kalland, "Deuteronomy," in *The Expositor's Bible Commentary*, ed. Frank E. Gaebelein (Grand Rapids, MI: Zondervan, 1992), Zondervan Interactive (Grand Rapids, MI: Zondervan, 2007), Pradis 6.0 software.

6. Matthew 28:18–20; Mark 16:15; Luke 24:46–49; John 17:18; 20:21; Acts 1:8; 10:42.

7. *The New International Dictionary of Old Testament Theology and Exegesis,* ed. Willem A. VanGemeren (Grand Rapids, MI: Zondervan, 1997, 2002), s.v. "*Shaba*," Zondervan Interactive, (Grand Rapids, MI: Zondervan, 2007), Pradis 6.0 software.

Chapter Three: Leadership and Growth

1. *The New International Dictionary of Old Testament Theology and Exegesis,* ed. Willem A. VanGemeren (Grand Rapids, MI: Zondervan, 1997, 2002), s.v. "*Masa'*," Zondervan Interactive (Grand Rapids, MI: Zondervan, 2007), Pradis 6.0 software.

2. Peter C. Craigie, *The Book of Deuteronomy*, The New International Commentary on the Old Testament (Grand Rapids, MI: Eerdmans, 1976).

3. Eugene Merrill, *Deuteronomy,* The New American Commentary, vol. 4 (Nashville, TN: B&H, 1994), WORDsearch 7.0 (Austin, TX: WORDsearch, 2005), software.

4. From W. T. Purkiser, *The New Testament Image of the Ministry* (1974; repr., Grand Rapids, MI: Baker, 1969), p. 64.

5. *The New International Dictionary of Old Testament Theology and Exegesis,* s.v. "*Yada'*."

Chapter Four: Basic Training for Judges

1. J. G. McConville, *Deuteronomy*, Apollos Old Testament Commentary (Leicester, UK and Downers Grove, IL: InterVarsity Press, 2002).

2. *The New International Dictionary of Old Testament Theology and Exegesis,* ed. Willem A. VanGemeren (Grand Rapids, MI: Zondervan, 1997, 2002),

s.v."*Tsavah*," Zondervan Interactive (Grand Rapids, MI: Zondervan, 2007), Pradis 6.0 software.

3. *Hebrew-English Lexicon of the Old Testament*, Zondervan Interactive (Grand Rapids, MI: Zondervan, 2007), Pradis 6.0 software.

4. From A. Skevington Wood, *Captive to the Word: Martin Luther, Doctor of Sacred Scripture* (Grand Rapids, MI: Eerdmans, 1969), p. 72.

Chapter Five: Faith versus Fear

1. Deuteronomy 1:21, 29; 3:2, 22; 7:18; 20:1, 3, 8; 31:6, 8.

2. Taken from Doug McIntosh, *Deuteronomy*, Holman Old Testament Commentary 3 (Nashville, TN: B&H, 2002).

3. Taken from "The Martyrdom of Polycarp," in *The Ante-Nicene Fathers*, vol. 1, ed. Alexander Roberts and James Donaldson, pp.83–86, Ages Digital Library (Rio, WI: Ages Library, 1996, 1997), software. I did some minimal modernizing of archaic words.

4. Exodus 14:14, 25; Deuteronomy 1:30; 3:22; 20:4; Joshua 10:14; 23:3, 10; 2 Chronicles 20:29; Nehemiah 4:20; Psalm 35:1; Isaiah 42:13.

Chapter Seven: Provision in the Wilderness

1. Ronald B. Allen, "Numbers," in *The Expositor's Bible Commentary*, ed. Frank E. Gaebelein, (Grand Rapids, MI: Zondervan, 1992), Zondervan Interactive (Grand Rapids, MI: Zondervan, 2007), Pradis 6.0 software.

2. *The New International Dictionary of Old Testament Theology and Exegesis,* ed. Willem A. VanGemeren (Grand Rapids, MI: Zondervan, 1997, 2002), s.v. "*Shamar*," Zondervan Interactive (Grand Rapids, MI: Zondervan, 2007), Pradis 6.0 software.

3. Edwin Yamauchi, "Nehemiah," in *The Expositor's Bible Commentary*, ed. Frank E. Gaebelein (Grand Rapids, MI: Zondervan, 1992), Zondervan Interactive (Grand Rapids, MI: Zondervan, 2007), Pradis 6.0 software.

4. From Sherwood Eliot Wirt and Kersten Beckstrom, ed., *Living Quotations for Christians* (New York: HarperCollins, 1974), p. 266.

Chapter Eight: Doing Battle with God's Help

1. Exodus 7:13, 14, 22; 8:15, 19, 32; 9:7, 34, 35; 13:15.

2. Exodus 4:21; 7:3; 9:12; 10:1, 20, 27; 11:10; 14:4, 8, 17.

3. Cleon L. Rogers Jr. and Cleon L. Rogers III, *The New Linguistic and Exegetical Key to the Greek New Testament* (Grand Rapids, MI: Zondervan, 1998), Zondervan Interactive (Grand Rapids, MI: Zondervan, 2007), Pradis 6.0 software.

4. A. Morgan Derham, "Carey, William," in *The New International Dictionary of the Christian Church*, ed. J. D. Douglas (Grand Rapids, MI: Zondervan, 2007), Zondervan Interactive (Grand Rapids, MI: Zondervan, 2007), Pradis 6.0 software.

5. Numbers 21:28–33, 34; Deuteronomy 1:4; 3:2, 21; 29:7, 8; 31:4; Joshua 2:10; 9:10; Judges 11:19–21; Nehemiah 9:22; Psalm 135:10–12; 136:17–22.

Chapter Nine: Preparing a Community to Live Harmoniously

1. J. L. Kelso, "Wealth," in *The Zondervan Pictorial Encyclopedia of the Bible*, ed. Merrill C. Tenney (Grand Rapids, MI: Zondervan, 1975), Zondervan Interactive (Grand Rapids, MI: Zondervan, 2007), Pradis 6.0 software.

2. *Hebrew-English Lexicon of the Old Testament*, Zondervan Interactive (Grand Rapids, MI: Zondervan, 2007), Pradis 6.0 software.

3. Ibid.

4. This information is from *The New International Dictionary of Old Testament Theology and Exegesis,* ed. Willem A. VanGemeren (Grand Rapids, MI: Zondervan, 1997, 2002), s.v. *"Tsavah,"* Zondervan Interactive (Grand Rapids, MI: Zondervan, 2007), Pradis 6.0 software.

5. Taken verbatim from Raymond McHenry, *McHenry's Quips, Quotes, & Other Notes* (Peabody, MA: Hendrickson, 1999), software.

6. Taken from Warren W. Wiersbe and Lloyd M. Perry, *Wycliffe Handbook of Preaching and Preachers* (Chicago: Moody Publishing, 1984), p. 195.

Chapter Ten: Nurturing People Who Cling to God and His Word

1. Actually 4:41–43 is something like a parenthesis about the cities of refuge.

2. Raymond McHenry, *McHenry's Quips, Quotes, & Other Notes* (Peabody, MA: Hendrickson, 1999), software.

3. This story is recounted in William Mitchell Ramsay, *The Bearing of Recent Discovery on the Trustworthiness of the New Testament* (Grand Rapids, MI: Baker, 1979). Reprinted from the 1915 edition.

4. William Mitchell Ramsay, *St. Paul the Traveler and Roman Citizen* (Grand Rapids, MI: Baker, 1949). First published in 1895.

5. *The New International Dictionary of Old Testament Theology and Exegesis,* ed. Willem A. VanGemeren (Grand Rapids, MI: Zondervan, 1997, 2002), Zondervan Interactive (Grand Rapids, MI: Zondervan, 2007), Pradis 6.0 software.

6. Peter Toon, *Heaven and Hell: A Biblical and Theological Overview* (Nashville, TN: Thomas Nelson, 1986), pp. 29–46.

7. Ajith Fernando, *Crucial Questions about Hell* (Wheaton, IL: Crossway, 1994), pp. 126–128.

8. Cited in Martin E. Marty, "Hell Disappeared. No One Noticed. A Civic Argument," *Harvard Theological Review*, vol. 78, 3–4 (1985), p. 204.

9. J. Oswald Sanders, *Enjoying Intimacy with God* (Grand Rapids, MI: Discovery House, 2000), p. 100.

Chapter Eleven: How to Prevent Idolatry

1. Deuteronomy 4:12, 15, 33, 36; 5:4, 22, 23, 24, 26; 9:10; 10:4.

2. John Pollock, *Amazing Grace: John Newton's Story* (London: Hodder & Stoughton, 1981), p. 182.

3. Exodus 20:5; 34:14 (2x); Deuteronomy 4:24; 5:9; 6:15; 29:20; 32:16, 21; Joshua 24:19; 1 Kings 14:22; Psalm 79:5; Ezekiel 5:13; 8:3 (2x), 5; 16:38, 42; 23:25; 38:19.

4. Ezekiel 36:5, 6; 39:25; Joel 2:18; Zechariah 1:14; 8:2 (x2).

5. *Hebrew-English Lexicon of the Old Testament*, Zondervan Interactive, (Grand Rapids, MI: Zondervan, 2007), Pradis 6.0 software.

Chapter Twelve: Returning to God after Disobedience

1. See John Pollock, *Amazing Grace: John Newton's Story* (London: Hodder & Stoughton, 1981) and Jonathan Aitken, *John Newton: From Disgrace to Amazing Grace* (Wheaton, IL: Crossway, 2007).

2. This point is made by Chitra Chhetri in *The New International Dictionary of Old Testament Theology and Exegesis,* ed. Willem A. VanGemeren (Grand Rapids, MI: Zondervan, 1997, 2002), Zondervan Interactive (Grand Rapids, MI: Zondervan, 2007), Pradis 6.0 software, who expresses indebtedness to Brevard S. Childs, *The Book of Exodus: A Critical, Theological Commentary* (Philadelphia, PA: Westminster, 1974), p. 592.

3. Taken from William Barclay, *The Gospel of Luke*, The Daily Study Bible (Philadelphia, PA: Westminster/John Knox, 1975), p. 205, WORDsearch (Austin, TX: WORDsearch, 2005), software.

Chapter Thirteen: Believing and Obeying the Bible

1. John Wesley, *The Works of John Wesley*, 3rd ed., vol. 3, *Journal*, June 5, 1766 (Grand Rapids, MI: Baker, 1984), p. 251.

2. I have argued for the uniqueness and authority of the words of Jesus using John 14:6–11 in Ajith Fernando, *The Supremacy of Christ* (Wheaton, IL: Crossway, 1995; London: Hodder & Stoughton, 1997; Secundarabad, India: OM Books, 2005).

3. *Merriam-Webster's Collegiate Dictionary Tenth Edition on CD-ROM* (Springfield, MA: Merriam-Webster, 2000), version 2.5 software.

4. Raymond McHenry, *McHenry's Quips, Quotes, & Other Notes* (Peabody, MA: Hendrickson, 1999), software.

5. See Donald W. Dayton, *Discovering an Evangelical Heritage* (Peabody, MA: Hendrickson, 1988).

Chapter Fourteen: How to Think about the Law

1. Dennis F. Kinlaw, *This Day with the Master* (Nappanee, IN: Francis Asbury Press of Evangel Publishing House, 2002), September 26.

2. Christopher J. H. Wright, "Law and Legal System," chap. 9 in *Old Testament Ethics for the People of God* (Leicester, UK and Downers Grove, IL: InterVarsity Press, 2004), especially pp. 321–324 in the U.S. edition.

3. J. G. McConville, *Deuteronomy*, Apollos Old Testament Commentary (Leicester, UK and Downers Grove, IL: InterVarsity Press, 2002).

4. Deuteronomy 1:6; 4:6, 10, 12, 33, 36; 5:1, 23, 24, 25, 26, 27, 28 (2x); 6:3, 4; 9:1; 19:20; 30:17; 31:11, 12, 13; 32:1.

5. Colin Brown, ed., *The New International Dictionary of New Testament Theology* (Grand Rapids, MI: Zondervan, 1986), Zondervan Bible Study Library: Scholars Edition (Grand Rapids, MI: Zondervan, 2007), Pradis 6.0 software.

6. Anne Bradstreet quoted in Larry Sibley, ed., *Classic Quotes on Contemporary Issues* (Wheaton, IL: Harold Shaw, 1997), p. 69.

7. *The New International Dictionary of Old Testament Theology and Exegesis,* ed. Willem A. VanGemeren (Grand Rapids, MI: Zondervan, 1997, 2002), Zondervan Interactive (Grand Rapids, MI: Zondervan, 2007), Pradis 6.0 software.

8. Ibid.

9. Psalm 119:14, 16, 24, 35, 47, 70, 77, 92, 143, 174; see also Psalm 1:2.

10. This point is from Kinlaw, *This Day with the Master*, May 4–5.

11. Wright, *Old Testament Ethics*, pp. 290–302.

Chapter Fifteen: Exclusive Loyalty to God

1. On this see Ajith Fernando, "The God of the Bible and Other Gods" chap. 7 in *Sharing the Truth in Love: How to Relate to People of Other Faiths* (Grand Rapids, MI: Discovery House, 2001), pp. 95–112.

2. Wesley Ariarajah, *The Bible and People of Other Faiths* (Geneva: World Council of Churches, 1985 and Maryknoll, NY: Orbis Books).

3. On this see Fernando, *Sharing the Truth in Love*, pp. 125–129.

4. On this whole topic see Fernando, *Sharing the Truth in Love*.

5. Italics are the author's.

6. Jay Kesler, *Being Holy, Being Human: Dealing with the Expectations of Ministry* (Carol Stream, IL: Christianity Today and Nashville, TN: Word, 1988), pp. 144, 145.

7. Roger Steer, *Hudson Taylor: Lessons in Discipleship* (Crowborough, UK: Monarch Publications, 1995), pp. 56, 57.

Chapter Sixteen: Honoring God's Name

1. Robert P. Gordon, "Leviticus," in *New International Bible Commentary* (Grand Rapids, MI: Zondervan, 1979), Zondervan Interactive (Grand Rapids, MI: Zondervan, 2007), Pradis 6.0 software.

2. Michael G. Moriarty, *The Perfect 10: The Blessings of Following God's Commandments in a Postmodern World* (Grand Rapids, MI: Zondervan, 1999), p. 89.

3. Cited in Philip Graham Ryken, *Written in Stone: The Ten Commandments and Today's Moral Crisis* (Wheaton, IL: Crossway, 2003), p. 97.

Chapter Seventeen: Sabbath-Keeping

1. Exodus 3:5 note, *The New International Version Study Bible*, ed. Kenneth Barker (Grand Rapids, MI: Zondervan, 1995), Zondervan Interactive (Grand Rapids, MI: Zondervan, 2004), Pradis 6.0 software.

2. David C. McCasland, *Eric Liddell: Pure Gold* (Grand Rapids, MI: Discovery House, 2001), p. 91.

3. Ibid., p. 94.

4. Philip Graham Ryken, *Written in Stone: The Ten Commandments and Today's Moral Crisis* (Wheaton, IL: Crossway, 2003), p. 105.

5. Cited in Christopher J. H. Wright, *Deuteronomy*, The New International Biblical Commentary (Peabody, MA: Hendrickson, 1996), p. 76.

6. See Earle E. Cairns, *An Endless Line of Splendor: Revivals and Their Leaders from the Great Awakening to the Present* (Wheaton, IL: Tyndale House, 1986), p. 305.

7. Blaise Pascal, *The Mind on Fire: An Anthology of the Writings of Blaise Pascal*, ed. James M. Houston (Sisters, OR: Multnomah, 1989), p. 97.

8. Ibid., p. 96.

9. Quoted in W. T. Purkiser, *The New Testament Image of the Ministry* (Grand Rapids, MI: Baker, 1974), p. 132.

10. Acts 2:32–36; 4:2, 10, 33; 10:40; 13:33–38; 17:18; Romans 10:9; 1 Corinthians 15:1–19; 1 Thessalonians 1:9.

11. George Eldon Ladd, *A Commentary on the Revelation of John* (Grand Rapids, MI: Eerdmans, 1972), p. 31.

12. Craig L. Blomberg, *1 Corinthians*, The NIV Application Commentary (Grand Rapids, MI: Zondervan, 1994), p. 324.

13. To the Magnesians, 9:1; see also Epistle of Barnabas, 15:9, cited in Murray J. Harris, *From Grave to Glory: Resurrection in the New Testament* (Grand Rapids, MI: Zondervan, 1990), p. 152.

14. This point is made by Michael G. Moriarty, *The Perfect 10: The Blessings of Following God's Commandments in a Postmodern World* (Grand Rapids, MI: Zondervan, 1999), p. 100.

Chapter Eighteen: Honoring Parents

1. Craig S. Keener, *IVP Bible Background Commentary: New Testament* (Downers Grove, IL: InterVarsity Press, 1997), Logos Library System: The Essential IVP Reference Collection (Bellingham, WA: Logos, 1985–2002), software.

2. See John H. Walton, Victor H. Matthews, and Mark W. Chavalas, *The IVP Bible Background Commentary: Old Testament* (Leicester, UK and Downers Grove, IL: InterVarsity Press, 2000), Logos Library System, The Essential IVP Reference Collection (Bellingham, WA: Logos, 1985–2002), software, on Exodus 20:12.

3. Annie Gottlieb, *Do You Believe in Magic?* (New York: Time, 1987), pp. 234, 235; quoted in Philip Graham Ryken, *Written in Stone: The Ten Commandments and Today's Moral Crisis* (Wheaton, IL: Crossway, 2003), p. 117.

4. H. Norman Wright, *The Premarital Counseling Handbook* (Chicago: Moody Publishing, 1981), p. 118.

5. Gaius Davies, *Genius, Grief and Grace: A Psychiatrist Looks at Suffering and Success* (Ross-shire, UK: Christian Focus Publications, 2002).

6. W. F. Batt, *Christian Witness in the Home and in the World* (London: InterVarsity Press, 1970), p. 19.

7. We had the privilege of having Samuel Ganesh live in our home while he was on a preaching mission in Sri Lanka. This story was related to me by him.

8. Adam Clarke's comments on 1 Timothy 5:8 in *A Commentary and Critical Notes on the Holy Bible: Old and New Testaments*, WORDsearch 7.0 (Austin, TX: WORDsearch, 2005).

9. I received this insight from Leon Morris's *Testaments of Love: A Study of Love in the Bible* (Grand Rapids, MI: Eerdmans, 1981).

10. A. Skevington Wood, "Ephesians," in *The Expositor's Bible Commentary*, ed. Frank E. Gaebelein (Grand Rapids, MI: Zondervan, 1992), Zondervan Interactive (Grand Rapids, MI: Zondervan, 2007), Pradis 6.0 software, on Ephesians 6:3.

11. Klyne Snodgrass, *Ephesians*, NIV Application Commentary (Grand Rapids, MI: Zondervan, 1996), Zondervan Interactive (Grand Rapids, MI: Zondervan, 2007), Pradis 6.0 software.

12. George E. Harpur, "Ephesians," *New International Bible Commentary*, ed. F. F. Bruce (Grand Rapids, MI: Zondervan, 1979), Zondervan Interactive (Grand Rapids, MI: Zondervan, 2007), Pradis 6.0 software. See also Peter T. O'Brien, *The Letter to the Ephesians*, The Pillar New Testament Commentary (Grand Rapids, MI: Eerdmans, and Leicester, UK: InterVarsity Press, 1999), p. 444. This was also the view of classic commentators such as Albert Barnes and John Calvin.

13. A. Skevington Wood, "Ephesians," in *The Expositor's Bible Commentary*, ed. Frank E. Gaebelein (Grand Rapids, MI: Zondervan, 1992), Zondervan Interactive (Grand Rapids, MI: Zondervan, 2007), Pradis 6.0 software, on Ephesians 6:3.

Chapter Nineteen: The Sanctity of Life

1. See Thomas R. Schreiner, *Romans*, Baker Exegetical Commentary on the New Testament (Grand Rapids, MI: Baker, 1998), p. 684, note 23. Here Schreiner gives an impressive list of scholars who affirm this point.

2. See B. Harris, "Suicide," in *The New Dictionary of Christian Ethics and Pastoral Theology*, ed. David J. Atkinson, et al. (Leicester, UK and Downers Grove, IL: InterVarsity Press, 1995), pp. 825, 826.

3. *Merriam-Webster's Collegiate Dictionary Tenth Edition on CD-ROM* (Springfield, MA: Merriam-Webster, 2000), version 2.5 software.

4. Michael G. Moriarty, *The Perfect 10: The Blessings of Following God's Commandments in a Postmodern World* (Grand Rapids, MI: Zondervan, 1999), p. 131.

5. See Henry Rack, *Reasonable Enthusiast: John Wesley and the Rise of Methodism* (Nashville, TN: Abingdon, 1992), pp. 379, 380.

6. D. Partner, "John Wesley," in *Who's Who in Christian History*, ed. J. D. Douglas, Philip W. Comfort, and Donald Mitchell (Wheaton, IL: Tyndale House, 1992), p. 712.

7. Philip Graham Ryken, *Written in Stone: The Ten Commandments and Today's Moral Crisis* (Wheaton, IL: Crossway, 2003), p. 139.

8. Ibid., p. 140.

Chapter Twenty: The Sanctity of Marriage

1. For a listing of the types of relationships included under adultery in the Old Testament see Allan Harmon, *Deuteronomy: The Commands of a Covenant God* (Ross-shire, UK: Christian Focus, 2001), p. 79.

2. On this see the comments of Peter C. Craigie, *The Book of Deuteronomy*, The New International Commentary on the Old Testament (Grand Rapids, MI: Eerdmans, 1976) and Christopher J. H. Wright, *Deuteronomy*, The New International Biblical Commentary (Peabody, MA: Hendrickson, 1996), p. 76.

3. Herbert J. Miles, *Sexual Understanding before Marriage* (Grand Rapids, MI: Zondervan, 1971).

4. Roger Steer, *Inside Story: The Life of John Stott* (Leicester, UK: InterVarsity Press, 2009).

5. From David Murray's testimony before the Senate Subcommittee on Oversight of Government Management, Restructuring, and the District of Columbia (May 8, 1997), quoted in Philip Graham Ryken, *Written in Stone: The Ten Commandments and Today's Moral Crisis* (Wheaton, IL: Crossway, 2003), p. 157.

6. Terry Fisher as quoted in Michael Medved, *Hollywood vs. America: The Explosive Bestseller that Shows How–and Why– the Entertainment Industry Has Broken Faith with its Audience* (New York: HarperCollins, 1992), pp. 111, 112; cited in Ryken, *Written in Stone*, p. 157.

7. Sharmila Mandre, "Bangalore Times," *The Times of India*, March 25, 2007.

8. From Larry Sibley, ed., *Classic Quotes on Contemporary Issues* (Wheaton, IL: Harold Shaw, 1997), p. 94.

9. Ibid., p. 92.

10. Ibid., p. 96. Hermas is known to us exclusively for his work *The Shepherd*. This quote is probably taken from that.

Chapter Twenty-one: Respect for Property and Truth

1. I read this about forty years ago in an article in *Christianity Today*.

2. John H. Walton, Victor H. Matthews, and Mark W. Chavalas, *The IVP Bible Background Commentary: Old Testament* (Leicester, UK and Downers Grove, IL: InterVarsity Press, 2000), Logos Library System: The Essential IVP Reference Collection (Bellingham, WA: Logos, 1985–2002), software, on Exodus 20:15.

3. From George W. Robertson, "The Eighth Commandment," *Leader to Leader*, July/August 1997, p. 3. Cited in Philip Graham Ryken, *Written in Stone: The Ten Commandments and Today's Moral Crisis* (Wheaton, IL: Crossway, 2003), p. 170.

4. From Michael S. Horton, *The Law of Perfect Freedom: Relating to God and Others through the Ten Commandments* (Chicago: Moody Publishing, 1993), p. 206. Quoted in Ryken, *Written in Stone*, p. 173.

5. For a discussion on how pantheism influences one's understanding of spirituality and holiness, see chapters 8 and 11 of Ajith Fernando, *Sharing the Truth in Love: How to Relate to People of Other Faiths* (Grand Rapids, MI: Discovery House, 2001).

6. From John Wesley, *Notes on the Old Testament* (1765), WORDsearch (Austin, TX: WORDsearch, 2005), software.

7. Warren W. Wiersbe and Lloyd M. Perry, *Wycliffe Handbook of Preaching and Preachers* (Chicago: Moody Publishing, 1984), p. 184. Taken from Bramwell Booth, *Echoes and Memories* (New York: George H. Doran, 1925), p. 27.

8. Johannes P. Louw and Eugene A. Nida, ed., *NT Greek-English Lexicon* (New York: United Bible Societies, 1989), WORDsearch (Austin, TX: WORDsearch, 2005), software.

Chapter Twenty-two: Covetousness versus Contentment

1. Ingvar Haddal, *John Wesley: A Biography* (Nashville, TN: Abingdon, 1961), p. 28.

2. This story is taken almost verbatim from Jay W. Marshall, *The Ten Commandments and Christian Community* (Scottsdale, PA and Waterloo, Ontario: Herald, 1996), pp. 103, 107. Marshall got this story from Paul Lee Tan, ed. *Encyclopedia of 7700 Illustrations*, (Rockville, MD: Assurance Publishers, 1979), pp. 288–299.

Chapter Twenty-three: A Conversation between God, Moses, and the People

1. John H. Walton, Victor H. Matthews, and Mark W. Chavalas, *The IVP Bible Background Commentary: Old Testament* (Leicester, UK and Downers Grove, IL: InterVarsity Press, 2000), Logos Library System: The Essential IVP Reference Collection (Bellingham, WA: Logos, 1985–2002), software.

2. Constance E. Padwick, *Henry Martyn: Confessor of the Faith* (New York: George H. Doran Company, 1922), p. 167.

3. G. B. Funderburk, "Fear," *The Zondervan Pictorial Encyclopedia of the Bible*, ed. Merrill C. Tenney (Grand Rapids, MI: Zondervan, 1975), Zondervan Interactive (Grand Rapids, MI: Zondervan, 2007), software.

4. E. Stanley Jones, *The Word Became Flesh* (Nashville, TN: Abingdon, 1963), p. 356.

5. Deuteronomy 4:10; 5:29; 6:2, 24; 8:6; 10:12, 20; 13:4; 14:23; 17:19; 28:58; 31:12, 13.

6. Deuteronomy 5:29; 6:2, 24; 8:6; 10:12–13; 13:4; 17:19; 28:58; 31:12.

7. *Hebrew-English Lexicon of the Old Testament*, Zondervan Interactive (Grand Rapids, MI: Zondervan, 2007), Pradis 6.0 software.

Chapter Twenty-four: How Fear and Love Can Make Us Holy

1. Laurence W. Wood, "Telling the Old, Old Story in the Postmodern Age," *The Asbury Herald*, Autumn 1996, p. 3.

2. *Hebrew-English Lexicon of the Old Testament*, Zondervan Interactive (Grand Rapids, MI: Zondervan, 2007), Pradis 6.0 software.

3. Ibid.

4. Christopher J. H. Wright, *Ambassadors to the World: Declaring God's Love* (Leicester, UK: InterVarsity Press, 1998), p. 43.

5. Ibid., pp. 49, 50.

6. John Piper, *Think: The Life of the Mind and the Love of God* (Wheaton, IL: Crossway, 2010), p. 87.

7. Deuteronomy 5:10; 6:5; 7:9; 10:12; 11:1, 13; 13:3; 30:6.

Chapter Twenty-five: How the Word Can Make Us Holy

1. Raymond McHenry, *McHenry's Quips, Quotes, & Other Notes* (Peabody, MA: Hendrickson, 1999), software.

2. Iva Hoth and Andre Le Blanc, *The Picture Bible: God's Word Brought to Life in Pictures* (Colorado Springs, CO: David C. Cook, 1998).

3. *The New International Dictionary of Old Testament Theology and Exegesis,* ed. Willem A. VanGemeren (Grand Rapids, MI: Zondervan, 1997, 2002), Zondervan Interactive (Grand Rapids, MI: Zondervan, 2007), Pradis 6.0 software.

4. John Goldingay, "Proverbs," in *New Bible Commentary: 21ˢᵗ Century Edition*, ed. G. J. Weham, J. A. Motyer, D. A. Carson, and R. T. France (Leicester, UK and Downers Grove, IL: IVP Academic, 1994), Logos Library System: The Essential IVP Reference Collection (Bellingham, WA: Logos, 1985–2002), software.

5. Joseph T. Bayly, *Out of My Mind: The Best of Joe Bayly*, ed. Timothy Bayly (Grand Rapids, MI: Zondervan, 1993), p. 101. The wording here is Bayly's.

6. C. S. Lewis, *The Four Loves* (London: Geoffrey Bles, 1960).

7. C. S. Lewis quoted in *The Quotable Lewis: An Encyclopedic Selection of Quotes from the Complete Published Works of C. S. Lewis*, ed. Wayne Martindale and Jerry Root (Wheaton, IL: Tyndale House, 1989), p. 233.

8. Harry Blamires, *The Christian Mind: How Should a Christian Think?* (London: SPCK, 1963; Ann Arbor, MI: Servant, 1978).

9. *New International Bible Dictionary*, ed. J. D. Douglas and Merrill C. Tenney (Grand Rapids MI: Zondervan, 1987), s.v. "Incense," Zondervan Interactive (Grand Rapids, MI: Zondervan, 2007), Pradis 6.0 software.

10. A. W. Morton, "Education in Biblical Times," *The Zondervan Pictorial Encyclopedia of the Bible*, ed. Merrill C. Tenney (Grand Rapids, MI: Zondervan, 1975), Zondervan Interactive (Grand Rapids, MI: Zondervan, 2007), Pradis 6.0 software.

11. On this see Ajith Fernando, "Sensitivity to Others," chap. 4 in *Sharing the Truth in Love: How to Relate to People of Other Faiths* (Grand Rapids MI: Discovery House, 2001).

12. See Morton, "Education in Biblical Times."

Chapter Twenty-six: How to Avoid the Pitfalls of Prosperity

1. Edythe Draper, *Draper's Book of Quotations for the Christian World* (Wheaton, IL: Tyndale House, 1992).

2. Note the titles of the following studies on Deuteronomy: J. G. McConville, *Grace in the End: A Study of Deuteronomic Theology* (Grand Rapids, MI: Zondervan; Carlisle, UK: Paternoster, 1993); Paul A. Barker, *The Triumph of Grace in Deuteronomy: Faithless Israel, Faithful Yahweh in Deuteronomy* (Carlisle, UK: Paternoster Press, 2004).

3. Howard Hendricks, "The Problem of Discrimination," *Preaching Today*, tape no. 76; http://www.preachingtoday.com/sermons/outlines/2007/january/problemof-discrimination.html.

4. Oswald Chambers in *Run Today's Race: A Word for Every Day in the Year from Oswald Chambers*. Cited in *Christianity Today*, vol. 35, no. 11.

5. *Hebrew-English Lexicon of the Old Testament*, Zondervan Interactive (Grand Rapids, MI: Zondervan, 2007), Pradis 6.0 software.

6. Ibid.

7. Haddon Robinson in *Leadership*, vol. 9, no. 4.

Chapter Twenty-seven: Show Them No Mercy

1. This wording is from the NIV translation of Deuteronomy 7:2 and is the title of an excellent book discussing some of the issues brought up in this chapter: C. S. Cowles, Eugene H. Merrill, Daniel L. Gard, and Tremper Longman III, *Show Them No Mercy: 4 Views on God and Canaanite Genocide*, ed. Stanley N. Gundry, (Grand Rapids, MI: Zondervan, 2003). See also Herman A. Hoyt, Myron S. Augsburger, Arthur F. Holmes, and Harold O. J. Brown, *War: Four Christian Views*, ed. Robert G. Clouse (Downers Grove, IL: InterVarsity Press, 1981); Peter C. Craigie, *The Problem of War in the Old Testament* (Grand Rapids, MI: Eerdmans, 1978); and Christopher J. H. Wright, *Old Testament Ethics for the People of God* (Downers Grove, IL: InterVarsity Press, 2004), pp. 272–280.

2. J. A. Thompson, *Deuteronomy: An Introduction and Commentary*, Tyndale Old Testament Commentaries (Leicester, UK and Downers Grove, IL: InterVarsity Press, 1974), Logos Bible software (Bellingham, WA: Logos, 2002–2009), software.

3. Wright, *Old Testament Ethics*, p. 476.

4. Craigie, *The Problem of War*, p. 52.

5. Microsoft Encarta Encyclopedia 2005, © 1993–2004 by Microsoft Corporation, CD-ROM.

6. Craigie, *The Problem of War*, p. 53.

7. Microsoft Encarta Encyclopedia.

8. Craigie, *The Problem of War*, pp. 98, 99.

9. For many points in this section I am indebted to an article by G. P. Hugenberger, "Some Introductory Notes on the Biblical Ethics of War" (Boston, MA: Park Street Church, September 23, 2001).

Chapter Twenty-eight: How Not to Forget God

1. For fearing God, see the discussions on 5:23–27, 29; 6:1–3, 13–15. For care in keeping the Law, see the discussions on 4:2; 5:32, 33.

2. See Adam Clarke's comments on Deuteronomy 6:12, in *A Commentary and Critical Notes on the Holy Bible: Old and New Testaments*, WORDsearch 7.0 (Austin, TX: WORDsearch, 2005), software.

3. Andre Crouch, "Through it All" (Burbank, CA: Manna Music, 1971).

4. Peter C. Craigie, *The Book of Deuteronomy*, The New International Commentary on the Old Testament (Grand Rapids, MI: Eerdmans, 1976).

5. Jane Stuart Smith and Betty Carlson, *The Gift of Music: Great Composers and their Influence* (Wheaton, IL: Crossway, 1987), p. 52.

6. Ajith Fernando, *Crucial Questions about Hell* (Eastbourne, UK: Kingsway Publications, 1991 and Wheaton, IL: Crossway, 1994).

Chapter Twenty-nine: God Wins in Spite of Us

1. E.g., Christopher J. H. Wright, *Deuteronomy*, The New International Biblical Commentary (Peabody, MA: Hendrickson, 1996), p. 76; and J. G. McConville, *Deuteronomy*, Apollos Old Testament Commentary (Leicester, UK and Downers Grove, IL: InterVarsity Press, 2002).

2. Cited in John R. W. Stott, *I Believe in Preaching* (London: Hodder, 1998).

3. Raymond McHenry, "Humility," in *McHenry's Quips, Quotes, & Other Notes* (Peabody, MA: Hendrickson, 1999), software.

4. See chapter 10 of Ajith Fernando, *Crucial Questions about Hell* (Wheaton, IL: Crossway, 1994).

Chapter Thirty: A Rebellious People and a Praying Leader

1. Cited in Wesley L. Duewel, *Ablaze for God* (Grand Rapids, MI: Zondervan, 1989).

2. D. R. Bowes, "Gold," in *The Zondervan Pictorial Encyclopedia of the Bible*, ed. Merrill C. Tenney (Grand Rapids, MI: Zondervan, 1975), Zondervan Interactive (Grand Rapids, MI: Zondervan, 2007), Pradis 6.0 software.

3. Samuel Chadwick, *The Path of Prayer* (Kansas City, MO: Beacon Hill Press, 1931), p. 68. Quoted in Wesley L. Duewel, *Mighty Prevailing Prayer* (Grand Rapids, MI: Zondervan, 1990), p. 76.

4. Chadwick, *Path of Prayer,* pp. 81, 82. Quoted in Duewel, *Mighty Prevailing Prayer*, p. 76.

5. Roger Steer, *George Mueller: Delighted in God* (Wheaton, IL: Harold Shaw, 1975), p. 267.

Chapter Thirty-one: Powerful Prayer

1. Wesley L. Duewel, *Mighty Prevailing Prayer* (Grand Rapids, MI: Zondervan, 1990), p. 297.

2. *My Path of Prayer*, ed. David Hanes (West Sussex, UK: Henry E. Walter, 1981), p. 59. Cited in Duewel, *Mighty Prevailing Prayer*, p. 216.

3. Raymond E. Brown, *The Gospel According to John I–XIII*, The Anchor Bible (New York: Doubleday, 1966), p. 124. See also F. F. Bruce, *The Gospel of John* (Grand Rapids, MI: Eerdmans, 1983), p. 75.

4. Constance E. Padwick, *Henry Martyn: Confessor of the Faith* (New York: George H. Doran, 1922), p. 264.

5. For the full story see Wesley L. Duewel, *Revival Fire* (Grand Rapids, MI: Zondervan, 1995), pp. 306–318.

6. J. A. Thompson, *Deuteronomy: An Introduction and Commentary*, Tyndale Old Testament Commentaries (Leicester, UK and Downers Grove, IL: InterVarsity Press, 1974), p. 144, Logos Bible software (Bellingham, WA: Logos, 2002–2009), software.

7. M. J. Evans, "Blessing and Cursing," *The New Dictionary of Christian Ethics and Pastoral Theology*, ed. David J. Atkinson and David H. Field (Leicester, UK and Downers Grove, IL: InterVarsity Press, 1995), p. 197.

8. See Ajith Fernando, *Jesus Driven Ministry* (Wheaton, IL: Crossway, 2002; Leicester, UK: InterVarsity Press, 2003), pp. 219–221.

Chapter Thirty-two: A Vision of God Fosters Heart Religion

1. John Calvin, *Calvin's Commentaries*, WORDsearch (Austin, TX: WORD-search, 2005), software, comment on Romans 3:18.

2. Deuteronomy 4:10; 5:29; 6:2, 13, 24; 10:12, 20; 13:4; 14:23; 17:19; 25:18; 28:58; 31:12, 13.

3. Deuteronomy 5:33; 8:6; 10:12; 11:22; 13:4, 5; 19:9; 26:17; 28:9; 30:16.

4. Deuteronomy 5:10; 6:5; 7:9; 10:12; 11:1, 13; 13:3; 30:6.

5. Deuteronomy 6:13; 10:12, 20; 11:13; 13:4; 28:47.

6. Deuteronomy 4:9, 29, 39; 6:5, 6; 8:5; 10:12, 16; 11:13, 16, 18; 13:3; 15:10; 17:17; 26:16; 28:47; 30:2, 6, 10, 14, 17; 32:46. Other texts marginally carry this idea.

7. See the discussions on Deuteronomy 4:2; 5:12, 32, 33; 6:12, 17.

8. Matthew 28:18–20; Mark 16:15, 16; Luke 24:45–49; John 17:18; 20:21; Acts 1:8; 10:42. We are not told when the statement in Acts 10:42 was made.

9. Numbers 14:8; Deuteronomy 30:9; Psalm 37:23; 41:11; 147:11; 149:4; Isaiah 62:4.

10. *Hebrew-English Lexicon of the Old Testament*, Zondervan Interactive (Grand Rapids, MI: Zondervan, 2007), Pradis 6.0 software.

11. *New International Encyclopedia of Bible Words*, ed. Lawrence O. Richards (Grand Rapids, MI: Zondervan, 1985, 1991), Zondervan Interactive (Grand Rapids, MI: Zondervan, 2007), Pradis 6.0 software.

12. J. W. Mieklejohn, "David Livingstone," *New International Dictionary of the Christian Church*, ed. J. D. Douglas (Grand Rapids, MI: Zondervan, 2002), Zondervan Interactive (Grand Rapids, MI: Zondervan, 2007), Pradis 6.0 software.

13. Steve May, *The Story File: 1,001 Contemporary Illustrations for Speakers, Writers and Preachers,* vol. 1 (Peabody, MA: Hendrickson), CD-ROM (Raleigh, NC: HeavenWord, 2000), software.

14. Taken from Kenneth J. Collins, *A Real Christian: The Life of John Wesley* (Nashville, TN: Abingdon, 1999), p. 158.

Chapter Thirty-three: Seven Motivations to Obedience

1. *The New International Dictionary of Old Testament Theology and Exegesis,* ed. Willem A. VanGemeren (Grand Rapids, MI: Zondervan, 1997, 2002), Zondervan Interactive (Grand Rapids, MI: Zondervan, 2007), Pradis 6.0 software.

2. *Hebrew-English Lexicon of the Old Testament*, Zondervan Interactive (Grand Rapids, MI: Zondervan, 2007), Pradis 6.0 software.

3. Deuteronomy 5:33; 8:6; 10:12; 11:22; 13:4, 5; 19:9; 26:17; 28:9; 30:16.

4. William Barclay, *Acts*, The Daily Study Bible (Louisville, KY: Westminster/ John Knox, 1976), WORDsearch 7.0, (Austin, TX: WORDsearch, 2005), software, on Acts 4:23–31.

5. J. A. Thompson, *Deuteronomy: An Introduction and Commentary*, Tyndale Old Testament Commentaries (Leicester, UK and Downers Grove, IL: InterVarsity Press, 1974), Logos Bible Software (Bellingham, WA: Logos, 2002–2009), software.

6. J. Allan Petersen, *The Myth of Greener Grass* (Wheaton, IL: Tyndale House, 1992).

Chapter Thirty-four: Worshipping God's Way

1. Cited in Kenneth L. Woodward, "The Other Jesus," *Newsweek*, March 27, 2000, p. 80.

2. Donald Guthrie, "John," in *New Bible Commentary: 21ˢᵗ Century Edition*, ed. G. J. Weham, J. A. Motyer, D. A. Carson, and R. T. France (Leicester, UK and Downers Grove, IL: IVP Academic, 1994), Logos Library System: The Essential IVP Reference Collection (Bellingham, WA: Logos, 1985–2002), software.

3. *The New International Dictionary of Old Testament Theology and Exegesis*, ed. Willem A. VanGemeren (Grand Rapids, MI: Zondervan, 1997, 2002), Zondervan Interactive (Grand Rapids, MI: Zondervan, 2007), Pradis 6.0 software.

4. J. Navone, "The Lukan Banquet Community," *Bible Today* 51 (1970): pp. 155–161; cited in John Koenig, *New Testament Hospitality: Partnership with Strangers as Promise and Mission* (Philadelphia, PA: Fortress Press, 1985), p. 89.

Chapter Thirty-five: Encountering Occult Power

1. John H. Walton, Victor H. Matthews, and Mark W. Chavalas, *The IVP Bible Background Commentary: Old Testament* (Leicester, UK and Downers Grove, IL: InterVarsity Press, 2000), p.183, Logos Library System: The Essential IVP Reference Collection (Bellingham, WA: Logos, 1985–2002), software.

2. Christopher J. H. Wright, *Deuteronomy*, The New International Biblical Commentary (Peabody, MA: Hendrickson, 1996), p. 173.

3. Peter C. Craigie, *The Book of Deuteronomy*, The New International Commentary on the Old Testament (Grand Rapids, MI: Eerdmans, 1976), p. 224.

4. Deuteronomy 13:5; 17:7, 12; 19:13, 19; 21:21; 22:21, 22, 24; 24:7.

5. Craigie, *The Book of Deuteronomy*, p. 224.

6. Walton, Matthews, Chavalas, *The IVP Bible Background Commentary*, p. 183.

7. See J. G. McConville, *Deuteronomy*, Apollos Old Testament Commentary (Leicester, UK and Downers Grove, IL: InterVarsity Press, 2002), pp. 240, 241.

8. Samuel Kamaleson, "The Local Church and World Evangelism," in *Christ the Liberator*, ed. John R. W. Stott (Downers Grove, IL: InterVarsity Press, 1971), pp. 158, 159.

Chapter Thirty-six: We Will Be Different from Others

1. I discovered the adoption, sanctification, and election terminology in Matthew Henry, *Matthew Henry's Commentary on the Whole Bible* (Grand Rapids, MI: Zondervan, 1999), Zondervan Interactive (Grand Rapids, MI: Zondervan, 2007), Pradis 6.0 software.

2. Most of this information is from R. K. Harrison's article "Funerary Customs: Palestinian," in *New International Dictionary of Biblical Archaeology*, ed. E. M. Blaiklock and R. K. Harrison (Grand Rapids, MI: Zondervan, 1983), Zondervan Interactive (Grand Rapids, MI: Zondervan, 2007), Pradis 6.0 software.

3. Eugene Merrill, *Deuteronomy*, The New American Commentary, vol. 4 (Nashville, TN: B&H, 1994), WORDsearch 7.0 (Austin, TX: WORDsearch, 2005), software.

4. J. G. McConville, "Deuteronomy," in *New Bible Commentary: 21ˢᵗ Century Edition*, ed. G. J. Weham, J. A. Motyer, D. A. Carson, and R. T. France (Leicester, UK and Downers Grove, IL: IVP Academic, 1994), Logos Library System: The Essential IVP Reference Collection (Bellingham, WA: Logos, 1985–2002), software.

5. Gordon J. Wenham, *The Book of Leviticus*, The New International Commentary on the Old Testament (Grand Rapids, MI: Eerdmans, 1979), p. 184.

6. See Merrill, *Deuteronomy*, for an explanation.

7. T. D. Alexander gives this as one possibility in his comment on Exodus 23:19 in *New Bible Commentary: 21ˢᵗ Century Edition*, ed. G. J. Weham, J. A. Motyer, D. A. Carson, and R. T. France (Leicester, UK and Downers Grove, IL: IVP Academic, 1994), Logos Library System: The Essential IVP Reference Collection (Bellingham, WA: Logos, 1985–2002), software.

Chapter Thirty-seven: Giving to God

1. Taken from Paul Lee Tan, ed., *Encyclopedia of 15,000 Illustrations*, WORDsearch (Austin, TX: WORDsearch, 2004), software.

2. Microsoft Encarta Encyclopedia 2005, © 1993–2004 by Microsoft Corporation, CD-ROM.

3. Related in Randy Alcorn, *Money, Possessions, and Eternity* (Wheaton, IL: Tyndale House, 2003), p. 173.

4. Ibid., p. 186.

5. Brian K. Morley, "Tithe, Tithing," in *Evangelical Dictionary of Biblical Theology*, ed. Walter A. Elwell, (Grand Rapids, MI: Baker, 1996), p. 779.

6. C. L. Feinberg, "Tithe," in *The Zondervan Pictorial Encyclopedia of the Bible*, ed. Merrill C. Tenney (Grand Rapids, MI: Zondervan, 1975), Zondervan Interactive (Grand Rapids, MI: Zondervan, 2007), Pradis 6.0 software.

7. Cited in Alcorn, *Money, Possessions, and Eternity*, p. 185.

8. Cited in ibid.

9. From Raymond McHenry, *McHenry's Quips, Quotes, & Other Notes*, ed. Raymond McHenry (Peabody, MA: Hendrickson, 1998, 1999), *Stories for Preachers and Teachers* (Raleigh, NC: HeavenWord, 1999), software.

10. The Barna Update, June 5, 2001. Cited in Alcorn, *Money, Possessions, and Eternity*, p. 180.

11. All of the above statistics have been gleaned from Alcorn, *Money, Possessions, and Eternity*, p. 180.

12. See Christopher J. H. Wright's comments on this in his discussion of this passage, in *Deuteronomy*, The New International Biblical Commentary (Peabody, MA: Hendrickson, 1996).

13. Taken from Paul S. Rees, *The Adequate Man: Paul in Philippians* (Westwood, NJ: Fleming H. Revell, 1959), p. 118.

Chapter Thirty-eight: Special Consideration for the Poor

1. J. C. Pollock, *Shaftesbury: The Poor Man's Earl* (London: Falcon Booklets, 1961), p. 3.

2. Donald B. Kraybill, *The Upside-Down Kingdom* (Scottsdale, PA and Waterloo, Ontario: Herald, 2003), p. 87.

3. Matthew 19:19; 22:39; Mark 12:31, 33; Luke 10:27; Romans 13:9; Galatians 5:14; James 2:8.

4. Tertullian, *Apology 39*; cited in Rodney Stark, *The Rise of Christianity: How the Obscure, Marginal Jesus Movement Became the Dominant Religious Force in the Western World in a Few Centuries* (San Francisco: HarperOne, 1997), p. 87.

5. Cited in Justo L. Gonzalez, *Faith and Wealth: A History of Early Christian Ideas on the Origin, Significance and Use of Wealth* (San Francisco: HarperCollins, 1990), p. 206.

6. Cited in ibid., p. 216.

7. See also Psalm 112:5, 9; Proverbs 11:24, 25; 14:21; 22:9; 28:27; Isaiah 58:10–12; Ezekiel 18:7–16; Hebrews 6:10.

8. See Proverbs 6:6–11; 10:4, 5, 26; 12:24, 27; 13:4; 15:19; 18:9; 19:15, 24; 20:4; 21:25; 24:30–34; 26:13–16; Ecclesiastes 10:18; Matthew 25:26, 27; Hebrews 6:12.

9. See Leviticus 6:2–7; 19:13, 35, 36; Deuteronomy 25:13–16; Psalm 5:6; 62:10; Proverbs 3:27, 28; 11:1; 20:10, 17, 23; Jeremiah 9:4–8; Hosea 4:1–3; 12:7; Micah 6:10, 11; Zephaniah 1:9; 1 Thessalonians 4:6.

10. See Proverbs 24:28; Mark 7:22; Romans 3:13; 1 Timothy 1:10; Titus 1:12; 1 Peter 3:10; Revelation 21:8.

11. From Larry Sibley, ed., *Classic Quotes on Contemporary Issues* (Wheaton, IL: Harold Shaw, 1997).

12. John Wesley, "The Use of Money," *The Works of John Wesley*, vol. 6 (Grand Rapids, MI: Baker, 1984), pp. 124–136.

13. John H. Walton, Victor H. Matthews, and Mark W. Chavalas, *The IVP Bible Background Commentary: Old Testament* (Leicester, UK and Downers Grove, IL: InterVarsity Press, 2000), Logos Library System: The Essential IVP Reference Collection (Bellingham, WA: Logos, 1985–2002), software.

Chapter Thirty-nine: Pilgrimage Festivals

1. Doug McIntosh, *Deuteronomy*, Holman Old Testament Commentary 3 (Nashville, TN: B&H, 2002).

2. Earl S. Kalland, "Deuteronomy," in *The Expositor's Bible Commentary*, ed. Frank E. Gaebelein (Grand Rapids, MI: Zondervan, 1992), Zondervan Interactive (Grand Rapids, MI: Zondervan, 2007), Pradis 6.0 software.

3. In Robert C. Shannon, *1000 Windows* (Cincinnati, OH: Standard, 1997), Bible Illustrator (Austin, TX: FindEx, 1998), software.

4. In James S. Hewett, *Illustrations Unlimited: A Topical Collection of Hundreds of Stories, Quotations, and Humor for Speakers, Writers, Pastors, and Teachers* (Wheaton, IL: Tyndale House, 1988), p. 462.

5. In Paul Lee Tan, ed., *Encyclopedia of 15,000 Illustrations*, WORDsearch 7.0 (Austin, TX: WORDsearch, 2005), software.

Chapter Forty: Principles of Leadership and Justice

1. This use of two words together to refer to the same thing is called a hendiadys.

2. Edythe Draper, *Draper's Book of Quotations for the Christian World* (Wheaton, IL: Tyndale House, 1992), # 5863. From Bible Illustrator (Austin, TX: FindEx, 1998), software.

3. Draper, *Book of Quotations*, # 5875.

4. From John H. Walton, Victor H. Matthews, and Mark W. Chavalas, *The IVP Bible Background Commentary: Old Testament* (Leicester, UK and Downers Grove, IL: InterVarsity Press, 2000), Logos Library System: The Essential IVP Reference Collection (Bellingham, WA: Logos, 1985–2002), software.

5. Christopher J. H. Wright, *Deuteronomy*, The New International Biblical Commentary (Peabody, MA: Hendrickson, 1996), p. 76.

6. Walton, Matthews, and Chavalas, *The IVP Bible Background Commentary: Old Testament*.

7. Deuteronomy 13:5; 17:7, 12; 19:19; 21:21; 22:21, 22, 24; 24:7.

Chapter Forty-one: How to Be a Good King

1. John H. Walton, Victor H. Matthews, and Mark W. Chavalas, *The IVP Bible Background Commentary: Old Testament* (Leicester, UK and Downers Grove, IL: InterVarsity Press, 2000), Logos Library System: The Essential IVP Reference Collection (Bellingham, WA: Logos, 1985–2002), software.

2. Gleason L. Archer, *New International Encyclopedia of Bible Difficulties* (Grand Rapids, MI: Zondervan, 1982), Zondervan Interactive (Grand Rapids, MI: Zondervan, 2007), Pradis 6.0 software, on Exodus 20:14.

3. Walton, Matthews, and Chavalas, *The IVP Bible Background Commentary: Old Testament*.

4. Ibid.

5. Bob Phillips, *Phillips' Book of Great Thoughts & Funny Sayings: A Stupendous Collection of Quotes, Quips, Epigrams, Witticisms, and Humorous Comments for Personal Enjoyment and Ready Reference* (Wheaton, IL: Tyndale House, 1993), p. 39.

6. Paul Lee Tan, ed., *Encyclopedia of 15,000 Illustrations*, WORDsearch 7.0 (Austin, TX: WORDsearch, 2005), software.

7. Waylon B. Moore, "Mentoring Your Pastor," www.mentoring-disciples.org/Pastor.html.

Chapter Forty-two: Priests and Prophets: The Good, the Bad, the Best, and the False

1. J. G. McConville, "Deuteronomy," in *New Bible Commentary: 21ˢᵗ Century Edition*, ed. G. J. Weham, J. A. Motyer, D. A. Carson, and R. T. France (Leicester, UK and Downers Grove, IL: IVP Academic, 1994), Logos Library System: The Essential IVP Reference Collection (Bellingham, WA: Logos, 1985–2002), software.

2. James Orr in *Deuteronomy*, Pulpit Commentary: Old Testament, ed. H. D. M. Spence and Joseph Exell, Ages Digital Library: Christian Library Series (Rio, WI: Ages Library, 2002), software.

3. John H. Walton, Victor H. Matthews, and Mark W. Chavalas, *The IVP Bible Background Commentary: Old Testament* (Leicester, UK and Downers Grove, IL:

InterVarsity Press, 2000), Logos Library System: The Essential IVP Reference Collection (Bellingham, WA: Logos, 1985–2002), software.

4. J. G. McConville, *Deuteronomy*, Apollos Old Testament Commentary (Leicester, UK and Downers Grove, IL: InterVarsity Press, 2002).

5. For a fuller discussion on this topic, see Ajith Fernando, "Protection, Help, and Guidance from the Divine," chap. 10 in *Sharing the Truth in Love: How to Relate to People of Other Faiths* (Grand Rapids, MI: Discovery House, 2001).

6. Dennis F. Hester, *The Vance Havner Quote Book* (Grand Rapids, MI: Baker, 1986), p. 124.

7. Walter C. Kaiser Jr., *The Messiah in the Old Testament* (Grand Rapids, MI: Zondervan, 1995), p. 61.

8. See 1 Kings 22; Isaiah 44:25; Jeremiah 13:14–22; 23:16–22, 33–39; 28:1–17; Lamentations 2:14; Ezekiel 13:1–23; 22:28; Matthew 7:15–19; 24:23–26; Mark 13:21–23; Luke 6:26; Acts 13:6–11; 2 Peter 2:1–3; 1 John 4:1–3.

9. See especially Acts 11:27; 13:1; 15:32; 21:9, 10; Romans 12:6; 1 Corinthians 12; 14; Ephesians 4:11; 1 Timothy 4:14.

10. *Hebrew-English Lexicon of the Old Testament*, Zondervan Interactive (Grand Rapids, MI: Zondervan, 2007), Pradis 6.0 software.

11. See "False Prophet Alert!" http://www.aloha.net/~mikesch/tbn.htm.

Chapter Forty-three: Legal Protection for the Vulnerable

1. *Merriam-Webster's Collegiate Dictionary Tenth Edition on CD-ROM* (Springfield, MA: Merriam-Webster, 2000), version 2.5 software.

2. Microsoft Encarta Encyclopedia 2005, © 1993–2004 by Microsoft Corporation, CD-ROM, s.v. "Manslaughter."

3. Taken from "George W. Truett, 1867–1944, Baptist Pastor," http://www.believersweb.net/view.cfm?ID=93.

4. John H. Walton, Victor H. Matthews, and Mark W. Chavalas, *The IVP Bible Background Commentary: Old Testament* (Leicester, UK and Downers Grove, IL: InterVarsity Press, 2000), Logos Library System: The Essential IVP Reference Collection (Bellingham, WA: Logos, 1985–2002), software.

5. Warren W. Wiersbe and Lloyd M. Perry, *The Wycliffe Handbook of Preaching and Preachers* (Chicago: Moody Publishing, 1984), p. 184. Taken from Bramwell Booth, *Echoes and Memories* (New York: George H. Doran, 1925), p. 8.

Chapter Forty-four: Rules for Warfare

1. Cited in *Daily Readings from F. W. Boreham*, ed. Frank Cumbers (London: Hodder & Stoughton, 1976), p. 320.

2. From *Speeches That Changed the World: The Stories and Transcripts of the Moments That Made History*, rev. ed. (London: Quercus Publishing, 2010), pp. 93, 94.

3. Roger Steer, *Hudson Taylor: Lessons in Discipleship* (Crowborough, UK: Monarch Publications, 1995), pp. 56, 57.

4. Christopher J. H. Wright, *Deuteronomy*, The New International Biblical Commentary (Peabody, MA: Hendrickson, 1996), p. 230.

Chapter Forty-five: Respect for Life and Land

1. Eugene Carpenter, *Zondervan Illustrated Bible Backgrounds Commentary: Old Testament*, ed. John H. Walton (Grand Rapids, MI: Zondervan, 2009), Logos Library System: The Essential IVP Reference Collection (Bellingham, WA: Logos, 1985–2002), software.

2. Ibid.

3. David F. Payne, *Deuteronomy*, The Daily Study Bible (Edinburgh, UK: The Saint Andrew Press and Philadelphia, PA: Westminster, 1985).

4. "Abortion Data from Reports of the Alan Guttmacher Institute," www.reli gioustolerance.org/abo_fact3.htm.

5. "Facts on Induced Abortion in the United States," Guttmacher Institute, 2008; www.guttmacher.org/pubs/fb_induced_abortion.html.

6. "Abortion Facts," The Center for Bio-Ethical Reform, www.abortionno.org/ Resources/fastfacts.html. They report, "All abortion numbers are derived from pro-abortion sources courtesy of The Alan Guttmacher Institute and Planned Parent-hood's *Family Planning Perspectives.*"

7. See http://nobelprize.org/nobel_prizes/peace/laureates/1964/king-lecture. html.

8. Christopher J. H. Wright, *Deuteronomy*, The New International Biblical Commentary (Peabody, MA: Hendrickson, 1996), p. 76.

9. John H. Walton, Victor H. Matthews, and Mark W. Chavalas, *The IVP Bible Background Commentary: Old Testament* (Leicester, UK and Downers Grove, IL: InterVarsity Press, 2000), Logos Library System: The Essential IVP Reference Collection (Bellingham, WA: Logos, 1985–2002), software.

10. There have been several good biographies of John Newton published recently, including Jonathan Aitken, *John Newton: From Disgrace to Amazing Grace* (Wheaton, IL: Crossway, 2007). An older influential biography was John Pollock, *Amazing Grace: John Newton's Story* (London: Hodder & Stoughton, 1981).

11. Walton, Matthews, and Chavalas, *The IVP Bible Background Commentary: Old Testament*.

12. J. Wolfendale, *Biblical Illustrator: Old Testament: Deuteronomy*, ed. Joseph Exell, Ages Digital Library: Christian Library Series (Rio, WI: Ages Library, 2002), software.

13. J. Orr, *Deuteronomy*, Pulpit Commentary: Old Testament, ed. H. D. M. Spence and Joseph Exell, Ages Digital Library: Christian Library Series (Rio, WI: Ages Library, 2002), software.

14. Walter C. Kaiser, *Hard Sayings of the Bible* (Downers Grove, IL: Inter-Varsity Press, 1996), Libronix Digital Library System, p. 174.

Chapter Forty-six: Rules for an Orderly and Healthy Society

1. "WordNet: A Lexical Database for the English Language," http://wordnet. princeton.edu.

2. *Merriam-Webster's Collegiate Dictionary Tenth Edition on CD-ROM* (Springfield, MA: Merriam-Webster, 2000), version 2.5 software.

3. P. M. Forni, *Choosing Civility: The Twenty-Five Rules of Considerate Conduct* (New York: Macmillan, 2003).

4. Taken from John T. Seamands, *Daybreak: Daily Devotions from Acts and Pauline Epistles* (privately printed, 1993), November 11.

5. Leviticus 9:18; Matthew 19:19; 22:39; Mark 12:31, 33; Luke 10:27; Romans 13:9; Galatians 5:14; James 2:8. (See also Matthew 5:43.)

Chapter Forty-seven: Upholding the High Value of Sex

1. Leland Ryken, *Worldly Saints: The Puritans as They Really Were* (Grand Rapids, MI: Zondervan, 1986), p. 2.

2. See, e.g., Proverbs 5:15–20.

3. See, e.g., Song 4:1–7; 7:1–10.

4. This explanation was presented by G. J. Wenham in "Betulah: A Girl of Marriageable Age," *Vetus Testamentum* 22 (1972): 326–348 and then used in several commentaries.

5. Marshall Shelley, "Ruth Graham Dies at 87," June 2007, http://www.christianitytoday.com/ct/2007/juneweb-only/124-43.0.html.

6. Chuck and Barb Snyder, *Incompatibility: Still Grounds for a Great Marriage* (Sisters, OR: Multnomah, 2006).

7. See "Incompatiblitiy: Still Grounds for a Great Marriage," http://www.chucksnyder.org/materials/incompatibility.htm.

8. William J. Bennett, *The Death of Outrage: Bill Clinton and the Assault on American Ideals* (New York: Free Press, 1999).

9. Deuteronomy 13:5; 17:7, 12; 19:13, 19; 21:9, 21.

10. Cited in Timothy F. Tennant, *Theology in the Context of World Christianity* (Grand Rapids, MI: Zondervan, 2007), p. 78.

11. Carrie Doan, "Incest in Film: Evasions, Postponements, and the Therapeutic Response," paper presented at the annual meeting of The Law and Society, Las Vegas, Nevada, May 25, 2009; http://www.allacademic.com/meta/p17679_index.html.

12. From the report "Changing Patterns of Nonmarital Childbearing in the United States," released by the National Center for Health Statistics. Reported by Gardiner Harris, *New York Times News Service* and printed in *Bakersfield Californian*, May 14, 2009.

13. Cited in Ted Olson, "Go Figure," *Christianity Today*, May 2009, p. 16.

14. I owe this insight to my pastor friend Dr. Matthew Ristuccia.

15. This story was related by Becky Pippert at the InterVarsity Urbana Student Missionary Conference in December 1987.

16. See *Why Wait? 24 Reasons to Wait until Marriage to Have Sex* (Torrance, CA: Rose Publishing, 2005), p. 6.

17. Daniel R. Heimbach, *True Sexual Morality: Recovering Biblical Standards for a Culture in Crisis* (Wheaton, IL: Crossway, 2004), p. 178.

18. Ibid., p. 181.

Chapter Forty-eight: Rules for a Holy Society

1. See also Exodus 12:6; Leviticus 16:17; Numbers 14:5; Deuteronomy 31:30; etc.

2. John H. Walton, Victor H. Matthews, and Mark W. Chavalas, *The IVP Bible Background Commentary: Old Testament* (Leicester, UK and Downers Grove, IL: InterVarsity Press, 2000), Logos Library System: The Essential IVP Reference Collection (Bellingham, WA: Logos, 1985–2002), software.

3. See Exodus 34:15, 16; Deuteronomy 7:3, 4; Joshua 23:12, 13; Judges 3:5, 6; 1 Kings 11:2; Ezra 9; Nehemiah 13:13–27.

4. See note 12 on virginity in chap. 47, "Upholding the High Value of Sex."

5. Leviticus 19:18–19; 22:39; Mark 12:31, 33; Luke 10:27; Romans 13:9; Galatians 5:14; James 2:8. (See also Matthew 5:43.)

6. Paul Lee Tan, ed., *Encyclopedia of 15,000 Illustrations*, WORDsearch 7.0 (Austin, TX: WORDsearch, 2005), software, # 5058.

7. Leviticus 11:44, 45; 19:2; 20:7, 26; 21:8.

8. Miroslav Volf, *The End of Memory: Remembering Rightly in a Violent World* (Grand Rapids, MI: Eerdmans, 2006).

Chapter Forty-nine: Rules for a Considerate Society

1. On slavery, see Murray J. Harris, *Slave of Christ: A New Testament Metaphor for Total Devotion to Christ* (Downers Grove, IL: InterVarsity Press, 2001).

2. Eugene Merrill, *Deuteronomy,* The New American Commentary, vol. 4 (Nashville, TN: B&H, 1994), WORDsearch 7.0 (Austin, TX: WORDsearch, 2005), software.

3. Janet and Geoff Benge, *Hudson Taylor: Deep in the Heart of China* (Seattle, WA: YWAM, 1998), pp. 49–58.

4. Frank Greve, "Neediest People Are Most Generous," *The Fresno Bee*, May 24, 2009, pp. A1, A14.

5. Cleon L. Rogers Jr. and Cleon L. Rogers III, *The New Linguistic and Exegetical Key to the Greek New Testament* (Grand Rapids, MI: Zondervan, 1998), Zondervan Interactive (Grand Rapids, MI: Zondervan, 2007), Pradis 6.0 software.

6. Cited in Warren W. Wiersbe and Lloyd M. Perry, *The Wycliffe Handbook of Preaching and Preachers* (Chicago: Moody Press, 1984), pp. 216, 217.

Chapter Fifty: Generous Justice

1. Timothy Keller, *Generous Justice: How God's Grace Makes Us Just* (New York: Dutton, 2010).

2. Christopher J. H. Wright, *Deuteronomy*, The New International Biblical Commentary (Peabody, MA: Hendrickson, 1996).

3. J. A. Thompson, *Deuteronomy: An Introduction and Commentary*, Tyndale Old Testament Commentaries (Leicester, UK and Downers Grove, IL: InterVarsity Press, 1974), Logos Bible Software (Bellingham, WA: Logos, 2002–2009), software.

4. Ibid.

5. The Barna Group, "New Marriage and Divorce Statistics Released" (Ventura, CA: The Barna Group, 2008), http://www.barna.org/barna-update/article/15-familykids/42-new-marriage-and-divorce-statistics-released?q=marriage+divorce+statistics+released.

6. See H. Norman Wright, *The Pre-Marital Counseling Handbook* (Chicago: Moody Publishers, 1981), pp. 104, 105.

7. Wright, *Deuteronomy*.

8. Peter C. Craigie, *The Book of Deuteronomy*, The New International Commentary on the Old Testament (Grand Rapids, MI: Eerdmans, 1976).

9. Deuteronomy 1:30; 4:20, 34, 37; 5:6, 15; 6:12, 21; 7:8, 18; 8:14; 9:26; 10:19, 22; 11:3, 4; 13:5, 10; 15:15; 16:1–12; 20:1; 23:4; 24:18, 22; 26:8; 29:2, 16, 25; 34:11.

10. John H. Walton, Victor H. Matthews, and Mark W. Chavalas, *The IVP Bible Background Commentary: Old Testament* (Leicester, UK and Downers Grove, IL: InterVarsity Press, 2000), Logos Library System: The Essential IVP Reference Collection (Bellingham, WA: Logos, 1985–2002), software.

11. Cited in PBS *Frontline* report, http://www.pbs.org/wgbh/pages/frontline/slaves/etc/stats.html.

12. Deann Alford, "Sex Slaves' Slow Freedom: Sometimes It Takes Years to Negotiate Their Release," *Christianity Today*, June 15, 2009, http://www.christianitytoday.com/ct/2005/february/19.22.html.

13. Eugene Merrill, *Deuteronomy*, The New American Commentary, vol. 4 (Nashville, TN: B&H, 1994), WORDsearch 7.0 (Austin, TX: WORDsearch, 2005), software.

14. Wright, *Deuteronomy*.

Chapter Fifty-one: Concern for Humans and Animals and Honesty

1. John H. Walton, Victor H. Matthews, and Mark W. Chavalas, *The IVP Bible Background Commentary: Old Testament* (Leicester, UK and Downers Grove, IL: InterVarsity Press, 2000), Logos Library System: The Essential IVP Reference Collection (Bellingham, WA: Logos, 1985–2002), software.

2. David F. Payne, *Deuteronomy*, The Daily Study Bible (Edinburgh, UK: The Saint Andrew Press and Philadelphia, PA: Westminster, 1985).

3. *Theological Wordbook of the Old Testament*, ed. R. Laird Harris, Gleason L. Archer Jr., Bruce K. Waltke (Chicago: Moody Publishers, 1980), WORDsearch 7.0 (Austin, TX: WORDsearch, 2004), software.

4. John H. Walton, Victor H. Matthews, and Mark W. Chavalas, *The IVP Bible Background Commentary: Old Testament* (Leicester, UK and Downers Grove, IL: InterVarsity Press, 2000), Logos Library System: The Essential IVP Reference Collection (Bellingham, WA: Logos, 1985–2002), software.

5. See Earle E. Cairns, *An Endless Line of Splendor: Revivals and Their Leaders from the Great Awakening to the Present* (Wheaton, IL: Tyndale House, 1986), p. 305.

6. Walton, Matthews, and Chavalas, *The IVP Bible Background Commentary: Old Testament*.

7. Payne, *Deuteronomy*.

8. Gary H. Hall, *The College Press NIV Commentary: Deuteronomy* (Joplin, MO: The College Press Publishing Co., Inc., 2000), Logos Bible Software (Bellingham, WA: Logos 2002–2009), software.

9. Christopher J. H. Wright, *Deuteronomy*, The New International Biblical Commentary (Peabody, MA: Hendrickson, 1996).

10. Paul Lee Tan, ed., *Encyclopedia of 15,000 Illustrations*, WORDsearch 7.0 (Austin, TX: WORDsearch, 2005), software, #5755.

11. Wright, *Deuteronomy*.

12. J. A. Thompson, *Deuteronomy: An Introduction and Commentary*, Tyndale Old Testament Commentaries (Leicester, UK and Downers Grove, IL: InterVarsity Press, 1974), Logos Bible Software (Bellingham, WA: Logos, 2002–2009), software.

13. Earl Kalland, "Deuteronomy," in *The Expositor's Bible Commentary*, ed. Frank E. Gaebelein (Grand Rapids, MI: Zondervan, 1992), Zondervan Interactive (Grand Rapids, MI: Zondervan, 2007), Pradis 6.0 software.

Chapter Fifty-two: The Heart of a Biblical Giver

1. J. G. McConville, "Deuteronomy," in *New Bible Commentary: 21st Century Edition*, ed. G. J. Weham, J. A. Motyer, D. A. Carson, and R. T. France (Leicester, UK and Downers Grove, IL: IVP Academic, 1994), Logos Library System: The Essential IVP Reference Collection (Bellingham, WA: Logos, 1985–2002), software.

2. Luciano C. Chianeque and Samuel Ngewa, "Deuteronomy," in *Africa Bible Commentary: A One-Volume Commentary Written by 70 African Scholars*, ed. Tokumbo Adyemo (Nairobi, Kenya: WordAlive Publishers and Grand Rapids, MI: Zondervan, 2006).

3. Christopher J. H. Wright, *Deuteronomy*, The New International Biblical Commentary (Peabody, MA: Hendrickson, 1996). (Italics his.)

4. Darrell W. Johnson, *The Glory of Preaching: Participating in God's Transformation of the World* (Downers Grove, IL: IVP Academic, 2009).

5. Wright, *Deuteronomy*.

Chapter Fifty-three: Acts that Help Refresh Commitment

1. Eugene Merrill, *Deuteronomy*, The New American Commentary, vol. 4 (Nashville, TN: B&H, 1994), WORDsearch 7.0 (Austin, TX: WORDsearch, 2005), software.

2. *The ESV Study Bible* (Wheaton, IL: Crossway, 2008), WORDsearch (Austin, TX: WORDsearch, 2008), software.

3. John H. Walton, Victor H. Matthews, and Mark W. Chavalas, *The IVP Bible Background Commentary: Old Testament* (Leicester, UK and Downers Grove, IL: InterVarsity Press, 2000), Logos Library System: The Essential IVP Reference Collection (Bellingham, WA: Logos, 1985–2002), software.

4. Genesis 8:20; 12:7, 8; 22:9; 26:25; 33:20; 35:7; Exodus 17:15; 24:4. See *The Zondervan Pictorial Encyclopedia of the Bible*, ed. Merrill C. Tenney (Grand Rapids, MI: Zondervan, 1975), s.v. "Altar," Zondervan Interactive (Grand Rapids, MI: Zondervan, 2007), Pradis 6.0 software.

5. Ibid.

6. Warren W. Wiersbe, *Be Equipped: Acquiring the Tools for Spiritual Success (Deuteronomy)* (Colorado Springs, CO: Chariot Victor, 1999), Logos Bible Software (Bellingham, WA: Logos, 2002–2009), software.

Chapter Fifty-four: Can We Curse People Today?

1. Bruce K. Waltke and Charles Yu, *An Old Testament Theology: An Exegetical, Canonical, and Thematic Approach* (Grand Rapids, MI: Zondervan, 2007), p. 494.

2. See James Dobson, *Hide or Seek: Building Self-Esteem in Your Child* (Old Tappan, NJ: Revell, 1974), pp. 81–88.

3. *The ESV Study Bible* (Wheaton, IL: Crossway, 2008), WORDsearch (Austin, TX: WORDsearch, 2008), software.

4. John Piper, *Future Grace* (Sisters, OR: Multnomah, 1995), pp. 262–266.

Chapter Fifty-five: Kinds of Blessings and Curses

1. In *Deuteronomy*, Pulpit Commentary: Old Testament, ed. H. D. M. Spence and Joseph Exell, Ages Digital Library: Christian Library Series (Rio, WI: Ages Library, 2002), software.

2. R. E. Webber, "Marcion," in *Who's Who In Christian History*, ed. J. D. Douglas and Philip W. Comfort (Wheaton, IL: Tyndale House, 1992), WORDsearch 7.0 (Austin, TX: WORDsearch, 2007), software.

3. Anthony Tyrrell Hanson, *The Wrath of the Lamb* (London: SPCK, 1959), p. 69.

4. C. H. Dodd, *The Epistle of Paul to the Romans* (London: Hodder & Stoughton, 1932), p. 23.

5. Leon Morris, *The Atonement: Its Meaning and Significance* (Leicester, UK and Downers Grove, IL: InterVarsity Press, 1983), p. 173.

6. Leon Morris, *The Apostolic Preaching of the Cross* (Grand Rapids, MI: Eerdmans and London: The Tyndale Press, 1955), pp. 181, 182.

7. For more on this topic, see Ajith Fernando, "Wrath versus God's Love," chap. 10 in *Crucial Questions about Hell* (Wheaton: Crossway, 1991, 1994). Much of the material in this section has been taken from there.

Chapter Fifty-six: Keys to Renewal

1. Christopher J. H. Wright, *Deuteronomy*, The New International Biblical Commentary (Peabody, MA: Hendrickson, 1996).

Chapter Fifty-seven: The Path of Repentance

1. Both quotations are from David McKee, *The Wonder of Worship* (Ahmedabad, India: Jiwan Sahitya Sanstha, 1967), p. 16.

2. Robert G. Tuttle Jr., *Sanctity without Starch: A Layperson's Guide to a Wesleyan Theology of Grace* (Anderson, IN: Bristol Books, 1992), p. 127.

3. J. T. Seamands, *Tell It Well: Communicating the Gospel Across Cultures* (Kansas City, MO: Beacon Hill Press, 1981), p. 62.

4. *Theological Wordbook of the Old Testament*, ed. R. Laird Harris, Gleason L. Archer Jr., Bruce K. Waltke (Chicago: Moody Publishers, 1980), s.v. "*Raham*," WORDsearch 7.0 (Austin, TX: WORDsearch, 2004), software.

5. Numbers 14:8; Deuteronomy 30:9c; Psalm 37:23; 41:11; 147:11; 149:4; Isaiah 62:4.

6. Taken from the Bible Society Record and cited in Paul Lee Tan, ed., *Encyclopedia of 15,000 Illustrations*, WORDsearch (Austin, TX: WORDsearch, 2004), software.

7. David F. Payne, *Deuteronomy*, The Daily Study Bible (Edinburgh, UK: The Saint Andrew Press and Philadelphia, PA: Westminster, 1985).

8. Acts 17:4; 18:4; 19:8, 26; 26:28; 28:23 ("convince"), 24 ("convince"); cf. 2 Corinthians 5:11. It appears six times in Acts before chapter 17, but 17:4 is the first time it appears in connection with Paul's evangelism.

Chapter Fifty-eight: How to Handle Leadership Succession

1. J. A. Thompson, *Deuteronomy: An Introduction and Commentary*, Tyndale Old Testament Commentaries (Leicester, UK and Downers Grove, IL: InterVarsity

Press, 1974), Logos Bible Software (Bellingham, WA: Logos, 2002–2009), software, on 28:6.

2. Matthew 28:18–20; Mark 16:15; Luke 24:26–48; John 17:18; 20:21; Acts 1:8.

3. The story is vividly described in J. Edwin Orr, "The Korean Pentecost," chap. 22 in *The Flaming Tongue: The Impact of Twentieth Century Revivals* (Chicago: Moody Publishers, 1973), pp. 165–172.

4. Patrick Fung, *Live to Be Forgotten* (Hong Kong: OMF, 2008).

5. Ibid., p. 6.

6. Dennis F. Kinlaw, *How to Have the Mind of Christ* (Nappanee, IN: Evangel, 1998), pp. 72, 73.

7. Thompson, *Deuteronomy: An Introduction and Commentary.*

8. Wilbur M. Smith, *Therefore Stand: Christian Apologetics* (New Canaan, CT: Keats Publishing, 1981), p. 448.

Chapter Fifty-nine: Moses' Song I: Scandalous Disobedience

1. Gary H. Hall, *The College Press NIV Commentary: Deuteronomy* (Joplin, MO: The College Press Publishing Co., Inc., 2000), Logos Bible Software (Bellingham, WA: Logos, 2002–2009), software.

2. A. W. Tozer, *The Knowledge of the Holy* (New York: HarperCollins, 1961), p. 9.

3. David F. Payne, *Deuteronomy*, The Daily Study Bible (Edinburgh, UK: The Saint Andrew Press and Philadelphia, PA: Westminster, 1985).

4. *Hebrew-English Lexicon of the Old Testament*, Zondervan Interactive (Grand Rapids, MI: Zondervan, 2007), Pradis 6.0 software.

5. John Piper, *Future Grace* (Sisters, OR: Multnomah, 1995), pp. 262, 263.

6. Ibid., pp. 31–49.

7. *Hebrew-English Lexicon of the Old Testament.*

8. John H. Walton, Victor H. Matthews, and Mark W. Chavalas, *The IVP Bible Background Commentary: Old Testament* (Leicester, UK and Downers Grove, IL: InterVarsity Press, 2000), Logos Library System: The Essential IVP Reference Collection (Bellingham, WA: Logos, 1985–2002), software.

Chapter Sixty: Moses' Song II: Judgment and Restoration

1. *Deuteronomy*, Pulpit Commentary: Old Testament, ed. H. D. M. Spence and Joseph Exell, Ages Digital Library: Christian Library Series (Rio, WI: Ages Library, 2002), software.

2. *The ESV Study Bible* (Wheaton, IL: Crossway, 2008), WORDsearch (Austin, TX: WORDsearch, 2008), software.

3. Psalm 6:3; 13:1; 35:17; 79:5; 80:4; 89:46; 90:13; 94:3.

4. From the Bible Society Record, cited in Paul Lee Tan, ed., *Encyclopedia of 15,000 Illustrations*, WORDsearch (Austin, TX: WORDsearch, 2004), software.

5. John Wesley, *The Works of John Wesley, Sermons*, vol. 1(Grand Rapids, MI: Baker 1984), p. 2.

Chapter Sixty-one: The Art of Blessing People

1. J. G. McConville, *Deuteronomy*, Apollos Old Testament Commentary (Leicester, UK and Downers Grove, IL: InterVarsity Press, 2002).

2. Earl Kalland, "Deuteronomy," in *The Expositor's Bible Commentary*, ed. Frank E. Gaebelein (Grand Rapids, MI: Zondervan, 1992), Zondervan Interactive (Grand Rapids, MI: Zondervan, 2007), Pradis 6.0 software.

3. Luke 16:29, 31; 24:27, 44; John 1:45; Acts 26:22; 28:23.

4. *The ESV Study Bible* (Wheaton, IL: Crossway, 2008), WORDsearch (Austin, TX: WORDsearch, 2008), software.

5. See McConville, *Deuteronomy*.

6. *Merriam-Webster's Collegiate Dictionary Tenth Edition on CD-ROM* (Springfield, MA: Merriam-Webster, 2000), version 2.5 software.

7. Gary H. Hall, *The College Press NIV Commentary: Deuteronomy* (Joplin, MO: The College Press Publishing Co., Inc., 2000), Logos Bible Software (Bellingham, WA: Logos, 2002–2009), software.

8. See Ruth Tucker, "From the Fringe to the Fold," *Christianity Today*, vol. 40, no. 8, July 1996.

9. Peter C. Craigie, *The Book of Deuteronomy*, The New International Commentary on the Old Testament (Grand Rapids, MI: Eerdmans, 1976).

10. Ibid.

11. Ibid.

12. Jennie Evelyn Hussey (1874–1958), "Lead Me to Calvary."

13. Hall, *The College Press NIV Commentary: Deuteronomy*.

14. McConville, *Deuteronomy*.

15. Craigie, *The Book of Deuteronomy*.

Chapter Sixty-two: Moses' Last Outburst of Praise

1. Herbert Lockyer, *Last Words of Saints and Sinners: 700 Final Quotes from the Famous, the Infamous, and the Inspiring Figures of History* (Grand Rapids, MI: Kregel, 1969).

2. J. A. Thompson, *Deuteronomy: An Introduction and Commentary*, Tyndale Old Testament Commentaries (Leicester, UK and Downers Grove, IL: InterVarsity Press, 1974), Logos Bible Software (Bellingham, WA: Logos, 2002–2009), software.

3. W. E. Sangster, *He Is Able* (Grand Rapids, MI: Baker, 1975). p. 58.

4. *Theological Wordbook of the Old Testament*, ed. R. Laird Harris, Gleason L. Archer Jr., Bruce K. Waltke (Chicago: Moody Publishers, 1980), WORDsearch 7.0 (Austin, TX: WORDsearch, 2004), software.

5. Taken from *Daily Readings from F. W. Boreham*, ed. Frank Cumbers (London: Hodder & Stoughton, 1976), p. 320.

6. Grant R. Osborne, *Revelation*, Baker Exegetical Commentary on the New Testament (Grand Rapids, MI: Baker Academic, 2002), p. 194.

7. William Barclay, *New Testament*, Daily Study Bible (Louisville, KY: Westminster/John Knox, 1976), WORDsearch 7.0 (Austin, TX: WORDsearch, 2007), software, on James 1:2–4.

Chapter Sixty-three: The Death of a Great Leader

1. Dietrich Bonhoeffer, *Letters and Papers from Prison*, translated from the German edition (London and Glasgow: Collins, 1959), p. 163.

2. J. Edwin Orr, *Campus Aflame: Dynamic of Student Religious Revolution* (Glendale, CA: Regal, 1971), pp. 217–219.

3. From Paul Lee Tan, ed., *Encyclopedia of 15,000 Illustrations*, WORDsearch (Austin, TX: WORDsearch, 2004), software.

4. These three possible interpretations are listed by Peter C. Craigie, *The Book of Deuteronomy*, The New International Commentary on the Old Testament (Grand Rapids, MI: Eerdmans, 1976).

5. From Patrick Kavanaugh, *The Spiritual Lives of Great Composers* (Nashville, TN: Sparrow Press, 1992), p. 13, Logos Bible Software (Bellingham, WA: Logos, 2002–2009), software.

6. Mary Artemisia Lathbury (1814–1913). Apparently she wrote the first verse of this hymn, and the other two verses were written by Alexander Groves (1842–1909).

Scripture Index

Judges

Ruth

1 Samuel

2 Samuel

1 Kings

2 Kings

General Index

Index of Sermon Illustrations

The Bible

Susanna Wesley tells her son John that sin will keep him from the Bible or the Bible will keep him from sin, 147

Mahatma Gandhi's indicting criticism of Christians who take the Bible casually: "you read it as if it were just good literature, and nothing else," 150

An African woman, asked if she enjoys reading her Bible, responds that her Bible is reading her, 624, 669

Calling

Religious leaders who think they shouldn't be given traffic tickets because of who they are don't understand their higher level of accountability, 58

An Asian pastor, trying to import goods not allowed, tells customs officials he is "the Billy Graham of Sri Lanka," to no avail, 663–664

Church Discipline

A man under discipline has time to do a tedious administrative task he wouldn't have had time to do otherwise, thanks to God, 302

Compromise

Christian leader tells author he exegetes society more than he does the Scriptures, 33

Albert Orsborn, Salvation Army hymnwriter, ministers during a time of great revival but later finds himself just going through the motions, 639–640

An Asian pastor, trying to import goods not allowed, tells customs officials he is "the Billy Graham of Sri Lanka," to no avail, 663–664

An evangelist who renounces the faith, asked about Christ when he is dying, answers, "I miss him," 694

Conversion

Skeptic scholar William Ramsey, on an archaeological dig, discovers evidence confirming the history in the book of Acts and later comes to Christ, 118

John Newton was formerly a slave trader but after coming to Christ wrote the now famous hymn "Amazing Grace," 131, 139

When Samuel Ganesh went to a Christian rally to disrupt it, along with a gang of Hindu militants, he received Christ and became a powerful evangelist, 201

Author's coworker in a drug rehabilitation center formerly robbed houses to fund his habit but is now a new man in Christ, 230

A woman formerly demon-possessed but now following Christ especially shows the reality of her conversion by her bright countenance, 382

When friends tell a Muslim convert he has changed religions, he explains that actually his religion changed him, 619

Courage

Martin Luther before the Diet of Worms refuses to recant, being bound by the Word of God, 61

Bishop Polycarp refuses to renounce Christ though that means his martyrdom, 70, 657–658

John and Betty Stam, martyred in China, valued walking with Christ above all else, 88